VOLUME II

ENCYCLOPEDIA
OF
CORPORATE MEETINGS, MINUTES, AND RESOLUTIONS, REVISED

NOTE

''This publication is designed to provide accurate and authoritative information in regard to the subject matter covered. It is sold with the understanding that the publisher is not engaged in rendering legal, accounting, or other professional service. If legal advice or other expert assistance is required, the services of a competent professional person should be sought.''

—From the Declaration of Principles jointly adopted by a Committee of the American Bar Association and a Committee of Publishers and Associations.

ENCYCLOPEDIA
OF
CORPORATE MEETINGS, MINUTES, AND RESOLUTIONS, REVISED

William Sardell, Revisor

VOLUME I

PRENTICE-HALL, INC.
Englewood Cliffs, New Jersey

Prentice-Hall International, Inc., *London*
Prentice-Hall of Australia, Pty. Ltd., *Sydney*
Prentice-Hall of Canada, Ltd., *Toronto*
Prentice-Hall of India Private Ltd., *New Delhi*
Prentice-Hall of Japan, Inc., *Tokyo*
Prentice-Hall of Southeast Asia Pte. Ltd., *Singapore*
Whitehall Books, Ltd., *Wellington, New Zealand*

Library of Congress Cataloging in Publication Data
Main entry under title:

Encyclopedia of corporate meetings, minutes, and
  resolutions.

  Includes index.
    1. Corporate meetings--United States. 2. Corporate
minutes--United States. 3. Corporation law--United
States. 4. Corporation law--United States--Forms.
I. Sardell, William.
KF1414.E48 1978   346'.73'0664   78-2723
ISBN 0-13-275305-7

Printed in the United States of America

PREFACE

The two volumes of this revised Encyclopedia constitute a legal and practical guide for all persons responsible for the conduct of corporate meetings and the preparation of the minutes of these meetings. Also any corporate officer, director, or attorney will find the Encyclopedia an extremely valuable reference book. Not only does it present the basic principles of law applicable to corporate meetings, but it supplies carefully drawn and legally tested forms to carry out all types of corporate activity that are considered at such meetings.

The legal principles take into account the numerous Federal statutes and state laws that affect corporate action. Citations to leading cases and to the most recent authorities buttress almost every statement. Particular care has been exercised to include new principles and trends.

The forms have been taken from court opinions, records of cases on appeal, records of investigating committees, and corporation minute books themselves, but always only after careful checking and, if necessary, editing. They were selected on the basis of their draftsmanship, conformity to legal requirements, and adaptability to the needs of the average corporation. When corporate activity must follow statutory procedure, several forms of resolutions are given. Thus the reader, after familiarizing himself with the applicable statute, may select, or readily adapt, a form suitable for his requirements.

The revisor is sincerely indebted to the editors of the previous edition, the late Lillian Doris, and Edith J. Friedman, for their careful planning and presentation which expedited the preparation of this revision.

William Sardell

CONTENTS—VOLUME I

ENCYCLOPEDIA
OF
CORPORATE MEETINGS,
MINUTES, AND RESOLUTIONS,
REVISED

Chapter 1

STOCKHOLDERS'
MEETINGS

Contents—Chapter 1

Conducting the Vote

Introduction. Generally, corporations organized for profit hold at least two kinds of meetings: (1) stockholders' meetings, sometimes called corporate meetings, and (2) directors' meetings. Particularly in large corporations, they may also hold meetings of committees of the board, like the executive, finance, or investment committee. The validity of the business transacted at these meetings ordinarily will depend on compliance with the statutes of the state in which the corporation is organized, the charter and by-laws of the corporation, or, in the absence of express regulations, upon the rules established through decisions of the courts. It is apparent, therefore, that officers of a corporation charged with the duty of calling and conducting meetings and recording action taken must be familiar with the elementary principles governing the legality of meetings. The purpose of this chapter and of the chapters immediately following is to present these principles, to show why the officers should keep an accurate account of the proceedings at a meeting, and to indicate how action taken at the meeting should be recorded.

Necessity for holding stockholders' meetings. The stockholders of a corporation are given certain rights and powers by the statute under which the corporation has come into existence, by the corporate charter, and by the by-laws.[1] These rights and powers can be exercised in one of three ways: (1) at a regular meeting of stockholders; (2) at a special meeting of stockholders; and (3) by written consent, without a meeting. The method by which the stockholders may exercise their rights—that is, whether at a meeting or by written consent—is in most instances prescribed by statute. When a statute says consent of the stockholders must be in writing, it is frequently good practice to hold a formal meeting to obtain this written consent. If the statute is not clear whether written consent may be obtained without a meeting, holding the meeting may avoid later legal attack against the action taken.

Generally, stockholders must act concurrently. They cannot bind the corporation if they act individually, even if a majority of the stockholders concur and express their consent in writing,[2] unless, of course, consent in

---

[1]For example, stockholders are given the right to elect annually a board of directors. However, when the action is one that is out of the ordinary, such as amending the corporate charter, mortgaging the corporate property, selling or leasing its entire assets, merging with another company, or dissolving the corporation—in general, any act that would tend to divert the use of stockholders' investment from its original purpose—a higher than normal proportion of shares must approve the action.

[2]Brewer v. Stoddard (1944) 309 Mich. 119, 14 N.W. 2d 804; Stott v. Stott (1932) 258 Mich. 547, 242 N.W. 747; Kappers v. Cast Stone Constr. Co., (1924) 184 Wis. 627, 200 N.W. 376. Corporation cannot provide in charter for action in writing by stockholders without meeting. Op., Att'y Gen., Fla., #056-197, July, 1956.

3

writing is sufficient under a governing statute.[3] To be sure, there are cases which show that the validity of a corporate act, even one of major importance, does not necessarily depend upon a meeting of the corporate body in a formal way.[4] Irregularities in the holding of meetings do not necessarily invalidate them; before an objecting stockholder can succeed in nullifying the proceedings at a meeting, he must show that the irregularity substantially affected his rights.[5] Stockholders participating in a meeting without claiming invalidity cannot thereafter deny the regularity of that meeting.[6]

Kinds of stockholders' meetings. Meetings of stockholders are either regular or special. However, some corporations, as part of a program for building better stockholder relations, have held informal regional meetings as a way to keep in touch with stockholders who could not attend the regular annual meeting. No official company business is transacted at these meetings.

The regular meeting is usually the annual meeting required to be held for the election of directors,[7] and the time for holding this meeting is generally fixed by the by-laws. Regular meetings are frequently called "general meetings" or "stated meetings." Special meetings are sometimes termed "general extraordinary meetings" or "called" meetings.

A corporation can transact ordinary business, as election of directors and consideration of the financial statement, at the regular stockholders' meeting,[8] but it cannot transact at a general meeting any business the statute says must be the subject of a special meeting. However, if not forbidden by statute, it can notice extraordinary action for a general meeting.[9]

At a special meeting of the stockholders, no business other than that

---

[3]Lohman v. Edgewater Holding Co., (1948) 227 Minn. 40, 33 N.W. 2d 842. See, for example, Calif., G.C.L. §2239; Del., G.C.L. §228; D.C., B.C.A. §136; Idaho, B.C.A. §133; Ill., B.C.A §147; Ky., G.C.L. §271.405; La., B.C.L. §64; Md., G.C.L. §43; Minn., B.C.A. §301.26; Neb., G.C.L. §21-1,153; Nev., G.C.L. §78.315; Ohio, G.C.L. §1701.54; Okla., B.C.A. §55; Ore., B.C.A. §57.791; Pa., B.C.L. §513; Tex., B.C.A. Art. 9.10; Va., S.C.A. §13.1-28; W. Va., G.C.L. §3080. (All statutory references may be found in Prentice-Hall *Corporation.*) The statutory trend seems to be towards dispensing with meetings in small or closely-held corporations.

[4]Kearneysville Creamery Co. v. American Creamery Co., (1927) 103 W. Va. 259, 137 S.E. 217

[5]Failure of stockholders to consent to an action is a matter about which only stockholders can complain, United States v. Jones (CA-10,1956) 229 F. 2d 84; Smith v. Hedenberg (1940) 189 Ga. 678, 7 S.E. 2d 243; Boston Acme Mines Development Co. v. Clawson (1925) 66 Utah 103, 240 P. 165; Beccio v. Tawnmoore Apartments (1972) 265 Md. 297, 289 A. 2d 311.

[6]In re Roosevelt Leather Handbag Co. (1947) 66 N.Y.S. 2d 735; State ex rel Blackwood v. Brast (1924) 98 W. Va. 596, 127 S.E. Beggs v. Myton Canal & Irrigation Co. (Utah, 1919) 179 P. 984; Smith v. Knauss (1918) 52 Utah 614, 176 P. 621; Hiles v. C.A. Hiles and Co. (1906) 120 Ill. App. 617.

[7]The election of directors at a special meeting is valid if the meeting is called in accordance with statute. In re Warns, (1941) N.Y.L.J., 11-10-41, p, 1448, col. 2.

[8]Frankel v. 447 Central Park West Corp., (1941) 176 N.Y. Misc. 701, 28 N.Y.S. 2d 505.

[9]Citrus Growers Div. Ass'n v. Salt River V.W. Users' Ass'n (Ariz., 1928) 268 P. 773; Da Prato v. Da Prato (1963) 346 Mass. 764, 190 N.E. 2d 869; Evans v. Boston Heating Co. (1892) 157 Mass. 37, 31 N.E. 698.

specified in the call for the meeting may be considered or transacted unless all the stockholders entitled to vote are present in person or represented by proxy, and unless all consent to the transaction of the business.[10]

The statute, charter, or by-laws may require that the consent of the stockholders to a particular transaction be given (1) in writing, (2) in writing expressed at a special meeting, (3) at any meeting called to consider the question, or (4) at any meeting. Under the first provision, no meeting is necessary, though, of course, consent may be given in writing at a meeting. Under the second provision, apparently, consent may be given only at a special meeting called for the purpose. Under the third provision, consent may be given at a regular or a special meeting, provided notice of the meeting contains a statement of the purpose of the meeting. Under the fourth provision, consent is sufficient if given at any meeting.

Calling stockholders' meetings. The by-laws generally indicate who may call regular and special meetings of stockholders. Occasionally, the provisions governing the calling of meetings are found in the certificate of incorporation. In many states, the manner of calling meetings is fixed by statute. If there is a conflict between the by-laws and the statute as to who shall make the call, the statute controls.[11] If neither the by-laws nor the statute designates who shall call meetings of the stockholders, the directors, acting as a board, are the proper officers to do so,[12] and they may call a meeting whenever they deem it necessary.

If the corporate officers have a duty to call a meeting, but wrongfully fail to do so, a stockholder may bring an action to compel the call.[13] A stockholder has a continuing right to insist that an annual stockholders' meeting be held.[14] Many of the statutes specifically provide that, in case the election of directors is not held on the day designated by the by-laws, a meeting for the election of directors may be called by a certain number of stockholders themselves, upon giving notice as prescribed in the statute. Where a special meeting of stockholders is called by a stockholder, strict compliance with the by-laws or statutes governing the calling of the meeting is particularly important.[15] It has been held that a stockholder who is not a stockholder of record can call a meeting.[16]

---

[10]Kersjes v. Metzger (1940) 292 Mich. 83, 290 N.W. 336.
[11]Grant v. Elder (1918) 64 Colo. 104, 170 P. 198.
[12]Walsh v. State ex rel. Cook (1917) 199 Ala. 123, 74 So. 45.
[13]Dedrick v. California Whaling Co. (1936) 16 Cal. App. 2d 284, 60 P. 2d 551; Michel v. Michel (1922) 151 La. 541, 92 So. 50. Under a by-law that gives a majority stockholder the right to call a meeting, the special administrator of a deceased majority stockholder could call such meeting, since he had duty to preserve deceased's property: Touchet v. Touchet (1928) 264 Mass. 499; 163 N.E. 184.
[14]Matter of Pioneer Drilling Co. (1967) 36 Del. Ch. 386, 130 A. 2d 559.
[15]Byrne v. Morley (1956) 78 Ida. 172, 299 P. 2d 758.
[16]Matter of Bloch (1947) 272 App. Div. 218, 70 N.Y.S. 2d 530.

In order to make the stockholders' meeting legal there must be substantial compliance with any mandatory provisions in the certificate of incorporation or by-laws of the corporation as to the method of call.[17] If the by-laws require that the meeting be called by the directors or by those stockholders holding a certain percentage of stock, it cannot be called by the president or by another officer;[18] nor may any other officer call a meeting when only the president is authorized to call it.[19] If the by-laws specify that a meeting be called in writing, an oral call is insufficient. However, attendance and participation in the meeting by all the stockholders constitute a waiver of any objection either to the regularity of the call or to the manner in which it is made.[20] Thus, those who are present and vote at a meeting cannot later attack its validity on the ground that those who called the meeting lacked the authority to do so.[21] Subsequent ratification by all the stockholders of the business transacted at a meeting that has been improperly called will also waive the irregularity.

Necessity for giving notice of stockholders' meetings. Notice of stockholders' meetings should be given exactly in the manner provided in the statute, charter, or by-laws.[22] However, substantial compliance with by-law requirements is sufficient.[23] Further, while the question is not free from doubt, a by-law can impose *more* stringent notice requirements than the statute itself calls for.[24] If no notice is required, and the charter or by-laws provide for the regular meeting, the by-laws themselves are

---

[17]Matter of Auer, (1954) 306 N.Y. 427, 118 N.E. 2d 590, in which the president of the corporation was compelled to call stockholders' meeting when stockholders requested one, pursuant to by-laws. See also Boericke v. Weise (1945) 68 Cal. App. 2d 407, 156 P. 2d 781. And once the directors had called stockholders' meeting as required by the charter, they could not postpone it without the stockholders' consent, even though the directors' motive was to complete an audit to present at the stockholders' meeting; otherwise, the court said, they could use delays to perpetuate themselves in office: Silverman v. Gilbert (La., 1966) 185 So. 2d 373, writ den. 249 La. 384, 186 So. 2d 630. Even though charter gives directors power to amend by-laws, they cannot use that power to change date of annual meeting to month later than generally held, since that would extend their term of office to 13 months, and so contravene the statutory mandate that term is for one year: Penn-Texas Corporation v Niles- Bement- Pond Co. (1955) 34 N.J. Super. 373, 112 A. 2d 302.

[18]Grant v. Elder (1918) 64 Colo. 104, 170 P. 198; Westcott v. Minnesota Mining Co. (1971) 23 Mich. 144. However, when corporate by-laws authorized president to call a stockholders meeting for any purpose, he could call one to fill vacancies on board, even though by-laws said stockholders could call meeting for that purpose: Campbell v. Loew's, Incorporated (Del., 1957) 134 A. 2d 852.

[19]A special meeting of stockholders called by a vice-president without authority is illegal: Kertjes v. Metzger (1940) 292 Mich. 83, 290 N.W. 336.

[20]Guaranty Loan Co. v. Fontanel (1920) 183 Cal. 1, 190 P. 177; First Mortgage Bond Homestead Ass'n v. Baker (1929) 157 Md. 309, 145 A. 876.

[21]Simon Borg & Co. v. New Orleans City R.R. (1917) 244 F. 617.

[22]Bryan v. Western Pac. R.R., (1944) 28 Del. Ch. 13, 35 A. 2d 909; In re J.A. Maurer, Inc. (1947) 77 N.Y.S. 2d 159.

[23]Boericke v. Weise (1945) 68 Cal. App., 2d 407, 156 P. 2d 781.

[24]See Kenton Furnace RR & M'fg Co. v. McAlpin S.D. Ohio, (1880) 5F. 737.

sufficient notice to all stockholders and no further notice is necessary.[25] However, if a statute requires that notice be given, the fact that the by-laws fix the time and place of the meeting does not dispense with the necessity for sending notice to stockholders.[26] If the time and place are not fixed, notice must be sent to the stockholders.[27] Special meetings, therefore, require that notice be given to the stockholders, and unless notice is so given, any action taken at the meeting is not binding.[28] This rule applies even to close corporations.[29] If stock is held by brokers in "street name" as nominees for their customers, sending the notice of meeting to these brokers is ordinarily considered adequate notice to the stockholders.[30] Unless a statute provides otherwise, notice need be given *only* to those stockholders who are *entitled to vote*.[31] Who is entitled to receive notice and to vote is determined by the list of stockholders.[32]

Great care should be exercised that notice is given in due time.[33] The by-laws and statutes usually provide how many days before the meeting notice must be given, and such requirements must be strictly observed. Thus, where the by-laws require thirty days' notice, a meeting will be invalid if only twelve days' notice is given,[34] even though the statute only calls for twelve days.[35]

---

[25]Morrill v. Little Falls Mfg. Co. (1893) 53 Minn. 371, 55 N.W. 547; State ex rel Carpenter v. Kreutzer (1919) 100 Ohio St. 246, 126 N.E. 54; State v. Kennedy (1962) 117 Ohio App. 248, 181 N.E. 2d 495 (Not-for-profit corporation). When no statute, charter or by-law provision fixes what notice must be given, common law principles say meeting must be called on "reasonable" notice to stockholders: Toombs v. Citizens Banks (1930) 281 U.S. 643, 50 S. Ct. 434.

[26]People v. Matthiessen, 269 Ill. 499 109 N.E. 1056, aff'g 193 Ill. App. 328.

[27]Close v. Brictson Mfg. Co., (1930) 43 F. 2d 869.

[28]Note, however, that statutes requiring notice of special meetings of stockholders are for the benefit of stockholders, and when all are present and acting, notice may be dispensed with. Dixie Cab Co. v. Black & White Cab Co., (1949) 214 Ark. 624, 217 S.W. 2d 602; Boswell v. Mt. Jupiter Mut. Water Co., (1950) 97 Cal. App. 2d 437, 217 P. 2d 980.

[29]Darvin v. Belmont Industries, Inc. (1972) 40 Mich App. 672, 190 N.W. 2d 542.

[30]But see American Hardware Corp. v. Savage Arms Corp. (1957) (Del.) 136 A. 2d 690, in which it was held that when a stockholder registers his stock in the name of a broker, he takes the risk of not receiving notice of meeting and proxy solicitation material in time.

[31]S. & S. Mfg. & Sales Co., N.D. Ohio, (1917) 246 F. 1005; Gray v. Bloomington & Normal Ry. (1905) 120 Ill. App. 159. Notice need not be given stockholders who owned shares only so they could qualify as directors, after demand made on them to give up stock to others. Guaranty Loan Co. v. Treadwell (1921) 53 Cal. App. 538, 200 P. 653. Nor need it be given to former stockholders who retained bare title only because transfer technically not fully correct. American National Bank v. Oriental Mills (1891) 17 R.I. 551, 23 A. 795.

[32]Schott v. Climax Molybdenum Co. (1959) 38 Del. Ch. 450, 54 A. 2d 221; In re Northwestern Water Co. (1944) 28 Del. Ch. 139, 38 A. 2d 818.

[33]Five days' notice of a special meeting of stockholders was held sufficient where an amendment of the by-laws changing the five days' notice requirement to ten days was invalid. Moon v. Moon Motor Car Co. (1930) 17 Del. Ch. 176, 151 A. 298. See also Hanrahan v. Andersen (1939) 108 Mont. 218, 90 P. 2d 494.

[34]In re Keller, (1906) 116 App. Div. 58, 101 N.Y. Supp. 133.

[35]Davison v. Parke, Austin & Lipscomb, Inc., (1937) 165 N.Y. Misc. 32, 299 N.Y Supp. 960, modified in other respects, (1939) 256 App. Div. 1071, 12 N.Y. Supp. 2d 358, companion case, (1940) 173 Misc. 782, 19 N.Y.S. 2d 117, rev'd, (1941) 285 N.Y. 500, 35 N.E. 2d 618.

The by-laws cannot provide for notice of less than the number of days called for by the statute; but the directors can fix a period of *more* than the statutory period.[36]

The day of mailing the notice and the day of the meeting are both excluded in counting the number of days.[37] If the statute requires publication of the notice for ten days, it means that the notice is to continue in the publication for a period of ten days. In a daily paper this would require ten different inserts; in a weekly paper, two inserts.[38]

Where the statute does not specifically require publication of the notice, newspaper notices are usually omitted.

Notice given respecting a meeting extends to all adjournments of the meeting, and, if proper notice of the original meeting has been given, notice of the adjourned meeting is unnecessary, unless the by-laws otherwise provide.[39] But notice of the prior meeting will apply to the adjourned meeting only if the latter is held for the same purpose as, and is virtually a continuation of, the first meeting.[40]

A stockholder who has not been given proper notice of a stockholders' meeting to which the law entitles him may be able to recover damages resulting from the breach of his right to notice.[41]

Contents of notice of stockholders' meeting. Notice of a meeting need not be in any particular form, unless the charter or by-laws prescribe one.[42] If should, however, specify the time, the place, and the hour at which the meeting is to be held,[43] and should show that it is being given by competent authority. Unless the notice shows who is calling the meeting, it is not a proper one.[44] The holding of the meeting should not be made conditional upon the happening of any event.

Notice of a regular meeting need not contain a statement of the business to be transacted at the meeting, unless the statute, charter, or

---

[36]MacCrone v. American Capital Corp., (D. Del., 1943) 51 F. Supp. 462.

[37]Ibid.

[38]State ex rel. Webber v. Shaw, (1921) 103 Ohio St. 550, 134 N.E. 643.

[39]People ex rel Loew v. Batchelor (1860) 22 N.Y. 128; In re Election of Directors of Bushwick S. & L. Ass'n (1947) 189 Misc. 316, 70 N.Y. S. 2d 478.

[40]Ibid.

[41]Mills v. Tiffany's, Inc., (1938) 123 Conn. 631, 198 A. 185.

[42]Citrus Growers' Development Ass'n v. Salt River Valley Water Users' Ass'n, (1928) 34 Ariz. 105, 268 P. 773.

[43]Boericke v. Weise, Matter of Auer, (1954) 306 N.Y. 427, 118 N.E. 2d 590, in which the president of the corporation was compelled to call stockholders' meeting when stockholders requested one, pursuant to by-laws. See also Boericke v. Weise (1945) 68 Cal. App. 2d 407, 156 P. 2d 781. (See Note 17.)

[44]Shell v. Conrad, (1941) (Mo. App.) 153 S.W. 2d 384.

by-laws require it.[45] Some corporations choose to include the purposes of a regular meeting in the notice. If so, a clause, such as "and to transact such other business as may properly come before the meeting," should follow the statement of purposes. This leaves the door open for consideration of business not included in the notice. If some unusual business is to be transacted at the regular meeting, such as a sale of all the corporate property or an amendment of the corporate charter[46] or a radical change in the method of electing directors,[47] notice of such unusual business should always be given. When ratification of specific acts is to come before the meeting, the notice should refer to the acts.[48] A statement of the object of the meeting is sufficient; details need not be specified.[49]

In the case of special meetings, the notice must state the purpose of the meeting in such a way that the stockholders will have a fair understanding of the business to be transacted.[50] A notice that the purpose of the meeting is to consider "all questions relating to the property, management and business policy of the corporation * * * and to take such action as may be deemed expedient and necessary in connection therewith," was held sufficient to notify stockholders that a change of officers and directors might be considered.[51] From the standpoint of policy, a clearer indication of the purpose would be advisable. Stockholders may not transact business

---

[45]Des Moines Life & Annuity Co. v. Midland Ins. Co., D. Minn., (1925) 6 F 2d 228; Koplar v. Warner Bros. Pictures, D. Del., (1937) 19 F. Supp. 173; Johnson v. Tribune Herald Co., (1923) 155 Ga. 204, 116 S.E. 810. It was held in Bushway Ice Cream Co. v. Fred H. Bean Co., (1933) 284 Mass. 239, 187 N.E. 537, that where the by-laws and the statute made imperative a statement in the call for the annual meeting, as well as for every other meeting of the stockholders, of the business to come before such meeting, a change in the by-laws could not properly be made at a meeting, the notice of which limited action to the election of officers and to action properly coming before the meeting in respect to such election.

[46]Des Moines Life & Annuity Co. v. Midland Ins. Co. (D. Minn.), (1925) 6F. 2nd 228; Johnson v. Tribune Herald Co., (1923) 155 Ga. 204, 116 S.E. 810.

[47]Klein v. Scranton Life Ins. Co., (1940) 139 P. Super. 369 11 A. 2d 770. Amendment proposed at 1938 meeting that tenure of directors should be changed in 1939 to election by classes. This made it impossible for minority stockholders to elect any directors, as they could when all members of the board were elected in a group. The call for the 1939 meeting contained no notice of the proposed amendment. The court held that the notice given to the stockholders was inadequate.

[48]For form of clause, see Index under "Forms, purpose clause in notice of meeting."

[49]Rogers v. Hill, (1932) 60 F. 2d 109, aff't (1933) 62 F. 2d 1097, rev'd on other grounds, (1933) 280 U.S. 582, 53 S. Ct. 731.

[50]Schwartz v. Inspiration Gold Mining Co., Brewer v. Stoddard (1944) 309 Mich. 119, 14 N.W. 2d 804; Stott v. Stott (1932) 258 Mich. 547, 242 N.W. 747; Kappers v. Cast Stone Constr. Co., (1924) 184 Wis. 627, 200 N.W. 376. Corporation cannot provide in charter for action in writing by stockholders without meeting. Op., Att'y Gen., Fla., #056-197, July, 1956: Klein v. Scranton Life Ins. Co., (1940) 139 P. Super. 369 11 A 2d 770. Amendment proposed at 1938 meeting that tenure of directors should be changed in 1939 to election by classes. This made it impossible for minority stockholders to elect any directors, as they could when all members of the board were elected in a group. The call for the 1939 meeting contained no notice of the proposed amendment. The court held that the notice given to the stockholders was inadequate. Notice of meeting which substantially informs stockholders of the purpose of the meeting is sufficient. Bruckmann v. Bruckmann Co., (1938) 12 Ohio Op. 44. See also Sutherland v. Garbutt, (1942) 132 F. 2d 208.

[51]Lawrence v. I.N. Parlier Estate Co., (1940) 15 Cal. 2d 220, 100 P. 2d 765.

not embraced in the notice of the meeting unless all the stockholders are present and give their consent.[52]

Proof of notice. Proof of the mailing of notice is established by an affidavit of the secretary, and where notice is required to be published in a newspaper, the affidavit of the publisher is sufficient.[53] (See pages 112 and 113 for a form of affidavit.) Proof of actual receipt is not necessary when evidence of the mailing of notices, properly addressed and stamped, is submitted.[54]

Waiver of notice of stockholders' meetings. Stockholders may waive notice of a meeting, whether required by the statute, charter, or by-laws.[55] Waivers may be either in writing or by action. A person who is present in person or by proxy, and who participates without dissent in a meeting, thereby waives defects in the notice.[56] But mere presence at the meeting without participation is not a sufficient waiver of notice.[57]

A stockholder may not participate in one matter of business and at the same time object to the legality of the meeting when another matter is considered.[58]

When all the stockholders are present at and participate in the meeting, that is tantamount to waiver of notice.[59] If no prior notice has been given, it is advisable to note such waiver in the minutes.

Most large corporations give notice of meetings and therefore find it unnecessary to obtain waivers from the stockholders. In small, close

[52]Vogtman v. Merchants' Mortgage & Credit Co., (1935) 20 Del. Ch. 364, 178 A. 99; 99; Asbury v. Mauney (1917) 173 N.C. 454, 92 S.E. 267; cf. Logie v. Mother Lode Copper Mines Co., (1919) 106 Wash. 208, 179 P. 835. Note that notice specifically addressed to holders of common stock isn't proper notice to owners of preferred: Liese v. Jupiter Corporation (Del., 1968) 241 A 2d 492.

[53]Callahan v. Chilcott Ditch Co. (1906) 37 Colo. 331, 86 P. 123.

[54]Ashley Wire Co. v. Illinois Steel Co., (1895) 60 Ill. App. 179. The ABA Model Business Corporation Act makes it a statutory presumption that notices properly addressed and with postage prepaid are deemed delivered when deposited in the mail (Section 27). Many states have adopted this provision as a part of their state statutes. Check these in the state statute sections of P-H *Corporation*.

[55]In re Hammond, (1905) 139 F. 898; In re Goldville Mfg. Co., (1902) 118 F. 892; Kenton Furnace R.R. & Mfg. Co. v. McAlpin (1880) 5 F 737; Camps v. Shannon (1961) 162 Tex. 515, 348 S.W. 2d 517.

[56]Sherrard State Bank v. Vernon, (1926) 243 Ill. App. 122; in re Electric Meter Corp., (1942) N.Y.L.J., 10-9-42, P, 972, col. 5; Frankel v. 447 Central Park West Corp., (1941) 176 N.Y. Misc. 701, 28 N.Y.S. 2d 505; Beggs v. Myton Canal & Irrigation Co., (1919) 54 Utah 120, 179 P. 984.

[57]People v. Matthiessen, (1915) 269 Ill. 499, 109 N.E. 1056, aff'g 193 Ill. App. 328. A stockholder who attends an annual meeting merely to demand that no business be transacted and then withdraws from the meeting after failing to secure a pledge from the chairman that no business will be transacted will not be deemed to have participated in the meeting to the extent of waiving his right to statutory notice.

[58]Frankel v. 447 Central Park West Corp., (1941) 176 N.Y. Misc. 701, 28 N.Y.S. 2d 505. In this case a stockholder objected to the election of directors on the ground that he had not received sufficient notice, but later took part in the consideration of the financial statement.

[59]Guaranty Loan Co. v. Treadwell, (1921) 53 Cal. App. 538, 200 P. 653; Larkin v. Maclellan, (1922) 140 Md. 570, 118 A. 181; Scranton Axle & Spring Co. v. Scranton Bd. of Trade, (1921) 271 Pa. 6, 113 A. 838; Camp v. Shannon (1961) 162 Tex. 515 348 S.W. 2d 517.

corporations, however, notice of the meeting is frequently waived. Where the meeting is held pursuant to waiver of notice, a form of waiver is prepared and signed by all the stockholders present at the meeting, and is inserted either before or after the minutes of the meeting.

Statutes in some states expressly provide that a waiver may be signed after the meeting. Even in the absence of such a statutory provision, a waiver signed after the meeting would be effective on the general principles applicable to waiver. The better practice, however, is to obtain the signature of stockholders on the waiver either before or at the meeting. Stockholders can waive notice of the meeting by proxy.[60] Business transacted at a meeting for which notice has not been properly given may be ratified subsequently by the stockholders at a legal meeting called by proper notice.[61]

Place of stockholders' meetings. If no statute provides otherwise, stockholders' meetings must be held within the state of incorporation.[62] The statutes in many states permit the stockholders to hold their meetings outside the state. Under some statutes, meetings may be held outside the state only if the charter or by-laws so provide. Under other statutes, they may be held within or without the state unless restricted by the charter or by-laws. The statutes in some states merely provide that the place for holding stockholders' meetings shall be fixed by the by-laws.[63]

Statutory directions as to the place of stockholders' meetings must be followed. If the statute prohibits the corporation from holding meetings outside the state, proceedings at a meeting held outside the state are void, and a board of directors elected at such a meeting will have no more power than if no election had been held.[64] The prohibition as to the performance of acts outside the state of incorporation refers to acts of a strictly corporate character, such as the original organization and the election of directors.[65]

In the absence of statutory provisions, the place at which a stockholders' meeting and an incorporators' meeting (sometimes called the "first meeting of stockholders") is to be held is determined by common law principles. The common law rule is that both stockholders'[66] and

---

[60]See, for example, New York Business Corporation Law Sec. 606. Check other state statutes in Prentice-Hall *Corporation*.

[61]Howard v. Tatum, (1918) 81 W. Va. 561, 94 S.E. 965.

[62]In re Wilson's Estate, (1917) 85 Ore. 604, 167 P. 580.

[63]For statutory provisions in each state, see Prentice-Hall *Corporation*.

[64]Franco-Texan Land Co. v. Laigle (1883) 59 Tex. 339; Op. Atty. Gen., Mont, (1939) 18 Ops. Atty. Gen. No. 68 (stockholders' meetings, whether regular or special, must be held within the state); but see Montana Business Corporation Act §5-2226.

[65]Franco-Texan Land Co. v. Laigle, (1883) 59 Tex. 339. See also Hening & Hadedorn v. Glanton, (1921) 27 Ga. App. 339, 108 S.E. 256.

[66]Jones v. Pearl Mining Co., (1894) 20 Colo. 417, 38 P. 700; Harding v. American Glucose Co., (1899) 182 Ill. 551, 55 N.E. 577; Hodgson v. Duluth, H. & D. R.R., (1891) 46 Minn. 454 49 N.W. 197.

incorporators'[67] meetings must be held within the state of incorporation.[68]

If the charter or statute makes no specific provision that the meeting must be held within the state, action taken at a meeting held outside the state will be valid if all the stockholders participate in the meeting.[69] Those who are present and take part in the meeting, or who accept the benefits of the meeting, may not deny the validity of the proceedings of such meeting.[70] Furthermore, informalities of meetings held outside the state may be waived by the stockholders, or the acts done at the meeting may be ratified by their subsequent consent and acquiescence.[71] Persons who have dealt with a corporation on the basis of the validity of such acts cannot afterwards set up their invalidity.[72]

Where a corporation is chartered in more than one state, a meeting in any one of the states is valid for all of them, and there is no necessity to repeat the meeting in the other states.[73]

Time of stockholders' meetings. The regular annual meetings of stockholders should be held on the day fixed by the by-laws or charter. Generally, the by-laws indicate when such meetings shall be held, and the time so fixed can be changed only by a proper amendment of the by-laws.[74] If the date is fixed in the by-laws adopted by the stockholders, and no authority is conferred upon the directors to change it, the directors cannot change the date of the annual meeting by passing a resolution or a by-law.[75]

The statutes of many states provide that if the regular annual meeting of stockholders is not held at the time specified, directors may call a meeting within a reasonable time thereafter,[76] and they must call it whenever it is demanded by any stockholder.[77]

The meeting should be held at the place designated in the notice and at the time specified, but it is not essential that it start on the stroke of the

---

[67]See Hasbrouck v. Rich, (1905) 113 Mo. App. 389, 88 S.W. 131.

[68]See Gorman v. Leach & Co., (1926) 11 F. 2d 454; Boyette v. Preston Motors Corp., (1921) 206 Ala. 240, 89 So. 746; Fowler V. Chillingworth, (1927) 94 Fla. 1, 113 So. 667.

[69]Handley v. Stutz, (1890) 139 U.S. 417, 11 S. Ct. 530. See also American Clearing Co. v. Walkill Stock Farms Co., (1923) 293 F. 58; Ellsworth v. National Home and Town Builders, (1917) 33 Cal. App. 1, 164 P. 14.

[70]Handley v. Stutz (1890) 139 U.S. 417, 11 S. Ct. 530.

[71]In re Wilson's Estate, (1917) 85 Ore. 604, 167 P. 580. (1917) 85 Ore. 604, 167 P. 580. See also Smith v. Hadenberg, (1940) 189 Ga. 678, 7 S.E. 2d 234.

[72]Hasbrouch v. Rich, (1905) 113 Mo. App. 88 S.W. 131.

[73]Graham v. Boston, H & E R.R. (1886) 118 U.S. 161, 6 S. Ct. 1009.

[74]Walsh v. State ex rel. Cook (1917) 199 Ala. 123, 74 So. 45. State ex rel. Carpenter v. Kreutzer, (1919) 100 Ohio St. 246, 126 N.E. 54.

[75]Ibid.

[76]Walsh v. State ex rel. Cook, Del. Ct. of Ch., Civ. Action No. 4427, 3-4-74; see also Del.; Tweedy, Browne & Knapp v. The Cambridge Fund, Inc. (1974) G.C.L. §211.

[77]Walsh v. State ex rel. Cook, (1917) 199 Ala. 123, 74 So. 45; State v. Wright, (1897) 10 Nev. 167.

clock; it is sufficient if it convenes within a reasonable time after the hour fixed in the notice.[78]

The meeting cannot legally be convened before the hour specified in the notice,[79] unless, of course, all the stockholders are present.

Quorum at stockholders' meetings. Generally, the by-laws fix how much stock must be represented at a meeting of the stockholders for the transaction of business,[80] though frequently the statute or charter designates the amount required. If the statute fixes the amount of stock necessary to constitute a quorum, a by-law that conflicts with the statute is void;[81] otherwise, the by-law provision is valid.[82]

Where the statute, charter, or by-laws expressly provide for a quorum, a valid meeting cannot be held unless a quorum is present.[83] If after a reasonable time no quorum appears, the chairman merely adjourns the meeting;[84] that is the only action that legally can be taken.[85]

In some states the statutes are silent on the question of what constitutes a quorum. Where this is the case, and neither the charter nor the by-laws make any provision for a quorum, it is not necessary that a majority of the stockholders or a majority of the stock be present for the transaction of business. If proper notice of the meeting has been given, any number present, provided there are at least two, may proceed with the meeting.[86] Note that this rule is different from that governing meetings of the board of directors or of the executive committee.[87]

---

[78]Michel v. Michel; People v. Albany, etc., R.R. (1869) 55 Barb. N.Y. 334.

[79]People v. Albany, etc., R.R., (1869) 55 Barb. (N.Y.) 344.

[80]Where a corporation by its by-laws defines what shall constitute a quorum, it means a quorum for the transaction of business. Beale v. Columbia Securities Co., (1926) 256 Mass. 326, 152 N.E. 703.

[81]Webb v. Morehead (1959) 251 N.C. 394, 111 S.E. 2d 586; Globe Slicing Machine Co. v. Hasner (SD N.Y., 1963) 223 F. Supp 589; Gentry-Futch Co. v. Gentry, (1952) 90 Fla. 595, 106 So. 473; Benintendi v. Kenton Hotel, (1945) 294 N.Y. 112, 60 N.E. 2d 829, See also In re William Faehndrich, (1957) 2 N.Y. 2d 468, 141 N.E. 2d 597, showing remedial legislation following Benintendi case does not affect result if articles aren't also amended.

[82]In re Warns, (1941) N.Y. L.J. 11-10-41, P. 1448, col. 2.

[83]Morton v. Talmadge, (1928) 166 Ga. 620, 144 S.E. 111; Hill v. Town, (1912) 172 Mich. 508, 138 N.W. 334.

[84]See page 000 for discussion of adjourned meetings.

[85]Kauffman v. Meyberg, (1943) 59 Cal. App. 2d 730, 140 P. 2d 210.

[86]Green v. Felton, (1908) 42 Ind. App. 675, 84 N.E. 166; Gilcrist v. Collopy, (1904) 119 Ky. 110, 82 S.W. 1018. See also Morrill v. Little Falls Mfg. Co., Morrill v. Little Falls Mfg. Co. (1893) 53 Minn. 371, 55 N.W. 547; State ex rel Carpenter v. Kreutzer (1919) 100 Ohio St. 246, 126 N.E. 54; State v. Kennedy (1962) 117 Ohio App. 248, 181 N.E. 2d 495 (Not-for-profit corporation). When no statute, charter or by-law provision fixes what notice must be given, common law principles say the meeting must be called on ''reasonable'' notice to stockholders: Toombs v. Citizens Bank (1930) 281 U.S. 643, 50 S. Ct. 434, holding that, where the person present held the proxies for other stockholders and voted their shares as well as his own, it was immaterial whether the number present was one or more than one.

[87]See page 000.

The term "majority," used in defining a quorum, means more than one-half. In determining the quorum, stockholders represented by proxy are included.[88] Where the statute states that a quorum is present when members owning a majority of the stock are present or are represented, except when otherwise specially provided by law or by the articles of incorporation, any subscribed but unpaid-for stock is not included in determining whether a majority of the stock is present. Only issued stock is taken into consideration.[89] A provision in a by-law that "three-fifths of all the stockholders shall constitute a quorum" applies to stockholders per capita, and not stockholders in interest.[90] And a by-law provision that "a majority of the stock issued and outstanding shall constitute a quorum, and all questions shall be decided by a majority of the votes cast," means that quorum members must be voting members.[91] The stock of a parent corporation registered in the name of a subsidiary cannot be counted in determining a quorum,[92] nor can treasury stock.[93]

The rule of parliamentary law that a quorum will always be presumed unless it is questioned at the meeting, or unless the record shows that a quorum in fact is not present, applies to corporate meetings.[94] When inspectors of an election[95] report that a quorum is not present, they may amend their report at an adjourned meeting if a quorum was actually present on the previous occasion.[96]

Whatever quorum is specified in the statute, charter, or by-laws, must be present not only to begin a meeting but to transact business.[97] Thus, if, during the meeting, a number of the stockholders depart, leaving less than a quorum present, the meeting must be discontinued by adjournment. However, once the meeting is organized and all the parties have participated, no person or faction, by withdrawing capriciously and for the sole purpose of breaking a quorum, can then render the subsequent proceedings invalid.[98]

---

[88]Franklin Trust Co. v. Rutherford Elec. Co., (1898) 57 N.J. Eq. 42, 41 A. 488, 58 N.J. Eq. 584, 43 A. 1098.

[89]Schwemer v. Fry, (1933) 212 Wis. 88, 249 N.W. 62.

[90]State ex rel. Schwab v. Price, (1929) 121 Ohio 114, 167 N.E. 366.

[91]Ibid.

[92]Italo Petroleum Corp. v. Producers' Oil Corp., (1934) 20 Del. Ch. 283, 174 A. 276. See also Kemp v. Levinger. (1934) 162 Va. 685, 174 S.E. 820.

[93]Atterbury v. Consolidated Coppermines Corp., (1941) 26 Del. Ch. 1, 20 A. 2d 743.

[94]Coombs v. Harford, (1904) 99 Me. 426, 59 A. 529.

[95]See pages 48-49.

[96]Atterbury v. Consolidated Coppermines Corp., (1941) 26 Del. Ch. 1, A. 2d 743.

[97]In re Gulla, (1921) 13 Del. Ch. 23, 115 A. 317, 13 Del. Ch. 1, 114 A. 596.

[98]See Potter v. Patee (1973) (Mo. App.) 493 S.W. 2d 58 holding that where some officers and members voluntarily leave a duly called annual meeting at which there is a quorum, any purported corporate acts undertaken by those officers and members, who subsequently met elsewhere, are a nullity. Commonwealth ex rel. Sheip v. Vandegrift, (1911) 232 Pa. 53, 81 A. 153. But see Textron, Inc. v. American Woolen Co., (1954) 122 F. Supp. 305, questioning soundness of Vandegrift case, and holding that where a stockholder, present in person or by proxy, leaves a meeting *before* a quorum exists, even though for a capricious reason, he cannot be counted for quorum purposes later.

If stockholders have withdrawn for the purpose of breaking a quorum, because of whim, caprice, or chagrin, the law will consider the action as unavailing, and will permit the meeting to proceed.[99]

The persons conducting a meeting should establish at the outset of such meeting the number present either in person or by proxy and not wait until the votes have been cast for the election of directors, or on some other question, to determine how many shares are represented.[100] Those present at a meeting solely for the purpose of protesting against its legality, and who do not otherwise take part in it, should not be counted to determine whether the quorum, called for by the statute, charter, or by-laws, is present.[101]

Who has the right to be present at stockholders' meetings. The general rule is that only those who have the right to vote have the right to be present at a meeting. Thus, holders of nonvoting stock would not be entitled to be present at a meeting. To be sure, persons may be permitted to attend even though they have no legal right to do so. If an objection is made to outsiders attending, the matter is generally put to a vote and decided in the same way that other questions are settled. Some corporations feel that it is better to permit holders of nonvoting stock to attend meetings, for the administration may be able to convince such stockholders at a meeting that its viewpoint is correct, and thus avoid subsequent opposition.

If it is anticipated that nonvoting stockholders will object at the meeting to action in which they have no voice, the meeting can be adjourned and a subsequent meeting called at which only stockholders having the right to vote may be admitted. In the meantime, the objections of the nonvoting stockholders can be carefully weighed.

A stockholder who has the right to be at a meeting as a voting stockholder and also in another capacity must be regarded as present in both capacities.[102]

Officer presiding at stockholders' meetings. Ordinarily, the president or some other officer has the power to preside at all stockholders' meetings. Most often, the by-laws give this power; sometimes it appears in the corporate charter. Provisions in the charter or in the by-laws as to who

---

[99]Duffy v. Loft, Inc., (1930) 17 Del. Ch. 376, 152 A. 849, aff'g, 17 Del. Ch. 140, 151 A. 223; Hexter v. Columbia Baking Co., (1929) 16 Del. Ch. 263, 145 A. 115. But see Textron, Inc. v. American Woolen Co., (1954) 122 F. Supp. 305, questioning soundness of Vandergrift case, and holding that where a stockholder, present in person or by proxy, leaves a meeting *before* a quorum exists, even though for a capricious reason, he cannot be counted for quorum purposes later.

[100]Commonwealth ex rel. Sheip v. Vandegrift, (1911) 232 Pa. 53, 81 A. 153. But see In re Gulla, (1921) 13 Del. Ch. 23, 115 A. 317, 13 De. Ch. 1, 114 A. 596.

[101]Leamy v. Sinaloa Exploration and Development Co., (1925) 15 Del. Ch. 28, 130 A. 282.

[102]Atterbury v. Consolidated Coppermines Corp., (1941) 26 Del. Ch. 1, 20 A. 2d 743. Duffy v. Loft, Inc., (1930) 17 Del. Ch. 376, 152 A. 849, aff'g, 17 Del. Ch. 140, 151 A. 223.

shall preside at a meeting of stockholders must be observed.[103] If no provision is made either in the charter or in the by-laws, anyone has the right to call the meeting to order and to preside until a chairman is elected.[104]

Stockholders present at a meeting may select a chairman or a presiding officer by a viva voce vote. A stock vote is not required unless a statute or by-law otherwise provides.[105] Where a valid by-law states that ''at stockholders' meetings each stockholder shall cast one vote for each share of stock owned by him,'' the by-law applies to the election of a chairman as well as to the proceedings after the meeting has been regularly organized.[106]

Selection of secretary for stockholders' meetings. When a secretary must be selected because the person or persons designated by the by-laws to act as secretary at stockholders' meetings are not present, the chairman may appoint a secretary. Any stockholder may, however, call for the motion to be put to a vote.

Conduct of stockholders' meeting. In the absence of express regulation by statute or by-law, stockholders' meetings, including those for the election of directors, are controlled largely by accepted usage and custom. The fundamental rule is that all who are entitled to take part shall be treated with fairness and good faith.[107] Most corporations conduct their meetings with considerable informality. The rules of parliamentary law need not be observed, but generally the ordinary parliamentary usages are applied.[108] Thus, the chairman recognizes members who are entitled to address the meeting, states the questions and puts them to a vote, calls for nominations in elections, announces the results of all votes, preserves order, and has the right to refuse to put a motion to a vote if the matter proposed by the motion is not within the legal powers of the meeting.[109] If the by-laws provide that the meetings shall be conducted according to the rules prescribed by a manual of parliamentary procedure, the requirement must be enforced.[110]

---

[103]People v. Peck, (1834) 11 Wend. (N.Y.) 604.

[104]See Cavender v. Curtiss-Wright Corp., (1948) 30 Del. Ch. 314, 60 A. 2d 102.

[105]Commonwealth ex rel. Sheip v. Vandegrift, (1911) 232 Pa. 53, 81 A. 153. However, if there is any question or dissent concerning the selection of a chairman by the stockholders, the safer method is to take a stock vote. Cavender v. Curtiss-Wright Corp.

[106]Proctor Coal Co., v. Finley, (1895) 98 Ky. 405, 33 S.W. 188.

[107]Washington State Labor Council v. Federated American Insurance Co. (1970) (Wash. Sup. Ct.) 474 P 2d 98. In re Dollinger Corporation (1966) 51 Misc. 2d 802, 274 N.Y.S. 2d 285. Young v Jebbett, (1925) 213 App. Div. 774, 211 N.Y. Supp. 61.

[108]Commonwealth ex rel. Sheip v. Vandergrift, (1911) 232 Pa. 53, 81 A. 153.

[109]Alliance Co-operative Ins. Co. v. Gasche, (1914) 93 Kan. 147, 142 P. 882.

[110]People v. American Institute of N.Y., (1873) 44 How. Pr. (N.Y.) 468.

While formality is not essential, some method of obtaining the assent of the stockholders is necessary in order to bind the corporation.[111]

It is advisable to have an executive officer present at the meeting, but there is no requirement that the directors or officers attend. In large corporations, general counsel usually attends the meetings to act as adviser to the chairman. Several clerks (or sometimes the inspectors) act as ushers. As each person arrives, a clerk asks his name and address, whether he is a stockholder, or whether he has been appointed proxy for a stockholder. The clerk immediately checks the information with the transfer agent or from the list of stockholders and filed proxies that have been brought to the meeting room.

Adjourned meetings of stockholders. If the holders of the amount of stock necessary to constitute a quorum fail to attend, the meeting must adjourn to another time, in the manner fixed by the statute, charter, or by-laws. In the absence of provision in the statute, charter, or by-laws to the contrary, a meeting that has been regularly convened is not legally adjourned unless the motion to adjourn has been passed by a majority of the stock represented at the meeting, even though passed by a majority of those present.[112] At any adjourned meeting at which a quorum is present, unless all the stockholders are present and consent to the transaction of other business, only such business may be transacted as might have come before the meeting as originally notified, since an adjourned meeting is but a continuation of the original meeting.[113] Business begun but not concluded at the original meeting may be considered at the adjourned meeting.[114]

Meetings may be adjourned to a day certain, or they may be adjourned *sine die*—that is, without naming a day and finally terminating the meeting—or they may be adjourned subject to the call of the chair. The

---

[111]Landers v. Frank St. Methodist Episcopal Church, (1899) 114 N.Y. 626, 21 N.E. 420. However, see Op. of Att'y. Gen. to Sec. of State (Fla.), #056-197, 7-5-56 (stockholders cannot act without a formal meeting; charter provision for informal written action will not be accepted).

[112]State v. Gray, (1925) 20 Ohio App. 26, 153 N.E. 187. See also State ex rel. Webber v. Shaw, (1921) 103 Ohio St. 550, 134 N.E. 643., holding that, in the interim between the annual meeting and the adjourned meeting, stockholders may not legally call another meeting.

[113]A meeting of stockholders was adjourned to a named date for the express purpose of putting into effect a resolution increasing the capital stock. It was held that at the adjourned meeting the resolution could not lawfully be rescinded by a majority of the stockholders only, since the business thereof, by the terms of the adjournment, was limited to such acts as would carry out and effectuate the purpose of the resolution but would not repeal or rescind. The rescinding resolution was subject to ratification at a subsequent general meeting of the corporation, provided the substantial rights of objecting or minority stockholders were not materially prejudiced thereby. Naftalin v. La Salle Holding Co., (1922) 153 Minn. 482, 190 N.W. 887.

[114]Sagness v. Farmers Co-operative Creamery Co., (1940) 67 S.D. 379, 293 N.W. 365.

motion to adjourn specifies which form of adjournment will be taken, and if none is specified, the adjournment is final.[115]

As to voting at adjourned meetings of stockholders, see page 19. As to notice of adjourned meetings, see page 17.

Revocation and reconsideration of action by stockholders. The stockholders, while they are still in session, may alter or change any resolution or motion adopted by them at the meeting.[116] They may also undoubtedly reconsider and repeal any vote or any resolution after the meeting, unless such action will disturb rights that have vested as a result of the action.

Order of business at stockholders' meeting. The business to be transacted at a meeting need not follow any particular order, even though one is prescribed by the by-laws. A logical order of business, however, expedites the meeting. The order generally followed at an annual meeting of stockholders is:

1. Call to order.
2. Election of a chairman and appointment of a temporary secretary, if necessary.
3. Presentation of proofs of the due calling of the meeting.
4. Presentation of list of stockholders.
5. Presentation and examination of proxies.
6. Announcement of a quorum present.
7. Reading and settlement of the minutes of the previous meeting.
8. Reports of officers and committees.
9. Appointment of inspectors of election.
10. Opening of polls
11. Election of directors.
12. Closing of polls.
13. Report of inspectors.
14. Declaration of election of directors.
15. Ratification of directors' and executive committee's acts.
16. New business.
17. Adjournment.

---

[115]The motions will be made thus: Move to adjourn without further notice, to ...., 19.., at .... o'clock .. M. at (state place of meeting). Move to adjourn, or more to adjourn *sine die*. Move to adjourn without further notice subject to the call of the chairman. It would seem that although the latter form of motion provides that no notice need be given, the call of the chair must be communicated in some way; the effect of the motion therefore is to waive strict compliance with statutory or by-law requirements, but not to dispense with whatever is reasonable in communicating the call of the meeting.

[116]Cumberland Coal & Iron Co. v. Sherman, (1863) 20 Md. 117.

VOTING AT STOCKHOLDERS' MEETINGS

Who may vote at stockholders' meetings. The right to vote capital stock is incident to ownership of the shares, so the owner can vote his stock at all meetings of the stockholders unless this right is denied by some statutory or charter provision or by an agreement under which he holds his shares.[117] For example, a stockholder who receives his shares without consideration and for qualifying purposes only will be barred from voting them,[118] and delivery of stock in escrow contingent on certain earnings is not delivered for voting purposes,[119] nor is delivery to escrow agent to hold until full purchase price is paid.[120]

This right attaches to preferred as well as to common stock, unless the voting power is expressly withheld by the terms under which the stock is issued.[121] The right of the corporation to place restrictions on the voting power of the stock issued by the corporation is discussed on page 442.

The right to vote belongs to the one who holds legal title to the shares.[122] It follows that if title is transferable, without reference to the recording thereof on the books of the company, evidence of ownership of the legal title is all that is required to enable the owner to establish his right to vote.[123] Since the need to determine ownership in a questionable case might place the officers of the corporation in the embarrassing position of having to decide a judicial question, generally the by-laws provide that the right to vote rests with the person who appears as the registered owner of the stock on the books of the corporation. In some instances, the statutes or charter make this provision. Under such circumstances, the right to vote is determined by looking at the books of the company.[124]

---

[117]Pennwood Corp. v. Ladner, ED Pa. (1937) 21 F. Supp. 575; Personal Industrial Bankers v. Citizens Budget Co., (1935) 80F 2d 327; Drob v National Memorial Park, Inc., (1945) 28 Del. Ch. 254, 41A. 2d 589; State ex rel. Johnson v. Heap, (1939) 1 Wash. 2d 316, 95 P. 2d 1039.

[118]Larkin v. Enright (1941) 312 Ill. App. 184, 37 N.E. 2d 905.

[119]Norton v. Digital Applications, Inc., Del. Ch. 1973 305 A 2d 656.

[120]Kim v. N.C.D. Industries, Inc. Del. Ch. 1973.

[121]Williams v. Davis (1944) 279 Ky. 626, 180 S.W. 2d 874; Millspaugh v. Cassedy, (1920) 191 App. Div. 221, 181 N.Y. Supp. 276. A corporation's charter may contain any provision with respect to voting rights of its stock that is not against public policy. Ellingwood v. Wolf's Head Oil Refining Co., (1944) 27 Del. Ch. 356, 38 A. 2d 743. See also Metzger v. George Washington Memorial Park, Inc., (1954) 70 Mont. Co. (Pa.) Rep. 30.

[122]Dedrick v. California Whaling Co., (1936) 16 Cal. App. 2d 284, 60 P. 2d 551; People ex rel. Courtney v. Botts, (1941) 376 Ill. 476, 34 N.E. 2d 403; State ex rel. Johnson v. Heap, (1939) 1 Wash. 2d 316, 95 P. 2d 1039.

For right to create voting trusts, see page 36.

[123]Tracy v. Brentwood Village Corp., (1948) 30 Del. Ch. 296, 59 A. 2d 708; People ex rel. Pickering v. Devin, (1855) 17 Ill. 84.

[124]Dedrick v. California Whaling Co., (1936) 16 Cal. App. 2d 284, 60 P. 2d 551; State ex rel. Breger v. Rusche, (1942) 219 Ind. 559, 39 N.E. 2d 433.

A mere record holder, without any beneficial interest in the stock, can vote it without instructions from the real owner, even if the record holder is a brokerage house[125] that holds the stock in "street name." However, if the legal owner delivers the stock to the record holder for a limited use, to be returned upon request, the record holder cannot vote the stock over the legal owner's objection.[126] Without some provision to the contrary, a stockholder's right to vote at a meeting is to be determined as of the time when the meeting is held.[127]

List of stockholders to determine eligibility to vote—Closing transfer books. Corporations used to be inundated with demands for transfers of stock just before their meetings, so that the owners might assert their right to be present and to vote at a meeting. This often meant that the corporation could not prepare its list of stockholders who were entitled to vote until the last moment. To avoid this difficulty the statutes in the various states now provide either for: (1) closing the stock transfer books a certain number of days before the meeting of stockholders and allowing only stockholders of record at the time the books are closed to vote, or (2) keeping the stock transfer books open, but permitting only stockholders of record upon a certain day, generally a week or more before the meeting, to vote at the meeting.

The officer or agent of the corporation having charge of the transfer of stock prepares a list of the stockholders, showing the number and class of shares held by each as shown on the books on the day fixed for the closing of the books of transfer, or, if the books are not closed, a list of the stockholders on record on the day fixed for determining the stockholders eligible to vote. So far as the corporation is concerned, the record owner has the conclusive right to vote stock standing in his name.[128]

Some states require the corporation to prepare a complete alphabetical list of the stockholders a certain number of days before the meeting and to file the list in the principal office of the corporation for inspection by the stockholders. The corporation may even be required to have such a list at the place where the voting is to take place and to disclose the addresses of its stockholders and the number of shares held by each of them.[129] The

---

[125]In re Pressed Steel Car Co., (1936) 16 F. Supp. 329; McLain V. Lanova Corp., (1944) 28 Del. Ch. 176, 39 A. 2d 209. In the latter case, the court allowed a New York brokerage house to vote its stock even though Rule 452 of the New York Stock Exchange required that when the meeting's business relates to certain matters, the brokerage firm may not give a proxy to vote without instructions from the true owner.

[126]Larkin v. Enright, (1941) 312 Ill. App. 184, 37 N.E. 2d 905.

[127]Bernheim v. Louisville Property Co., (1914) 221 F. 273; McLain v. Lanova Corp., (1944) 28 Del. Ch. 176, 39 A. 2d 209.

[128]In re Giant Portland Cement Co., (1941) 26 Del. Ch. 32, 21 A. 2d 697.

[129]Magill v. North American Refractories Co., (1956) (Del.) 128 A. 2d 233. In a later decision in the same case, (1957) 129 A 2d 411, the court held that where the list was not wilfully withheld, election will not be set aside if new annual meeting is imminent and other relief would be futile.

books of the corporation, or the list prepared, are considered prima facie evidence of the ownership of the stock;[130] they are binding upon inspectors of elections as to who has the right to vote. However, they are not binding upon the courts.[131] Thus, courts have frequently held that a duly qualified stockholder does not lose his right to vote if his name fails to appear on the proper stock record book or on the list of stockholders because of negligence or ignorance of the corporation in maintaining its records.[132]

Also, of course, if the corporation or its transfer agent deliberately and for an ulterior purpose prevents registration of a transfer on the books of the corporation, the right to vote at the meeting is not lost.[133]

Who may vote at adjourned meetings of stockholders. Directors can fix a record date for determining stockholders entitled to vote at an adjourned meeting, even a date later than the date of the adjourned meeting itself.[134] New stockholders of record and stockholders who were not present or represented at the original meeting, but who are present or represented at the adjourned meeting, will be permitted to vote.[135] This is because a stockholder's right to vote at a meeting generally is determined as of the time the meeting is held.[136]

Right of subscribers to vote at meetings. The fact that a stockholder has not paid in full for his shares,[137] or that no certificate of stock has been issued to him,[138] does not disenfranchise him, unless there is a provision to that effect in the charter or by-laws. Thus, if there is no provision to the contrary, subscribers to the capital stock of a corporation who are deemed to be stockholders are entitled to vote at a meeting of the stockholders, even though no certificates of stock have been issued to them.[139] However, if the subscription to the stock is such that it does not make the subscriber a

---

[130]Swaim v. Martin, (1946) 302 Ky. 381, 194 S.W. 2d 855.

[131]Lawrence v. I. N. Parlier Estate Co., (1940) 15 Cal. 2d 220, 100 P. 2d 765.; Double O Mining Co. v. Simrak, (1942) 61 Nev. 431, 132 P. 2d 605. See also Tracy v. Brentwood Village Corp., (1948) 30 Del. Ch. 296, 59 A. 2d 708.

[132]Hall v. Woods, (1937) 316 Ill. 183, 156 N.E. 258; Swaim v. Martin, (1946) 302 Ky. 381, 194 S.W. 2d 855.; In re Timen, (1923) 120 N.Y. Misc. 815, 200 N.Y. Supp. 488.

[133]Italo Petroleum Corp. v. Producers' Oil Corp., (1934) 20 Del. Ch. 283, 174 A. 276; Beck v. Beck Investment Co., (1946) 249 Wis. 5, 23 N.W. 2d 454.

[134]McDonough v. Foundation Co., (1956) 155 N.Y.S. 2d 267.

[135]Ibid.

[136]Bonheim v. Louisville Property Co., (W.D. Ky. 1917) 221 F 273.

[137]Georgia Life Ins. Co. v. Bell, (1914) 141 Ga. 502, 80 S.E. 765; Cummings v. State ex rel. Wallower, (1915) 47 Okla. 627, 149 P. 864.

[138]Beckett v. Houston, (1869) 32 Ind. 303; Swaim v. Martin, (1946) 302 Ky. 381, 194 S.W. 2d 855; Sherburne v. Meade, (1939) 303 Mass. 356, 21 N.E. 2d 946 (stock was paid for but was not issued until after the meeting).

[139]Kauffman v. Meyberg (1943) 59 Cal. App 2d 730, 140 P 2d 210; Swaim v. Martin, (1946) 302 Ky. 381, 194 S.W. 2d 855; In re Timen, (1923) 120 N.Y. Misc. 815, 200 N.Y. Supp. 488.

stockholder—for example, where the subscription is merely a contract with the corporation to purchase stock—he is not entitled to vote.[140]

Right of transferee to vote. If a stockholder has sold his shares to another, and the transfer has not been registered, the transferee may not vote until the transfer has been entered on the books of the corporation.[141] The purchaser, however, although not registered as a stockholder, may get a proxy from the seller and thus obtain the right to vote.[142] In fact, he can *compel* the transferor to give him a proxy.[143] Failure to register the stock in his name indicates that the transferee is willing to have the record holder vote the stock.[144]

A transferee who comes into possession of stock otherwise than by sale and purchase should also have the stock transferred to his name on the corporate records. Provisions of the bankruptcy act that require the trustee to make all necessary transfers do not, by themselves, take away the right of the bankrupt to vote stock still standing in his name.[145]

The majority rule is that the voting power may be separated from the ownership of a stock by agreement without violating public policy, provided there is a legitimate purpose behind such agreement—for example, to assure continuity of policy and management.[146] If a transferee of the stock who waives his right to vote is considered to have given his proxy to the transferor for such a purpose, he cannot cancel the proxy since it is coupled with an interest.[147]

A mere option to purchase stock does not give the optionee the right to vote it.[148]

Right of minors and incompetents to vote their stock. The general rule is that minors cannot personally vote their shares. This rule appears to have been so generally accepted that it has not been questioned in

[140]Owensboro Seating & Cabinet Co. v. Miller (1908) 130 Ky. 310, 113 S.W. 423. See also Goodisson v. North American Securities Co., (1931) 40 Ohio App. 85, 178 N.E. 29: The distinction between subscribers who become shareholders and those who do not is brought out in Baltimore City Passenger Ry. v. Hambleton (1893) 77 Md. 341, 26 A. 279.

[141]Morril v. Little Falls Mfg. Co., (1893) 53 Minn. 371, 55 N.W. 547; Double O Mining Co. v. Simrak, (1942) 61 Nev. 431, 132 P. 2d 605.

[142]Commissioner v. Southern Bell Tel. Co., (1939) 102 F. 2d 397; McLain v. Lanova Corp. (1944) 28 Del. Ch. 176, 39A. 2d 209; Thomson v. Blaisdell, (19191) 93 N.J.L. 31, 107 A. 405. But see Notes 147, 148, below.

[143]In re Giant Portland Cement Co., (1941) 26 Del. Ch. 32, 21 A. 2d 697.

[144]In re D.J. Salvator, Inc., (1944) 268 Ap. Div. 919, 51 N.Y.S. 2d 342.

[145]Kresel v. Goldberg, (1930) 111 Conn. 475, 150 A. 693.

[146]Ecclestone v. Indialantic, Inc., (1947) 319 Mich. 248, 29 N.W. 2d 679; Trefethen v. Amazeen, (1944) 93 N.H. 110, 36 A. 2d 266.

[147]Ecclestone v. Indialantic, Inc., (1947) 319 Mich. 248, 29 N.W. 2d 679. See also pg. 35.

[148]Martindell v. Fiduciary Counsel, Inc., (1943) 133 N.J. Eq. 408, 30 A. 2d 281; Stoelting Bros. Co. v. Stoelting, (1944) 246 Wis. 109, 16 N.W. 2d 367.

litigation.[149] The right of a stockholder in a private business corporation to vote his shares of stock at a stockholders' meeting is in the nature of a property right. Like other property rights of minors, it is generally exercised by the guardian and not by the minor.[150] Statutes on the point are all to this effect.

A stockholder who has been adjudged mentally incompetent should be represented at corporate meetings by his guardian.[151] A guardian who has stock in his own name can vote it in addition to the stock he votes in his capacity as guardian.[152]

Right to vote, as between pledgor and pledgee. As between the pledgor and the pledgee, the pledgor has the right to vote, since he retains legal title to the stock pledged.[153] That principle has been specifically laid down by state statutes.[154]

A pledgor may imply by his acts that the pledgee has authority to vote the stock. For example, if the pledgor attends the meetings year after year and lets the pledgee vote the stock, he cannot later say that the pledgee did not have the right to vote.[155] Or if the pledgor permits the pledgee to register the latter's name on the books of the corporation as the owner of the stock without reservation, the corporation will be justified in recognizing the pledgee as having the right to vote.[156] It has been held that if the pledgor fails to appear at a meeting in person or by proxy, the pledgee has the right to be represented at the meeting.[157]

Who may vote at death of owner of stock. Property cannot exist without a legal owner, and therefore, when an owner of stock dies, title to

[149]But see the following cases suggesting that a minor can personally vote his shares. Chicago Mut. Life Indemnity Ass'n v. Hunt (1899) 127 Ill. 257, 20 N.E. 55; In re United Towns Bldg. and Loan Ass'n, (1909) 79 N.J.L. 31, 74 A. 310. Neither of these cases involved a private business corporation, nor were they decided under provisions of a general corporation law.

[150]Where the statute provides that the shares of stock of an estate of a minor or insane person may at all elections and meetings of corporations be represented by his guardian, it refers to the guardian appointed by law. State v. Farmers' Bank, (1931) 61 N.D. 427, 238 N.W. 122.

[151]State v. Farmers' Bank, (1931) 61 N.D. 427, 238 N.W. 122.

[152]Gow v. Consolidated Coppermines Corp., (1933) 19 Del. Ch. 172, 165 A. 136.

[153]Lawrence v. I.N. Parlier Estate Co., (1940) 15 Cal. 2d 220, 100 P. 2d 765; Fisk Discount Corp. v. Brooklyn Taxicab Trans. Co., (1946) 270 App. Div. 491, 60 N.Y.S. 2d 453.

[154]Crest Finance Co. v. First State Bank of West Mont. (1967) 387 Ill., 2d 243, 226 N.E. 2d 369.

[155]Carter v. Curlew Creamery Co., (1943) 16 Wash. 2d 476, 134 P. 2d 66.

[156]Italo Petroleum Corp. v. Producers' Oil Corp., (1934) 20 Del. Ch. 283, 174; In re Argus Printing Co., (1891) 1 N.D. 435, 48 N.W. 347. But see Benkard v. Leonard, (1931) 231 App. Div. 625, 248 N.Y. Supp. 497, where the court said: "Undoubtedly, for the mere purpose of voting the stock at an election, the inspectors of the election do not inquire into any equity under which the shares were held, or look behind what the corporate books disclose, but where it appears, as appears by the agreed statement of facts, that the pledgee of this stock in question held the same under a limited authority, the Court may properly determine as to where the voting power of said stock rests."

[157]Michaels v. Pacific Soft Water Laundry, (1930) 104 Cal. App. 366, 286 P. 172.

the stock passes immediately to the deceased owner's legal representatives. When the representatives are able to establish their appointment, for example, as administrator or executor, they may vote the stock even without causing a change in the corporate records.[158] When the legal title to shares is vested in more than one executor, they can vote only as co-owners,[159] or as a unit.[160] Stock voted by one executor over the protest of another is illegal and should not be counted.[161] (For right of co-owners to vote, see below.) After delivery of the shares to the heirs, the administrator does not have the right to vote the stock in defiance of the transferees' wishes, even though the transferees failed to register the transfer of the stock to themselves.[162]

Right of trustee or beneficiary to vote. On the basis of the fundamental rule that the right to vote stock follows the legal title thereto, the trustee, not the beneficiary, has the voting power.[163] Even if the statute gives the right to vote to the beneficiary, his right will not accrue unless his name appears on the company's records as a stockholder.[164] The instrument creating the trust may give voting power to one trustee, but if it simply provides that one trustee shall get proxies from the other trustees, the instrument will not be binding on the corporation if the proxies are not in fact executed and delivered.[165] Where there is more than one trustee, the trustees hold title to stock jointly. To vote such stock, they must act jointly, either in person or by proxy.[166] A trust instrument requiring the trustee to give an unrestricted proxy to the president has been upheld.[167] Income beneficiaries of testamentary trust cannot petition for dissolution of a corporation in which the trust owns shares, since only holders of shares with voting rights can file such a petition; they are not such shareholders.[168]

---

[158]Market St. Ry. v. Hellman, (1895) 109 Cal. 571, 42 P. 225; Investment Associates, Inc. v. Standard Power & Light Corp., (1946) 29 Del. Ch. 225, 48 A. 2d 501, aff'd, Standard Power & Light Corp. v. Investment Associates, Inc., (1947) 29 Del Ch. 593, 51 A. 2d 572; In re Schirmer's Will, (1931) 231 App. Div. 625, 248 N.Y. Supp. 497. An executor who obtains control of a corporation because the decedent owned all the stock of the corporation can vote the stock without the formality of a transfer of the shares to his name on the books of the company. In re Steinberg's Estate, (1934) 153 N.Y. Misc. 339, 274 N.Y. Supp. 914.

[159]Townsend v. Winburn, (1919) 107 N.Y. Misc. 443, 177 N.Y. Supp. 757.

[160]Sellers v. Joseph Bancroft & Sons Co., (1941) 25 Del. Ch. 268, 17 A 2d 831.

[161]Ibid.

[162]In re Canal Constr. Co., (1936) 21 Del. Ch. 155, 182 A. 545.

[163]Lawrence v. I.N. Parlier Estate Co., (1940) 15 Cal. 2d 220, 100 P. 2d 765; Sutliff v. Aydelott, (1940) 373 Ill. 633, 27 N.E. 2d 529.

[164]People ex rel. Courtney v. Botts, (1941) 376 Ill. 476, 34 N.E. 2d 403.

[165]Lafferty's Estate, (1893) 154 Pa. St. 430, 26 A. 388; Tunis v. Hestonville, M. & F.R.R., (1892) 149 Pa. St. 70, 24 A. 88.

[166]People ex rel. Courtney v. Botts, (1941) 376 Ill. 476, 34 N.E. 2d 403.

[167]Edson v. Norristown-Penn Trust Co., (1948) 359 Pa. 386, 59 A. 2d 82.

[168]Turner v. Flynn & Emrich Co. of Baltimore City (1973) Md. Ct. of Appeals, 306 A. 2d 218.

Right of co-owners to vote. Co-owners of stock must unanimously agree as to the manner in which the stock shall be voted; otherwise their vote will not count.[169] But one co-owner may vote the stock if the other owner does not object.[170] In actual practice, one co-owner may present proxies from the other co-owners and exercise the right to vote on that basis. (See pages 27-28 to validity of partnership proxies.) Where one partner alone attends a meeting, he may vote the stock in behalf of his partner. Upon the death of a partner, the surviving partner may vote the stock standing in the name of the partnership.[171]

Corporation's right to vote. The right of a corporation to vote stock in another corporation depends upon its authority to hold such stock.[172] In practice, where stock appears in the name of a corporation, it is voted by proxy authorized by the corporation owning the stock. A corporation's directors cannot vote the company's own treasury stock, either directly or indirectly;[173] nor can they vote stock in the company held by one of the corporation's subsidiaries, for this is a mere circumvention of the rule that a corporation cannot vote its own stock.[174] However, the fact that the parent and subsidiary's respective boards of directors consist basically of the same individuals does not preclude the parent from voting its shares in the subsidiary's election for new directors.[175]

Right of interested stockholders to vote. A stockholder is not disqualified from voting on a question because he has a personal interest in the subject matter that is opposed to or different from the interests of the company.[176] This rule applies to a corporate as well as an individual stockholder[177] A director, on the other hand, occupies a fiduciary relation to the corporation and may not vote at directors' meetings on matters in which he is personally interested. (See page 137 for a further discussion of

---

[169]See Townsend v. Winburn, (1919) 107 N.Y. Misc. 443, 177 N.Y. Supp. 757.

[170]Sellers v. Joseph Bancroft & Sons Co. (1941) 25 Del. Ch. 268, 17A. 2d 831.

[171]Kenton Furnace R.R. & Mfg. Co. v. McAlpin, (1880) 5F. 737.

[172]Rogers v. Nashville, etc. Ry., (1898) 91 F. 299; Aldridge v. Franco Wyoming Oil Co., (1939) 24 Del. Ch. 126, 7 A. 2d 753, aff'd (1940) 24 Del. Ch. 349, 14 A 2d 380. A corporation owned 78 per cent of the stock in another corporation; it had the right to vote that stock. Blaustein v. Pan American Petroleum & Transport Co., (1941) 263 App. Div. 97, 31 N.Y.S. 2d 934, aff'd, (1944) 293 N.Y. 281, 56 N.E. 2d 705. See also Adams v. Clearance Corp., (1955) (Del.) 116 A. 2d 893; 69 Harv. L. Rev. 1321.

[173]Lawrence v. I.N. Parlier Estate Co., (1940) 15 Cal. 2d 220, 100 P. 2d 765; Vanderlip v. Los Molinos Land Co., (1943) 56 Cal. App. 2d 747, 133 P. 2d 467.

[174]Italo Petroleum Corp. v. Producers' Oil Corp., (1934) 20 Del. Ch. 283, 174 A.; O'Connor v. International Silver Co., (1904) 68 N.J. Eq. 67, 59 A. 321. But see Vanderlip v. Los Molinos Land Co., (1943) 56 Cal. App. 2d 747, 133 P. 2d 467, where it was held that shares in a parent corporation acquired in good faith by a subsidiary are not "treasury shares" of the parent.

[175]State of Tennessee v. Shacklett (1974) Tenn. S. Ct., 7-15-74.

[176]Wilson v. Rennselaer & Saratoga R.R., (1945) 184 N.Y. Misc. 218, 52 N.Y.S. 2d 847.

[177]Ibid.

this subject.) If the interested director is also a stockholder, he may vote at a stockholders' meeting upon a matter in which he has a personal interest.[178] On the general principle that courts of equity will defend minorities from the self-seeking practices of large and centralized majorities, the courts will scrutinize carefully the actions of a corporation owning a majority of the stock of another corporation.[179] However, a majority stockholder is not a fiduciary of the other stockholders.[180]

PROXIES AND VOTING TRUSTS

Validity of proxies. Absent stockholders are generally given the right, by statute, charter, or by-laws, to vote at a meeting by written proxy.[181] The statutory provisions concerning voting by proxy vary throughout the states. The usual provisions are (1) that the proxy shall be in writing; (2) that it is revocable at the pleasure of the person executing it; (3) that it will expire after a certain number of months or years from the date of its execution unless the stockholders executing the proxy indicate the length of time it is to continue in force; and (4) that the term of the proxy shall be limited to a definite period.

At common law, a proxy was not recognized.[182] Voting by stockholders must therefore be in person unless the right to vote by proxy is granted by statute, charter, or by-laws.[183]

The word ''proxy'' is applied both to the document evidencing the authority of another person to vote for a stockholder, and to the person acting as representative. The relationship created is governed generally by the rules of principal and agent.[184] Unless the statute or by-laws otherwise

[178]Gamble v. Queens County Water Co., (1890) 123 N.Y. 91, 25 N.E. 201.

[179]Case v. Los Angeles Lumber Products Co., (1939) 308 U.S. 106, 60 S. Ct. 1; Wool Growers Service Corp. v. Ragan, (1943) 18 Wash. 2d 655, 140 P. 2d 512; 17 N.Y.U.L.Q. Rev. 287, 54 Harv. L. Rev. 488.

[180]Wilson v. Rensselaer & Saratoga R.R., (1945) 184 N.Y. Misc. 218, 52 N.Y.S. 2d 847.

[181]Right to vote by proxy is property right which courts will protect by injunction if necessary. Mayberg v. Superior Ct., (1942) 19 Cal. 2d 336, 121 P. 2d 685.

[182]Perry v. Tuskaloosa Cotton-Seed Oil-Mill Co., (1891) 93 Ala. 364, 9 So. 217; Manson v. Curtis, (1918) 223 N.Y. 313, 119 N.E. 559.

[183]Walker v. Johnson, (1900) 17 App. Cas. (D.C.) 144; McKee v. Home Sav. & Trust Co., (1904) 122 Iowa 731. 98 N.W. 609; Sagness v. Farmers Cooperative Creamery Co. (1940) 67 S.D. 379, 293 N.W. 365.

[184]In re Morse, (1928) 247 N.Y. 290, 160 N.E. 374. For the distinction between revocable proxy and stock pooling agreement, see Ringling v. Ringling Bros., Inc., (1946) 29 Del. Ch. 318, 49 A 2d 603, modified (1947) 29 Del. Ch. 610, 53 A. 2d 441. For the distinction between a proxy holder and a trustee under a voting trust agreement, see Tompers v. Bank of America, (1926) 217 App. Div. 691, 217 N.Y. Supp. 67, and also 247 N.Y. 290, 160 N.E. 374, wherein it was pointed out that the usual proxy merely establishes the relation of principal and agent, terminable by the principal at will, either through revocation or through the sale of his stock, whereas a voting trust agreement vests the trustee with the title to the stock, which the original owner obviously is unable to nullify by any sale of stock, and which he cannot otherwise cancel except through an attempted breach of contract. On the other hand, the holder of a proxy has no control over the stock itself, whereas the voting trustee has not only the possession of the stock but the legal title to it as well. See also Chandler v. Bellance Aircraft Corp., (1932) 19 Del. Ch. 57, 162 A. 63; Johnson v. Spartanburg County Fair Ass'n, (1947) 210 S.C. 56, 41 S.E. 2d 599.

provide, it is not essential that the person to whom the proxy is given should himself be a stockholder.[185] Proxies need not be drawn up in any particular form,[186] nor need they be witnessed,[187] or sealed,[188] unless otherwise provided by the statute, charter, or by-law provision. Moreover, in the absence of any statutory or corporate requirement, oral authorization of a proxy may be recognized.[189]

A proxy presented in defiance of an injunction against the stockholder forbidding a vote of the stock is invalid.[190] Likewise a proxy is invalid if it is voted for more shares than the stockholder owns. If the vote was counted and was a crucial one, it may also invalidate the election.[191]

It is generally considered contrary to public policy for a stockholder to sell his right to vote for a consideration by which he alone will benefit.[192] In some states, it is a crime for a stockholder to sell a proxy.

Since the proxy was not recognized at common law, statutory, charter, or by-law provisions permitting the appointment of a proxy must be strictly observed.[193] Care should be taken to see that all proxies comply with the statutes and by-law regulations. Ordinarily the presiding officer makes this decision,[194] although in large corporations the power to pass on the validity of proxies is frequently delegated to a special committee of inspectors.[195]

Who may vote by proxy. The right to vote by proxy may be exercised by an individual, a corporation owning stock in another

---

[185]Gentry-Futch Co. v. Gentry, (1952) 90 Fla. 595, 106 So. 473. In West Virginia, a by-law provision requiring a proxy to be a stockholder has been held void because it can destroy his right to vote if the stockholder has to give his proxy to a fellow stockholder whose interests are hostile to his own. State ex rel. Syphers v. McCune, (1958) W.Va. 101 S.E. 2d 834.

[186]White v. N.Y., etc. Soc., (1887) 45 Hun. N.Y. 580. There is not reason for requiring the execution of a proxy by a corporation to be effected with all the formalities required for the execution of corporate acts. Gow v. Consolidated Coppermines Corp., (1933) 19 Del. Ch. 172, 165 A. 136.

[187]Ibid.

[188]Hankins v. Newell, (1907) 75 N.J.L. 26, 66 A. 929.

[189]Hoene v. Pollack, (1897) 118 Ala. 617, 24 So. 349. While there appears to be no case directly in point, it has been stated that Gow v. Consolidated Coppermines Corp., (1933) 19 Del. Ch. 172, 165 A. 136, is probably some authority for the proposition that telegraphic proxies are valid. JUSTINIAN, Brooklyn Law School, Nov. 16, 1933.

[190]Clarke v. Central R.R. & Banking Co., (1892) 50 F. 338.

[191]In re Topping Bros., (1949) 121 N.Y.L.J. 2022, 6-7-49.

[192]Macht v. Merchants Mortgage & Credit Co., (1937) 22 Del. Ch. 74, 194 A. 19; Stott v. Stott, (1932) 258 Mich. 547, 242 N.W. 747.

[193]Machen, "Modern Law of Corporations," §1256. See also Wellington Bull & Co. v. Morris, (1928) 132 N.Y. Misc. 509, 230 N.Y. Supp. 122.

[194]People v. Crossley, (1873) 69 Ill. 195. In New York, the rule seems to be that inspectors can pass only on forgery and the regularity of the face of the document; other questions are judicial in their nature and can be passed upon only by the courts. For an extensive discussion of various questions as to the regularity of proxies, see Young v. Jebbett, (1925) 213 App. Div. 774, 211 N.Y.S. 61, and Gow v. Consolidated Coppermines Corp., (1933) 19 Del. Ch. 172, 165 A. 136.

[195]Standard Power & Light Corp. v. Investment Associates, (1947) 29 Del. Ch. 593, 51 A. 2d 572 Atterbury v. Consolidated Coppermines Corp., (1941) 26 Del. Ch. 1, 20 A.2d 743. The inability to examine proxies of an opposing faction at the meeting should not in itself invalidate the election of directors held at such a meeting, if a majority of the stock is represented. Duffy v. Loft, Inc., (1930) 17 Del. Ch. 376, 152 A. 849, aff'g, 17 Del. Ch. 140, 151 A. 223.

corporation,[196] a partnership, or a fiduciary.[197] (See page 30 as to the right of a fiduciary to vote by proxy.) The stockholder of record, not the beneficial owner, appoints the proxy.[198] For example, often the record holder is a brokerage house without beneficial interest; in that situation, the brokerage house gives the proxy.[199] If a stockholder sells his stock, he cannot later give a valid proxy, except to the purchaser, even if the stock was not transferred on the corporate books.[200]

The holder of a proxy to vote corporate stock is an agent of the record owner and, within scope of his authority, has certain fiduciary relations towards his principal.[201]

Designations and signatures. The person who is to act as proxy may be designated, as, for example, "any member of the firm of A, B, and Co.," without being specifically named.[202] A proxy is not invalid merely because the name of the corporation is incorrectly given, if it agrees with the name given in the notice of meeting.[203]

If a proxy is authentic on its face, it should be counted although the signature differs from the name as registered on the corporate books, or if only one of the two joint owners signs it.[204] But a proxy in which the name of the stockholder is written in the body but not at the close of the proxy is void, and should not be accepted.[205]

The mere fact that the signature on a proxy is not in the handwriting of the shareholder does not invalidate the proxy. There is no statute or rule of law that prevents a shareholder from authorizing a third party to sign his name to a proxy.[206] Where stock is registered in the name of both husband and wife, the proxy should be signed in the name of both. However, if it is signed as the names appear on the books, although both names are signed by the same person, the proxy should be counted.[207] Proxies signed by

---

[196]Gow v. Consolidated Coppermines Corp., (1933) 19 Del. Ch. 172, 165 A. 136.; see also Bouree v. Trust Francais des Actions de La Franco-Wyoming Oil Co., (1924) 14 Del. Ch. 332, 127 A. 56.

[197]Gow v. Consolidated Coppermines Corp., (1933) 19 Del. Ch. 172, 165 A. 136.

[198]Dougherty v. Cross, (1944) 65 Cal. App. 2d 687. 151 P. 2d 654.

[199]McLain v. Lanova Corp., (1944) 28 Del. Ch. 176, 39 A. 2d 209.

[200]Swaim v. Martin, (1946) 302 Ky. 381, 194 S.W. 2d 855. This rule should be applied only as between the parties personally involved. The corporation and inspectors of election are ordinarily entitled to honor proxies signed by the record stockholder. Hall v. Woods, (1937) 316 Ill. 183, 156 N.E. 258.

[201]McLain v. Lanova Corp., (1944) 28 Del. Ch. 176, 39 A. 2d 209.

[202]MACHEN, MODERN LAW OF CORPORATIONS, §1255.

[203]In re Election of Directors of St. Lawrence Steamboat Co., (1882) 44 N.J.L. 529.

[204]Atterbury v. Consolidated Coppermines Corp., (1941) 26 Del. Ch. 1, 20 A. 2d 743.

[205]Schilling v. Car Lighting & Power Co., (1922) 289 F. 489.

[206]Standard Power & Light Corp. v. Investment Associates, Inc., (1947) 29 Del. Ch. 593, 51 A. 2d 572.

[207]Ibid.

executors, administrators, agents, or attorneys, without other authority attached, are recognized, but the better practice is to attach a short certificate showing the appointment.[208]

More than two proxies from the same stockholder. A corporation will sometimes receive more than one proxy from the same stockholder. In that case, the execution date and the postmark date become important.

Where execution and postmark dates are not in conflict, the execution date controls.[209] If two proxies are received from the same stockholder, and neither is dated, the one with the latest postmark date is counted. If both are mailed the same day, the one bearing the latest time of day on the postmark is counted.[210]

Suppose one proxy is dated and the other is not. The undated proxy with a postmark date later than the postmark of the dated proxy should be counted, if the dated proxy is postmarked *prior* to its execution date. This is true even though the undated proxy was mailed prior to the execution date of the other proxy.[211]

If a proxy without a postmark date has a later execution date than any of the postmark dates on other proxies given by the same stockholder, the one with the later execution date should be counted.[212] Inspectors of election must reject conflicting proxies submitted by a broker-dealer holding shares in "street name," and they cannot consider evidence, in the form of an affidavit from a broker-dealer's office, that stock should be voted saying the conflict was the result of clerical error in the broker's office. This is so, because conflict cannot be resolved from the face of proxies themselves or from a corporation's regular books and records.[213]

Proxies in the name of several persons. In some of the larger corporations, a proxy committee is selected at the annual meeting of stockholders. This committee, in effect, represents those who control the corporation. The names of members of the proxy committee are placed on what is known as the official proxy, which is sent out with notices of meetings during the course of the year.[214] The management has the right to prevent others from soliciting proxies on its behalf.[215] Where several persons are named to act as proxy, and they are not named in the alterna-

---

[208]Ibid., citing Atterbury v. Consolidated Coppermines Corp., (1941) 26 Del. Ch. 1, A. 2d 743.
[209]Investment Associates, Inc., v. Standard Power & Light Corp., (1947) 29 Del. Ch. 593, 51 A. 2d 572.
[210]Ibid.
[211]Ibid.
[212]Ibid.
[213]Williams v. Sterling Oil of Oklahoma, Inc. (1971) Del. S. Ct., 273 A. 2d 264.
[214]Lawyers Advertising Co. v. Consolidated Ry. Lighting & Refrigerating Co., (1907) 187 N.Y. 395, 80 N.E. 199.
[215]Empire Southern Gas Co. v. Gray, (1946) 29 Del. Ch. 95, 46 A. 2d 741.

tive, all those named must agree as to the vote; otherwise their vote will not be received.[216] A proxy given to the "board" can be voted by majority of the board; it need not be unanimous.[217]

Proxies given by fiduciaries. The general rule is that a fiduciary cannot delegate his authority. So a trustee or an executor or administrator cannot vote by general proxy unless he has specifically been given that power in the instrument creating his office, or unless the statute so provides.[218] However, a fiduciary can give a proxy that specifically directs how a vote shall be cast.[219] When there are several trustees or executors or administrators, each one of them should sign the proxy; but even though only one signs, the proxy should be accepted.[220]

Some statutes specifically authorize substitution of proxies. That is, they let a proxyholder name another person to actually vote the proxy. Of course, they let the proxy provide otherwise. In the absence of statute, a proxy can provide for substitution of proxies. When a proxy authorizes substitution, and the proxy giver has struck the names of those originally named as proxies on the proxy form, and inserted the names of others, those others can in turn substitute the originally named persons as the proxies.[221]

Restrictions on solicitation of proxies. The Securities Exchange Act of 1934, as amended, prohibits the solicitation of proxies in respect of registered securities (other than exempted securities) in contravention of rules and regulations of the Securities and Exchange Commission. Under the authority granted to it by the Act, the Commission has issued regulations governing the solicitation of proxies by management or stockholders, designed to assure that the security holder whose proxy or consent is solicited will be afforded adequate information as to the action proposed to be taken, and as to the source of the solicitation and the interest of the solicitor.[222] Proxies solicited in violation of Securities Exchange Commis-

---

[216]Sullivan v. Parkes, (1902) 69 App. Div. 221, 74 N.Y. Supp. 787.

[217]Keough v. Kittleman (1968) Wash. S, Ct., No. 39845, 11-17-68.

[218]Edson v. Norristown-Penn Trust Co., (1948) 359 Pa. 386, 59 A. 2d 82; Noremac, Inc. v. Centre Hill Court, (1935) 164 Va. 151, 178 S.E. 877. Unless specifically authorized, a voting trustee may not exercise his right through another, but only in person. In re Green Bus Lines, Inc., (1937) 166 N.Y. Misc. 800, 2 N.Y.S. 2d 556. See also Gans v. Delaware Terminal Corp., (1938) 23 Del. Ch. 69. 2 A. 2d 154, in which it was held that voting trustees could vote through proxies the shares held by them in trust.

[219]State v. Voight, (1913) 2 Ohio App. 145. In Gans v. Delaware Terminal Corporation, (1938) 23 Del. Ch. 69, 2 A. 2d 154, the court held that "though the fiduciaries, the trustees, are not stockholders of record, yet, the stock having been assigned to and held by them subject to the trust, they were entitled to vote through their proxies."

[220]Atterbury v. Consolidated Coppermines Corp., (1941) 26 Del. Ch. 1, 20 A. 2d 743.

[221]McGoldrick v. Rotwein, (S. Ct.), (1952) 127 N.Y.L.J. 508, 2-6-52.

[222]See Aranow & Einhorn, "Proxy Contests for Corporate Control," Columbia University Press, 1973; "Proxy Contests," 41 Calif. L. Rev. 393-438; "The Va-Carolina Chem. Corp. Proxy Contest," 57 Colum. L. Rev. 801-844. SEC Rule 14a governs solicitations.

sion regulations are counted at meetings—it is not for the inspectors of elections to determine their validity.[223] If they are secured by false or misleading statements, the courts will, at the SEC's request, enjoin their use.[224]

There is a question whether a stockholder may enjoin the use of proxies at a stockholders' meeting on the basis that management violated the Securities Exchange Commission's rule X-14A-9 in soliciting the proxies. In the federal courts, the right of a stockholder to enjoin the use of proxies obtained by a false and misleading proxy statement remains a problem since the Securities Exchange Act does not expressly give a stockholder the right to institute a court action to enforce the proxy rules.[224A]

Even if it is assumed that a private remedy is created by the statute, there remain several formidable barriers to injunctive relief. Such relief has been denied where it has not been shown that a technical violation of the proxy rules materially influenced the stockholders' voting.[224B] Furthermore, "a certain amount of innuendo, misstatement, exaggeration and puffing"[225] is allowed as a natural by-product of a bitter proxy fight before proxy solicitation is considered materially false and misleading.[226] Moreover an injunction will only be granted upon a showing that irreparable harm will otherwise result and that there is no adequate remedy at law.[227]

However, stockholders have cause for action for money damages or to set aside a merger, or both, when it is shown that the proxy statement failed to disclose that directors of merging corporations were controlled by a third corporation; stockholders need not prove that such a statement caused submission of sufficient proxies to approve the merger.[228] Further, a minority stockholder can bring derivative action in Federal District Court to rescind a transaction between a majority stockholder and the corporation, previously approved at the stockholders' meeting, on the alleged ground that proxy material for the meeting was false and misleading, even though the majority vote needed for approval of transaction was brought about not through use of such proxy material but by a majority stockholder exercising his voting power.[229]

---

[223]Standard Power & Light Corp. v. Investment Associates, Inc., (1947) 29 Del. Ch. 593, 51A. 2d 572.

[224]S.E.C. v O'Hara Re-election Committee, (1939) 28 F. Supp. 523.

[224a]Howard v. Furst (1956) 140 F. Supp. 507.

[224b]Textron, Inc. v. American Woolen Co., (see Note 98.)

[225]Matter of Hoe and Co., (1954) 137 N.Y.S. 2d 142, aff'd 285 App. Div. 927, 139 N.Y.S. 2d 883, aff'd (1955) 309 N.Y. 719, 128 N.E. 2d 420.

[226]See also Kerbs v. California Eastern Airways, Inc. (1953) 33 Del. Ch. 395, 94 A. 2d 217, recognizing an area of "permissible puffing."

[227]Lyon v. Holton, (1938) 167 N.Y. Misc. 585, 4 N.Y.S. 2d 538.

[228]Mills v. The Electric Auto-Lite Co. (1970) Us. S. Ct., 90 S. Ct. 616.

[229]Laurenzano v. Einbender (1966) DC, E.D.N.Y., 264 F. Supp. 356.

The regulations require that a written "proxy statement" be furnished concurrently with or before the solicitation of the proxy, containing the items of information set forth in the regulations. (In an election contest, or "proxy battle," a solicitation may be made in advance of furnishing the formal proxy statement under certain special conditions, including the withholding of the actual proxy form.) The proxy statement need not be contained in a single document. Every proxy statement must state whether or not the proxy is revocable and, if revocable subject to conditions, what the conditions are. The required information also includes a statement of the names of the persons by whom, directly or indirectly, the cost of the solicitation is to be borne, the method of solicitation used, the names and interest of the persons soliciting the proxy, and a concise description of the substance of each of the various matters which, at the time of solicitation, are intended for consideration by the meeting at which the proxy is to be exercised. The proxy itself must contain a space wherein the person solicited may specify how his vote shall be cast on each matter or group of matters described in the proxy statement. However, the person to whom the proxy is given may have conferred upon him discretionary authority with respect to matters as to which no specification has been made by the person solicited, with respect to matters not known or determined at the time of the solicitation, and with respect to the election of directors or other officers.

The SEC has recently adopted extensive amendments to its Rules relating to the solicitation of proxies and to the contents of annual reports that have to be included with proxy statements.[230] In essence, the amendments require that annual reports to security holders include at least the following information, all of which may be set forth in any form deemed suitable by management: (1) certified financial statements for the issuer corporation's last two fiscal years; (2) a summary of the issuer's operations for the last five fiscal years and a management analysis of these operations; (3) a brief description of the issuer's business; (4) a lines of business breakdown for the issuer's last five fiscal years; (5) the identification of the issuer's directors and executive officers and the disclosure of each such person's principal occupation or employment and of the name and principal business of any organization by which such person is so employed; and (6) the identification of the principal market in which securities entitled to vote at the meeting are traded and a statement of the market price ranges of such securities and dividends paid on such securities for each quarterly period during the issuer's two most recent fiscal years.

---

[230]Securities Exchange Act of 1934, Release No. 11079, Public Utility Holding Company Act of 1935, Release No. 18638, Investment Company Act of 1940, Release No. 8563, all dated 10/31/74 and all effective 12/20/74; for adaptable Form to comply with the new Rules, see page 60.

The amendments to the Rules also require an issuer to undertake to furnish without charge to persons whose proxies are solicited or who are furnished an information statement, upon the written request of any such person, a copy of the issuer's Form 10-K or 12-K, including the financial statements and their schedules, that are required to be filed with the SEC for the issuer's most recent fiscal year and to provide copies of the exhibits to such reports upon payment of a reasonable fee. This fee is limited to the issuer's reasonable expenses in furnishing such exhibits.

Finally, the amendments require that, if an issuer knows certain of its securities are held of record by a broker, dealer, bank, voting trustee, or their nominees, the issuer must inquire as to whether such record holder is holding on behalf of one or more beneficial owners and, if so, the number of copies of the proxy and proxy soliciting materials (or of the information statement) and, in the case of an annual meeting at which directors are to be elected, the number of copies of the annual report to security holders necessary to supply such material to the beneficial owners. The issuer must then furnish such record holders with an appropriate number of copies assembled in such a form and at such a place as each record holder may reasonably request, and must pay the reasonable expenses of each such record holder, if so requested, for mailing such material to the beneficial owner.

Expenses of proxy solicitation. Solicitation of proxies, particularly in a proxy battle, can be very expensive. The costs generally include fees and expenses for attorneys, accountants, public relations firms, printing, advertising, transportation, litigation and other costs incidental to the solicitation. Although there is no statutory provision for reimbursement, management, by custom and usage, can pay its expenses of a proxy fight out of the corporate treasury regardless of the result of the fight, if the contest is over corporate policy and the amount is reasonable.[231] It is doubtful, however, that it can spend corporate funds for the sole purpose of perpetuating its control over the corporation.

A successful insurgent enjoys the same privilege. The corporation will be permitted to reimburse the successful insurgent if the contest was

---

[231]See Friedman, "Expenses of Corporate Proxy Contests," 51 COLUMBIA L. REV. 951; Aranow and Einhorn, "Corporate Proxy Contests: Expenses of Management and Insurgents," 42 CORNELL L.Q. 4, Compare Kaufman v. Wolfson, (1957) 153 F. Supp. 253, holding that directors are personally liable for corporate funds to be used to help finance a proxy fight in another corporation.

See also Campbell v. Loew's Inc., (1957) (Del. Ch) 134 A. 2d 852, holding that if, due to resignation of some directors, a minority of directors is in control of management, the minority is entitled to expend reasonable amounts of corporate funds in solicitation of proxies, though it will be enjoined from using corporate facilities and the services of the corporation's employees for such solicitation.

over the corporate policy,[232] although it may have to get the approval of the stockholders.[233] But note that a stockholder's attorney who conducted the stockholder's proxy contest cannot be reimbursed by the corporation, even though his efforts defeated the corporation's proposed sale of certain assets and allegedly saved the corporation millions of dollars; this is so, because he was a full time salaried employee of the stockholder, and the contest was conducted for the stockholder's own purposes and not over matters of policy.[234] There is no precedent for paying a losing insurgent's proxy solicitation expenses. However, some writers have suggested that unsuccessful insurgents should be proportionally reimbursed.[235]

Powers of proxies. Proxies may be either general or limited. A general proxy is one that does not specifically limit the holder in his right to vote. A general proxyholder may vote only on ordinary corporate business.[236] He cannot vote on extraordinary matters[237] unless they are specifically mentioned in the proxy. When an unrestricted proxy is given, it is presumed that what the proxy does in the proper exercise of the power granted to him expresses the will of the stockholder.[238]

A limited proxy gives the holder the right to vote on a specific subject only, or according to, specific instructions.[239] The holder must not act outside the scope of his authority, otherwise the vote is declared invalid. However, it would seem that the secretary cannot alter the proxy's vote to make it conform to the instructions contained in the proxy, for the vote is cast not by the written authorization but by the person. If the administration wants the vote to be in accordance with the instructions, the correct practice would be to adjourn the meeting, notify the stockholder to revoke the proxy, send a new proxy, and get the vote at the adjourned meeting. To save the time of the other stockholders, their proxies could be taken immediately, so that they might be voted at the adjourned meeting in accordance with the administration's desires.

---

[232]Steinberg v. Adams, (1950) 90 F. Supp. 604. See, however, Cullom v. Simmonds, (1955) 285 App. Div. 1051, 139 N.Y.S. 2d 401, in which the successful insurgents were denied reimbursement because the expenses were incurred not for policy purposes but for the purpose of changing the personnel, and the amount was unreasonable.

[233]Rosenfeld v. Fairchild Engine and Airplane Corp., (1955) 309 N.Y. 168, 128 N.E. 2d 291, discussed in 43 CALIF. L. REV. 893, 41 CORNELL L.Q. 714-26; 23 U. CHI. L. REV. 682.

[234]Groddetsky v. McCrory Corporation (1966) N.Y.S. Ct., 267 N.Y.S. 2d 356, aff'd (1966) App. Div. N.Y.L.J., 12-2-66.

[235]See 41 CALIF. L. REV. 393, 496. For a complete discussion of this problem, see Aranow and Einhorn, "Proxy Contests for Corporate Control," Columbia University Press, 1973.

[236]Gottleib v. McKee, (1954) (Del. Ch.) 107 A. 2d 240; Hauth v. Giant Portland Cement Co., (1953) 33 Del. Ch. 496, 96 A. 2d 233.

[237]McKee v. Board of Directors, (1941) 60 Nev. 382, 110 P. 2d 212.

[238]Hauth v. Giant Portland Cement Co., (1953) 33 Del. Ch. 496, 96 A. 2d 233.

[239]McKee v. Board of Directors, (1941) 60 Nev. 382, 110 P. 2d 212.

May a proxy waive irregularities in a meeting, such as a defect in the notice of meeting? The answer is that in connection with matters upon which the proxy has the power to vote, he may act in respect to subsidiary questions, such as the waiving of irregularities in form.[240]

Where stockholders merely give a proxyholder the right to vote stock at an election, this does not imply that the latter has the authority to call a special stockholders' meeting.[241]

Effect of vote by proxy. A vote by proxy is as effective as though the stockholder had voted in person.[242] The stockholder is bound by the proxy's acts[243] even if the former had no knowledge of the matter acted upon, for knowledge of the proxy is chargeable to the stockholder.[244] The stockholder, however, may repudiate acts of the proxy committed in bad faith or in the exercise of unauthorized powers, if the interests of third parties are not adversely affected.[245] If he fails to repudiate such acts within a reasonable time, he is presumed to have ratified the vote of the proxy.[246] The stockholder is also bound by his proxy's ratification of action taken at a meeting.[247]

Duration and revocation of proxies. Some state statutes provide that proxies shall be limited in duration to a definite period of time.[248] In other states the statutes provide that a proxy shall expire after a designated period from the date of its execution, unless it expressly designates the length of time it is to continue in force. A proxy is, however, always revocable unless it is (1) coupled with an interest,[249] or (2) given as part of a security.[250] An irrevocable proxy or power of attorney to vote stock, if not coupled with an interest, is contrary to public policy.[251] And even though it

---

[240]Columbia Nat'l Bank v. Mathews, (1898) 85 F. 934.

[241]Josephson v. Cosmocolor Corp., (1949) 31 Del Ch. 46, 64 A. 2d 35.

[242]Goldboss v. Reimann, (1943) 55 F. Supp. 811, aff'd, memo dec., (1944) 143 F. 2d 594.

[243]Holmes v. Republic Steel Corp., (1946) 69 N.E. 2d 396, aff'd, (1948) 84 Ohio App. 442, 84 N.E. 2d 508.

[244]Gray v. Aspironal Laboratories, (1928) 24 F. 2d 97. See also McLean v. Bradley, (1924) 299 F. 379; Gottlieb v. McKee, (1945) Del. Ch. 107 A. 2d 240; Wellington Bull & Co. v. Morris, (1928) 132 N.Y. Misc. 509, 230 N.Y. Supp. 122; Chounis v. Laing, (1942) 125 W. Va. 275, 23 S.E. 2d 628.

[245]Blair v. F.H. Smith Co., (1931) 18 Del. Ch. 150, 156 A. 207; Lowman v. Harvey R. Pierce Co., (1923) 276 Pa. 382, 120 A. 404.

[246]Fidelity Bldg. & Loan Ass'n Thompson, (1930) (Tex. Civ. App.) 25 S.W. 2d 247. See also Rossing v. State Bank, (1917) 181 Iowa 1013. 165 N.W. 254.

[247]Chounis v. Laing, (1942) 125 W. Va. 275, 23 S.E. 2d 628.

[248]See Simpson v. Nielson, (1926) 77 Cal. App. 297, 246 P. 342.

[249]State ex rel. Everett Trust & Sav. Bank v. Pacific Waxed Paper Co., (1945) 22 Wash. 2d 844, 157 P. 2d 707; Stoelting Bros. Co. v. Stoelting, (1944) 246 Wis. 109, 16 N.W. 2d 367. See also Abercrombia v. Davies, (1956) (Del.) 123 A. 2d 893, modified, 125 A. 2d 588.

[250]State ex rel. Everett Trust & Sav. Bank v. Pacific Waxed Paper Co., (1945) 22 Wash. 2d 844, 157 P. 2d 707

[251]Roberts v. Whitson, (1945) (Tex. Civ. App.) 188 S.W. 2d 875.

is coupled with an interest, a statute can limit its duration to say, 10 years.[252]

Revocation need not be expressed or in writing. A proxy which is last given is deemed to be a revocation of all former proxies.[253] The voluntary dissolution of a corporation does not revoke an irrevocable proxy given by it as stockholder in another corporation.[254]

If a stockholder who executed a proxy attends the meeting and asserts his right to vote, the proxy is considered revoked, unless it is irrevocable because it is coupled with an interest.[255] If any question arises between a stockholder and his proxy, the corporation should always recognize the stockholder.[256] Irrevocable proxies can also give rise to tax problems. For example, a question arose whether a stockholder's grant of an irrevocable proxy affecting his voting power resulted in creation of a second class of shares so as to cause the corporation to lose its Subchapter S eligibility; the Tax Court held no, since the proxy did not change the reporting of relative shares of profits by stockholders.[257]

Voting trusts. A voting trust is the accumulation in a few hands of shares of stock belonging to many owners, in order to control the business of the corporation.[258] Such centralization of control of the affairs of a corporation may be found necessary or desirable upon organization, upon reorganization, upon merger or consolidation, in raising capital, or in carrying out any other corporate plan. It is used as a means of securing continuity of both management and company policy.[259]

Voting trusts are usually recognized as valid,[260] provided the trust is based upon a sufficient consideration, does not contravene public policy[261]

---

[252]Stein v. Capital Outdoor Advertising Inc. (1968) 273 N.C. 77, 159 S.E. 2d 351.

[253]Pope v. Whitridge, (1909) 110 Md. 468, 73 A. 281.

[254]State ex rel. Everett Trust & Sav. Bank v. Pacific Waxed Paper Co., (1945) 22 Wash. 2d 844, 157 P. 2d 707

[255]State ex rel. Breger v. Rusche, (1942) 219 Ind. 559, 39 N.E. 2d 433.

[256]Sylvania & Girard R.R. v. Hoge, (1907) 129 Ga. 734, 59 S.E. 806.

[257]Parker Oil Co., Inc. v. C.I.R. (1972) 58 T.C. No. 95.

[258]Alderman v. Alderman, (1935) 178 S.C. 9, 181 S.E. 897. For a discussion of the subject of voting trusts, see Finkelstein, "Voting Trust Agreements," 24 Mich. L. Rev. 344; Cushing, "Voting Trusts," 40 Harv. L. Rev. 106; Case, "Legal Characteristics and Consequences of Voting Trusts," 20 Wash. L. Rev. 129.

Whether a particular agreement is a voting trust must ordinarily be determined from the provisions of the instrument, read, as a whole. Aldridge v. Franco Wyoming Oil Co., (1939) 24 Del. Ch. 126, 7A. 2d 753, aff'd (1940) 24 Del. Ch. 349, 14A 2d 380. See also Peyton v. William C. Peyton Corp., (1937) 22 Del. Ch. 187, 194 A. 106. A voting trust agreement is distinguished from a stock-pooling agreement in Ringling v. Ringling Bros., Inc. (1946) 29 Del. Ch. 318, 49 A. 2d 603, modified (1947) 29 Del. Ch. 610, 53 A. 2d 441.

[259]In rel Election of Directors of Baldwinsville Federal Sav. & Loan Ass'n (1944) 268 App. Div. 414, 1024, 51 N.Y.S. 2d 816.

[260]Mackin v. Nicollet Hotel, Inc., (1928) 25 F. 2d 783, cert. den., 278 U.S. 618, 45 Sup. Ct. 22; Odman v. Odman, (1946) 319 Mass 24, 26, 64 N.E. 2d 439, 440. See also Delaney, "The Corporate Director," 50 Colum. L. Rev. 240.

[261]Chandler v. Bellanca Aircraft Corp., (1932) 19 Del. Ch. 57, 162 A. 63; Alderman v. Alderman, (1935) 178 S.C. 9, 181 S.E. 897.

or a positive prohibitory statute,[262] and is made in good faith.[263] The statutes of several states specifically authorize the creation of voting trusts by stockholders. These statutes vary in their provisions and should be consulted when a voting trust is being created, for it has been held that a trust which is not within the terms of the statute is not valid.[264] Even in states where the voting trusts are not specifically sanctioned by statute, they have been recognized by the courts.[265]

Voting trust agreement and rights of parties to the voting agreement. The voting trust is generally organized and operated under a voting trust agreement. No particular form of agreement is required, though statutes generally provide they must be in writing.[266] Also, nearly every statute imposes one formal requirement for the creation of a voting trust: a record of the agreement must be filed with the corporation. The statute must be carefully followed as to the kind of record to be filed. Thus, if the statute says that a duplicate of the agreement must be filed, a photostatic copy will not do.[267] Even when failure to file does not void a voting trust, the trust will be inoperative while that failure persists.[268] However, under a more lenient view, failure to file will not invalidate the voting trust agreement, as long as that failure does not adversely affect parties outside the agreement.[269]

The voting trust agreement is entered into between the stockholders of the corporation and the voting trustees, irrevocably conferring upon the voting trustees the right to vote the stock for the period fixed in the agreement.[270] The stock is transferred to the trustees, and the names of the trustees are entered on the books of the corporation as the owners entitled to vote.[271] The trustees, in turn, issue to the stockholders certificates of beneficial interest, and the stockholders are entitled to the cash dividends, if any, paid on the stock.[272] The holder of a voting trust certificate does not

---

[262]Abercrombia v. Davies, (1957) (Del.) 130 A. 2d 338.

[263]Perrine v. Pennroad Corp., (1934) 20 Del. Ch. 106, 171 A. 733.

[264]Abercrombie v. Davies, (1957) Del. 130 A. 2d 338; Gertenbach v. Rodnon, (1939) 171 N.Y. Misc. 302, 12 N.Y.S. 2d 518 N.Y. Misc. 302, 12 N.Y.S. 2d 518. See also Prentice-Hall *Corporation*. Prentice-Hall *Corporation*.

[265]Gumbiner v. Alden Inn, Inc., (1945) 289 Ill 273, 59 N.E. 2d 648.

[266]See Wygood v. Makewell Hats, Inc., (1942) 265 App. Div. 286, 38 N.Y.S. 2d 587; see also Prentice-Hall *Corporation*.

[267]State v. Keystone Life Ins. Co. (1957) La. Ct. of App., 93 So. 2d 565.

[268]De Marco v. Paramount Ice Corp. (1950) N.Y.S. Ct., 102 N.Y.S. 2d 692.

[269]In the Matter of Farm Industries, Inc. (1963) Del. Ch. Ct., Civ. No. 1824, 11-20-63.

[270]Stockholders may tell the trustees for whom they should vote, but a voting trust agreement executed by common stockholders cannot provide for alteration of voting rights of preferred stockholders fixed by the charter, by-laws, and statute. Seward v. American Hardware Co., (1933) 161 Va. 610, 171 S.E. 650.

[271]Smith v. First Personal Bankers' Corporation, (1934) 20 Del. Ch. 89, 171 A. 839.

[272]These certificates are sometimes called "capital stock trust certificates." For the necessity of registering voting trust certificates with the Securities and Exchange Commission under the Securities Act of 1933, as amended, and for official forms required for registration, see Prentice-Hall *Securities Regulation*.

The certificates also represent the holder's equitable interest in any stock dividends subsequently allotted.

have the rights of a stockholder and is bound by the acts of the voting trustees executed in good faith and within the scope of their authority.[273] The right to vote is thereby separated from the beneficial ownership of the stock, but not from the legal or registered ownership.[274]

Legal title to the shares and the right to vote them are in the trustees as owners, not as proxies.[275] Further, a voting trustee can validly vote Class A voting stock that is converted from Class B non-voting stock for election of directors: delivery of B shares to the trustee makes the corporation no longer the beneficial owner, so later conversion is permitted under the charter.[276] Failure to deliver the stock to the trustees does not invalidate the voting trust.[277] After a voting trust is terminated, the trustees cannot take any action under it.[278]

Provisions of the voting trust agreement; termination. Provision may be made for the appointment of a depositary[279] to receive the deposited stock, and for the appointment of a transfer agent and registrar to effect transfers[280] of the voting trust certificates. Other provisions regulating the rights, duties, and liabilities of the various parties to the agreement are also found in the voting trust agreement.

When the duration of a voting trust is regulated by statute, a trust agreement for a longer period is usually invalid,[281] but the agreement may fix a time shorter than that allowed by statute.[282] A state law limiting the duration applies to reorganizations under the Bankruptcy Act as well as to reorganizations under state law.[283] The statement in a voting trust agreement that it is irrevocable does not prevent its revocation;[284] nor does the power to amend include the power to extend the life of the voting trust

---

[273]Scott v. Arden Farms Co., (1942) 26 Del. Ch. 283, 28 A. 2d 81. The voting trust certificate holder cannot inspect corporate books unless the right is specifically given. State ex rel. Crowder v. Sperry Corp., (1940) 41 Del. Ch. 84, 15 A. 2d 661. But see Brentmore Estates, Inc. v. Hotel Barbison, Inc., (1942) 263 App. Div. 389, 33 N.Y.S. 2d 331.

[274]Kann v. Rossett, (1940) 307 Ill. App. 153, 30 N.E. 2d 204; Ecclestone v. Indialantic, Inc., (1947) 319 Mich. 248, 29 N.W. 2d 679., comment, 61 HARV. L. REV. 1062; 47 MICH. L. REV. 547.

[275]Dougherty v. Cross, (1944) 65 Cal. App. 2d 654; Johnson v. Spartanburg County Fair Ass'n, (1947) 210 S.C. 56, 41 S.E. 2d 599.

[276]Sundlum v. Executive Jet Aviation, Inc. (1970) Del. Ch. Ct., 273 A. 2d 282.

[277]Boericke v. Weise, (1945) 68 Ca. App. 2d 407, 156 P. 2d 781.

[278]Brown v. McLanahan, (1945) 148 F. 2d 703; Clemmer v. Morgan, (1951) 77 Pa. D. & C. 405.

[279]The depositary may be a party to the agreement.

[280]As to the transferability of voting trust certificates, see Union Trust Co. v. Oliver, (1915) 214 N.Y. 517, 108 N.E. 809. An unreasonable restriction on the transfer of a voting trust certificate is void. Tracey v. Franklin, (949) 31 Del. Ch. 477, 67 A. 2d 56, companion case, (1949) 31 Del. Ch. 510, 70 A. 2d 250.

[281]In re Elless, (1949) 174 F. 2d 926; Brown v. McLanahan, (1945) 148 F. 2d 703; Olson v. Rossetter, (1948) 399 Ill. 232 77 N.E. 2d 652.

[282]In re Elless, (1949) 174 F. 2d 926.

[283]Bakers Share Corp. v. London Terrace, Inc., (1942) 130 F. 2d 157.

[284]H.M. Byllesby & Co., v. Doriot, (1940) 25 Del. Ch. 46, 12 A. 2d 603.

agreement.[285] If money is loaned on faith of the voting trust agreement, it cannot be terminated before its expiration date.[286]

CONDUCTING THE VOTE

Methods of taking the vote—Ballot. A vote is merely a means of ascertaining the will of the body casting the vote. Where the statute requires a ballot,[287] this should be provided.[288] Otherwise the consensus of the meeting may be taken either by a showing of hands or by a viva voce vote. Where there is a dissent, neither a showing of hands nor a viva voce vote is satisfactory, for they indicate the per capita desires of the stockholders but not the per share determination of the question. The will of the shareholders may be taken by a reading of the roll, and a count of the per share vote may be made in that way. (See page 119 for form of demand that a vote be taken by ballot.)

Where a ballot is used, any form is satisfactory if it shows the number of shares voted, the persons for whom they are voted, and the name of the person casting the ballot. For forms of ballots, see pages 120-121.

Where the written consent of stockholders to any action is required, a document setting forth the consent should be prepared and signed by the stockholders, with an indication of the shares held by each stockholder.

Per capita and stock vote. At common law, each member of a corporation was entitled to one vote. Today, however, the general rule is that each stockholder is entitled to one vote for each share of stock that he owns,[289] unless the statute, charter, or by-laws provide otherwise. But income beneficiaries of a testamentary trust cannot petition for dissolution of a corporation in which the trust owns shares, since only holders of shares with voting rights can file such a petition; they are not such shareholders.[290] A by-law provision that no stockholder shall vote for more than one director is void, if the statute gives the stockholder the right to cast one vote for each of his shares for each director to be elected.[291] The holder of a fractional share cannot vote it in the absence of a specific statutory

---

[285]Olson v. Rossetter, (1948) 399 Ill. 232, 77 N.E. 2d 652.

[286]Hearst v. American Newspaper, Inc., (1943) 51 F. Supp. 171; Thomas v. Kliesen, (1949) 166 Kan. 337, 201 P. 2d 663.

[287]As used in the statutes, a ballot is a "paper so prepared by printing or writing thereon as to show the voter's choice." In re Mathiason Mfg. Co., (1907) 122 Mo. App. 437, 99 S.W. 502.

[288]A ballot is specifically required by statute in some states for the election of directors. See Prentice-Hall *Corporation*.

[289]State ex rel. Cullitan v. Campbell, (1939) 135 Ohio St. 238, 20 N.E. 2d 366; State ex rel. Chapman v. Urschel, (1922) 104 Ohio St. 172, 135 N.E. 630; State ex rel. Fritz v. Gray, (1925) 20 Ohio App. 26, 153 N.E. 187.

[290]Turner v. Flynn & Emrich Co. of Baltimore City (1973) Md. Ct. of Appeals, 306 A. 2d 218.

[291]In re Crown Heights Hospital, Inc., (1944) 183 N.Y. Misc. 563, 49 N.Y.S. 2d 658.

provision.[292] In some states, a corporation may be organized with shares that carry multiple voting rights.[293]

See voting restrictions on stock, on page 442 in Chapter 15.

Cumulative voting. Since a stockholder is entitled to cast a number of votes equal to the number of shares he owns, it would be possible for a single stockholder owning a majority of stock to elect all the directors. To avoid such a situation, and to give the minority the opportunity to be represented on the board of directors, a system known as cumulative voting has been devised. Under this plan, each shareholder is entitled to as many votes as are equal to the number of shares he owns multiplied by the number of directors to be elected. He may cumulate the votes—that is, cast all the votes for one candidate—or he may distribute his votes among the candidates in any way he sees fit.

To illustrate, let us take as an example a corporation with 100 shares of which the majority controls 51 shares and the minority 49 shares. The faction strength is nearly equal. If 5 directors are to be elected, the majority is entitled to 255 votes (51 × 5) and the minority to 245 votes (49 × 5). If the majority contents itself with casting this cumulative vote for three out of five directors, it can secure their election by giving each director 85 votes. The minority may elect only two directors by giving one of the directors 122 votes and another 123 votes. In this case, if the majority frittered away its strength among the five directors, while the minority concentrated its strength upon four, the minority would gain control of the board.[294]

The right to cumulative voting cannot be claimed unless that method of voting is provided for by law, or unless the statute permits the corporation's charter or by-laws to make such a provision.[295] In some states, the law requires that directors be elected by cumulative voting. Such a "mandatory" provision secures the right of cumulative voting to the stockholder regardless of any provision to the contrary in the corporate charter or by-laws.[296] In other states, cumulative voting is permitted when the certificate of incorporation or the by-laws so provide.[297] A corporation that renewed articles under an old statute providing for cumulative voting,

---

[292]Commonwealth ex rel. Cartwright v. Cartwright, (1944) 350 Pa. 638, 40 A. 2d 30; Op. Atty. Gen., (N.Y.) to Sec'y of State, 12/9/46; Op. Atty. Gen. (Pa.) to Sec'y of Banking, 11/30/46, 94 PITTSBURGH LEG. J. 458.

[293]Op. Atty. Gen. (Minn.) to Sec'y of State, 3/30/44; Op. Atty. Gen. (N.C.) to Sec'y of State, 3/25/44.

[294]See State ex rel. Price v. Du Brul, (1919) 100 Ohio St. 272, 126 N.E. 87.

[295]Brooks v. State ex rel. Richards, (1911) 26 Del. 1, 79 A. 790; A by-law is ineffective to confer cumulative voting on the stockholders if the statute requires that the charter make provision therefor. In re Brophy, (1935) 13 N.J. Misc. 462, 179 A. 128. All by-laws with regard to voting rights must be consistent with the statute and with provisions in the articles of incorporation on the subject. In re American Fibre Chair Seat Corp., (1934) 241 App. Div. 532, 272 N.Y. Supp. 206, aff'd, 265 N.Y. 416, 193 N.E. 253; State v. Perham, (1948) 30 Wash. 2d 368, 191 P. 2d 689.

[296]Commonwealth ex rel. Laughlin v. Green, (1945) 351 Pa. 170, 40 A 2d 492.

[297]Quilliam v. Hebbronville Utilities, (1951) (Tex. Civ. App.) 241 S.W. 2d 225.

but failed to amend articles under a new statute to eliminate cumulative voting by simple majority vote instead of unanimous vote required under the new statute, could not take away the shareholder's right to cumulate votes at the election of officers.[298]

The chairman should announce at the beginning of the meeting whether or not cumulative voting is permitted.[299] It is not necessary for a stockholder, or a director, to inform the other stockholders that he intends to cumulate his vote.[300]

Classification of directors. Classification of directors, or a "staggered directorate," occurs when the directors of a corporation are divided into two or more classes with terms of office expiring at different times. A staggered directorate is designed to provide corporations with experienced personnel and to preserve stability and continuity of management.[301] The statutes of a majority of the states permit classification. Many statutes also require classification of directors in certain types of corporations.[302]

Conflict between classification and cumulative voting. The effect of staggering the terms of directors is to reduce the number of director-candidates to be elected at any given time. Hence it may be employed as a device to "dilute" the stockholders' cumulative voting right and to make it more difficult for minority stockholders to be represented on the board. In jurisdictions where the annual election of all directors is required by statute, this problem does not arise.[303] But in jurisdictions where the state constitution makes cumulative voting mandatory, but the statutes also provide for classification of directors, an unresolved conflict has occurred.[304] Some state courts have reached the conclusion that the cumulative voting right is designed to give the minority representation on the board proportional to its strength, and thus a constitutional provision for cumulative voting nullifies statutory provision for classification.[305] Yet another state high court has interpreted the constitutional provision for cumulative voting as only granting the right of cumulative voting but not purporting to insure the maximum effectiveness of the exercise of that right.[306] This latter result was also reached in a state with *statutes* making

---

[298]Golconda Mining Corp. v. Helca Mining Co. (1972) Wash. S. Ct., 80 Wash. 2d 372.

[299]See Zachary v. Milin, (1940) 294) 294 Mich. 622, 293 N.W. 770.

[300]Commonwealth ex rel. Laughlin v. Green, (1945) 351 Pa. 170, 40 A. 2d 492.

[301]Janney v. Philadelphia Transp. Co., (1956) 387 Pa. 282, 128 A. 2d 76.

[302]Matter of Baldwinsville Fed. Sav. & Loan Ass'n, (1944) 268 App. Div. 414, 51 N.Y.S. 2d 816.

[303]Alabama, California and Wyoming.

[304]See Sell and Fuge, "Impact of Classified Corporate Directorates on the Constitutional Right of Cumulative Voting," 17 U. Pitt. L. Rev. 151. See also Prentice-Hall *Corporation*.

[305]Wolfson v. Avery, (1955) 6 Ill. 2d 78, 126 N.E. 2d 701; State ex rel. Syphers v. McCune, (1958) (W.Va.) 101 S.E. 2d 834.

[306]Janney v. Philadelphia Transp. Co., (1956) 387 Pa. 282, 128 A. 2d 76. See Williams, "Cumulative Voting for Directors," 50 HARV. BUS. REV. 48; 22 U. CHI. L. REV. 751.

cumulative voting mandatory but at the same time permitting classification.[307]

Method of determining shares needed to elect certain number. Often it becomes necessary to determine how many shares one should hold or control under the system of cumulative voting to insure the election of a certain number of directors. The following method may be used: (1) Multiply the total number of shares entitled to vote by the number of directors it is desired to elect; (2) divide this product by one more than the total number of directors to be elected; (3) add one to the quotient. The result will be the least number of shares of stock that must be held or controlled in order to elect the desired number of directors. Thus, if a company has outstanding 1,000 voting shares, 5 directors are to be elected, and it is desired to elect 2 out of the 5, the least number of shares that it will be necessary to hold or to control in order to accomplish this result will be found by multiplying 1,000 by 2, and dividing the product (2,000) by one more than the number of directors to be elected (5 + 1, or 6), giving a result of 333⅓. To this is added 1, giving 334⅓. The desired result, therefore, will be actually accomplished only if 335 shares are held or controlled. (Where there is a fraction, it is to be counted as an extra share.)[308]

Other methods of voting. Methods of voting other than those described above may be prescribed by the certificate of incorporation.[309] For example, the holders of a certain class of stock may be given ten votes for the first ten shares and one vote for each ten shares thereafter, until a maximum of one hundred shares is reached, whereupon voting rights in respect to shares cease.

Sometimes the statutes make special provisions regarding the right to vote, as, for example, that stockholders who are in arrears or who are in debt to the company may not vote, or that stockholders whose stock has been attached may vote until title is divested.

Votes necessary for an election of directors. In the absence of special provision in the statute, charter, or by-laws, a majority of the votes cast, as distinguished from a majority of those present, will decide the result of an election.[310] This rule applies even if those voting do not

---

[307]Humphrey v. Winous Co., (1956) 165 Ohio St. 45, 133 N.E. 2d 780.

[308]The result can be obtained by algebra if the following formula is used:

$$x = \frac{ac}{b+1} + 1$$

where x is the number of shares required, a the total voting shares, c the number of directors it is desired to elect, and b the number of directors to be elected.

[309]Op. Att'y Gen. (Minn.) to Sec'y of State, 3/30/44.

[310]Investment Associates, Inc. v. Standard Power & Light Corp., (1946) 29 Del. Ch. 225, 48 A. 2d 501; Stratford v. Mallory, (1904) 70 N.J.L. 294, 58 A. 347; Beardsley v. Johnson, (1890) 121 N.Y. 224, 241 N.E. 380. Contra: Commonwealth v. Wickersham, (1870) 66 Pa. 134.

constitute a majority of all the stockholders, or do not represent a majority of the stock.[311] A charter provision that is intended to abrogate the general rule must be clear and explicit.[312] A statutory provision permitting cumulative voting takes precedence over a statutory provision requiring the vote of a majority of the number of shares for election of directors; the latter provision must be considered to apply only where the shares are voted without cumulating.[313]

Votes necessary to decide questions other than election. A majority of those present at a legal meeting may generally take action at the meeting, even though this majority may be less than a majority in number of stockholders and less than a majority in amount of stock.[314] This rule does not hold, of course, if the statute, charter, or by-laws require a specific number of votes to decide a question. In such cases, the express requirement must be met.[315] Charter or by-law provisions calling for a greater vote than the statutes require have been upheld.[316]

Where the consent of the stockholders is being obtained in accordance with a statutory requirement, care should be exercised to determine just what proportion of the corporate stock is necessary to carry the proposal. A provision in the statute or by-laws requiring the approval of "a majority of the stockholders" upon a particular question has been held to mean a majority in interest of the stockholders, and not a majority in number only.[317] But the more general view is that the term "a majority of the stockholders," as ordinarily used, means a per capita majority when the right to vote is per capita, and a stock majority when each share of stock is entitled to vote.[318] Stock that is void because it has been illegally issued cannot be counted when determining whether a proposition has been carried by the required vote.[319]

---

[311]In re Rapid Transit Ferry Co., (1897) 15 App. Div. 530, 44 N.Y. Supp. 539.

[312]A charter requirement that directors shall be elected by the "vote of the majority in number of shares issued and outstanding" is not clear enough to abrogate the general rule. Standard Power & Light Corp. v. Investment Associates, Inc., (1947) 29 Del. Ch. 593, 51 A. 2d 572.

[313]Schwartz v. State, (1900) 61 Ohio St. 497, 56 N.E. 201.

[314]Green v. Felton, (1908) 42 Ind. App. 675, 84 N.E. 166; Green River Mfg. Co. v. Bell, (1927) 193 N.C. 367, 137 S.E. 132, and cases there cited.

[315]In re Boulevard Theatre & Realty Co., (1921) 195 App. Div. 518, 186 N.Y. Supp. 430.

[316]Sellers v. Joseph Bancroft & Sons Co., (1938) 23 Del. Ch. 13.2 A 2d 108, comment 37 MICH. L. REV. 803, aff'd, (1941) 25 Del. Ch. 268, 17 A. 2d 831.

In N.Y. a by-law requiring the unanimous vote of stockholders for certain corporate acts was invalidated because it was inconsistent with statutory provisions giving a prescribed percentage of stockholders the control of those matters. Benintendi v. Kenton Hotel, Inc., (1945) 294 N.Y. 112, 60 N.E. 2d 829. (The statute was subsequently amended to permit charter provisions calling for greater percentage.)

[317]Bank of Los Banos v. Jordan, (1914) 167 Cal. 327, 139 P. 691.

[318]Simon Borg & Co. v. New Orleans City R.R., (1917) 244 F. 617., following Mower v. Staples, (1884) 32 Minn. 284, 20 N.W. 225.

[319]Bentley v. Zelma Oil Co., (1919) 76 Okla. 116, 184 P, 131.

In some cases, the statute is so worded that the percentage of consent required is a percentage of the total amount of stock outstanding, irrespective of the classes into which the stock is divided. In other cases, certain percentages of each of the several classes of stock are required. Sometimes the statutes require that the consent be obtained from stockholders having the right to vote. In other cases, the statutes provide that the consent be obtained from the stockholders, and the question as to whether stock which is ordinarily nonvoting has the right to participate in the action is left open. It would seem that nonvoting stock should have the right to vote in any matter specifically affecting the rights of the holders thereof, unless the statute is very clear in indicating that their consent is not required.

Tie votes. The following illustration explains the effect of a tie vote. Five directors, let us say, are to be elected by cumulative voting. Six candidates have been named. Four hundred votes have been cast. Suppose that candidates A and B each receives 80 votes, and candidates C, D, E, and F each receives 60 votes. What is the result of the election? The chairman of the meeting may not declare that no board has been elected and that the old directors shall continue in office.[320] A and B will be considered elected,[321] and the chairman must permit the stockholders to vote again and again, if necessary, until it is demonstrated that further balloting is futile.

The same rules apply in the following situation: Suppose there are 100 shares of stock to be voted by straight voting, that is, one vote for each share. These shares are divided among four stockholders as follows: Jones, 2 shares; Smith, 25 shares; Brown, 40 shares; and Grey, 33 shares. The by-laws require that directors must be elected by a majority of the votes cast. Three directors are to be elected and there are six candidates. Each stockholder would have as many votes for each of three directors as he has shares. The votes cannot be split among the six candidates. The voting shows the following results: A, 100 votes; B, 100 votes; C, 2 votes; D, 25 votes; E, 40 votes; and F, 33 votes. A and B are considered elected and the balloting continues for the election of a third director.

Where the votes are divided between two factions, it is inadvisable for either faction to remain silent or to refuse to vote while the other faction votes, for by so doing the voting group is enabled to carry the election.[322]

If less than a majority of the board is elected, those elected cannot be inducted into office, and the old directors hold over until their successors

---

[320]State ex rel. Price v. Du Brul, (1919) 100 Ohio St. 272, 126 N.E. 87.
[321]Ibid.
[322]Ibid.

are elected.[323] But if a majority of the board has been elected, this number is sufficient to constitute a new board of directors, provided that the election is valid. The entire old board steps out, the elected majority assumes the duties of the board, and the places of directors not filled at the election are considered vacant.[324] The manner of electing directors to fill such vacancies in the board is discussed on page 275.

Election of directors. The statutes generally vest in the stockholders the right to elect a board of directors annually.[325] When the charter or a statute requires an annual election of directors by the stockholders, the election must in that case take place once a year.[326] The right to elect directors cannot be taken away from the stockholders by any act of either the directors or the officers.[327] Stockholders, however, may agree to vote for certain persons as directors.[328]

In some of the states, the statutes regulate the manner of electing directors. Where this is the case, the statutory direction cannot be modified by charter or by-law or by any other regulation. Thus, if the statute provides that directors shall be chosen at the time and place of meeting fixed by the by-laws, by a plurality of the votes at such meeting, the corporation cannot, by a charter provision or by-law, require that the vote of a majority of the total stock shall be necessary to elect directors; or that a majority of the stock shall vote at the election; or that directors can be elected only by unanimous vote of the stockholders.[329] Neither may the corporation, under such a statute, by fixing the amount of stock necessary to constitute a quorum, enable stockholders to defeat an election by staying away from the meeting.[330]

---

[323]Freidus v. Kaufman, (1955) 35 N.J. Super. 601, 114 A 2d 751, aff'd, memo dec., 36 N.J. Super. 321, 115 A 2d 592.

[324]State v. Gray, (1925) 20 Ohio App. 26, 153 N.E. 187, State ex rel. Price v. Du Brul, (1919) Ohio St. 272, 126 N.E. 87.

[325]See Finkelstein, "The Conduct of Corporate Elections," 17 St. John's L. Rev. 75.

[326]State ex rel. Curtis v. McCullough, (1867) 3 Nev. 202. Where the by-laws set the election date, the directors empowered to change the by-laws may postpone the election. Barker v. National Life Ins. Ass'n, (1918) 183 Iowa 966, 166 N.W. 597.

[327]State v. Cronan, (1897) 23 Nev. 437, 49 P. 41. The refusal of the president to preside at the meeting or to permit the stockholders to use the office of the company for the meeting was illegal. The stockholders had the right to proceed with the business of the meeting without the president, and to adjourn the meeting to another room.

[328]Davis v. Arguls Gas & Oil Sales Co., (1938) 167 N.Y. Misc. 377, 3 N.Y.S. 2d 241; Williams v. Fredericks, (1937) 187 La. 987, 175 So. 642; Benintendi v. Kenton Hotel, (1945) 294 N.Y. 112, 60 N.E. 2d 829.

[329]In re Boulevard Theatre & Realty Co., (1921) 195 App. Div. 518, 186 N.Y. Supp. 430.; Benintendi v. Kenton Hotel, (1945) 294 N.Y. 112, 60 N.E. 2d 829.

[330]Matter of P.F. Keogh, Inc., (1920) 192 App. Div. 624, 183 N.Y. Supp. 408.

It is not necessary to elect all of the required number of directors at one meeting.[331] In electing directors nominations need not be seconded. A motion to close the nominations may be made and put to a vote at any time. No person has the right to make nominations after they have been voted closed,[332] but this does not prevent the casting of ballots for other persons. Ordinarily a person can be elected to office through "write-ins" of his name on the ballot.[333] Where the election is unanimous, the secretary may cast a ballot for the slate. The ballot is deemed a vote from all voting stock represented at the meeting, and the election is recorded accordingly.

Effect of announcing the vote. The polls may be kept open for a prescribed period during which votes will be taken. After the polls are closed and the vote is announced, they cannot be reopened to receive additional votes.[334] The election is not vitiated, however, if, after the polls are closed, additional votes are received, provided that the election results have not been announced.[335] This means a formal announcement by the chairman or secretary.[336] Thus, an announcement by another stockholder, or by the teller to a majority stockholder, does not prevent a stockholder from changing his vote or from voting additional proxies.[337]

The final results of an election may not be announced until the time has arrived for the closing of the polls, unless a majority of all voting stock has been voted in favor of a slate. Any stockholder may change his vote at any time before the results of the election are announced.[338] If cumulative voting is permitted, a stockholder may change his vote to vote cumulatively.[339] No election can be declared closed until the presiding officer so announces.[340] Further, a minority of stockholders can not call a new meeting and elect directors after the annual meeting has adjourned for lack of quorum; the by-law that lets them adjourn to a future date applies

---

[331] Great Falls, etc. Ry. v. Ganong, (1913) 48 Mont. 54 136 P. 390; State ex rel. Price v. Du Brul, (1919) 100 Ohio St. 272, 126 N.E. 87. See also page 41.

[332] This rule carries with it the corollary that no person can thereafter address the assemblage on the merits of any candidates. See Moon v. Moon Motor Car Co., (1930) 17 Del. Ch. 176, 151 A. 298.

[333] Commonwealth ex rel. Laughlin v. Green, (1945) 351 Pa. 170, 40 A 2d 492.

[334] State ex rel. David v. Dailey, (1945) 23 Wash. 2d 25. 158 P. 2d 330.

[335] Ibid.

[336] Zachary v. Milin, (1940) 290 Mich. 622, 293 N.W. 770.

[337] State ex rel. David v. Dailey, (1945) 23 Wash. 2d 25, 158 P. 2d 330; Zachary v. Milin, (1940) 290 Mich. 622, 293 N.W. 770. See also Young v. Jebbett, (1925) 213 App. Div. 774, 211 N.Y. Supp. 61, in which it was held that proxies which had been overlooked through error, and had not therefore been voted, could be accepted after the polls were closed, but during the time the meeting was still in existence awaiting the report of the judges, there having been no indication that the proxies were irregular.

[338] Young v. Jebbett, (1925) 213 App. Div. 774, 211 N.Y. Supp. 61: Zachary v. Milin. (1940) 294 Mich. 622, 293 N.W. 770.

[339] Zachary v. Milin, (1940) 294 Mich. 622, 293 N.W. 770.

[340] Ibid.

only when a stockholder has moved to set a new date before the presiding officer declares the annual meeting over.[341]

Effect of failure to elect directors. The statutes generally provide that if no election is held on the day designated for the election of directors, the corporation is not thereby dissolved, but the directors continue to hold office and must discharge their duties until their successors have been elected. A hold-over director, in the absence of any resignation, is deemed a director to the same extent as during the year for which he was elected.[342] His term of office ends when his successor is elected.[343] The statutes generally direct that another meeting for the election of directors be held as soon after the day fixed by the by-laws for election as may be convenient, or within a certain number of days thereafter.[344]

Disputes as to result of election of directors. Disputes as to the result of the election of directors frequently involve disputes concerning the eligibility of voters. Where the power is not given to him by the charter or by-laws,[345] the president or chairman of the meeting has no right to determine who shall vote. Where no provision is made, the stockholders may determine the eligibility of voters by a vote. Their decision, of course, may be reviewed by the court.[346] (In regard to the right of inspectors of election to determine the eligibility of voters, see page 49.) An election or other action at a corporate meeting is not considered void unless the votes illegally cast change the result.[347]

In settling disputes between stockholders claiming the right to vote, the meeting must be guided by the corporate records or the list of stockholders prepared for the meeting. The officers of the corporation need not look beyond the books to ascertain who are the real owners of the shares, although a court of equity will do so in a dispute in which it is seeking to settle rights between the claimants as such.[348] If one of the stockholders claims that the record is not correct, he may apply to a court of equity for a writ compelling the acceptance of his vote. This writ must be obtained

---

[341]State ex. rel. Industrial Finance Limited v. Yanagawa (1971) Haw. S. Ct., No. 5098, 5-3-71.

[342]Turp v. Dickinson, (1926) 100 N.J. Eq. 41, 134 A. 888. (1941) N.Y.L.J., 11-10-41, P. 1448, col. 2.

[343]In re Warns, see Note 7. But see Note 331.

[344]This is also the rule by judicial opinion. See Dowdle v. Central Brick Co., (1934) 206 Ind. 242, 189 N.E. 145; Estel v. Midgard Inv. Co., (1932) (Mo.) 46 S.W. 2d. 193.

[345]In re Robert Clarke, Inc., (1919) 186 App. Div. 216, 174 N.Y. Supp. 314.

[346]State ex rel. Martin v. Chute, (1885) 34 Minn. 135, 24 N.W. 353.

[347]Vanderlip v. Los Molinos Land Co., (1943) 56 Cal. App. 2d 747, 133 P. 2d 467; Beutelspacher v. Spokane Sav. Bank, (1931) 164 Wash. 227, 2 P. 2d 729. When votes cast under an invalid voting trust decided the result of an election, the election was void. Appon v. Belle Isle Corp., (1946) 29 Del. Ch. 122, 46 A. 2d 749.

[348]Application of Sugarman, (1954) 133 N.Y.S. 2d 754.

before the meeting and must be presented to the chairman; in the absence of such writ, the stockholders of record on the books of the corporation will be given the right to vote.

In some states, disputed elections are regulated by law. Where a dispute arises over the ownership of shares and hence over the right to vote, a court of equity will take jurisdiction to enjoin an election pending settlement of the dispute.[349] Where two elections are held by rival factions, the first faction that regularly organizes and carries its election will prima facie be recognized; the other faction is, of course, entitled to its day in court on the question of irregularities.[350] It has been held, however, that the courts may decide a dispute of this kind by considering the effect of the votes at the two meetings as though they were combined.[351] Moreover, in a proper case, an equity court will appoint a master to conduct the election.[352]

Inspectors of election. Many states have statutes calling for the election of directors to be conducted by appointed inspectors or judges of election. If the inspectors are absent or refuse to act, it is lawful for the stockholders or the proxies present to appoint inspectors by a per capita vote.[353] In the absence of a statutory, charter, or by-law requirement, inspectors are not essential, although the stockholders present or represented at the meeting may appoint such at their discretion.[354] Unless the statutes or by-laws otherwise provide, an inspector need not be a stockholder, nor is he disqualified because he is a candidate for office or holds an office. However, in New Jersey and Pennsylvania, a candidate for office cannot be an inspector.[355] An election is not void if the inspectors are not sworn, even if they are required by statute to be sworn.[356]

The by-laws may provide that inspectors shall conduct the vote not only for the election of directors, but for other questions that are put to vote. If the appointment of inspectors of election is not specifically required by the statute, charter, or by-laws, and a division of the vote is expected, the chairman generally appoints tellers to count the ballots. Since tellers are not required to report the results of election under oath, it is advisable for the chairman to permit anyone who disputes the count to examine the ballots in

[349]Villamil v. Hirsch, (1905) 138 F. 690, 143 F. 654.

[350]Commonwealth ex rel. Sheip v. Vandergrift, (1911) 232 Pa. 53, 81 A. 153.

[351]In re Cedar Grove Cemetery Co., (1898) 61 N.J.L. 422, 39 A. 1024.

[352]Tunis v. Hestonville, etc. R.R. (1892) 149 Pa. St. 70, 24 A. 88. Bartlett v. Gates, (1902) 118 F. 66. See also Wyatt V. Armstrong, (1945) 186 N.Y. Misc. 216, 59 N.Y.S. 2d 502.

[353]Gow v. Consolidated Coppermines Corp., (1933) 19 Del. Ch. 172, 165 A. 136; In re Remington Typewriter Co., (1922) 234 N.Y. 296, 137 N.E. 335

[354]In re Remington Typewriter Co., (1922) 234 N.Y. 296, 137 N.E. 335.

[355]N.J.G.C.L. 14-10-14; Pa. B.C. L.S. 512.

[356]In re Zenitherm Co., (1921) 95 N.J.L. 297, 113 A. 327. But if the right of the inspector to act is questioned at the time, he must be sworn, or all his actions are invalid. State v. Merchant, (1881) 37 Ohio 251.

the company of the tellers. If any stockholder who is present at the meeting objects to the way in which the votes are being counted, he may always make a motion directing that inspectors administer the election; and then the will of the meeting as expressed in the result of the motion will be binding, provided that the transaction is not tainted with fraud.

Powers of inspectors of election. Where an election of directors is conducted by inspectors of election, the latter distribute the ballots, collect them, count the vote, and report the result of the election under oath. The inspectors are ministerial, not judicial, officers.[357] Ordinarily they are bound by the corporate records and cannot question the right of a registered owner to vote stock standing in his name on the books of the corporation.[358] Within the scope of their function, inspectors may exercise some discretion.[359] For example, they may pass upon the eligibility of voters, but they may not determine the eligibility of candidates, and their decisions are subject to review by the courts.[360] The inspectors may reject votes,[361] and they may keep the polls open for a reasonable time after the hour fixed for closing them, if the extra time is needed to give all stockholders who are ready and who wish to vote an opportunity to do so.[362]

A vote can always be challenged.[363] If it is, the person presenting the ballot is entitled to defend his right to vote.[364] If the vote is not challenged, the inspectors' duty is to count it. After learning the result of the election, inspectors cannot decide that some of the ballots cast for the successful candidate were illegal, and thus cause the minority to win.[365]

Report of election of directors. In some states, the statutes require the filing, within a specified time, of a report showing, among other things, those persons who were elected. Of course, the mandatory effect of such statutes will depend upon their wording. The courts seem disposed to construe such requirements very liberally in favor of the corporation.[366]

---

[357]Standard Power & Light Corp. v. Investment Associates, Inc., (1947) 29 Del. Ch. 593, 51 A. 2d 572; Young v. Jebbett, (1925) 213 App. Div. 774, 211 N.Y. Supp. 61.

[358]In re Giant Portland Cement Co., (1941) 26 Del. Ch. 32, 21 A 2d 697.

[359]For a case in which the inspectors acted beyond their powers. See Gow v. Consolidated Coppermines Corp., (1933) 19 Del. Ch. 172, 165 A. 136.

[360]McGoldrick v. Rotwein, (1952) 127 N.Y.L.J. 508.

[361]Ibid.

[362]In re Gulla, (1921) 13 Del. Ch. 23, 115 A. 317, 13 Del. Ch. 1, 114 A. 596.; In re Schirmer's Will, (1931) 231 App. Div. 625, 248 N.Y. Elevator Supplies Co. v. Wylde, (1930) 106 N.J. Eq. 163, 150 A. 347.

[363]Petition of Serenbetz, (1943) 46 N.Y.S. 2d 475.

[364]Kauffman v. Mayberg, (1943) 59 Cal. App. 2d 730, 140 P. 2d 210.

[365]Ibid.

[366]Where officers are ineligible for reelection, if they "shall wilfully refuse to comply with the provisions" respecting the filing of a report, neglect will not be construed as wilful if there has been no demand or request on the directors to file. In re Zenitherm Co., (1921) 95 N.J.L. 297, 113 A. 327.

Chapter 2

FORMS RELATING TO STOCKHOLDERS' MEETINGS

Contents—Chapter 2

51

CONTENTS

CALLS, NOTICES, AND WAIVERS OF NOTICE OF STOCKHOLDERS' MEETINGS

CALL OF REGULAR ANNUAL MEETING OF STOCKHOLDERS BY PRESIDENT

To ....,

Secretary of ....Corporation:
    The regular annual meeting of stockholders of the.....
................Corporation is hereby called for .... *(Day of Week)*, ...,
19.., at ..... A.M., to be held at the principal office of the Corporation at .....
.... *(Street)*, ... *(City)*, ... *(State)*, for the following purposes:

(Here insert purposes; see special purpose clauses form on page 73.)

    You are hereby directed, as Secretary of the Corporation, to give proper notice of said meeting to the stockholders of said Corporation, as prescribed by the By-laws thereof.

....
President

Dated ...., 19..

REQUEST BY STOCKHOLDERS TO SECRETARY TO GIVE NOTICE OF SPECIAL BUSINESS TO BE TRANSACTED AT ANNUAL STOCKHOLDERS' MEETING

To the Secretary of ....Corporation:

    We, the undersigned, stockholders of ....Corporation, holding the number of shares hereinafter set opposite our respective names, do hereby request that you give notice to the stockholders of the .... Corporation that the following proposal will be presented for consideration and vote at the annual meeting of stockholders of the Corporation, to be held at the office of the Corporation, ... *(Street)*, ... *(City)*, ... *(State)*, on ...., 19.., at ....M.—to wit:

(Here insert special business proposed to be considered at the meeting.)

...., holding ..... shares
...., holding ..... shares
...., holding ..... shares

CALL OF SPECIAL MEETING OF STOCKHOLDERS
BY PRESIDENT

To ....,

Secretary of ....Corporation:

Pursuant to the provisions of the By-laws of the ....
Corporation, I hereby call a special meeting of the stockholders of said Corporation, to be held at the principal office of the Corporation, ... *(Street)*,
.... *(City)*, ... *(State)*, on ...., 19.., at .....A.M., for for
following purposes:

(Here insert purposes; see form on page 73.)

You are hereby authorized and directed, as Secretary of the Corporation, to
give notice to the stockholders of said special meeting, as required by the By-laws
of the Corporation.

....
President

CALL OF SPECIAL MEETING OF STOCKHOLDERS
BY THE STOCKHOLDERS

Dated ...., 19..

To ....,

Secretary of ....Corporation:

The undersigned, stockholders of the ....Corporation,
owning at least ....*(insert fractional part)* of the outstanding capital stock of
said Corporation, do hereby call a special meeting of the stockholders of the
Corporation, to be held at the principal office of the Corporation, ... *(Street)*,
.... *(City)*, ... *(State)*, on ...., 19.., at .....P.M., for the following purposes:

(Here insert purposes; see form on page 73.)

We hereby direct you, as Secretary, to give notice to the stockholders of the
Corporation of such meeting, as prescribed by the By-laws.

Name of Stockholder   Number of Shares Owned

....	....
....	....
....	....

CALL OF SPECIAL MEETING OF STOCKHOLDERS BY DIRECTORS, ADDRESSED TO PRESIDENT

...., 19..

To the President of the ....Corporation:

We, the undersigned, directors of the ....Corporation, pursuant to the provisions of the By-laws of said Corporation, do hereby authorize and direct you to call a special meeting of the stockholders of the Corporation, to be held on ...., 19.., at .....P.M., at the principal office of the Corporation, ... *(Street)*, ... *(City)*, ... *(State)*, for the purpose of:

(Here insert purpose of meeting.)

....

....

....

(Signatures of directors)

CALL OF SPECIAL MEETING OF STOCKHOLDERS BY THE DIRECTORS, ADDRESSED TO THE SECRETARY

To ....,

Secretary of ....Corporation:

We, the undersigned, directors of the ....Corporation, pursuant to the provisions of the By-laws of this Corporation, do hereby call a special meeting of stockholders of the Corporation, to be held at the office of the Corporation, ... *(Street)*, ... *(City)*, ... *(State)*, on ...., 19.., at .....A.M., for the purpose of considering and voting upon the following proposal submitted to this Board—.......... *(insert subject matter of proposal)*, and for the transaction of any further business that may be necessary and proper in connection therewith.

We direct you, as Secretary of the Corporation, to give notice to the stockholders of the special meeting, pursuant to the provisions of the By-laws of said Corporation.

Dated ...., 19 ..

....

....

.,...............................

(Signatures of directors)

REQUEST BY STOCKHOLDERS FOR SPECIAL MEETING OF STOCKHOLDERS

...., 19..

To the President of the ....Corporation:

We, the undersigned, holding at least ..... (.....) per cent of the capital stock of the .... Corporation entitled to vote, pursuant to the provisions of the laws of the State of .... and of the By-laws of this Corporation, do request you to call a special meeting of the stockholders of the Corporation, to be held at the office of the Corporation, ... *(Street)*, ... *(City)*, ... *(State)*, on ...., 19.., at .....A.M., for the purpose of .... *(insert purpose)*, and for the transaction of such other business as may be necessary and proper in connection therewith.

...., holding ..... shares
...., holding ..... shares
...., holding ..... shares
...., holding ..... shares

PRESIDENT'S INSTRUCTIONS TO SECRETARY INDORSED ON STOCKHOLDERS' REQUEST TO CALL SPECIAL MEETING

...., 19..

To the Secretary of ....Corporation:

You are hereby authorized and directed to serve notice of a special meeting of the stockholders of the .... Corporation, to be held at the office of the corporation, ... *(Street)*, ... *(City)*, ... *(State)*, on ...., 19.., at .....A.M., called by me pursuant to the within request of stockholders for the purpose therein set forth.

....
President

CALL OF SPECIAL MEETING OF STOCKHOLDERS BY ONE STOCKHOLDER, UPON FAILURE TO ELECT DIRECTORS

To the Stockholders of ....Corporation:

PLEASE TAKE NOTICE That the annual meeting of stockholders of ....
..... Corporation for the election of directors, provided by the By-laws to be held on the first .... *(Day of Week)* in ...., 19.., was not held, and that the

directors have failed and omitted for a period of more than one month thereafter to call a meeting for such purpose. Therefore, the undersigned stockholder hereby calls a special meeting of the stockholders of .... Corporation, pursuant to the provisions of the laws of the State of ...., to be held at the principal office of the Corporation, ... *(Street)*, ... *(City)*, ... *(State)*, on ...., 19.., at .....P.M., for the purpose of electing directors and for the further purpose of transacting all business which may properly come before said meeting.

    Dated at ....*(City)*, ... *(State)*, ..., 19..

....
A Stockholder of ....Corporation

NOTICE OF ANNUAL MEETING OF STOCKHOLDERS

.... COMPANY

...., 19..

    The Annual Meeting of the stockholders of the .... Company, for the election of directors and the transaction of such other business as may be brought before the meeting, will be held at its principal office, ... *(Street)*, ... *(City)*, ... *(State)*, on .... *(Day of Week)*, ..., 19.., at .......P.M.

    No stock can be voted at the election of directors which has been transferred within ..... (....) days prior thereto.

....
Secretary

If you are unable to be personally present at the meeting, please sign the attached [or enclosed] proxy and return it in the enclosed envelope.

    [Note. For proxies, see forms on page 00. et seq.]

NOTICE OF ANNUAL MEETING OF STOCKHOLDERS THAT DOES NOT SOLICIT PROXIES

    The Annual Meeting of the Shareholders of .... Corporation, will be held at the ....Hotel, ... *(City)*, ...*(State)*, on .... *(day of week)*, ..., 19.., at ..... (Eastern Standard Time), for the election of directors and for the transaction of such other business as may properly come before the meeting or any adjournment thereof.

    The stock transfer books of the Corporation will not be closed, but only shareholders of record, as of the close of business ...., 19.., will be entitled to vote at the meeting.

The above notice is given pursuant to the By-laws of the Corporation. No solicitation is hereby made on behalf of any person for any proxy, consent or authorization, in respect of any securities of ....Corporation.

....
Secretary

.... *(City)*, ... *(State)*
...., 19..

NOTICE OF ANNUAL MEETING OF STOCKHOLDERS, INCLUDING NOTICE OF SPECIAL BUSINESS TO BE TRANSACTED

...., 19..

To the Stockholders of
......................, Inc.:
The Annual Meeting of Stockholders of ...., Inc., will be held in Room ..... at the principal office of the Company, at ..... *(Street)*, ... *(City)*, ... *(State)*, on .... *(day of week)*, ..., 19.., at ..... A.M., Eastern Standard Time, for the following purposes:

1. To elect a Board of ..... Directors, each to serve for the term of one year and until his successor shall have been elected and have duly qualified;
2. To .... *(include here any special purpose)*.

[See purpose clauses on page 73.]

3. To transact such other business as may properly come before the meeting or any adjournment thereof.
In accordance with the By-laws, the close of business on ....
.., 19.. has been fixed as the record date for the determination of the Stockholders entitled to notice of and to vote at such meeting and any adjournment thereof.

By order of the Board of Directors,

....
Secretary

IMPORTANT

All stockholders who do not expect to attend in person are urged to fill in, date, sign and return the enclosed proxy promptly in the envelope herewith to which no additional postage need be affixed if mailed in the United States.

NOTICE OF ANNUAL MEETING OF STOCKHOLDERS, WITH PROXY STATEMENT COMPLYING WITH REGULATIONS UNDER SECURITIES EXCHANGE ACT OF 1934

.... Corporation

NOTICE OF ANNUAL MEETING OF STOCKHOLDERS

NOTICE IS HEREBY GIVEN That the annual meeting of stockholders of the (insert name of company) will be held at the principal office of the Corporation, at *(insert street address, city and state)*, on the (instert date of meeting), at *(insert the time of day)*, for the following purposes:

1. To elect two directors of the Corporation;
2. To consider and act upon the approval of A, J & Co., as auditors for the Corporation for the ensuing year; and
3. To transact such other business as may properly come before the meeting.

Only stockholders of record at the close of business on *(insert record date)* will be entitled to vote at the meeting.

If you do not expect to be present in person at the meeting, please sign, date and fill in the enclosed proxy and return it by mail.

....
           Secretary

(Here insert date of notice)

PROXY STATEMENT

(For use only if there is no contest with respect to election or removal of directors.)

[*Note*: Rule X-14A-3 requires that a written proxy statement be furnished each person whose proxy is solicited. The proxy statement must contain the information enumerated in Schedule 14A. The references throughout this suggested form are to the particular items of Schedule 14A which require the information given. Responses to items 1, 3, and 5 of Schedule 14A must be included in every proxy statement. Schedule 14B sets forth special information required to be included in the statement if there is a contenst.]

The enclosed proxy is solicited by the management of ....
Corporation for use at the Annual Meeting of the Stockholders to be held on ....
.., 19.., at ...... *(Street Address)*, ... *(City)*, ... *(State)* [*Item 3(a) (1)*]. Any stockholder giving a proxy has the power to revoke it at any time before it is voted [*Item 1*].

[*Note: If the right to revoke a proxy is subject to conditions, state the conditions.*]

The Annual Reports and certified financial statements for the last two fiscal years ending and .... 19.., are enclosed herewith.

(Note: See pages 30-33 for summary of SEC's new Rules on annual reports and proxy statements. Also, for details on the new SEC Rules 14a-3, 14c-3 and 14c-7, as amended and analyzed indetail, see Prentice-Hall "Securities Regulation.")

Costs and Method of Solicitation

The cost of soliciting proxies will be borne by the Corporation [*Item 3(a)(4)*].

Arrangements may be made with brokerage houses, custodians, nominees and other fiduciaries to send proxy material to their principals, and the Corporation may reimburse them for their expenses, estimated not to exceed $500. In addition to solicitation by mail, certain oficers and employees of the Corporation, who will receive no compensation for their services other than their regular salaries, may solicit proxies by telephone, telegraph and personally. These persons may be reimbursed for their expenses, estimated not to exceed $200 [*Item 3(a)(3)*].

[*Note: If solicitation of proxies will also be made by paid solicitors, include the additional information required by Item 3(a)(3).*]

Voting Rights

The outstanding voting securities of the Corporation (entitled to one vote per share irrespective of class) is ..... shares, consisting of ..... shares of Common Stock, and ..... shares of Preferred Stock [*Item 5(a)*].

Only stockholders of record at the close of business ...., 19.. will be entitled to vote at the meeting [*Item 5(b)*].

[*Note: If stockholders other than those of record on the record date are entitled to vote at the meeting, give the additional information required by Item 5(b). If, with respect to the election of directors, shareholders have cumulative voting rights, give the information required by Item 5(c). If any person owns of record or beneficially more than 10% of the outstanding voting securities, include the information required by Item 5(d).*]

Election of Directors

Two directors are to be elected to serve for a term of four years and until the election and qualification of their successors. It is the intention of the persons named in the proxy to vote the proxies for the election as directors of N. Hiram-Shore and Jon Van Keck, who are at present directors of the Corporation [*Item 6(a)*]. In the event, however, either of the nominees refuses or is unable to serve as a director (which is not now anticipated), the persons named as proxies reserve full discretion to vote for such other persons as may be nominated.

[*Note: If the candidacy of any nominee for election as a director is the subject of an arrangement or understanding between the nominee and any other person, furnish the information required by Item 6(b).*]

Information Regarding Nominees

The following information is submitted concerning the present directors of the Corporation, including those who are nominees for reelection [*Item 6*]:

Nominees	Principal Occupation	Director since	Term of office expires	Securities of the Company bene-ficially owned as of ...., 19..*	
				Common	Preferred
N. Hiram-Shore	President				
Jon Van Keck	Chairman of Executive Committee—Member of firm, B, C, P & G, Attorneys				

Directors whose terms continue after the meeting	
John L'Amery	Chairman of the Board ....
Thomas Caldwell	Attorney, member of Caldwell & Agnew ....
Taylor Clemons	President, Foto Co. ....
John Rooney	CPA, Armstrong & Ott ....
Anton Karl	Consulting engineer, Video Tube Corp. ....
William Silvio	Investment manager, Providence Investors ....

* Based on information furnished by the respective directors.

[Note: *Information regarding the business experience of a nominee for election as director must be furnished, unless such nominee meets the conditions specified in Item 6(a)(2).*]

Remuneration of Officers and Directors

The table below gives the remuneration paid by the Corporation and its subsidiary, during the fiscal year ended *(insert date)*, to each of the following persons whose aggregate remuneration was more than $40,000, and who (1) was a director at any time during the year, or (2) was one of the three highest paid officers of the Corporation, and to all persons, as a group, who were directors or officers of the Corporation during the last fiscal year [*Item 7(a)*].

(1) Name of individual or identity of group	(2) Capacity in which remuneration was received	(3) Aggregate remuneration
Allen A. Dale	Vice-President	$ 46,325
N. Hiram-Shore	Director and President	98,030
John L'Amery	Chairman of the Board	71,020
Martin Vance	Treasurer	44,125
Robert Pratt	Secretary and General Counsel	41,500
8 directors and 5 officers, as a group	As directors and officers	371,835

Estimated Annual Benefits Payable Under Annuity Plan

Effective April 20, 1968, the Corporation adopted an Annuity Plan for salaried employees receiving $250 or more per month. Each participant contributes 4% of his monthly base salary in excess of $250 for a maximum period of 30 years and the Corporation contributes the balance of the funds necessary to provide future service benefits under the Plan.

It is not possible to determine which of the Corporation's officers or directors will eventually receive an annuity or, as to those who will receive them, what the amount of such annuity will be. No specific amount is paid or set aside by the Corporation for the account of any individual employee or officer prior to retirement date. Retirement benefits have not at this date vested in any person who is mentioned in the preceding tabulation and who is a participant in the Plan.

Based on the assumption that the Annuity Plan will be continued in its present form, and based on certain assumptions as to an employee's (including participating officers and directors) earnings and years of credited service, there is shown in the table below, for purposes of illustration, the approximate annuity to which participating employees may become entitled upon retirement [*Item 7(b)*].

Average annual earnings while a contributor under the Plan	20 years	Total annuity payable at normal retirement date based on average annual earnings	
		25 years	30 years
$6,000	$ 1,200	$ 1,500	$ 1,800
12,000	2,400	3,000	3,600
24,000	4,800	6,000	7,200
40,000	8,000	10,000	12,000

[Note: *Item 7(b) requires information, in tabular form, regarding the estimated annual benefits payable to each person named in response to Item 7(a) pursuant to any pension or retirement plan. In lieu of this, however, it is permitted by the Instruction to Item 7(b) to substitute a table showing the annual benefits payable to persons in specified salary classifications. If such a table is used, make certain to give the name and amount of benefits for each person named in response to Item 7(a) whose retirement benefits have already vested.*]

Transactions Between the Corporation and Directors and Officers

During the fiscal year, the Corporation paid $12,000 as rent for a warehouse to the Z Corp. This company is wholly owned by Allen A. Dale, Vice President of the Corporation, and members of his family [*Item 7(f)*].

The Corporation paid $48,925 to the law firm of B, C, P & G of which Jon Van Keck, a director and the chairman of the executive committee, is a member. The amount of Mr. Van Keck's interest in the firm is not known [*Item 7(f)*].

Election of Auditors

Upon the approval of a majority of the stockholders, the Board of Directors proposes to adopt a resolution appointing A, J & Co. as auditors of the Corporation for the ensuing year. A, J & Co. have audited the Corporation's books for the past 10 years. The Corporation has been advised by A, J & Co. that neither that firm nor any of its associates had any material relationship with the Corporation or any affiliate of the Corporation [*Item 8*].

Other Matters

The management of the Corporation knows of no other matters which may come before the meeting. However, if any matters other than those referred to above should properly come before the meeting, it is the intention of the persons named in the enclosed proxy to vote such proxy in accordance with their best judgment.

By order of the Board of Directors,

....,
Secretary.

Dated: ...., 19..

NOTICE OF ADJOURNED STOCKHOLDERS' ANNUAL MEETING

.... COMPANY

The annual meeting of the stockholders called for ...., 19.., was adjourned until ...., 19...

The adjourned meeting will reconvene at the office of the Company, ...*(Street)*, ... *(City)*, ... *(State)*, ... *(day of week)*, ..., 19.. at ..... A.M., for the purposes set forth in the original notice of ...., 19...

The Annual Report of the Company is enclosed.

....

Clerk

.... (City), ...*(State)*
...., 19...

NOTICE OF ADJOURNED ANNUAL MEETING OF STOCKHOLDERS

To Stockholders of ....Corporation:

NOTICE IS HEREBY GIVEN That, pursuant to the laws of the State of .... and to the By-laws of the .... Corporation, the adjourned annual meeting of the stockholders of the Corporation will be held at its principal office, ...*(Street)*, ... *(City)*, ... *(State)*, on ...., 19.., at .....P.M., for the purpose of:

(Here insert purposes set forth in notice of original meeting; see forms on pages 59 and 73.)

Dated ...., 19 ..

....

Secretary

NOTICE OF ANNUAL MEETING OF STOCKHOLDERS FOR ELECTION OF DIRECTORS; SPECIFIED PROPORTION OF DIRECTORS TO BE ELECTED BY VARIOUS CLASSES OF STOCK

The annual meeting of the stockholders of ....Corporation for the purpose of electing directors, and for the transaction of such other business as may properly come before the meeting, is to be held at the office of the Corporation in the City of ...., State of ...., on ...., 19.., at .....P.M.

Stockholders of record at the close of business twenty (20) days prior to ...., 19.., are entitled to vote for the election of directors at that meeting. Holders of Common Stock have the right to vote for and to elect one third of the directors of the Corporation, and the holders of Management Stock have the right to vote for and to elect two thirds of the directors of the Corporation. Nine directors are to be elected. The Certificate of Incorporation of the Corporation contains the following provisions:

At each annual meeting, the common stockholders and the holders of Management Stock shall separately nominate directors, and each holder of Common Stock shall be entitled to vote for a number of directors from those nominated by the common stockholders equal to one third of the total number of directors to be elected, and each holder of Management Stock shall be entitled to vote for a number of directors from those nominated by the holders of Management Stock equal to two thirds of the total number of directors to be elected. The nominees of the common stockholders (not exceeding one third of the total number of directors to be elected at any such meeting) receiving the largest number of votes of the holders of Common Stock shall be elected directors of the Corporation, and the nominees of the holders of Management Stock (not exceeding two thirds of the total number of directors to be elected at any such meeting) receiving the largest number of votes of the holders of Management Stock shall also be elected directors of the Corporation. All directors so chosen shall hold office until the next annual meeting of the stockholders of the Corporation and until their successors shall be duly elected.

If you are unable to be present at the meeting, please sign and return the enclosed proxy, authorizing Messrs. ...., ..., ..., ..., and ...., or a majority of them that may be present at such meeting (or if only one be present and act, then that one), to nominate three (3) directors in behalf of the common stockholders, and to vote as your proxy the number of shares of Common Stock held by you for the election of such directors so nominated. The proxy should be signed and returned in the stamped envelope enclosed for that purpose to ...., Secretary of the Corporation ....(Street), ... (City), ... (State).

Your truly,

.... Corporation

By ....

Secretary

COMBINED NOTICE OF ANNUAL MEETING, AND OF SPECIAL MEETING; MAJORITY OF DIRECTORS TO BE ELECTED BY PREFERRED STOCK

TAKE NOTICE that the Annual General Meeting of .... Company will be held at the Head Office of the Company, ... (Street), ... (City), ... (State), on .... (Day of Week), ..., 19.., at .....A.M., Eastern Daylight Saving Time, to receive the report of the Directors for the year ending ...., 19.., to appoint Auditors, and to transact such other business as may properly come before the meeting;

AND FURTHER TAKE NOTICE that the meeting is also called as a Special General Meeting of the Shareholders for the purpose of electing the Board of Directors of the Company, and that at such meeting the holders of preference shares are entitled to elect a majority of the members of the Board, and the holders of the common shares are entitled to elect the remaining members of the Board.

DATED at .... (City), ... (State), this .... day of ....., 19...

By Order of the Board.

.............................,

Secretary

PUBLISHED NOTICE OF RECORD DATE FOR NOTICE OF ANNUAL MEETING OF STOCKHOLDERS

RECORD DATE FOR NOTICE OF ANNUAL MEETING

The Board of Directors of ....Company, has, in accordance with the By-laws of the Company, fixed ...., 19.., as the day as of which stockholders entitled to notice of and to vote at the annual meeting, to be held on ...., 19.., shall be determined, and only stockholders of record at the close of business on ...., 19.. will be entitled to notice of or to vote at such annual meeting.

....
Secretary

COMBINED NOTICE OF ANNUAL MEETING OF COMMON STOCKHOLDERS AND SPECIAL MEETING OF PREFERRED STOCKHOLDERS, INDICATING PURPOSE OF MEETING (AUTHORIZATION OF DEBENTURES) AND SHOWING MANNER IN WHICH HOLDER OF PROXY WILL VOTE

NOTICE IS HEREBY GIVEN That the annual meeting of the stockholders of .... Company, Inc., a .... (insert state) corporation, will be held on ...., 19.., at ..... P.M., at the offices of the Company at .... (Street), ... (City), ... (State), for the following purposes:

1. To elect a Board of Directors for the ensuing year.
2. To approve the form of the enclosed annual report for the year 19...
3. To transact such other business as may properly come before the meeting.

Pursuant to the Amended Certificate of Incorporation of the Company, as last Amended, and the By-laws of the Company, only the holders of record of Common Stock of the Company at the close of business on ...., 19.. shall be entitled to vote for the election of directors at said meeting.

NOTICE IS ALSO HEREBY GIVEN That a Special Meeting of the Preferred Stockholders of the Company will be held on ...., 19.., at .....P.M., at the offices of the Company at .... (Street), ... (City), ... (State), for the following purposes:

1. To consider and take action, pursuant to the provisions of Subdivision ..... of Article ..... of the Amended Certificate of Incorporation of the Company, as last amended, upon a proposal to authorize the Board of Directors of the Company to create and issue ..... Dollars ($.....) principal amount of Ten-Year 5% Sinking Fund Debentures of the Company, with Common Stock Purchase Warrants attached, a description of certain provisions of the Indenture under which such Debentures and Warrants will be issued being printed on the reverse side of this notice. The net proceeds of these Debentures, if and when sold, will be used together with additional funds of the Company, to redeem and retire all of the Ten-Year 6% Sinking Fund Debentures of the Company now outstanding in the principal amount of .... Dollars ($.....), which are due ...., 19...

2. To transact such other business as may properly come before the Special Meeting.

Pursuant to a resolution of the Board of Directors, only the holders of record of the Preferred Stock of the Company at the time of the meeting shall be entitled to vote at said special meeting.

By order of the Board of Directors.

Dated ...., 19 ..

....
Secretary

Notice. If you cannot attend, please sign the attached form of proxy designating the officers named therein to act as your proxy at the Annual Meeting and/or Special Meeting, as the case may be, the proxy having been approved by the Board of Directors of the Company, and being forwarded in behalf of the management of the Company. In the exercise of the said proxy, it is intended that at the Annual Meeting, the holders of the proxy, in behalf of the Common Stockholders, will consider and vote upon the election of directors and the approval of the form of the Annual Report for the year 19.., and that at the Special Meeting, the holders of the proxy, in behalf of the Preferred Stockholders, will consider and vote in favor of a resolution authorizing the Company to create and issue the Debentures above referred to.

[*reverse side of notice*]

Outline of certain provisions of the proposed Indenture (hereinafter called the "Indenture"), to be dated on or about ...., 19.., between .... Company, Inc. (hereinafter called the "Corporation"), and .... Trust Company, Trustee:

(Here follows the outline referred to.)

NOTICE OF SPECIAL BUSINESS TO BE CONSIDERED AT ANNUAL MEETING OF STOCKHOLDERS

Special Notice to Stockholders:

Pursuant to the requirements of the laws of the State of ...., and by order of the Board of Directors of the ....Corporation, notice is hereby given that, in addition to the usual business to be transacted at the annual meeting of the stockholders of the Corporation, to be held on ...., 19.., at .....A.M., at the office of the Corporation, ... *(Street)*, ... *(City)*, ... *(State)*, said meeting is specially called for the purpose of:

(Here insert special business to be considered.)

....
Secretary

NOTICE OF SPECIAL MEETING OF STOCKHOLDERS TO ACT UPON RESOLUTION OF DIRECTORS

To the Stockholders of ....Corporation:

NOTICE IS HEREBY GIVEN That a special meeting of the stockholders of the .... Corporation will be held at its office at .... *(Street)*, ... *(City)*, ... *(State)*, on ...., 19.., at ..... A.M., pursuant to a resolution of the Board of Directors of said Corporation, adopted at a special meeting of the Board on ...., 19.., for the purpose of considering and voting upon the following resolution also adopted by the said Board at the said meeting:

(Here insert resolution of directors.)

The meeting of stockholders is also called for the purpose of transacting such other business as may properly come before the meeting or any adjournment thereof.

By order of the Board of Directors.

....
Secretary

(Should you be unable to attend said meeting, please sign the enclosed proxy, have your signature witnessed, and return the same in the enclosed stamped envelope.)

NOTICE OF SPECIAL MEETING OF STOCKHOLDERS, INDICATING PURPOSE OF THE MEETING (SALE OF ASSETS, CHANGE OF NAME, DISSOLUTION OF COMPANY)

NOTICE IS HEREBY GIVEN That a special meeting of stockholders of .... Company will be held at .... *(Street)*, ... *(City)*, ... *(State)*, on ..... *(Day of Week)*, ..., 19.., at .....P.M., for the following purposes:

1. To consider and act upon the matter of authorizing the sale of all the property and assets, including the goodwill of this Company, to .... Corporation, a .... *(insert state)* Corporation, or its nominee, upon the terms of an offer from .... Corporation, dated ...., 19.., which terms include the assumption by .... Corporation, or its nominee, of the liabilities of this Company and the delivery to the Company of common capital stock of .... Corporation, on the basis of six (6) shares of the latter for each share of stock of this Company, or upon substantially the above terms.

2. To consider and act upon the matter of changing the name of this Company and the matter of voting to liquidate and wind up the affairs of this Company in such manner as may be determined at the meeting; and, particularly, but without limiting the generality of the foregoing, to authorize the distribution of

the proceeds of any sale of this Company's property and assets authorized at the meeting of stockholders by the payment of a dividend in liquidation on such terms and in such manner as may be determined at the meeting; and to authorize a reduction of the capital stock accordingly.

3. To consider and act upon the matter of voting to dissolve this Company and all details in any way relating thereto, or in furtherance thereof.

4. To authorize, empower, and direct the Board of Directors and/or any officers of this Company to carry into effect and take such action as, in the opinion of the directors or of the officers acting, may become necessary or desirable to carry into effect all action taken at the meeting and every adjournment thereof.

5. To consider and act upon any other matters which may properly come before the meeting.

By order of the Board of Directors.

....
Secretary

......................................, City, ... State
...., 19..

Notice. If you cannot be present at the meeting, YOU ARE RESPECTFULLY URGED TO SIGN AND RETURN THE ENCLOSED PROXY, which will be voted in favor of the proposal of .... Corporation. The directors desire as large a representation of stockholders at the meeting as possible, since A VOTE OF EIGHT-FIVE PER CENT OF THE STOCK IN FAVOR OF ACCEPTANCE IS REQUIRED as a condition of the offer.

SECOND NOTICE OF SPECIAL MEETING OF STOCKHOLDERS

...., 19..

To the Stockholders of ....Corporation (a ....
corporation):

Under date of ...., 19.., there was sent to you a notice of a Special Meeting of Stockholders of your Corporation to be held in the City of ....,
State of ...., on ...., 19.., for the purpose of voting upon the question of whether or not the Corporation should be dissolved. This notice was accompanied by a proxy, to be executed by you and returned in the event that you did not expect to be personally present at the meeting, and was enclosed with a letter explaining the circumstances leading up to the calling of the meeting. To date your proxy has not been received.

At the Special Meeting of the Stockholders held pursuant to said notice, in the City of ...., State of ...., on ...., 19.., ... (.....) shares of the capital stock of the Corporation were represented at the meeting. There are outstanding ..... (.....) shares of the capital stock of the Corporation. Under the General Corporation Law of the State of ...., since two thirds of the number of shares of stock of the Corporation were not represented at the meeting, no action could be taken except to adjourn to a later date. The meeting was therefore adjourned to reconvene on ...., 19.., at the same hour and place.

A further adjournment of the meeting would involve considerable expense to the Corporation, in addition to the delay. As has been previously explained to you, the Board of Directors feels it desirable that the stockholders express their wishes on the proposed dissolution. This cannot be done unless the required number of shares are represented.

Accordingly, if you do not expect to attend the adjourned meeting, will you kindly execute the enclosed proxy and return it in the enclosed return envelope. A copy of the original notice of the Special Meeting of Stockholders is enclosed herewith.

Very truly yours,

....

Secretary

NOTICE OF ADJOURNED SPECIAL
MEETING OF STOCKHOLDERS

...., 19..

To the Stockholders of ....Corporation:

The special meeting of stockholders of the ....Cor-poration, which was called to be held at the office of the Corporation, ...(Street), ...(City), ...(State), on ...., 19.., at .... P.M., has been adjourned to ...., 19.., to be held at the same hour and place.

We are enclosing a copy of the call of the meeting, indicating the purposes thereof, as well as another proxy covering representation of your stock at the meeting.

(Here insert, if desired, explanation of importance of action to be taken at meeting.)

If you are unable to be present at the adjourned meeting in person, will you please execute and return the enclosed proxy promptly in order to have your stock represented at the adjourned meeting.

.... Corporation

By ....

Secretary

MISCELLANEOUS ITEMS APPEARING IN NOTICES
OF STOCKHOLDERS' MEETINGS

[*Note.* Statements similar to those appearing below often appear in the form of proxy accompanying the notice of meeting; see proxy forms, page 92 et seq.]

Right to vote vested in preferred stockholders because of default in dividend payments

Because the accumulated and unpaid dividends on the Preferred Stock of the Corporation outstanding amount to ..... per cent (....%) and more of the par value of such stock, the right to vote at said meeting is vested exclusively in the holders of Preferred Stock, each such holder having one vote for each share of such stock held by him.

Note as to voting rights of different classes of stock

At this meeting the $7 Preferred Stock, the $6 Preferred Stock, and the Common Stock will have the right to vote equally, share for share (and the $4 Preferred Stock will have the right to cast 5 votes for each 8 shares, or ⅝ of 1 vote for each share) upon the election of all directors, and upon any other matters which may properly come before the meeting.

Tickets of admission required to stockholders' meeting

Tickets of admission, as prescribed by the By-laws, will be required for attendance at this meeting, and may be obtained by personal application to the undersigned, or by letter addressed to him at .... *(Street)*, ... *(City)*, ... *(State)*.

Time for election specified

The election of ..... (....) directors to serve for the ensuing year will be held between the hours of ..... A.M. and ..... P.M.

Transfer books to be closed

The transfer books for all classes of preferred and common stock will be closed at ..... P.M., on ...., 19.., and will be reopened at ..... A.M., on ...., 19...

Transfer books not to be closed

The board of directors has fixed ...., 19.., as the record date for the determination of the stockholders entitled to notice of, and to vote at, the special meeting, and all persons who are holders of record of common or preferred stock at the close of business on that date (but only such persons) will be entitled to vote at such meeting and any adjournment thereof. The stock transfer books will not be closed.

Copy of annual report being mailed

A copy of the annual report will be mailed to each stockholder of record, under separate cover, and will be submitted at the meeting.

Copy of annual report to be mailed if requested

The annual report for 19.., which will be ready for distribution on or about ...., 19.., will be sent only to those stockholders who request it. If you desire that the report be sent you, please indicate this fact on the accompanying proxy card. If no response is received, it will be assumed that the report is not desired.

Minutes of meetings open for inspection

The minutes of the meetings of the Board of Directors and of the Finance Committee will be open to inspection by stockholders of record during business hours at the principal office of the Corporation, ... *(Street)*, ... *(City)*, ... *(State)*, until after the close of the meeting.

Offer of trustees to issue proxy to stockholders of affiliated corporation whose shares are held under trust agreement

Referring to the foregoing notice of the annual meeting of the stockholders of .... Company, the undersigned, as Trustees under the Trust Agreement dated ...., 19.., relating to stock of said .... Company, in accordance with the provisions of said Trust Agreement, will issue to any shareholder in the .... Corporation, upon timely and written request by such shareholder, addressed to the undersigned at the principal office of said .... Company stated in said notice, a proxy to enable such shareholder or his substitute to vote at said meeting upon the number of shares of stock of said .... Company corresponding to such shareholder's proportionate beneficial interest in the total number of shares of the stock of said .... Company held by the undersigned; but no such proxy will be given in respect of any fraction of a share of stock of said .... Company.

....
....
....
Trustees under said Trust Agreement

Note requesting stockholders to return proxy promptly, and showing who is soliciting proxy

If you do not expect to be present at the meeting, please execute the attached proxy and return it promptly, as it is important that the presence of a quorum be secured. No postage is required to return the proxy. Said proxy is being solicited in behalf of the management of the Company. It is intended that the holders of the proxy will consider and vote upon the election of directors.

Note indicating how proxy will be used

Unless instructions to the contrary are given, all proxies sent in will be voted in favor of the proposed amendment to the By-laws.

Note indicating that annual meeting is to be adjourned pending preparation of annual report

Because of the fact that the auditors of your Company have been unable to complete their audit in time to have the annual report of your Company sent to you with this notice, it is contemplated that the meeting, when convened, will be adjourned to ...., 19.., at ..... A.M., and at the same place, in order that you may receive the annual report in ample time before the meeting. Proxies will be enclosed with the annual report.

[*Note.* A notice such as the above may be included with the notice of annual meeting where the annual meeting must be called for a certain date to meet the by-law requirements but where, for some reason, an adjournment is desirable.]

SPECIAL PURPOSE CLAUSES IN NOTICES OF STOCKHOLDERS' MEETINGS

To authorize attendance by proxy at stockholders' meetings

To authorize directors and officers of the Company to attend in person or by proxy any annual and/or special meetings of corporations in which .... Company is a stockholder, with authority to vote stock in said corporations standing in the name of .... Company or owned by it, and to provide for the execution of proxies.

To change date of annual meeting of stockholders

To authorize the change of the date for the holding of the annual meeting of stockholders of the Corporation from the second .... *(Day of Week)* in .... of each year to the third .... *(Day of Week)* in .... of each year, and to that end to authorize the necessary amendment to Section .... of Article .... of the By-laws of the Corporation.

To consider annual report

To consider, approve, and ratify any and all matters that may be referred to in the annual report to the stockholders.

To consider officers' reports

To receive and act upon the reports of the officers of the corporation.

To elect directors for varying terms

To elect thirty-six (36) directors of the Company, twelve (12) to be elected for three (3) years, twelve (12) to be elected for two (2) years, and twelve (12) to be elected for one (1) year, and/or until their respective successors shall have been elected and qualified.

To fill vacancies in board

To elect directors to fill vacancies created by resignations, prior to said meeting, of previously elected directors.

To elect inspectors of election

To elect Inspectors of Election to serve until the close of the next annual meeting of stockholders.

or

To elect two (2) Inspectors of Election to serve at the next annual meeting.

To hear report

To hear the report of the .... *(Insert title of officer or other person making report)* and act thereon.

To remove directors

To consider and act upon the proposal to remove the present Board of Directors of this Corporation and to elect a new Board of Directors in case the present Board is removed.

To remove named directors for cause

To remove for cause .... *(Name)* and .... *(Name)* as directors, and to fill the vacancy created by the removal of each.

To approve transactions of corporations and acts of directors, executive committee, and officers since last annual meeting

To consider and vote upon the approval and ratification of all contracts and transactions of the Corporation and all acts and proceedings of the Board of Directors, the Executive Committee, and the officers since the last annual meeting of the Corporation, including contracts and transactions of this Corporation with individual directors and with partnerships in which a director of this Corporation is a member, and with corporations of which directors of this Corporation are directors. The contracts, transactions, acts, and proceedings are set forth in the minute book of the Corporation, which will be presented to the meeting and be open to the inspection of stockholders.

[*Note.* To meet the requirements of the Securities Exchange Act of 1934, the notice of meeting should contain a brief description of the various acts and proceedings to be approved or ratified at the meeting.]

To approve sale of treasury stock

To consider and vote upon the ratification of the action of the Board of Directors in effecting the sale of ..... (....) shares of treasury stock.

To vote upon the question of investment of corporate funds

To vote upon the following question: "Shall the .... Corporation continue to invest substantial portions of the cash funds of the Corporations in stocks and/or bonds of corporations not allied with the .... industry?"

To approve contract in which directors are interested

To approve the contract entered into on ...., 19.., between this Corporation and the .... Company for the .... *(state subject matter of contract)*, in which contract .... and ...., directors of this Corporation, have a personal interest, said directors being holders of stock in the .... Company.

To consider sale of an asset (stock in another corporation) to a director

To consider the question of approving or disapproving the proposed sale to ...... of *(City)*, ... *(State)*, a director of this Corporation, of the ..... shares of Capital Stock of .... Company owned by this Corporation, upon the terms and conditions set forth in that certain contract dated ...., 19.. between this Corporation and .... which, among other things, provides that the consideration to be paid by .... is the sum of $....., plus the sum of $....., being an amount equal to the net current assets of said Company as of ....., 19.., plus an amount equal to the earnings of said Company from ...., 19.., to the date of the consummation of the sale and that such purchase price is based upon the acquisition by purchaser of ..... shares, or all of the outstanding Capital Stock of .... Company, and is to be adjusted proportionately to the actual number of shares owned by this Corporation.

To approve lease between a director as landlord, and the company as tenant

To consider and vote upon the ratification of the action of the Board of Directors in effecting a lease for further factory space between one of the directors, as landlord, and this company, as tenant.

To ratify specific contract

To ratify, confirm, and approve the contract entered into on ...., 19.., with the .... Company, by the officers of this Corporation in its name and in its behalf, to ..... *(state subject matter of contract)*.

To authorize directors and officers to carry out authorized changes

To authorize and empower the Board of Directors and the officers of the Corporation to effectuate the foregoing proposal, if adopted by the stockholders, and to authorize and empower the Board of Directors and the officers to amend the Charter and the By-laws of the Corporation to conform therewith.

To ratify additional compensation of officers and employees

To vote upon a proposal to ratify the action of the Board of Directors, taken at a meeting duly held on ...., 19.., authorizing payment to the officers and employees of the Corporation of the sum of ...... ($.....) Dollars, as additional compensation for their services.

To elect auditors

To elect independent auditors to audit the books and accounts of the Corporation at the close of the current fiscal year.

To select committee to employ auditor

To select a committee of three (3) stockholders of the Corporation who are not directors to employ an auditor for the Corporation, *in accordance with the statutory requirements*.

To adjourn meeting

To adjourn said meeting from time to time to a date or dates to be fixed at said meeting or any adjournment thereof, for the purpose of considering and acting upon any of the foregoing matters or any modifications thereof.

To approve acts of board of directors and executive committee

To consider and vote upon the approval and ratification of all purchases, contracts, contributions, compensations, acts, proceedings, elections, and appointments by the Board of Directors, or by the Finance Committee since the .... Annual Meeting of the Stockholders of the Corporation on .... , 19.., and all matters referred to in the .... Annual Report to stockholders for the fiscal year ending ...., 19... The minutes of the Board of Directors and of the Finance Committee will be open to inspection by stockholders of record during business hours at the *(City)* office of the Corporation, No. ...., City of ...., State of .... until after the close of the meeting.

To consider employees' stock subscription plan

To consider and vote upon the revised Employees' Stock Subscription Plan of the Corporation formulated and declared advisable by the Board of Directors pursuant to Chapter .... of the Laws of the State of ...., a copy of which revised Plan is inclosed.

To issue stock to employees

To vote upon the question of reserving for, and selling to, the employees of the Company and of its subsidiaries, through the agency of the Savings Fund Committee of the Company under the rules governing the Employees' Savings Fund, without first being offered for subscription to the Stockholders of the Company, ... shares of the Common Stock of the par value of .... Dollars ($.....) each of this Company heretofore authorized but at present unissued, and of selling the shares reserved by the Company at .... Dollars ($.....) per share or at such higher price as may from time to time be determined by the Board of Directors.

To issue stock to employees engaged in important capacities

The stockholders will consider and vote on a proposal to authorize the Board of Directors to issue, or set apart for issue, to persons now engaged or employed, or hereafter to be engaged or employed by the company in important capacities, not more than ..... shares of the now authorized and unissued common stock; the Directors to be authorized to sell shares or to grant non-assignable options of the same, in lots of not more than ..... shares to any one person, either in connection with an employment contract of ..... years or more or upon the basis of service in the employ of the company for a period exceeding ..... years, upon such prices, terms and conditions as said Board of Directors shall in their discretion determine.

To consider employee insurance and pension benefit plans

To consider and take action upon the proposed .... Corporation Plan for Employee Insurance Benefits and that part of the proposed .... Corporation Plan for Employee Pension Benefits relating to new noncontributory pension benefits for employees, the plans being attached to and described in the proxy statement dated ...., 19.., copies of which plans and proxy statement are being mailed to all stockholders of .... Corporation with this notice.

To elect committee

To elect a committee of three stockholders to administer the Corporation Profit Sharing Plan adopted at the Annual Meeting, ..., 19...

To fill vacancies

To elect new directors to fill the .... vacancies which exist in the Board of Directors by reason of the resignation of Messrs. .... and ....

To ratify all contributions up to a limited amount

To consider, and, if deemed advisable, to ratify, all contributions made by the officers of the Company to an amount not exceeding .... Dollars ($......).

To vote upon resolution passed by board of directors

The following resolution, which was duly passed at the regular meeting of the Board of Directors on ...., 19.., will serve to explain the purpose of the special meeting and the matters which will be submitted to the stockholders for action thereon:

(Insert here the resolutions passed at the meeting of the Directors, to be approved by the stockholders.)

Authorizing board of directors and officers to do all necessary acts to carry out changes authorized by stockholders

Authorizing the Board of Directors and officers of the Company to effectuate the foregoing propositions if adopted by the stockholders and authorizing the Board of Directors and officers to amend the Charter and the By-laws of the Company to conform thereto.

To ratify compensation

To vote upon a proposition to ratify the action of the Board of Directors, taken at a meeting duly held on ...., 19.., in authorizing and paying $........... to the officers and employees as a part of their compensation.

To authorize sale of stock below par value

To authorize the sale and issuance of stock below par value.

To approve the issuance of stock

To approve the issuance of .... additional shares of the Common Stock of the Company.

To authorize sale of stock to stockholders, and approve under-writing agreement for shares not taken by stockholders

1. Authorizing the sale of .... shares of the present authorized but unissued Common Stock pro rata to the stockholders at a price of $.......... per share.

2. Approving a certain underwriting agreement entered into between the Company and Messrs. .... & Company and .... & Company as bankers, whereby the bankers agree to underwrite the sale of all or any part of said .... shares that is not subscribed for by the stockholders, at $....... per share, upon the terms and conditions therein set forth.

To authorize issuance of convertible preferred stock

To consider and act upon a proposition to authorize the issue of not exceeding five hundred thousand (500,000) shares of cumulative preferred stock of the par value of One Hundred Dollars ($100) each, the holders of which shall be entitled to receive out of the annual net income of the Company dividends of not exceeding five (5) per cent per annum, with the privilege of exchanging said preferred stock for common stock par for par; also to authorize the issue from time to time of common stock to be available for exchange for said preferred stock par for par; also to fix a price and time at which said preferred stock may be called and retired; also to determine any other rights and privileges which may pertain to said preferred stock when issued; and also to authorize an underwriting to purchase such of said preferred stock as shall not be taken by those entitled to subscribe for the same.

To vote upon options to officers to purchase stock

To consider and vote upon the grant of options to certain other officers and employees of the Company and of its subsidiaries, for the purchase of stock of the Company.

To consider employees' stock subscription plan
(First Form)

To consider and act upon a resolution or resolutions authorizing the amendment of the Certificate of Incorporation of said Corporation (as amended by Certificate of Amendment of its Certificate of Incorporation filed in the office of the Secretary of State of the State of .... on ...., 19..):

First: By striking out the .... paragraph of Article ...., which now reads as follows:

(Insert the clause.)

and by inserting in lieu thereof the following:

(Insert the clause.)

To consider amendment of certificate of incorporation
(Second Form)

To consider and vote upon an amendment to Article .... of the Certificate of Incorporation, which amendment has been declared advisable by resolution of the Board of Directors of the Company. The .... paragraph of Article .... of Certificate of Incorporation as per the proposed amendment shall read as follows:

(Insert clause.)

To amend certificate and by-laws to provide for electiⴠn annually of all directors

To consider and act upon a proposal to amend Article Sixth of the Certificate of Incorporation, as restated, and to amend Section 1 of Article IV of the By-laws, so as to eliminate the present classification of the directors and to provide for the election annually of all directors, as recommended by the Board of Directors.

To change the name of a bank

To vote upon a resolution to change the name of this Company to "..........." and to authorize the President or a Vice President and the Secretary or an Assistant Secretary of the Company to execute the certificate required for such purpose pursuant to Section 40 of the General Corporation Law of the State of New York and to make and annex to such certificate the affidavit required by said section and to cause such certificate, with the approval of the Superintendent of Banks indorsed thereon, to be filed as required by said section on ...., 19.., or such later date as shall be determined by the Board of Directors of the Company.

To adopt state business corporation act and restate articles of incorporation

1. To consider and act upon a proposal that the Company voluntarily adopt the .... *(State)* Business Corporation Act as set forth in the resolution numbered ..... in the Proxy Statement below.

If the above resolution is not adopted, no vote will be taken on the resolution to amend, supplement, and restate the articles of incorporation.

If the above resolution No. 1 is adopted by the affirmative vote of the holders of at least two-thirds of the outstanding shares entitled to vote thereon, vote will be taken upon the following:

2. A proposal to amend, supplement, and restate the articles of incorporation of the Company as set forth in the resolution numbered ..... in the Proxy Statement below.

To enlarge purposes

To enlarge the objects for which said company was formed.

To extend corporate existence

To consider and act upon a proposition to extend the term of the corporate existence of this corporation for .... years.

To change location

To act upon a proposition to change the location of the office of the corporation.

To increase number of directors, and to elect additional directors

To consider and act upon a proposition to increase the number of directors from .... to ...., and to elect such additional members to the Board as may be provided for at said meeting.

To increase capital stock without par value and to authorize issuance

1. To consider and act upon a proposal to increase the authorized number of shares of the Corporation from 500,000 shares without par value to 1,500,000 shares without par value.

2. To authorize the issuance and/or sale of said additional shares of Common Stock for such consideration as from time to time may be fixed by the Board of Directors.

3. To authorize the execution and filing of such certificate or certificates as may be necessary or advisable to effect any of the changes herein referred to.

To authorize increase of stock having par value; approve an offer to stockholders; and to approve sale to trustees for benefit of employees

1. To increase the authorized capital stock of the Company from $1,000,000 divided into 10,000 shares of the par value of $100 each to $4,000,000 divided into 40,000 shares of the par value of $100 each.

2. To approve of an offer of 27,000 shares of the par value of $100 each, of such increase of stock, for subscription by stockholders at $200 per share, each-stockholder of record at the close of business on a date to be determined by the Board of Directors or Executive Committee (which date it is anticipated will be ...., 19..), to have the right to subscribe to two and seven-tenths (2-7/10) shares for each share then held by him, any shares so offered but not subscribed for within a time to be fixed by the Board of Directors or Executive Committee to be sold or disposed of as the Board of Directors or Executive Committee may determine, but at a price of not less than $200 per share.

3. To approve of the issue and sale of 3,000 shares of the par value of $100 each, of such increase of stock, at $200 per share to trustees, to be selected by the

Board of Directors, to be held for the benefit of officers and employees of the Company under such plan and/or agreement and subject to such terms and conditions as may be determined by the Board of Directors.

4. To authorize, ratify, and approve all acts and proceedings necessary or proper fully to perform and carry into effect any of the above matters.

In the event that the increase of stock and the offer of shares for subscription by stockholders above mentioned shall be approved by the stockholders at the meeting and such consents as are necessary from public authorities obtained, warrants representing such subscription rights will be mailed to stockholders of record entitled thereto with an appropriate letter of instructions.

To authorize increase of stock and amendment of certificate of incorporation

1. To consider and act upon the proposition of increasing the capital stock of the Corporation from $.........., as at present authorized, to $.........., and of amending Article .... of the Certificate of Incorporation so as to provide that the capital stock shall be $.........., divided into .... shares of the par value of $.......... each.

2. To authorize *(indicate officer or officers designated by statute)* of the Corporation to file the required certificate of the foregoing increase in the office of the Secretary of State of the State of ....

3. To prescribe, authorize, or approve the terms and conditions upon which subscriptions for the increased stock shall be received and upon which such stock shall be issued.

To increase stock, provide for convertible notes, and ratify contract with banking syndicate

1. Considering and voting upon an increase in the number of the authorized shares of the Cumulative 7% Preferred Stock of the Company by 250,000 shares and an increase in the number of authorized shares of Common Stock of the Company by 250,000 shares so that, including those previously authorized, the total authorized number of shares of the Company will be 2,250,000 shares divided as follows:

One million (1,000,000) shares of Cumulative 7% Preferred Stock of the par value of $100 each.

Two hundred fifty thousand (250,000) shares of Cumulative 6% Preferred Stock of the par value of $100 each.

One million (1,000,000) shares of Common Stock without par value.

2. Considering and voting upon a proposal authorizing the Board of Directors of the Company to issue $25,000,000 principal amount of convertible notes or debentures of the Company, such notes or debentures to be dated October 1, 19.., to mature October 1, 19.., to bear interest at the rate of 6% per annum, and to have such other terms and provisions as the Board of Directors in their absolute discretion may determine; and to authorize the Board of Directors of the Company, under such regulations as they may adopt, to confer upon the holder of each of said notes or debentures the right to convert the principal thereof within such period and upon such terms and conditions as may be fixed by the resolution of the Board of Directors conferring the right of conversion, into Cumulative 7% Preferred Stock of the Company at the rate of $100 principal amount of such notes or debentures for

$100 par value of such Stock. Such notes or debentures may further provide that the holder shall have the right, upon conversion of the same, to purchase within such period or periods and at such price or prices as the Board of Directors may determine (not less than $50 a share) one share of Common Stock for each $1,000 principal amount of such notes or debentures so converted.

3. Considering and voting upon such variations of and additions to the above as may be deemed advisable at said meeting, and the giving of full authority to the agents and officers of the Company to make, execute, and file such certificates and documents and to do such acts as may be necessary, convenient, or advisable to carry into effect such actions as may be adopted at said meeting.

4. Taking action upon the approval and ratification of a contract by the Company with a group or syndicate to purchase or effect the sale of the $25,000,000 principal amount of convertible notes or debentures, if authorized at the meeting to be issued. The group or syndicate will include banks and banking or security houses which have handled former issues of the Company and in which some directors of the Company are interested as directors or otherwise.

5. Taking action upon any other matter relative to the foregoing that properly may come before the meeting.

To increase stock and reclassify stock authorized but not issued

1. To vote in favor of or against an amendment declared by vote of the Board of Directors of the Company by resolution to be advisable, to the Charter or Certificate of Incorporation of the Company (as heretofore amended), the purpose and effect of which amendment is:

    a. To increase the total number of authorized shares of 7% series preferred stock of the Company from 20,000 to 60,000 shares.

    b. To change the authorized 6% series preferred stock of the Company (none of which stock has been issued) to 6½% series preferred stock, and thereby to create a 6½% series preferred stock and set forth the designations, preferences, and voting powers or restrictions or qualifications thereof.

2. To approve the resolutions of the Board of Directors of the Company respecting such amendment to the Charter or Certificate of Incorporation of the Company, and to authorize the directors and officers of the Company to take all action necessary or proper to make such amendment (or any modification thereof) effective.

To increase capital stock and to acquire stock of another corporation in exchange for stock

1. To authorize the increase of the number of shares of Common Stock, without par value, of this Company from 4,320.000 shares, the number heretofore authorized, to 12,000,000 shares, and the change of all the previously authorized shares of Common Stock, now issued, into twice the number of shares of the same class, and to prescribe the terms upon which such change is to be made.

2. To authorize the acquisition by this Company, subject to authorization by the Public Service Commission, of all or any part (but not less than 70 per cent) of the outstanding capital stock of the . . . . .Company, Inc., a New York corporation, by the issue, in exchange therefor, of one share of the $5 Cumulative Preferred Stock and two shares of the Common Stock, as increased, of this Company, for each share of the capital stock of the . . . . Company, Inc., so acquired.

To increase par value of stock, and reduce the number of shares

To increase the par value of the shares of . . . . .Company from Dollars ($ . . . .) each to . . . . .Dollars ($ . . . .) each, and effect a corresponding reduction in the number of shares.

To increase number of shares, to reduce par value, and to exchange new for old

To consider and act upon a proposition to increase the number of shares of capital stock of the Company from 40,000 shares to 200,000 shares and to amend the Charter of the Company accordingly, and to consider and act upon a proposition to reduce the par value of the shares of capital stock of the Company from $25 each to $5 each and to amend the Charter of the Company accordingly, so that hereafter all shares, including those now issued and those to be hereafter issued, shall have a par value of $5 each; and that the holders of all outstanding shares having a par value of $25 each shall receive five shares of stock having a par value of $5 each in exchange for each share of stock held by them.

To authorize change from stock with par value to stock without par value and exchange of stock

To consider and act upon a proposed amendment to the Certificate of Incorporation changing the authorized Common Stock of the Company from shares of the par value of $ . . . . each, to . . . . .shares of Common Stock without par value; and to authorize the issue of . . . . .(. . . . .) shares of such stock without par value for each share of the existing Common Stock of the par value of $ . . . . . outstanding.

To reduce capital stock by reducing par value, and to authorize distribution of surplus

1. To consider and act upon a proposition to reduce this Company's capital stock from $. . . . . to $. . . . ., such decrease to be effected by reducing the par value of each share from $. . . . . to $. . . . . .

2. To consider and act upon a proposition to authorize the Board of Directors to distribute in whole or in part to the stockholders pro rata, at such times and in such manner as the Board shall determine, any surplus in excess of the amount to which the capital stock is reduced.

To reduce capital by retiring stock held in the sinking fund.

To consider and act upon a resolution which will be presented to said meeting reducing the capital of the Corporation by retiring . . . . . shares of its preferred stock without nominal or par value, owned by the Corporation and now held in the sinking fund.

To amend the certificate of incorporation to provide for a recapitalization

1. Considering and voting upon proposed amendments to the Certificate of Incorporation of the Corporation to effect a recapitalization thereof, by decreasing its authorized capital stock by changing the number of shares from . . . . . shares to . . . . . shares, and reclassifying the authorized capital stock of the Company so that there shall be one class of stock, Common Stock, and so that the total number of shares that may be issued by the Company shall be . . . . . shares, all of which are to

be without nominal or par value and are to be Common Stock. This change will be effected by (1) the amendment of Article ''Fourth'' of the Certificate of Incorporation by striking out all of the said Article ''Fourth'' and inserting in lieu thereof the following:

(Insert new article.)

(2) The amendment of Article ''Fifth'' of the Certificate of Incorporation, by striking out all of the said Article ''Fifth,'' which article now sets forth the distinguishing rights, privileges, restrictions, classifications, and voting powers of the Common Stock and the Management Stock of the Company.

2. Taking action upon a resolution, in the event of the adoption of the aforesaid proposed amendments, authorizing the exchange of all the present issued and outstanding ..... shares of Management Stock of the Corporation, for ..... shares of presently authorized and unissued Common Stock of the Corporation, in the ratio of ..... shares of such Management Stock for each ..... shares of such Common Stock, and the cancellation and retirement of such Management Stock upon the said exchange.

To amend by-laws or adopt new by-laws
To amend the By-laws of the Company or to adopt new By-laws.

To amend the by-laws to change annual meeting date
To amend the By-laws of the Company so as to change the date of the annual meeting of stockholders from the first Tuesday in March in each year to the first Tuesday in April in each year.

To amend the by-laws to fix date for determining stockholders entitled to vote, or to receive dividends or rights
To amend the By-laws of the Company so as to fix, or authorize the Board of Directors to fix, a date, not exceeding twenty days preceding the date of any meeting of stockholders, any dividend payment date or any date for the allotment of rights, as a record date for the determination of the stockholders entitled to notice of and to vote at such meeting, or entitled to receive such dividends or rights, as the case may be.

To amend by-laws to permit facsimile signatures
To consider and act upon a proposal to amend the By-laws so as to permit facsimile signatures of officers and facsimile corporate seal upon stock certificates.

To amend a certain section of the by-laws
To take action upon the amendment of Section ..... of Article ..... of the By-laws of the Corporation, adopted by the Board of Directors at a Special Meeting thereof held on ...., 19.., by adding thereto a provision reading as follows:

(Insert new provision.)

To amend by-laws to increase number of directors
To amend the Company's By-laws to increase the number of directors from ..... to .... and to increase the quorum necessary for a meeting of the directors from ..... to ....., and to elect ..... additional directors.

To amend by-laws as to closing transfer books
(First Form)

To consider and act upon a proposal to alter and amend Article ....., Section ..... of the Company's By-laws by striking out in such section reference to the closing of the transfer books for purposes of stockholders' meetings and substituting therefor a date of record to be fixed by the Board of Directors for determination of stockholders entitled to notice of and to vote at any such meetings. A copy of the proposed amendment will be mailed at least ..... days prior to the meetings in a postage prepaid envelope, addressed to each stockholder at his address as entered upon the books of the Company.

To amend by-laws as to closing transfer books
(Second Form)

To permit the taking of a record date (not more than .... days prior to any meeting) for determining stockholders entitled to notice of and to vote at meetings to avoid the necessity of closing stock transfer books prior to meetings.

To adopt amended by-laws adopted by the board of directors

Considering and voting upon the adoption of amended By-laws of the company heretofore adopted by the Directors of the Company on ...., 19..; a printed copy of the amended By-laws, the adoption of which is proposed, is enclosed.

To borrow money to finance building, and to authorize
lease of land and building

1. To borrow money for the purpose of financing in part the erection of the proposed clubhouse of the Corporation, and to that end to authorize the execution and delivery of a bond of the Corporation in the principal amount of $3,400,000, maturing fifteen years after its date and bearing interest at the rate of 5½% per annum for five years and 5% per annum thereafter; and to secure the payment of the principal and interest of said bond by authorizing the execution, acknowledgement, and delivery of a first mortgage upon the land of the Corporation known as *(insert description)*, and the building proposed to be erected thereon.

2. To borrow additional money for the purpose of financing in part the erection and equipment of the proposed clubhouse of the Corporation, and to that end to authorize the execution and issuance of coupon bonds of the Corporation in an aggregate principal amount not exceeding $1,500,000, maturing twenty-five years after their date and bearing interest at the rate of 8½% per annum; each of said bonds to have attached a warrant entitling the holder thereof to purchase shares of the fully paid and nonassessable common stock of the Corporation at any time within ten years on payment in New York funds of the purchase price to be therein stated, but not less than par, at the rate of ten shares for each $1,000 bond, and to secure the payment of the principal and interest of said bonds by authorizing the execution, acknowledgement, and delivery to some Bank or Trust Company of the City of New York, N.Y., as trustee, of a second mortgage upon the land of the Corporation, above described, and the building proposed to be erected thereon, and also of a chattel mortgage upon the furnishings and equipment to be placed in said proposed building.

3. To authorize the execution, acknowledgement, and delivery of all other

mortgages, building loan agreements, assignments, pledges, transfers, leases, conveyances, assurances, and instruments of whatever nature that may reasonably be required to carry out any of the purposes set forth above.

4. To lease the above described land of the Corporation, together with the clubhouse proposed to be erected thereon, and the furnishings and equipment to be placed therein, to .... Association, Inc., for a term of twenty-five (25) years, said term to commence when said proposed clubhouse shall have been erected, furnished, and equipped, and to authorize the execution, acknowledgement, and delivery of any and all leases, agreements, contracts, and assignments that may reasonably be necessary to carry out such a purpose.

To authorize execution of a mortgage

a. The execution of a first mortgage in the sum of $300,000 to .... Trust Company, of ...., as Mortgagee, upon the real property, together with the buildings and improvements thereon, owned by the Company and located at Nos. .... Street, in the city of ...., situated at the .... corner of .... and .... Streets; said mortgage to be payable at the expiration of five (5) years from the date thereof or at any semiannual date for the payment of interest prior thereto, on six (6) months' notice from the Company to the Mortgagee, with interest at the rate of 8 per cent (8%) per annum, payable semiannually, and to contain such other terms and conditions as the Board of Directors of the Company may deem advisable;

b. The execution of a first mortgage or deed of trust in the sum of $560,000 to .... Trust Company of ...., ..., as Trustee, upon the real property, together with the buildings and improvements thereon, and the machinery, fixtures, and other permanent property now or hereafter owned by the Company on the premises located at the corner of .... Street and .... Avenue in the city of ...., County of ...., State of ....; said mortgage to be payable at the expiration of ten (10) years from the date thereof; and the issue and sale, on such terms and conditions as the Board of Directors of the Company may determine, of bonds to be secured by said mortgage or deed of trust to an amount not exceeding in the aggregate $560,000; said bonds to become due and payable at the expiration of ten (10) years from the date of issuance, or, at the option of the Company, one (1) per cent of the principal amount thereof to become due and payable on any semiannual date for the payment of interest thereon, with interest at a rate not in excess of 8 per cent (8%) per annum; and said mortgage or deed of trust and said bonds to contain such terms and conditions as the Board of Directors of the Company may deem advisable.

To authorize creation and issue of mortgage bonds

1. To consent to, direct, approve, sanction and authorize the creation and issue of Refunding and Improvement Mortgage Bonds of the Company limited to an aggregate principal amount equal to three times the par value of the capital stock of the Company; such bonds to mature at such date or dates, not later than April 1, ..., to bear interest from such date or dates, not earlier than April 1, 19.., and at such rate or rates as the Board of Directors or the Executive Committee of the Company may determine; to be issuable from time to time in such series, for such purposes, upon and subject to such terms and conditions and in such denominations, to be payable, both principal and interest, at such place or places, in such

currency or currencies and at such rate or rates of exchange, and to be in such form and to contain such additional terms and provisions, as said Board or Committee may determine.

2. To consent to, direct, approve, sanction, and authorize the execution and delivery to secure such bonds of a mortgage and deed of trust (or other proper instrument) on and of all or any part of the railroads, equipment, franchises, and property, including corporate stocks and obligations, owned by the Company at the date of the execution and delivery of such mortgage and deed of trust or at any time thereafter acquired by it, as in such mortgage and deed of trust shall be provided.

3. To make and approve any changes or alterations in the foregoing that may be brought before the meeting.

4. To determine and approve in the foregoing as set out in (1) and (2) and in all other particulars the form and terms of such mortgage and deed of trust (or other proper instrument), or to authorize the Board of Directors in its discretion to determine the same.

5. To approve, ratify, and confirm and to authorize and consent to any action thereto foretaken or authorized by the Board of Directors or by the Executive Committee of the Company, whether for the purposes of or in connection with or in contemplation of any of the matters aforesaid or otherwise which may be submitted to the meeting.

To vote upon creation of indebtedness

To consider and vote upon the proposition to create an original bonded indebtedness of and by the .... Corporation, in the principal sum of ..... Dollars ($.....), and to take such other and further action and proceedings as properly and usually pertain thereto.

To authorize corporate mortgage and refunding of bonds

To consider and act upon a proposal to authorize a mortgage of all or part of the Corporation's properties and franchises to secure an issue of bonds, in the aggregate amount of ..... Dollars ($.....), and to authorize the issuance of such bonds in order to retire existing bonds which will mature on ...., 19...

To consent to mortgage and issuance of convertible bonds

To vote on a proposition to mortgage the franchises and property of said Corporation and to consent to said mortgage and to the conversion of bonds that may be issued thereunder into capital stock of such corporation.

To execute and deliver bonds, and to sell same

To authorize the directors and officers of the Company to execute and deliver an issue of ..... Dollars ($.....) par value of *(insert description)* bonds of the Company and a Debenture Bond Agreement securing the same, and to dispose of said bonds or any part thereof at such prices and on such terms as the Board of Directors may determine; also for the purpose of authorizing the directors and officers of the Company to pay off and retire the unpaid bonds of the present *(insert description)* bonds amounting to ..... Dollars ($.....).

To authorize pledge of stock

To authorize the deposit and pledge by .... Corporation of the whole or any part of its holdings of the capital stock of subsidiary companies as security for a guaranty by .... Corporation of the payment of the principal and interest of a proposed issue of '..., face value, of Seven Per Cent Fifteen Year Sinking Fund Bonds of .... Company.

To consider proposition that trustee deliver securities when trust indenture terms are satisfied

To consider and vote upon the proposition that the ....Company of New York, Trustee under the Indenture, dated ...., 19.., securing the Fifty-Year Five Per Cent Bonds of the .... Corporation, and under the Indenture, dated ...., 19.., securing the Ten-Sixty-Year Five Per Cent Sinking Fund Bonds of said .... Corporation, be authorized, in case both of said Indentures are satisfied in accordance with their terms, to deliver to said .... Corporation any or all shares of stock, bonds, and other securities held thereunder by said Trustee (except stocks, bonds, and other securities held in the Sinking Fund, which shall be delivered to said .... Corporation in accordance with the provisions of said Indentures), in accordance with the request of said .... Corporation approved by two-thirds of the members of its Board of Directors.

To act upon sale of part of the corporate business

Voting and taking action upon and consenting to the sale and conveyance of the shipbuilding business of the Corporation, or any interest therein or any part thereof, together with the properties of the Corporation, real, personal, or mixed, in any way used, acquired, or held by the Corporation in connection with said business, or any interest therein or any part thereof, upon such terms and conditions as may be consented to by vote of the stockholders at such meeting or any adjournments thereof, or upon such terms and conditions as such meeting may authorize the Board of Directors to settle and determine, or taking such action upon the foregoing proposition or any modification thereof, as may be submitted to such meeting (or any adjournment thereof).

To sell stock holdings of the corporation

Taking such action as may be advisable to consummate the sale of the stock holdings of the Corporation in the .... Company, or any interest therein or any part thereof.

To authorize sale of property

To authorize the Board of Directors to sell the property of the Corporation known as .... Street, City of ...., State of ....

Sale of entire property

To consider and act upon a proposed agreement for the sale of the entire property and assets of the said .... Company.

To lease property from a corporation

A proposition will be presented for the approval of the stockholders to lease from the .... Company, for the use and operation by this Company, the portion of the railroad of the .... Company on .... Avenue between the town line separating the former Town of ...., and the former Town of ...., and .... Avenue, in the Borough of ...., City of ...., and State of ....., for a term of ..... (.....; years.

To lease property jointly with another from a corporation

One of the purposes of said meeting will be the approval of and consent to a lease for a term of 999 years proposed to be made by .... Railroad Company, as lessor, to this company and the .... Company jointly and severally as lessees, of the line of railroad proposed to be constructed by the lessor in the State of ....., together with appurtenant properties and franchises and all extensions and branches that may be constructed, acquired, or leased by the lessor with the approval of the lessees.

.... Railroad Company has been organized in the interest of the proposed lessee, each of which will own one half of its capital stock, to construct a line of railroad extending from .... to ...., in the counties of .... and ...., in the State of .... The Board of Directors has authorized the proposed lease subject to the approval of the stockholders.

To lease entire assets of a corporation

To authorize, approve, and consent to a lease proposed to be taken by the Company of the lines of railroad, rights, interests, powers, privileges, immunities, and appurtenant franchises and other properties of the .... Company, such lease to be for a term of ..... (.....) years.

To lease property to a corporation

A proposition will be presented for the approval of the stockholders to lease that portion of the railroad of the Company on .... Avenue from, at, or near .... Street, to .... Street, to the .... Company for a term of ..... (.....) years.

To approve of merger agreement

To consider and act upon approving the agreement made and entered into between the .... Company and the .... Corporation for the merger of the .... Company into the .... Corporation, and to take any and all other proceedings necessary or advisable in connection with such merger.

To act upon reorganization of the corporation

To consider and pass upon the recommendation of the Board of Directors that this Company be reorganized, either by consolidation or by transfer to another corporation of all the assets of the Company, to the end that the business of this Company and its Subsidiaries shall be conducted as one enterprise and be owned and operated by one corporation. Appended hereto is a letter addressed to the stockholders by the President of the .... Company containing information with reference to such proposal.

To act upon consolidation agreement

To take action upon the proposal to consolidate said .... Company and .... Corporation into a corporation to be known as ...., Inc., in accordance with and upon the terms and conditions set forth in a certain Agreement between said .... Company and .... Corporation, dated ...., 19.., or upon such other terms as may be approved by the stockholders at said meeting or any adjournment thereof.

To approve of agreement of consolidation

To consider and act upon an Agreement of Consolidation, dated ...., 19.., between the .... and the .... Corporation, a *(State)* Corporation, which has been entered into and signed by the Directors or a majority of them, of the corporations, and to transact such other business in connection with the foregoing as may come before the meeting.

The Agreement of Consolidation is on file and may be inspected at any time during business hours at the office of the Corporation, No. ...., ... *(City)*, ... *(State);* and a copy thereof will be furnished to any stockholder upon application to the Secretary.

To act upon a merger or consolidation

To consider and act upon a proposition to merge or to consolidate this Company with the A Company by this Company transferring substantially all its assets to: (1) a new company which shall also acquire all the assets of the A Company, the consideration to be paid to each constituent company for its assets so transferred to be a number of shares of the capital stock of the new company equal to the number of outstanding shares of such constituent company, or (2) the A Company, in exchange for a number of shares of the capital stock of the company last mentioned equal to the number of outstanding shares of this Company.

To acquire stock of another corporation

To consider and act upon the acquisition of shares of the capital stock of the .... Corporation.

To acquire entire assets and capital stock of a corporation

To approve or disapprove a written agreement for the sale of the .... Corporation, as vendor, to this corporation as vendee, of all the outstanding and issued capital stock, and of all the franchises, corporation property, rights, and credits of the .... Corporation, subject to all the debts, liabilities, duties, and obligations of the .... Corporation, the purchasing corporation to pay to the .... Corporation the sum of .... Dollars ($.....).

To acquire capital stock of another corporation

To authorize the directors and officers of the Company to acquire by purchase the entire capital stock of ...., a corporation organized and existing under the laws of the state of ...., and engaged in the business of ....

To acquire property

To vote upon a proposal to acquire the railroad, property, and franchise of the .... Railroad Company upon such terms as the Board of Directors shall determine and to approve and ratify any such acquisitions.

To approve purchase of property of another corporation

To approve the purchase of the plant and property of the .... Corporation at *(City)*, State of ....

To consider dissolution
(First Form)

To consider and act upon a proposition to dissolve this corporation and to distribute its assets according to law.

To consider dissolution
(Second Form)

To consider and act upon the proposed dissolution of the .... Corporation and the surrender and abandonment of its corporate authority and franchises and to transact any and all business necessary or incident thereto.

To consider dissolution
(Third Form)

The proposition of dissolving the .... Company will be considered and voted upon. The proposed resolution, which will be introduced at this annual meeting, will direct that, in the event said dissolution is authorized by the stockholders, a proportionate distribution of substantially all the cash on hand of the corporation be presently made to the stockholders of said corporation by way of liquidating dividend; and that the remainder of the assets of said corporation, which will consist of a small cash balance, second mortgages, and other securities, be transferred to a Trustee or Trustees in liquidation for the purpose of thereafter liquidating said assets of the corporation. The plan of dissolution so to be voted upon will involve a surrender by the stockholders of their stock upon the distribution to them of the cash above mentioned, together with certificates of beneficial interest in said trust, which certificates of beneficial interest will ultimately be surrendered upon the distribution of proceeds realized from the liquidation of the assets of the corporation so turned over to the Trustees.

To dissolve a trust, and organize a corporation to take over the property and assets of the trust

1. To pass a resolution or resolutions authorizing ...., ..., ... and ...., or one or more of them, as agent of the certificate holders voting therefor, to convey all such certificate holders' right, title, and interest in and to the property and assets of .... Trust as beneficial and equitable part owners thereof and their certificate or certificates of beneficial interest representing said ownership and the legal ownership and title in and to such property and assets held by the Trustees corresponding to their right, title, and interest therein, to .... Corporation, a corporation of Delaware (such conveyance to be made in connection and contemporaneously with a general conveyance by the Trustees of said Trust of all the property, property interests, securities, and moneys constituting the entire trust fund and assets of the Trust to said corporation), in exchange for the delivery to said four persons as individuals, or any one or more of them, acting as agents of such certificate holders, such certificate holders' due proportion of the entire authorized Special Stock of said .... Corporation, which entire authorized Special Stock consists of 208,433 shares without nominal or par value;

2. To pass a resolution or resolutions authorizing ...., ..., ..., and ...., or one or more of them, to receive from said corporation as the agent of certificate holders voting in favor thereof, for such certificate holders' use and benefit and in their name and behalf, their due proportion of the said 208,433 shares of Special Stock of said corporation issued in exchange for said certificates (and assets), consisting of one share of said Special Stock for each share of beneficial interest represented by certificate or certificates of beneficial interest in said Trust so held and conveyed, such receipt of shares of said corporation to be in connection and contemporaneously with the receipt by said persons as individuals and/or as Trustees of the entire authorized Special Stock of said corporation on the acquisition by it of the entire property, estate and assets of said Trust;

3. To pass a resolution or resolutions authorizing ...., ..., ..., and ...., or one or more of them, to distribute among the Trust

beneficiaries and certificate holders, upon the surrender by them, respectively, of their certificates of beneficial interest, the certificates of stock of said corporation so received by said persons as individuals or as Trustees representing all the shares of the Special Stock thereof in accordance with the respective interests of the said beneficiaries therein and in the ratio of one share of said Special Stock for each one share of beneficial interest;

4. To authorize the Trustees of .... Trust, after such distribution has been completed and the Trust estate fully disposed of, to terminate and dissolve the Trust as provided in the trust deed by which it was created; and

5. To authorize the Trustees of .... Trust, acting as Trustees and/or as individuals, to enter into such contracts, execute such conveyances and transfers and perform such other acts and deeds as may be necessary or appropriate to carry out the plan of replacing the Trust by a corporation, and of terminating and dissolving the Trust, recommended by the Trustees in their statement to certificate holders, dated ...., 19.., according to the intent thereof.

WAIVER OF NOTICE OF MEETING OF STOCKHOLDERS

We, the undersigned, being all the stockholders of .... Corporation, a corporation organized under the laws of the State of ...., do hereby waive any and all notice as provided by the laws of the State of ...., or by the Articles of Incorporation or By-laws of said Corporation, and do hereby consent to the holding of a .... *(insert annual or special)* meeting of stockholders of said Corporation, on ...., 19.., at ..... P.M., or any adjournment or adjournments thereof, at the principal office of the Corporation, ... *(Street)*, ... *(City)*, ... *(State)*, for the purpose of .... *(insert purposes; see form No. 26)*, and we do hereby consent to the transaction of any business, in addition to the business herein noticed to be transacted, that may come before the meeting.

Dated at the City of ...., State of ...., this .. day of ...., 19...

...., holding ..... shares

...., holding ..... shares

...., holding ..... shares

(Signatures of all stockholders)

WAIVER OF NOTICE AND OF PUBLICATION OF NOTICE OF STOCKHOLDERS' MEETING

The undersigned, being all the stockholders of .... Corporation, a corporation organized under the laws of the State of ...., hereby assent and agree that a meeting of the stockholders of said Corporation be held at the office of the Corporation, ... *(Street)*, ... *(City)*, ... *(State)*, on ...., 19.., at ...... A.M., for the purpose of .... *(insert purposes; see form on page 73)*, and for the transaction of such other business as may come before the meeting.

We do hereby waive any and all notice of the said meeting and publication of the said notice which may be required by the statutes of the State of ...., or by the Articles of Incorporation by By-laws of the said Corporation, and agree that any business transacted at such meeting shall be as valid and effective as though held after notice duly given and published.

Dated at the City of ...., State of ...., this .. day of ......, 19...

...., holding .... shares
...., holding .... shares
...., holding .... shares

WAIVER OF NOTICE OF SPECIAL MEETING SIGNED BY INDIVIDUAL STOCKHOLDER

I, the undersigned, being a stockholder of the .... Corporation, a corporation organized under the laws of the State of ...., holding ..... (....) shares of the stock of the Corporation, do hereby waive any and all notice required by the laws of the State of ...., or by the Articles of Incorporation or By-laws of said Corporation, and do hereby consent to the holding of a special meeting of stockholders of said Corporation, on ...., 19.., at ..... P.M., or any adjournment or adjournments thereof, at the office of the Corporation, ... *(Street)*, ... *(City)*, ... *(State)*, for the following purposes:

(Here insert purposes; see form on page 73.)

I do further consent to the transaction of any business, in addition to the business noticed to be transacted, that may come before the meeting.

Dated at the City of ...., State of ...., this .. day of ...., 19...

....
(Signature of Stockholder)

PROXIES FOR STOCKHOLDERS' MEETINGS

PROXY APPOINTING INDIVIDUAL PROXY FOR ANNUAL MEETING

Know All Men By These Presents, That ...., the undersigned, being the owner(s) of ..... (.....) shares of the capital stock of the .... Corporation do .. hereby constitute and appoint .... of .... *(City)*, ... *(State)*, true and lawful attorney, for and in ..... name, place, and stead, to vote upon the stock owned by ..... or standing in ...... name, as ..... proxy, at the annual meeting of the stockholders of the said company, to be held at the company's office, No. .., ..., City of ...., State of .... on ...., 19.., or on such other day as the meeting may be thereafter held by adjournment or otherwise. according to the number of votes ..... now or may then be entitled to cast, hereby granting the attorney full power and authority to act for ..... and in ..... name at the meeting or meetings, in voting for directors of the company or otherwise, and in the transaction of such other business as may come before the meeting, as fully as ..... could do if personally present, with full power

of substitution and revocation, hereby ratifying and confirming all that ..... said
attorney or substitute may do in ..... place, name, and stead.

In Witness Whereof, ... have hereunto set ..... hand and seal this ...... day
of ...., 19...

                                                    .... (L.S.)
                                                    .... (L.S.)

PROXY FOR FIRST ANNUAL MEETING OF STOCKHOLDERS

Know All Men By These Presents. That the undersigned stockholder of
.... Corporation, a corporation of the State of ...., does hereby
constitute and appoint Messrs. ...., ..., ..., and .... the
attorneys and proxies, and each of them attorney and proxy, irrevocable, of the
undersigned, with full power of substitution, for and in the name, place, and stead
of the undersigned, to vote upon all the stock held by the undersigned in
.... Corporation, according to the number of votes and shares of stock
which the undersigned would be entitled to vote if personally present at the firs
annual meeting of the stockholders of .... Corporation, to be held at the
principal office of the Corporation, ... *(Street)*, ... *(City)*, ...
(State), ... *(Day of Week)*, ..., 19.. at ..... A.M., and at any adjournment or adjournments thereof, for the following purposes:

(Here insert purpose clauses.)

as fully and with the same effect as the undersigned might or could do if personally
present at said meeting; hereby ratifying and confirming all that said attorneys and
proxies, and each of them, or their or his substitutes or substitute, may lawfully do
or cause to be done by virtue hereof; hereby revoking any proxies or proxy to vote
said shares heretofore given by the undersigned to any person or persons whom-
soever.

In Witness Whereof, the undersigned stockholder has executed this proxy,
this .. day of ...., 19...
                                                    .... (L.S.)

Notice. A proxy to be executed by a corporation should be signed in its name by its President or
one of its Vice-presidents, and its corporate seal should be affixed and attested by its Secretary or one of
its Assistant Secretaries or other proper officer.

PROXY FOR ANNUAL MEETING OF STOCKHOLDERS; PURPOSES
OF MEETING INDICATED BY REFERENCE TO NOTICE

.... Corporation
.... Street
.... City, ... State

Know All Men By These Presents. That I, the undersigned, do hereby constitute and appoint .... and .... with power to be exercised by

them or either of them, for me and in my name, place, and stead, to vote as my proxy at the annual meeting of the stockholders of .... Corporation, to be held on ...., 19.., at ..... P.M., at the office of said Corporation, ... *(Street)*, ... *(City)*, ... *(State)*, and at all adjournments of said meeting, upon all the matters referred to in the notice of the meeting dated ...., 19.., to which notice this proxy was attached at the time of the receipt thereof by me, according to the number of votes I should be entitled to vote if then personally present, with full power of substitution and revocation, hereby ratifying and confirming all that my proxies, or either of them, or their substitutes, may do by virtue hereof, and I do hereby revoke all proxies heretofore given by me for use at said meeting or at any adjournment thereof.

IN WITNESS WHEREOF, I have hereunto set my hand and seal, this .. day of ...., 19...

.... (L.S.)

Please sign, detach, and return in the enclosed envelope.

PROXY FOR ANNUAL MEETING OF STOCKHOLDERS OF CORPORATION AFFECTED BY SECURITIES EXCHANGE ACT OF 1934

[NOTE: Stockholders who do not expect to attend the meeting are requested to sign and return this Proxy in the enclosed stamped envelope, addressed to Secretary, ... Company, No. .. .. Avenue, ... *(City)*, ... *(State)*.]

.... COMPANY
PROXY

KNOW ALL MEN BY THESE PRESENTS, That the undersigned hereby constitutes and appoints ...., ..., and ...., or any of them, with power of substitution, attorneys and proxies to appear and vote all of the shares of stock standing in the name of the undersigned, at the annual meeting of stockholders of the .... Corporation, to be held at No. .... *(Street)*, ... *(City)*, ... *(State)*, on 19.., at ..... A.M., and at any and all adjournments thereof; and the undersigned hereby instructs said attorneys to vote:

1. To elect two Directors for the ensuing year.

2. To authorize the Board of Directors to select the firm of ...., as auditors of the .... Corporation for the ensuing year ....**Yes No**
☐ ☐

3. Upon any other business which may properly come before the meeting or any adjournment thereof.

IF NO INSTRUCTIONS ARE GIVEN ABOVE, THE UNDERSIGNED HEREBY AUTHORIZES THE PROXIES NAMED HEREIN TO VOTE IN FAVOR OF THE MATTER SET FORTH IN PARAGRAPH 2.

The undersigned hereby acknowledges receipt of the Proxy Statement dated
...., 19...

Dated this .... day of ....., 19...

.... (L.S.)

This Proxy Is Solicited on Behalf of the Management
of the Corporation.

PROXY FOR ANNUAL MEETING, GIVING DISCRETION
TO PROXIES AS TO HOW TO VOTE

Know All Men By These Presents. That the undersigned hereby constitutes and appoints ....., ..., and ....., and each of them, attorneys and agents, with power of substitution in each of them for and in behalf of the undersigned, to vote as proxy at the annual meeting of the stockholders of .... Company, to be held at the main office of the Company, ... *(Street)*, ... *(City)*, ... *(State)*, on ...., 19.., at ..... P.M., and at any adjournment or adjournments thereof, according to the number of shares that the undersigned would be entitled to vote if then personally present, upon the matters and proposals set forth in the Notice of said meeting, dated ...., 19.., and the Proxy Statement, dated ...., 19.. furnished therewith, copies of which have been received by the undersigned.

The undersigned agrees that said proxies and each of them may vote in favor of the directors named in said Proxy Statement, or, in their discretion, in favor of the election as directors of any other persons, and may vote in accordance with their discretion on all matters, not known or determined at the time of the solicitation of this proxy, which may legally come before the meeting.

Dated ...., 19...

....

When signing as attorney, executor, administrator, trustee or guardian,
please give your full title as such.

PROXY FOR ANNUAL MEETING OF
STOCKHOLDERS, INDICATING VOTE IN FAVOR OF ONE OF THE
SPECIAL PURPOSES OF THE MEETING

Know All Men By These Presents. That the undersigned, a stockholder of .... Company, does hereby constitute and appoint ....,
..............., ..., and ...., or a majority of them, true and lawful attorneys, agents, and proxies, with full power of substitution, for and in his name, place, and stead, to vote upon all of the shares of stock standing in his name at the annual meeting of stockholders of .... Company, to be held at .....
.... *(Street)*, ... *(City)*, ... *(State)*, on .... *(Day of Week)*,
...., 19.. at ..... P.M., and at any or all adjournments thereof, with all the powers the undersigned would possess if then personally present, and especially

(but without limiting the general authorization of power hereby given) to vote in favor of amending the charter of the Corporation by increasing the common capital stock from ..... Dollars ($.....) to ..... Dollars ($.....).

Witness my hand and seal, this .. day of ...., 19...

.... (L.S)

PROXY FOR ANNUAL MEETING, INDICATING PERSONS FOR WHOM PROXIES ARE TO VOTE

Know All Men By These Presents. That I, the undersigned, do hereby constitute and appoint ...., ..., ..., ..., and ...., or any one or more of them, with power of substitution, my true and lawful attorney, or attorneys, for me and in my name and stead, to vote as proxy or proxies upon all shares of stock of .... Company, entitled to vote, owned by me or standing in my name on the books of the company, at the close of business on ...., 19.., at the annual meeting of the stockholders of .... Company to be held at the office of the Company, ... *(Street)*, ... *(City)*, ... *(State)*, on ...., 19.., at ..... A.M., or at any adjournment thereof, for the following purposes;

(Here insert purposes.)

Witness my hand and seal, this .. day of ...., 19...

.... (L.S.)

(In order for this proxy to be effective, your name must be signed on this line exactly as stenciled below.)

I hereby request my attorney, or attorneys, above named, in casting any vote as my proxy, to vote for the following persons as directors of .... Company:

1.	7. ....
2.	8. ....
3.	9. ....
4.	10. ....
5.	11. ....
6.	

.... (L.S.)

(If you fill in names in the above spaces, also sign here, exactly the same as above.)

Many stockholders knowing the personnel of the Company will desire to have their votes cast for particular persons. They may fill in any number of names on the lines above up to 11. Where names are not filled in, the proxies above named will select the directors for whom they, or any one or more of them, will vote.

Notice. In preparing proxy for return, be sure to fill in date, and mail promptly in enclosed envelope.

PROXY FOR ANNUAL MEETING AND ANY MEETINGS HELD DURING THE YEAR FOR ELECTION OR REMOVAL OF DIRECTORS; MAJORITY PRESENT AT MEETING TO ACT

KNOW ALL MEN BY THESE PRESENTS, That the undersigned stockholder of ...., a Corporation organized under the laws of the State of ...., does hereby constitute and appoint ...., ..., and ...., and each or any of them, the true and lawful attorney or attorneys, agent or agents, and proxy or proxies of the undersigned, with power of substitution, for and in the name, place, and stead of the undersigned, to attend the annual meeting of stockholders of the .... Corporation, to be held at the principal office of the Corporation, ... *(Street)*, ... *(City)*, ... *(State)*, on ...., 19.., and any and all adjournments thereof, and to attend any and all other meetings of the stockholders of the Corporation held during the calendar year ending ...., 19.., for the election or removal of directors of the .... Corporation, and any and all adjournments thereof, and then and there to vote all stock held or owned by the undersigned or standing in his name, for the transaction of any and all business that may come before such meeting or meetings, and any and all adjournments thereof, including the election or removal of directors; and upon all matters and in all things that may come before such meeting or meetings and any and all adjournments thereof, to represent and to vote all shares of stock of the undersigned, according to the number of votes which the undersigned would be entitled to cast if personally present, hereby revoking any proxy or proxies heretofore given to vote such stock, and ratifying and confirming all that said attorneys, agents, and proxies may do by virtue hereof.

The said proxies are hereby authorized and empowered to act in the following manner:

If all three proxies be present at such meeting or meetings or any adjournments thereof, according to the determination of a majority; if only two of the three proxies be present, according to the determination of such two; and if only one proxy be present, according to the determination of such one; and thus to exercise all the powers of all of said attorneys, agents, and proxies hereunder.

WITNESS my hand, this ..day of ...., 19...

....
(Signature of stockholder)

PROXY FOR ANNUAL MEETING OF COMMON STOCKHOLDERS AND SPECIAL MEETING OF PREFERRED STOCKHOLDERS; PURPOSES SPECIFIED IN NOTICE REPEATED IN PROXY

Annual Meeting, ..., 19.. ..... Shares of Common Stock
        (Common Stockholders)
Special Meeting, ..., 19.. ..... Shares of Preferred Stock
        (Preferred Stockholders)

KNOW ALL MEN BY THESE PRESENTS, That the undersigned, the holder of Common Stock and/or Preferred Stock in .... Company, Inc., a corporation of the state of ...., hereby irrevocably constitutes and appoints ...., ..., ..., and .... the attorneys and proxies, and each of them, with full power to act without the others, the attorney and proxy of the undersigned, for and in the name, place, and stead of the undersigned: (1) to vote upon all shares of Common Stock held by the undersigned in said Company at the annual meeting of stockholders of the Company, to be held at the office of the Company, ... *(Street)*, ... *(City)*, ... *(State)*, on ...., 19.., at .... P.M., for the election of directors, for the approval of the form of the annual report of the Company for the year 19.., and for or against the adoption of resolutions and all acts and proposals that may properly come before the meeting, or any adjournment or adjournments thereof; and (2) to vote upon all shares of Preferred Stock held by the undersigned in the Company at the special meeting of Preferred Stockholders of the Company, to be held at the office of the Company, ..., *(Street)*, ... *(City)*, ... *(State)*, on ...., 19.., at ...... P.M., or at any adjournment or adjournments thereof, in favor of a proposal to authorize the Board of Directors of the Company to create and issue ...... Dollars ($.....) principal amount of Ten-Year 8% Sinking Fund Debentures of the Company, a description of certain provisions of the Indentures under which the Debentures will be issued being printed on the reverse side of the Notice of Meeting to which this proxy was attached, the receipt of which Notice of Meeting is hereby acknowledged; according to the number of votes present at the annual meeting and the special meeting, or any adjournment or adjournments of either or both of the meetings, and the undersigned does hereby ratify and confirm all that said attorneys and proxies, or any of them, or their or his substitutes or substitute, may do in the premises.

WITNESS the hand and seal of the undersigned, this .. day of ...., 19...

.... (L.S.)

PROXY FOR SPECIAL MEETING OF STOCKHOLDERS; PURPOSES OF MEETING NOT INDICATED

KNOW ALL MEN BY THESE PRESENTS. That ...., the undersigned, stockholder in the .... Company, does hereby appoint .... and ...., or either of them, true and lawful attorneys, with power of substitution for ..... and in ..... name to vote, as ..... proxy, at the Special Meeting of the Stockholders in said Company, to be held at the City of ...., State of ...., on ...., 19.., or at any adjournment thereof, with all the powers which ...... would possess if personally present.

Dated this .. day of ...., 19...

.... (L.S.)

PROXY FOR SPECIAL MEETING OF STOCKHOLDERS; PURPOSES INDICATED BY REFERENCE TO NOTICE OF MEETING

KNOW ALL MEN BY THESE PRESENTS:

That the undersigned stockholder of .... Company hereby appoints and constitutes ...., ..., ..., and ...., and each of them, the true and lawful attorneys and proxies of the undersigned, with several power of substitution, for and in the name of the undersigned, to vote at the special meeting of the stockholders of said Company, to be held at .... *(Street)*, ... *(City)*, ... *(State)*, on ...., 19.., at ..... P.M., Eastern Standard Time, or at any adjournment thereof, with all the powers which the undersigned would possess if personally present, including the power of voting in favor of the propositions referred to in the notice of the meeting, hereby revoking any proxy or proxies heretofore given to vote upon such stock, and ratifying and confirming all that said attorneys or proxies may do by virtue hereof. A majority of such of my attorneys or proxies as shall be present and shall act at the meeting (or if only one be present and act, then that one) shall have and may exercise all of the powers of all of said attorneys or proxies hereunder.

WITNESS my hand and seal, this .. day of ......, 19...

....

PROXY FOR SPECIAL MEETING OF STOCKHOLDERS; PURPOSES SPECIFIED IN NOTICE REPEATED IN PROXY

KNOW ALL MEN BY THESE PRESENTS. That I, the undersigned, being the owner of ..... (.....) shares of the Preferred Stock and ..... (.....) shares of the Common Stock of the Corporation, do hereby constitute and appoint ...., ..., and ...., or one or more of them, my true and lawful attorney or attorneys, in my name, place, and stead to vote all the stock owned by me or standing in my name as my proxy at a special meeting of the stockholders of said Corporation, to be held at .... *(Street)*, ... *(City)*, ... *(State)*, at ..... A.M., ..., 19.., or on such other day as the meeting may be thereafter held by adjournment or otherwise, according to the number of votes I am now or may then be entitled to cast, hereby granting said attorney or attorneys full power and authority to act for me and in my name at the meeting or meetings, for the purpose of considering and acting upon the following propositions recommended by the Board of Directors of the Corporation:

(Here list purposes of meeting.)

and for the transaction of such other business as may lawfully come before the meeting, as fully as I could do if personally present, with full power of substitution and revocation, hereby ratifying and confirming all that my attorney or attorneys may do in my name, place and stead.

In Witness Whereof, I have hereunto set my hand and seal, this .. day of ...., 19...

.... (Seal)

PROXY FOR SPECIAL MEETING OF STOCKHOLDERS, WAIVING NOTICE OF MEETING AND GIVING AUTHORITY TO SIGN CONSENT TO PROPOSED ACTION

Know All Men By These Presents. That the undersigned, stockholder of .... Corporation does hereby constitute and appoint .... and ...., attorneys, agents, and proxies, and each of them attorney, agent, and proxy, with power of substitution, to vote as proxy for and in behalf of the undersigned, at a special meeting of stockholders of said Corporation, to be held at the principal office of the Corporation, at *(Street)*, ... *(City)*, ... *(State)*, on ...., 19.., hereby waiving all requirements of the State of .... and of the Articles of Incorporation and By-laws of said Corporation as to service of notice of said meeting and publication thereof, and on such other day or days as the meeting may thereafter be held by adjournment or otherwise, according to the number of votes which the undersigned may now or may then be entitled to cast; and the undersigned hereby grants to said attorneys, agents, or proxies, and each of them, full power and authority to act for the undersigned at said meeting or meetings; and as fully as the undersigned could do if personally present, to vote upon any and all matters which may come before said meeting, including all matters mentioned in the call for said meeting dated ...., 19.., a copy of which has been received by the undersigned, and especially to vote in favor of the proposal to .... *(insert subject matter of proposal)*, mentioned in said notice, and in the name and in behalf of the undersigned to consent to such proposed .... and to sign the name of the undersigned to such consent; hereby ratifying and confirming all that said attorneys, agents or proxies, and each of them, may do in the name, place, and stead of the undersigned.

In Witness Whereof, the undersigned stockholder has hereunto set his hand and seal, this ... day of ...., 19...

.... (L.S.)

PROXY FOR SPECIAL MEETING OF STOCKHOLDERS; AUTHORITY TO SIGN CONFIRMATION OF RECORD OF MEETING

Know All Men By These Presents:

That I ...., the holder of ..... shares of Common Stock in the .... Company, do hereby appoint ...., ..., and ...., or any of them, my true and lawful attorney, with power of substitution, for me and in my name, to vote as my proxy at the meeting of the stockholders of said Company to be held at the office of the Company, ... *(Street)*, ... *(City)*, ... *(State)*, on ...., 19.., at ..... A.M., or at any adjournment thereof, with all the powers which I would possess if personally present, and particularly to vote as my proxy in favor of any and all of the propositions referred to in the notice of said meeting and/or in the President's letter accompanying said notice, and also, if necessary, to sign my name to any confirmation of the record of said meeting.

Wɪᴛɴᴇss my hand and seal, this .. day of ...., 19...

.... (L.S.)

PROXY FOR SPECIAL MEETING OF STOCKHOLDERS, GIVING INSTRUCTIONS TO VOTE IN FAVOR OF PROPOSED RESOLUTIONS; PROXY TO AN INDIVIDUAL

Kɴᴏᴡ Aʟʟ Mᴇɴ Bʏ Tʜᴇsᴇ Pʀᴇsᴇɴᴛs,That the undersigned, being the owner of ..... (.....) shares of the capital stock of the .... Corporation, does hereby constitute and appoint ...., of ....*(Street)*, ... *(City)*, ... *(State)*, ... true and lawful attorney, in .... name, place, and stead, to vote upon the stock owned by ..... or standing in ..... name, as ..... proxy, at the special meeting of the stockholders of the said Corporation to be held at the Corporation's office, on ...., 19.., or on such other day as the meeting may be thereafter held by adjournment or otherwise, according to the number of votes ..... may now or may then be entitled to cast, hereby granting the attorney full power and authority to vote in favor of the four resolutions described in the notice of meeting as follows:

(Here indicate resolutions by title or number as they appear in the notice.)

and to vote to consent to the proposition described in paragraph .. of the notice of meeting, with full power of substitution and revocation.

Iɴ Wɪᴛɴᴇss Wʜᴇʀᴇᴏғ, ... have hereunto set ..... hand and seal, this .. day of ...., 19..,

....

[*Note*. See also form on page 96.]

PROXY FOR SPECIAL MEETING, ON WHICH STOCKHOLDER INDICATES HOW TO VOTE ON THE SPECIAL PURPOSE OF MEETING

Kɴᴏᴡ Aʟʟ Mᴇɴ Bʏ Tʜᴇsᴇ Pʀᴇsᴇɴᴛs,That the undersigned stockholder in .... Company hereby constitutes and appoints ...., ..., and ...., attorneys, with power of substitution to each, for and on behalf of the undersigned, and with the powers the undersigned would possess if personally present, to vote all stock of the undersigned in .... Company at the special meeting of stockholders of said Company to be held on ...., 19.., and at any adjournments of said meeting, upon the matter set forth in the notice of said meeting and proxy statement, dated ...., 19.., and upon such other matters as may properly come before the meeting. Copies of such notice of meeting and proxy statement have been received by the undersigned. A majority of such of said attorneys as shall be present and shall act at said meeting shall have and may exercise all the powers of all said attorneys hereunder.

Without limiting the general authorization and power hereby given, said attorneys are specifically directed to vote as indicated below on the resolution to be submitted to the meeting:

☐ *FOR (The management recommends a vote FOR).*
☐ *AGAINST*

Said Attorneys Are Authorized to Vote This Proxy FOR Such Resolution Unless a Contrary Direction Is Indicated.

Dated ...., 19 ..
Please sign here

....

Please sign as name appears on stock certificate (as indicated above). When signing as attorney, executor, administrator, trustee, guardian, etc., give full title as such. For joint accounts, each joint owner should sign.

PROXY APPOINTING TWO PERSONS TO ACT AS ALTERNATES; PROXY GIVEN WITHOUT SOLICITATION

I hereby nominate and appoint ...., if present, and if said .... is not present, then ...., as my attorney, or proxy, in the order herein named, to represent me and cast my vote by proxy at the annual meeting of the stockholders of .... Corporation, to be held at the principal office of the Corporation, on ...., .., 19.., or at any adjournment thereof, as fully and with the same effect as I might or could do if personally present at such meeting, hereby ratifying and confirming all that my attorney may legally do by virtue hereof.

This proxy is given voluntarily and without any solicitation by an agent of the Corporation. Any proxy heretofore given by me for said meeting is hereby revoked.
Dated ...., 19 ...

....

PROXY FOR A SPECIFIED PERIOD

Know All Men By These Presents, That I, the undersigned, of ...... *(Street)*, ... *(City)*, ... *(State)*, do hereby irrevocably constitute and appoint .... of .... *(Street)*, ... *(City)*, ... *(State)*, my true and lawful attorney, in my name, place, and stead, for a period of ....,

beginning ...., 19.., to vote upon the stock owned by me or standing in my name, as my proxy, at any and all meetings of the stockholders of ....
Corporation held within the period, upon any and all matters which may be presented, considered, and voted upon at any annual or special meeting of stockholders of the Corporation, including the election of directors, as fully and with like effect as I might or could have done if personally present, hereby ratifying and confirming all that my attorney may do in my name, place, and stead.

WITNESS my hand and seal, this .. day of ...., 19...

.... (L.S.)

PROXY FOR SPECIFIED PERIOD UNLESS SOONER REVOKED; AUTHORITY TO SIGN CONSENT CERTIFICATE

KNOW ALL MEN BY THESE PRESENTS:
That I/we, ..., do hereby constitute and appoint ...., ..., and ...., jointly and severally, my/our true and lawful attorneys for me/us and in my/our name and stead, to attend all meetings whatsoever of the stockholders of the .... Company, and to vote any and all shares of the capital stock of the .... Company, at the time standing in my/our name on the books of said Company, at any meeting of the stockholders, and also to sign my/our name as such stockholder to any consent certificate or other document relating to said Company which the laws of the State of .... may require or permit.
This proxy is to continue in force for the period of ..... (.....) years from the date hereof, BUT MAY BE REVOKED AT ANY TIME BY NOTICE THEREOF IN WRITING, FILED WITH THE SECRETARY.
Date at ....(L.S.)
...., 19..,   Address ....

PROXY COUPLED WITH AN INTEREST

KNOW ALL MEN BY THESE PRESENTS, That I, a stockholder of the ....
Corporation, holding ..... (.....) shares of stock of the said Corporation, do hereby make, constitute, and appoint ...., and/or ...., and/or ...., or any of them, with full power of substitution, and during and for the period of .... *(insert months or years)* from the date hereof, the true and lawful attorneys and proxies of the undersigned for and in my name, place, and stead in respect to such stock or any other stock received by the attorney or attorneys, or his or their substitute or substitutes, in said Corporation, or any other corporation or corporations in respect thereof, for the following purposes: to represent and vote for the undersigned at all meetings, regular or special, of said Corporation, or said other corporation or corporations; to consent to and waive notice of all special or regular meetings; to consent to and enter into any transactions, contracts, reorganizations, recapitalizations, dissolutions, changes of name,

or other acts of whatsoever kind or nature requiring the consent of stockholders or for which the consent of stockholders is requested by the Corporation, or any other corporation or corporations whose stock is received in respect of the stock of said Corporation, or by the directors or officers thereof; to receive dividends; to accept in lieu of the stock of the Corporation cash, and/or new stock, and/or other securities in the same Corporation, or any other corporation or corporations, and/or other securities, and/or other consideration, whether in a single or in several transactions; to transfer, indorse, or otherwise deal with the stock, and/or cash, and/or other securities, and/or other consideration, and to execute a deed, bill of sale, receipt, discharge, release, or other agreement or other instrument in respect of the interest of the undersigned in such stock, cash, securities, and/or other consideration; and generally and without limitation because of the above specific enumeration of authority hereby conferred, to do any and all acts and things which the undersigned might or could do in respect to such stock, cash, securities, and/or other consideration. And the undersigned hereby agrees that, in consideration of the acceptance of the authority hereby conferred and of the undertaking of the attorney or attorneys, or his or their substitute or substitutes, to act uniformly in behalf of all the stockholders, subject to their instructions designating persons to receive new stock, cash, securities, and/or other consideration, this power of attorney and proxy is coupled with an interest and is irrevocable, and the undersigned hereby ratifies and confirms all that said attorney or attorneys and proxy or proxies, or their substitute or substitutes, may lawfully do or cause to be done by virtue hereof.

IN WITNESS WHEREOF, I have hereunto set my hand and seal, this .. day of ...., 19..

.... (L.S.)

PROXY FROM ADMINISTRATOR OR INDIVIDUAL EXECUTOR

KNOW ALL MEN BY THESE PRESENTS, That ...., as .... *(insert administrator or executor)* of the Estate of ...., deceased, hereby constitutes and appoints .... his true and lawful attorney, for him and in his name, place, and stead to attend the special meeting of stockholders of .... Corporation, to be held at the principal office of the corporation, ... *(Street)*, ... *(City)*, ... *(State)*, ..., 19.., at ..... A.M., and all adjournments thereof, and then and there to vote all of the stock of the .... Corporation now standing in the name of ...., as .... *(insert administrator or executor)* of the Estate of .... deceased, in favor of a proposed .... *(insert subject matter on which vote is to be taken)*.
Dated this .... day of .., 19 ..

....
As ....
(administrator or executor)
of the Estate of ....,
Deceased

PROXY FROM GUARDIAN OF AN INCOMPETENT

KNOW ALL MEN BY THESE PRESENTS, That ...., as Guardian of the Estate of ...., an incompetent person, hereby constitutes and appoints .... his true and lawful attorney, for him and in his name, place, and stead to attend the annual meeting of the stockholders of .... Corporation, at the office of the Corporation, ... *(Street)*, ... *(City)*, ... *(State)*, on ...., 19.., at ..... P.M., and at any and all adjournments thereof, and then and there to vote all stock of the .... Corporation now standing in the name of .... as Guardian of the Estate of ...., an incompetent person.
Dated this .... day of .., 19 ..

....
As Guardian of the Estate of
....., an Incompetent Person

PROXY FROM CORPORATE EXECUTOR

KNOW ALL MEN BY THESE PRESENTS, That .... Trust Company, as Executor of the Last Will and Testament of ...., deceased, hereby constitutes and appoints .... its true and lawful attorney, for it and in its name, place, and stead to attend the annual meeting of stockholders of the .... Corporation, to be held at the principal office of the Corporation, ... *(Street)*, ... *(City)*, ... *(State)*, on ...., 19.., at ..... P.M., and all adjournments thereof, and then and there to vote all the stock of the .... Corporation standing the name of the .... Trust Company, as Executor of the Last Will and Testament of ...., deceased.

IN WITNESS WHEREOF, the ....Trust Company, as Executor of the Last Will and Testament of ...., deceased, has hereunto caused its corporate name and seal to be affixed by its officers thereunto duly authorized this .. day of ...., 19...
(Corporate Seal)
Attest:
Secretary

.... Trust Company
As Executor of the Last Will and
Testament of ....
Deceased
            By ....
                            President

PROXY FROM A TRUSTEE

KNOW ALL MEN BY THESE PRESENTS, That .... Trust Company, as trustee for .... under a certain Trust Agreement dated ...., 19.., between it and ...., hereby constitutes and appoints .... its true and lawful attorney, for it and in its name, place, and stead to attend the .... meeting of the stockholders of the .... Corporation, to be held at the principal office of the Corporation, at .... *(Street)*, ... *(City)*, ... *(State)*, on ...., 19.., at ..... P.M., and all adjournments thereof, and then and there to vote all stock of the .... Corporation now or hereafter standing in the name of the .... Trust Company, as trustee under the Trust Agreement, provided, however, that this proxy shall not be used for the purpose of voting said stock in any way not consistent with the provisions of said Trust Agreement.

In Witness Whereof, the .... Trust Company, as trustee under the said Trust Agreement, has caused these presents to be signed by its President and Secretary, and its corporate seal to be hereto affixed this .. day of ...., 19...

> .... Trust Company
> As Trustee under Trust Agreement
> with ...., dated
> ...., 19..
> By ....
> President
> By ....
> Secretary

(Corporate Seal)

PROXY FROM A CORPORATION

Know All Men By These Presents, That .... Corporation, a corporation organized and existing under and by virtue of the laws of the State of ...., owning and holding ..... (....) shares of the capital stock of the .... Company, does hereby appoint and constitute .... of .... *(City)*, ... *(State)*, its true and lawful attorney, to attend the annual meeting of the stockholders of the .... Company, to be held at the principal office of the company, ... *(Street)*, ... *(City)*, ... *(State)*, on ...., 19.., at ..... A.M., and all adjournments thereof, and then and there to vote in behalf of this Company, and in its name, place, and stead, as its proxy and representative, the number of votes which this Corporation would be entitled to cast if actually present; and full power and authority are hereby conferred upon said attorney, in the name of this Corporation and in its behalf, and as its corporate act and deed, to consent in writing, and upon the records of the meeting, to any and all votes and proceedings thereof, and to do all such other things within the power of a stockholder of said .... Company as may, in his judgment, be necessary or advantageous for the interests of this Corporation.

IN WITNESS WHEREOF, this Corporation has hereunto caused its corporate name and seal to be affixed by its President and its Secretary, thereunto duly authorized by a resolution of its Board of Directors, duly passed and adopted on the .. day of ...., 19...

.... Corporation

By ....
President

By ....
Secretary

(Corporate Seal)

SUBSTITUTION OF PROXY

KNOW ALL MEN BY THESE PRESENTS:

That the undersigned attorney and proxy for the stockholders of .... Corporation, under certain proxies and powers of attorney given to .... and ...., with power of substitution to each attorney and substitute, which proxies and powers of attorney are filed with the Assistant Secretary of said Corporation, hereby by virtue and in exercise of the powers therein contained and every other power, substitute, constitute, and appoint .... and .... as attorneys and proxies for the stockholders, with all the powers of the undersigned, for and in the name of said stockholders, to call and waive notice of said Corporation, and at any and all adjournments thereof, with all the powers which the stockholders or the undersigned would have if personally present.

The undersigned hereby ratifies and confirms all that shall be done in accordance with the foregoing.

Dated ...., 19.. .... (L.S.)

APPOINTMENT OF ASSOCIATE PROXY AS SUBSTITUTED PROXY

WHEREAS ...., ..., ..., and ...., or a majority of them, are duly appointed as proxies of certain stockholders of .... Corporation, with full power of substitution in the premises (including appointment of one of said associate proxies as substituted proxy), to vote and act in behalf of said stockholders at the annual meeting of stockholders of said Corporation, to be held at .... *(Street)*, ... *(City)*, ... *(State)*, on .... *(day of week)*, ..., 19 .., at ..... P.M., or at any adjournment or adjournments thereof:

Now, THEREFORE, we, the undersigned, do hereby severally constitute and appoint our associate proxy, ..., as our substituted proxy to vote and act in our place and stead at said meeting, or any adjournment or adjournments thereof. We do severally give to our said substituted proxy all the rights and powers which we, and each of us, as original proxies, would have had if present, under every original proxy running to the above-named proxies, or a majority of them, in respect of such meeting, or any adjournment or adjournments thereof. We hereby ratify and confirm the acts of our substituted proxy hereunder.

In Witness Whereof, the undersigned have hereunto set their hands and seals, this .. day of ...., 19...

.... (L.S.)
.... (L.S.)
.... (L.S.)

REVOCATION OF PROXY

Know All Men By These Presents, That the undersigned, ..., being the owner of ..... (.....) shares of stock of the .... Corporation, a corporation organized and existing under and by virtue of the laws of the State of ...., does hereby revoke, countermand, and declare null and void the proxy and power of attorney heretofore executed by him on ...., 19.., whereby the undersigned did constitute and appoint ...., of .... *(City)*, ...*(State)*, his true and lawful attorney for him and in his name, place, and stead, to vote upon the stock owned by him or standing in his name, as his proxy, at the .... meeting of the stockholders of the Corporation, to be held at the office of the Corporation, ... *(Street)*, ... *(City)*, ... *(State)*, on ...., 19.., at ..... P.M.

In Witness Whereof, the undersigned has hereunto set his hand and seal, this .. day of ...., 19...

.... (Seal)

REVOCATION OF PROXY AND CONSENT

The undersigned hereby revokes and cancels the Proxy and Consent given to ...., ..., and ...., to vote his stock at the special meeting of the stockholders of the Company, to be held on ...., 19.., and at adjournments thereof, and at any other meeting of the shareholders called for the purpose of authorizing a new first mortgage on the property of the Company.

The undersigned also hereby revokes his consent to the execution of such mortgage.

Witness the hand and seal of the undersigned, this .. day of ...., 19...

.... (L.S.)
Stockholder

LETTER TO STOCKHOLDERS REQUESTING
EXECUTION OF PROXY

...., 19..

Messrs. ....and ....
.... Street
.... *(City)* .... *(State)*

Dear Sirs:

In the event that you do not expect to be present in person or otherwise represented at the annual meeting of stockholders of .... Company in the City of .... on ...., 19.. (a notice of which was mailed to you some days ago), will you please sign and return to us the enclosed proxy, to the end that there may be a full representation of the stock at the meeting.

Very truly yours,

....
Secretary

NOTICE URGING EXECUTION OF PROXY

...., 19..

Dear Sir:

On ...., 19.., we mailed you notice of the Annual and Special Meetings of the stockholders of this Company, to be held ...., 19.., and ...., 19.., respectively, and enclosed a form of proxy for execution by you as a stockholder.

In going over the stockholders' list, we find that your proxy has not been received.

By referring to the notice of these meetings, you will see that a number of important matters are to be presented for the consideration of the stockholders. Four of them involve amendments to the Articles of Consolidation, and one relates to the proposed issue of Convertible Bonds, in connection with which Subscription Warrants representing valuable rights to subscribe to the bonds have been mailed to you.

All of the foregoing matters require the affirmative vote of the holders of two thirds of the total outstanding preferred and common stock. It is important, therefore, if you are unable to attend the meeting, that you sign and return the enclosed proxy at your earliest convenience, using the enclosed stamped and addressed envelope.

Yours truly,

....
Assistant Secretary

ACKNOWLEDGEMENT AND THANKS BY MANAGEMENT FOR PROXY FOR ANNUAL MEETING OF STOCKHOLDERS

...................................., 19..

Dear Sir:

We acknowledge and thank you for your proxy to be voted at the Annual Meeting of Stockholders of the Company to be held on ...., 19.., which evidence of confidence is not only appreciated by the management but serves as a constant encouragement to it for the exercise of the utmost diligence in the promotion of the Company's interests.

Very truly yours,

....

Secretary

RESOLUTION EXTENDING DURATION OF VOTING TRUST AGREEMENT

RESOLVED, That the duration of the Voting Trust Agreement relating to all of the common capital stock without nominal or par value of .... Company, dated ...., 19.., is hereby extended from twelve o'clock noon on ...., 19.. to twelve o'clock noon on ...., 19.., subject to the written consent of the registered holders of voting trust certificates representing not less than sixty per cent of the common stock deposited under said Voting Trust Agreement.

AFFIDAVITS, CERTIFICATES, OATHS, BALLOTS, ETC. RELATING TO STOCKHOLDERS' MEETINGS

AFFIDAVIT OF SECRETARY THAT NOTICE OF ANNUAL MEETING OF STOCKHOLDERS WAS MAILED

State of ....
} ss:
County of ....

................, being duly sworn, on oath deposes and says that he is the Secretary of the .... Corporation, a corporation organized and existing under the laws of the State of ...., having its principal office in the State of ....; and that on ...., 19.., he caused notice of the annual meeting of the stockholders of the Corporation, a copy of which is hereto attached and is hereby made a part of this affidavit, to be deposited in the United States Post Office at the City of ...., in a sealed envelope, postage prepaid, duly addressed to each stockholder of record of the Corporation at his last-known post-office address as the same appeared on the books of the Corporation.

Subscribed and sworn to before me   ....
this .. day of ...., 19..   Secretary
                           ....
                      Notary Public

PROOF OF SERVICE OF NOTICE OF STOCKHOLDERS' MEETING PERSONALLY ON INDIVIDUAL STOCKHOLDER

State of ....⎫
                                                            ⎬ ss:
County of ....⎭

..............., being duly sworn, deposes and says that he is the Secretary of .... Corporation; and that on ...., 19.., at .... *(Street)*, ...*(City)*, ...*(State)*, he served notice of the meeting of stockholders, a copy of which is annexed hereto and made a part of this affidavit as if herein fully set forth, on ...., a stockholder holding ..... (.....) shares of stock of the Corporation, by delivering to and leaving personally with .... a true copy thereof.

Sworn to before me this   ....
.. day of ...., 19..   Secretary
        ....
                      Notary Public

CERTIFICATE OF SECRETARY THAT ALL STOCKHOLDERS HAVE WAIVED NOTICE OF MEETING

I, ..., Secretary of the .... Corporation, do hereby certify that .... *(insert number)* waivers of notice of the special meeting of stockholders, to be held on ...., 19.., at ...... P.M., at the office of the Corporation, ... *(Street)*, ... *(City)*, ... *(State)*, attached hereto, have been signed in the aggregate by all the stockholders of the .... Corporation.

WITNESS my hand and seal, this .. day of ...., 19...

                                                 ....
                                                                        Secretary

                      (Corporate Seal)

PROOF OF SERVICE OF NOTICE OF SPECIAL MEETING OF STOCKHOLDERS BY MAIL; NAMES AND ADDRESSES OF STOCKHOLDERS LISTED

State of ....
County of ....
} ss:

............., being first duly sworn, on oath deposes and says:

That he is the duly elected, qualified, and acting Secretary of .... Corporation.

That, pursuant to an order of the Board of Directors passed at a meeting of said Board at the office of said Corporation, on ...., 19.., ordering and directing that the Secretary cause notice of the special meeting of stockholders of this Corporation on ...., 19.., to be given to the stockholders of this Corporation in the manner prescribed by the By-laws, he personally served the notice, a copy of which is hereto attached, upon each of the stockholders of said Corporation in the manner required by the By-laws for giving notice of special meetings of stockholders—to wit: by sending a copy of the notice through the mail, by depositing a full, true, and correct copy thereof in the post office of the United States Mail, City of ...., State of ...., postage prepaid, to each of the stockholders of this Corporation at his last-known place of residence, being the address left by him with the Secretary of the Corporation.

The following is a list of stockholders to whom notice was sent, being a list of all of the stockholders of this Corporation as shown by the books of this Corporation, and to whom such notices were respectively addressed:

Name	*Address*
....	....
....	....
....	
	....

Subscribed and sworn to before me
this .. day of ...., 19..
....
Notary Public

PROOF OF SERVICE OF NOTICE OF STOCKHOLDERS' MEETING, PERSONALLY AND BY MAIL ON STOCKHOLDERS INDICATED BY NAME

State of ....
County of ....
} ss:

............., being duly sworn, deposes and says that he is Secretary of the .... Corporation, a corporation organized under the laws of the State of ....; that pursuant to the call of the President, he served written notice of a special meeting of stockholders, a copy of which is annexed hereto and made a part of this affidavit, upon ...., ..., and ...., *(insert names of all stockholders served personally)*, by delivering to and leaving a true copy of said notice personally with each of them;

That on ...., 19.., he served written notice of the meeting upon ...., ..., and ...., *(insert names of all stockholders served by mail)*, by mailing to each of them a true copy thereof, enclosed in a sealed and post-paid wrapper, directed to each of the stockholders at his last-known post-office address, and deposited in a post-office box in the City of ....

Sworn   to   before   me   this
.. day of ...., 19..

....
Notary Public

....
Secretary

AFFIDAVIT OF SECRETARY OF PUBLICATION OF NOTICE OF STOCKHOLDERS' MEETING

State of ....
$\left.\right\}$ ss:
County of ....

.............., being duly sworn, on his oath says that he is the Secretary of .... Corporation, a corporation organized and existing under the laws of the State of ....; that pursuant to the order of the Board of Directors of said Corporation, he caused the notice of the .... *(insert annual or special)* meeting of stockholders, a copy of which is hereto annexed and made a part of this affidavit, to be published in the ...., a newspaper published in the City of ...., and circulating in the County of ...., being the county in which said Corporation is located, for a period of ...., beginning ...., 19.., as required by ..... *(insert words "the laws of the State of ....," or, "the By-laws of the Corporation")*.

Sworn   to   before   me   this
.. day of ...., 19..
....
Notary Public

....
Secretary

AFFIDAVIT OF PUBLISHER OF PUBLICATION OF NOTICE OF STOCKHOLDERS' MEETING

State of ....
$\left.\right\}$ ss:
County of ....

.............., being duly sworn, deposes and says that he is of lawful age; that he is the chief clerk of the printer and publisher of ...., a newspaper of general circulation, printed and published .... *(daily or weekly)* in the County of ....; and that the notice of meeting of the stockholders of .... Corporation, of which the annexed slip is a printed and true copy, was duly published ..... (.....) *(insert number of times)* in the above-named newspaper—to wit: on the ....*(insert dates of publication of notice).*

Sworn to before me this   ....
.. day of ...., 19..

....
Notary Public

AFFIDAVIT OF NO CHANGE OF STOCKHOLDERS' ADDRESSES

State of .... ⎫
                                                ⎬ ss:
County of .... ⎭

.............., being duly sworn, deposes and says that he is the Secretary of .... Corporation; and that no stockholder of said Corporation has filed with the Secretary thereof a written request (other than such written request or requests as may have heretofore expired or been withdrawn) that notices intended for him shall be mailed to some address other than his address as it appears on the stock book of the Corporation.

Sworn to before me this   ....
.. day of ...., 19..   Secretary

....
Notary Public

CERTIFICATION OF MINUTES OF STOCKHOLDERS' MEETING

I, ..., Secretary of .... Corporation, a corporation organized under the laws of the State of ...., hereby certify that the foregoing is a full, true, and complete copy of the minutes of the .... *(insert annual or special)* meeting of the stockholders of the Corporation, held at the office of said Corporation at .... *(Street)*, ... *(City)*, ... *(State)*, on ...., 19.., at ..... A.M.

IN WITNESS WHEREOF, I have hereunto set my hand and caused the seal of the Corporation to be affixed hereto, this .. day of ...., 19...

(Corporate Seal)

....
Secretary

SECRETARY'S CERTIFICATE OF LIST OF HOLDERS OF STOCK

I, ..., Secretary of the .... Corporation, a corporation organized and existing under the laws of the State of ...., do hereby certify that the attached list of holders of the Common Stock of this Corporation, with the number of shares owned by each, represents the total issued and outstanding Common Stock of the Corporation as shown by the books of the Corporation on ...., 19.., and on ...., 19...

I further certify that with the exception of ..... shares of Treasury Common Stock owned by the Corporation, said holders of the Common Stock are entitled to vote at the special meeting of this Corporation on ...., 19.., and to cast the number of votes indicated respectively by the number of shares on said statement.

WITNESS my hand and seal of said Corporation this .. day of ...., 19...

(Corporate Seal)

....
Secretary

LIST OF STOCKHOLDERS

The following is a list of stockholders of the .... Corporation at the closing of books on ...., 19..:

			SHARES HELD
Name of Stockholder	*Address*	*Common*	*Preferred*
....	....		
....	....	....	....
....	....	....	....

OATH OF INSPECTORS OF ELECTION

State of ....
County of ....
} ss:

We, ... and ...., the undersigned, duly appointed Inspectors of Election of .... Corporation, being severally and duly sworn, do solemnly swear that we will fairly and impartially perform our duties as Inspectors of Election at the election to be held this ...., 19.., for directors of the Corporation, and will faithfully and diligently canvass the votes cast at such election and honestly and truthfully report the result of said election.

Sworn to before me this
.. day of ...., 19..
....
Notary Public

....
Secretary

JUDGES' OATH

State of ....
County of ....
$\Big\}$ ss:

We, ..., ..., and ...., the undersigned, duly appointed Judges for the purpose of conducting the vote at the special meeting of holders of the Common Stock of .... Corporation, a corporation organized and existing under the laws of the State of ...., being severally duly sworn, do solemnly swear that we will fairly and impartially perform our duties as such Judges at the meeting to be held this ...., 19.., and will faithfully and diligently canvass the votes cast at such election and honestly and truthfully report the result of said election.

....
....
....

Subscribed and sworn to before me this .. day of ...., 19.

....
Notary Public

CERTIFICATE AND REPORT OF INSPECTORS OF ELECTION

We, the undersigned, duly appointed Inspectors of election of the .... Corporation, a stock corporation of the State of ...., do hereby certify as follows:

That a meeting of the stockholders of the Corporation was held at the office of the Corporation, ... (Street), ... (City), ... (State), on ...., 19.., at ..... P.M., pursuant to due notice.

That before entering upon the discharge of our duties, we were severally sworn, and the oath so taken by us is hereto annexed.

That we inspected the signed proxies used at the meeting and found the same to be in proper form.

That we did receive the votes of the stockholders by ballot for the election of ..... (.....) directors of the Corporation, to serve for ..... (.....) years, did canvass the votes cast, and that the result of the vote taken at such meeting was as follows:

| Directors | Votes | CONSISTING OF | |
		Preferred	Common
"A"	280,370	9,500	270,870
"B"	280,370	9,500	270,870
"C"	280,370	9,500	270,870
"D"	280,370	9,500	270,870
"E"	280,370	9,500	270,870
"F"	280,370	9,500	270,870

That the said "A," "B," "C," "D," "E," and "F," having received the number of votes above set opposite their respective names, being a majority of the votes cast, were declared by us duly elected directors of the Corporation, as successors to the class of directors whose terms expire with this annual election, to hold office for the term of ..... (....) years.

IN WITNESS WHEREOF, we have made this certificate and have hereunto set our hands, this .. day of ...., 19...

....
....

CERTIFICATE AND REPORT OF INSPECTORS OF ELECTION (SHORT FORM)

We, the undersigned, Inspectors of Election, duly appointed by the stockholders of the .... Corporation, at the meeting held ...., 19.., do report that, having taken the oath to conduct the election of directors impartially, we did receive the votes of the stockholders by ballot.

We report that ..... (....) votes were cast, and that the following persons received the number of votes set opposite their respective names:

Directors	*Number of Votes*
....	....
....	....

INSPECTORS' REPORT OF STOCK REPRESENTED AT MEETING

We, the undersigned, duly appointed and qualified Inspectors at the annual meeting of the stockholders of .... Company, held in the City of ...., State of .... on ...., 19.., do hereby certify that we have examined the list of stockholders of that Company, dated ...., 19.., properly certified; that we have received and taken in charge the proxies presented at said meeting; and have taken a poll of the stockholders present in person; and we do further certify that there are represented at said meeting, by proxy, stockholders of said Company shown by said list to be the holders of ..... (.....) shares of Common Stock and ..... (.....) shares of Preferred Stock, a total of ..... (.....) shares of stock of both classes, of which ..... (.....) shares are represented by proxies other than the official Proxy Committee, and the remainder are represented by the Proxy Committee, or a member thereof. There are present in person stockholders holding together ..... (.....) shares of Preferred Stock, making the total number of shares represented:

Common	.......shares
Preferred	.......shares
Both Classes	.......shares

or ..... (....%) per cent of the total stock outstanding.

....
....
....

Inspectors

CERTIFICATE OF JUDGES ON SPECIFIC QUESTION
CONSIDERED AT MEETING

We, the undersigned, duly appointed Judges for the purpose of conducting the vote at the special meeting of the holders of Common Stock of .... Corporation, do hereby certify as follows:

That a special meeting of the holders of the Common Stock of said Corporation was held at Room ....., No. .... (Street), ... (City), ..., on ...., 19.., at ..... P.M., by adjournment from ...., 19.., pursuant to the call of the President as authorized by the Board of Directors of the Corporation and written notice thereof given by the Secretary:

That before entering upon the discharge of our duties, we were severally duly sworn and the oath so taken by us is hereto annexed.

That we inspected the signed proxies and the credentials presented to the meeting and we found the same to be in proper form; that at said meeting we did receive the votes by ballot of the holders of the Common Stock upon the following resolutions:

(Here insert resolutions in full.)

That we did canvass the votes so cast and that the result of such voting was as follows:

That the number of shares of stock issued and outstanding and entitled to vote on said resolutions were ..... shares of the Common Stock (exclusive of ..... shares of Treasury Common Stock owned by the Corporation); that ..... shares of Common Stock voted in favor of said resolutions; and that no shares of Common Stock were voted against them.

In Witness Whereof, we have made this certificate and have hereunto set our hands this .. day of ...., 19...

....
....
....

INSPECTORS' CERTIFICATE OF VOTES ON A RESOLUTION RATIFYING THE ACTS OF THE DIRECTORS, COMMITTEES, AND OFFICERS

We, the undersigned, duly appointed Inspectors of stockholders' votes and elections of .... Company, to act at a meeting of stockholders held on ...., 19.., having taken an oath faithfully, honestly, and impartially to perform the duties of said Inspectors, do hereby certify that we did receive the votes of the stockholders of said Company by ballot in person and by proxy for and against the following resolution:

RESOLVED, That all contracts, acts, proceedings, elections, and appointments by the Board of Directors, Executive Committee, and officers of this Company from ...., 19.., as shown by the minutes of meeting of said Board of Directors and Executive Committee since that date, be and they hereby are approved, ratified, and confirmed.

and that the holders of ..... (.....) shares of the capital stock of said Company voted in person and by proxy in favor of said resolution, and that no holders of shares of the capital stock of said Company voted in person or by proxy against said resolution.

PROTEST OF STOCKHOLDERS AGAINST A MEETING TO ELECT DIRECTORS AND OFFICERS

We, the undersigned, stockholders of the .... Company, protest against this meeting and object to its validity as a meeting to elect directors or other officers of the .... Company, on the following grounds:

1. This meeting was not called by any member of the Company.

2. The meeting was not advertised as required by the laws of the State of ....

3. Notice of the meeting has not been served personally or by mail upon each member of the Company.

4. This meeting is called to be held at a place other than the office of the Company.

5. Directors and other officers of the Company were duly elected at a stockholders' meeting held at the offices of the Company on ...., 19.., and the directors and officers so elected have qualified and are discharging the duties of their offices, and their term of office has not expired.

Filed ...., 19..

....
Clerk

DEMAND FOR A VOTE BY BALLOT

To the Secretary of the .... Corporation:
We, the undersigned, being holders of the shares of stock of the .....
.... Corporation hereinbelow set opposite our respective names, do hereby demand that a vote by ballot be taken on the following resolution, which you declared to have been duly carried by a show of hands:

(Here set forth resolution.)

..........., holding ..... shares
..........., holding ..... shares
..........., holding ..... shares

BALLOT UPON ELECTION OF DIRECTORS: STRAIGHT VOTING; STOCKHOLDERS ENTITLED TO ONE VOTE FOR EACH SHARE

.... CORPORATION

Annual meeting of Stockholders, ..., 19..

I, the undersigned, hereby vote ..... (.....) shares of stock for the following-named persons to serve as directors for the ensuing year:

....

....

....

....

By ....

Proxy

[*Note*. If a stockholder votes personally, his signature must be placed on the first line. If the ballot is cast by proxy, the proxy must sign the name of the stockholder on the first line, and his own name on the second line. If several stockholders are represented by one proxy, the proxy may sign on the second line and write on the first line the words "Proxies filed."]

BALLOT UPON ELECTION OF DIRECTORS WHERE CUMULATIVE VOTING IS USED

EELECTION OF DIRECTORS OF .... CORPORATION

at

Annual Meeting of Stockholders, ..., 19..

Names of stockholder ....

Name of proxy ....

Number of shares ....

Directors to be elected ....

Number of votes to which entitled ..... (multiply number of directors to be elected by number of shares)

BALLOT FOR DIRECTORS

Names   *Votes*

....

....

....

....

(Stockholder signs here)

By ....

Proxy

BALLOT FOR VOTE ON RESOLUTION

.... CORPORATION
SPECIAL MEETING OF STOCKHOLDERS, HELD ...., 19..

for
The undersigned votes   the following resolution:
against

(Here follows resolution in full.)

Vote in person .... shares
Vote by proxy .... shares

....
(Stockholder or proxy
signs here)

BALLOT FOR VOTE ON RESOLUTION (ANOTHER FORM)

SPECIAL MEETING OF PREFERRED STOCKHOLDERS

OF

.... COMPANY
Held ...., 19..

In favor of:
Against:

the resolution with respect to the creation and issuance by the Company of its
Ten-Year 5% Sinking Fund Debentures in the principal amount of ..... ($....)
Dollars with Common Stock Purchase Warrants attached.

Holding ..... shares of Preferred Stock
Representing by proxy ..... shares of Preferred Stock

Dated at ...., (City), ... (State), .., 19...

....
(Stockholder or proxy
signs here)

Chapter 3

DIRECTORS' AND
COMMITTEE MEETINGS

Contents—Chapter 3

Necessity for holding directors' meetings. The sole authority to manage corporate affairs is vested in the board of directors, acting as a body. Generally directors can bind the corporation by their acts only when they are duly assembled at a meeting.[1] A casual and informal get-together of the directors, at which no record of the proceedings is kept, is not a legal meeting.[2] Nor is the gathering of the separate consents of each of the directors equivalent to board action, since directors, as individuals, cannot act for the board.[3] Even if they are majority stockholders, they are not authorized to bind the corporation in an informal manner.[4] Unless otherwise provided for in the charter, stockholders are not allowed to encroach upon the board's authority in the management of corporate affairs.[5] Indeed any agreement by the stockholders which substantially limits the freedom of each director to exercise his best judgment on policies of the board is invalid.[6]

Exceptions to rule that directors must act in meeting. The rule that directors can bind the corporation only when they are duly assembled is subject to certain exceptions. These are the exceptions: (1) if, by usage or custom, the directors have managed the corporate affairs without formal meetings, and the corporation and its stockholders have long acquiesced, the acts of the directors, within the scope of their powers, are valid;[7] (2) if stockholders or minority directors, with knowledge of the facts, have ratified, or acquiesced in, informal action taken by the directors, they are bound by that action;[8] (3) if the corporation or its stockholders retain or

---

[1]Schuckman v. Rubenstein, (1947) 164 F. 2d 952, cert. denied, (1948) 333 U.S. 875, 68 S. Ct. 905; In re Raljoed Realty Co., (1967) S.D.N.Y. 277 F. Supp. 225; In re Joseph Feld & Co., (1941) 38 F. Supp. 506; Branch v. Augusta Glass Works, (1895) 95 Ga. 573, 23 S.E. 128; Zachary v. Milin, (1940) 294 Mich. 622 293 N.W. 770; Farmers & Merchants Bank v. Boland, (1943) (Mo. App.) 175 S.W. 2d 939; Bayer v. Beran, (1944) 49 N.Y.S. 2d 2; Kelly v. Galloway, (1937) 156 Ore. 301, 68 P. 2d 474; Starring v. Kemp, (1936) 167 Va. 429, 188 S.E. 174; Trethewey v. Green River Gorge, (1943) 17 Wash. 2d 697, 136 P. 2d 999.

[2]Lycette v. Green River Gorge, (1944) 21 Wash. 2d 859, 153 P. 2d 873.

[3]Baldwin v. Canfield, (1879) 26 Minn. 43, 1 N.W. 261, 276; Coleman v. Northwestern Mut. Life Ins. Co., (1917) 273 Mo. 620, 201 S.W. 544.

[4]Rothberg v. Manhattan Coil Co., (1951) 84 Ga. App. 528, 66 S.E. 2d 390; Mosell Realty Corp. v. Schofield, (1945) 183 Va. 782, 33 S.E. 2d 774.

[5]Kaplan v. Block, (1944) 183 Va. 327, 31 S.E. 2d 893.

[6]Abercrombie v. Davies, (1956) (Del. Ch.) 123 A. 2d 893, rev'd on other grounds, (1957) (Del.) 130 A. 2d 338.

For the position of stockholders in the management of the corporation, see page 223, Chapter 9.

[7]Forrest City Box Co. v. Barney, (1926) 14 F. 2d 590; Holy Cross Gold Mining Milling Co. v. Goodwin, (1924) 74 Colo. 532, 223 P, 58; Kozy Theater Co. v. Love, (1921) 191 Ky. 595, 231 S.W. 249; Byron v. Byron Hefferman & Co., (1922) 98 N.J.L. 127, 119 A. 12; Bayer v. Beran, (1944) 49 N.Y.S. 2d 2; Baker v. Smith, (1918) 41 R.I. 17, 102 A. 721.

[8]Western Battery & Supply Co. v. Hazelett Storage Battery Co., (1932) 61 F. 2d 220; Hurley v. Ornsteen, (1942) 311 Mass. 477, 42 N.E. 2d 273; Clark Realty Co. v. Douglas, (1923) 46 Nev. 278, 212 P. 466.

accept the benefits of informal action, they are deemed to have ratified it;[9] (4) if the directors are themselves the only stockholders, action taken by all of them, informally, and without a meeting, is corporation action; [10] and, (5) if there is a statute, as in Delaware, Michigan, Pennsylvania and certain other states, permitting the directors, in advance of the action, to sign a unanimous consent and file it with the minutes of the board proceedings.

If all the directors are present when the terms of a contract with another party are agreed to, the corporation cannot deny the contract on the ground that it was not made at a legal meeting.[11]

Examples of acts held valid without formal meeting. The following illustrate acts that have been held not to require formal action by the board:

1. Making ordinary contract by agent.[12]
2. Entering into general contracts of employment.[13]
3. Chartering vessels to carry on the regular business of a corporation engaged in transporting passengers or freight.[14]
4. Purchasing radio time for advertising.[15]

Examples of acts held invalid without formal meeting. The following are examples of acts that have been held to require the vote of the board of directors:

1. Giving a mortgage of corporate property as security for a loan.[16]
2. Selling principal assets of the corporation.[17]
3. Authorizing bankruptcy proceedings.[18]
4. Instituting legal action in corporate name.[19]

---

[9]Noto v. Satloff, (1963) 32 Misc. 2d 915, 239 N.Y.S. 2d 324; Webb v. Duvall, (1940) 177 Md. 592, 11 A. 2d 446; Bayer v. Beran, (1944) 49 N.Y.S. 2d 2. Directors are obligated to repudiate unauthorized transactions of a single director in behalf of the corporation. Failure to do so implies ratification. Friend Lumber Co. v. Armstrong Building Finish Co., (1931) 276 Mass. 361, 177 N.E. 794. Further, an unauthorized act in the name of a corportion may be ratified later by the acceptance of the benefits of the act if acquiescence in or the receipt and retention of the proceeds is done with knowledge of the material facts concerning the transaction. Linden Homes, Inc. v. Larkin, (1963) 231 Md. 566, 191 A. 2d 441.

[10]Gerard v. Empire Square Realty Co., (1921) 195 App. Div. 244, 187 N.Y. Supp. 306; Temple Enterprises, Inc. v. Combs, (1940) 164 Ore. 133, 100 P. 2d 613.

[11]Thompson v. M.K. & T. Oil Co., (1935) 5 Cal. App. 117, 42 P. 2d 374

[12]Scholfield v. Parlin & Orendorff Co., (1894) 61 F. 804.

[13]Scott v. Superior Sunset Oil Co., (1904) 144 Cal. 140, 77 P. 817; Crowley v. Genesse Mining Co., (1880) 55 Cal. 273.

[14]Prentice v. United States & Central American S.S. Co., (1893) 58 F. 702.

[15]Bayer v. Beran, (1944) 49 N.Y.S. 2d 2.

[16]St. Joseph State Nat'l Bank v. Union Nat'l Bank, (1897) 168 Ill. 519, 48 N.E. 82; Currie v. Bowman, (1894) 25 Ore. 364 35 P. 848; Lycette v. Green River Gorge, (1944) 21 Wash. 2d 859, 153 P. 2d 873.

[17]Mosell Realty Corp. v. Schofield, (1945) 183 Va. 782, 33 S.E. 2d 774.

[18]In re Raljoed Realty Co. (1967) S.D.N.Y. 277 F. Supp. 225; In re Joseph Feld & Co., (1941) 38 F. Supp. 506.

[19]Douglas Development Corp. v. Carillo, (1946) 64 N.Y.S. 2d 747.

Kinds of directors' meetings. Meetings of directors may be either regular or special. Regular meetings are called at the time and place and in the manner provided for in the charter, by-laws or in the statutes. Special meetings may be called at any time and in the manner as provided in the charter, by-laws, or statutes. If there is no evidence as to whether the meeting was regular or special, it will be assumed to have been regular.[20]

Meetings held on Sundays or holidays. Meetings of directors are generally held on the date designated in the by-laws. If the designated date falls on Sunday or is a holiday, in the absence of a provision in the statutes, charter, or by-laws prohibiting a meeting on a Sunday or holiday, a notice of meeting must be given for any change of date.[21] Thus, a meeting held without notice on the day following the appointed date, which was a holiday, was not a legal meeting.[22]

A meeting of directors on Sunday is valid if affirmed at a weekday meeting.[23] If agreements or contracts entered into on Sunday are void under statutes, a board of directors cannot, at a Sunday meeting, amend or rescind a contract.[24]

Calling directors' meetings. The duty of calling a meeting of the board of directors is generally delegated by the charter or by-laws to the chairman of the board, or, in his absence, to the president. Provision is also frequently made that meetings may be called upon written direction of a certain number of the directors. If the provisions of the charter or by-laws are mandatory, they must be followed carefully to insure a valid meeting, but defects in the call of the meeting cannot defeat rights of innocent third persons dealing with the corporation.[25]

If the by-laws provide that special meetings of directors shall be called by the president, or, at his request, by the secretary, the secretary and a third member of the board, though constituting the majority of the board, have no authority to call a special meeting.[26] If the by-laws authorize the president or the secretary to call special meetings, the secretary can call the meeting without a request from the president.[27]

---

[20]Barrell v. Lake View Land Co., (1898) 122 Cal. 129, 54 P. 594.

[21]Cheney v. Canfield, (1910) 158 Cal. 342, 111 P. 92. This decision was made in the face of a statute providing that if an act, which by law or contract was to be performed on a particular day, fell on a holiday, it might be performed on the next business day. The court said, however, the statute is inapplicable since a by-law is not a contract within the meaning of the statute.

[22]Cheney v. Canfield, (1910) 158 Cal. 342, 111 P. 92.

[23]Flynn v. Columbus Club, (1900) 21 R.I. 534, 45 A. 551.

[24]Smith v. Mills, (1946) 199 Miss. 367, 24 So. 2d 864. See also Chapin v. Cullis, (1941) 299 Mich. 101, 299 N.W. 824. In this case the evidence was insufficient to show that the contract had been amended at a Sunday meeting; the added proviso was, therefore, not invalid.

[25]Bruch v. National Guarantee Credit Corp., (1922) 13 Del. Ch. 180, 116 A. 738; Morris v. Y. & B. Corp., (1930) 198 N.C. 705, 153 S.E. 327.

[26]Aetna Cas, and Surety Co. v. American Brewing Co., (1922) 63 Mont. 474, 208 P. 921.

[27]Jackson v. Dillehay, (1946) 209 Ark. 707, 192 S.W. 2d 354

The manner of calling directors' meetings is controlled by the charter and by-laws, and cannot be changed by an agreement among the stockholders.[28] In the absence of provisions in the statute or by-laws of the corporation, the meeting need not be called in any particular manner; if all the directors receive proper notice, the meeting will be valid.[29]

Necessity for giving notice of directors' meetings. The general rule of law is that no power or function entrusted to a body consisting of a number of persons can be legally executed unless notice of the meeting at which such power or function is to be exercised is given to all the members of that body.[30] Directors, as representatives of the stockholders, have the right to consult with each other and to be heard upon all questions considered during the meeting.[31] A lawful meeting, therefore, requires due notice to all of the directors, unless there is a waiver of notice.[32] Notice may be either implied or express.

No notice of regular meetings need be given where the by-laws, charter, or a resolution of the board of directors specify the time and place of the regular meeting.[33] Notice is implied and the directors are chargeable with such knowledge.[34] Nor is the validity of a regular meeting impaired by failure to give notice, even if the by-law or charter requires such notice, when all the directors attend the meeting and do not object.[35] This is particularly true when the members of the board not only are present, but also participate in the discussion and action taken by the board.[36] If the directors establish the custom of meeting at a regular time, such as on the first Monday of every month, action taken at such a meeting is valid even though one director is not notified of the meeting.[37]

In the case of meetings for special purposes or for business not pertaining to the ordinary affairs of the corporation, express notice must be given of the time and place and the object or purpose of the meeting.[38]

Notice of a special meeting must be given, unless it may be waived or unless there is some express provision in the charter or by-laws or estab-

---

[28]In re Allied Fruit & Export Co., (1934) 243 App. Div. 52, 276 N.Y. Supp. 153.

[29]Bell v. Standard Quicksilver Co., (1905) 146 Cal. 699, 81 P. 17.

[30]People v. Batchelor (1860) 22 N.Y. 128; Lycette v. Green River Gorge, (1944) 21 Wash. 2d 859, 153 P. 2d 873.

[31]Holcombe v. Trenton White City Co., (1912) 80 N.J. Eq. 122, 82 A. 618, aff'd, memo dec., (1913) 82 N.J. Eq. 364, 91 A. 1069.

[32]In re Joseph Feld & Co., (1941) 38 F. Supp. 506.

[33]Seal of Gold Mining Co. v. Slater, (1911) 161 Cal. 621, 120 P. 15; Whitehead v. Hamilton Rubber Co., (1893) 52 N.J. Eq. 78, 27 A. 897.

[34]Gumaer v. Cripple Creek Tunnel Transportation & Mining Co, (1907) 40 Colo. 1, 90 P. 81.

[35]Thompson v. M.K, & T. Oil Co., (1935) 5 Cal. App. 117, 42 P. 2d 374.; Ney v. Eastern Iowa Tel. Co., (1919) 185 Iowa 610, 171 N.W. 26; Zachary v. Milin, (1940) 294 Mich. 622, 293 N.W. 770; Minneapolis Times Co. v. Nimocks, (1893) 53 Minn. 381, 55 N.W. 546.

[36]Darvin v. Belmont Industries, Inc.,(1972) 40 Mich. App. 672, 199 N.W. 2d 542.

[37]White v. Penelas Mining Co., (1939) 105 F. 2d 726.

[38]Whitehead v. Hamilton Rubber Co., (1893) 52 N.J. Eq. 78, 27 A. 897.

lished usage to the contrary, or unless it is impractical or impossible to do so.[39] Presence at a special meeting waives notice.[40] But a special meeting attended by only two of the corporation's four directors is invalid and so cannot approve sale of stock to the corporation, when charter and by-laws require three directors for both quorum and corporate action.[41] And a by-law amendment adopted at a special stockholders' meeting is invalid, since notice of the meeting failed to state its purpose and so a stockholder was reinstated as director; his attendance at a meeting without actual participation did not constitute a waiver of defect in notice.[42] Otherwise, the meeting is illegal, and all actions taken are invalid[43] unless later ratified.[44] Thus, an assessment levied at a special meeting held without notice is void.[45] The fact that a director might object to the proposed action is no excuse for not sending him a notice of the meeting.[46]

But elections held at two special directors' meetings to replace an opposing faction were both void, since as to the first meeting, the organizers failed to give required notice of special meeting to the directors, and as to the second meeting, another director's absence was secured through misrepresenting the date of the meeting; thus, the board was constituted by those that served before the special meetings and compromise directors were elected to fill vacancies on the board after the opposing factions enlarged the number to provide continuity and regularity in the corporation's management.[47]

Failure to give notice is excused when an emergency demands immediate action, and the directors who were not given notice could not have been notified in time to attend the meeting.[48] An example of such an emergency is when all the property of a corporation is about to be sold at public auction for a fraction of its value, and the corporation wishes to postpone the sale.[49] Where the exceptions are not present, a special meeting held in the absence of some of the directors and without any notice to

---

[39]American Exchange Nat'l Bank v. First Nat'l Bank, (1897) 82 F. 961 (Wash. law); Colcord v. Granzow, (1929) 137 Okla. 194, 278 P. 654; McCay v. Luzerne & Carbon County Motor Transit Co., (1937) 125 Pa. Super. 217, 189 A. 772.

[40]Ney v. Eastern Iowa Tel. Co., (1919) 185 Iowa 610, 171 N.W. 26; Minneapolis Times Co. v. Nimocks (1893) 53 Minn. 381, 55 N.W. 546.

[41]Lewis v. Steinhart, (1972) N.Y.S. Ct., 338 N.Y.S. 2d 552.

[42]Darvin v. Belmont Industries, Inc., (1972) CA-6, Mich., 459 F. 2d 584.

[43]Rapoport v. Schneider, (1972) 29 N.Y. 2d 431, 328 N.Y.S. 2d 431, 278 N.E. 2d 645; Shelton v. Second Judicial Dist. Co., (1947) 64 Nev. 487, 185 P. 2d 320.

[44]Defanti v. Allen Clark Co., (1921) 45 Nev. 120, 198 P. 549.

[45]Boswell v. Mt. Jupiter Mut. Water Co., (1950) 97 Cal. App. 2d 437, 217 P. 2d 980.

[46]Lycette v. Green River Gorge, (1944) 21 Wash. 2d 859, 153 P. 2d 873.; Troy Mining Co. v. White, (1898) 10 S.D. 475, 74 N.W. 236.

[47]Schroder v. Scotten, Dillon Co., (1972) Del. Ct. of Ch., Civ. Action No. 3793, 11-9-72.

[48]Stafford Springs St. Ry. v. Middle River Mfg. Co., (1907) 80 Conn. 37, 66 A. 775; National Bank of Commerce v. Shunway, (1892) 49 Kan. 224, 30 P. 411.

[49]Paducah & Illinois Ferry Co. v. Robertson, (1914) 161 Ky. 485, 171 S.W. 171.

them is illegal, and the action of such a meeting, although affirmed by a majority of the directors, is invalid.[50] But a corporation can repurchase stock from a director-employee under an option agreement, even though the option period to repurchase has already expired, since the director's conduct in requesting from the corporation terms of payment that would give him favorable tax treatment, and in agreeing to return the contract embracing those terms to it barred him from denying timely exercise and from the right to object to no notice of a special directors' meeting when the resolution to repurchase was approved.[51] However, a director, officer and half-owner of stock in a close corporation who refuses to attend a stockholders' meeting cannot be compelled to attend it or refrain from establishing a terminal date for exercising of preemptive rights for a new issue of stock, or cease to continue as director and officer, pending a stockholders' meeting, since a stockholder (even though also a director) is not under any legal obligation to participate in corporate affairs.[52]

If notice is required, it must be sent to all directors.[53] In the absence of proof to the contrary, notice will be presumed to have been given and received.[54] One who attacks the validity of a directors' meeting on the ground that there was no notice has the burden of proving failure to give such notice. The testimony of two directors that they received no notice of a meeting of the board of directors was held sufficient to show that no written notice was given.[55]

Rights of innocent third persons who deal with the corporation are not affected by failure to give directors notice of a special meeting, because they are justified in assuming that the meeting is a lawful one.[56]

Necessity for giving notice of adjourned meetings of directors. In the absence of contrary by-law requirements, notice of an adjourned meeting is not necessary if notice of the original meeting was given.[57] Thus, if all the directors agree to adjourn to a date and hour named, a meeting held by a majority of directors at such a time is a legal meeting

---

[50]Farwell v. Houghton Copper Works, (1881) 8 F. 66; State v. Kylmanen, (1930) 180 Minn. 486, 231 N.W. 197.

[51]State ex. rel. Howeth v. D.A. Davidson & Co., (1973) Mont. S. Ct., 517 P. 2d 722.

[52]Hall v. Hall, (1974) Mo. Ct. of App., No. KCD 26131, 2-4-74.

[53]Richman v. Bank of Perris, (1929) 102 Cal. App. 71, 282 P. 801; Doernbecher v. Columbia City Lumber Co., (1892) 21 Ore. 573, 28 P. 899.

[54]Stockton Combined Harvesting & Agricultural Works v. Houser, (1895) 109 Cal. 1, 41 P. 899; Ashley Wire Co. v. Illinois Steel Co., (1896) 164 Ill. 149, 45 N.E. 410.

[55]Lowe v. Los Angeles Suburban Gas Co., (1914) 24 Cal. App. 367, 141, P. 399.

[56]Morris v. Y. & B. Corp., (1930) 198 N.C. 705, 153 S.E. 327.; Colcord v. Granzow, (1929) 137 Okla. 194, 278 P. 654.

[57]Clark v. Oceano Beach Resort Co., (1930) 106 Cal. App. 574, 289 P. 946; Withcomb v. Giannini, (1919) 43 Cal. App. 229, 184 P. 887; Seal of Gold Mining Co. v. Slater (1911) 161 Cal. 621, 120 P. 15.

though no notice is given.[58] Directors who receive the original notice of a special meeting are bound to know that the meeting may be adjourned for a quorum and that business which could have been transacted at the original meeting may be transacted at the adjourned meeting.[59] However, notice of an adjourned meeting must be given to any absentees, if, at the original meeting, no hour is set at which the adjourned meeting will be held.[60] The adjourned meeting is in fact a special meeting.

Contents of notice of directors' meetings. Unless a statute, the charter, or a by-law prescribes a particular form of notice of directors' meeting, any form will be satisfactory. Thus, if the custom is to hold meetings without written notice, oral notice is sufficient.[61] If written notice is prescribed, oral notice may not be sufficient unless all the directors do not object and attend the meeting.

The notice should contain the exact time and place of the meeting,[62] but it need not state the purpose of the meeting unless it is expressly required by statute, charter, or by-law.[63] If a special meeting is called by a general notice without specifying the business to be transacted, the meeting will be presumed to have been called to consider and act upon any general business matters that may come before it.[64] If the notice of a special meeting states a purpose, the courts are likely to hold that any extraordinary business outside of that stated in the notice cannot be transacted unless all the directors are present.[65] References to an oral stock option in the minutes of the board meeting may be an exception to this general rule, since the minutes satisfy the requirement for written proof of a valid stock option and that requirement does not call for a "complete memorialization" of stock option agreements.[66]

Delivery of notice of directors' meetings. If written notice must be sent to each director, the secretary of the board of directors generally has the duty to see that such notice is delivered to each director sufficiently prior to the meeting. If the director receives the notice, or if he attends the meeting, it is immaterial by what means notice was conveyed to him. The manner of serving notice becomes important when the director is absent from the meeting and the question arises whether notice was properly

---

[58]Bank of National City v. Johnston, (1900) (Cal) 60 P. 776.
[59]Seal of Gold Mining Co. v. Slater, (1911) 161 Cal. 621, 120 P. 15.
[60]Thompson v. Williams, (1888) 76 Cal. 153, 18 P. 153.
[61]O'Rourke v. Grand Opera House Co., (1913) 47 Mont. 459, 133 P. 965.
[62]Hackler v. International Traveler's Ass'n, (1914) (Tex. Civ. App.), 165 S.W. 44.
[63]Homan v. Fir Products Co., (1923) 123 Wash. 260, 212 P. 240.
[64]In re Argus Co., (1893) 138 N.Y. 557, 34 N.E. 388.
[65]Bourne v. Sanford, (1950) 327 Mich. 175, 41 N.W. 2d 515; Mercantile Library Hall Co. v. Pittsburgh Library Ass'n, (1896) 173 Pa. 30, 33 A. 744.
[66]Tripp v. Pay 'N Pak Stores, Inc., (1974) Ore. S. Ct., 98 Ore. Adv. Sh. 1039.

served upon him. If the by-laws are silent as to the manner in which written notice shall be served, it is best to mail the notice to each director at his last known address. Receipt of the notice by mail will be presumed in the absence of proof to the contrary.[67] Further, if the by-laws or statutes prescribe the length of notice, of course, they should be followed. To avoid doubt, the by-laws should read that notice must be mailed a certain number of days before the meeting. If they say that a certain number of days' notice must be given, the question may arise as to whether the day on which the notice is mailed or that on which it is received governs. In such case, the safer principle to follow is that notice is not given until it is received.[68]

Waiver of notice of directors' meeting. Directors may waive the notice of meeting required by by-laws.[69] To be effective, a waiver of notice must be executed before the meeting.[70] The principles underlying the decisions regarding notice of directors' meetings are explained as follows:

Each member of a corporate body has the right to consultation with the others, and has the right to be heard upon all questions considered. It is presumed that if the absent members had been present, they might have dissented, and their arguments might have convinced the majority of the wisdom of their proposed action, thus producing a different result. If, however, they had notice and failed to attend, they waived their rights. Likewise, they lose this right if they sign a waiver of notice prior to the meeting. But consent given subsequent to the meeting, looking to the ratification of what was done, cannot validate the action taken.[71] However, under special fact situations, courts have held a subsequent waiver to be valid.[72]

Ratification of action taken at improperly called meetings. Action taken by the directors at a meeting for which proper notice has not been given may be ratified at a subsequent meeting properly called.[73] If the subsequent meeting is called upon proper notice to ratify or adopt the action taken at the previous meeting, it is immaterial whether the previous

---

[67]Stockton Combined Harvesting & Agricultural Works v. Houser, (1895) 109 Cal. 1, 41 P. 899; Ashley Wire Co. v. Illinois Steel Co., (1896) 164 Ill. 149, 45 N.E. 410.

[68]Ibid.

[69]Colcord v. Granzow, (1929) 137 Okla. 194, 278 P. 654.

[70]United States v. Interstate R.R., (1926) 14 F. 2d 328; Lippman v. Kehoe Stenograph Co., (1915) 11 Del. Ch. 80, 95 A. 895; Holcombe v. Trenton White City Co.; Hill Dredging Corp. v. Risley, (1955) 18 N.J. 501, 114 A. 2d 697. But see Stafford Spring St. Ry. v. Middle River Mfg. Co., (1907) 80 Conn. 37, 66 A. 775., in which waiver of notice subsequent to a meeting was considered effective, the meeting being necessary and an attempt being made to reach all directors. Furthermore, the corporation had acquiesced in what was done at the meeting.

[71]Holcombe v. Trenton White City Co., (1912) 80 N.J. Eq. 122, 82 A. 618.

[72]Smith v. Sinaloa Land and First Co., (1913) 42 Utah 445, 132 P. 556.

[73]United States v. Interstate R.R., (1926) 14 F. 2d 328; McCay v. Luzerne & Carbon County Motor Transit Co., (1937) 125 Pa. Super. 217, 189 A. 772.

meeting has been properly called.[74] Ratification may also be effected by the subsequent acquiescence of the board of directors in action taken or authorized by the illegal board meeting, if such action was within the power of the board in the first instance.[75] Directors who attend the meeting and know the nature of the meeting cannot later claim that the meeting is illegal, when an action is voted over their objections.[76] If all the directors attend and participate in the meeting, it is immaterial that notice has not been given as provided in the by-laws.[77]

Place of directors' meetings. The directors' meeting should be held at the place designated in the notice[78] in compliance with the requirements of the statute, charter, or by-laws. When the statute says meetings shall be held at the office or principal place of business, the certificate of incorporation calls for meetings at the principal place of business, and the by-laws call for meetings at the office of the company, the statute governs, and a meeting held at the office of the company is legal.[79] Where by-laws require a board of directors to hold regular meetings in a specified place, special meetings, which are not within such restriction, may be held any place.[80] In the absence of an express provision naming a particular place, the directors are not bound to meet at the principal place of business[81] and they may designate any reasonably convenient place within the state.[82]

The statutes of most of the states authorize the holding of directors' meetings, as provided in the by-laws, either within or without the state of incorporation. If the statute specified that meetings of directors shall be held within the state, a meeting outside the state will not be legal, and the action taken by the directors at such a meeting will not be binding.[83] Where the statute requires the written consent of all the directors if meetings are to be held outside the state, a valid meeting cannot be held outside the state

---

[74]County Court v. Baltimore & Ohio R.R., (1888) 35 F. 161.

[75]Clark Realty Co. v. Douglas, (1923) 46 Nev. 278, 212 P. 466. But mere approval of the minutes of the prior illegal meeting does not constitute ratification. In re Chelsea Exchange Corp., (1932) 18 Del. Ch. 287, 159 A. 432.

[76]Zachary v. Milin, (1940) 294 Mich. 622, 293 N.W. 770.

[77]Clark v. Mutual Loan & Investment Co., (1937) 88 F. 2d 202; Minneapolis Times Co. v. Nimocks, (1893) 53 Minn. 381, 55 N.W. 546.; Homan v. Fir Products Co., (1923) 123 Wash. 260, 212 P. 240.

[78]A meeting held in the hall outside the office, because the directors found the office locked, was valid, although the statute required the meeting to be held at the principal office. Seal of Gold Mining Co. v. Slater, see Note 33.

[79]Moreno Mut. Irrigation Co. v. Jordan, (1925) 197 Cal. 69, 239 P. 716.

[80]Ashley Wire Co. v. Illinois Steel Co., (1896) 164 Ill. 149, 45 N.E. 410.

[81]Hackler v. International Traveler's Ass'n, (1914) Tex. Civ. App., 165 S.W. 44.

[82]Corbett v. Woodward, (1879) 5 Sawyer (U.S.) 403, Fed. Cas. No. 3233; Russian Reinsurance Co. v. Stoddard, (1925) 211 App. Div. 132, 207 N.Y. Supp. 574.

[83]State Nat'l Bank v. Union Bank, (1897) 168 Ill. 519, 48 N.E. 82.

without such written consent.[84] But those who attend the meeting and participate in the action cannot object to the validity of the meeting on the ground that it was improperly held outside the state.[85] Also a meeting is valid, though not held at the place specified in the by-laws, when all the directors waived notice of the meeting, and the attending directors owned almost all the stock.[86]

Quorum at directors' meetings. Since directors can act only as a board, the presence of a quorum at a board's meeting is necessary to transact corporate business.[87] Generally a majority of the directors constitutes a quorum.[88] A majority of a quorum has authority to transact any corporate business upon which the board may act.[89]

A quorum is presumed to be present unless it is questioned.[90] The presence and vote at a meeting of directors owning a majority of the stock is not a substitute for quorum requirements.[91] Corporations can fix their own quorum requirements, as long as they do not conflict with statutory requirements.[92]

A director cannot be tricked into attendance at a meeting against his will in order to obtain a quorum.[93] For example, if the directors come together accidentally, some of them cannot declare, over the protests of others, that the persons gathered together are in a "meeting." But if all the members of the board are present at the meeting and understand it to be a directors' meeting, then the gathering is a legal meeting.[94]

Quorum requirements for ratification are the same as those for original authorization.[95] Thus, a special meeting attended by only two of a corporation's four directors is invalid and cannot approve sale of stock to

---

[84]A. Lorenze Co. v. Penn-Louisiana Oil & Gas Co., (1924) 155 La. 749, 99 So. 586. See Illig v. Chartiers Ry., (1920) 268 Pa. 467, 112 A. 116, in which it was held that the board had authority to carry out a resolution to change the route of the road, passed at a meeting of the board held outside the state of domicile.

[85]Lippman v. Kehoe Stenograph Co., (1915) 11 Del. Ch. 80, 95 A. 895.

[86]Freeman v. King Pontiac, (1960) 236 S.C. 335, 114 S.E. 2d 478.

[87]Cleburne County Bank v. Butler Gin Co., (1931) 184 Ark. 503, 42 S.W. 2d 769; Parucki v. Polish Nat'l Catholic Church, (1920) 114 N.Y. Misc. 6, 186 N.Y. Supp. 702; Federal Mining & Engineering Co. v. Pollak, (1939) 59 Nev. 145, 85 P. 2d 1008.

[88]Calumet Paper Co. v. Haskell Show-Printing Co., (1898) 144 Mo. 331, 45 S.W. 1115.

[89]Leavitt v. Oxford & Geneva Silver Mining Co., (1883) 3 Utah 265, 1 P. 356.

[90]Coombs v. Harford, (1904) 99 Me. 426, 59 A. 529.

[91]Belle Isle Corp. v. MacBean, (1946) 29 Del. Ch. 261, 49 A. 2d 5; comment, 45 MICH. L. REV. 630.

[92]Matter of Auer, (1954) 306 N.Y. 427, 118 N.E. 2d 590; Benintendi v. Kenton Hotel, (1945) 294 N.Y. 112, 60 N.E. 2d 829.

[93]Zachary v. Milin, (1940) 294 Mich. 622, 293 N.W. 770; Trendley v. Illinois Traction Co., (1912) 241 Mo. 73, 145 S.W. 1.

[94]Zachary v. Milin, (1940) 294 Mich. 622, 293 N.W. 770.

[95]Belle Isle Corp. v. MacBean, (1946) 29 Del. Ch. 261, 49 A. 2d 5.

the corporation when the charter and by-laws require three directors for both quorum and corporate action.[96] In regard to the necessity for a continuance of a quorum during a meeting, see page 14.

Quorum when board has vacancies. In the absence of a provision to the contrary in the statutes, charter, or by-laws, a majority of the authorized number of directors is necessary to constitute a quorum. This is true even when there are vacancies on the board.[97] Thus, if the by-laws provide that the board shall consist of seven directors and a majority shall constitute a quorum, the unanimous vote of three directors is insufficient even though there are four vacancies on the board.[98] Unfilled directorships are distinguished from vacant directorships for quorum purposes.[99] Thus where by-laws are changed to increase the number of directors from five to nine, though no actual change in the number has been effected, three of the five directors would constitute a quorum.[100] Unfilled positions must be voted in by stockholders while vacancies may be filled by directors in office. Although the charter provides that the corporation shall be managed by a certain number of directors, the by-laws can provide that a majority of the directors in office at that time shall constitute a quorum.[101] Under such a by-law, if a corporation is required by its charter to provide for a board of from three to seven directors, and seven directors are elected but two decline to serve, any three of the remaining five directors constitute a quorum and may hold a legal meeting.[102]

The fact that there are vacancies on the board does not prevent the remaining directors from holding meetings and transacting business, when they constitute a majority of the entire board as it would be constituted if all the vacancies were filled.[103] If the number of members of the board is less than the quorum requirement, the board cannot transact any business other than the filling of vacancies except, perhaps, to adjourn the meeting to another day. (See page 138 on adjournment.) Some states, however, permit the remaining directors to fill vacancies even when they do not have a quorum, unless charter or by-laws provide otherwise.[104] However, the

---

[96]Lewis v. Steinhart, (1972) S. Ct., 338 N.Y.S. 2d 552.

[97]Hotaling v. Hotaling, (1924) 193 Cal. 368, 224 P. 455; Belle Isle Corp. v. MacBean, (1946) 29 Del. Ch. 261, 49 A. 2d 5.

[98]Bruch v. National Guarantee Credit Corp. (1922) 13 Del. Ch. 180, 116 A. 738.

[99]Belle Isle Corp. v. MacBean, (1948) 30 Del. Ch. 373, 61 A. 2d 699; Freidus v. Kaufman, (1955) 35 N.J. Super. 601, 114 A. 2d 751.

[100]Robertson v. Hartman, (1936) 6 Cal. 2d 408, 57 P. 2d 1310.

[101]Twisp Mining & Smelting Co. v. Chelan Mining Co., (1943) 16 Wash. 2d 264, 133 P. 2d 300.

[102]Blish v. Thomspon Automatic Arms Corp., (1948) 30 Del. Ch. 538, 64 A. 2d 581.

[103]Currie v. Matson, (1940) 33 F. Supp. 454.

[104]In re Chelsea Exchange Corp., (1932) 18 Del. Ch. 287, 159 A. 432. Bruch v. National Guarantee Credit Corp., (1922) 13 Del. Ch. 180, 116 A. 738; But see Friedus v. Kaufman, (1955) 35 N.J. Super. 601, 114 A. 2d 751.

directors' power to *fill* vacancies on the board does not mean that they can *create* a new seat on the board and elect a new director to fill it; so, any action taken hinging on the director's vote is invalid.[105] Also, newly created vacancies on a corporation's board of directors, until filled, are not counted in determining a majority.[106]

Interested directors, for quorum purposes. Frequently, a quorum is present, but one of the directors necessary to make a quorum is personally interested in the business before the meeting. The general rule is that a director who is disqualified from voting because he is *personally* interested in the matter under consideration *cannot be included* in determining whether a quorum is present.[107] The reason for this rule is that the director, in acting for the corporation, must do so in the best interests of the corporation. His duty is first to the corporation. However, unless prohibited by statute, a corporation's charter can provide that an interested director may be counted for quorum purposes.[108] There is some authority for including such a director even in the absence of express charter provision but it represents a minority view.[109]

The widespread practice of having corporate attorneys and employees on boards of directors indicates a fairly universal acceptance of the proposition that such relationships do not necessarily disqualify a director from being counted in determining the existence of a quorum. Thus, a director who was an attorney and expected compensation for negotiating a contract has been counted for quorum purposes; also, a director who was an employee and participant in a bonus plan.[110]

For voting by interested directors, see page 137.

Conduct of directors' meetings. In the case of small corporations, meetings of the board of directors are usually conducted in an informal manner. Larger corporations, however, generally conduct their directors' meetings with considerable formality. The chairman of the board sits at the head of the directors' table. The president sits at the right of the chairman,

---

[105]Hackett v. Diversified Chemicals, Inc., (1965) La. Ct. of App., 180 So. 2d 831.

[106]Rocket Mining Corporation v. Gill, (1971) Utah S. Sct., 483 P. 2d 897.

[107]Goldie v. Cox, (1942) 130 F. 2d 695; In re Lone Star Shipbuilding Co., (1925) 6 F. 2d 192; McLean v. Bradley, (1922) 282 F. 1011; In re Fergus Falls Woolen Mills Co., (1941) 41 F. Supp. 355; Holcomb v. Forsyth, (1927) 216 Ala. 484, 113 So. 516; Mortensen v. Ballard, (1951) 218 Ark. 653, 236 S.W. 2d 1006; Hill Dredging Corp. v. Risley, (1955) 18 N.J. 501, 114 A. 2d 697.; Cardin Bldg. Co. v. Smith, (1927) 125 Okla. 300, 258 P. 910; Marcuse v. Broad-Grace Arcade Corp., (1935) 164 Va. 553, 180 S.E. 327; Hein v. Gravelle Farmers Elevator Co., (1931) 164 Wash. 309, 2 P. 2d 741. But see Fountain v. Oreck's Inc., (1955) 245 Minn. 202, 71 N.W. 2d 646.

[108]Piccard v. Sperry Corp., (1943) 48 F. Supp. 465, aff'd (1946) 152 F. 2d 462, cert. denied, 328 U.S. 845, 66 S. Ct. 1024.

[109]Buell v. Buckingham, (1864) 16 Iowa 284; Gumaer v. Cripple Creek Tunnel Transportation & Mining Co., (1907) 40 Colo. 1, 90 P. 81.

[110]Piccard v. Sperry Corp., (1943) 48 F. Supp. 465, aff'd (1946) 152 F. 2d 462, cert. denied, 328 U.S. 845, 66 S. Ct. 1024.

or if the office of chairman of the board does not exist, the president sits at the head of the table. Usually the secretary sits next to the chairman, often at his left, so that he can be consulted conveniently on any matter in the order of business and hand documents and records to him with a minimum of disturbance. The chairman generally presides at meetings of the directors, unless some other provision is made by the by-laws.[111]

Votes are usually taken in an informal manner, generally by a call for "yes" and "no" answers.[112] The usual order of business is as follows:

1. Call to order.
2. Announcement of a quorum present.
3. Reading and approval of the minutes of the previous meeting. (It is the practice of some secretaries to prepare a copy of the minutes for each director in order that he may peruse it at his leisure before the meeting is called to order and to note on the margin thereof any exceptions or amendments he may wish to move).
4. Reports of officers and committees.
5. Unfinished business.
6. Election of officers, if there is to be an election.
7. Declaration of dividend, if there is to be a dividend declared.
8. Other new business.
9. Adjournment.

Voting at directors' meetings. Unless expressly provided otherwise in the statutes, charter, or by-laws, a majority vote of the directors present at a meeting, as distinguished from a majority of the full board, is sufficient to authorize action.[113] A majority of the board is a quorum and the board can act by a majority of a quorum present *and voting*, irrespective of the number of other directors who may be present at the meeting.[114] The by-laws or articles of incorporation can, of course, require a greater number in both instances.

A director has no additional authority because he is the representative of the majority stockholder.[115] Voting by directors is not on the basis of stock ownership.[116] In all jurisdictions, except Arkansas and Louisiana, directors cannot vote by proxy.[117]

---

[111]See Benson v. Keller, (1900) 37 Ore. 120, 132, 60 P. 918.

[112]A chairman was justified in declaring a resolution unanimously adopted, where one of the directors who did not answer "no" denied that he voted in the affirmative, and did not dispute the declaration of unanimous adoption. Herring-Curtiss Co. v. Curtiss, (1923) 120 N.Y. Misc. 733, 200 N.Y. Supp. 7.

[113]Kaplan v. Block (1944) 183 Va. 327, 31 S.E. 2d 893.

[114]Crowley v. Commodity Exchange, Inc., (1944) 141 F. 2d 182.

[115]Trethewey v. Green River Gorge, (1943) 17 Wash. 2d 697, 136 P. 2d 999.

[116]Geiman-Herthel Furniture Co. v. Geiman, (1945) 160 Kan. 346, 161 P. 2d 504.

[117]Perry v. Tuscaloosa Cotton-Seed Oil-Mill Co., (1891) 93 Ala. 364, 9 So. 217; Greenberg v. Harrison, (1956) 143 Conn. 519, 124 A. 2d 216; Stevens v. Acadia Dairies, Inc., (1927) 15 Del. Ch. 248, 135 A. 846; Lippman v. Kehoe Stenograph Co., (1915) 11 Del. Ch. 80, 95 A. 895; First Nat'l Bank v. East Omaha Box Co., (1902) 2 Neb. Unof. 820, 90 N.W. 223; Craig Medicine Co. v. Merchants' Bank, (1891) 59 Hun. (N.Y.) 561, 14 N.Y. Supp. 16.

In Arkansas and Louisiana, written proxies may be authorized by by-laws or charter respectively. See Ark. Acts of 1955, Act 83, Sec. 1; and La. B.C.L. Sec. 35 (F).

Voting by interested directors. A director who is present at a meeting may vote on any subject in which he is not directly or personally interested.[118] If a meeting is called to vote on matters in which he is directly involved or has a personal interest, his presence at the meeting will not be counted for the purpose of quorum,[119] nor his vote taken if necessary and essential to the passage of the resolution.[120] His fellow directors who are disinterested in the matter, however, may vote. If the "interested" director does vote, the resolution becomes voidable at the instance of the corporation or its stockholders regardless of its fairness.[121] Further, directors can sue fellow directors for knowingly voting on a resolution that authorized payment of an alleged duplicate claim to the corporation they are interested in; while interested directors can vote on such a resolution without invalidating it when the majority of disinterested directors voted in favor of it, they are personally liable for waste of corporate assets.[122]

A director who is an attorney for a person having a claim against the corporation is not qualified to vote on the settlement of the claim,[123] nor may directors against whom the corporation is bringing suit vote on that question.[124] But a wife is not disqualified at a directors' meeting fixing the sum due her husband under a contract with the corporation.[125] Likewise, a director will not be considered an "interested" director if his wife owns stock in another company with which the corporation is contracting.[126] Also, directors validly allotted corporate stock when all shareholders knew of the allotment and did not object, and it was made in consideration of their valuable services in organizing corporations.[127] (See "Voting on contracts by interested directors," page 247; also, "Right of interested directors to vote on compensation," page 349.

Irregularity of directors' meetings. The principles expressed under irregularities of stockholders' meetings apply generally to directors' meetings. Ratification by directors at a subsequent legal meeting, or by stock-

---

[118]Alward v. Broadway Gold Mining Co., (1933) 94 Mont. 45, 20 P. 2d 647; Sacajawea Lumber & Shingle Co. v. Skookum Lumber Co., (1921) 116 Wash. 75, 198 P. 1112.

[119]Goldie v. Cox, (1942) 130 F. 2d 695; Bovay v. Byllesby & Co., (1944) 27 Del. Ch. 381, 38 A. 2d 808; Fields v. Victor Bldg. & Loan Co., (1918) (Okla.) 175 P. 529.

[120]Rocket Mining Corporation v. Gill (1971) Utah S. Ct., 483 P. 2d 897; In re Franklin Brewing Co., (1920) 263 F. 512.

[121]Cathedral Estates, Inc. v. Taft Realty Corp., (1955) 228 F. 2d 85; Bates Street Shirt Co., v. Waite, (1931) 130 Me. 352, 156 A. 293; Standard Furniture Co. v. Hotel Butler Co., (1931) 161 Wash. 109, 296 P. 153.

[122]Rapoport v. Schneider, (1972) 29 N.Y. 2d 431, 328 N.Y.S. 2d 431, 278 N.E. 2d 645.

[123]North Confidence Mining & Development Co. v. Fitch, (1922) 58 Cal. App. 329, 208 P. 328.

[124]Anderson v. Gailey, (1929) 33 F. 2d 589.

[125]Cuneo v. Giannini, (1919) 40 Cal. App. 348, 180 P. 633.

[126]Piccard v. Sperry Corp., (1943) 48 Supp. 465, aff'd (1946) 152 F. 2d 462, cert. Denied, 328 U.S. 845, 66 S. Ct. 1024.

[127]Eastern Oklahoma Television Co. v. Ameco, Inc., (1971) CA-10, 437 F. 2d 138.

holders through express ratification or through acquiescence with knowledge of the facts, may confirm illegal or irregular proceedings of the directors and give the action validity.[128]

Adjournment of directors' meeting for lack of quorum. The principles governing adjournment of stockholders' meetings apply to directors' meeting as well (see page 17). If there is less than a quorum present, the meeting must necessarily adjourn. To avoid interference with the conduct of the business through repeated failure of a quorum to attend, some corporations include in their by-laws a provision that, if a meeting adjourns for lack of a quorum, the president may send out notices, setting forth the failure of the meeting to convene for want of a quorum, and calling another meeting, at which a quorum shall consist of two or more directors, instead of the larger number ordinarily required.

The by-laws usually provide that a majority of those present at a meeting which fails because of the absence of a quorum may adjourn the meeting to another day. Unless authorized by statute, charter, or by-laws, less than a quorum of directors have no power to adjourn a meeting to another day.[129] At an adjourned meeting, such business may be transacted as might have been transacted at the original meeting. (See page 129 for necessity of notice of adjourned meetings.)

Rescission of action taken at previous directors' meetings. The directors have the right to repeal any resolution passed at previous meetings, or to rescind any previous action, provided that the repeal or rescission does not involve a breach of contract or disturb a vested right.[130] Thus, the directors cannot rescind or modify their action in calling stock for redemption or retirement.[131] The right of the directors to revoke declared dividends is treated separately on page 716, in Chapter 23. The right of the directors to revoke declared dividends is treated on pages 716-717 in Chapter 23.

Notification of action at directors' meetings. Provision is often made in the by-laws that notification regarding action taken at directors' meetings shall be given by the secretary. He is sometimes directed to notify the auditor of expenditures authorized at meetings, or to advise other officers or persons of any business transacted in which they are concerned. Usually copies of resolutions are distributed after meetings to interested persons who request them, to directors who were absent from the meeting,

---

[128] Caminetti v. Prudence Mut. Life Ins. Ass'n, (1944) 62 Cal. App. 2d 945, 146 P. 2d 15; Bates Street Shirt Co. v. Waite, (1931) 130 Me. 352, 156 A. 293.

[129] Cheney v. Canfield, (1910) 158 Cal. 342, 111 P. 92.; Noremac, Inc. v. Centre Hill Court, (1935) 164 Va. 151, 178 S.E. 877.

[130] Staats v. Biograph Co., (1916) 236 F. 454.

[131] Taylor v. Axton-Fisher Tobacco Co., (1943) 295 Ky. 226, 173 S.W. 2d 377.

and to officers or executives who have been directed to take the action called for by the resolution.

Meetings of finance and executive committees. In many corporations, the executive and finance committees are the most active bodies. They are created generally in accordance with the provisions of the by-laws, or by resolution of the board of directors. The by-laws usually prescribe the manner of calling committee meetings, the number of persons necessary to constitute a quorum, the method of filling vacancies, the number of votes necessary to take action, and similar regulations. The by-laws or resolution creating the committee may provide that the committees shall set up their own rules of procedure. In the absence of special rules governing the conduct of committee meetings, the rules governing meetings of directors apply. Thus, the executive or other committee must act as a whole. In the absence of specific requirements, a majority of the committee will constitute a quorum and a majority of those present at any meeting will have power to decide questions that come before the meeting. Committee meetings are ordinarily not conducted with as much formality as meetings of the board of directors.

The function of the executive committee generally is to exercise all the powers of the board of directors, in accordance with the policy of the corporation, during intervals between formal meetings of the board of directors (see page 258). Frequently, the minutes of meetings of the executive committee, held since the last meeting of the board of directors, are read at each directors' meeting, and a motion to approve and ratify is passed.

Chapter 4

FORMS RELATING TO DIRECTORS'
AND COMMITTEE MEETINGS

Contents—Chapter 4

CALLS, NOTICES, AND WAIVERS OF NOTICE OF DIRECTORS' MEETINGS

CALL OF REGULAR MEETING OF DIRECTORS BY CHAIRMAN OF THE BOARD

...., 19..

To the Directors of ....Corporation:

The undersigned, Chariman of the Board of the ....Corporation, hereby calls the regular monthly meeting of the Board of Directors of said Corporation, to be held at the office of the Corporation, ...*(Street)*, ... *(City)*, ... *(State)*, on ...., 19.., at ...... A.M.

....
Chairman of the Board

REQUEST OF DIRECTORS TO PRESIDENT TO CALL SPECIAL MEETING OF BOARD

.... *(City)*, ... *(State)*
...., 19..

Mr. ...., President of .... Corporation
.... *(Street)*
.... *(City)*, ... *(State)*

Dear Sir:

The undersigned, being a majority of the Board of Directors of the .... Corporation, hereby request you to call a special meeting of said Board, to be held at the office of the Corporation, ... *(Street)*, ... *(City)*, ... *(State)*, on ...., 19.., at ..... A.M. for the purpose of:

(Here insert purposes of meeting; see form on page 146.)

and for the transaction of any and all business necessary in connection therewith that may properly come before said meeting.

....
....
....
Directors of ....Corporation

CALL OF SPECIAL MEETING OF DIRECTORS BY PRESIDENT

To ....,
Secretary of ....Corporation:

The undersigned, President of .... Corporation, pursuant to authority vested in him by Article ....., Section ..... of the By-laws of said Corporation, hereby calls a special meeting of the Board of Directors of the Corporation, to be held on ...., 19.., at ..... P.M., at the office of the Corporation at .... *(Street)*, ... *(City)*, ... *(State)*, for the purpose of:

(Here insert purposes of meeting; see form on page 146.)

As Secretary of the .... Corporation, you are hereby authorized and directed to give written notice, personally or by mail, of the time, place, and purpose of the meeting to each member of the said Board of Directors, as required by Article ....., Section ..... of the By-laws of the said Corporation.

Dated at .... *(City)*, ... *(State)*, this .. day of ...., 19...

....
President

CALL OF SPECIAL MEETING OF BOARD OF DIRECTORS
BY THE DIRECTORS

To ....,
Secretary of ....Corporation:

We, the undersigned, directors of .... Corporation, pursuant to the authority vested in us by Article ....., Section ..... of the By-laws of said Corporation, do hereby call a special meeting of the Board of Directors of the Corporation, to be held on ...., at ..... A.M., at the office and principal place of business of said Corporation, at .... *(Street)*, ... *(City)*, ... *(State)*, for the purpose of:

(Here insert purposes of meeting; see form on page 146.)

We hereby authorize and direct you, as Secretary of the Corporation, to give written notice of the time, place, and purpose of the said meeting to each member of the Board of Directors of the said Corporation, in accordance with the By-laws.

Dated at .... *(City)*, ... *(State)*, this .. day of ...., 19...

....
....
....
Directors of ....Corporation

NOTICE OF ANNUAL MEETING OF DIRECTORS

To the Board of Directors of ....Corporation:

NOTICE IS HEREBY GIVEN That, pursuant to Article ....., Section ..... of the By-laws of the .... Corporation, the annual meeting of the Board of Directors of said Corporation will be held at the office of the Corporation, located at .... *(Street)*, ... *(City)*, ... *(State)*, on ...., 19.., at ..... P.M.

.... Secretary

Dated ...., 19 ..

NOTICE OF DIRECTORS' MEETING TO BE HELD IMMEDIATELY FOLLOWING ANNUAL STOCKHOLDERS' MEETING

NOTICE IS HEREBY GIVEN That, pursuant to Section ..... of Article ..... of the By-laws of the .... Corporation, the annual meeting of the Board of Directors of the Corporation will be held at the offices of the Corporation, ... *(Street)*, ... *(City)*, ... *(State)*, on ...., 19.., immediately after the annual meeting of the stockholders, the stockholders' meeting to be held at ..... A.M. on the said day.
Dated ...., 19 ..

....
Secretary

PRINTED NOTICE OF REGULAR MEETING OF DIRECTORS

A regular meeting of the Board of Directors of The .... Corporation will be held on ...., 19.., at ..... A.M., at .... *(Street)*, ... *(City)*, ... *(State)*.
Business: ....
....

....
Secretary

PRINTED NOTICE OF REGULAR OR SPECIAL MEETING OF DIRECTORS

On .... *(Day of Week)*, ..., 19.., at ..... P.M., a .... *(insert regular or special)* meeting of the Board of Directors of .... Manufacturing Company will be held at the .... office of the Company.

....
Secretary

To ....
    City of ...., State of ...., ..., 19..

NOTICE OF SPECIAL MEETING OF DIRECTORS
(PURPOSES NOT SPECIFIED)

Notice Is Hereby Given That, pursuant to the call of the President of ....
Corporation, a special meeting of the Board of Directors of the Corporation will be
held at the office of the Corporation at .... *(Street)*, ... *(City)*,
.... *(State)*, on ...., at ..... P.M.
Dated ...., 19 ..

....
Secretary

NOTICE OF SPECIAL MEETING OF DIRECTORS
(SPECIFYING PURPOSES)

.... *(City)*, ... *(State)*
To ...., ..., and ....,
Directors of .... Corporation:

Notice Is Hereby Given That, in accordance with the provisions of Article .....,
Section ..... of the By-laws of the .... Corporation, and in accordance with
the requirements of the laws of the State of ...., a special meeting of the
Board of Directors of the said Corporation will be held at its office and principal
place of business, ... *(Street)*, ... *(City)*, ... *(State)*, on
...., 19.., at ..... A.M., for the purpose of:

1. *(Here insert particular purposes of meeting)*
2. To transact such other business as may lawfully come before said
meeting.
Dated this .. day of ...., 19..

....
Secretary

NOTICE OF DIRECTORS' MEETING WITH REPLY CARD

To the members of the Board of Directors of ....Corporation:

You are requested to attend a .... *(insert regular or special)* meeting
of the Board of Directors at the office of the Corporation at ....
(Street), ... *(City)*, ... *(State)*, on ...., 19.., at ..... P.M.
Please use the attached card to notify me whether or not you will be present.

Respectfully,
....
Secretary

....

To the Secretary of the .... Corporation:

      will
I   be present.
      will not

....
Director

PURPOSE CLAUSES FOR NOTICES OF DIRECTORS' MEETINGS

To employ accountants

To employ accountants to audit the books and accounts of the corporation at the close of the fiscal year on ...., 19...

To ratify charitable and other contributions

To consider and pass upon the ratification and confirmation of charitable and other lawful contributions made by any of the officers of this corporation during the year ending ...., 19.., in an amount not in excess of ..... Dollars ($.....).

To fill vacancies in board of directors

To elect ..... (.....) directors to fill the vacancies in the membership of the Board of Directors due to the resignations of .... and ....

To consider removal of director

To consider whether sufficient cause exists for the removal of .... from the office of director of the corporation, and to remove him if such cause exists.

To consider annual report of officers

To receive and hear the annual report of the officers of the corporation, and to consider its confirmation and ratification.

NOTICE OF ADJOURNED MEETING OF DIRECTORS

To the Directors of ....Corporation:

PLEASE TAKE NOTICE That the meeting of the Board of Directors, held at the office of the Corporation at .... *(Street)*, ... *(City)*, ... *(State)*, on ...., 19.., at ..... P.M., has been adjourned to and will be held on ...., 19.., at the same place.

....
President

...., 19..

NOTICE OF FAILURE OF DIRECTORS' MEETING TO CONVENE FOR LACK OF QUORUM AND CALLING OF ANOTHER MEETING

...., 19..

To the Directors of the ....Corporation:

PLEASE TAKE NOTICE That the special meeting of directors of the .... Corporation, called to be held at the office of the Corporation, ... *(Street)*, ...*(City)*, ...*(State)*, on ...., 19.., at ..... A.M., failed to convene for lack of a quorum, and that, pursuant to the provisions of the By-laws of the Corporation, another special meeting of the directors is hereby called to be held on ...., 19.., at the same place, at which ..... or more directors will constitute a quorum for the transaction of business.

....
President

WAIVER BY ALL DIRECTORS OF NOTICE OF MEETING (REGULAR OR SPECIAL)

We, the undersigned, being all the directors of .... Corporation, a corporation organized and existing under the laws of the State of ...., do hereby waive all notice as provided by the laws of the State of ...., or by the Articles of Incorporation by By-laws of the Corporation, of the time, place, and purpose of a .... *(insert regular or special)* meeting of the Board of Directors of said Corporation, and do hereby fix the .. day of ...., 19.., at ..... A.M., as the time, and the office of the Corporation, ... *(Street)*, ... *(City)*, ... *(State)*, as the place, and the following as the purposes of the said meeting:

(Here insert purposes of meeting; see page 146.)

We hereby consent to the transaction of any business, in addition to the business herein noticed to be transacted, that may come before the meeting. Dated ...., 19..

....
....
....
(To be signed by all the directors)

WAIVER BY CERTAIN DIRECTORS OF NOTICE OF MEETING

We, ..., ..., and ...., directors of the .... Corporation, a corporation organized under the laws of the State of ...., hereby waive notice of the time, place, and purpose of a .... *(insert regular or special)* meeting of the Board of Directors of the Corporation, to be held at the office of the Corporation, ... *(Street)*, ... *(City)*, ... *(State)*, on ...., 19.., at ..... P.M., for the purpose of:

(Here insert purposes of meeting.)

....
....
....
Directors

AFFIDAVITS AND CERTIFICATES RELATING TO DIRECTORS' MEETINGS

AFIDAVIT OF SECRETARY THAT PERSONAL NOTICE OF MEETING WAS SERVED

State of ....

} ss:

County of ....

................, being duly sworn, on oath deposes and says that he is the Secretary of the .... Corporation, a corporation organized and existing under the laws of the State of ....; and that on ...., 19.., he served notice of a directors' meeting of the said Corporation, a copy of which is hereto attached and is hereby made a part of this affidavit, upon the following members of the Board of Directors: .... *(insert names of members)*, by handing personally to each of them a copy thereof.

....
Secretary

Subscribed and sworn to before me
this .. day of ...., 19..

....
Notary Public

AFFIDAVIT OF SERVICE OF NOTICE OF DIRECTORS' MEETING BY MAIL

State of ....

} ss:

County of ....

................, being duly sworn, deposes and says that he is Secretary of .... Corporation, a corporation existing under the laws of the State of ....

That on ...., 19.., at the order and direction of the President of the Corporation, he caused the notice of the .... *(insert regular or special)* meeting of the directors of the Corporation, a copy of which is hereunto annexed and made a part of this affidavit as if herein fully set forth, to be deposited in a United States post-office box at the City of ...., in a sealed and post-paid wrapper, duly addressed to each member of the Board of Directors of the Corporation, at his last-known post-office address.

....
Secretary

Sworn to before me
this .. day of ...., 19..

....
Notary Public

AFFIDAVIT OF SECRETARY OF PUBLICATION OF NOTICE OF DIRECTORS' MEETING

State of ....
County of .... } ss:

............., being duly sworn, deposes and says that he is Secretary of .... Corporation, a corporation existing under the laws of the State of ....; that the notice of which the annexed printed slip is a true copy has, by order of the Board of Directors of the Corporation, been published in the ...., a newspaper printed and published in the City of ...., County of ...., State of ...., for a period of .... *(insert number of days or weeks)*, commencing on ...., 19...

Sworn to before me this ....
day of ...., 19..   Secretary
....
Notary Public

[*Note*. Notice of directors' meeting need not be published unless required by the by-laws, by statute, or by the articles of incorporation.].

AFFIDAVIT OF SERVICE OF NOTICE OF DIRECTORS' MEETING BY MAIL SETTING FORTH NAMES AND ADDRESSES OF DIRECTORS SERVED

State of ....
County of .... } ss:

............., being first duly sworn upon oath, deposes and says that he is the duly elected, qualified, and acting Secretary of the .... Corporation.

That pursuant to an order of .... as President of said Corporation, he personally gave notice to each and every director of said Corporation of the special meeting of the Board of Directors, to be held at ..... P.M. on ...., 19.., at the office of said Corporation, by depositing in the post office of the United States Mail, in the City of ...., State of ...., on ...., 19.., a notice to each of said directors, specifying the time, place, and objects for which said meeting was called (a full, true, and accurate copy of which notice is hereto attached), addressed to each of said directors at the address of each as shown by the books of said Corporation—to wit:
..... notices addressed as follows, respectively:

Name	Address
....	....
....	....
....	....

Sworn to before me this ....
day of ...., 19..   Secretary
....
Notary Public

AFFIDAVIT OF PUBLISHER OF PUBLICATION OF NOTICE OF DIRECTORS' MEETING

State of ....
County of .... } ss:

................, being duly sworn, deposes and says that he is and was at all the times hereinafter mentioned over the age of eighteen (18) years and a citizen of the United States; that he is not a party to and is not interested in the matter herein; that he is and was during all the time hereinafter mentioned the chief clerk of the printers and publishers of ...., a newspaper of general circulation printed and published daily (or weekly) in the City of ...., County of ...., State of ...., in charge of all advertisements in said newspaper; and that the notice, of which the annexed printed slip is a true copy, was published in said newspaper ..... (.....) times, commencing on ...., 19.., and ending on ...., 19.., (both days inclusive), and as often as said newspaper was regularly issued during said time.

Sworn to before me this
.. day of ...., 19..
....
Notary Public

....

[*Note.* This form may be used for proof of publication of other notices. As to necessity of publication of notice of directors' meetings, see note to form on page 149.]

CERTIFICATION OF MINUTES OF DIRECTORS' MEETING

State of ....
County of .... } ss:

................, being duly sworn, deposes and says that he is the Secretary of the .... Corporation, a corporation organized and existing under the laws of the State of ...., and having its principal place of business at .... *(Street)*, ... *(City)*, ... *(State)*; that he has custody of the books of the Corporation; and that the foregoing is a full, true and correct copy of the minutes of a .... *(insert regular or special)* meeting of the Board of Directors of the Corporation, held on ...., 19.., at its said principal place of business.

Wɪᴛɴᴇss my hand and the seal of the said Corporation this .. day of ...., 19...

Sworn to before me this
.. day of ...., 19..
....
Notary Public

....
Secretary

(Corporate Seal)

CERTIFICATE OF PASSAGE OF RESOLUTION AT DIRECTORS' MEETING, WITH ACKNOWLEDGMENT

....CORPORATION

...., 19..

At a duly constituted meeting of the Board of Directors of the ....
Corporation, held on ...., 19.., the following resolutions were adopted:

(Here insert resolutions.)

I, the undersigned, hereby certify that the foregoing is a true copy of the resolutions adopted by the Board of Directors of the abovementioned Corporation at a meeting of the said Board held on the aforementioned date, and entered upon the regular minute book of the said Corporation, and now in full force and effect, and that the Board of Directors of the Corporation has, and at the time of the adoption of the said resolutions had, full power and lawful authority to adopt the said resolutions and to confer the powers thereby granted to the officers therein named, who have full power and lawful authority to exercise the same.

....
Secretary of the Board of Directors

(Corporate Seal)

State of ....
County of .... } ss:

On ...., 19.., in the County of ...., before me, a Notary Public duly commissioned and qualified, in and for the state and county aforesaid, personally came ...., personally known to me, and known to me to be the person described in and who executed the foregoing certificate, and acknowledged to me that he executed the same; and being by me duly sworn, did depose and say that he is the Secretary of the Board of Directors of the .... Corporation; that, as such officer, he keeps the corporate minute books and seal of the Corporation; and that the foregoing certificate is true to his own knowledge.

Subscribed and Sworn to before me
this .. day of ...., 19..
....
Notary Public

CERTIFICATE OF PASSAGE OF RESOLUTION SIGNED BY SECRETARY AND CERTIFIED BY DIRECTOR

I, ..., do hereby certify that I am the duly ${\left\{{\text{elected} \atop \text{appointed}}\right\}}$ and qualified Secretary and the keeper of the records and corporate seal of

................, a corporation organized and existing under the laws of the State of ...., and that the following is a true and correct copy of certain resolutions duly adopted at a meeting of the Board of Directors thereof, convened and held in accordance with law and the By-laws of said Corporation on ...., 19.., and that such resolutions are now in full force and effect:

(Here insert copy of resolution.)

IN WITNESS WHEREOF, I have affixed my name as Secretary and have caused the corporate seal of said Corporation to be hereunto affixed, this .. day of ...., 19...

....
Secretary

Affix corporate seal below:
(Here insert seal)

I, ..., a director of said Corporation, do hereby certify that the foregoing is a correct copy of certain resolutions passed as therein set forth.

....
Director

Chapter 5

MINUTES OF MEETINGS

Contents—Chapter 5

Necessity for keeping minutes of all meetings. The purpose of minutes is to preserve a permanent, official record of the actions taken at meetings of stockholders, directors, or committees.[1] The duty of keeping minutes is usually imposed on the secretary, or some other officer, by statute, or by the charter or by-laws of the corporation. As a practical matter minutes should be kept even without an express duty to do so. A corporation speaks through its records and the minutes are a part of such records.[2] Accurate minutes avoid future misunderstandings, are useful in litigation, and serve as a guide to the directors in carrying out their own decisions and those of the stockholders. For example, a former employee cannot share in the bonus for the year in which he left the job, when the corporate minutes show that the directors' resolution authorized a bonus only if employees continued employment until the end of the year.[3]

Minutes as evidence. The minutes of meetings are presumed to be correct.[4] They are prima facie evidence of the facts they recite.[5] Together with the by-laws, minutes are the highest proof of the powers of corporate officers,[6] and the minutes are the best evidence of the events or decisions they record.[7] For example, a major stockholder could not enjoin officers from exercising a stock option allegedly granted when he was mentally ill, since the court had to presume that statements in the minutes of directors' and stockholders' meetings authorizing the option were correct.[8]

In general, minutes are presumed to cover the entire subject or transaction recorded,[9] but, if the record is incomplete or ambiguous, other evidence may be submitted to supply the omission or explain the intent of a motion and overcome the presumption attached to the written record.[10]

---

[1]Chapin v. Cullis, (1941) 299 Mich. 101, 299 N.W. 824.

[2]Stipe v. First Nat'l Bank, (1956) 208 Ore. 251, 301 P. 2d 175.

[3]Doberrer v. Harris Industries, Inc., (1971) 28 Ohio App. 2d 71, 274 N.E. 2d 575.

[4]Young v. Janas, (1954) (Del. Ch.) 103 A. 2d 299.

[5]Santa Fe Hills Golf and Country Club v. Safelic Realty Co., (1961) S. Ct. Mo., 349 S.W. 2d 27; Hopewell Baptist Church v. Craig, (1956) 143 Conn. 593, 124 A. 2d 220; Stipe v. First Nat'l Bank, (1956) 208 Ore. 251, 301 P. 2d 175.; Wear v. Harrisburg Steel Corp., (1956) 70 Dauph. (Pa.) 83.

[6]Gentry-Futch Co. v. Gentry, (1925) 90 Fla. 595, 106 So. 473; Supreme Kingdom, Inc. v. Fourth Nat'l Bank, (1932) 174 Ga. 779, 164 S.E. 204.

[7]American & British Mfg. Corp. v. New Idria Quicksilver Mining Co., (1923) 293 F. 509; Central Clay Drainage Dist. v. Hunter, (1927) 174 Ark. 293, 295 S.W. 19; Kilsby v. Aero-Test Equipment Co., (1957) (Tex. Civ. App.) 301 S.W. 2d 703.

[8]My Florist, Inc. v. Harris, (1973) N.Y. S. Ct. N.Y.L.J. 6-6-73.

[9]Sweitzer v. Land, (1963) Pa. Com. Pls., Berks Co. L.J. 8-22-63, p. 209; Wenban Estate v. Hewlett, (1924) 193 Cal. 675, 227 P. 723; Green River Mfg. Co. v. Bell, (1927) 193 N.C. 367, 137 S.E. 132. See also Wright v. Phillips Fertilizer Co., (1927) 193 N.C. 305, 136 S.E. 716.

[10]Hopewell Baptist Church v. Craig, (1956) 143 Conn. 593, 124 A. 2d 220; Teiser v. Swirsky, (1931) 137 Ore. 595, 2 P. 2d 920, aff'd on rehearing, 137 Ore. 595, 4 P. 2d 322; Wear v. Harrisburg Steel Corp., (1956) 70 Dauph. Pa. 83.

Oral testimony about the circumstances of a meeting may be used to explain the purpose of a recorded transaction,[11] or to interpret a resolution.[12] However, the plain terms of a resolution cannot be varied by the corporate secretary's interpretation.[13]

The record of the written minutes sometimes may be successfully contradicted by oral testimony.[14] If the record is false or fraudulent it may be denied even by one who has certified the record.[15] The form of the record does not affect its validity or usefulness as evidence.[16]

Effect of failure to keep minutes. The failure to record acts done, or authority given, by the board of directors or the stockholders does not make these actions invalid, unless a record is required by statute, charter, or by-laws.[17] The transactions and decisions of the meeting may be proved by oral evidence.[18] Frequently, in close corporations, there is not even a formal meeting of directors when a decision is made.[19] A corporation cannot avoid its obligations because of a failure to keep records.[20] Thus a mortgage given in accordance with a resolution bound the corporation although minutes were not written up and attested by the officers of the corporation.[21]

Necessity for adopting resolutions. It is clear that a formal resolution is not necessary in law to bind the corporation or to give authority to bind the corporation. As a practical matter, however, resolutions are essential in the conduct of the corporate business. Directors may be personally liable for failure to follow the terms of a resolution.[22] A resolu-

---

[11]In re Norton's Will (1927) 129 N.Y. Misc. 875 224 N.Y. Supp. 77; Teiser v. Swirsky, (1931) 137 Ore. 595, 2 P. 2d 920, aff'd on rehearing, 137 Ore. 595, 4 P. 2d 322.

[12]Oakland Scavenger Co. v. Gandi, (1942) 51 Cal. App. 2d 69, 124 P. 2d 143.

[13]Kilsby v. Aero-Test Equipment Co., (1957) (Tex. Civ. App.) 301 S.W. 2d 703.

[14]Hopewell Baptist Church v. Craig, (1956) 143 Conn. 593, 124 A. 2d 220; Kelly-Koett Mfg. Co. v. Goldenberg, (1924) 207 Ky. 695, 270 S.W. 15; Keough v. St. Paul Milk Co., (1939) 205 Minn. 906, 285 N.W. 809; Koeune v. State Bank, (1939) 134 Pa. Super. 108, 4 A. 2d 234.

[15]Charles R. Heddon Co. v. Dozier, (1926) 99 N.J. Eq. 543, 133 A. 857, aff'd, 100 N.J. Eq. 560, 135 A. 915.

[16]Brown v. Ramsdell, (1931) 139 N.Y. Misc. 360, 249 N.Y. Supp. 387.

[17]Altavista Cotton Mills, Inc. v. Lane, (1922) 133 Va. 1, 112 S.E. 637. See also Wright v. Phillips Fertilizer Co., (1927) 193 N.C. 305, 136 S.E. 716.

[18]Cary v. Hoffman Mach. Corp., (1957) 148 F. Supp. 748; Alabama City G. & A. Ry. Co. v. Kyle, (1918) 202 Ala. 552, 81 So. 54; Redstone v. Redstone Lumber & Supply Co., (1931) 101 Fla. 226, 133 So. 882; Norelli v. Mutual Sav. Fund Harmonia, (1938) 121 N.J.L. 60, 1 A. 2d 440; Wright v. Phillips Fertilizer Co., (1927) 193 N.C. 305, 136 S.E. 716.; McCay v. Luzerne & Carbon County Motor Transit Co., (1937) 125 Pa. Super. 217, 189 A. 772; First Nat'l Bank v. Frazier, (1933) 143 Ore. 662, 22 P. 2d 325.

[19]In re Stylemaster Dep't. Store, (1956) 154 N.Y.S. 2d 58.

[20]Cary v. Hoffman Mach. Corp., (1957) 148 F. Supp. 748; Redstone v. Redstone Lumber & Supply Co., (1931) 101 Fla. 226, 133 So. 882; Webb v. Duvall, (1940) 177 Md. 592, 11 A. 2d 446.

[21]Sorge v. Sierra Auto Supply Co., (1923) 47 Nev. 217, 218 P 735. See also Emmert v. Drake, (1955) 224 F. 2d 299.

[22]Emmert v. Drake, (1955) 224 F. 2d 299.

tion is the best way to revoke action taken by a prior resolution.[23] A clear, concise statement of the action of the directors or stockholders in a formal resolution minimizes misunderstandings.[24]

Motions and resolutions. Most business matters that come before a meeting are introduced by a motion recommending that the body assembled express an opinion, take certain action, or order something to be done. A motion, in other words, is a proposal, and the expression "I move" is equivalent to "I propose." A resolution is adopted by a motion, made and seconded, that the resolution be adopted. Every motion need not be followed by a resolution. For example, someone may move that the meeting be adjourned, that a particular discussion be postponed, or that the report of a committee be accepted. Action frequently takes place with neither motion nor resolution. For example, the report of the inspectors of election may be unanimously approved and the secretary directed to file a duplicate in the office of the county court in the state and to attach another to the minutes of the meeting.

No hard and fast rules specifying when action should be taken by resolution can be drawn. All that can be said is that, under the following circumstances, resolutions are either required or appropriate: (1) if the matter is one that the statute, charter, or by-laws require to be covered by a resolution; (2) if a certificate showing that the authority granted by stockholders or directors to perform a certain act is required to be filed, or likely to be required at some future time; (3) if the matter regulates the management of the corporation and is meant to be permanent until changed; (4) if the matter is one of importance; (5) if the matter is one that is likely to be referred to from time to time; and (6) if the matter consists of amendments to the charter or by-laws.

By-laws and resolutions. The by-laws of a corporation are the rules adopted to govern the corporation, its officers, directors, and stockholders. They are the private statutes of the corporation to regulate its affairs.[25] They are permanent and continuing, except insofar as they may be amended.[26] A resolution, on the other hand, applies to a single act, and may be passed at any valid meeting of the directors or stockholders. It may change a previous resolution if it does not interfere with the rights of persons who claim protection under the previous resolution.[27] If a resolution conflicts with a

---

[23]Wear v. Harrisburg Steel Corp., (1956) 70 Dauph. (Pa.) 83.

[24]Kilsby v. Aero-Test Equipment Co., (1957) (Tex. Civ. App.) 301 S.W. 2d 703.

[25]Wear v. Harrisburg Steel Corp., (1956) 70 Dauph. (Pa.) 83.

[26]For power to amend the by-laws, see pages 796-797 in Chapter 25.

[27]Rosenfeld v. Inland Iron Works, (1932) 267 Ill. App. 254; Schlens v. Poe, (1916) 128 Md. 352, 97 A. 649.

by-law, the by-law prevails. For example, a resolution raising an officer's salary above the limit set in the by-laws is ineffective, unless the by-law is repealed or amended.[28]

When should an action be embodied in the by-laws, and when should it be recorded as a simple resolution? If the decision is to become a permanent, controlling policy, it should be incorporated in the by-laws. If notice of the action is intended to be conveyed to all the stockholders and directors of the corporation, it should be embodied in the by-laws. On the other hand, if it is likely that the future conduct of the corporation will be subject to changing conditions, a resolution will be a more appropriate form of recording the decision. Indeed, many corporations gain flexibility by passing a by-law permitting action to be determined by resolution. In such cases, provision is made in the by-laws to safeguard the interests of the corporation. For example, the by-laws may state that regular meetings of directors shall be held at the time fixed by resolution of the directors, but provision is made in the same by-laws that no meeting held in pursuance of such general resolution shall be valid unless a copy of the resolution is sent to each director at least five days before the first meeting to be held pursuant to the resolution fixing the date, or unless all the directors are present at the meeting at which the general resolution is passed.

Secretary's duty to keep minutes. The by-laws generally provide that the secretary of the corporation shall act as secretary of all meetings of the directors or stockholders, and shall keep minutes of such meetings. The secretary must therefore note carefully all discussions that take place at the meeting, and all action taken, in order that his minutes may constitute an accurate and full report of the proceedings. The secretary may adopt the record as written by someone else.[29] The minutes should be clear and concise, complete and accurate. The importance of simple, unambiguous language is apparent from the fact that the minutes are legal evidence of action taken. The contents of the minutes should be considered in the light of possible development in the future, and all language which might be used or construed to the company's disadvantage at some time in the future should be eliminated. The secretary should bear in mind that the directors of the corporation stand in a fiduciary relation which requires them to exercise the utmost good faith in managing the business affairs of the company. He should remember, in preparing his minutes, that acts of the directors are subject to the closest scrutiny.

---

[28]Hingston v. Montgomery, (1906) 121 Mo. App. 451, 97 S.W. 202.

[29]Teiser v. Swirsky, (1931) 137, Ore. 595, 2 P. 2d 920, aff'd on rehearing, 137 Ore. 595, 4 P.2d 322.

The importance of using simple, unambiguous language in recording the minutes of the meeting cannot be too strongly emphasized. The courts have repeatedly held that a resolution of the directors or stockholders may constitute a contract.[30] The importance of carefully drawing a contract is obvious. In writing up his minutes the secretary should use words in their ordinary and general sense. When taking action pursuant to a statute, it is a good plan, in framing the necessary resolutions, to follow as nearly as possible the wording of the statute.

<table>
<tr><td></td><td colspan="3">SECRETARY'S MEMORANDUM</td></tr>
<tr><td></td><td colspan="3">MEETING OF BOARD OF DIRECTORS</td></tr>
<tr><td></td><td></td><td>Stated
Annual
Special</td><td>Reg. Notice
Personal
Waiver</td></tr>
<tr><td>ORGANIZATION</td><td></td><td></td><td></td></tr>
<tr><td>DATE</td><td>19__</td><td>Hour</td><td>Standard</td></tr>
<tr><td>PRESENT
CHAIRMAN
SECRETARY
MINUTES
STATEMENTS
RESOLUTIONS</td><td>No. Present</td><td>Necessary for quorum</td><td></td></tr>
<tr><td>#1</td><td>Proposed by

Votes</td><td>Seconded by
For
Against</td><td></td></tr>
<tr><td>#2</td><td>Proposed by

Votes</td><td>Seconded by
For
Against</td><td></td></tr>
<tr><td>#3</td><td>Proposed by

Votes</td><td>Seconded by
For
Against</td><td></td></tr>
</table>

Secretary's Memorandum for Entering Notes of Minutes at Meeting (Page 1).

Preparation for taking minutes of meetings. The secretary will find himself better able to perform his duties in connection with meetings if he will make the following preparations before attending the meeting:

1. Prepare in advance a statement of the order of business and the agenda. The agenda is a digest of action to be taken at the meeting. In some cases,

[30]Central Clay Drainage Dist. v. Hunter (1927) 174 Ark. 293, 295 S.W. 19; Wright v. Phillips Fertilizer Co., (1927) 193 N.C. 305, 136 S.E. 716.

a copy of the agenda of the directors' meeting is given to each director as well as to the presiding officer.

2. If important matters are to be considered, indicate on the outline the names of those who are to present the business to the meeting.

3. Have with him all books, papers, contracts, and reports that are likely to be called for at the meeting.

4. Draft, in advance, motions or resolutions for the business that is to come before the meeting, if the subject has been thoroughly worked out and is ready for the vote of the directors or stockholders. Resolutions prepared in advance save the time of the meeting, clarify the propositions, and simplify the entries in the minute book.

RESOLUTIONS CONTINUED		
#4	Proposed by	Seconded by
		For
	Votes	Against
#5	Proposed by	Seconded by
		For
	Votes	Against
#6	Proposed by	Seconded by
		For
	Votes	Against
#7	Proposed by	Seconded by
		For
	Votes	Against
NOTES		
ADJOURNMENT		
	Fees	Per member present
DISBURSEMENT	Expenses	" " present Sundries Total
	(Signed)................................	
	Secretary	

Secretary's Memorandum for Entering Notes of Minutes at Meeting (Page 2).

5. If payment is to be made immediately to the directors for attendance at the meetings, the secretary should have with him the necessary funds.

6. Bring with him to the meeting a memorandum form for entering the notes of the minutes of the meeting.

Taking notes at meetings. Secretaries equipped to take shorthand notes usually find this training valuable in reporting minutes of meetings. Many secretaries take notes in longhand during the meetings. These notes are condensed, and no attempt is made to put everything down in full. Occasionally comments are inserted which may explain statements and decisions made. Frequently, proposals are made in an informal way, and a vote is taken with the understanding that the secretary will frame the proposition into a clear statement. The secretary should not permit the meeting to proceed to the next subject unless he has a clear understanding of what has been done. If a point is not clear to him at the time of the meeting, it is not likely to become clear after the meeting, when he prepares the minutes. If necessary, the secretary should ask for a formal wording of the proposition at the meeting.

Many secretaries destroy the typewritten notes dictated from memoranda taken at the meetings after entries are made in the minute book, but preserve the original notes as unofficial memoranda of what has taken place. Where the secretary prepares a memorandum (see illustrations on pages 158 and 159), outline, digest, or rough draft of minutes in advance of the meeting, he usually fills in the information blanks left for that purpose as each matter is concluded.

Recording discussions at meetings. Generally, the argument on particular questions and the discussion that takes place at meetings are not made a part of the record, unless some member present specifically requests that his view be made a matter of record. Frequently, however, it is advisable to include a statement explaining the resolution or motion in order to clarify the proposal. Where this is necessary, the statement might well become a part of the resolution by being included in the preamble, under the "whereas" clauses. The secretary should not hesitate to record in his minutes full details of the transaction; too many secretaries err on the side of brevity in preparing minutes. However, not every detail need be included. In one case, a director sued to compel the secretary to include certain matters in the minutes. These were the matters he wanted included, and the court's holding on each:

(1) That the director requested that a report on the appointment of new counsel be made a part of the minutes. *Court:* The minutes show that the director dissented to the report. That is enough.

(2) That the director asked a question about the payment of fees to new counsel and that it wasn't answered nor the name of counsel given. *Court*: The minutes were later corrected to show the director had asked the question. The answer to his question and the name of counsel did not have to be recorded.

(3) That the director had written letters to the corporation about the deficiency of the minutes. *Court*: The minutes did not have to show this.
(4) That the minutes show the reason for the directors' objection to the reelection of an officer to an outside directorship. *Court*: The fact that he objected was recorded; his reason for objecting did not have to be.[31]

The practice followed by some secretaries is to report fully the discussions at committee meetings, but to limit the minutes of directors' meetings to a record of the motions and resolutions upon which action has been taken. Others, however, include in the minutes of the directors' meetings considerable matter in explanation of the resolutions. This not only serves to interpret the resolutions but may help to refresh the recollection of directors on points of fact that may become the subject of future controversy.

Drafting resolutions. The drafting of resolutions is generally done by the secretary. Frequently, resolutions are drafted in advance of a meeting in order to clarify the subject matter and to facilitate discussions. The secretary may submit the draft of the resolution to the officer or department which originated the proposition to make sure that the resolution expresses the wishes of those sponsoring the matter. Resolutions involving routine matters are usually drafted by the secretary without the aid of counsel. Resolutions relating to matters that involve legal technicalities are generally drafted by counsel. However, the secretary sometimes prepares the initial draft of a resolution requiring legal knowledge, and then refers it to the legal department, with appropriate oral or written explanation. In some organizations, the resolutions are submitted to the president for his approval after they have been examined by counsel.

Certain action may require the passage of resolutions in a form satisfactory to some outside person or organization. For example, a resolution to amend the charter may have to be in a form prepared by the Secretary of State; in such cases counsel for the corporation or the secretary may obtain an official printed form and complete it as required. Resolutions relating to the cancellation of mortgages are frequently drawn in whole or in part by the trustee; the mortgagor corporation, in voting upon cancellation, simply follows the form required by the trust company which has acted as trustee for the bond issue. The appointment of a transfer agent is usually made by a resolution prepared by the transfer agent. The opening of a bank account generally calls for passage of a resolution in the form furnished by the bank.

---

[31]Field v. Oberwortman, (1958) Ill. Ct. App. 16 Ill. App. 2d 376.

Where new topics are brought up unexpectedly at a corporate meeting for discussion, and the secretary has had no opportunity before the meeting to draft a resolution, he may immediately write out the resolution in full and have it approved by the chairman, or he may follow the practice of writing out the resolution after the meeting. The resolution, under the second plan, is accurately worded in the typewritten minutes, but is not read until the succeeding meeting. This practice is more suitable for directors' than for stockholders' meetings. At stockholders' meetings, it is advisable that adequate time be taken to frame an exact resolution to be voted upon at the meeting.

Manner of recording motions, resolutions, and votes taken. The names of proposers and seconders of motions are generally omitted, although in some cases it may be advisable to show by whom a proposal was introduced. In most cases, it is not necessary that the names of those voting for or against a proposition be recorded, unless the statute, charter, or by-laws require this information to be shown. It is generally sufficient, in the case of stockholders' meetings, to show the number of shares voting for and against a proposition. Furthermore, by recording the vote in this way, the minutes show that a quorum was present when the business was authorized. Where a special request is made for the recording of dissenting votes by a minority, the entries should be so made by the secretary.[32] It is advisable to indicate in the minutes that a director personally interested in a particular transaction did not vote, or that he left the room. In matters of great importance, such as sales of the corporation's property, consolidations, and like transactions, in addition to the exact wording of resolutions, the names of the proposers and seconders of the motions, and the names of those voting in favor of or contrary to the resolution, should be recorded.

If no vote is taken on a certain question, and the chairman obtains the consensus of the directors in an informal manner, it is sufficient to note in the minutes that "it was the consensus that," or that "each director present expressed his approval of," or that "doubt was expressed as to," and to follow with a statement of the facts. This puts on record some evidence of the points covered and the general reaction.

All important written proposals, contracts, or other papers brought before the meeting may be ordered "spread upon the minutes"—that is, written out in full in the minute book (see, however, pages 167-168).

In certain actions, dissenting directors should be particularly careful to have their opposition noted.[33] For example, when the statute places a

---

[32]See page 000 in regard to noting dissent generally.
[33]Field v. Oberwortman, (1958) Ill. Ct. App. 16 Ill. App. 2d 376.

personal liability upon directors who consent to the issuance of stock for property in excess of the actual value of the property, the minutes should show the names of the directors concurring in the judgment of the value of the property. In connection with the declaration of dividends, recording of dissent may be necessary to save the directors from personal liability for dividends illegally declared (see pages 713-715 in Chapter 23).

Arrangement of minutes. The secretary is not required to write the minutes out in his own handwriting. The general form of minutes is fairly well standardized. The minutes usually begin with the time and place of meeting, establish that the meeting was properly called and that notice was given or waived, give the names of the chairman and the secretary of the meeting, and state the amount of stock represented in person or by proxy, thus indicating whether a quorum was present. The minutes then state that the minutes of the previous meeting were read.[34] The additional subject matter of the minutes consists of a clear, accurate, and complete report of all business transacted. With respect to subject matter, the minutes of most companies are carefully arranged in accordance with the established order of business.

Some of the larger corporations have strict rules as to uniformity of arrangement, especially where frequent tabulations or enumerations appear. Independently of such rules, some secretaries take particular pains with details such as the arrangement, typing, spacing, and general appearance of the minute book.

The following is a suggested list of rules that may be followed by those who typewrite the minutes in the minute book.

1. Capitalize and center the heading designating the meeting held.
2. Indent paragraphs ten spaces.
3. Indent names of attending directors and absentees, or similar lists, fifteen spaces.
4. Double space the text of the minutes.
5. Double space between each paragraph and triple space between each item in the order of business.
6. Indent resolutions fifteen spaces and type in single space.
7. Use initial capitals for the words "Board of Directors" and "Corporation" when it is the board and corporation whose minutes are being typed.
8. Leave an inch and one-half to two inch margin on the left- or right-hand side of the page, depending on whether it is a left- or right-hand page, for captions, if desired, and indexing.
9. Use capital letters or red type for marginal captions, when they are desired.

10. Capitalize the words "WHEREAS" and "RESOLVED", and place a comma following each; start the word "That" with a capital "T".
11. When sums of money are mentioned in a resolution, first spell out the amount, then put the figures in parentheses.

Approval of minutes. To speed up the approval of minutes, one company sends a copy of the minutes of each directors' meeting to the chairman of the board, the president, and the general counsel; other members of the board have access to any of these copies. Thus, there are seldom any changes to be made in the minutes at the following board meeting. (See page 165 as to correction of errors in minutes.)

Another company follows the practice of attaching to the directors' agenda copies of the previous minutes of the Board of Directors and of the Executive Committee. When the meeting is called to order, sufficient time is given for the directors to digest the agenda and to read the minutes of the previous meeting prior to any discussion of the agenda itself.

It is the practice of some corporations to send copies of minutes of the previous meeting to all directors prior to the meeting at which the minutes are to come up for approval. The minutes can then be "approved without reading," thus saving considerable time.

The minutes of a meeting of an old board of directors, held just before the election of a new board, should be read at the first meeting of the new board, not for the purpose of approval by that board, but to inform the new board of what took place. The new board does not need to approve the minutes of the last meeting of the old board, for the new directors were probably not present at this meeting, and thus they cannot tell whether the minutes record accurately what occurred there. The outgoing directors, for their own protection, should read over the minutes of their last meeting even though no opportunity is given them to do so at a subsequent meeting. For example, a director who has dissented from some business that he believed was not for the best interests of the company should be sure to examine the minutes and note whether his dissent was entered.

Although a director is not present at a meeting, if he signs the minutes, he is bound by them.[35] The time when he signs is immaterial.[36] Ordinarily,

---

[34]Stockholders and directors of a corporation are entitled to have the minute book before the meeting, and the president may not refuse to produce it. State ex rel. Dendinger v. J.D. Kerr Gravel Co., (1925) 158 La. 324, 104 So. 60. The reading of minutes of a previous meeting is a mere acknowledgment that the secretary has correctly recorded what occurred at the meeting. Hornady v. Goodman, (1928) 167 Ga. 555, 146 S.E. 173. See also Teiser v. Swirksy, (1931) 137 Ore. 595, 2 P. 2d 920, aff'd on rehearing, 137 Ore. 595, 4 P. 2d 322; in which it was held that failure to read the minutes before they were signed by the secretary did not invalidate the record.

[35]Vance v. Mutual Gold Corp., (1940) 6 Wash. 2d 466, 108 P. 2d 799.

[36]Ibid.

officers who certify to minutes cannot later challenge them.[37] (See form on page 150, Chapter 4, for certification of minutes of directors' meeting.)

Correction of errors in minutes. One of the purposes of reading the minutes of a previous meeting is to offer an opportunity to make corrections of any misstatements or errors that may have crept into the record.[38]

The manner of correcting errors depends upon the importance of the matter to be changed. The chairman may informally direct correction of simple errors such as mistakes in the spelling of names. If a dispute arises as to the correctness of a statement, motion, or resolution reported in the minutes, it may be necessary to put the matter to a vote to determine how the minutes shall read. If the error can be corrected immediately, the correction may be made at the meeting, and the minutes, as changed, may then be offered for approval. If the correction involves a revision of the minutes, the minutes of the current meeting will report the corrections of the minutes of the previous meeting.

The methods of inserting corrections in the minute book vary. One way is to strike out the erroneous matter by drawing a red line through each line of the incorrect material, and to write in between the red lines the correct minutes. Reference should be made in the margin of the minutes to the minutes of the following meeting, showing when the correction was ordered. If it is impractical to make the correction in this way, the erroneous material may be stricken out in red, and a note made in the margin showing where the revised minutes appear. The correct minutes may then be inserted at the end of the original minutes. Where loose-leaf books are used, it is inadvisable to throw away the pages that were incorrectly written. The better practice is to retain the original pages, to indicate that the minutes are obsolete by reference to the minutes of the meeting at which the errors were discussed, and to insert the corrected minutes in a subsequent page.

If the effect of a resolution adopted at a meeting is to create a contract between the corporation and some other party, the resolution cannot be changed by a memorandum entered on the records after the adjournment of the meeting, without the knowledge or consent of the parties to the agreement.[39] Clerical errors in the writing of minutes are immaterial where the proof is clear that the entry is erroneous. Thus, where it is evident that

---

[37]Wright v. Phillips Fertilizer Co., (1927) 193 N.C. 305, 136 S.E. 716. Compare Charles R. Heddon Co. v. Dozier, (1926) 99 N.J. Eq. 543, 133 A. 857, aff'd, 100 N.J. Eq. 560, 135 A. 915.

[38]Directors may properly correct minutes to show actual official action. Bown v. Ramsdell, (1931) 139 N.Y. Misc. 360, 249 N.Y. Sup. 387.

[39]Schlens v. Poe, (1916) 128 Md. 352, 97 A. 649.

the directors met on the same day as the stockholders, immediately after the stockholders' meeting adjourned, and that both meetings were held on a certain day, a different date at the head of the minutes of the directors' meeting is simply a clerical error and is immaterial.[40] The fact that corrections are made after the minutes are prepared is comparatively unimportant, from a legal standpoint, if the entry faithfully shows what was done.[41] But if there are two sets of minutes with contrary facts the one that shows evidence of tampering will be rejected.[42]

Indexing of minutes. Large corporations usually have their minutes carefully indexed so that any business which has been passed upon at a formal meeting, however remote in time, may be referred to and reviewed easily and quickly. Some corporations do not index the directors' meetings, but keep a complete index of the minutes of the executive committee. Card indexes, loose-leaf binder indexes, or bound books may be used for the purpose. Many of the larger corporations have a separate index at the beginning of each minute book.

The making of the index is facilitated by the use of captions in the minutes. The index card contains the subject matter taken from the captions and a reference to the page on which the caption appears. If a more detailed index is desired, the captions appearing on the page may bear a number, and reference on the card may be made to the number rather than to the page. The numbers, of course, run consecutively through the minute book.

Systems of handling minutes. The usual practice is for the secretary to dictate the minutes immediately after the meeting while events are still fresh in his mind. The assistant secretary of one company, the secretary of which is a practicing attorney, takes shorthand notes during the meeting and dictates the minutes to a stenographer, who indexes them and numbers and files any reports submitted at the meeting. The assistant secretary makes up the marginal notes, indicates the persons to be notified of action taken at the meeting, and attends to other similar details. His draft of the minutes is sent to the law offices of the secretary, where they are reviewed carefully by the secretary for omissions and inaccuracies of expression before they are copied by a stenographer into the minute book.

The practice followed by the secretary of one large corporation is typical of that of many others. This secretary personally takes down the minutes at all meetings upon loose sheets. Immediately after each meeting, he prepares the minutes, keeping the typewritten original in a book which

---

[40]Hatcher-Powers Shoe Co. v. Bickford, (1925) 212 Ky. 163, 278 S.W. 615.

[41]Caldwell v. Dean, (1926) 10 F. 2d 299.

[42]Rice & Hutchins v. Triplex Shoe Co., (1929) 16 Del. Ch. 298, 147 A. 317, aff'd without discussion of this point, 17 Del. Ch. 356, 152 A. 342.

he calls his "blotter." At the next meeting he reads the minutes of the previous meeting from his blotter, and only after approval are the actual minutes carefully typewritten and locked in the current minute book. Some secretaries who follow this plan include in the blotter minutes a record of the maker and seconder of each resolution, but eliminate such details in the minute book proper. The blotter minutes are either kept in a loose-leaf binder or filed in a meeting folder.

In many corporations, a duplicate of the minute book is made and is kept apart from the original; in this way, in case of mishap to one copy, there is always another one available.

Resolutions book. Some companies follow the practice of keeping a copy of all resolutions in a separate book, properly indexed. This avoids the inconvenience of having to leaf through pages of minutes of unrelated matter when reference is made to a particular action authorized by resolution. Furthermore, by keeping the resolutions in a separate place, the minute book is preserved, and perusal of confidential matters contained in the minute book by someone interested only in a particular resolution is prevented.

In some companies the set of resolutions is preceded by a copy of the by-laws, and the resolutions and by-laws are kept up-to-date in the following way: ample margin is provided at the left of each page, in which subsequent actions affecting a section or sub-section of a by-law or a resolution can be indicated by cross referencing to the minutes where the actions are recorded. A more convenient way is to enter a copy of the actions on numbered supplementary sheets to which reference is made in the margin of the affected by-law provision or resolution. The marginal note may read "Repealed. Sup. p. 7" or "Changed to 15 days. Sup. p. 10." The latter note shows immediately what the change is and refers to supplementary p. 10. At supplementary page 10, the minutes which changed the notice, for example, required to be given for a certain purpose from 20 days to 15 days, will be found, as well as a cross reference to the minutes of the meeting from which the excerpt is taken. The purpose of the supplementary sheets is to obviate hunting through the series of books in which minutes are recorded; the by-laws and resolutions book forms a single complete record.

Permanent records of reports. The methods of preserving reports submitted and discussed at meetings vary considerably. In some corporations, only very important reports that have been ordered by formal resolution to be spread on the minutes are bound in the minute book. In numerous other corporations, whether or not a motion is made to spread such reports on the minutes, the reports are bound in with the minutes, and immediately follow the last page of minutes of the meeting in which the report was discussed or formally accepted. Some corporations have inaugurated the system of binding with the minutes only bulky reports and the annual reports to stockholders containing the audited certified balance sheet. The test adopted by many secretaries to determine whether a report should be incorporated in the minutes is to ascertain whether the report is directly referred to in the resolution in such a way as to make it part of the resolution. If reports are not included in the minutes, they may be bound separately, filed in the meeting folders with other papers relating to action taken, or placed in a special locked report file. Where reports are bound or filed separately, the necessity for a carefully prepared cross-index system that will permit instant reference from the reports to the minutes, and vice versa, is obvious.

Chapter 6

FORMS OF MINUTES
OF MEETINGS

Contents—Chapter 6

MINUTES OF STOCKHOLDERS' MEETINGS

MINUTES OF ANNUAL MEETING OF STOCKHOLDERS

[*Note*. The headings in brackets sometimes appear in the minute book as marginal notes.]

[Time and place of meeting]

The annual meeting of the stockholders of .... Corporation was held at the principal office of the Corporation at .... *(Street)*, ... *(City)*, ... *(State)*, on ...., 19.., at ..... A.M., pursuant to a call made by the President and written notice given by the Secretary.

[Presiding officer; Secretary]

Pursuant to the provisions of the By-laws, Mr. ...., President of the Corporation, presided over the meeting, and Mr. ...., Secretary of the Corporation, acted as secretary of the meeting.

or

Pursuant to the provisions of the by-laws, in the absence of the President, the meeting was called to order by Mr. ...., Chairman of the Board, who acted as Chairman of the meeting, and Mr. ...., Secretary of the Corporation, acted as secretary of the meeting.

[List of stockholders]

The Chairman announced that the transfer books and the stock books of the Corporation, together with a full, true, and complete list in alphabetical order of all the stockholders entitled to vote at the ensuing election, with the residence of each, and the number of shares held by each (which list has been on file at this office of the Corporation continuously since ...., 19..), were before the meeting and would remain open for inspection during the election.

[Proxies; quorum]

The Chairman stated that he was acting as proxy and representative of the holders of record of ..... (.....) shares of the Preferred Stock, and ..... (.....) shares of the Common Stock of this Corporation, as shown by the certificate of the Secretary, made under the By-laws of the Corporation, and by the original powers of attorney and substitutions and the list of the stockholders now filed and deposited with the Secretary.

The Chairman then asked if there were any stockholders present in person, or any persons present as attorneys or proxies for stockholders.

The following stockholders then appeared:

In Person	*Preferred*	*Common*
....	....	....
....	....	....
....	....	....
By Proxy		
....	....	....
....	....	....
....	....	....

The Chairman requested the Secretary to report the number of shares represented either by proxy, or in person, or by attorney.

The Secretary reported as follows:

Preferred:	....	shares
Common:	....	shares
Total:	....	shares

Thereupon the Chairman announced that the holders of stock in excess of the amount necessary to constitute a quorum were present in person or represented by proxy.

The proxies presented were ordered to be filed with the Secretary of the meeting.

[Proof of notice of meeting]

The Secretary presented and read a copy of the notice of the meeting, together with proof that the same had been published as required by the By-laws once in each of the ..... (.....) calendar weeks next preceding the meeting—to wit: On the .. day of ...., and the .., .., .., and .. days of ...., in at least one newspaper in each of the following cities: ...., ..., and .....[1] The Secretary further presented proof that copy of this notice, and also a copy of the annual report to stockholders for the year 19.., had been duly mailed, postage prepaid, to every stockholder of record at the closing of the books for this election on ...., 19...

or

The Secretary presented an affidavit, duly signed and sworn to by himself, showing that notice of the meeting had been mailed to each stockholder, addressed to such stockholder at the address given by him to the Corporation, postage prepaid, as required by the By-laws of the corporation. The affidavit was approved and ordered attached to these minutes.

(Insert affidavit: see form on page 110, Chapter 2.)

[Inspectors of election]

Upon motion duly seconded, Messrs. ...., ..., and ...., (none of whom were candidates for the office of director), who had been duly appointed inspectors by the Board of Directors, pursuant to the By-laws, were duly sworn.

or

Upon motion duly made and seconded, ..., ..., and ...., were unanimously elected Inspectors of Election to count the votes presented to the meeting in person or by proxy. The Inspectors of Election thereupon submitted their oaths as such Inspectors, duly subscribed by them, and the Secretary was directed to attach the same to these minutes.

[Approval of minutes]

The Secretary then presented the minutes of the annual meeting of stockholders held in ...., 19.., which were read and approved.

---

[1] If the notice is not published, omit the statement as to publication.

[Approval of acts of directors and annual report]

Thereupon the Chairman presented to the meeting the following papers and documents, all of which were laid upon the table and were publicly declared by the Chairman to be open for inspection by any stockholder:

1. The minutes of the Board of Directors, covering all purchases, contracts, contributions, compensations, acts, decisions proceedings, elections, and appointments by the Board of Directors since the annual meeting held on ...., 19...

2. The ..... *(insert number)* annual report, a copy of which has been mailed to every stockholder of record.

Upon motion duly made and seconded, it was unanimously

RESOLVED, That all purchases, contracts, contributions, compensations, acts, decisions proceedings, elections, and appointments by the Board of Directors since the Annual Meeting of Stockholders of the Corporation on ...., 19.., and all matters referred to in the Annual Report to Stockholders for the fiscal year ending ...., 19.., be and the same hereby are approved and ratified.

[Nomination of directors]

The meeting then proceeded to the election of ..... (.....) directors as successors to the directors whose terms expire with this annual meeting, to hold office for a term [expiring in 19..][2] of ..... (.....) year(s), and until their successors shall be elected and shall qualify.

The following were nominated and seconded to be directors:

....
....
....

There were no other nominations.

Upon motion duly made, seconded, and unanimously carried, the nominations were closed.

The meeting then proceeded to the election of a director to the vacancy on the Board of Directors caused by .... *(insert reason for vacancy, such as "the death of Mr. Blank")*, such director to hold office for the remainder of the term expiring in 19.. and until his successor shall be elected and shall qualify.[3]

(Insert nominations and closing of nominations.)

[Request for election by ballot]

Mr. .... then asked that a ballot be taken upon the foregoing nominations, and on motion duly seconded, it was so ordered.

[Polls open]

The Chairman, before finally declaring the polls open, asked if there were any other nominations. Hearing none, he thereupon declared the polls open at .....

---

[2]For meetings at which directors from more than one class are elected.

[3]For meetings at which directors from more than one class are elected.

P.M., and stated that they would remain open for at least one hour for the receipt of ballots upon the nominations made.

[Polls closed]

At ..... P.M., the Chairman stated that the polls had now been open for over one hour, and he inquired whether there were any who had not voted and who desired to vote. No one requesting further opportunity to vote, the polls were then declared closed.

[Report of inspectors of election]

The Inspectors of Election thereupon inspected the proxies and counted the ballots, and submitted their report in writing.

Upon motion duly made and seconded, the report of the Inspectors of Election was unanimously approved, and the Secretary was directed to file the original report and to attach a copy to the minutes of this meeting.

[Declaration of election]

The Chairman thereupon declared that the ..... persons receiving the highest number of votes, namely *(insert names)*, had been duly elected directors of the Corporation, to serve for the term [expiring in 19..] of ..... year(s), and until their successors shall be elected and shall qualify.[4]

(Insert declaration of election of directors of other classes.)

[Insert of papers in minutes]

The Secretary was directed to insert in the minute book, for the purpose of reference, a copy of each of the following papers:

1. Notice of meeting and proof of service thereof.
2. Form of proxy.
3. Certificate of the Secretary as to the regularity of the powers of attorney and the number of shares represented by the Proxy Committee.
4. Inspectors' oath and report.

(Insert any other business before the meeting.)

No other business coming before the meeting, it was, on motion duly made and seconded, adjourned.

....
President

....
Secretary

MINUTES OF SPECIAL MEETING OF STOCKHOLDERS

[*Note.* The headings in brackets sometimes appear in the minute book as marginal notes.]

[Time and place of meeting]

A special meeting of the stockholders of .... Corporation was held

---

[4] For meetings at which directors from more than one class are elected.

at the office of the Corporation at .... *(Street)*, ... *(City)*, ... *(State)*, on ...., 19.., at ..... P.M., pursuant to a call made by .... *(state how call was made)*.

[Presiding officer; Secretary]

Mr. ...., President of the Corporation, presided at the meeting, and Mr. ...., Secretary of the Corporation, acted as Secretary of the meeting, as provided by the By-laws.

[Roll call]

The Secretary called the roll of stockholders, and all the stockholders were found present either in person or by proxy.[5]

The following notice of the meeting was read by the Secretary and ordered spread upon the minutes of this meeting:

(Insert notice of special meeting indicating purpose; page 68, Chapter 2.)

[Proof of mailing of notice of meeting]

The Secretary then presented an affidavit, showing that the notice of meeting had been duly mailed to each stockholder at his last-known address, more than ..... (.....) weeks (or days) preceding this meeting.

(Insert affidavit)

[Proof of publication of notice of meeting]

The Secretary also presented an affidavit of publication of the notice of meeting in the ...., a newspaper published and having a circulation in the county where the principal business office of the corporation is located, on the .. day of ...., 19.., and on the .., .., and .. days of ...., 19.., as required by law and by the By-laws of this Corporation.[6]

(Insert affidavit)

[Inspectors of election]

The President stated that the Board of Directors had heretofore chosen two Inspectors, Messrs. ...., and ...., and that it was desirable that their appointment be confirmed at the meeting.

Upon motion duly made and seconded, the appointment of .... and .... as Inspectors was unanimously confirmed, and they and each of them took and subscribed to the prescribed oath.

(or)

The President stated that Messrs. ...., and ...., elected Inspectors of elections at the last annual stockholders' meeting, were present.

The Inspectors thereupon took charge of the proxies, and upon examination thereof and of the stock books, reported that there were present in person or by proxy stockholders of record owning ..... (.....) shares of stock, being the entire outstanding capital stock of the Corporation.

---

[5]If less than all the stockholders are present, insert statement as in minutes of annual meeting, page 000.

[6]If publication is not required, omit this clause.

[Vote on resolutions]

On motion duly made and seconded, and after due deliberation, the following resolution was voted upon:

(Insert resolutions covering matters considered at meeting.)

The Inspectors of Election canvassed the votes and reported that the aforesaid resolution had been adopted by the affirmative vote of all the stockholders of the Corporation.

[Adjournment]

No other business coming before the meeting, the meeting was thereupon adjourned.

....
President
....
Secretary

EXCERPT OF MINUTES SHOWING VOTES FOR AND AGAINST MOTION

Mr. .... thereupon moved that ....*(state subject matter of motion)*. The motion was seconded by Mr. .... A vote was taken which showed:

In Favor of Motion
...................., representing ..... shares
...................., representing ..... shares
...................., representing ..... shares
...................., representing ..... shares

Opposed to Motion
...................., representing ..... shares
...................., representing ..... shares

Not Voting on Motion
...................., representing ..... shares

EXCERPT OF MINUTES SHOWING ADOPTION OF MINUTES OF PREVIOUS MEETING AS CORRECTED

The Secretary then presented and read the minutes of the previous meeting of the stockholders *(or* directors),[7] held on ...., 19...

Upon motion duly made and seconded, it was

RESOLVED, That the minutes of the meeting of ...., held on ....
.., 19.., are hereby adopted and approved in their entirety, except that the words

---

[7]This form may be used either for stockholders' or directors' meeting. See also form showing approval of minutes as corrected, page 178.

"................" be eliminated from the resolution .... *(specify subject matter of resolution for identification)* contained therein.

EXCERPT OF MINUTES SHOWING DEFEAT OF MOTION TO AMEND MINUTES OF PREVIOUS MEETING

The minutes of the previous meeting were read. Mr. "C" made a motion that the minutes be amended by striking out from the last paragraph the words "................" The motion was not seconded and therefore not put to a vote. Mr. "A" then moved that the minutes be adopted as read. The motion having been duly seconded by Mr. "B," the Chairman called for a vote on the motion for approval of the minutes as read, which resulted as follows:

In Favor of Motion	*Opposed*
"A"	"C"
"B"	

The Chairman thereupon declared the minutes approved as read.

EXCERPT OF MINUTES SHOWING AMENDMENT OF MOTION

The following motion was presented by "A" and seconded by "B."

(Insert motion.)

After considerable discussion, "C" moved that the said motion be amended by striking out (or by adding) the following: "................"

The motion to amend was accepted by "A" and "B." The Chairman then called for a vote on the motion as amended. The motion as amended was carried by a unanimous vote.

EXCERPT FROM MINUTES OF ANNUAL STOCKHOLDERS' MEETING APPOINTING COMMITTEE TO ASCERTAIN AND REPORT ATTENDANCE OF STOCKHOLDERS IN PERSON AND BY PROXY

Upon motion duly seconded, ..., and ...., were appointed a committee to ascertain and report what stockholders were present in person, and the number of shares owned by them, respectively, and to canvass the proxies of stockholders presented at the meeting, and to ascertain and report the number of shares owned by stockholders present by proxy.

The committee, after ascertaining the facts, announced that there were present more than a quorum of the stockholders of the Company, and presented their formal report, which is as follows:

.... *(City)*, ... *(State)*
...., *19..*

To the Meeting of Stockholders of the .... Corporation:

Gentlemen:

The undersigned, having been appointed a committee for the purpose of ascertaining the stockholders of the Company present in person or by proxy at the meeting, with the number of shares owned by them, respectively, report that there are present in person at such meeting the following-named persons, owning the number of shares of stock of the par value of .... Dollars ($.....) each set opposite their respective names—viz.:

Name of Stockholder	Number of Shares
....	....
....	....
....	....

Total .... shares

We have examined the proxies presented at the meeting and in the hands of the Secretary, and find that there are present by such proxies stockholders owning the number of shares of .... Dollars ($.....) par value hereinafter indicated, and that their respective proxies are as follows—viz.:

Name of Proxy	Number of Shares
....	....
....	....
....	....

Total .... shares

Summarizing, we therefore report that there are stockholders present in person, owning ..... shares; that there are stockholders present by proxies, owning ..... shares; total, ... shares.

There being outstanding ..... shares of such stock of ..... Dollars ($.....) par value, and ..... shares being necessary for a quorum, we report that a quorum of stockholders is present.

Respectfully submitted,

....
....
Committee

EXCERPT FROM MINUTES OF STOCKHOLDERS' MEETING
SHOWING ADOPTION OF MINUTES OF THE PRESENT MEETING

The foregoing minutes of this meeting were then read by the Secretary to the stockholders, and, on motion duly made, seconded, and carried, they were adopted as and for the record of this meeting.

EXCERPT OF MINUTES OF STOCKHOLDERS' MEETING
SHOWING RATIFICATION OF ACTS OF DIRECTORS AND OFFICERS

The Secretary then presented to the meeting the minute book of the Corporation containing a record of the decisions, contracts, acts, and commitments of the Board of Directors and officers of the Corporation since the last annual meeting of the stockholders.

After consideration thereof, on motion duly made and seconded, the following resolution was unanimously adopted:

RESOLVED, That the minutes of the meetings of the Board of Directors of this Corporation since the last annual meeting of the stockholders be and they hereby are in all respects approved; that the resolutions therein set forth are hereby severally adopted, approved, ratified, and confirmed; and that all action of every kind taken by officers of the Corporation, pursuant to any such resolution, action, decision, or authorization, be and it hereby is authorized, adopted, approved, ratified, and confirmed.

MINUTES OF DIRECTORS' AND
COMMITTEE MEETINGS

MINUTES OF ANNUAL MEETING OF DIRECTORS, FOLLOWING
ADJOURNMENT OF ANNUAL STOCKHOLDERS' MEETING

[*Note*. The headings in brackets sometimes appear in the minute book as marginal notes.]

[Time and place of meeting]

The annual meeting of the Board of Directors of .... Corporation was held at the principal office of the Corporation, at .... *(Street)*, ... *(City)*, ... *(State)*, on ...., 19.., at ..... P.M., immediately after the adjournment of the annual meeting of the stockholders.

[Attendance of directors]

The following directors were present:

....

....

The following directors were absent:

....

....

or, if all were present, say:

The following directors were present:

....

....

....

being all of the directors of the said Corporation.

[Presiding officers]

Mr. ...., President of the Corporation, called the meeting to order and acted as Chairman thereof, and Mr. ...., Secretary of the Corporation, acted as Secretary of the meeting.

[Quorum]

The Chairman announced that a quorum of the directors was present, and that the meeting, having been duly convened, was ready to proceed with its business.

[Proof of service of notice of meeting]

The Secretary presented to the meeting a copy of the notice of this meeting, sent to all of the directors of the Corporation, with proof of due service thereof upon each of them. The notice, with proof of service thereof, which read as follows, was thereupon ordered to be spread upon the minutes of this meeting:

(Insert form of notice of meeting; see second form on page 144, Chapter 4. Insert also form of proof of service; see forms on page 148 et seq.)

[Presentation of minutes of stockholders' annual meeting]

The Chairman presented and read to the meeting the minutes of the Stockholders' annual meeting held at the principal office of the Corporation, at .... *(Street)*, ...*(City)*, ...*(State)*, on ...., 19.., at ..... A.M., at which the following persons were elected to act as members of the Board of Directors of the said Corporation, for a period of ..... (.....) year(s), commencing ...., 19.., and until their successors shall be duly elected:

....

....

....

(Names of directors elected.)

[Election of officers]

Mr. .... moved to proceed with the election of officers for the ensuing year. The motion was duly seconded and carried.

Mr. .... was nominated for the office of President. There being no further nomination, Mr. .... was, upon motion duly made, seconded, and unanimously carried, duly elected and declared President of the Corporation.

(Insert similar statement for election of every other officer.)

(If more than one nomination is made for any particular office, use the following form:)

The names of Mr. .... and Mr. .... were placed in nomination as candidates for the office of President. No other names being proposed, the nominations were closed and a ballot taken. The Chairman announced that the result of the vote taken was as follows: Mr. ...., ... votes, and Mr. ...., ... votes, and declared Mr. .... the duly elected President for the ensuing year.

[Acceptance of office]

Each of the officers so elected thereupon accepted the office to which he was elected as aforestated.

[Salaries of officers]

Mr. .... moved to consider the salaries of the officers of the

Corporation for the year commencing ...., 19... The motion was duly seconded and carried. The Chairman announced that the officer whose salary was under consideration would not participate in the vote, and that the salary of each officer would be considered separately.

Mr. ...., President, having left the room, it was on motion duly made, seconded, and carried:

RESOLVED, That the salary of Mr. .... as President of the .... Corporation, beginning ...., 19.., and ending with the ...., 19.., be fixed at ..... Dollars ($.....) per year, payable in ..... *(insert weekly, semi-monthly, or monthly)* installments of ..... Dollars ($.....) on the .. day (and the .. day) of each and every .... *(insert week or month)*.

The salary of Mr. .... as President to the .... Corporation, having been duly voted upon, Mr. .... was recalled to the meeting.
Mr. ...., Vice-president of the Corporation, then left the room.

(Insert similar paragraphs fixing salary of each officer.)

[Adjournment of meeting]
There being no further business, on motion duly made, seconded, and carried, the meeting was thereupon adjourned.

....
President
....
Secretary

EXCERPT FROM MINUTES OF ANNUAL DIRECTORS' MEETING, SHOWING ELECTION OF OFFICERS BY BALLOT

The following persons were nominated for officers of the corporation to serve until their respective successors are chosen and qualify:

Chairman of the Board of Directors, ...

President, ...

Vice-president, ...

Treasurer, ...

Secretary, ...

Ballots being duly cast by all the directors present, the Chairman announced that the aforenamed persons had been unanimously elected to the offices set before their respective names, to assume the duties and responsibilities fixed by the By-laws.

The Chairman of the Board of Directors [or the President] thereupon took the chair.

The Secretary was then sworn to the faithful discharge of his duties, and he immediately assumed the discharge thereof. The Secretary's oath was ordered filed.

EXCERPT FROM MINUTES OF ANNUAL DIRECTORS' MEETING, SHOWING ELECTION OF OFFICERS (SHORT FORM)

The following were duly elected officers of the company, to serve for one year, or until their successors are elected and qualify:

President, ...

Vice-president, ...

Secretary, ...

Treasurer, ...

MINUTES OF REGULAR MEETING OF DIRECTORS

[*Note.* The headings in brackets sometimes appear in the minute book as marginal notes.]

[Time and place of meeting]
A regular meeting of the Board of Directors of the .... Corporation was held at the office of the Corporation, at .... *(Street)*, ... *(City)*, ... *(State)*, on ...., 19.., ... A.M..

[Attendance of quorum]
There were present and participating at the meeting:

....

....

....

being all the directors of the Corporation.

[Presiding officers]
Mr. ...., President of the Corporation, acted as Chairman of the meeting, and Mr. ...., Secretary of the Corporation, acted as Secretary of the meeting.

[Proof of service of notice of meeting]
The Secretary presented to the meeting the following notice of the regular directors' meeting, a copy of which had been mailed on ...., 19.. to each of the directors of the Corporation, at his last-known post-office address as it appears on the books of the Corporation, as provided in the By-laws.

(Insert notice of regular directors' meeting; see form on page 144, Chapter 4.)

A quorum of the directors being present and the meeting having been duly called, the President announced that the meeting would proceed with the transaction of business.

[Approval of minutes of preceding regular directors' meeting]
The minutes of the regular meeting of the directors held on ...., 19.. were read and approved.

(Insert business transacted at the meeting.)

[Adjournment of meeting]

There being no further business, the meeting was, upon motion duly made, seconded, and carried, adjourned.

....
Secretary

MINUTES OF SPECIAL MEETING OF DIRECTORS

[*Note.* The headings in brackets sometimes appear in the minute book as marginal notes.]

[Time and place of meeting]

A special meeting of the Board of Directors of the .... Corporation was held at the office of the Corporation, ... *(Street)*, ... *(City)*, ... *(State)*, on ...., 19.., at ..... P.M., pursuant to the call of .... *(insert who called meeting)*.

[Attendance and quorum]

The following directors, being all the directors of the Corporation, were present:

....
....
....

[Presiding officers]

Mr. ...., President of the Corporation, acted as Chairman of the meeting, and Mr. ...., Secretary of the Corporation, acted as Secretary of the meeting.

[Waiver of notice of meeting]

The Secretary presented to the meeting the original call therefor, and the original waivers of notice of said meeting, signed by all the directors of the Corporation. Upon motion duly made, seconded, and carried, the call and waiver of notice were made a part of the records of this meeting, and the Secretary was instructed to spread the same upon the minutes. The call and waiver of notice read as follows:

(Insert call and waiver; see forms on pages 143 and 147.)

[Approval of minutes of previous meeting]

The minutes of the meeting of directors held ...., 19.., were read and approved.

[Business of meeting]

The President stated that the purpose of the special meeting was to .... *(insert purpose of meeting)*, and that discussion of the proposed action was in order.

(The discussion may be set forth in full, or may be summarized, or the minutes may simply state: "After a general discussion and careful consideration of the proposed .... *(insert nature of business)*, upon motion duly made and seconded, the following resolution was unanimously adopted: RESOLVED, etc.'')

[Adjournment]

There being no further business before the meeting, the same was, on motion duly made, seconded, and carried, adjourned.

....

Secretary

EXCERPT FROM MINUTES OF ADJOURNED MEETING OF DIRECTORS

An adjourned meeting of the Board of Directors of .... Corporation was held at the office of the Corporation, at .... *(Street)*, ... *(City)*, ... *(State)*, on ....., 19.., at ..... P.M., pursuant to an adjournment of a meeting held on ...., 19.., at the same time and place.

(The rest of the minutes are the same as for an originally called meeting of directors. See forms on page 178 et seq.)

EXCERPT FROM MINUTES OF DIRECTORS' MEETING DISPENSING WITH READING OF MINUTES

Copies of minutes of the meeting of the Board of Directors held on ...., 19.., having been mailed to each director ..... (......) days before the meeting, the directors present agreed to dispense with the reading of the minutes, and approved and adopted them as they appeared in the copies received by them.

EXCERPT FROM MINUTES OF DIRECTORS' MEETING CORRECTING MINUTES OF PREVIOUS MEETING

The minutes of the previous meeting were read. Mr. .... moved that the minutes be corrected and amended by striking out, from the next to the last paragraph, the words ''..............,'' and by substituting in lieu thereof· the following: ''..............,'' and that as thus corrected the minutes be approved as read.

The motion was seconded by Mr. .... and unanimously carried.

EXCERPT OF MINUTES SHOWING APPROVAL OF MINUTES WITH CORRECTIONS[8]

The minutes of the previous meeting were read. Mr. .... moved that they be adopted with the elimination of the words ''and Executive Committee'' from the resolution ratifying and confirming the acts of the Board of Directors for

---

[8]This form may be used either for directors' or stockholders' meetings. See also form on page 175.

the previous year. The motion was seconded by Mr. .... A vote was taken which showed:

In Favor of Adoption as Amended	Opposed to Adoption	Not Voting
....	None	....
....		....

The chairman declared the minutes approved as corrected.

EXCERPT OF MINUTES SHOWING AMENDMENT OF MOTION

The following motion was presented by Mr. A, and seconded by Mr. B:

"RESOLVED, That the Secretary is hereby requested to read the minutes of meetings of the Board of Directors and the Executive Committee held since the last meeting of stockholders."

After considerable discussion, it was moved by Mr. C that the motion be amended by adding: "So far as they are applicable to any matters mentioned in the report which the stockholders are asked to approve."

The motion to amend was accepted by Mr. A and Mr. B.

The motion as amended was carried by a unanimous vote.

MINUTES OF MEETING OF DIRECTORS ADJOURNED FOR LACK OF QUORUM

A regular meeting of the Board of Directors of the .... Corporation was scheduled to be held at the office of the Corporation, at .... (Street), ... (City), ... (State), on ...., 19.., at ..... A.M.

The following directors appeared at the time and place set for the said meeting:

....

....

No quorum being present, the meeting was duly adjourned, as provided by the By-laws of the Corporation, to ...., 19.., at the same hour and place.

....

Secretary

EXCERPT FROM MINUTES OF DIRECTORS' MEETING DISPENSING WITH NEXT REGULAR MEETING

A resolution was adopted by the Board of Directors to dispense with the next regular meeting of the Board of Directors, which was scheduled to be held on .... (day of week), ..., 19...

MINUTES OF REGULAR MEETING OF EXECUTIVE COMMITTEE

[*Note.* The headings in brackets sometimes appear in the minute book as marginal notes.]

[Time and place of meeting]

A regular meeting of the Executive Committee of the .... Corporation was held at the office of the Corporation .... *(Street)*, ... *(City)*, ... *(State)*, on ...., 19.., at ..... P.M., notice of the said meeting having been duly given by the Secretary of the Corporation as prescribed by the By-laws.

[Presiding officers]

Mr. ...., Chairman of the Executive Committee, acted as Chairman of the meeting, and Mr. ...., Secretary of the Executive Committee, acted as Secretary of the meeting.

[Quorum]

The following members of the Committee were present at the meeting:

....
....
....

The following members of the Committee were absent from the meeting:

....
....
....

A majority being represented, a quorum was declared to be present.

[Business of meeting]

The Chairman stated that the Board of Directors, by resolution adopted at a regular meeting of the Board held on ...., had approved the Committee's resolution passed on ...., 19.., for the appointment of ...., as Assistant to the President, and had authorized the Executive Committee to fix the salary of the said .... as such Assistant.

Upon motion duly made, seconded, and unanimously carried, it was

"RESOLVED, That pursuant to the resolution of the Executive Committee adopted the .. day of ...., 19.., appointing .... as Assistant to the President, and pursuant to the resolution of the Board of Directors adopted the .. day of ...., 19.., approving the said appointment and authorizing the Executive Committee to fix the salary of the said .... as Assistant to the President, the Executive Committee does hereby fix the salary of the said ...., as such Assistant, at the sum of ..... Dollars ($.....) per year, payable monthly on the last day of each and every month."

(Insert any other business of the meeting.)

There being no further business before the meeting, on motion duly made, seconded, and carried, it was adjourned.

....
Secretary

MINUTES OF MEETING OF INVESTMENT COMMITTEE

[Note. The headings in brackets sometimes appear in the minute book as marginal notes.]

[Time and place of meeting]

A meeting of the Investment Committee of the Board of Directors of .... Corporation was held at the office of the Corporation, at ....*(Street)*, ...*(City)*, ...*(State)*, on ...., 19.., at ..... P.M., pursuant to notice duly given to each member of the Committee.

[Attendance]

All the members of the Committee were present.

[Presiding officers]

Mr. ....acted as Chairman of the meeting.

Mr. ....acted as Secretary of the meeting.

[Approval of minutes of previous meeting]

The minutes of the previous meeting of the Investment Committee, held on ...., 19.., were read and approved.

[Business of meeting]

The Chairman of the meeting reported that an offer had been made by the .... Company to sell to the .... Corporation ..... (.....) shares of common stock of the .... Company, at a price of ..... Dollars ($.....) per share.

Since the said stock so offered represented more than a majority of the total number of shares of stock of the .... Company issued and outstanding, and the purchase of the said stock would involve the active participation of the .... Corporation in the management of the business of the .... Company, the Chairman stated that it would be necessary to obtain the approval of the Board of Directors of the .... Corporation before finally accepting the said offer. However, the Chairman recommended that the Investment Committee pass upon the advisability of accepting the offer aforesaid, subject to the approval of the Board of Directors of the .... Corporation.

Upon motion duly made, seconded, and unanimously carried, it was

RESOLVED, That the offer of .... Company to sell to the .... Corporation ..... (.....) shares of its common stock, at a price of ..... Dollars ($.....) per share, be accepted subject to approval by the Board of Directors, and that the Chairman of the Investment Committee convey to the next meeting of the Board, to be held on ...., 19.., the Committee's recommendation that the Board approve the purchase.

(Insert any other business of meeting.)

There being no further business before the meeting, the same was, on motion duly made, seconded, and carried, adjourned.

....
Secretary

EXCERPT FROM MINUTES OF EXECUTIVE COMMITTEE; REGULAR MEETING NOT HELD BECAUSE OF FAILURE OF MEMBERS TO ATTEND

All the members of the Executive Committee having failed to appear at the regular meeting of the Committee, scheduled to be held at the office of the Corporation, at .... (Street), ... (City), ... (State), on ...., 19.., ... P.M., no meeting of the Committee was held and no business transacted thereat.

A true record.

....
Secretary

EXCERPT FROM MINUTES OF MEETING OF EXECUTIVE COMMITTEE ACCEPTING RESIGNATION OF DIRECTOR AND MEMBER OF COMMITTEE

The Secretary read a letter addressed to him on ...., 19.., by Mr. ...., and, on motion duly made, seconded, and unanimously passed, it was

Resolved, That the Committee hereby accepts the resignation of Mr. .... from the Board of Directors of this Corporation, and greatly regrets that the pressure of other business necessitates the termination of his long and valuable service to the Corporation as a director and as a member of the Executive Committee.

DIRECTORS' RATIFICATION OF MINUTES

We, the undersigned, being all of the directors of .... Corporation, do hereby ratify, approve, and confirm all that has occurred at the foregoing meeting, the minutes of which we have read, and in signification of such approval, ratification, and confirmation, and of our assent to any and all acts at the said meeting, do hereby sign our names and affix our seals this ..... day of ...., 19...

.... [Seal]
.... [Seal]
.... [Seal]

Chapter 7

ORGANIZATION MEETING

Contents—Chapter 7

189

Necessity for organization meeting. As a practical matter, an organization meeting must be conducted to complete the corporate structure. It is at the organization meeting that some of the steps essential for corporate recognition are usually taken.[1] These steps usually include the election and qualification of directors and officers,[2] the adoption of by-laws, and an authorization for the issuance of stock.[3]

Failure to take such organizational action may prevent the organization from enjoying benefits of the corporate form of doing business.[4] Persons who act for the unorganized corporation may be personally liable for contracts made by them,[5] and for personal injuries resulting in the course of the business.[6] Shareholders in an unorganized corporation may be held personally liable as if they were partners.

Organization meeting—procedure. The organization meeting may be (1) a meeting of the incorporators, (2) a meeting of the subscribers or shareholders,[7] or (3) a meeting of the directors named in the certificate of incorporation. Organization procedure depends upon the statutory requirements in the state in which the corporation is organized and upon the practice that has grown up in the particular state. Generally, as a matter of

---

[1]Murdock v. Lamb, (1914) 92 Kan. 857, 142 P. 961. See also Baum v. Baum Holding Co., (1954) 158 Neb. 197, 62 N.W. 2d 864; Petition of Plantz, (1950) 282 App. Div. 552, 125 N.Y.S. 2d 750.

A corporation, though imperfectly organized, may attain the advantages of corporate form, if there has been a good faith attempt to incorporate, substantial compliance with the statute of incorporation, and a use of the corporate powers. This is called a de facto corporation as contrasted with a de jure corporation, which is one that is perfectly organized. A de facto corporation's existence can be challenged only by the state, and not by individuals. Baum v. Baum Holding Co., (1954) 158 Neb. 197, 62 N.W. 2d 864.

[2]First Nat'l Bank v. Henry, (1906) 159 Ala. 367, 49 So. 97.

[3]Murdock v. Lamb, (1914) 92 Kan. 857, 142 P. 961.

[4]Walton v. Oliver, (1892) 49 Kan. 107, 30 P. 172; Hammond v. Williams, (1939) 215 N.C. 657, 3 S.E. 2d 437.

[5]Geisenhoff v. Mabrey, (1943) 58 Cal. App. 2d 481, 137 P. 2d 36; Southern Cotton Oil Co. v. Duskin, (1956) 92 Ga. App. 288, 88 S.E. 2d 421; Culkin v. Hillside Restaurant, (1939) 126 N.Y. Eq. 97, 8 A. 2d 173.

[6]Beck v. Stimmel, (1931) 39 Ohio App. 510, 177 N.E. 920.

[7]The states do not all use the same terminology as to who participates in the organization meeting of a corporation. There are at least three variations of terminology among the statutes:

(1) In states that do not require each incorporator to be a subscriber to capital stock of the corporation (for example, Delaware), the incorporators are properly called "incorporators."

(2) In states that require each incorporator to subscribe for at least one share of the capital stock of the corporation (for example, Illinois), the incorporators are properly designated "subscribers and incorporators."

(3) In states that do not require each incorporator to be a subscriber to the capital stock of the corporation, and where the incorporators all subscribe to (sign) the articles of incorporation (for example, Massachusetts), "subscribers" may be used.

convenience, if an incorporators' or subscribers' meeting is held, it is followed immediately by a meeting of the directors.

Time for organization meeting. The statutes of a few states require that a meeting of incorporators be held within a certain period after filing the certificate of incorporation. Where no time for the meeting is specified in the statute, the organization meeting should be held within a reasonable time after the certificate of incorporation has been filed.[8]

Place of organization meeting. Corporate organization must, of course, be completed in accordance with the provisions of the law of the state of incorporation. State law may direct that the meeting must be completed within the state. It has been held that a meeting outside the state will be wholly void[9] but, in general, this defect can only be attacked by the state in a direct action.[10]

If, by reason of failure to hold the meeting within the state, defective organization results, it may be legalized by a subsequent meeting within the state, and acts done and contracts made prior to such meeting may be ratified.

Call and notice of incorporators' meeting—conduct of meeting. The statutes that make provision for the holding of an incorporators' meeting designate who shall call the meeting, what notice of the meeting shall be given, who shall sign the notice, and how the notice shall be transmitted to the incorporators. Where no statutory provisions are found for the calling of an incorporators' meeting, the incorporators should be guided by the general rules governing the calling of stockholders' meetings.[11] The prescribed procedure must, of course, be followed.

Organization meetings are conducted in the same manner as are other stockholders' or directors' meetings.[12]

Purposes of "dummy" incorporators. Organizers of a corporation are frequently far removed from the state selected for incorporation.[13] This

---

[8]Bonaparte v. Baltimore, H. & L. R.R., (1892) 75 Md. 340, 23 A. 784.

[9]Hening & Hagedorn v. Glanton, (1921) 27 Ga. App. 339, 108 S.E. 256.

[10]McKee v. Title Ins. & Trust Co., (1911) 159 Cal. 206, 113 P. 140; see also p. 190.

[11]See page 5, Chapter 1.

[12]See page 16, et seq. (Chapter 1) and page 135 et seq. (Chapter 3).

[13]If the statute requires the first directors to be named in the articles of incorporation and dummy incorporators have been used, it is entirely likely that the dummy incorporators will also have been named as the directors. In that case, the dummy incorporators will hold three meetings: (1) a first meeting of incorporators; (2) a first meeting of directors; and (3) a special meeting of the incorporators. At the first two meetings, all of the organizational matters will be attended to. At the third meeting, the dummy directors will resign, the actual directors will be elected, and the incorporators will transfer their shares to the real parties in interest.

is so because, in choosing a state for incorporation, the organizers take into consideration the cost of incorporating, the annual taxes, and the general requirements of the corporation laws of the state. Proximity of operations to the state of incorporation is only a minor consideration in the selection of an incorporating state.

Suppose the statute requires that all or a certain number of the incorporators shall be residents of the state of incorporation and that the incorporators' meeting shall be held within the state. The persons interested in the corporation, let us say, are nonresidents. How are the statutory requirements met? Temporary or "dummy" incorporators who meet the requirements of the statute subscribe to the shares necessary to qualify them as incorporators. They sign the certificate of incorporation and hold the incorporators' meeting. At the meeting, the qualifying shares subscribed for by the incorporators are transferred to the actual stockholders and the dummy incorporators fade from the picture entirely.

However, every "dummy" incorporator should be aware of the danger involved if, as an incorporator, he does not in fact transfer to the actual stockholders the qualifying shares and does not actually fade from the picture. In most instances, these "dummy" incorporators are attorneys in the state the shareholders-to-be wish to incorporate in when the shareholders, for various reasons, are unable to attend an incorporators' meeting within the state of incorporation as that particular state statute may require. If the attorney acts as an incorporator to "accommodate" his out-of-state clients, he should make it his business to divorce himself from the corporation as a stockholder or a director after incorporation has been completed. Otherwise, he opens the door to personal liability, particularly if he takes stock in the corporation in payment for his fee. The possible business failure of the corporation at a later date may make him personally liable to the corporation's creditors.[14]

And, of course, if he is also a director he is even more exposed to liability. He cannot excuse himself by arguing that he was acting only as an accommodator and that he received no personal gain from the corporation, or that his services were gratuitous.[15] Further, recent case holdings have expanded directors' liabilities so much that it is wise to think before

---

[14]Minton v. Cavaney, (1961) S. Ct., 15 Cal. Rptr. 641, 364 P. 2d 473.
[15]McGlynn v. Schultz, (1966) N.J. S. Ct., 218 A. 2d 408, aff'd. (1967) Super. Ct. App. Div., 231 A. 2d 386; Heit v. Bixby, (1967) DC E.D. Mo., 276 F. Supp. 217. See also Prentice-Hall *Corporation.*

deciding to change from a "dummy" director to a "real" director with all its responsibilities and possible unfavorable results.[16]

Suppose the statute specifies that two of the three incorporators shall be residents of the state and that the incorporators' meeting shall be held within the state. The corporation is organized, let us say, with three actual incorporators, two of whom are residents of the state and the third a nonresident. If any of the incorporators finds it inconvenient to attend the incorporators' meeting held within the state of incorporation, he may be represented at such a meeting by proxy.

Business transacted at organization meeting. The business transacted at an organization meeting depends largely upon whether it is a meeting of incorporators, subscribers, or directors. It is therefore impracticable to list the business generally transacted at the organization meetings. The following list, however, may be helpful in checking the organization record to see that those items usually covered in the organization meetings are included in the minutes of the meetings.

1. Election of temporary chairman and secretary of the meeting.
2. Oath of office of temporary officers.
3. Presentation of notice of meeting or waiver if notice has been waived.
4. Report that certificate of incorporation has been filed as required by statute. This report should include date or dates (if the certificate is required to be filed in two places) of filing.
5. Order that certificate of incorporation be made a part of the record of the meeting.
6. Adoption of by-laws, or appointment of committee to draft by-laws.
7. Fixing number of directors (if not determined in the certificate of incorporation), and election of directors. Generally, where the board of directors is named in the certificate of incorporation, no election takes place at the first incorporators' meeting. If "dummy" directors have been named in the certificate of incorporation, these directors resign at the special incorporators' meeting and an election is held by the incorporators to fill the vacancies, as described on page 272-273.

---

[16]Escott v. BarChris Construction Corporation (1968) DC S.D.N.Y., 283 F. Supp. 643; Globus v. Law Research Service, Inc., (1968) DC.S.D.N.Y., 287 F. Supp. 188, aff'd, CA-2, 418 F. 2d 1276, cert. den. 409 S. Ct. 913; SEC v. Texas Gulf Sulphur Co., (1968) CA-2, 401 F. 2d 833, cert. den. Coates v. SEC and Kline v. SEC, 394 U.S. 976; SEC v. Great American Industries, Inc., (1968) CA-2, 407 F. 2d 453, cert. den. 395 U.S. 920; Mitchell (Reynolds) v. Texas Gulf Sulphur Company (1971) CA-10, 446 F. 2d 90, cert. den. 92 S. Ct. 564; Diamond v. Oreamuno, (1968) N.Y. App. Div., 287 N.Y.S. 2d 300, 248 N.E. 2d 910, aff'd, (1969) Ct. of App., 24 N.Y. 2d 494, 301 N.Y.S. 2d 78. For extended discussion of this problem see Prentice-Hall *Corporation* and Prentice-Hall *Securities Regulation*.

8. Authorization for opening the books for subscriptions.
9. Report of subscriptions to capital stock.
10. Order that subscriptions be made a part of the record of the meeting.
11. Presentation of transfers of subscriptions. This step is necessary where temporary or "dummy" incorporators have been used in incorporating the company, and also where the state statute requires directors to own stock and the person to be elected is to acquire the qualifying shares of the incorporators.
12. Fixing capitalization and describing stock (if not determined in the certificate of incorporation). Authorization for board of directors to issue stock.
13. Election of officers.
14. Oath of office of permanent officers.
15. Call for bond from treasurer. (Bonds may, of course, be required from other officers.)
16. Approval of bond.
17. Adoption of corporate seal.
18. Adoption of form of corporate stock certificate.
19. Authority to purchase corporate record books.
20. Designation of principal office and appointment of resident agent in the state of incorporation, if one is required by statute, or appointment of agent for service of process.
21. Order that proper officers or directors execute and file any reports or records that the statute requires.
22. Appointment of regular date for directors' meeting, if by-laws do not provide for one.
23. Fixing the fiscal period.
24. Authorization for treasurer to open a bank account. If by-laws do not provide for the signing of checks and other instruments, the directors by resolution will assign the duty to some officer or officers.
25. Authorization for treasurer to pay the expenses incident to the organization of the company.
26. Transaction of any other business that is within the power of the persons meeting to transact, such as acquisition of property.

What the minute book contains upon completion of the organization. After the organization meetings have been held, the minute book of the corporation will contain the following information, subject, of course, to such variations as are made necessary by the requirements of the statute under which the corporation is organized and by the circumstances surrounding each particular case. The preservation of all the various documents listed below may become important in preventing subsequent disputes or as evidence in the event of litigation.[17]

---

[17]See page 154 in Chapter 5.

1. Certificate of incorporation, articles of association, articles of agreement, certificate of organization, and any other documents filed by the incorporators or officers in a public office. The minute book need not reproduce, however, the first annual tax report, or the first annual financial statement, where one is required to be filed upon organization of the company.
2. Pre-organization agreements and application for charter.
3. By-laws. It is well to annotate the copy of the by-laws that appears in the minute book, with references to the statute. The purpose of the annotation is to call to the attention of the officers sections of the by-laws which are subject to statutory provisions. The officers will thus avoid falling into the error of recommending amendments to the by-laws that conflict with the statutory requirements.
4. Receipt from the state treasurer, secretary of state, tax commissioner, or other official to whom the organization and filing fees have been paid. Some corporations prefer to file the receipt in their regular files. The better practice is to paste the receipt into the minute book.
5. The certificate issued by the secretary of state, or other official, showing that the charter has been filed.
6. Affidavit of publication of articles of incorporation; or other notice of organization.
7. Affidavit or certificate of paid-in capital, or certificate of initial payment of capital stock.
8. Notice or waiver of notice of the meeting of incorporators or stockholders.
9. Minutes of the first meeting of incorporators or stockholders.
10. Proxies used at the first meeting of incorporators or stockholders.
11. Subscription agreements.
12. Specimen forms of stock certificates.
13. Transfers of subscriptions.
14. Inspectors' oath and report.
15. Resignations of directors.
16. Notice or waiver of notice of first meeting of directors.
17. Minutes of first meeting of directors.
18. Oaths of secretary and other officers.
19. Oath of directors.
20. Bonds of treasurer and other officers.
21. Certificate of appointment of resident agent and location of principal office.

The original documents, rather than duplicates, should be retained whenever it is possible to do so.

Chapter 8

CERTIFICATE OF INCORPORATION, BY-LAWS, AND ORGANIZATION

RECORD OF A
DELAWARE CORPORATION

Contents—Chapter 8

CERTIFICATE OR ARTICLES OF INCORPORATION[1]

CERTIFICATE OF INCORPORATION
OF

....

(Incorporated under the Laws of Delaware)

The undersigned, a natural person, for the purpose of organizing a corporation for conducting the business and promoting the purposes hereinafter stated, under the provisions and subject to the requirements of the laws of the State of Delaware (particularly Chapter 1, Title 8 of the Delaware Code and the acts amendatory thereof and supplemental thereto, and known, identified and referred to as the "General Corporation Law of the State of Delaware"), hereby certifies that:

FIRST: The name of the corporation (hereinafter called the "corporation") is....

SECOND: The address, including street, number, city, and county, of the registered office of the corporation in the State of Delaware is 229 South State Street, City of Dover, County of Kent; and the name of the registered agent of the corporation in the State of Delaware at such address is The Prentice-Hall Corporation System, Inc.

THIRD: The nature of the business and of the purposes to be conducted and promoted by the corporation, which shall be in addition to the authority of the corporation to conduct any lawful business, to promote any lawful purpose, and to engage in any lawful act or activity for which corporations may be organized under the General Corporation Law of the State of Delaware, is as follows:

To purchase, receive, take by grant, gift, devise, bequest or otherwise, lease, or otherwise acquire, own, hold, improve, employ, use and otherwise deal in and with real or personal property, or any interest therein, wherever situated, and to sell, convey, lease, exchange, transfer or otherwise dispose of, or mortgage or pledge, all or any of its property and assets, or any interest therein, wherever situated.

To engage generally in the real estate business as principal, agent, broker, and in any lawful capacity, and generally to take, lease, purchase, or otherwise acquire, and to own, use, hold, sell, convey, exchange, lease, mortgage, work, clear, improve, develop, divide, and otherwise handle, manage, operate, deal in

---

[1]In several states, blank forms of certificates of incorporation may be procured from some public office, generally that of the secretary of state. Since these forms have official sanction it is usually safe to follow them, unless they contain objectionable matter. Even if the forms are not used they may serve as models and their acceptable provisions may be incorporated into the certificate actually drawn. In some states, the secretary of state will not accept a certificate of incorporation for filing unless it is drawn on the statutory form. It has been ruled that the secretary of state may inquire into the legal form of the articles of incorporation of a domestic corporation, but not into the propriety of the provisions of the articles, before filing [Op. Atty. Gen., Idaho, 12-19-41]. Secretary of State of Idaho has no discretion to inquire into propriety of provisions of articles of incorporation before filing them. He must file the articles under Idaho Business Corporation Act, § 30-108, if he finds the articles are in legal form. The distinction is a matter of degree. Secretary could not lawfully file articles of a corporation having only one incorporator. However, he would have no function to ascertain whether or not each of several incorporators was a citizen, or was of age.

and dispose of real estate, real property, lands, multiple-dwelling structures, houses, buildings and other works and any interest or right therein; to take, lease, purchase or otherwise acquire, and to own, use, hold, sell, convey, exchange, hire, lease, pledge, mortgage, and otherwise handle, and deal in and dispose of, as principal, agent, broker, and in any lawful capacity, such personal property, chattels, chattels real, rights, easements, privileges, choses in action, notes, bonds, mortgages, and securities as may lawfully be acquired, held, or disposed of; and to acquire, purchase, sell, assign, transfer, dispose of, and generally deal in and with, as principal, agent, broker, and in any lawful capacity, mortgages and other interests in real, personal, and mixed properties; to carry on a general construction, contracting, building, and realty management business as principal, agent, representative, contractor, subcontractor, and in any other lawful capacity.

To carry on a general mercantile, industrial, investing, and trading business in all its branches; to devise, invest, manufacture, fabricate, assemble, install, service, maintain, alter, buy, sell, import, export, license as licensor or licensee, lease as lessor or lessee, distribute, job, enter into, negotiate, execute, acquire, and assign contracts in respect of, acquire, receive, grant, and assign licensing arrangements, options, franchises, and other rights in respect of, and generally deal in and with, at wholesale and retail, as principal, and as sales, business, special, or general agent, representative, broker, factor, merchant, distributor, jobber, advisor, and in any other lawful capacity, goods, wares, merchandise, commodities, and unimproved, improved, finished, processed, and other real, personal, and mixed property of any and all kinds, together with the components, resultants, and by-products thereof.

To apply for, register, obtain, purchase, lease, take licenses in respect of or otherwise acquire, and to hold, own, use, operate, develop, enjoy, turn to account, grant licenses and immunities in respect of, manufacture under and to introduce, sell, assign, mortgage, pledge or otherwise dispose of, and, in any manner deal with and contract with reference to:

(a) inventions, devices, formulae, processes and any improvements and modifications thereof;

(b) letters patent, patent rights, patented processes, copyrights, designs, and similar rights, trademarks, trade names, trade symbols and other indications of origin and ownership granted by or recognized under the laws of the United States of America, the District of Columbia, any state or subdivision thereof, or and any commonwealth, territory, possession, dependency, agency or instrumentality of the United States of America and of any foreign country, and all rights connected therewith or appertaining thereunto;

(c) franchises, licenses, grants and concessions.

To guarantee, purchase, take, receive, subscribe for, and otherwise acquire, own, hold, use, and otherwise employ, sell, lease, exchange, transfer, and otherwise dispose of, mortgage, lend, pledge, and otherwise deal in and with, securities (which term, for the purpose of this Article THIRD, includes, without limitation of the generality thereof, any shares of stock, bonds, debentures, notes, mortgages, other obligations, and any certificates, receipts or other instruments representing rights to receive, purchase or subscribe for the same, or representing any other rights or interests therein or in any property or assets) of any persons, domestic and foreign firms, associations, and corporations, and by any government or agency or instrumentality thereof; to make payment therefor in any lawful manner; and, while owner of any such securities, to exercise any and all rights, powers and privileges in respect thereof, including the right to vote.

To make, enter into, perform and carry out contracts of every kind and description with any person, firm, association, corporation or government or agency or instrumentality thereof.

To acquire by purchase, exchange or otherwise, all, or any part of, or any interest in, the properties, assets, business and good will of any one or more persons, firms, association or corporations heretofore or hereafter engaged in any business for which a corporation may now or hereafter be organized under the laws of the State of Delaware; to pay for the same in cash, property or its own or other securities; to hold, operate, reorganize, liquidate, sell or in any manner dispose of the whole or any part thereof; and in connection therewith, to assume or guarantee performance of any liabilities, obligations or contracts of such persons, firms, associations or corporations, and to conduct the whole or any part of any business thus acquired.

To lend money in furtherance of its corporate purposes and to invest and reinvest its funds from time to time to such extent, to such persons, firms, associations, corporations, governments or agencies or instrumentalities thereof, and on such terms and on such security, if any, as the Board of Directors of the corporation may determine.

To make contracts of guaranty and surety-ship of all kinds and endorse or guarantee the payment of principal, interest or dividends upon, and to guarantee the performance of sinking fund or other obligations of, any securities, and to guarantee in any way permitted by law the performance of any of the contracts or other undertakings in which the corporation may otherwise be or become interested, of any persons, firm, association, corporation, government or agency or instrumentality thereof, or of any other combination, organization or entity whatsoever.

To borrow money without limit as to amount and at such rates of interest as it may determine; from time to time to issue and sell its own securities including its shares of stock, notes, bonds, debentures and other obligations, in such amounts, on such terms and conditions, for such purposes and for such prices, now or hereafter permitted by the laws of the State of Delaware and by this Certificate of Incorporation, as the Board of Directors of the corporation may determine; and to secure any of its obligations by mortgage upon, pledge or other encumbrance of all or any of its property, franchises and income.

To be a promoter or manager of other corporations of any type or kind; and to participate with others in any corporation, partnership, limited partnership, joint venture, or other association of any kind, or in any transaction, undertaking or arrangement which the corporation would have power to conduct by itself, whether or not such participation involves sharing or delegation of control with or to others.

To draw, make, accept, endorse, discount, execute, and issue promissory notes, drafts, bills of exchange, warrants, bonds, debentures, and other negotiable or transferable instruments and evidences of indebtedness whether secured by mortgage or otherwise, as well as to secure the same by mortgage or otherwise, so far as may be permitted by the laws of the State of Delaware.

To purchase, receive, take, reacquire or otherwise acquire, own and hold, sell, lend, exchange, reissue, transfer or otherwise dispose of, pledge, use, cancel, and otherwise deal in and with its shares and its other securities from time to time to such an extent and in such manner and upon such terms as the Board of Directors of the corporation shall determine; provided that the corporation shall not use its funds or property for the purchase of its own shares of capital stock when its capital is impaired or when such use would cause any impairment of its capital, except to the extent permitted by law.

To organize, as an incorporator, or cause to be organized under the laws of the State of Delaware, or of any other State of the United States of America, or of the District of Columbia, or of any commonwealth, territory, dependency, colony, possession, agency or instrumentality of the United States of America, or of any foreign country, a corporation or corporations for the purpose of conducting and promoting any business or purpose for which corporations may be organized, and to dissolve, wind up, liquidate, merge or consolidate any such corporation or corporations or to cause the same to be dissolved, wound up, liquidated, merged or consolidated.

To conduct its business, promote its purposes, and carry on its operations in any and all of its branches and maintain offices both within and without the State of Delaware, in any and all States of the United States of America, in the District of Columbia, in any or all commonwealths, territories, dependencies, colonies, possessions, agencies or instrumentalities of the United States of America, of foreign governments.

To promote and exercise all or any part of the foregoing purposes and powers in any and all parts of the world, and to conduct its business in all or any of its branches as principal, agent, broker, factor, contractor, and in any other lawful capacity, either alone or through or in conjunction with any corporations, associations, partnerships, firms, trustees, syndicates, individuals, organizations, and other entities in any part of the world, and, in conducting its business and promoting any of its purposes, to maintain offices, branches and agencies in any part of the world, to make and perform any contracts and to do any acts and things, and to carry on any business, and to exercise any powers and privileges suitable, convenient, or proper for the conduct, promotion, and attainment of any of the business and purposes herein specified or which at any time may be incidental thereto or may appear conducive to or expedient for the accomplishment of any of such business and purposes and which might be engaged in or carried on by a corporation incorporated or organized under the General Corporation Law of the State of Delaware, and to have and exercise all of the powers conferred by the laws of the State of Delaware upon corporations incorporated or organized under the General Corporation Law of the State of Delaware.

The foregoing provisions of this Article THIRD shall be construed both as purposes and powers and each as an independent purpose and power. The foregoing enumeration of specific purposes and powers shall not be held to limit or restrict in any manner the purposes and powers of the corporation, and the purposes and powers herein specified shall, except when otherwise provided in this Article THIRD, be in no wise limited or restricted by reference to, or inference from, the terms of any provision of this or any other Article of this certificate of incorporation; [provided, that the corporation shall not conduct any business, promote any purpose, or exercise any power or privilege within or without the State of Delaware which, under the laws thereof, the corporation may not lawfully conduct, promote, or exercise.]

FOURTH: [Adapt following for par shares.] The total number of shares of stock which the corporation shall have authority to issue is.... The par value of each of such shares is.....

All such shares are of one class and are shares of Common Stock.

[Adapt following for no par shares.] The total number of shares of stock which the corporation shall have authority to issue is ...., all of which are without par value. All such shares are of one class and are Common Stock.

[Adapt following for grant of pre-emptive rights.] Each share of stock of the corporation shall entitle the holder thereof to a pre-emptive right, for a period of thirty days, to subscribe for, purchase, or otherwise acquire any shares of stock of the same class of the corporation or any equity and/or voting shares of stock of any class of the corporation which the corporation proposes to issue or any rights or options which the corporation proposes to grant for the purchase of shares of stock of the same class of the corporation or of equity and/or voting shares of any class of stock of the corporation or for the purchase of any shares of stock, bonds, securities, or of the corporation or for the purchase of any shares of stock, bonds, securities, or obligations of the corporation which are convertible into or exchangeable for, or which carry any rights, to subscribe for, purchase, or otherwise acquire shares of stock of the same class of the corporation or equity and/or voting shares of stock of any class of the corporation, whether now or hereafter authorized or created, whether having unissued or treasury status, and whether the proposed issue, reissue, transfer, or grant is for cash, property, or any other lawful consideration; and after the expiration of said thirty days, any and all of such shares of stock, rights, options, bonds, securities or obligations of the corporation may be issued, reissued, transferred, or granted by the Board of Directors, as the case may be, to such persons, firms, corporations and associations, and for such lawful consideration, and on such terms, as the Board of Directors in its discretion may determine. As used herein, the terms "equity shares" and "voting shares" shall mean, respectively, shares of stock which confer unlimited dividend rights and shares of stock which confer unlimited voting rights in the election of one or more directors.

FIFTH: The name and the mailing address of the incorporator are as follows:

SIXTH: The corporation is to have perpetual existence.

SEVENTH: Whenever a compromise or arrangement is proposed between this corporation and its creditors or any class of them and/or between this corporation and its stockholders or any class of them, any court of equitable jurisdiction within the State of Delaware may, on the application in a summary way of this corporation or of any creditor or stockholder thereof or on the application of any receiver or receivers appointed for this corporation under the provisions of section 291 of Title 8 of the Delaware Code or on the application of trustees in dissolution or of any receiver or receivers appointed for this corporation under the provisions of section 279 of Title 8 of the Delaware Code order a meeting of the creditors or class of creditors, and/or of the stockholders or class of stockholders of this corporation, as the case may be, to be summoned in such manner as the said court directs. If a majority in number representing three-fourths in value of the creditors or class of creditors, and/or of the stockholders or class of stockholders of this corporation, as the case may be, agree to any compromise or arrangement and to any reorganization of this corporation as consequence of such compromise or arrangement, the said compromise or arrangement and the said reorganization shall, if sanctioned by the court to which the said application has been made, be binding on all the creditors or class of creditors, and/or on all the stockholders or class of stockholders, of this corporation, as the case may be, and also on this corporation.

EIGHTH: For the management of the business and for the conduct of the affairs of the corporation, and in further definition, limitation and regulation of the powers of the corporation and of its directors and of its stockholders or any class thereof, as the case may be, it is further provided:

1. The management of the business and the conduct of the affairs of the corporation shall be vested in its Board of Directors. The number of directors which shall constitute the whole Board of Directors shall be fixed by, or in the manner provided in, the By-Laws. The phrase "whole Board" and the phrase "total number of directors" shall be deemed to have the same meaning, to wit, the total number of directors which the corporation would have if there were no vacancies. No election of directors need be by written ballot.

2. After the original or other By-Laws of the corporation have been adopted, amended, or repealed, as the case may be, in accordance with the provisions of Section 109 of the General Corporation Law of the State of Delaware, and, after the corporation has received any payment for any of its stock, the power to adopt, amend, or repeal the by-Laws of the corporation may be exercised by the Board of Directors of the corporation; provided, however, that any provision for the classification of directors of the corporation for staggered terms pursuant to the provisions of subsection (d) of Section 141 of the General Corporation Law of the State of Delaware shall be set forth in an initial By-Law or in a By-Law adopted by the stockholders entitled to vote of the corporation unless provisions for such classification shall be set forth in this certificate of incorporation.

3. Whenever the corporation shall be authorized to issue only one class of stock, each outstanding share shall entitle the holder thereof to notice of, and the right to vote at, any meeting of stockholders. Whenever the corporation shall be authorized to issue more than one class of stock, no outstanding share of any class of stock which is denied voting power under the provisions of the certificate of incorporation shall entitle the holder thereof to the right to vote, at any meeting of stockholders except as the provisions of paragraph (c)(2) of the General Corporation Law of the State of Delaware shall otherwise require; provided, that no share of any such class which is otherwise denied voting power shall entitle the holder thereof to vote upon the increase or decrease in the number of authorized shares of said class.

NINTH: The corporation shall, to the fullest extent permitted by Section 145 of the General Corporation Law of the State of Delaware, as the same be amended and supplemented indemnify any and all persons whom it shall have power to indemnify under said section from and against any and all of the expenses, liabilities or other matters referred to in or covered by said section, and the indemnification provided for herein shall not be deemed exclusive of any other rights to which those indemnified may be entitled under any By-Law, agreement, vote of stockholders or disinterested directors or otherwise, both as to action in his official capacity and as to action in another capacity while holding such office, and shall continue as to a person who has ceased to be director, officer, employee or agent and shall inure to the benefit of the heirs, executors and administrators of such a person.

TENTH: From time to time any of the provisions of this certificate of incorporation may be amended, altered or repealed, and other provisions authorized by the laws of the State of Delaware at the time in force may be added or inserted in the manner and at the time prescribed by said laws, and all rights at any time conferred upon the stockholders of the corporation by this certificate of incorporation are granted subject to the provisions of this Article TENTH.

[Adapt following if effective date of certificate of incorporation is to be a date which is subsequent to the "filing date," but not later than 90 days thereafter. "Filing date" is defined as the date upon which Secretary of State endorses the word "Filed" on the Certificate. G.C.L. 103(c)(3) and (d).]

_____: The effective date of the certificate of incorporation of the corporation, and the date upon which the existence of the corporation shall commence, shall be ...., 19...

Signed on ...., 19..

....
Incorporator

LONG FORM OF BY-LAWS

BY-LAWS
OF
(A Delaware Corporation)
ARTICLE I
STOCKHOLDERS

1. CERTIFICATES REPRESENTING STOCK. Every holder of stock in the corporation shall be entitled to have a certificate signed by, or in the name of, the corporation by the Chairman or Vice-Chairman of the Board of Directors, if any, or by the President or a Vice-President and by the Treasurer or an Assistant Treasurer or the Secretary or an Assistant Secretary of the corporation certifying the number of shares owned by him in the corporation. Any and all signatures on any such certificate may be facsimiles. In case any officer, transfer agent, or registrar who has signed or whose facsimile signature has been placed upon a certificate shall have ceased to be such officer, transfer agent, or registrar before such certificate is issued, it may be issued by the corporation with the same effect as if he were such officer, transfer agent, or registrar at the date of issue.

Whenever the corporation shall be authorized to issue more than one class of stock or more than one series of any class of stock, and whenever the corporation shall issue any shares of its stock as partly paid stock, the certificates representing shares of any such class or series or of any such partly paid stock shall set forth thereon the statements prescribed by the General Corporation Law. Any restrictions on the transfer or registration of transfer of any shares of stock of any class or series shall be noted conspicuously on the certificate representing such shares.

The corporation may issue a new certificate of stock in place of any certificate theretofore issued by it, alleged to have been lost, stolen, or destroyed, and the Board of Directors may require the owner of any lost, stolen, or destroyed certificate, or his legal representative, to give the corporation a bond sufficient to indemnify the corporation against any claim that may be made against it on account of the alleged loss, theft, or destruction of any such certificate or the issuance of any such new certificate.

2. FRACTIONAL SHARE INTERESTS. The corporation may, but shall not be required to, issue fractions of a share. If the corporation does not issue fractions of a share, it shall (1) arrange for the disposition of fractional interests by those entitled thereto, (2) pay in cash the fair value of fractions of a share as of the time when those entitled to receive such fractions are determined, or (3) issue scrip or warrants in registered or bearer form which shall entitle the holder to receive a certificate for a full share upon the surrender of such scrip or warrants aggregating a full share. A certificate for a fractional share shall, but scrip or warrants shall not unless otherwise provided therein, entitle the holder to exercise voting rights, to receive dividends thereon, and to participate in any of the assets of the corporation in the event of liquidation. The Board of Directors may cause scrip or warrants to be issued subject to the conditions that they shall become void if not exchanged for certificates representing full shares before a specified date, or subject to the conditions that the shares for which scrip or warrants are exchangeable may be sold by the corporation and the proceeds thereof distributed to the holders of scrip or warrants, or subject to any other conditions which the Board of Directors may impose.

3. STOCK TRANSFERS. Upon compliance with provisions restricting the transfer or registration of transfer of shares of stock, if any, transfers or registration of transfers of shares of stock of the corporation shall be made only on the stock ledger of the corporation by the registered holder thereof, or by his attorney thereunto authorized by power of attorney duly executed and filed with the Secretary of the corporation or with a transfer agent or a registrar, if any, and on surrender of the certificate or certificates for such shares of stock properly endorsed and the payment of all taxes due thereon.

4. RECORD DATE FOR STOCKHOLDERS. For the purpose of determining the stockholders entitled to notice of or to vote at any meeting of stockholders or any adjournment thereof, or to express consent to corporate action in writing without a meeting, or entitled to receive payment of any dividend or other distribution or the allotment of any rights, or entitled to exercise any rights in respect of any change, conversion, or exchange of stock or for the purpose of any other lawful action, the directors may fix, in advance, a record date, which shall not be more than sixty days nor less than ten days before the date of such meeting, nor more than sixty days prior to any other action. If no record date is fixed, the record date for determining stockholders entitled to notice of or to vote at a meeting of stockholders shall be at the close of business on the day next preceding the day on which notice is given, or, if notice is waived, at the close of business on the day

next preceding the day on which the meeting is held; the record date for determining stockholders entitled to express consent to corporate action in writing without a meeting, when no prior action by the Board of Directors is necessary, shall be the day on which the first written consent is expressed; and the record date for determining stockholders for any other purpose shall be at the close of business on the day on which the Board of Directors adopts the resolution relating thereto. A determination of stockholders of record entitled to notice of or to vote at any meeting of stockholders shall apply to any adjournment of the meeting; provided, however, that the Board of Directors may fix a new record date for the adjourned meeting.

5. MEANING OF CERTAIN TERMS. As used herein in respect of the right to notice of a meeting of stockholders or a waiver thereof or to participate or vote thereat or to consent or dissent in writing in lieu of a meeting, as the case may be, the term "share" or "shares" or "share of stock" or "shares of stock" or "stockholder" or "stockholders" refers to an outstanding share or shares of stock and to a holder or holders of record of outstanding shares of stock when the corporation is authorized to issue only one class of shares of stock, and said reference is also intended to include any outstanding share of shares of stock and any holder or holders of record of outstanding shares of stock of any class upon which or upon whom the certificate of incorporation confers such rights where there are two or more classes or series of shares of stock or upon which or upon whom the General Corporation Law confers such rights notwithstanding that the certificate of incorporation may provide for more than one class or series of shares of stock, one or more of which are limited or denied such rights thereunder; provided, however, that no such right shall vest in the event of an increase or a decrease in the authorized number of shares of stock of any class or series which is otherwise denied voting rights under the provisions of the certificate of incorporation.

6. STOCKHOLDER MEETINGS.

Time. The annual meeting shall be held on the date and at the time fixed, from time to time, by the directors, provided, that the first annual meeting shall be held on a date within thirteen months after the organization of the corporation, and each successive annual meeting shall be held on a date within thirteen months after the date of the preceding annual meeting. A special meeting shall be held on the date and at the time fixed by the directors.

Place. Annual meetings and special meetings shall be held at such place, within or without the State of Delaware, as the directors may, from time to time, fix. Whenever the directors shall fail to fix such place, the meeting shall be held at the registered office of the corporation in the State of Delaware.

Call. Annual meetings and special meetings may be called by the directors or by any officer instructed by the directors to call the meeting.

Notice or Waiver of Notice. Written notice of all meetings shall be given, stating the place, date, and hour of the meeting and stating the place within the city or other municipality or community at which the list of stockholders of the corporation may be examined. The notice of an annual meeting shall state that the meeting is called for the election of directors and for the transaction of other business which may properly come before the meeting, and shall, (if any other action which could be taken at a special meeting is to be taken at such annual meeting) state the purpose or purposes. The notice of a special meeting shall in all instances state the purpose or purposes for which the meeting is called. The notice of any meeting shall also include, or be accompanied by, any additional statements, information, or documents prescribed by the General Corporation Law. If any action is proposed to be taken which would, if taken, entitle stockholders to receive payment for their shares of stock, the notice shall include a statement of that purpose and to that effect. Except as otherwise provided by the General Corporation Law, a copy of the notice of any meeting shall be given, personally or by mail, not less than ten days nor more than fifty days before the date of the meeting, unless the lapse of the prescribed period of time shall have been waived, and directed to each stockholder at his record address or at such other address which he may have furnished by request in writing to the Secretary of the corporation. Notice by mail shall be deemed to be given when deposited, with postage thereon prepaid, in the United States mail. If a meeting is adjourned to another time, not more than thirty days hence, and/or to another place, and if an announcement of the adjourned time and/or place is made at the meeting, it shall not be necessary to give notice of the adjourned meeting unless the directors, after adjournment, fix a new record date for the adjourned meeting. Notice need not be given to any stockholder who submits a written waiver of notice signed by him before or after the time stated therein. Attendance of a stockholder at a meeting of stockholders shall constitute a waiver of notice of such meeting, except when the stockholder attends a meeting for the express purpose of objecting, at the beginning of the meeting, to the transaction of any business because the meeting is not lawfully called or convened. Neither the business to be transacted at, nor the purpose of, any regular or special meeting of the stockholders need be specified in any written waiver of notice.

Stockholder List. The officer who has charge of the stock ledger of the corporation shall prepare and make, at least ten days before every meeting of stockholders, a complete list of the stockholders, arranged in alphabetical order, and showing the address of each stockholder and the number of shares registered in the name of each stockholder. Such list shall be open to the examination of any stockholder, for any purpose germane to the meeting, during ordinary business hours, for a period of at least ten days prior to the meeting, either at a place within the city or other municipality or community where the meeting is to be held, which place shall be specified in the notice of the meeting, or if not so specified, at the place where the meeting is to be held. The list shall also be produced and kept at the time and place where the meeting is to be held. The list shall also be produced and kept at the time and place of the meeting during the whole time thereof, and may be inspected by any stockholder who is present. The stock ledger shall be the only evidence as to who are the stockholders entitled to examine the stock ledger, the list required by this section or the books of the corporation, or to vote at any meeting of stockholders.

Conduct of Meeting. Meetings of the stockholders shall be presided over by one of the following officers in the order of seniority and if present and acting—the Chairman of the Board, if any, the Vice-Chairman of the Board, if any, the President, a Vice-President, or, if none of the foregoing is in office and present and acting, by a chairman to be chosen by the stockholders. The Secretary of the corporation, or in his absence, an Assistant Secretary, shall act as secretary of every meeting, but if neither the Secretary nor an Assistant Secretary is present the Chairman of the meeting shall appoint a secretary of the meeting.

Proxy Representation. Every stockholder may authorize another person or persons to act for him by proxy in all matters in which a stockholder is entitled to participate, whether by waiving notice of any meeting, voting or participating at a meeting, or expressing consent or dissent without a meeting. Every proxy must be signed by the stockholder or by his attorney-in-fact. No proxy shall be voted or acted upon after three years from its date unless such proxy provides for a longer period. A duly executed proxy shall be irrevocable if it states that it is irrevocable and, if, and only as long as, it is coupled with an interest sufficient in law to support an irrevocable power. A proxy may be made irrevocable regardless of whether the interest with which it is coupled is an interest in the stock itself or an interest in the corporation generally.

Inspectors. The directors, in advance of any meeting, may, but need not, appoint one or more inspectors of election to act at the meeting or any adjournment thereof. If an inspector or inspectors are not appointed, the person presiding at the meeting may, but need not, appoint one or more inspectors. In case any person who may be appointed as an inspector fails to appear or act, the vacancy may be filled by appointment made by the directors in advance of the meeting or at the meeting by the person presiding thereat. Each inspector, if any, before entering upon the discharge of his duties, shall take and sign an oath faithfully to execute the duties of inspector at such meeting with strict impartiality and according to the best of his ability. The inspectors, if any, shall determine the number of shares of stock outstanding and the voting power of each, the shares of stock represented at the meeting, the existence of a quorum, the validity and effect of proxies, and shall receive votes, ballots or consents, hear and determine all challenges and questions arising in connection with the right to vote, count and tabulate all votes, ballots or consents, determine the result, and do such acts as are proper to conduct the election or vote with fairness to all stockholders. On request of the person presiding at the meeting, the inspector or inspectors if any, shall make a report in writing of any challenge, question or matter determined by him or them and execute a certificate of any fact found by him or them.

Quorum. The holders of a majority of the outstanding shares of stock shall constitute a quorum at a meeting of stockholders for the transaction of any business. The stockholders present may adjourn the meeting despite the absence of a quorum.

Voting. Each share of stock shall entitle the holder thereof to one vote. In the election of directors, a plurality of the votes cast shall elect. Any other action shall be authorized by a majority of the votes cast except where the General Corporation Law prescribes a different percentage of votes and/or a different exercise of voting power, and except as may be otherwise prescribed by the provisions of the certificate of incorporation and these By-Laws. In the election of directors, and for any other action, voting need not be by ballot.

7. STOCKHOLDER ACTION WITHOUT MEETINGS. Any action required by the General Corporation Law to be taken at any annual or special meeting of stockholders, or any action which may be taken at any annual or special meeting

of stockholders, may be taken without a meeting, without prior notice and without a vote, if a consent in writing, setting forth the action so taken, shall be signed by the holders of outstanding stock having not less than the minimum number of votes that would be necessary to authorize or take such action at a meeting at which all shares entitled to vote thereon were present and voted. Prompt notice of the taking of the corporate action without a meeting by less than unanimous written consent shall be given to those stockholders who have not consented in writing.

ARTICLE II
DIRECTORS

1. FUNCTIONS AND DEFINITION. The business and affairs of the corporation shall be managed by or under the direction of the Board of Directors of the corporation. The Board of Directors shall have the authority to fix the compensation of the members thereof. The use of the phrase ''whole board'' herein refers to the total number of directors which the corporation would have if there were no vacancies.

2. QUALIFICATIONS AND NUMBER. A director need not be a stockholder, a citizen of the United States, or a resident of the State of Delaware. The initial Board of Directors shall consist of ..... persons. Thereafter the number of directors constituting the whole board shall be at least one. Subject to the foregoing limitation and except for the first Board of Directors, such number may be fixed from time to time by action of the stockholders or of the directors, or, if the number is not fixed, the number shall be ...... The number of directors may be increased or decreased by action of the stockholders or of the directors.

3. ELECTION AND TERM. The first Board of Directors, unless the members thereof shall have been named in the certificate of incorporation, shall be elected by the incorporator or incorporators and shall hold office until the first annual meeting of stockholders and until their successors have been elected and qualified or until their earlier resignation or removal. Thereafter, directors who are elected at an annual meeting of stockholders, and directors who are elected in the interim to fill vacancies and newly created directorships, shall hold office until the next annual meeting of stockholders and until their successors have been elected and qualified or until their earlier resignation or removal. In the interim between annual meetings of stockholders or of special meetings of stockholders called for the election of directors and/or for the removal of one or more directors and for the filling of any vacancy in that connection, newly created directorships and any vacancies in the Board of Directors, including unfilled vacancies resulting from the removal of directors for cause or without cause, may be filled by the vote of a majority of the remaining directors then in office, although less than a quorum, or by the sole remaining director.

4. MEETINGS.

Time. Meetings shall be held at such time as the Board shall fix, except that the first meeting of a newly elected Board shall be held as soon after its election as the directors may conveniently assemble.

Place. Meetings shall be held at such place within or without the State of Delaware as shall be fixed by the Board.

Call. No call shall be required for regular meetings for which the time and place have been fixed. Special meetings may be called by or at the direction of the Chairman of the Board, if any, the Vice-Chairman of the Board, if any, of the President, or of a majority of the directors in office.

NOTICE OR ACTUAL OR CONSTRUCTIVE WAIVER. No notice shall be required for regular meetings for which the time and place have been fixed. Written, oral, or any other mode of notice of the time and place shall be given for special meetings in sufficient time for the convenient assembly of the directors thereat. Notice need not be given to any director or to any member of a committee of directors who submits a written waiver of notice signed by him before or after the time stated therein. Attendance of any such person at a meeting shall constitute a waiver of notice of such meeting, except when he attends a meeting for the express purpose of objecting, at the beginning of the meeting, to the transaction of any business because the meeting is not lawfully called or convened. Neither the business to be transacted at, nor the purpose of, any regular or special meeting of the directors need be specified in any written waiver of notice.

QUORUM AND ACTION. A majority of the whole Board shall constitute a quorum except when a vacancy or vacancies prevents such majority, whereupon a majority of the directors in office shall constitute a quorum, provided, that such majority shall constitute at least one-third of the whole Board. A majority of the directors present, whether or not a quorum is present, may adjourn a meeting to another time and place. Except as herein otherwise provided, and except as otherwise provided by the General Corporation Law, the vote of the majority of the directors present at a meeting at which a quorum is present shall be the act of the Board. The quorum, and voting provisions herein stated shall not be construed as conflicting with any provisions of the General Corporation Law and these By-Laws which govern a meeting of directors held to fill vacancies and newly created directorships in the Board of action of disinterested directors.

Any member or members of the Board of Directors or of any committee designated by the Board, may participate in a meeting of the Board, or any such committee, as the case may be, by means of conference telephone or similar communications equipment by means of which all persons participating in the meeting can hear each other.

Chairman of the Meeting. The Chairman of the Board, if any and if present and acting, shall preside at all meetings. Otherwise, the Vice-Chairman of the Board, if any and if present and acting, or the President, if present and acting, or any other director chosen by the Board, shall preside.

5. REMOVAL OF DIRECTORS. Except as may otherwise be provided by the General Corporation Law, any director or the entire Board of Directors may be removed, with or without cause, by the holders of a majority of the shares then entitled to vote at an election of directors.

6. COMMITTEES. Whenever its number consists of three or more, the Board of Directors may, by resolution passed by a majority of the whole Board, designate one or more committees, each committee to consist of two or more of the directors of the corporation. The Board may designate one or more directors as alternate members of any committee, who may replace any absent or disqualified

member at any meeting of the committee. In the absence or disqualification of any member of any such committee or committees, the member or members thereof present at any meeting and not disqualified from voting, whether or not he or they constitute a quorum, may unanimously appoint another member of the Board of Directors to act at the meeting in the place of any such absent or disqualified member. Any such committee, to the extent provided in the resolution of the Board, shall have and may exercise the powers and authority of the Board of Directors in the management of the business and affairs of the corporation with the exception of any authority the delegation of which is prohibited by Section 141 of the General Corporation Law, and may authorize the seal of the corporation to be affixed to all papers which may require it.

7. WRITTEN ACTION. Any action required or permitted to be taken at any meeting of the Board of Directors or any committee thereof may be taken without a meeting if all members of the Board or committee, as the case may be, consent thereto in writing, and the writing or writings are filed with the minutes of proceedings of the Board or committee.

ARTICLE III

OFFICERS

The officers of the corporation shall consist of a President, a Secretary, a Treasurer, and, if deemed necessary, expedient, or desirable by the Board of Directors, a Chairman of the Board, a Vice-Chairman of the Board, an Executive Vice-President, one or more other Vice-Presidents, one or more Assistant Secretaries, one or more Assistant Treasurers, and such other officers with such titles as the resolution of the Board of Directors choosing them shall designate. Except as may otherwise be provided in the resolution of the Board of Directors choosing him, no officer other than the Chairman or Vice-Chairman of the Board, if any, need be a director. Any number of offices may be held by the same person, as the directors may determine, except that no person may hold the offices of President and Secretary simultaneously.

Unless otherwise provided in the resolution choosing him, each officer shall be chosen for a term which shall continue until the meeting of the Board of Directors following the next annual meeting of stockholders and until his successor shall have been chosen and qualified.

All officers of the corporation shall have such authority and perform such duties in the management and operation of the corporation as shall be prescribed in the resolutions of the Board of Directors designating and choosing such officers and prescribing their authority and duties, and shall have such additional authority and duties as are incident to their office except to the extent that such resolutions may be inconsistent therewith. The Secretary or an Assistant Secretary of the corporation shall record all of the proceedings of all meetings and actions in writing of stockholders, directors, and committees of directors, and shall exercise such additional authority and perform such additional duties as the Board shall assign to him. Any officer may be removed, with or without cause, by the Board of Directors. Any vacancy in any office may be filled by the Board of Directors.

ARTICLE IV
CORPORATE SEAL

The corporate seal shall be in such form as the Board of Directors shall prescribe.

ARTICE V
FISCAL YEAR

The fiscal year of the corporation shall be fixed, and shall be subject to change, by the Board of Directors.

ARTICLE VI
CONTROL OVER BY-LAWS

Subject to the provisions of the certificate of incorporation and the provisions of the General Corporation Law, the power to amend, alter or repeal these By-Laws and to adopt new By-Laws may be exercised by the Board of Directors or by the stockholders.

I HEREBY CERTIFY that the foregoing is a full, true and correct copy of the By-Laws of ...., a Delaware corporation, as in effect on the date hereof.

WITNESS my hand and the seal of the corporation.

Dated:

....
Secretary

(SEAL)

SHORT FORM OF BY-LAWS

ARTICLE 1—STOCKHOLDERS' MEETINGS

SECTION 1. THE ANNUAL MEETING OF STOCKHOLDERS of the Corporation shall be held each year at the principal office of the Corporation in the City of ...., State of ....., on the .... day in ...., at ...... o'clock in the .... noon, for the purpose of election of directors, and for the transaction of such other business as may properly come before the meeting. Notice of the time and place of the annual meeting of stockholders shall be given to each stockholder of record of the Corporation entitled to vote at such meeting, by mailing to such stockholder, at least ..... (.....) days prior to said meeting, a notice thereof, postage prepaid, addressed to his last-known post-office address.

SECTION 2. SPECIAL MEETINGS OF STOCKHOLDERS shall be held as provided in the Certificate of Incorporation, or if not so provided, then such meetings shall be called by the Board of Directors, or by the President, to be held at the principal office of the Corporation in the City of ...., State of .... Notice of such special meetings shall be given in the same manner as is provided in the case of annual meetings.

ARTICLE 2—BOARD OF DIRECTORS

SECTION 1. THE MANAGEMENT AND CONTROL of the business of the corporation shall be vested in a Board of Directors, consisting of ..... (.....) persons, who shall be elected at the annual meeting of stockholders from among the stockholders, for a term of one year, and who shall hold office until their successors are elected and qualify. The Board of Directors may employ such agents as it deems advisable.

SECTION 2. ANY VACANCIES IN THE BOARD OF DIRECTORS caused by resignation, death, or otherwise may, except as may be otherwise provided in the Certificate of Incorporation, be filled by the remaining directors, at a special meeting called for that purpose, or by the stockholders at any regular or special meeting held prior to the filling of such vacancy by the Board as above provided. The person so chosen as director shall hold office until the next annual meeting of stockholders, or until his successor is elected and qualifies.

ARTICLE 3—DIRECTORS' MEETINGS

SECTION 1. REGULAR MEETINGS OF THE BOARD OF DIRECTORS shall be held on the .... day in each month, at ..... o'clock, ..M., at the principal office of the Corporation, in the city of ...., State of .... No notice of regular meetings need be given to the directors.

SECTION 2. SPECIAL MEETINGS OF THE BOARD OF DIRECTORS may be called at any time by the President, or, in his absence, by the Vice-president, or by any two directors, to be held at the principal office of the Corporation in the City of ...., State of ...., or at such other place or places as the directors may from time to time designate. Notice of special meetings of the Board of Directors shall be given to each director by ..... (.....) days' service of the same by telegram, letter or personally.

ARTICLE 4—OFFICERS

SECTION 1. THE OFFICERS OF THE CORPORATION shall consist of a President, a Vice-president, a Secretary, and a Treasurer, who shall be elected for one year by the Board of Directors at its first meeting after the annual meeting of stockholders, and who shall hold office until their successors are elected and qualify. The office of Secretary and Treasurer may be held by the same person. Any vacancies in office arising from death, resignation, or otherwise may be filled by the Board of Directors at any regular or special meeting. The duties of the officers shall be such as are usually imposed upon such officials of corporations and as are required by law, and such as may be assigned to them, respectively, by the Board of Directors from time to time.

ARTICLE 5—AMENDMENT OF BY-LAWS

SECTION 1. THESE BY-LAWS MAY BE AMENDED or repealed, or new By-laws may be made and adopted, at any annual or special meeting of stockholders called for that purpose, by the vote or written assent of the holders representing .... (*insert fractional part*) of the subscribed capital stock, or by a vote of .... (*insert fractional part*) of the Board of Directors at a regular or special meeting of the Board.

MINUTES OF FIRST MEETING OF INCORPORATORS

[*Note*. This form, together with all the following forms in this chapter, constitutes the organization record of a Delaware corporation. The headings in brackets may appear as marginal notes in the minute book.]

[Time and place of meeting]

The first meeting of incorporators of the .... was held at ...., in the City of ...., State of ...., on ...., 19.., at ..... A.M., pursuant to a written waiver of notice signed by all of the incorporators, fixing said place and time.

The following incorporators were present in person or by proxy:

Name of Incorporator	Name of Proxy [2]
....	....
....	....
....	....

being all of the incorporators named in the Certificate of Incorporation.

[Temporary officers]

On motion unanimously carried, Mr. .... was elected Chairman, and Mr. .... Secretary of the meeting.

[Waiver of notice]

The Secretary presented the waiver of notice of the meeting signed by all of the incorporators, and it was filed as part of the minutes. The Secretary was ordered to file as a part of the minutes any proxies which had been accepted.

[Certificate of incorporation reported filed]

The Chairman reported that the Certificate of Incorporation of the corporation was filed in the office of the Secretary of State of the State of Delaware on ...., 19.., and a certified copy thereof was filed for record in the office of the Recorder of Deeds in the County of ...., on ...., 19.., and a copy of said Certificate of Incorporation was ordered to be inserted in the minute book as a part of the records of the meeting.

[Adoption of By-laws]

The Secretary presented a proposed form of By-laws for the regulation and management of the affairs of the Corporation, which was read, section by section, and unanimously adopted and ordered to be made a part of the permanent records to follow the Certificate of Incorporation in the minute book.

---

[2]If the incorporator was present in person, write "In person" in this column. If not, write the name of the person who represented him as proxy.

[Election of directors]

Motions were then declared by the Chairman to be in order for the nomination of directors of the Corporation to hold office for the ensuing year and until their successors are elected and qualify, and the following gentlemen were nominated: *(insert names of nominees)*.

No further nominations having been made, a ballot was taken and all of the incorporators having voted, and the ballots having been duly canvassed, the Chairman declared that the above-named persons were elected directors of the Corporation by the unanimous vote of all the incorporators.

Upon motion duly made, seconded and unanimously carried, it was

[Issuance of capital stock]

RESOLVED, That the Board of Directors be and it hereby is authorized in its discretion to issue the capital stock of this Corporation to the full amount or number of shares authorized by the Certificate of Incorporation, in such amounts and for such considerations[3] as from time to time shall be determined by the Board of Directors and as may be permitted by law.

[Adjournment]

There being no other business to be transacted, the meeting was, upon motion duly made, seconded, and carried, adjourned.

....
Secretary of the Meeting

WAIVER OF NOTICE OF MEETING OF
INCORPORATORS

We, the undersigned, being all of the incorporators of the ...., a corporation organized under the laws of the State of Delaware, do hereby severally waive all the statutory requirements as to notice of the time, place, and purpose of the first meeting of incorporators of the said Corporation and the publication thereof, and consent that the meeting shall be held at ...., in the City of ...., State of ...., on ...., 19.., at ..... A.M., and we consent to the transaction of any and all business that may properly come before the meeting.

Dated ...., 19..

....
....
....

PROXY FOR FIRST MEETING OF INCORPORATORS

KNOW ALL MEN BY THESE PRESENTS:

That I, the undersigned, being an incorporator (and a subscriber for shares of the capital stock)[4] of the above-named Corporation, do hereby constitute and

---

[3]Stock with par value cannot be issued for less than par.
[4]If incorporators subscribe for shares, the words in parentheses should be included in the proxy.

appoint .... as my true and lawful attorney to vote for me in my name, place, and stead (the stock subscribed for by me or standing in my name) and to act as my proxy at the first meeting of the incorporators to be held at .... in the City of ...., State of ...., on ...., 19.., or on such other day as the meeting may be thereafter held by adjournment or otherwise (according to the number of votes I am now or may then be entitled to cast).

I hereby grant to the said attorney full power and authority to act for me and in my name at the said meeting or meetings in voting for directors of the Corporation, adopting the By-laws, and in the transaction of such other business as may come before the meeting, as fully as I could do if present in person. I hereby expressly ratify and confirm all that my said attorney or substitute may do in my place, name, and stead.

In Witness Whereof, I have hereunto set my hand and seal this .. day of ...., 19...

Witness: .... (Seal)

....

TRANSFER OF SUBSCRIPTION

Know All Men By These Presents:

That I, ..., in consideration of ....'s agreement to fulfill the obligation of my subscription for ..... shares, contained in the original Certificate of Incorporation of ...., a corporation organized under the laws of Delaware, have assigned and transferred and by these presents do assign and transfer unto said ...., all my right, title, and interest in said subscription, and I do hereby authorize and empower the proper officers to issue the certificates for the said shares to the order of said transferee.

In Witness Whereof, I have hereunto set my hand and seal this .. day of ...., 19..

In presence of: .... (Seal)

....

MINUTES OF FIRST MEETING OF DIRECTORS

[*Note.* The headings in brackets may appear as marginal notes in the minute book.]

[Time and place of meeting]

The first meeting of the Board of Directors of .... was held at ...., in the City of ....., State of ....., on ...., 19.., at ..... P.M.

Present: Messrs. ...., ..., and ...., constituing[5] .... of the Board.

[Temporary officers]

Mr. .... was unanimously chosen temporary Chairman, and Mr. .... was unanimously chosen temporary Secretary of the meeting.

---

[5]Insert "a quorum" or "the full membership."

[Waiver of notice]

The Secretary presented and read a waiver of notice of the meeting signed by all the directors, which was ordered filed.

[Approval of minutes]

The minutes of the first meeting of incorporators were read and approved.

[Election of officers]

The following persons were nominated for officers of the Corporation to serve until their respective successors are chosen and qualify:

Chairman of the Board of Directors,[6] ....

President, ...

Vice-president, ...

Treasurer, ...

Secretary, ...

Ballots being duly cast by all the directors present, the Chairman announced that the aforenamed persons had been unanimously elected to the offices set before their respective names to assume the duties and responsibilities fixed by the By-laws.

The Chairman of the Board of Directors (*or* the President) thereupon took the chair.[7] and the Secretary immediately assumed the discharge of his duties.

On motion duly made, seconded, and unanimously adopted, it was

[Adoption of Seal]

RESOLVED, That a corporate seal, the impression of which is affixed in the margin hereof, be and the same shall be the corporate seal of the Corporation.

[Approval of form of stock certificate]

A form of stock certificate was presented, and upon motion duly made, seconded, and adopted, was unanimously approved.

[Treasurer's Bond]

The Treasurer was then called upon to give a bond in the sum of ..... Dollars ($.....) with one surety. The form of the bond and the name of the surety were presented at this meeting for the approval of the Board, to determine the sufficiency of the surety, said bond being signed by .... as principal and by .... as surety, and both the form and the surety of the bond were approved and accepted. The Treasurer's bond was then ordered filed.[8]

Upon motion duly made, seconded, and unanimously carried, it was

[Resident agent and office]

RESOLVED, That the office of .... Corporation, ... *(Street)*, in the City of ...., County of ....., in the State of Delaware, is hereby designated as the principal office of this Corporation within the State of Delaware,

---

[6]If the by-laws so provide, the chairman may be omitted.

[7]This clause may be omitted if the temporary officers are the same as the permanent officers.

[8]The directors may or may not require a bond to be given by the treasurer. If the bond is not to be required, this paragraph will be omitted.

and that .... Corporation is hereby appointed the Resident Agent of this Corporation, in charge of the Principal Office in Delaware and custodian of the books required by law to be kept in that office, and the agent upon whom process against this Corporation may be served in accordance with the laws of Delaware, and

FURTHER RESOLVED, That .... Corporation, may look for advice and follow the instructions of ...., Esq., counsel of this Corporation, on legal questions arising in connection with such agency, and

FURTHER RESOLVED, That the Secretary is hereby instructed to prepare and execute a certificate, sealed with the corporate seal, authorizing the .... Corporation, to act in the capacity heretofore set forth, and

FURTHER RESOLVED, That an office of the Corporation be established and maintained at ...., in the City of ...., State of ...., and that meetings of the Board of Directors from time to time may be held either at such office in the City of ...., or elsehere, as the Board of Directors shall from time to time order, or at the Registered Office in ...., Delaware.

[Meetings of directors]

FURTHER RESOLVED, That until otherwise ordered, regular meetings of the Board of Directors be held at said office in the City of ...., on the .. day of each month at ....M.

The following motion was made, seconded, and unanimously carried:

[Purchase of property for stock]

WHEREAS, ... has offered to sell to this Corporation the following property (*insert description of property*) in consideration that this Corporation will issue to the order of said ...., ... (.....) shares of capital stock of this Corporation, fully paid and non-assessable, as follows:[9] ...., and

WHEREAS, it appears to the Board of Directors that said property is necessary for the business of this Corporation, that the same is of a fair value at least equal to the[10] .... value of the stock to be issued therefor,[11] be it

RESOLVED, That the offer of said .... to sell to this Corporation said property (which property the Board of Directors does hereby declare in its best judgment to be of the vlaue above set forth and necessary for the business of this Corporation) is hereby accepted, that the proper officers are authorized and directed to execute, issue, and deliver in the name and on behalf of this Corporation, and under its corporate seal, certificates of stock for ..... shares to the order of ...., and

RESOLVED FURTHER, That of the consideration received or to be received for such stock, the sum of ..... Dollars ($.....) is hereby specified as capital.[12]

Upon motion duly made, seconded, and unanimously carried, it was

---

[9]Insert here a description of the shares and the number to be issued.

[10]If the stock has no par value, insert here, "fair"; if it has par value, insert "par"; if two classes are to be issued, one without par value and the other with par value, insert here "fair and par" and add an "s" to the succeeding word "value."

[11]If the whole or part of the stock to be issued has no par value and it is desired to place a dollar value on the property for future bookeeping, balance sheet, or other purposes, there may be added here, "that is, $.........," stating here the reasonable cash value.

[12]In the case of par stock, the amount may not be less than par. In the case of no-par stock, any amount may be specified as capital.

[Opening of bank account]

RESOLVED, That the Treasurer be authorized and directed to open a bank account for the Corporation with the ...., in the City of ...., which bank be and it hereby is authorized to honor from the deposits of the Corporation, checks drawn against such deposits signed by[13] ...., as long as there is a balance in favor of the Corporation.

Upon motion duly made, seconded, and unanimously carried, it was

[Qualification in other states]

RESOLVED, That the proper officers of this Corporation be and they hereby are authorized and directed, in behalf of the Corporation, and under its corporate seal, to make and file such certificate or certificates, report or reports, or other instrument or instruments as may be required by law to be filed in any State, territory, colony, or dependency of the United States, or in any foreign country in which said officers shall find it necessary or expedient to file the same to authorize the Corporation to transact business in such State, territory, colony, dependency, or foreign country.

Upon motion duly made, seconded, and unanimously carried, it was

[Payment of organization fees]

RESOLVED, That the Treasurer is hereby authorized to pay all fees and expenses incident to and necessary for the organization of this Corporation.

[Adjournment of meeting]

Upon motion duly made, seconded, and unanimously carried, the meeting was adjourned.

....
Secretary

WAIVER OF NOTICE OF FIRST MEETING
OF DIRECTORS

We, the undersigned, duly elected directors of ...., do hereby severally waive notice of time, place, and purpose of the first meeting of directors of said Corporation, and consent that the meeting be held at ...., in the City of ...., State of ....., on ...., 19.., at ..... A.M., and we do further consent to the transaction of any business requisite to complete the organization of the Corporation and to any and all business which may properly come before the meeting.

Dated ...., 19..   ....
....
....

Signed, sealed, and delivered   .... (L.S.)
in the presence of: .... (L.S.)
....

---

[13]Designate the officer or officers; a convenient and not unusual provision is the following: "any two of the following officers: President, Vice President, Treasurer, Secretary."

CERTIFICATE OF APPOINTMENT OF RESIDENT
AGENT AND OF LOCATION OF PRINCIPAL OFFICE

This is to certify that the Board of Directors of .... Corporation, on ...., 19.., upon motion duly made, seconded, and unanimously carried,

RESOLVED, That the office of .... Corporation, ... *(Street)*, in the City of ...., County of ...., in the State of Delaware, be and is hereby designated as the principal office of this Corporation within the State of Delaware, and that .... Corporation, be and is hereby appointed the Resident Agent of this Corporation, in charge of the principal office and custodian of the books required by law to be kept in that office, and the agent upon whom process against this Corporation may be served in accordance with the laws of Delaware.

FURTHER RESOLVED, That said .... Corporation may look for advice and follow the instructions of ...., Esq., counsel of this Corporation, on legal questions arising in connection with such agency.

IN WITNESS WHEREOF, I have hereunto by order of the Board of Directors, set my official hand, in behalf of the Corporation, and have hereunto affixed the corporate seal, this .. day of ...., 19...

....
By ....
Secretary

Chapter 9

MANAGEMENT OF
THE CORPORATION

Contents—Chapter 9

Scope of chapter. This chapter is devoted to a discussion of the place of the stockholders in the management of the corporation, the general powers of directors and officers in conducting the ordinary corporate affairs, the appointment of committees and agents, the execution of corporate instruments, and the resignation and removal of directors and officers. Forms of resolutions relating to these subjects are presented in Chapter 10. The principles governing compensation of directors, officers, and employees for their services to the corporation are discussed in Chapter 11.

POWERS OF STOCKHOLDERS

Position of stockholders in management of the corporation. The business management of a corporation is specifically entrusted by the statutes of the various states to the board of directors, sometimes called the board of trustees. Stockholders do not participate in management of the business,[1] nor do they vote on questions of management.[2] Their consent is not necessary in the conduct of the ordinary affairs of the corporation.[3] However, when a corporation makes a contract subject to stockholder approval, the contract is unenforceable, when the stockholders consent to it either in their capacity as officers or as directors, but *not* in their capacity as stockholders.[4] The stockholders ordinarily may not, by agreement among themselves, control the directors in the exercise of their judgment to elect corporate officers.[5] (But where the directors are the sole stockholders[6] or where it does not injure the corporation or a third party,[7] such an agreement may be valid.) The stockholders' power to control the corporation rests largely in the fact that they have the right to elect directors.[8] However, they also have the power to approve or reject propositions that, according to statute, charter, or by-laws, cannot be undertaken without their approval. (See page 225.)

Stockholders cannot exercise the powers that are vested in the

[1]SEC v. Transamerica Corp., (1946) 67 F. Supp. 326, aff'd, (1947) 163 F. 2d 511; Fowler v. Shaw, (1925) 119 Kan. 576, 240 P. 970; Hanrahan v. Andersen, (1939) 108 Mont. 218, 90 P.2d 494.

[2]Geiman-Herthel Furniture Co. v. Geiman, (1945) 160 Kan. 346, 161 P.2d 504.

[3]Warren v. Fitzgerald, (1948) 189 Md. 476, 56 A.2d 827; Hayes v. St. Louis Union Trust Co., (1927) 317 Mo. 1028, 298 S.W. 91.

[4]Salton v. Seaporcel Metals, Inc., (1960) N.Y.S. Ct. 208 N.Y.S. 2d 60.

[5]McQuade v. Stoneham, (1934) 263 N.Y. 326, 189 N.E. 234. See Delaney, "The Corporate Director: Can His Hands Be Tied In Advance," 50 COLUM. L. REV. 52.

[6]Clark v. Dodge, (1936) 269 N.Y. 410, 199 N.E. 641.

[7]E.K. Buck Retail Stores v. Harkert, (1954) 157 Neb. 867, 62 N.W. 2d 288.

[8]Prince George's Country Club, Inc. v. Carr. (1964) Md. Ct. of App., Balt. Daily Record, 9-28-64, p.9; Elevator Supplies Co. v. Wylde, (1930) 106 N.J. Eq. 163, 150 A. 347; Dunlay v. Avenue M. Garage & Repair Co., (1930) 253 N.Y. 274, 170 N.E. 917; Adams v. Farmers Gin Co., (1938) Tex. Civ. App. 114 S.W. 2d 583.

directors,[9] nor the powers that are delegated to the company's officers and agents.[10] They do not instruct the directors in the management of the corporation.[11] It has been held, however, that selection of independent auditors to audit the corporate books is a proper subject for stockholder consideration.[12]

Stockholders in close corporations frequently want to control the policies and actions of the directors. Their attempt at control usually takes the form of a provision in the charter or by-laws removing certain areas of management from the directors' responsibility or discretion. The courts, when called upon to decide the legality of such a provision, will base their decisions on whether or not the directors are unduly deprived of independent judgment and responsibility.[13]

Power of stockholders to make contracts. Stockholders cannot bind the corporation by the simplest contract, either individually or while acting together at a stockholders' meeting,[14] without authority from the corporation.[15] For example, a contract of employment made by the owners of a majority of the stock is not binding on the corporation.[16] While, strictly speaking, this is the rule where management of the corporation has been vested in the board of directors, there are many exceptions. Action taken by the stockholders, that should have been authorized by the board of directors, will be binding on the corporation under the following circumstances: (1) if it has been the custom of the corporation to act through the authority of the stockholders; (2) if the corporation has acquiesced in, or the directors have ratified, the action taken by the stockholders; (3) if the corporation has accepted and retained the benefits of the transaction; (4) if the stockholders and the directors are the same people and all the directors were present and participated in the meeting at which the action was taken by the

---

[9]Bodell v. General Gas & Elec. Corp., (1926) 15 Del. Ch. 119, 132 A. 442; Charlestown Boot & Shoe Co. v. Dunsmore, (1880) 60 N.H. 85.

[10]Klein v. Journal Square Bank Bldg. Co., (1932) 110 N.J. Ch. 607, 160 A. 812.

[11]Commissioner v. Laughton, (1940) 113 F. 2d 103; Ayres v. Hadaway, (1942) 303 Mich, 589, 6 N.W. 2d 905.

[12]SEC v. Transamerica Corp., (1946) 67 F. Supp. 326, aff'd, (1947) 163 F. 2d 511.

[13]In Abercrombie v. Davies, (1956) Del. Ch. 123 A. 2d 893, rev'd on other grounds, (1957) 130 A.2d 338, the court invalidated an agreement among stockholders as an unlawful attempt to encroach upon the statutory powers and duties imposed on the directors, and in Long Park, Inc. v. Trenton-New Brunswick Theatres Co., (1948) 297 N.Y. 174, 77 N.E.2d 633, an agreement among the stockholders vesting sole management of the corporation on one of them was also held invalid. But see Clark v. Dodge, (1936) 269 N.Y. 410, 199 N.E. 641; where it was held a "slight infringement" on the directors' authority will be upheld. See also Hornstein, "Stockholders' Agreements in the Closely Held Corporation," 59 YALE L.J. 1040, 1045.

[14]Fowler v. Shaw, (1925) 119 Kan. 576, 240 P. 970; Manufacturers' Exhibition Bldg. Co. v. Landay, (1905) 219 Ill. 168, 76 N.E. 146; Sellers v. Greer, (1898) 172 Ill. 549, 50 N.E. 246; Ayres v. Hadaway, (1942) 303 Mich. 589, 6 N.W. 2d 905.

[15]Jones v. Williams, (1897) 139 Mo. 1, 39 S.W. 486; MacBrine-McAdams Realty Co. v. Morris, (1938) 129 Pa. Super. 604, 196 A. 511.

[16]D'Arcangelo v. D'Arcangelo, (1945) 137 N.J. Eq. 63, 43 A.2d 169.

stockholders;[17] (5) if the stockholders and the directors are the same people and they acted in writing, signed by them all;[18] and (6) if all the stockholders were present or represented at the meeting.[19]

The stockholders cannot by their consent give the corporation power to do something which the corporation has not the power to do under its charter. But, if they do consent, they are estopped from objecting that the corporation acted beyond its powers.

Acts requiring consent of stockholders. Consent of all or a certain proportion of the stockholders is generally required in the following matters: (1) acceptance of the corporate charter; (2) amendment of the corporate charter; (3) adoption of by-laws, unless this power is expressly vested in the governing board by statute or charter; (4) amendment of by-laws if the stockholders have the right to adopt them and if the power to amend them is not expressly given to the governing board; (5) removal of directors; (6) merger of the corporation with another company, or consolidation; (7) transfer of all the property of the corporation by sale or lease;[20] (8) voluntary dissolution of the company; (9) assessments on fully paid stock; and (10) all other matters where approval of the stockholders is required by statute, charter, or by-laws.

The extent of the right of stockholders to control the actions of the corporate officers or agents is determined by the law of the state of incorporation.[21]

POWERS OF DIRECTORS AND OFFICERS

Management by the board of directors. The corporate powers are exercised, the corporate business conducted, and the corporate property controlled by the board of directors, acting as a body.[22] The directors must direct.[23] It is no defense that stockholders gave blanket ratification to

---

[17]First Trust Co. v. Miller, (1915) 160 Wis. 336, 151 N.W. 813.

[18]Hotard v. Fleitas, (1953) La. App. 67 So. 2d 345; Lohman v. Edgewater Holding Co., (1948) 227 Minn. 40, 33 N.W. 2d 842.

[19]Colorado Springs Co. v. American Publishing Co., (1899) 97 F. 843.

[20]Prince George's Country Club Inc. v. Carr, (1964) Md. Ct. of App., Balt. Daily Record, 9-28-64, p. 9.

[21]Farmers Educational & Co-operative Union, Minn. Div. v. Farmers Educational & Co-operative Union, (1940) 207 Minn. 80, 289 N.W. 884.

[22]Western Battery & Supply Co. v. Hazelett Storage Battery Co., (1932) 61 F. 2d 220, cert. den., (1933) 288 U.S. 608, 53 S. Ct. 399; United States v. Interstate R.R., (1926) 14 F. 2d 328; In re Joseph Feld & Co., (1941) 38 F. Supp. 506; Walker v. Detroit Transit Ry., (1882) 47 Mich. 338, 11 N.W. 187; Brown v. Citizens' State Bank, (1939) 345 Mo. 480, 134 S.W. 2d 116.

[23]Larisey v. Hill, (1968) Ga. Ct. of App., 159 S.E. 2d 843; Warren v. Fitzgerald (1948) 189 Md. 476, 56 A. 2d 827; D'Arcangelo v. D'Arcangelo, (1945) 137 N.J. Eq. 63, 43 A. 2d 169. Petition of Binder, (1939) 172 N.Y. Misc. 634, 15 N.Y.S. 2d 4. See also "Directors Who Do Not Direct," 47 HARV. L. REV. 1305; "A Defense of Non-Managing Directors," 5 U. CHI. L. REV. 668.

directors' acts at annual meetings.[24] Also, a director's limited business experience does not excuse him from leaving management to two executives, if such management leads to company losses; the director is personally liable for such losses.[25] Further, directors who do not know about secret commission payments being made by the corporation to other directors, are personally liable for these payments, since if they themselves had properly participated in the management of the corporation they could have discovered those secret arrangements.[26]

In essence, therefore, the basic rule is that directors cannot agree among themselves or with other stockholders to abdicate their duties themselves or with other stockholders to abdicate their duties of management.[27] Thus, it has been held illegal for the controlling stockholders of a corporation to agree to elect certain directors who would act as nominal directors and who would not take part in the management of the corporation.[28] An agreement to take authority away from the directors and place it in the hands of a stockholder, or one class of stockholders, is also illegal.[29] However, a corporation that is equally owned by two groups of stockholders can create a new class of non-participating voting stock, and issue one share to an odd-numbered new director able to break a deadlock; such an arrangement is not an unlawful delegation of directors' duties, if it was approved by the unanimous vote of stockholders and effected through a charter amendment.[30] Some states have specific statutes which let a court appoint a tie-breaking "provisional director" when a corporation's board is equally divided in running the corporation so that the corporation's business suffers.[31] (In most states, the only judicial remedies are a receivership or a dissolution.[32]) The provisional director is an impartial stranger to the corporation. He has all the rights of a regularly elected director until the deadlock is broken or until he is removed by court order or by majority stockholder consent. At least one court, even without a specific statute, but with the consent of the two sole stockholder-directors of a solvent corpora-

---

[24]Nesse v. Brown, (1964) Tenn. S. Ct. 405 S.W. 2d 577.

[25]McDonnell v. American Leduc Petroleum, Ltd., (1974) CA-2 Dkt. No. 73-1172, 1-21-74.

[26]Heit v. Bixby, (1967) DC E.D. Mo. 276 F. Supp. 217.

[27]Ashman v. Miller, (1939) 101 F. 2d 85; Field v. Carlisle Corp., (1949) 31 Del. Ch. 227, 68 A.2d 817, comment, 34 MARQ. L. REV. 48; Wheeler v. Layman Foundation, (1939) 188 Ga. 267, 3 S.E. 2d 645; Long Park, Inc. v. Trenton-New Brunswick Theatres Co., (1948) 297 N.Y. 174, 77 N.E. 2d 633; Keolbel v. Tecktonius, (1938) 228 Wis. 317, 280 N.W. 305.

[28]Jackson v. Hooper, (1910) 76 N.J. Eq. 592, 75 A. 568.

[29]Abbey v. Meyerson, (1948) 274 App. Div. 389, 83 N.Y.S. 2d 503, aff'd, (1949) 299 N.Y. 557, 85 N.E.2d 789; Hamblen v. Horwitz-Texan Theatres Co., (1942) Tex. Civ. App. 162 S.W. 2d 455. See also Long Park, Inc. v. Trenton-New Brunswick Theatres Co., (1948) 297 N.Y. 174, 77 N.E. 2d 633; comment, 14 BROOKLYN L. REV. 282; 61 HARV. L. REV. 1251; 47 MICH. L. REV. 119.

[30]Lehrman v. Cohen, (1966) Del. S. Ct., 222 A.2d 800.

[31]E.g., Calif. G.C.L. §819; Del. G.C.L. §353; Mo. G. & B.C.L. §351.323.

[32]E.g., Ill. B.C.A. §86; N.Y.B.C.L. §1104; Wis. B.C.L. §180.771.

tion, has appointed a tie-breaking director.[33] Contracts providing for the election of a designated person as an officer have been held void,[34] because they take from the directors the right to exercise their own judgment in the management of the corporation's affairs.[35]

The directors must consider conscientiously every question involving the interests of the company.[36] They must act in good faith and with reasonable care,[37] and must use that prudence in the handling of the affairs of the corporation that an ordinary, prudent man would use.[38] They are presumed to know everything concerning corporate affairs that they might have learned by the use of reasonable care and diligence.[39] Although each director must use his independent judgment upon every problem that comes before the board,[40] he can take into consideration the views and arguments advanced by others, and can be guided by information supplied by others.[41]

Directors as fiduciaries. Directors are fiduciaries.[42] They occupy a position of trust and confidence and are considered by the courts as trustees for the stockholders,[43] although they cannot be held to the standard of a trustee of an express trust.[44] They must represent fully the interests of the corporation,[45] and must not use their positions of trust and confidence to further their own private interests.[46] They must use their powers for the

[33]In re Hickory House, Inc., (1958) N.Y.S. Ct., 13 Misc. 2d 761, 177 N.Y.S. 2d 356, following the dictum of the New York Court of Appeals. In re Radom & Neidorff, Inc., (1954) 307 N.Y. 1, 8, 119 N.E. 2d 563.565.

[34]Kennerson v. Burbank Amusement Co., (1953) 120 Cal. App. 2d 157, 260 P.2d 823; Williams v. Fredericks, (1937) 187 La. 987, 175 So. 642; Goldfarb v. Dorset Products, Inc., (1948) 82 N.Y.S. 2d 42; Roberts v. San Jacinto Shipbuilders, Inc., (1946) (Tex. Civ. App.) 198 S.W. 2d 488.

[35]Lockley v. Robie, (1950) 276 App. Div. 291, 94 N.Y.S. 2d 335.

[36]Ames v. Goldfield Merger Mines Co., (1915) 227 F. 292; Walker v. Man, (1931) 142 N.Y. Misc. 277, 253 N.Y. Supp. 458.

[37]People's Bank & Trust Co. v. Thibodaux, (1930) 170 La. 969, 129 So. 547; Peabody v. Interborough Rapid Transit Co., (1923) 121 N.Y. Misc. 647, 202 N.Y. Supp. 287; State ex rel. Blackwood v. Brast, (1925) 98 W. Va. 596, 127 S.E. 507.

[38]Ames v. Goldfield Merger Mines Co., (1915) 227 F. 292. See also Sternberg v. Blaine, (1929) 179 Ark. 448, 17 S.W. 2d 286.

[39]Leterman v. Pink, (1936) 249 App. Div. 164, 291 N.Y. Supp. 249.

[40]Marvin v. Solventol Chemical Products, Inc., (1941) 298 Mich. 296, 298 N.W. 782.

[41]Miller v. Vanderlip, (1941) 285 N.Y. 116, 33 N.E.2d 51.

[42]Pepper v. Litton, (1939) 308 U.S. 295, 60 S. Ct. 238.

[43]Pepper v. Litton, (1939) 308 U.S. 295, 60 S. Ct. 238; Arn v. Bradshaw, (1939) 108 F.2d 125; Howell v. Poff, (1932) 122 Neb. 793, 241 N.W. 548.

[44]Manufacturers Trust Co. v. Becker, (1949) 338 U.S. 304, 70 S. Ct. 127, aff'g In Re Calton Crescent, Inc., (1949) 173 F.2d 944, comment, 59 YALE L.J. 151.

[45]American Trust Co. v. California Western States Life Ins. Co., (1940) 15 Cal.2d 42, 98 P.2d 497; Lyon v. Holton, (1938) 167 N.Y. Misc. 585, 4 N.Y.S. 2d 538.

[46]Kaufmann v. Commissioner, (1949) 175 F.2d 28; In re Norcor Mfg. Co., (1940) 109 F.2d 407; Mothershead v. Douglas, (1949) 215 Ark. 519, 221 S.W.2d 424, comment, 4 Sw. L. J. 285; Angelus Securities Corp. v. Ball, (1937) 20 Cal. App. 2d 423, 67 P. 2d 158; Guth v. Loft, Inc., (1939) 23 Del. Ch. 255, 5 A.2d 503; Lydia E. Pinkham Medicine Co. v. Gove, (1937) 298 Mass. 59, 9 N.E. 2d 573; Bailey v. Jacobs, (1937) 325 Pa. 187, 189 A. 320. See also Knox Glass Bottle Co. v. Underwood, (1956) (Miss.) 89 So.2d 799.

benefit of all the stockholders and not for only a few.[47] Thus, for example, when an individual who served as president, treasurer, and chairman of the board was offered shares of a corporation's stock, he had a duty to offer it on a pro-rata basis to all the other stockholders before purchasing it himself.[48] Directors are personally liable for secret commissions they receive for business they bring to the corporation, even though there is no evidence that the corporation itself suffered any financial loss.[49]

Directors who dominate both corporations involved in a merger, and use that domination to buy and sell among themselves stock in the surviving corporation at prices pegged artificially high, are guilty of self-dealing, and must pay the excess over the stock's book value to the surviving corporation; however, that self-dealing does not vitiate the actual merger, and a court will not set it aside on that ground.[50] And, it is worth noting that executives who were part of the old management of corporations and also were former partners in a law firm retained as counsel for such corporations could participate with corporate principals in an action charging former officers and directors of the corporations prevailed over the ethics of an attorney-client relationship.[51] Also, issuance of authorized shares which diluted the power of a principal shareholder was not improper action by directors; courts will not interfere with the good faith judgment of directors in managing a corporation.[52]

But a dominant stockholder and director is not bound by a contract with a third party obliging him to qualify other directors' shares for sale to the public. When such action is not, in his judgment, in the corporation's best interests, since the director's duty to the corporation supersedes his contractual obligations—even though he was not a director when he made the contract—no agreement may bind the director to any future course of action that violates his judgment or discretion.[53] Also, the board has no authority to issure an extra bonus to the corporation's president in order for the latter to repay to the corporation what he owes from short-swing profits he received on the sale of his stock; that is illegal siphoning of corporate funds.[54] The corporation and its stockholders have a primary right to expect the directors to perform their duties honestly and efficiently.[55] Thus, directors cannot issue a new class of voting stock to themselves in order to

---

[47]Atkins v. Hughes, (1929) 208 Cal. 508, 282 P. 787.

[48]Irwin v. West End Development Co., (1973) CA-10 No. 72-1446, 6-27-73.

[49]Heit v. Bixby, (1967) DC, E.D. Mo., 1967, 276 F. Supp. 217.

[50]Klein v. Fisher Foods, Inc., (1965) Ohio C.P., 6 Ohio Misc. 84, 216 N.E.2d 647.

[51]Federal Savings & Loan Insurance Corp. v. Fielding, (1972) D. Nev., 343 F. Supp. 537.

[52]Tallant v. Executive Equities, Inc., (1974) Ga. S. Ct., No. 28951, 9-24-74.

[53]In re Glekel, (1971) N.Y. App. Div., 37 A.D.2d 1.

[54]Seilon, Inc. v. Hickman, (1972) N.Y.S. Ct., N.Y.L.J., 5-30-72, p. 19.

[55]Covey v. England & McCaffrey, Inc., (1931) 233 App. Div. 332, 253 N.Y. Supp. 340.

retain the control of the corporation,[56] nor can they issue stock for their own benefit against the interests of the stockholders as a whole,[57] nor secretly set up a competing business.[58]

Directors, however, do not have a fiduciary duty to stockholders that keeps them from buying and selling the corporation's stock.[59] Their fiduciary duty is to the stockholder, not to his stock.[60] They can buy this stock on any terms they can get.[61] While they should not withhold facts that might influence the stockholder to demand a higher price,[62] they are not under obligation to disclose inside information as long as they do not actively mislead the seller, or resort to fraud.[63] They are, however, liable for any fraud, misrepresentation of fact, or withholding of material information while transacting a deal,[64] and they have the burden of proving that the transaction is fair and reasonable.[65]

Directors do not violate their fiduciary duty to the corporation by selling their shares to it at a slight premium, when (1) they did not vote on the resolution approving the purchase, (2) they made full disclosure, (3) other shareholders could sell on the same terms and (4) the corporation wanted to keep the shares out of undesirable hands.[66] Also, directors do not breach their fiduciary duty and are not personally liable because they take over corporate property in exchange for loans they made to the corporation, when there was no overreaching as to price and, after full disclosure, the majority stockholder had acquiesced in the transaction and himself took over the business to avoid threatened dissolution.[67]

---

[56]Rosenthal v. Four Corners Oil & Minerals Co., (1965) Colo. S. Ct. 403 P. 2d 762; Kahn v. Schiff, (1952) 105 F. Supp. 973.

[57]First Mortgage Bond Homestead Ass'n v. Baker, (1929) 157 Md. 309, 145 A. 876.

[58]Areo Drapery of Kentuck, Inc. v. Engdahl, (1974) Ky. Ct. of App., 507 S.W. 2d 166; Dretzin v. Alson, (1967) N.Y.S. Ct., N.Y.L.J., 8-3-67, p.8.

[59]SEC v. Chenery Corp., (1943) 317 U.S. 80, 63 S. Ct. 454. But see SEC v. Chenery Corp., (1947) 332 U.S. 194, 67 S. Ct. 1575, in which the Supreme Court upheld the SEC in its refusal to grant certain voting rights to stock purchased by directors while reorganization of the company was pending, although purchased in good faith. The court based its opinion on the SEC's administrative right, without approving the decision reached by the SEC.

It has been held that a director may, ordinarily, deal in securities of his corporation without subjecting himself to any liability to account for profits. Hauben v. Morris, (1938) 255 App. Div. 35, 5 N.Y.S. 2d 721.

[60]Llewellyn v. Queen City Dairy, (1946) 187 Md. 49, 48 A.2d 322.

[61]SEC v. Chenery Corp., (1943), (1943) 317 U.S. 80, 63 S. Ct. 454.

[62]Barnes v. Eastern & Western Lumber Co., (1955) 205 Ore, 553, 287 P.2d 929.

[63]Llewellyn v. Queen City Dairy, (1946) 187 Md. 49, 48 A. 2d 322.

[64]Ohio Drill & Tool Co. v. Johnson, (1974) CA-6, 498 F.2d 186; Talbot v. James, (1972) S.C.S. Ct. No. 19460, 8-1-72; Blazer v. Black, (1952) 196 F.2d 139; Jaynes v. Jaynes, (1950) 98 Cal. App. 2d 447, 220 P.2d 598; Hotchkiss v. Fischer, (1932) 136 Kan. 530, 16 P.2d 531; Sher v. Sandler, (1950) 325 Mass. 348, 90 N.E.2d 536.

[65]Fountain v. Oreck's Inc., (1955) 245 Minn. 202, 71 N.W.2d 646; Solimine v. Hollander, (1940) 128 N.J. Eq. 228, 16 A.2d 203. See also Miller v. Wahyou, (1956) 235 F.2d 612.

[66]Borden v. Guthrie, (1965) N.Y. App. Div., 260 N.Y.S. 2d 769, aff'd., (1966) Ct. of App., 17 N.Y.2d 571.

[67]Power-Oil Mfg. Co., Inc. v. Carstense, (1966) Wash. S. Ct., 69 Wash.2d 681, 419 P.2d 793.

What duty does a director have to his corporation's stockholders when he offers to buy their shares? An increasing number of courts are now taking the position that a director has a fiduciary duty to disclose any facts he knows that may affect the value of the stock he is buying, which are not within the stockholder's knowledge, nor accessible to him. For example, a sale will be rescinded when a director knows that the value of the stock he wants to buy is much greater than what he is offering to pay, because he is negotiating a sale of the corporation's assets at a high price, but says nothing about it to the stockholders.[68] Also, a stockholder can recover the true value of stock he was induced to sell to a director by the latter's misrepresentations that the corporation was in a poor financial condition and had no prospects for improvement, when, in fact, (1) a stockholders' special meeting, notice of which was not given to the complaining stockholder, had voted to have the corporation ''go public'' because of its success in developing overseas markets and (2) the director had refused to allow the stockholder to inspect the corporation's books, so that he was unable to check its true condition.[69] Action of directors in hiding behind the veil of a dummy corporation to conceal from the stockholders the true identity of the buyer violates their fiduciary duty.[70] Directors are liable for the profits they make.[71]

Of course, if it is shown that when the directors buy stock from its holders, they have no knowledge of its appreciation possibilities they are not liable.[72] A director violates no fiduciary duty when he accepts an option to buy a stockholder's shares at book value, but does not mention an outside offer to purchase the corporate assets at a higher price, since the stockholder had previously voted to approve the proposed sale of the assets at that higher price and so he knew that the book value was not the shares' true worth when he gave the option.[73] Also, a director is not liable to minority stockholders when he causes the corporation to distribute shares it owns in another corporation as a stock dividend, and then makes a tender offer for these shares at a price allegedly below another offer, since the other offer is for the purchase of net assets for liquidation purposes, not for the going concern value of the shares, even though the director did become the owner of 90% of the other corporation's stock, and can, if he wishes, effect a short form merger or liquidation.[74] Further, a director can buy from

---

[68]Low v. Wheeler, (1962) Calif. Dist. Ct. of App., 24 Cal. Rptr. 538.
[69]Quinn v. Forsyth, (1967) Ga. Ct. of App., 158 S.E. 2d 686.
[70]Barnes v. Eastern & Western Lumber Co., (1955) Ore. S. Ct., 287 P.2d 929.
[71]International Bankers Life Insurance Company v. Holloway, (1963) Texas S. Ct., 368 S.W. 2d 567.
[72]Kors v. Carey, (1960) Del. Ch. Ct., 158 A.2d 136.
[73]Lank v. Steiner, (1965) Del. Ch. Ct., 213 A.2d 848.
[74]Epstein v. The Celotex Corporation, (1968) 238 A. 2d 843.

his corporation shares in its subsidiary, even though his motive was to secure a position with the subsidiary, when the price he paid for the shares was based on an arm's length negotiation.[75]

In addition, when a director is dealing in his own corporation's stock, not only must he keep in mind this common law fiduciary duty doctrine, but he also must be on the alert for his possible violations of the Federal securities laws in the same area.[76] For example, stockholders and corporations can bring actions against directors under the anti-fraud rule,[77] and the rule against "short-swing" profits[78]

So long as the directors conduct the business of the corporation under the standards discussed above, they remain free from personal liability, even though the corporation suffers losses through their poor judgment.[79] If the directors prove to be incompetent to handle the affairs of the corporation, the stockholders' redress is to elect a new board at the next annual election.

Since directors owe undivided loyalty to the corporation, they must not divert a corporate opportunity for their own benefit.[80] Any secret profits realized from a corporate opportunity diverted to the directors' own business may be recovered.[81] For example, a director who secretly secures for himself a lease of property that his corporation has an interest in and is financially able to avail itself of, must hold it for the corporation's benefit.[82] The same result follows when a director procures such a lease for

---

[75]Lagrange v. Hoving, (1964) N.Y.S. Ct., N.Y.L.J., 12-28-64, p.13.

[76]For full discussion see Prentice-Hall *Securities Regulation.*

[77]Sec. 10(b) of Securities Exchange Act of 1934, 48 Stat. 891; Rule 10(b)-5, Exch. Act Release 3230, eff. 5-21-42.

[78]Sec. 16(b) of Securities Exchange Act of 1934, 48 Stat. 896.

[79]Perlman v. Feldmann (1955) CA-2, 219 F. 2d 173, cert. den., 349 U.S. 952, 75 S. Ct. 880.

[80]Abbott Redmont Thinlite Corp. v. Redmont (1973) CA-2 Dkt., No. 7-1565, 3-13-73; Italo Petroleum Corp v. Hannigan, (1940) 40 Del. 534, 14 A. 2d 401; Maclary v. Pleasant Hills, Inc., (1954) Del. Ch. 109 A. 2d 830; Production Machinery Co. v. Howe, (1951) 327 Mass. 372, 99 N.E. 2d 32; Lutherland, Inc. v. Dahlen, (1947) 357 Pa. 143, 53 A.2d 143. See also Notes, "A Survey of Corporate Opportunity," 45 Geo. L.J. 99. It is impossible to formulate an all-encompassing definition of an opportunity in the line of a corporation's business. But "where a corporation is engaged in a certain business, and an opportunity is presented to it embracing an activity as to which it has fundamental knowledge, practical experience, and ability to pursue, which logically and naturally is adaptable to its business having regard for its financial position, and is one that is consonant with its reasonable needs and aspirations for expansion, it may be properly said that the opportunity is in the line of the corporation's business." Guth v. Loft, Inc., (1939) 23 Del. Ch. 255, 5A.2d 503. There the court held that the opportunity to acquire cheaply the trademark, formula and good will of the then Pepsi-Cola Company belonged to Loft, Inc. and was wrongfully appropriated by Guth, Loft's president, when that opportunity came to Guth's attention at a time when Loft was seeking to replace Coca-Cola with another cola syrup at its soda fountains. Loft was already a substantial manufacturer of fountain syrup, and it had the resources to develop Pepsi-Cola. The Court ordered Guth to turn over to Loft all his stock in the new Pepsi-Cola Company he had formed.

[81]Uchida Investment Co. v. Igagiki, (1952) 108 Cal. App. 2d 647, 239 P.2d 644; Durfee v. Durfee & Canning, Inc., (1948) 323 Mass. 187, 80 N.E.2d 522; Arneman v. Arneman, (1953) 43 Wash. 2d 787, 264 P.2d 256. See also Amen v. Black, (1956) 234 F.2d 12, cert. granted, 352 U.S. 888; Western Grain Co. Cases, (1955) 264 Ala. 145, 85 So.2d 395.

[82]Schildberg Rock Products Co., Inc. v. Brooks, (1966) Iowa S. Ct., 140 N.W. 2d 132.

another corporation in which he is interested,[83] or when he buys such premises.[84] The doctrine has been extended even further. Thus, stockholders can compel the directors to account for profits they allegedly made when they sold their stock over-the-counter using knowledge they had of the corporation's reduced earnings and such information was not known to other stockholders and investors; this amounts to converting to themselves something that belongs to the corporation, even though there was no damage to the corporation, its assets were not wasted, and there actually was no diversion of corporate opportunity.[85] But officers who bought land available to their corporation and rented it profitably to the corporation are not liable for appropriating a corporate opportunity, when it is shown that the corporation was itself financially unable to make the purchase.[86] The right to recover, however, is vested in the corporation and not in the stockholders.[87] To recover secret profits from the directors, the stockholders must first demand that the corporation sue the faithless directors.[88] If the board of directors fails to institute an action,[89] if the demand on the directors to sue is clearly futile,[90] or if the directors have approved the wrong complained of,[91] any stockholder[92] may sue "derivatively"[93] on

---

[83]Gildener v. Lynch, (1945) N.Y. S. Ct., 54 N.Y.S. 2d 823.

[84]Paulman v. Kritzer, (1966) Ill. App. Ct., 219 N.E.2d 541.

[85]Diamond v. Oreamuno, (1968) N.Y. App. Div., 287 N.Y.S. 2d 300.

[86]A.C. Petters Co. v. St. Cloud Enterprises, (1974) Minn. S. Ct., 222 N.W. 2d 83.

[87]Orlando v. Nix, (1930) 171 La. 176, 129 So. 810. But see Perlman v. Feldmann, (1955) 219 F. 2d 173, cert. denied, 349 U.S. 952, 75 S. Ct. 880, noted in 40 CORNELL L.Q. 786; 60 HARV. L. REV. 1274.

[88]Mayer v. Adams, (1957) (Del. Ch.) 133 A.2d 138; Punch v. Hipsolite Co., (1936) 340 Mo. 53, 100 S.W.2d 878; Kowalski v. Nebraska-Iowa Packing Co., (1955) 160 Neb. 609, 71 N.W.2d 147.

[89]Findley v. Garrett, (1952) 109 Cal. App. 2d 166, 240 P. 2d 421.

[90]Pergament v. Frazer, (1949) 93 F. Supp. 9; American Life Ins. Co. v. Powell, (1955) 262 Ala. 560, 80 So. 2d 487. See, however, Mayer v. Adams, (1957) Del. Ch. 133 A.2d 138; comment in 33 N.Y.U.L. REV. 71, holding that where a demand on the directors to sue would have been futile, a stockholder must, nevertheless, make a demand on the other stockholders to sue, or show the futility of such a demand, before he can sue derivatively.

[91]Swanson v. Traer, (1957) 249 F.2d 854; Carroll v. New York, N.H. & Hartford R.R., (1956) 141 F. Supp. 456, American Life Ins. Co. v. Powell, (1955) 262 Ala. 560, 80 So. (2d) 487.

[92]Equitable stockholders, even though not record holders, may maintain derivative action. F.H.G. Co. v. Pioneer Publishing Co., (1947) 30 Del. Ch. 298, 60 A. 2d 106, comment, 49 COLUM. L. REV. 233. But stockholders cannot maintain a derivative action as to a transaction which took place before they became stockholders. Pergament v. Frazer, (1949) 93 F. Supp. 9; Newkirk v. W.J. Rainey, Inc., (1950) 31 Del. Ch. 433, 76 A.2d 121.

[93]A derivative suit is an action brought by a stockholder, usually against the directors or officers, to collect damages or enforce some other legal right on behalf of his corporation. It is distinguished from a representative suit which is an action brought by a stockholder against a corporation or its directors or officers to collect damages or enforce some other legal right on his own behalf and on behalf of all other stockholders who have the same claim. See Siegel v. Englemann, (1955) 1 N.Y. Misc. 2d 447, 143 N.Y.S. 2d 193; 32 N.Y.U.L. Rev. 980.

behalf of the corporation.[94] Stockholders, however, are estopped from suing the directors if they have acquiesced in the action of the directors, or have received any benefits from the action challenged,[95] or have deferred the action unreasonably.[96]

Although directors are required to be faithful to the corporation especially in business transactions, they may nevertheless take advantage of a business opportunity that comes to them in their individual capacity[97] or that comes to the corporation but which the corporation is legally and financially unable to perform.[98] Thus, directors of a corporation owning and operating low-rent apartment houses do not appropriate corporate opportunity by buying for themselves other similar property, when (1) they were engaged in such activities before the corporation was formed; (2) there was no agreement to offer all such property to the corporation; (3) they were not full-time employees of the corporation required to devote their business activities solely to the corporation; and (4) it was shown the complaining stockholder knew that the directors were engaging in this activity but did not object.[99] Further, a director who did not know that his corporation needed certain property at the time he bought it in his own name, did not breach his fiduciary duty to his corporation and he could sell

---

[94]Knutsen v. Frushour, (1968) Ida. S. Ct., 436 P. 2d 521; Ragnar Benson, Inc. v. Kassab, (1963) CA-3, 325 F. 2d 591, related case Kassab v. Ragnar Benson, Inc., (1966) DC W. D. Pa., 254 F. Supp. 830; Alvest, Inc. v. Superior Oil Corp., (1965) Alaska S. Ct., 398 P. 2d 213; Sequoia Vacuum Systems v. Stransky, (1964) Calif. Dist. Ct. of App., 40 Cal. Rptr. 203; Liddell v. Smith, (1965) Ill. App. Ct., 213 N.E. 2d 604; Hubbard v. Pape, (1964) Ohio Ct. of App., 203 N.E. 2d 365, aff'd., (1965) 2 Ohio App. 2d 326. For an account of some stockholder suits, see ''Striking Out Strike Suits,'' by Richard F. Wolfson, *Fortune*, March, 1949, p. 137. The title of this article has reference to the tendency for legislatures to pass laws that discourage such suits. Under these laws, generally, a complaining stockholder who does not own a specified dollar amount or percentage of the outstanding stock of the company must post a bond covering the costs and attorneys' fees of the corporation and the individual defendants. If the suit is unsuccessful, the defendants have recourse to the security.

See Gilbert v. Case, (1957) 3 App. Div. 2d 930, 163 N.Y.S. 2d 179, criticized in 32 N.Y.U.L. REV. 1388, suggesting N.Y. security statute is designed only to protect the corporation from liability for expenses of its officers and directors in defending themselves and not for the corporation's own defense expenses. However, under the present New York law (B.C.L.§627), a corporation can request a bond to cover its own expenses in any minority shareholders' action, and also can require a bond to be given to cover the individual defendants' expenses only when the corporation would be liable for their expenses by law, contract or otherwise. For full discussion of derivative suits, see Prentice-Hall *Corporation*.

[95]Griffin v. Smith, (1938) 101 F.2d 348; Uccello v. Gold'N Goods, Inc., (1950) 325 Mass. 319, 90 N.E. 2d 530. See page 000 as to ratification by stockholders of directors' unauthorized acts.

[96]Hill Dredging Corp. v. Risley, (1955) 18 N.J. 501, 114 A.2d 697.

[97]Johnston v. Green, (1956) Del. 121 A. 2d 919; Solimine v. Hollander, (1940) 128 N.J. Eq. 228, 16 A. 2d 203.

[98]Robinson v. Brier (1963) Pa. S. Ct., 194, A. 2d 204; Urban J. Alexander Co. v. Trinkle, (1949) 311 Ky. 635, 223 S.W. 2d 923.

[99]Burg v. Horn, (1967) CA-2, 380 F. 2d 897.

the property to the corporation at a profit.[100] Also, directors of a textile manufacturing corporation who set up related companies to absorb some of the first corporation's activities and develop new business areas for themselves were not liable for breach of fiduciary duty through appropriation of corporate opportunities, since these companies did not interfere with or unfairly divert the first corporation's business and the directors acted with due care and in good faith.[101]

Personal liability of directors in corporate management. In most states statutory provisions impose obligations, liabilities and penalties upon directors. In addition in most states there are other obligations and liabilities not spelled out in statutes, that are nonetheless imposed by the courts. These are discussed below.

Directors, of course, are liable to the corporation for any loss suffered by it as a result of their fraudulent design.[102] They are also liable to the corporation for gross negligence.[103] It is no excuse that they did no. benefit from their negligence and that their services were gratuitous.[104] They can also be held personally liable for secret commissions they receive for business they bring to the corporation, even though there is no showing that the corporation itself suffered any financial loss.[105] Directors' management of the corporation will be upheld so long as they exercise an honest discretion for a lawful purpose.[106] Usually personal liability of directors is imposed by law but it may be assumed by contract.

> *Example:* Where a director agreed to become responsible for a bill for services rendered and to be rendered to the corporation, it was held the director became personally liable for the payment of the bill.[107]

Directors are not liable for losses suffered by the corporation, if they have acted honestly and within their powers.

> *Examples:* Directors are not liable for abuse of discretion in refusing a higher offer for sale of a corporate asset, when (1) two of the directors made the offer at a special meeting called to consider lower offer and directors' higher offer was made on business card of one of

---

[100]Tower Recreation, Inc. v. Beard, (1967) Ind. App. Ct., 231 N.E. 2d 154.

[101]Miller v. Miller, (1974) Minn. S. Ct., No. 165, 9-20-74.

[102]Ohio Drill & Tool Co. v. Johnson, (1974) CA-6, 498 F.2d 186; Davidge v. White, (1974) DC S.C.N.Y., 377 F. Supp. 1084; Roman v. Kantron, Inc., (1967) N.Y.S. Ct., N.Y.L.J., 5-15-67, p. 17; Hoggan & Hall & Higgins, Inc. v. Hall, (1966) Utah S. Ct., 414 P. 2d 89.

[103]Selheimer v. Manganese Corporation of America, (1966) Pa. S. Ct., 224 A. 2d 634.

[104]McGlynn v. Schultz, (1966) N.J.S.Ct., 218 A. 2d 408, aff'd. (1967) Super. Ct. App., 231 A. 2d 386.

[105]Heit v. Bixby, (1967) DC E.D. Mo., 276 F. Supp. 217.

[106]Kalmanash v. Smith, (1943) N.Y. Ct. of App., 291 N.Y. 51 N.E. 2d 681.

[107]Ady v. Weicker Transfer & Storage Co., (1935 Colo. 5 Ct., 97) Colo. 230, 48 P.2d 807.

them, no deposit was offered, and no evidence of authority to make the offer was apparent; (2) the lower offer which was accepted had been pending for about a month and was conditioned on acceptance by the date of the meeting and would be withdrawn thereafter.[108]

Directors are not liable for having the corporation buy a block of its shares at premium prices to fend off purchase by outsiders that they believed posed a threat to the corporation's continued existence; their belief was reasonable when based on personal investigation and competent professional advice.[109]

Directors' decision (1) to issue stock rights to raise money needed by corporation, but preserving minority shareholders' preemptive rights, and (2) to sell some of the corporation's property to controlling stockholder in an arm's length transaction are matters of business judgment with which a court will not interfere; there is no showing of fraud, negligence or bad faith.[110]

However, if they act clearly beyond their powers, and the result is loss to the corporation, they are personally liable.[111] They are bound to care for the corporate property, and conduct and manage its affairs in good faith, and for a violation of these duties, resulting in waste or loss of its assets, they are liable and must account in the same manner as other trustees.

Examples: A Corporation cannot use its stated capital to buy its own shares from stockholders in order to resolve disputes among them; it can do that only to resolve controversies between corporation and its stockholders, and so corporation's creditor can hold directors liable, unless they show they voted for the purchase in good faith and with due care, and creditor can also hold selling stockholder liable if he sells to corporation knowing that payment is from stated capital.[112]

A Director who voted to sell his 10 percent to a company for $280,000, when it owed $60,000 to a creditor, and the effect of such sale impaired capital and rendered the corporation insolvent was properly sued in an action to recover the debt.[113]

Directors of a defunct corporation who alleged that all known corporate debts were paid, were liable to a creditor whose claim was in litigation during dissolution proceedings, when they distributed assets to themselves as stockholders without providing for payment of his claim.[114]

---

[108]Selama-Dindings Plantations, Ltd. v. Durham, (1963) DC S.D. Ohio 216 F. Supp. 104, aff'd., (1964) CA-6, 337 F. 2d 949.
[109]Cheff v. Mathes, (1964) Del. S. Ct., 41 Del. Ch. 494, 199 A. 2d 548.
[110]Greenbaum v. American Metal Climax, Inc., (1967) N.Y. App. Div., 278 N.Y.S. 2d 123.
[111]Borbein, Young & Co. v. Cirese, (1966) Mo. Ct. of App., 401 S.W. 2d 940; Sajer, Trustee v. Pitzer, (1964) Pa. Com. Pls., 36 D. & C. 2d 33.
[112]England v. Christensen, (1966) Calif. Dist. Ct. of App., 243 A.C.A. 478, 52 Cal. Rptr. 402.
[113]Patterson Heating v. Durable Construction, (1972) Ill. App. Ct., 3 Ill. App. 3d 437.
[114]Hoover v. Galbraith, (1972) Calif. S. Ct., 7 Cal. 3d 519.

However, creditors could not sue directors and officers for money damages for transferring all corporate assets to another corporation allegedly to wipe out their claims, when the statute under which suit was brought did not enumerate that type of action.[115]

Directors of a corporation are liable with the corporation for its torts in which they participate. They are not liable for torts in which they do not participate if they are not guilty of culpable negligence in allowing the commission of the torts.[116]

Knowledge of corporate affairs: Liability is imposed on a director for wrongful acts only if he has knowledge, actual or imputed, of such acts. Therefore, in order for a director to know what responsibility rests upon him, and to what extent care and diligence will be required of him, he must know to what extent he is charged with knowledge of the affairs of the corporation. Directors are charged with knowledge of the corporate charter and by-laws, and with such knowledge of the corporate affairs as they would have acquired by due attention to their duties.[117] Directors are not held as a matter of law to know all of the affairs of the corporation, or all the transactions or business conducted by the corporation, or at all times to know just what its books and papers contain, and such knowledge cannot be imputed to them for the purpose of charging them with liability.[118] In deciding upon corporate action to be taken, directors may rely upon data supplied by subordinates and employees.[119] But such reliance does not always excuse them from liability, if it is shown they did not rely in good faith and did not exercise due diligence in verifying the accuracy of the data.[120]

Nature of liability of directors: The liability of directors who have concurred in wrongful acts, or who are responsible for wrongful acts because of gross negligence or failure to object upon learning of a wrongful act, is joint and several for the loss suffered by the corporation. The general rule is that if a loss has been caused by misappropriation of the funds of a corporation to purposes unauthorized by its charter, or by culpable negligence, or by a conversion of funds, all the officers of the corporation who

---

[115]Ali Baba Creations, Inc. v. Congress Textile Printers, Inc., (1973) N.Y. App. Div., 343 N.Y.S. 2d 712.

[116]Aeroglide Corp. v. Zeh, (1962) CA-2, 301 F. 2d 420.

[117]Heit v. Bixby, (1967) DC E.D.Mo., 276 F. Supp. 217; Martin v. Webb, (1884) 110 U.S. 7; Folsom v. Smith, (1915) Me. S. Ct., 113 Me. 83, 92 A. 1003. But see Burt v. The Irvine Co., Calif. Dist. Ct. of App., 47 Cal. Rptr. 392.

[118]Goff v. Emde, (1928) Ohio App. Ct., 32 Ohio App. 216, 167 N.E. 698.

[119]Graham v. Allis-Chalmers Mfg. Co., (1963) Del. S. Ct., 188 A.2d 125.

[120]This is particularly true in fixing directors' liabilities under the federal securities laws. See full discussion in Prentice-Hall *Corporation* and Prentice-Hall *Securities Regulations*.

are chargeable with the fault which occasioned the loss are liable for the entire misappropriation without regard to the degree of dereliction of which each is guilty.[121]

Liability when directors act on professional advice: Directors sometimes must make decisions that call for specialized knowledge they do not have—for example, a business deal may raise a legal or accounting problem. If the directors get such advice, does reliance on it absolve them from personal liability if the advice turns out to be wrong? The answer is generally yes, provided the director acts in good faith.[122] And, as one authority points out, provided the advice given encompasses the whole problem.[123]

Statutes in most states specifically exonerate directors from liability for improperly declaring dividends if they, in good faith, rely on the books of account of the corporation, or statements prepared by its officers or by independent public accountants.[124] The American Bar Association Model Business Corporation Act recommends such a provision [§43].

In some states a director is not liable for damages resulting from his actions when he relies in good faith on the written opinion of counsel to his corporation.

Liability of directors resulting from improper accumulation of earnings under the Internal Revenue Code: Directors should have a general knowledge of the main principles of taxation; their decisions upon many of the financial problems which come before the board will have a material effect upon the tax liability of the company.

Under certain circumstances, directors may become personally liable to the corporation as a result of "unnecessary" taxes imposed upon the corporation. The danger of personal liability is particularly present where penalty taxes have been imposed upon the corporation under the Internal Revenue Code [Sec. 531, 1954 Code].[125]

Penalty tax liability: The above section of the Internal Revenue Code levies a penalty tax on corporations that keep more earnings than are reasonably needed in the business for the purpose of enabling their stock-

---

[121]Briggs v. Spaulding, (1891) 141 U.S. 132; Federbush v. Federbush, (1949) N.Y.S.Ct., 88 N.Y.S. 2d 185.

[122]Gilbert v. Burnside, (1962) N.Y. App. Div., 13 A.D. 2d 982, 216 N.Y.S. 2 2d 430, aff'd., (1962) Ct. of App., 11 N.Y. 2d 960, 229 N.Y.S. 2d 10, 183 N.E. 2d 325.

[123]"Personal Liabilities of Corporate officers and Directors," by Mortimer Feuer, Prentice-Hall, Inc., Englewood Cliffs, N.J. (1974), pages 97-99.

[124]E.g. Del G.C.L. secs. 172-174. This statute permits directors also to rely on reports of appraisers they select to determine the value of the corporation's assets and the amount of liabilities.

[125]J.K. Lasser and R.S. Holzman: "Personal Liability of Directors for Section 102 (now Sec. 531—*Ed.*) Surtaxes," in the July, 1948 issue of "The Controller" published by Controllers Institute of America, N.Y.; see also 61 HARVARD LAW REV. 1058 (1948).

holders to escape taxation on dividends. The fact that a corporation accumulates earnings instead of paying them out in dividends does not necessarily mean that the accumulated earnings tax will be incurred. Such accumulations may be justified, as, for example, to provide against contingencies or the hazards of the business, to set up necessary reserves, to finance an expansion program, to modernize or replace equipment and to increase inventory. But whether they are justified is a question of fact in each case.

If the corporation has to pay the tax there is a very definite possibility of personal liability of the directors to the corporation on the ground that they have been negligent in permitting the corporation to become liable. The case against the directors may be even stronger where they also are stockholders since the contention will be made that they benefited personally through lower personal income taxes. While the decision in a tax case, brought by the government against the corporation, will not be binding in an action by the corporation (or stockholders in a derivative action) against directors, as a practical matter the directors may be placed in a very vulnerable position. The government will have built up its case to show an unreasonable accumulation of earnings and Revenue Agents' reports generally will show what personal taxes would have had to be paid if dividends had been declared.[126]

Liability to creditors: The fact that directors have mismanaged the corporation does not render them liable to creditors, unless they are made liable by the provisions of the articles of incorporation or by statute.[127]

The reason for this is that directors are the agents of the corporation and not of creditors. However, some courts consider the relationship of directors to creditors as one similar to that of trustee and trust beneficiary, and on that basis they have permitted creditors to proceed directly against directors who are guilty of neglect of duty.[128] A waiver by a creditor of his right to have a receiver appointed for a corporation is a sufficient consideration for the promise of an officer, director and stockholder of a corporation to pay the debt of the corporation to the creditor.[129] The corporation is a necessary party in an action by a judgment creditor against directors for allegedly appropriating to themselves all the assets of the corporation to avoid paying a judgment debt, since it is the one primarily injured by the alleged fraudulent acts, and the court will appoint a receiver to protect the rights of stockholders and creditors.[130]

[126]See Prentice-Hall *Federal Taxes* for law, regulations and complete discussion of the tax on accumulated earnings under Sec. 531.
[127]Sutton v. Reagan & Gee, (1966) Texas Ct. of Civ. App., 405 S.W. 2d 828.
[128]Sternberg v. Blaine, (1929) Ark. S. Ct., 179 Ark. 448, 17 S.W. 2d 286; Webb v. Cash, (1926) Wyo. S. Ct., 35 Wyo. 398, 250 P. 1.
[129]Allanson v. Frieder, (1940) Ill. App. Ct., 305 Ill. App. 484, 27 N.E. 2d 307.
[130]Underwood v. Stafford, (1967) N.C. S. Ct., 155 N.E. 2d 211.

A director is personally liable to a bondholder when his solvent corporation refuses to pay the bond at maturity date, and fails to satisfy a judgment obtained against it after its refusal to pay, but instead pays a bank loan on which the director is an accommodation endorser.[131] Directors of an insolvent corporation are personally liable to the corporation's judgment creditor when they pay themselves excessive salaries that deplete the corporation's assets; the corporation's pending counterclaim against the same judgment creditor is not a corporate asset to be counted in determining its solvency, when the claim is inchoate, uncertain and contested.[132] A corporation's judgment creditor can hold former stockholder-directors personally liable, when they caused the corporation to mortgage its assets, and to use the proceeds of that loan to buy back directors' shares, thereby in effect dissolving the corporation, appropriating its assets and making it unable to pay its bills to creditors.[133]

A corporation cannot use its stated capital to purchase its own shares from stockholders in order to resolve disputes among them, but only to resolve controversies between the corporation and its stockholders, so a corporation's creditor can hold a selling stockholder liable if he sells to the corporation knowing that the payment is from stated capital, and can hold directors liable unless they show they voted for the sale in good faith and with due care.[134] A California judgment creditor can hold directors of an Oregon corporation doing business in-state personally liable when they approved a distribution of corporate assets without paying known debts, in violation of the Oregon statutes.[135]

Directors and officers are personally liable on their corporation's debts, incurred after the corporation forfeited its right to do business for failure to pay franchise taxes, when they approved invoices representing those debts.[136] But, if a corporation fails to file its annual reports on time, the directors' personal liability to the corporation's creditors is only for those debts the corporation incurs during the period of default, and they cannot be held liable on any contract the corporation made either before or after the default period.[137]

---

[131]Alberts v. Schneiderman, (1966) Fla. Dist. Ct. of App., 182 So. 2d 50.

[132]Glenmore Distilleries Company v. Seideman, (1967) DC E.D.N.Y., 267 F. Supp. 915; see also Patterson Heating v. Durable Construction, (1972) Ill. App. Ct., 3 Ill. App. 3d 437; Hoover v. Galbraith, (1972) Calif. S.Ct., 7 Cal. 3d 519; but see Ali Baba Creations, Inc. v. Congress Textile Printers, Inc., (1973) N.Y. App. Div., 343 N.Y.S. 2d 712, where use of improper statute by creditor as basis for his action barred suit against director.

[133]Burton Mill & Cabinet Works, Inc. v. Truemper, (1968) Texas Ct. of Civ. App., 422 S.W. 2d 825.

[134]England v. Christensen, (1966) Calif. Dist. Ct. of App., 243 A.C.A. 478.

[135]Barney v. Buswell, (1965) Calif. Dist. Ct. of App., 236 A.C.A. 230.

[136]First National Bank of Boston v. Silberstein, (1966) Texas S. Ct., 398 S.W. 2d 914.

[137]Mountain States Supply, Inc. v. Mountain States Feed and Livestock Company, (1967) Mont. S. Ct., 425 P. 2d 75.

This is particularly true in fixing directors' liabilities under the federal securities laws. See full discussion in Prentice-Hall *Corporation* and Prentice-Hall *Securities Regulation*.

Indemnification of directors and officers. Most states now have statutes permitting a corporation to indemnify the litigation expenses of its directors and officers in a successful defense of a derivative action against them. Even in the absence of such a statute, a corporation may be able to indemnify in some situations.[138]

The typical indemnification statute makes indemnification within certain limits an express power of the corporation. Thus, a corporation can indemnify within those limits whether or not it provides for indemnification in its charter, a by-law, or in a separate contract.

The limits are these: A corporation can indemnify its incumbent and former directors or officers and also persons who are serving or who have served at its request as directors or officers of other corporations in which it owns shares or of which it is a creditor. It has been held that the right to indemnify is not affected by the corporation's bankruptcy.[139] Indemnifiable expenses are those actually and reasonably incurred by the person indemnified in connection with the defense of any action, suit or proceeding, civil or criminal, in which he is made a party because he is or has been a director or officer. Such suits are sometimes termed suits questioning the director's or officer's official conduct. A suit did not question official conduct and thus indemnification was barred, when the suit questioned stock options and an employment contract granted a person before he became a director, and a by-law allowed indemnification only for litigation expenses in defending official conduct.[140] Also, a corporation need not indemnify directors and officers who incurred expenses in defending themselves in an action brought by the SEC alleging their violation of the Investment Act for personally dealing in stock held in their own company's portfolio, since indemnification only applies when they are defending themselves as directors or officers, not as individuals who allegedly personally profited from their own stock transactions.[141] A corporation does

---

[138]For example, indemnification has been allowed at common law even if there's no showing of any direct or tangible benefit to the corporation from the director's defense. In re E.C. Warner Co., (1950) Minn. S. Ct. 232 Minn. 207, 45 N.W. 2d 388. Some earlier cases, though, denied indemnification, absent benefit to the corporation or approval by the stockholders. Bailey v. Bush Terminal Co., (1944) N.Y. Ct. of App., 293 N.Y. 735, 56 N.E. 2d 739. In some states that have statutes covering the indemnification of directors and officers, there's a specific provision retaining the common law rights of indemnification as they apply to corporate personnel other than directors and officers. N.Y. B.C.L. sec. 721.

[139]Matter of R. & L. Engineering, (1961) DC S.D. Calif., Bankruptcy No. 94006-WB.

[140]Sorensen v. Overland Corp., (1957) Del. law, CA-3, 242 F. 2d 570.

[141]Tomash v. Midwest Technical Development Corporation, (1968) Minn. S. Ct., No. 160, 7-12-68.

not have to reimburse its directors for their litigation expenses, when it is shown their acts constituted misconduct.[142] Further, it has been held that a suit by a broker against an officer for preventing the broker from earning commissions on a sale of the corporation's stock did not question the officer's official conduct, and the officer's expenses thus were not indemnifiable.[143] Also, the defense of a right to an office, if successful, is indemnifiable.[144] A director can seek indemnification from his corporation for costs of defending a suit charging him with slander, even though the action has not yet been tried, when he claims that the alleged slanderous remarks were made by him while acting in the course of his duties.[145] In all instances, the directors must look to their corporation for indemnification; stockholders losing a derivative suit are not required to indemnify the directors.[146] And conversely, a corporation cannot recover from its directors for defending them in a stockholder's derivative action for fraud in which the corporation successfully resisted an attempt to upset a previous $1,100,000 settlement in its favor.[147]

The typical statute bars indemnification in relation to matters in which the director or officer is adjudged liable for negligence or misconduct in the performance of his duties to the corporation. On the other hand, it lets a corporation make indemnification arrangements that go beyond the statutory limits. For example, the new Delaware General Corporation Law allows a corporation to adopt special by-law provisions or enter into contracts providing that the statutory indemnification is not exclusive of any other rights to which those indemnified may be entitled.[148] Such arrangements, however, must be specifically provided for in the charter, a by-law, or in a resolution adopted by the shareholders after notice. Some statutes expressly bar any indemnification arrangements that go beyond the statutory limits.[149] In extreme situations, the courts may not permit indemnification: for example, when the person sought to be indemnified violated a statute that would be ineffectual unless a violator were personally liable.

Under a typical indemnification statute, the corporation should be able to indemnify the expenses of settling a suit, when the corporation has been advised by legal counsel that the suit was without substantial merit and that the settlement did not exceed the probable expenses of litigation.

---

[142]Teren v. Howard, (1963) CA-9, 322 F. 2d 949.
[143]Spring v. Moncrieff, (1958) N.Y.S. Ct., 10 Misc. 2d 731, 173 N.Y.S. 2d 86.
[144]Essential Enterprises Corp. v. Automatic Steel Products, Inc., (1960) 164 A 2nd 437, Del.
[145]Brokate v. Hehr Mfg. Co., (1966) Calif. Dist. Ct. of App., 243 A.C.A. 133, 52 Cal. Rptr. 672.
[146]De Mendez v. Davis, (1965) N.Y.S. Ct., N.Y.L.J., 6-4-65, p. 18.
[147]Alleghany Corp. v. Kirby, (1963) DC S.D.N.Y., 218 F. Supp. 164.
[148]Del. G.C.L. sec. 145(f).
[149]*E.g.*, N.Y. B.C.L. sec. 721.

However, when the statute does not spell out the power to indemnify upon a settlement, it may be advisable for the by-laws to provide for indemnification for settlement payments or expenses.

In some states, the indemnification statute is not self executing. That is, there is no right to indemnification unless the corporation itself provides for it in the charter, the by-laws, or in a specific resolution. In some states, a corporation *must* indemnify in certain circumstances. However, some of these states require court approval before indemnification becomes mandatory.

Courts in states with indemnification statutes have held that a corporation need not indemnify its president who successfully defended on the merits a suit for fraudulent sale of stock when his active participation in the sale showed lack of good faith;[150] that a corporation need not indemnify a director not accused of wrongdoing, but made a defendant only to permit an injunction against board action and who aided the suing stockholders;[151] and that a corporation need not indemnify a director when the complaint against him is dismissed, not on the merits, but because the suing stockholder participated with the director in the wrongs complained of.[152] On the other hand, the fact that plaintiffs have been reimbursed does not bar reimbursement of successful derivative defendants,[153] and the courts have permitted indemnification though the suit was dismissed for the suing stockholder's failure to post security for the corporation's costs,[154] and when the suit was partly dismissed because of the running of the statute of limitations and partly by consent.[155] The courts have also ruled that an attorney cannot sue for indemnification; for example, a corporation cannot pay counsel fees of an officer sued for breach of duty in a derivative suit, when it is not shown that counsel's services were of any benefit to the corporation.[156] Only the director can sue[157] and an ordinary employee has no right to indemnification under the statute, when the statute does not cover employees.[158]

Further, dismissal without prejudice of a stockholder's action against a director solely to avoid duplicity of actions did not entitle the officer to

[150]Peo. v. Ulran Min. Corp., (1961) N.Y. App. Div., 13 A.D. 2d 419, 216 N.Y.S. 2d 985.
[151]Warnecke v. 40 Wall St. Bldg., Inc., (1959) N.Y.S. Ct., 16 Misc. 2d 467, 183 N.Y.S. 2d 925.
[152]Diamond v. Diamond, (1954) N.Y. Ct. of App. 307 N.Y. 268, 120 N.E. 2d 819, rearg. den., 307 N.Y. 804, 121 N.E. 2d 626.
[153]Cohn v. Columbia Pictures Corp., (1952) N.Y.S. Ct., 117 N.Y.S. 2d 809.
[154]Tyler v. Consumers Ass'n., (1962) N.Y.S. Ct., N.Y.L.J., 6-21-62, p. 10.
[155]Dornan v. Humphrey, (1951) N.Y. App. Div., 278 A.D. 1010, 106 N.Y.S. 2d 142.
[156]Sandfield v. Goldstein, (1970) N.Y. App. Div., 308 N.Y.S. 2d 25, aff'd. (1970) N.Y. Ct. of App., 28 N.Y. 2d 794, 270 N.E. 2d 723.
[157]Buchman & Buchman v. Lanston Industries, Inc., (1960) N.Y.S. Ct., 25 Misc. 2d 8181, 200 N.Y.S. 2d 445.
[158]Gilbert v. Curtiss-Wright Corp., (1943) N.Y.S. Ct., 179 Misc. 641, 38 N.Y.S. 2d 548.

indemnification, since the dismissal was not a vindication on the merits, nor did it result from a technical defense that made it unnecessary to defend on the merits.[159] Also, a state law against contributions between tort-feasors does not apply to a director against whom damages are assessed for violating his fiduciary duty to his corporation by resigning rather than resisting a raid on the corporation; damages he pays belong to the corporation, so that he can get indemnity from other directors who were similarly passive.[160] In addition, it has also been held that while corporate directors are entitled to indemnity pendent lite in New Jersey, former directors of a Texas corporation cannot claim indemnity pending the outcome of a derivative action, when both Texas law and the corporation's by-laws provide indemnity only for actual and necessary expenses incurred.[161]

Indemnification insurance. During the past year many states have amended the indemnification sections of their corporation laws to permit a corporation to obtain insurance at its expense to protect anyone who might be indemnified under the state's statute, *and also* to insure against liabilities which it would be beyond the power of the corporation to indemnify against under the statute.[162] Thus, for example, a corporation may pay premiums on an insurance policy which indemnifies an executive against liability for negligence in the performance of his duty to the corporation.

Policies are available that cover suits against officers and directors for alleged wrongful acts in respect to duties owing to the corporation. These can be policies either directly insuring the officers and directors if there is no indemnification, or making payment to the corporation itself, if it has indemnified the officers and directors.

These latter policies ordinarily will call for the covered individual to pay some of the premiums, say 10%, and the corporation to pay the rest. They also have a deductible provision.

However, even when these policies cover against liability, they do not cover intentional wrongdoing or fraud. But the line between negligence and the kind of recklessness that can amount to fraud is very nebulous. The result is that although, for example, such policies cover actions brought under the securities laws from violation of either the antifraud or short-swing sections of those laws, recent decisions throw doubt on whether these policies will reimburse those found liable under these sections.[163] But

---

[159]Galdi v. Berg, (1973) DC D. Del., 359 F. Supp. 698.

[160]DePinto v. Landoe, (1969) Ariz., CA-9, 411 F. 2d 297.

[161]Gross v. Taxas Plastics, Inc., (1972) DC D.N.J., 344 F. Supp. 564.

[162]For example: Calif. G.C.L. sec 830(h); Del. G.C.L. sec 145(g); Ga. B.C.C. sec. 22-202; sec. 22-717; Kans. G.C.C. S.B. 500, L.'68 sec. (g); La. B.C.L. sec. 41; sec. 83; N.J. B.C.A. sec. 14A:3-5 (proposed); Pa. B.C.L. sec. 410; Va. S.C.A. sec. 13.1-3.1(g).

[163]Escott v. BarCris Construction Corporation, (1968) DC S.D.N.Y., 283 F. Supp. 643.

a corporation was liable for defense fees when a director was sued for statements he made against a competitor, since the director acted in good faith and for the best interest of the corporation and the corporation's by-laws provided for such indemnification; director's possession of liability insurance did not relieve the corporation of the duty to indemnify him against the cost of defending the suit, even though the corporation claimed that such cost was his insurer's primary obligation.[164]

Lloyds and some American companies also issue policies covering underwritings. One kind protects a specific underwriter for all issues in which the firm participates. Another kind covers those participating in a particular underwriting—but not accountants and lawyers. But even here coverage is in doubt. A court in a recent case threw out an indemnification agreement between the issuer and the underwriter. It said that kind of agreement violated public policy because it minimized the penalty for breaching the law and so lessened the deterrent effect.[165] Logically, that same argument could apply to insurance contracts that protect against the consequences of violation. No case has yet specifically so said—but that may be the next step.

In the light of increasing risks imposed by courts on corporate executives and directors, accountants and underwriters, more are turning to insurance for protection. But the increasingly expensive premiums, and the doubtful limits of the policies' coverage may make indemnification insurance economically unattractive.

Even when there is no specific statutory authority, it is advisable, if permissible, to include an indemnification or reimbursement provision in the articles of incorporation or in the by-laws. Whether this can be done depends upon: (1) policy of state departments in accepting articles of incorporation including the provision; and (2) attitude of the courts in sustaining the provision. Most of the state departments allow articles of incorporation to include an indemnification provision, even though the statutes are silent on the subject. Some courts have allowed reimbursement, particularly when the successful defense of the suit has preserved corporate property.[166] But the weight of authority, numerically at least, is against such reimbursement where there is no statute authorizing it.[167]

The by-law that permits indemnification of directors and officers usually provides:

1. They must not be guilty of negligence or misconduct in their duties.

---

[164]Dankoff v. Bowling Proprietors Ass'n. of America, Inc., (1972) N.Y.S. Ct., 331 N.Y.S. 2d 109.

[165]Globus v. Law Research Service, Inc., (1968) DC S.D.N.Y., 287 F. Supp. 188.

[166]Solimine v. Hollander, (1940) 128 N.J. Eq. 228, 16 A.2d 203.

[167]See Bailey v. Bush Terminal Co., (1944) 293 N.Y. 735, 56 N.E. 2d 739; New York Dock Co. v. McCollum, (1939) 173 N.Y. Misc. 106, 16 N.Y.S. 2d 844.

2. The liability against which they are indemnified includes attorney's fees and other expenses.
3. They are indemnified whether or not they are in office at the time the expenses are incurred.
4. Their right to indemnification passes to their heirs, executors, and administrators.
5. If the suit is compromised, it must be with the approval of the board of directors.
6. The indemnification may be against liability incurred for acts committed prior, as well as subsequent, to adoption of the by-laws.
7. The right to indemnificaiton is not exclusive of other rights the directors and officers may have as a matter of law.

Notation of director's dissent in minutes. A director who is present at a meeting at which some action is taken that he believes to be against the best interests of the corporation should see that his dissent is noted in the minutes, for, unless his disapproval is recorded, he will be deemed to have concurred in the action. He should read over the minutes of meetings held during his absence and request notation of any disagreement he may have with action taken at the meeting. If he remains a director some time after the action is taken without requiring his dissent to be entered in the minutes, he is deemed to have concurred in the action.

Contracts in which directors are interested. A director has the right to enter into a contract with the corporation, provided that he deals openly with the corporation and that the contract is properly authorized.[168] Thus, if a contract between a corporation and an interested director is authorized by a disinterested majority or quorum of the directors, it is valid, and is voidable only for unfairness, unreasonableness, or fraud.[169] The director has the right to lend money to the corporation and to take a mortgage as security.[170] While a contract between a director and the corporation is subject to severest scrutiny, it will be upheld if the director has been open, fair, and honest in his dealing with the corporation, and has gained no advantage that injures the corporation.[171] A contract between a director and the corporation will be presumed to be valid. But the burden of proof is on

---

[168]In re Country Club Bldg. Corp., (1937) 91 F. 2d 713; Barber v. Kolowich, (1938) 283 Mich. 97, 277 N.W. 189; Swenson v. G.O. Miller Tel. Co., (1937) 200 Minn. 354, 274 N.W. 222; Federal Mortgage Co. v. Simes, (1932) 210 Wis. 139, 245 N.W. 169.

[169]Lipkin v. Jacoby, (1964) Del. Ch. Ct., 222 A. 2d 572; McKittrick v. Ark. Central Ry. Co. (1894) 152 U.S. 473, 14 S. Ct. 661; Epstein v. U.S., (1949) CA-6, 174 F. 2d 754 (Mich. law).

[170]Arn v. Bradshaw, (1939) 108 F.2d 125; Scully v. Colonial Trust Co., (1929) 105 N.J. Eq. 309, 147 A. 776; Weissman v. Weissman, Inc., (1955) 382 Pa. 189, 114 A. 2d 797.

[171]Mayflower Hotel Stockholders' Protective Committee v. Mayflower Hotel Corp., (1951) 193 F.2d 666; Saunders v. Russell's Inc., (1939) 173 Va. 125, 3 S.E. 2d 198; Claus v. Farmers & Stockgrowers State Bank, (1936) 51 Wyo. 45, 63 P. 2d 781.

the director to show that it is fair and honest.[172] So, even though profits gained by a director in commercial dealings with his corporation can be held in constructive trust for the corporation, they will not be when it is shown the contract was fair, and, therefore, the director can keep the benefit of his bargain.[173] The courts will set aside contracts that violate the director's fiduciary duties and will hold the director accountable for the profit.[174] Thus, where a director purchased a plant, knowing that it was needed for corporate purposes, and thereafter sold it to the corporation at a profit, the corporation recovered the profit made by the director.[175]

Also, a corporate director was guilty of self-dealing when he gave a construction contract to a construction company of which he was sole shareholder without disclosing it to other officers; it was immaterial that a corporate resolution authorized him to negotiate the contract.[176] But a receiver cannot set aside a sale of a mining claim to the corporation by a director on the ground that she had made a profit on it, when (1) she had bought the claim long before the sale and (2) the price paid by the corporation was fair.[177]

In entering a contract with an interested director, authorization should only be given at a meeting of the directors at which there is a quorum present, not counting the interested director.[178] Thus, a contract with a retiring director to retain him as an independent consultant for life at an annual fee together with his covenant not to compete, also for life, is enforceable, since (1) there is adequate consideration, (2) it is fair to the corporation, (3) it was approved by a vote of disinterested directors and (4) it was of a kind directors had authority to make without shareholder approval.[179]

Further, a director who sublets restaurant premises to his own corporation is not barred from evicting it when it cannot pay its rent.[180] And an agreement is not void as against public policy because it provides that the president will resign and the other directors will assume his personal obligation, when that personal obligation is really a corporate one, being a guarantee of a corporate loan.[181] On the other hand, a director who returned to his corporation stock he received for sale to it of certain property because

[172]Epstein v. United States, (1949) 174 F. 2d 754; Gord v. Iowana Farms Milk Co.,(1953) 243 Iowa 1007, 60 N.W. 2d 820; Johnson v. Kaiser, (1937) 104 Mont. 261, 65 P. 2d 1179.
[173]The Tennessee Dressed Beef Co. v. Hall and Hall, (1974) Tenn. Ct. of App., 7-26-74.
[174]Knox Glass Bottle Co. v. Underwood, (1956) (Miss.) 89 So. 2d 799.
[175]Jno. Dunlop's Sons, Inc. v. Dunlop, (1939) 172 N.Y. Misc. 66, 14 N.Y.S. 2d 452.
[176]Talbot v. James, (1972) W. Va. S.Ct., 190 S.E. 2d 759.
[177]Schoff v. Clough, (1963) Nev. S.Ct., 380 P. 2d 464.
[178]Nicholson v. Kingery, (1927) Wyo. S.Ct., 37 Wyo. 299, 261 P. 122.
[179]Osborne v. The Locke Steel Chain Company, (1965) Conn. S. Ct., 218 A. 2d 526.
[180]Reed v. South Shore Foods, Inc. (1964) Calif. Dist. Ct. of App., 40 Cal. Rptr. 575.
[181]Cox v. Berry, (1967) Utah S.Ct., 431 P.2d 575

of his failure to disclose his interest in that property cannot later get back the stock.[182] Also, a court will set aside the sale of a corporation's real estate to a director who paid for it with a long-term, non-interest-bearing note; however, he can offset any taxes and other expenses he paid while he held the property.[183]

In cases involving contracts authorized by interlocking directorates, if the corporation entering into contracts with each other have only a minority on the board of directors in common, the rule, according to weight of authority, is that the transaction can only be voided upon a showing of unfairness or bad faith.[184] The Court would not enjoin a stockholders' meeting called to approve a merger on the ground of (1) director's alleged failure to disclose his interest in an investment banking firm that was promoting the merger, when it was shown he would not share in the banking firm's profit from the merger transaction, and (2) the alleged participation by the interlocking directors in the plan was merely one of discussion and they did not vote on it.[185]

Voting on contracts by interested director. If a director is personally interested in a matter that is being authorized by the board, he should not vote upon the question.[186] According to the decisions of most courts, where the director votes on a contract affecting his own private interest, and where his vote is necessary in order to carry the resolution or motion authorizing the action, the contract is voidable at the option of the corporation, regardless of whether or not the contract is fair or beneficial,[187] provided that the option to avoid the contract is exercised within a reasonable time.[188] For example, a director is an interested party to a resolution awarding him stock, and so his vote on such a resolution invalidates it if it was needed to pass it; however, he can vote as a stockholder to ratify the resolution, but if he does not and his abstention prevents approval by a

---

[182]Rosenthal v. Four Corners Oil & Minerals Co., (1965) Colo. S.Ct., 403 P. 2d 762.

[183]The House of Campbell, Inc. v. Campbell, (1965) La. Ct. of App., 172 So.2d 727.

[184]Geddes v. Anaconda Copper Min. Co., (1902) 254 U.S. 590, 41 S. Ct. 209.

[185]Evans v. Armour & Co., (1965) DC E.D. Pa., 241 F. Supp. 705.

[186]Sundlun v. Noank Shipbuilding Co., (1948) (R.I.) 61 A. 2d 665; Elggren v. Woolley, (1924) 64 Utah 183, 228 P. 906; Stoiber v. Miller Brewing Co., (1950) 257 Wis. 13, 42 N.W. 2d 144.

[187]Twin-Lick Oil Co. v. Marbury, (1875) 91 U.S. 329; Cathedral Estates, Inc. v. Taft Realty Corp., (1955) 228 F. 2d 85; Mobile Land Improvement Co. v. Goss, (1904) 142 Ala. 520, 39 So. 229; Landstreet v. Meyer, (1947) 201 Miss. 887, 29 So. 2d 653; Jones v. Morrison, (1883) 31 Minn. 140, 16 N.W. 854. In Sacajawea Lumber & Shingle Co. v. Skookum Lumber Co., (1921) 116 Wash. 75, 198 P. 112, it was held that the board of directors could not authorize the president to dismiss a legal action in which the corporation was plaintiff, where the vote of an interested director was necessary to pass the resolution. The interested director in this case was one of the defendants and a director in the plaintiff corporation.

[188]National Lock Co. v. Hogland, (1939) 101 F. 2d 576; New Blue Point Mining Co. v. Weissbein, (1926) 198 Cal. 261, 244 P. 325.

majority of the outstanding stock, the ratification is invalid and he must return the stock he received from the corporation.[189]

Where, however, a contract in which a director is interested is authorized by a disinterested majority or quorum of the directors, it is voidable, according to the weight of authority, only upon a showing of unfairness, unreasonableness, or fraud.[190] If the good faith of the director is challenged, the court will scrutinize the contract and its origin with extraordinary care.[191] (See "Rights of interested directors and officers to vote on compensation," page 349 in Chapter 11.)

Tests to determine whether directors are acting within their powers. In determining whether directors are acting within their powers, the following questions should be asked: (1) Is the act within the powers of the corporation? (2) Is the transaction prohibited by the charter or by-laws? (3) Is the transaction reasonably suitable and necessary for the conduct of the business for which the corporation was created and organized? (4) Is the act or transaction being performed in good faith, or as a mere cloak to cover some illegal or fraudulent act? (5) In carrying out the powers of the corporation, are the directors limited by a statutory or charter provision requiring the consent of the stockholders? (6) Is the act one conferred by statute on the stockholders?

General powers of board of directors. The board of directors, as the governing body of the corporation, has the power to transact any business which the corporation itself has the power to perform.[192] The board cannot increase or decrease corporate powers. Thus, a corporation does not lose the power to perform a certain act, merely because the board has declared by resolution that such action will not be taken.[193]

Generally, the board of directors has as much control over the affairs of the corporation as an individual has over his own business, but no more.[194] When directors act within the law, their authority in the conduct of

---

[189]Crass v. Budd, (1966) N.Y.S. Ct., N.Y.L.J., 12-5-66, p. 18, N.Y.S. Ct., (1967) N.Y.L.J., 3-10-67, p. 16.

[190]Todd v. Temple Hospital Ass'n, (1928) 96 Cal. App. 42, 273 P. 595; Nicholson v. Kingery, (1927) 37 Wyo. 299, 261 P. 122. See, however, an early New York case, holding that a contract made by an interested director is not enforceable against the corporation even if it is authorized by a disinterested majority, irrespective of whether or not the contract was a fair one. Munson v. Syracuse, Geneva & Corning R.R., (1886) 103 N.Y. 59, 8 N.E. 355.

[191]Pepper v. Litton, (1939) 308 U.S. 295, 60 S. Ct. 238; Hallam v. Indianola Hotel Co., (1881) 56 Iowa 178, 9 N.W. 111; Knudsen v. Burdett, (1939) 67 S.D. 20, 287 N.W. 673; Central Bldg. Co. v. Keystone Shares Corp., (1936) 185 Wash. 645, 56 P. 2d 697; Gall v. Cowell, (1937) 118 W. Va. 263, 190 S.E. 130.

[192]Templeman v. Grant, (1924) 75 Colo. 519, 227 P. 555; Henderson Lumber Co. v. Chatham Bank & Trust Co., (1924) 33 Ga. App. 196, 125 S.E. 867; Hall v. Woods. (1927) 325 Ill. 114, 156 N.E. 258; Elggren v. Woolley, (1924) 64 Utah 183, 228 P. 906.

[193]National Lock Co. v. Hogland, (1939) 101 F.2d 576; Riddle v. Riddle, (1948) 142 N.J. Eq. 147, 59 A. 2d 599.

[194]Merchants Life Ins. Co. v. Griswold, (1919) Tex. Civ. App. 212 S.W. 807; Berkeley County Court v. Martinsburg & Potomac Turnpike Co., (1922) 94 W. Va. 246, 115 S.E. 448.

the business is absolute.[195] Thus, only directors can authorize the filing of a petition in bankruptcy for their corporation, and so a 33-percent stockholders' petition will be dismissed if directors do not authorize it.[196] Questions of business policy must be determined by the judgment of a majority of the board of directors. In the absence of bad faith or abuse of powers, the courts will not interefere with the corporate management.[197] The directors are free to change the policies of the company, provided they keep within its charter powers and do not change the essential character of the business in which the stockholders have invested their money.[198] If there is no bad faith, breach of trust, or abuse of powers, the courts will not interfere with corporate management.[199] For example, directors and officers of a newspaper corporation were not guilty of misconduct, breach of trust, and misuse of corporate assets when they purchased a subsidiary's stock at $260 per share and sold it to the Employee Stock Trust at $130 per share, when the aim was to promote employee stock ownership, improve employee relationship and preclude takeover by outsiders; the transaction was lawful, approved by directors and majority stockholders as necessary to protect corporate policy, and benefited stockholders, employees and public.[200] Also, directors had authority to enter into a ten-year employment contract with a corporate employee, and when they discharged him after six months they breached such contract.[201]

Further, directors who in good faith believe that an attempt is being made to gain control of their corporation can incur reasonable expenses to investigate such information and to advise stockholders of the results of the investigation, even though no proxy contest has been started.[202] Minority stockholders of a parent corporation cannot bar it from settling claims made against its subsidiary even though there is no showing that the parent has any legal obligation to pay the subsidiary's debts, when (1) the parent's directors, in exercise of their business judgment, found that the parent's

---

[195]Price v. Gurney, (1945) 324 U.S. 100, 65 S. Ct. 513; SEC v. Transamerica Corp., (1946) DC D. Del., 67 F. Supp. 326; Ayres v. Hadaway, (1942) 303 Mich. 589, 6 N.W. 2d 905.

[196]Matter of Raljoed Realty Co., Inc. (1967) DC S.D.N.Y., 277 F. Supp. 225.

[197]Greenbaum v. American Metal Climax, Inc., (1967) N.Y. App. Div., 278 N.Y.S. 2d 123; D. Kaltman & Co., Inc. v. Burrows, (1967) Del. Ch. Ct., N.Y.L.J., 10-17-67, p.18, N.Y.L.J., 10-18-67, p. 17; Sunset Farms, Inc. v. Superior Ct., (1935) 9 Cal. App. 2d 389, 50 P. 2d 106; Brown v. Ins. Equities Corp., (1936) Del. Ct. Ch., 21 Del. Ch. 273, 187 A. 18: Chicago Bank of Commerce, (1932) CA-5, 61 F.2d 986.

[198]Solimine v. Hollander, (1940) 128 N.J. Eq. 228, 16 A. 2d 203.

[199]Feldman v. Pennroad Corp., (1946) 155 F. 2d 773; Regenstein v. J. Regenstein Co., (1957) (Ga.) 97 S.E. 2d 693; Carey v. Dalgarn Constr. Con., (1930) 171 La. 246, 130 So. 344; Warren v. Fitzgerald, (1948) 189 Md. 476, 56 A.2d 827; Smith v. Banister, (1940) 127 N.J. Eq. 385, 13 A. 2d 485; Chapman v. Troy Laundry Co., (1935) 87 Utah 15, 47 P. 2d 1054.

[200]The Herald Company, (1972) CA-10, 472 F. 2d 1081.

[201]Fulton v. Walking Horse Breeders Association of America, (1972) Tenn. Ct. of App., 476 S.W. 2d 644.

[202]Selama-Dindings Plantations, Ltd. v. Durham, (1963) DC S.D. Ohio, 216 F. Supp. 104, aff'd. (1964) CA-6, 377 F. 2d 949.

world-wide reputation and good will would be irreparably damaged by its subsidiary's failure to honor its obligations, and (2) the settlement of the subsidiary's debts would not in any way affect or impair the parent's ability to meet its own obligations.[203] Further, an employment agreement made by the board of directors to hire an individual as "general manager and chief operating officer" for five years is valid, even though the directors cannot bind a later board to continue him as president.[204] Minority stockholders cannot set aside a stock option granted to the corporation's chief executive officer on the ground that it was improvidently granted and gave him a windfall, when (1) the option was part of a plan applying to all other key officers, (2) it was granted by the board in the exercise of its discretion, and (3) the officer's services to the corporation furnished a sufficient consideration to negate any implication of fraud.[205]

Express, incidental, and implied powers of corporations. Every corporation has three classes of powers—express, incidental, and implied.

The express powers are those specifically given to it by the corporation laws or other applicable statutes of the state in which it is organized and by the provisions of its charter; they are concerned largely with the purposes and business for which the corporation was organized.[206]

The incidental powers are those that are customarily inherent in the very nature of corporate existence,[207] such as the power of corporate succession, or the right to continuing existence irrespective of changes in corporate membership;[208] the power to sue[209] and be sued;[210] the power to purchase, hold, and convey real and personal property for corporate objects;[211] the power to have a common seal;[212] the power to make by-laws to govern the corporation.[213]

---

[203]Helmann v. American Express Co., (1967) N.Y.S. Ct., N.Y.L.J., 3-29-67, p. 19.

[204]Streett v. Laclede-Christy Co., (1966) Mo.S. Ct., 409 S.W. 2d 691.

[205]Saigh v. Busch, (1966) Mo. S. Ct., 403 S.W. 2d 559.

[206]Heinz v. National Bank of Commerce, (1916) 237 F. 942; Joyce v. First Nat'l Bank, (1936) Tex. Civ. App. 99 S.W. 2d 1092.

[207]Jacksonville, M.P. Ry. & Navigation Co. v. Hooper, (1896) 160 U.S. 514, 16 S. Ct. 379

[208]Andrews Bros. Co. v. Youngstown Coke Co., (1898) 86 F. 585; People v. Wayman, (1912) 256 Ill. 151, 99 N.E. 941; State v. Scott County Macadamized Road Co., (1907) 207 Mo. 54, 105 S.W. 752.

[209]American Power & Light Co. v. SEC, (1944) 143 F.2d 250; New York Society for the Suppression of Vice v. MacFadden Publications, Inc., (1932) 260 N.Y. 167, 183 N.E. 284; Allis-Chalmers Mfg. Co. v. Asmussen, (1942) 14 Wash. 2d 242, 127 P. 2d 681.

[210]Monarch Refriegerating Co. v. Farmers' Peanut Co., (1935) 74 F.2d 790; Knight v. Industrial Trust Co., (1937) 38 Del. 480, 193 A. 723; Kell Cleaners & Laundry v. Commercial Standard Ins. Co., (1947) Tex. Civ. App. 199 S.W. 2d 673.

[211]Medlinsky v. Premium Cut Beef Co., (1944) 317 Mass. 25, 57 N.E. 2d 31; Stott v. Stott Realty Co., (1929) 246 Mich. 261, 224 N.W. 621; In re Koffend's Will, (1944) 218 Minn. 206, 15 N.W. 2d 590; Coates & Hopkins Realty Co. v. Kansas City T. Ry., (1931) 328 Mo. 1118, 43 S.W. 2d 817; Strong v. Efficiency Apartment Corp., (1929) 159 Tenn. 337, 17 S.W. 2d 1.

[212]Bank of United States v. Dandridge, (1827) 25 U.S. 552; Ransom v. Stonington Sav. Bank, (1860) 13 N.J. Eq. 212.

[213]Peterson v. Gibson, (1901) 191 Ill. 365, 61 N.E. 127; Engelhardt v. Dime Sav. & Loan Ass'n, (1896) 148 N.Y. 281, 42 N.E. 710.

Implied powers are those which are not only reasonably necessary to enable the corporation to accomplish its objects, but include those that are appropriate, convenient, and suitable in carrying out the express purposes of the corporation.[214] For example, a corporation has the implied power to do acts in the usual course of business, such as to borrow money,[215] make ordinary contracts,[216] execute promissory notes,[217] checks, and other bills of exchange, take notes or other securities, and perform acts to protect or aid employees, and so forth. An act done under an implied power must have a direct and immediate relation to the exercise of an express power.[218] For example, in the absence of express statutory provision, corporations generally cannot make gifts of their property.[219] However, it has been held that corporations may validly make gifts and contributions to educational, religious, and charitable institutions.[220]

General powers of officers. The officers of a corporation are merely its agents, vested only with authority given them by the corporation or by statute.[221] They can bind the corporation only when acting within the scope of their authority.[222] Authority may be presumed if they are acting in the regular course of business.[223]

An officer may derive his power in one of the following ways: (1) by express statute, charter, or by-law provisions;[224] (2) by resolution or act of the board of directors, where powers are subject to delegation by the

---

[214]American Surety Co. v. 14 Canal St., Inc., (1931) 276 Mass. 119, 176 N.E. 785; McCraith v. National Mohawk Valley Bank, (1887) 104 N.Y. 414, 10 N.E. 862; Malone v. Lancaster Gas Light & Fuel Co., (1897) 182 Pa. St. 309, 37 A. 932; Malone v. Republic Nat'l Bank & Trust Co., (1934) (Tex. Civ. App.) 70 S.W. 2d 809.

[215]J.K. Syphon Ventilator Co. v. Hutton, (1915) 116 Ark. 545, 175 S.W. 30; Alton Mfg. Co. v. Garrett Biblical Institute, (1910) 243 Ill. 298, 90 N.E. 704; Taylor Feed Pen Co., v. Taylor Nat'l Bank, (1915) Tex. Civ. App. 181 S.W. 534.

[216]Squaw Gulch Mining & Milling Co. v. Kollberg, (1930) 36 Ariz. 442, 286 P. 822.

[217]Burnett's Lumber & Supply Co. v. Commercial Credit Corp., (1951) 211 Miss. 53, 51 So. 2d 54; Granite Hall Farms Corp. v. Virginia Trust Co., (1930) 154 Va. 333, 153 S.E. 841. However, in Schloss Bros. & Co. v. Monongahela Nat'l Bank, (1932) 60 F. 2d 365, it was held that a corporation has no implied power to issue or indorse commercial paper.

[218]Nicollet Nat'l bank v. Frisk-Turner Co., (1898) 71 Min. 413, 74 N.W. 160.

[219]Brayton v. Welch, (1941) 39 F. Supp. 537. For the power of a corporation to make a gift of property where no objection is made by stockholders or creditors, see Southern Hide Co. v. Best, (1932) 174 La. 748, 141 So. 449; Harry R. Roeder, Inc. v. Roeder, (1932) 236 App. Div. 87, 258 N.Y. Supp. 44.

[220]A.P. Smith Mfg. Co. v. Barlow, (1953) 13 N.J. 145, 98 A. 2d 581. See also Memorial Hospital Ass'n v. Pacific Grape Products Co., (1955) 45 Cal. 2d 634, 290 P.2d 481, rev'g, (1954) 277 P.2d 878.

[221]Anderson-Tully Lumber Co. v. Gillett Lumber Co., (1922) 155 Ark. 224, 244 S.W. 26; Henderson Lumber Co. v. Chatham Bank & Trust Co., (1924) 33 Ga. App. 196, 125 S.E. 867; Moll v. Roth Co., (1915) 77 Ore. 593, 152 P. 235.

[222]Johnson v. Maryland Trust Co., (1939) 176 Md. 557, 6 A.2d 383; Klein v. Journal Sq. Bank Bldg. Co., (1932) 110 N.J. Ch. 607, 160 A. 812.

[223]Electronic Development Co. v. Robson, (1947) 148 Nev. 526, 28 N.W. 2d 130; Pegram-West, Inc. v. Winston Mut. Life Ins. Co., (1949) 231 N.C. 277, 56 S.E. 2d 607.

[224]Hale-Georgia Minerals Corp. v. Hale, (1951) 83 Ga. App. 561, 63 S.E. 2d 920.

board;[225] (3) by implication, that is, through powers which are incidental to express powers;[226] (4) by being clothed with power to act, that is, through apparent powers;[227] or (5) by virtue of the nature of his office, that is, through inherent powers.[228] The powers of a particular officer necessarily vary according to the nature of the business in which the corporation is engaged, and sometimes depend upon custom and usage of the business.[229] Whether or not an officer has exceeded his authority in a particular instance depends upon the facts and circumstances in the case.[230]

Persons dealing with corporate officers are generally chargeable with notice of limitations on their authority,[231] but a limitation contained in a by-law is not valid against an innocent person who has no knowledge of it.[232] Of course, an officer cannot bind a corporation beyond its charter powers,[233] nor can a corporation ratify an ultra vires act of an officer, that is, an act which is beyond the powers of the corporation.[234]

Meaning of express, implied, apparent and inherent powers of officers. Express powers are given by statutes, charter, by-laws or resolution of the board of directors.[235] Implied powers result from the general rule that every delegation of authority carries with it the power to do acts which

---

[225]No express written authority is necessary to empower a particular officer to do a particular act; an informal permission is sufficient. Alabama City G. & A. Ry. v. Kyle Co., (1918) 202 Ala. 552, 81 So. 54; Hartley v. Ault Woodenware Co., (1918) 82 W. Va. 780, 97 S.E. 137.

[226]Durfee & Canning, Inc. v. Canning, (1951) 78 R.I. 385, 82 A. 2d 615.

[227]Bodcan Oil Co. v. Atlantic Refining Co., (1950) 217 Ark. 50, 228 S.W. 2d 626; Sweeney v. Adam Groth Co., (1934) 269 Mich. 436, 257 N.W. 855; Meder v. Superior Oil Co., (1928) 151 Miss. 814, 119 So. 318; Van Duesen Aircraft Supplies, Inc. v. Terminal Constr. Corp., (1949) 3 N.J. 321, 70 A.2d 65, comment, 5 RUTGERS L. REV. 190; Uline Loan Co. v. Standard Oil Co., (1921) 45 S.D. 81, 185 N.W. 1012.

[228]Gignilliat v. West Lumber Co., (1949) 80 Ga. App. 652, 56 S.E. 2d 841.

[229]Richardson v. Taylor Land & Livestock Co., (1946) 25 Wash. 2d 518, 171 P.2d 703; Betz v. Tacoma Drug Co., (1942) 15 Wash. 2d 471, 131 P. 2d 183.

[230]Sacks v. Helene Curtis Industries, Inc., (1950) 340 Ill. App. 76, 91 N.E. 2d 127; Lewis v. Minnesota Mut. Life Ins. Co., (1948) (Iowa) 35 N.W. 2d 51.

[231]Federal Services Finance Corp. v. Bishop Nat'l Bank, (1951) 190 F. 2d 442; Alabama Nat'l Bank v. O'Neil, (1901) 128 Ala. 192, 29 So. 688; Winsted Hosiery Co. v. New Britain Knitting Co., (1897) 69 Conn. 565, 38 A. 310; Slattery v. North End Sav. Bank, (1900) 175 Mass. 380, 56 N.E. 606; First Nat'l Bank v. Asheville Furniture & Lumber Co., (1895) 116 N.C. 827, 21 S.E. 948.

[232]Bijur Motor Lighting Co. v. Eclipse Mach. Co., (1917) 243 F. 600; Western Inv. & Land Co. v. First Nat'l Bank, (1912) 23 Colo. App. 143, 128 P. 476; Arts, Inc. v. Bowles, (1944) D.C. 38 A.2d 660; Bennett v. Alumo Co., (1931) 277 Mass. 325, 178 N.E. 519; Meder v. Superior Oil Co., (1928) 151 Miss. 814, 119 So. 318; Bacon v. Montauk Brewing Co., (1909) 130 App. Div. 737, 115 N.Y. Supp. 617; Doehler v. Lansdon, (1931) 135 Ore. 687, 291 P. 392, 298 P. 200; W.C. Downey & Co. v. Kraemer Hosiery Co., (1939) 136 Pa. Super. 553, 7 A. 2d 492.

[233]Stephens v. Gall, (1910) 179 F. 938; McCorry v. Wiarda & Co., (1912) 149 App. Div. 863, 134 N.Y. Supp. 667.

[234]People's Bank v. Mobile Towing & Wrecking Co., (1924) 210 Ala. 678, 99 So. 87; State Exchange Bank v. Simms, (1924) Tex. Civ. App. 266 S.W. 1111.

[235]Petition of Mulco Products, Inc., (1956) Del. Super. 123 A.2d 95. See also Western Grain Co. Cases, (1955) 264 Ala. 145, 85 So.2d 395, holding that so far as officers' powers and duties are prescribed by statute, charter or by-laws, officers are chargeable with such knowledge.

are reasonably necessary to carry into effect the express power conferred.[236] They are, in effect, express powers.

Apparent powers[237] may result when: (1) a corporation holds an officer out as possessing certain powers;[238] (2) a corporation ratifies the unauthorized act of an officer by acquiescence,[239] and (3) the board of directors is inactive and the officer is left to take charge of all corporate transactions.[240] When innocent third parties rely upon the apparent authority of an officer and deal with him, his acts are binding on the corporation.[241] The corporation is even liable for his fraudulent acts, made within the apparent scope of his authority, though the corporation gets no benefit from them.[242]

Inherent powers are those that an officer has, by virtue of his holding office, to execute matters that arise in the ordinary course of business.[243] But a corporate officer has no inherent power, by virtue of his office, to dispose of corporate assets.[244]

Rules of agency applicable to officers of corporation. Rules of agency applicable to agents of individuals are also applicable to agents, or officers, of corporation.[245] (See authority of agents, other than officers, on page 260.) Knowledge acquired by an officer while acting for the corporation or in line of his official duty is generally chargeable to the corporation.[246] However, a corporation is not chargeable with knowledge of its officer in a transaction when he is not representing the corporation,

---

[236]New York Mortgage Co. v. Garfinkel, (1931) 258 N.Y. 5, 179 N.E. 33, holding that an officer with authority to loan money for a corporation is authorized to receive payment.

[237]American Trust & Sav. Bank v. de Jaeger, (1921) 191 Iowa 758, 183 N.W. 369; O'Donnell v. Union Paving Co., (1936) 121 Pa. Super. 68, 182 A. 709.

[238]Mahoney Mining Co. v. Anglo-Californian Bank, Ltd., (1881) 104 U.S. 707; Enterprise Foundry & Mach. Works v. Miners' Elkhorn Coal Co., (1931) 241 Ky. 779, 45 S.W. 2d 470; Forgeson v. Corey, Hill Garage, Inc., (1924) 249 Mass. 163, 144 N.E. 383; Fink v. Gregg Realty Co., (1927) (Mo. App.) 296 S.W. 838.

[239]Spain Management Co. v. Packs' Auto Sales, Inc., (1950) 54 N.W. 64, 213 P.2d 433; Scott v. Southwest Grease & Oil Co., (1949) 167 Kan. 171, 205 P.2d 914; Shaten v. American Nat'l Bank, (1931) 109 N.J. Eq. 307, 157 A. 128.

[240]Greenpoint Coal Docks, Inc. v. Newtown Creek Realty Corp., (1949) 91 N.Y.S. 2d 466; Nolan v. J. & M. Doyle Co., (1940) 338 Pa. 398, 13 A. 2d 59.

[241]O'Donnell v. Union Paving Co., (1936) 121 Pa. Super. 68, 182 A. 709; Betz v. Tacoma Drug Co., (1942) 15 Wash. 2d 471, 131 P. 2d 183.

[242]Morrison v. Bank of Mount Hope, (1942) 124 W. Va. 478, 20 S.E.2d 790.

[243]Warszawa v. White Eagle Brewing Co., (1939) 299 Ill. App. 509, 20 N.E. 2d 343, Lydia E. Pinkham Medicine Co. v. Gove, (1940) 305 Mass. 213, 25 N.E. 2d 332.

[244]Kagan v. Levenson, (1956) (Mass.) 134 N.E. 2d 415; Beck v. Edwards & Lewis, Inc., (1948) 141 N.J. Eq. 326, 57 A.2d 459.

[245]Cushman v. Cloverland Coal & Mining Co., (1908) 170 Ind. 402, 84 N.E. 759; Metzger v. Southern Bank, (1910) 98 Miss. 108, 54 So. 241; Gilbert v. Sharkey, (1916) 80 Ore. 323, 156 P. 789.

[246]Ohio Farmers Indemnity Co. v. Charleston Laundry Co., (1950) 183 F.2d 682; All Steel Engines, Inc. v. Taylor Engines, Inc., (1950) 88 F. Supp. 745; Nissen v. Nissen Trampoline Co., (1949) 241 Iowa 474, 39 N.W.2d 92; Knox Glass Bottle Co. v. Underwood, (1956) (Miss.) 89 So. 2d 799; New York Mortgage Co. v. Garfinkel, (1931) 258 N.Y. 5, 179 N.E. 33.

but is dealing as a private individual and in his own interest.[247] Nor is a corporation bound by an act of its officer if it has not held the officer out as having authority and if it has no knowledge that he, without authority, is presuming to act for it.[248]

An officer who contracts for his corporation may become personally liable if he is acting without authority,[249] or if he fails to disclose that he is acting for the corporation.[250]

Officers as fiduciaries. An official or executive of a corporation owes it a fiduciary as well as a contractual duty. Like a director, a corporate officer must represent fully the interests of the corporation and must not use his official position to advance his own interests. (See "Directors as fiduciaries," on page 227.) He is accountable for the profits from a diverted corporate opportunity[251] and he cannot recover on a contract with an outside party that involves a breach of duty to his corporation.[252] An officer who wrongfully purchases property in his own name with corporate funds may be made a "constructive trustee" for his corporation.[253]

Power of officers to delegate authority. An officer cannot delegate authority when the act to be done involves the use of discretion or implies that personal confidence and trust have been placed in him.[254] However, an officer may delegate authority insofar as it is necessary for the prosecution of his employment, or if the act to be done is merely ministerial.[255]

Regulatory laws require caution. In exercising their duties, directors and officers must bear in mind that many of the regulatory laws provide penalties in one form or another for violations. In some instances, as in the Securities Act of 1933, the Securities Exchange Act of 1934, (see pp. 426-427) and the Internal Revenue Code of 1954, civil and criminal liabilities can be imposed directly against directors and officers.[256] In other statutes, such as the Walsh-Healey Public Contracts Act, the penalty is

[247]York Livestock Commission Co. v. Northwestern Livestock Commission Co., (1939) 136 Neb. 716, 287 N.W. 94.
[248]Security Bldg. & Loan Ass'n v. Seibert, (1935) (Cal. App.) 41 P.2d 556.
[249]Vulcan Corp. v. Cobden Mach. Works, (1949) 336 Ill. App. 394, 84 N.E.2d 173.
[250]Carelesimo v. Schwebel, (1948) 87 Cal. App. 2d 482, 197 P.2d 167.
[251]Central Ry. Signal Co. v. Longden, (1952) 194 F.2d 310.
[252]Colonell v. Goodman, (1948) 78 F. Supp. 845, cert. denied, 335 U.S. 870, 69 S. Ct. 166.
[253]Central Bus Lines, Inc. v. Hamilton Nat'l Bank, (1951) 34 Tenn. App. 480, 239 S.W. 2d 583; Paddock v. Siemoneit, (1949) 147 Tex. 571, 218 S.W. 2d 428.
[254]Royal Theatre Corp. v. United States, (1946) 66 F. Supp. 301; Citizens Nat'l Bank v. Florida Tile & Lumber Co., (1921) 81 Fla. 889, 89 So. 139; Citizens' Development Co. v. Kypawva Oil Co., (1921) 191 Ky., 183 229 S.W. 88; Dewey v. National Tank Maintenance Corp., (1943) 233 Iowa 58, 8 N.W. 2d 593.
[255]Fowel v. Continental Life Ins. Co., (1947) D.C. 55 A. 2d 205; Gerrish Dredging Co. v. Bethleham Shipbuilding Corp., (1932) 247 Mass. 162, 141 N.E. 867.
[256]Penfield Co. v. Young, (1947) 330 U.S. 585, 67 S. Ct. 918; United States v. Fox, (1951) 95 F. Supp. 315.

applied against the corporation. Directors should be exceedingly cautious not to subject themselves to liability by authorizing or directing activities which might be violative of the laws. Resolutions authorizing the execution of contracts, or other action, which might be affected by such laws, should contain express provisions that the contract or other corporate action shall be in accordance with the applicable laws.

While an exhaustive list of the regulatory statutes cannot be given here, the following other acts may be mentioned as of great importance to directors and officers because of the penalty provisions against them or the corporation: Fair Labor Standards Act (the Federal Wage and Hour Law); the National Labor Relations Act; the Federal Trade Commission Act, as amended by the Wheeler-Lea Act against unlawful advertising of foods, drugs, devices, and cosmetics; the state unfair sales laws, and many state taxing and license laws.

APPOINTMENT OF COMMITTEES AND AGENTS

Delegation of authority by directors. Since the board of directors has sole authority to manage corporate affairs, it may be stated as a general rule that it also has the right to delegate to officers, agents,[257] and committees[258] the performance of corporate acts, especially those ministerial in character, which the board itself can legally perform.[259] Whether or not the directors can delegate a power or act requiring the exercise of discretion depends entirely upon the nature of the act and the reasonableness of the delegation of power involved.[260] They may intrust to agents, officers, and committee the conduct of the ordinary business affairs of the corporation.[261] They may delegate authority to execute leases and sub-leases;[262] and they may authorize an attorney to execute a deed in behalf of the corporation.[263] Also, directors can delegate authority to an officer to change the coverage of an insurance policy taken out by the corporation, since that type of obligation is within the statute granting

---

[257]For a discussion of the distinction between an officer and agent, see Colby v. Klune, (1949) 83 F. Supp. 159; Vardeman v. Pennsylvania Mut. Life Ins. Co., (1906) 125 Ga. 117, 54 S.E. 66.

[258]See "The Executive Committee in Corporate Organization—Scope of Powers," 42 MICH. L. REV. 133.

[259]Schulte v. Ideal Food Products Co., (1929) 208 Iowa 767, 226 N.W. 174.

[260]Under common law principles, directors can without statutory authority, delegate to officers, agents or executive committees the power to transact not only ordinary and routine business, but business requiring the highest degree of judgment and discretion. Social Security Board v. Warren, (1944) 142 F.2d 974.

[261]Wallace v. International Trade Exhibition, Inc., (1930) 170 La. 55, 127 So. 362; Boss v. Alms & Doepke Co., (1923) 17 Ohio App. 314.

[262]Holwick v. Walker, (1935) 6 Cal. App. 2d 669, 45 P. 2d 374.

[263]Federal Land Bank v. Bross, (1938) (Mo. App.) 122 S.W. 2d 35.

general management powers to directors.[264] Actually the complexity of modern corporate affairs is such that it has become impracticable for a corporation to function without vesting in its agents some authority to act in matters which may involve the exercise of discretion.[265]

A general agent has authority to act for the corporation in all matters pertaining to the business or a particular branch of the business. A special agent is authorized to act for the corporation only in a specific transaction.[266] Authority may be given to an agent in the following ways: (1) by appointment through a resolution of the board defining the powers of the agents; (2) by contract with the corporation; (3) by a power of attorney to act. Also, the board may be held to have authorized acts of an agent by implication from the acquiescence of the directors in a course of dealings by the agent, or by holding out the agent as possessing full power to act.[267] A revocation of an agent's authority cannot affect the rights of third parties who entered into agreements with the corporation before revocation of the agent's authority.[268]

An agency is irrevocable, whether so expressed in the appointment or not, when the authority is coupled with an interest, or is part of a security for the payment of money or the performance of some other lawful act. For an agency to be coupled with an interest, the agent must have an interest in the subject matter of the agency aside from an interest in the compensation he is to receive for his services. Merely calling an agency irrevocable will not make it so, if the nature of the agency is such that it would otherwise be revocable.[269]

Restrictions on delegation of authority. The right to delegate authority does not depend upon statutory authority.[270] However, it is limited by the statutes, the articles of incorporation, and the by-laws.[271]

Ordinarily, directors cannot bind the corporation by contracts of employment for a term beyond their tenure in office.[272] But where the services bargained for are peculiarly necessary to the corporation and cannot be obtained except for a stated term, such a contract of employment

[264]Mass. Mutual Life Ins. Co. v. Vogue, Inc., (1965) Tenn. S. Ct. 393 S.W. 2d 164.

[265]Wood Co. v. McCutcheon, (1939) 136 Pa. Super, 446, 7 A.2d 564; San Antonio Joint Stock Land Bank v. Taylor, (1937) 129 Tex. 335, 105 S.W. 2d 650.

[266]Fulton v. Des Jardins, (1950) Wyo. S. Ct., 67 Wyo. 517, 227 P. 2d 240; Murray v. Standard Pecan Co., (1923) Ill. S. Ct., 309 Ill. 226, 140 N.E. 834.

[267]Crown Zellerbach Corp. v. International Grain Corp, (1968) La. Ct. of App., 213 So. 2d 53; Long v. National Bank & Trust Co. of Central Pennsylvania, (1968) Pa. Orph. Ct. 89 Dauph. 238.

[268]Hansen v. Columbia Breweries, Inc., (1942) Wash. S. Ct., 12 Wash. 2d 554, 122 P. 2d 489.

[269]For a definition of an agency coupled with an interest, see Frink v. Roe, (1886) Calif. S. Ct., 70 Cal. 296, 11 P. 820. See also page 000 for further discussion of this subject.

[270]Social Security Board v. Warren, (1944) 142 F. 2d 974.

[271]Dewey v. National Tank Maintenance Corp., (1943) 233 Iowa 58, 8 N.W. 2d 593.

[272]Edwards v. Keller, (1939) Tex. Civ. App. 133 S.W. 2d 698.

may be valid.[273] (See revocation of contracts of employment on page. 261.)

The directors cannot completely delegate their authority, abandon their duties and have others act for them.[274] For example, they cannot make installment contracts with a provision that upon default the voting rights of the directors shall go to the other party to the contract.[275]

How authority is delegated. It is advisable that the appointment of committees, agents, officers, and employees who are to hold managerial positions, be made by resolution at a meeting of the board, and that special care be given to the preparation of resolutions authorizing the appointment and defining the powers of the appointees, since such resolutions have frequently been held by the courts to be contracts.[276] It is not essential, however, that the delegation of authority be made by formal action.[277] Frequently authority is implied from a course of conduct, or from a recognized practice of the corporation.[278] A corporation is bound by the act of an agent with apparent powers that third parties, in good faith, believe the corporation has delegated to the agent.[279]

Liability of directors after delegation of authority. Directors do not free themselves from responsibility by delegating the management of the business to someone else. They must always exercise a general supervision over it.[280] Circumstances may arise where directors, by their careless supervision or selection of subordinate officers, make themselves liable for the wrongful acts of such subordinate.[281] For example, if a subordinate officer makes a practice of committing wrongful acts that the directors can discover by proper supervision, the directors are liable for those acts. The courts, of course, are more lenient with a single act of wrongdoing. Thus, the directors were not liable where a subordinate officer made one fraudu-

---

[273]General Paint Corp. v. Kramer, (1932) 57 F. 2d 698.

[274]Royal Theatre Corp. v. United States, (1946) 66 F. Supp. 301; Lane v. Bogert, (1934) 116 N.J. Eq. 454, 174 A. 217; Farmers' Gin Co. v. Kasch, (1925) Tex. Civ. App. 277 S.W. 746. Divestment of control over property occasioned by leasing is not an abdication of duty which the law condemns as violative of the trusteeship of directors. Schneider v. Greater M. & S. Circuit, (1932) 144 N.Y. Misc. 534, 259 N.Y. Supp. 319.

[275]Wheeler v. Layman Foundation, (1939) 188 Ga. 267, 3 S.E. 2d 645.

[276]Houghtaling v. Upper Kittanning Brick Co., (1915) 92 N.Y. Misc. 228, 155 N.Y. Supp. 540.

[277]Covington v. Covington & C. Bridge Co., (1873) 73 Ky. 69.

[278]Stoneman v. Fox Film Corp., (1936) 295 Mass. 419, 4 N.E. 2d 63; Hahnemann Hospital v. Golo Slipper Co., (1939) 135 Pa. Super. 398, 5 A. 2d 605; Betz v. Tacoma Drug Co., (1942) 15 Wash. 2d 471, 131 P. 2d 183.

[279]Morris County Bldg. & Loan Ass'n v. Walters, (1938) 123 N.J. Eq. 548, 198 A. 756; Severance v. Heyl & Patterson, Inc., (1936) 123 Pa. Super. 553, 187 A. 53.

[280]Ames v. Goldfield Merger Mines Co., (1915) 227 F. 292; Martin v. Hardy, (1930) 251 Mich. 413, 232 N.W. 197.

[281]Lowell Hoit & Co. v. Detig, (1943) 320 Ill. App. 179, 50 N.E. 2d 602.

lent contract, without the directors' knowledge, and no corporate record came before them reflecting the transaction.[282]

Appointment of committees by directors. Permanent or temporary committees may be appointed by the board of directors, subject to limitations made by statute and by the charter or by-laws of the corporation.[283] These committees may be endowed with such ministerial duties as are granted to them by the board of directors or by the by-laws.[284] The executive committee of the board must consist of directors, appointed by the board. It cannot delegate its decision-making to a single committee member.[285]

Authority of committees between board meetings. The by-laws frequently provide that the board of directors may appoint from its members an executive committee to exercise the powers of the board in the management of the business of the corporation during intervals between meetings of the board.[286] The powers of the executive committee, however, are limited to those corporate affairs which are ministerial, current, ordinary and routine.[287] It does not have authority to inaugurate radical reversals of, or departures from, fundamental policies and methods of conducting the business prescribed by the board.[288] When the board reconvenes, the powers of the executive committee are automatically suspended.[289]

Limitations upon authority of committees. The authority of execu-

---

[282]Ibid.

[283]Dyer Bros. Golden West Iron Works v. Central Iron Works, (1920) 182 Cal. 588, 189 P. 445; New Mexico Potash & Chemical Co. v. Oliver, (1951) 123 Colo. 268, 228 P.2d 979; Haldeman v. Haldeman, (1917) 176 Ky. 635, 197 S.W. 376; Temple v. Dodge, (1895) 89 Tex. 69, 32 S.W. 514.

[284]Fensterer v. Pressure Lighting Co., (1914) 85 N.Y. Misc. 621, 149 N.Y. Supp. 49.

[285]Gumpert v. Bon Ami Co., (1958) CA-2, 251 F. 2d 735.

[286]Commercial Wood & Cement Co. v. Northampton Portland Cement Co., (1907) 190 N.Y. 1, 82 N.E. 730.

For a discussion of the extent to which a board of directors may entrust its powers to the executive committee, see 20 HARV. L. REV. 225, and, for a discussion of the length of time that a board of directors may delegate its powers to an executive committee, see Sherman & Illis, Inc. v. Indiana Mut. Cas. Co., (1930) 41 F. 2d 588, comment, 29 MICH. L. REV. 367.

[287]Tilden v. Goldy Mach. Co., (1908) 9 Cal. App. 9, 98 P. 39; Wallace v. International Trade Exhibition Inc., (1930) 170 La. 55, 127 So. 362; First Nat'l Bank v. Commercial Travelers Home Ass'n, (1905) 108 App. Div. 78, 95 N.Y. Supp. 454, aff'd, memo dec. 185 N.Y. 575, 78 N.E. 1103; Fensterer v. Pressure Lighting Co., (1914) 85 N.Y. Misc. 621, 149 N.Y. Supp. 49.

[288]Fensterer v. Pressure Lighting Co., (1914) 85 N.Y. Misc. 621, 149 N.Y. Supp. 49.

[289]Commercial Wood & Cement Co. v. Northampton Portland Cement Co., (1907) 190 N.Y. 1, 82 N.E. 730.

tive committees has been limited by statutes and by court rulings.[290] An executive committee may not perform acts specifically required by statute to be performed only by the directors. Thus, the committee cannot amend by-laws that only the directors, under the statute, are permitted to amend.[291] An executive committee cannot rescind a stock subscription agreement when the by-laws limit its authority to administrative and ministerial acts.[292]

If an executive committee is appointed for the purpose of making a report on an agreement, the committee has no authority to enter into a binding contract without reporting to the directors.[293] But where the board authorized the executive committee to determine what action should be taken when the corporation was unable to pay its obligations, the corporation was bound by the action of the committee when it filed a voluntary bankruptcy petition.[294]

---

[290]§38 of the Illinois Business Corp. Act was amended in 1957 to provide specifically that the board of directors cannot delegate to an executive committee its right to amend the articles and by-laws, declare dividends, elect or remove officers, fix the compensation of committee members, adopt mergers plans, and various other powers. Cases: Executive committee cannot change the number of its members, remove member by majority vote, or appoint or remove officers and fix their salaries. Hayes v. Canada, Atlantic & Plant S.S. Co., (1910) 181 F. 289. A corporation whose charter vests its management in the board of directors cannot by a by-law substitute an executive committee. Temple v. Dodge, (1896) 89 Tex. 69, 32 S.W. 514. But see Wallace v. International Trade Exhibition, Inc., (1930) 170 La. 55, 127 So. 362, holding that directors may delegate to executive committee the exercise of their powers, including the power to fix the president's salary.

§712 of the New York Business Corporation Law provides that:

(a) If the certificate of incorporation or the by-laws so provide, the board, by resolution adopted by a majority of the entire board, may designate from among its members an executive committee and other committees, each consisting of three or more directors, and each of which, to the extent provided in the resolution or in the certificate of incorporation or by-laws, shall have all the authority of the board, except that no such committee shall have authority as to the following matters: (1) The submission to shareholders of any action that needs shareholders' approval under this Business Corporation Law; (2) the filling of vacancies in the board of directors or in any committee; (3) the fixing of compensation of the directors for serving on the board or on any committee; (4) the amendment or repeal of the by-laws, or the adoption of new by-laws; (5) the amendment or repeal of any resolution of the board which by its terms shall not be so amendable or repealable.

(b) The board may designate one or more directors as alternate members of any such committee, who may replace any absent member or members at any meeting of such committee.

(c) Each such committee shall serve at the pleasure of the board. The designation of any such committee and the delegation thereto of authority shall not alone relieve any director of his duty to the corporation as such director.

[291]Hayes v. Canada, Atlantic & Plant S.S. Co., (1910) 181 F. 289.
[292]Doyle v. Chladek, (1965) Ore. S. Ct. 401P. 2d 18.
[293]Greensboro Gas Co. v. Home Oil & Gas Co., (1908) 222 Pa. 4, 70 A. 940.
[294]Lawrence v. Atlantic Paper & Pulp Corp., (1924) 298 F. 246.

A corporation is bound by an act of the committee outside of its authorized powers, if the corporation accepts the benefits of the act,[295] or legally ratifies the unauthorized act.[296]

The authority that can be delegated to an executive committee varies with the purpose for which the corporation was organized. For example, the executive committee of a corporation organized to deal in securities can sell stock held by the company.[297]

Appointment of agents by directors. The board of directors may appoint such agents as may be needed to conduct the ordinary affairs of the corporation. The agents appointed are either general or special. A general agent has the authority to act for the corporation in all matters pertaining to the management of the ordinary business of the corporation.[298] A special agent has the authority to act for the corporation only in a specific transaction.[299]

An agent, however, has apparent authority commensurate with the business entrusted to him.[300] A person may ordinarily deal with him in matters within such authority, without regard to limitations on his authority, if the limitations are not brought to the attention of outsiders.[301] Agents appointed by the directors become agents of the corporation and not of the directors.[302] But agents appointed by an officer of the corporation are not agents of the corporation. Their acts are not the acts of the corporation unless they are authorized by the corporation, or are for its benefit and are accepted by it.[303]

How agents are appointed. Authority may be given to an agent in any of the following ways: (1) by appointment by a resolution defining the powers of the agent; (2) by a contract with the corporation; (3) by a power of attorney to act; and (4) by implication from the acquiescence of the directors in a course of dealings by the agents. (See also page 256.)

A corporation may appoint agents by resolution or by a writing signed by a duly authorized officer, without using its corporate seal, just as an individual may do.[304] A person dealing with the corporation through its

---

[295]Respess v. Rex Spinning Co., (1926) 191 N.C. 809, 133 S.E. 391.

[296]The test of the effectiveness of the ratification of an unauthorized act is whether the corporation could have authorized the act in the first instance. Boyce v. Chemical Plastics, Inc., (1949) 175 F.2d 839.

[297]Wingate v. Bercut, (1945) 146 F.2d 725.

[298]Fulton v. Des Jardins, (1950) 67 Wyo. 517, 227 P. 2d 240.

[299]Murray v. Standard Pecan Co., (1923) 309 Ill. 226, 140 N.E. 834.

[300]Wood Co. v. McCutcheon, (1939) 136 Pa. Super, 446, 7 A.2d 564.

[301]W.C. Downey & Co. v. Kraemer Hosiery Co., (1939) 136 Pa. Super. 553, 7 A.2d 492; Dallas Joint Stock Land Bank v. Harrison, (1939) Tex. Civ. App. 135 S.W. 2d 573.

[302]Kidd v. N.H. Traction Co., (1907) 74 N.H. 160, 66 A. 127.

[303]Sells Petroleum, Inc. v. Victory Swabbing Co., (1948) Tex. Civ. App. 209 S.W.2d 199.

[304]North Carolina Mortgage Corp. v. Morgan, (1935) 208 N.C. 743, 182 S.E. 450.

agent is presumed to know the limitations of the agent's authority as defined in a directors' resolution filed with public records.[305]

Appointment of agents by power of attorney. A power of attorney is a written instrument giving authority to the agent appointed to perform a certain act in the name and on behalf of the corporation. Usually, where a power of attorney is to be given to an agent, the board of directors appoints the agent by resolution and authorizes the proper officers to execute and deliver a power of attorney to the agent appointed. (See Directors' resolution authorizing officers to execute power of attorney, page 298, Chapter 10.)

If a statute requires that an agent be appointed, for example, for the service of process, the appointment should be made in the form required by law. Thus, if the agent is required to be appointed by resolution, the form of resolution should meet the statutory requirements; if the agent is required to be appointed by a power of attorney, the proper resolutions should be passed authorizing the execution of a power of attorney. The blue-sky laws of some of the states, regulating the sale of securities in the state, require the corporation obtaining permission to market securities to appoint an agent for service of process in the state.[306] Many of the states furnish the form of resolution to be passed by the directors to appoint an agent for service of process. Most of the states also require the appointment of an agent for service of process when a corporation organized in another state makes application to do business as a foreign corporation.[307]

Revocation of agent's authority. Whoever has the power to appoint an agent has the power to revoke the agency unless it is irrevocable.[308] Thus the board of directors has the power to remove an agent appointed by it. The agent's authority may be revoked any time with or without cause, if the agency has no fixed term and is revocable. Even if the agent has been appointed for a definite term, the board still has the power to revoke his authority within the contract term, although the corporation may be liable for damages for the breach of contract.[309] If a corporate by-law gives the board authority to terminate the appointment of an agent at any time, and the agent is chargeable with knowledge of that by-law, the board can revoke the appointment without being liable on a contract of employment.[310]

If the agent has entered into contracts binding the corporation, the

---

[305]Standard Oil Co. v. Evans, (1950) 218 La. 590, 50 So.2d 203.
[306]See Prentice-Hall *Securities Regulation*.
[307]See Prentice-Hall *Corporation*.
[308]Stott v. Stott Realty Co., (1929) 246 Mich. 261, 224 N.W. 621.
[309]Hansen v. Columbia Breweries, Inc., (1942) 12 Wash. 2d 554, 122 P. 2d 489.
[310]Cohen v. Camden Refrigerating & Terminals Co., (1943) 129 N.J.L. 519, 30 A. 2d 428.

revocation of his authority cannot affect the rights of third persons. A change of the directors does not abrogate the authority of the agent.[311]

Agency coupled with an interest. An agency is coupled with an interest[312] when the agent has an interest in the subject matter of the agency aside from an interest in the compensation he is to receive for his services. Following is an example of an agency "coupled with an interest." An agent for the corporation has advanced money for the corporation; to protect the agent, the corporation has given him the power to sell certain property and to reimburse himself out of the proceeds. The agency is irrevocable because of the interest of the agent in the subject matter.

Ratification of unauthorized acts of directors, officers, and agents. Unauthorized acts of directors, officers, and agents taken without the corporation's knowledge are not binding,[313] unless the corporation expressly or impliedly ratifies the acts.[314] Ratification of an unauthorized act validates it and makes it binding on the corporation to the same extent as if it had been expressly authorized.[315]

Ratification[316] will be implied from the adoption of the unauthorized act,[317] from acquiescence by those who had power to grant authority in the first place,[318] from the failure to repudiate the unauthorized act in due time,[319] or from enjoyment by the corporation of the benefits of the acts.[320] A corporation is estopped from denying that a contract was made without authority by its agent, if it had impliedly ratified the unauthorized act.[321] If only a part of the unauthorized act is ratified, the effect of the ratification,

---

[311]Kidd v. N.H. Traction Co., (1907) 74 N.H. 160, 66 A. 127.

[312]For a definition of an agency coupled with an interest, see Frink v. Roe, (1886) 70 Cal. 296, 11 P. 820.

[313]Wilmington Provision Co. v. Sinskey, (1950) 31 Del. Ch. 311, 72 A.2d 446; Murray v. Standard Pecan Co., (1923) 309 Ill. 226, 140 N.E. 834.

[314]Hennessey v. Nelen, (1938) 299 Mass. 569, 13 N.E. 2d 431.

[315]Eastern Pub. Serv. Corp. v. Funkhouser, (1929) 153 Va. 128, 149 S.E. 503.

[316]Ratification dates from the time the unauthorized agent made the proposed contract; adoption dates from the time the principal adopts the contracts. Consequently, acts of promoters may ordinarily be adopted, but not ratified, because ratification would date back to a time when the corporation did not exist.

[317]Stoneman v. Fox Film Corp., (1936) 295 Mass. 419, 4 N.E. 2d 63.

[318]Fayette Lumber Co. v. Faught, (1936) 102 Ind. App. 686, 5 N.E. 2d 132; Bates Street Shirt Co. v. Waite, (1931) 130 Me. 352, 156 A. 293.

[319]Santarsiero v. Green Bay Transport, Inc., (1946) 249 Wis. 308, 24 N.W. 2d 659.

[320]Coldiron v. Good Coal Co., (1939) 276 Ky. 833, 125 S.W. 2d 757; Farmers & Merchants Bank v. Burns & Hood Motor Co., (1956) (Mo.), 295 S.W. 2d 199; Reynier v. Associated Dyeing & Printing Co., (1936) 116 N.J.L. 481, 184 A. 780; Magruder v. Hagen-Ratcliff & Co., (1948) 131 W. Va. 679, 50 S.E. 2d 488.

[321]In Colorado Industrial Loan & Inv. Co. v. Clem, (1927) 82 Colo. 399, 260 P. 1019, it was held that the corporation could not question the validity of a contract made in disagreement with its charter, where the corporation had retained the benefits of the contract, provided that the contract was not forbidden by statute and was not immoral or contrary to public policy. See also Royal Blue Coaches, Inc. v. Delaware River Coach Lines, Inc., (1947) 140 N.J. Eq. 19, 52 A. 2d 763.

nevertheless, extends to the whole.[322] Sometimes the statutes, charter, by-laws, or terms of a contract may require the ratification of the agent's act by a certain body, for instance, the board of directors. In this case, a contract will not be binding until it is approved by the board of directors, even though signed with authority.[323]

Essentials of valid ratification. In order for a ratification to be valid, the following elements must be present:

1. The ratification must be made by those who had authority in the first instance to authorize the acts to be done.[324] For example, stockholders cannot ratify an act which they cannot authorize.[325] and therefore cannot, by a general resolution ratifying the acts of directors, validate action taken by the directors in violation of express statutory provision.[326] A corporation cannot ratify any acts of its directors, officers, or agents which it has not the power to perform.[327]
2. The ratification must be the voluntary act of the principal.
3. Those ratifying an unauthorized act must, at the time of ratification, be fully informed of all material facts and circumstances attending the unauthorized act.[328] The knowledge needed for ratification of an agent's unauthorized act is ordinarily actual knowledge such as may be acquired from direct evidence or may be inferred from other facts and circumstances.[329]

There can be no implied ratification of unauthorized acts unless there is evidence showing ratification, such as acceptance of benefits, knowledge of the transaction, a failure to protest, and acts of like character.[330] Nor is the knowledge that a corporate agent has of his own unauthorized act imputable to the corporation so as to result in ratification.[331]

Corporate officers cannot ratify their own wrongful acts.[332]

---

[322]Webb v. Duvall, (1940) 177 Md. 592, 11 A.2d 446.

[323]Barnes v. Red Bayou Oil Co., (1921) 271 F. 297; McCray v. Sapulpa Petroleum Co., (1923) 102 Okla. 108, 226 p. 875.

[324]Baltimore & O.R.R. v. Foar, (1936) 84 F. 2d 67; Lammers v. Arkansas Power & Light Co., (1938) 196 Ark. 108, 116 S.W. 2d 361.

[325]Hotaling v. Hotaling, (1924) 193 Cal. 368, 224 P. 455; Elward v. Peabody Coal Co., (1956) 9 Ill. App. 2d 234, 132 N.E. 2d 549.

[326]Fidanque v. American Maracaibo Co., (1952) 33 Del. Ch. 522, 92 A.2d 311; Shickel v. Berryville Land & Improvement Co., (1901) 99 Va. 88, 37 S.E. 813.

[327]People's Bank v. Mobile Towing & Wrecking Co., (1924) 210 Ala. 678, 99 So. 87; State Exchange Bank v. Simms, (1924) Tex. Civ. App. 266 S.W. 1111.

[328]Bowen v. Trust Co., (1948) 166 F. 2d 264; Baltimore & O.R.R. v. Foar, (1936) 84 F.2d 67; Old Mortgage & Finance Co. v. Pasadena Land Co., (1928) 241 Mich. 426, 216 N.W. 922; Barclay v. Dublin Lake Club, (1938) 89 N.H. 500, 1 A.2d 633; Union Discount Co. v. MacRobert, (1929) 134 N.Y. Misc. 107, 234 N.Y.S. 529; Greensboro Gas Co. v. Home Oil & Gas Co., (1908) 222 Pa. 4, 70 A. 940, Richardson v. Taylor Land & Livestock Co., (1946) 25 Wash. 2d 518, 171 P. 2d 703.

[329]Scrivner v. American Car & Foundry Co., (1932) 330 Mo. 408, 50 S.W. 2d 1001.

[330]Betz v. Tacoma Drug Co., (1942) 15 Wash. 2d 471, 131 P. 2d 183.

[331]Scrivner V. American Car & Foundry Co., (1932) 330 Mo. 408, 50 S.W. 2d 1001.

[332]McCray v. Sapulpa Petroleum Co., (1923) 102 Okla. 108, 226 P. 875.

EXECUTION OF CORPORATE INSTRUMENTS

Manner of executing corporate instruments. In the execution of corporate instruments, a corporation need observe only such formalities as are required of individuals under similar circumstances, unless the statute or charter otherwise provides.[333] A contract or instrument, to be binding on the corporation, should be executed in the name of the corporation by the person or persons authorized to execute the instrument. Ordinarily, the agent or officer should name the corporation as the contracting party, at the bottom of the contract, and sign as its agent or officer.[334] The signature should appear as follows:

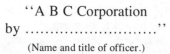

"A B C Corporation

by ...."

(Name and title of officer.)

Other forms of execution. While the above form of execution is technically correct, it is not the only one that the courts recognize as sufficient to bind the corporation.[335] Where the body of an agreement or instrument indicates that it is the instrument of the corporation and not of the signer, and the signature itself indicates that the execution was made in a representative capacity, the instrument will be regarded as binding on the corporation, provided, of course, that the signer was acting within the scope of his authority.[336] The official designation of the one who signs is not absolutely necessary, for it may be otherwise established.[337] The use of a commonly understood abbreviation to designate the office of the person signing a corporate instrument is sufficient, since the abbreviation is suggestive of his official position.[338] For example, where the name of the corporation is typed on a note, followed by the name of the secretary and an abbreviation of his official capacity, written in ink, the signing is sufficient to bind the corporation, provided the secretary is authorized to execute the note on its behalf.[339]

---

[333] Altavista Cotton Mills v. Lane, (1922) 133 Va. 1, 112 S.E. 637.

[334] Gottfried v. Miller, (1881) 104 U.S. 521, 26 L. Ed. 851; Mastin Realty & Mining Co. v. Commssioner, (1942) 130 F.2d 1003. To avoid personal liability, the corporate officer who signs the note must clearly show that he is acting on behalf of the corporaiton. Betz v. Bank of Miami Beach, (1957) (Fla.) 95 So. 2d 891.

[335] Bickart v. Henry, (1947) 67 Ind. App. 493, 116 N.E. 15.

[336] Cochran v. Grand Theater Co., (1923) 29 Ga. App. 481, 115 S.E. 926; Bickart v. Henry, (1947) 67 Ind. App. 493, 116 N.E. 15; Harris v. Fielding, (1921) 109 Kan. 491, 199 P. 467; De Maria & Janssen v. Baum, (1932) 227 Mo. App. 212, 52 S.W. 2d 418; Atlanta & C.A. L. Ry. v. Limestone-Globe Land Co., (1918) 109 S.C. 444, 96 S.E. 188.

[337] Greve v. Taft Realty Co., (1929) 101 Cal. App. 343, 281 P. 641.

[338] Santa Marina Co. v. Canadian Bank of Commerce, (1918) 254 F. 391; Griffin v. Erskine, (1906) 131 Iowa 444, 109 N.W. 13.

[339] Reifeiss v. Barnes, (1946) Mo. App. 192 S.W. 2d 427.

The corporation may adopt or authorize the execution of documents by a typewritten, printed, or rubber-stamped signature, and, if the adoption or the authority to use such a signature is shown, the corporation is bound by it.[340]

The contract must indicate that it is made in behalf of the corporation.[341] If the name of the corporation is placed on an agreement by an agent who is authorized to execute the instrument, even though the agent does not sign his own name, the contract will be considered the act of the corporation.[342] But where the instrument does not purport to be made by the corporation, the persons who subscribe to it, and not the corporation, are responsible even though the signers have added to their signatures a profession of some official title.[343]

Acknowledgment. If an instrument requires an acknowledgment, the acknowledgment must conform with mandatory statutory requirements.[344] It is, however, not necessary to follow them word for word; substantial compliance is sufficient.[345] If there is no statutory form to be followed, any form of acknowledgment will do since it will be liberally construed.[346] The acknowledgment must, however, associate the acknowledgor with the corporation. Thus, a certificate of acknowledgment is not sufficient when it does not recite that the acknowledging officer is an officer of the corporation named in the instrument.[347]

Corporate name in instrument. A corporation, like an individual, can do business and contract in a name other than its legal name.[348] A misnomer of the corporation will not affect the validity of its contracts,[349] but if the name is not the corporation's regular name, and no agency to make the contract is disclosed, it is prima facie not a contract of the corporation.[350] The omission of the word "Company" from the corporate

---

[340]Tabas v. Emergency Fleet Corp., (1926) 9 F.2d 648, aff'd in Emergency Fleet Corp. v. Tabas, (1927) 22 F. 2d 398, in which case no evidence of adoption or of authority in anyone to bind the United States was shown.

[341]Hasenfratz v. Berger Apartments, Inc., (1946) 61 N.Y.S. 2d 12.

[342]Kull v. Dierks Lumber & Coal Co., (1927) 173 Ark, 445, 292 S.W. 695; Dougherty v. Becklenberg, (1917) 205 Ill. App. 491.

[343]Birum Olson Co. v. Johnson, (1931) 213 Iowa 439, 239 N.W. 123; Casco Nat'l Bank v. Clark, (1893) 139 N.Y. 307, 34 N.E. 908.

[344]Dream Homes, Inc. v. Kessler, (1949) 196 N.Y. Misc. 808 93 N.Y.S. 2d 144; Bank of Commerce v. Kelpine Products Co., (1932) 167 Wash. 592, 10 P.2d 238.

[345]In re Atlantic Smokeless Coal Co., (1952) 103 F. Supp. 348; Fidelity & Deposit Co. v. Rieff, (1930) 181 Ark. 798, 27 S.W.2d 1008.

[346]Lenhart v. Grace Constr. & Supply Co., (1950) 20 Ind. App. 41, 89 N.E. 2d 627.

[347]Haverell Distributors v. Haverell Mfg. Corp., (1944) 115 Ind. App. 501, 58 N.E.2d 372, citing First Nat'l Bank v. Baker, (1895) 62 Ill. App. 154.

[348]Butler Mfg. Co. v. Elliott & Cox, (1930) 211 Iowa 1068, 233 N.W. 669; Spain Management Co. v. Pack's Auto Sales, Inc., (1950) 54 N.M. 64, 213 P.2d 433. See discussion of use of trade or fictitious names by corporations and statutes governing them in Prentice-Hall *Corporation*.

[349]H.W. Underhill Constr. Co. v. Nilson, (1928) Mo. App. 3 S.W. 2d 399.

[350]Stephens v. Brackin, (1931) 16 La. App. 272, 134 So. 326.

name is generally of no effect, so far as the corporation's liability is concerned.[351]

Necessity for seal on corporate instruments. The corporation is required to use its seal in executing an instrument only when a seal is required by statute[352] or charter, or when an individual executing a similar document would be required to do so under seal.[353] If a corporation intends to seal an instrument, it cannot avoid its obligation merely because it has not adopted and used a corporate seal of its own.[354] It can use a scroll, or the word ''Seal,'' or any other device, just as individuals do.[355]

In the absence of statutory prohibition, a corporation may enter into contracts[356] and may convey and mortgage land without the use of its corporate seal.[357] Even where a seal is required to convey property, a deed that cannot convey legal title for want of a seal can pass equitable title.[358]

Seal as evidence of authority. It is generally held that a seal on a corporate instrument is prima facie evidence that the instrument was executed by authority of the corporation.[359] The burden of showing lack of authority is upon the person attacking the instrument.[360]

Who may sign corporate instruments. The authority to sign rests in the person or persons who are given that power in any of the following ways: (1) by statute, charter, or by-law provision; (2) by resolution conferring the power; or (3) by assumption and exercise of the authority in the past with the apparent consent and acquiescence of the corporation. If the corporation has not delegated to any particular person the power to sign,

---

[351]Houston Press Co. v. Bawden Bros., (1932) Tex. Civ. App. 51 S.W. 2d 438.

[352]Garrett v. Belmont Lane Co., (1895) 94 Tenn. 459, 29 S.W. 726.

[353]Alabama Fidelity & Cas. Co. v. Jefferson County Sav. Bank, (1917) 198 Ala. 557, 73 So. 918; Caruthers v. Peninsular Life Ins. Co., (1942) 150 Fla. 467, 7 So. 2d 841. Some states have relaxed the common law as to seals with respect to natural persons but not as to corporations. Covington Virginian, Inc. v. Woods, (1944) 182 Va. 538, 29 S.E. 2d 406.

[354]Collins v. Tracy Grill & Bar Corp., (1941) 144 Pa. Super. 440, 19 A.2d 617.

[355]Ismon v. Loder, (1904) 135 Mich. 345, 97 N.W. 769; Collins v. Tracy Grill & Bar Corp., (1941) 144 Pa. Super 440, 19 A.2d 617.

[356]Gottfried v. Miller, (1881) 104 U.S. 521, 26 L. Ed. 851; Leinkauf v. Calman, (1880) 110 N.Y. 50, 17 N.E. 389.

[357]Armstrong v. Home Service Stores, (1932) 203 N.C. 499, 166 S.E. 321; O'Neal v. Upton, (1950) 202 Okla. 403, 214 P.2d 712.

[358]Harris v. Zeuch, (1931) 103 Fla. 183, 137 So. 135.

[359]Port of Palm Beach Dist. v. Goethals, (1939) 104 F.2d 706; Central Hanover Bank & Trust Co. v. United Traction Co., (1938) 95 F.2d 50; H.G. Hill Co. v. Taylor, (1936) 232 Ala. 471, 168 So. 693; Thomas v. Peterson, (1931) 213 Cal. 672, 3 P.2d 306; Italo-Petroleum Corp. v. Hannigan, (1940) 40 Del. 534, 14 A. 2d 401; Henderson Lumber Co. v. Chatham Bank & Trust Co., (1924) 75 Colo. 519, 227 P. 555; 192; Bonninghausen v. Roma, (1939) 291 Mich. 603, 289 N.W. 921; York Ice Machinery Corp. v. Robbins, (1936) 323 Pa. 369, 185 A. 626; May Tire & Service, Inc. v. Sinclair Refining Co., (1942) 240 Wis. 260, 3 N.W. 2d 347. See also Ransom, ''Corporate Seal—When Affixing Seal Makes the Instrument a Specialty,'' 36 MICH. L. REV. 839.

[360]Bethel Methodist Episcopal Church v. Dagsboro Council, (1943) 27 Del. Ch. 64, 30 A. 2d 273; Robertson v. Burstein, (1929) 105 N.J.L. 375, 146 A. 355.

and the authority has not been assumed by usage, the person or persons who have power to enter into the contract and bind the corporation have the power to sign for the corporation.[361]

General authority of officers and agents to sign corporate instruments. The president of a corporation in active charge of the corporate business has the authority to sign the corporate name to any instrument executed in the course of the regular business.[362] Thus, if the corporation is created for the purpose of engaging in the business of buying and selling real estate, the president can make a contract for the sale of the corporation's realty, without special authorization.[363] If an instrument is signed by the vice president, and impressed with the corporation's seal, it is presumed that the vice president is acting in place of the president, in the absence of evidence to the contrary.[364]

A general manager who can exercise general authority has authority to sign a contract[365] and any provisions incidental to the contract itself.[366] But a corporation will not be bound by a contract signed by its general manager which is outside of its ordinary business.[367]

The secretary is often a ministerial officer, not an executive officer as are the president and vice president. Therefore, an instrument signed by the secretary should recite that he has the authority to execute it.[368]

Limitations on authority to sign corporate instruments. Authority given to a corporate officer or agent to sign and execute all documents does not mean that the officer or agent thus empowered has the further power to make any contract that he pleases.[369]

If authority to execute an instrument is specifically given by a corporate resolution, that authority is limited by the resolution. Thus, if an officer or agent is given authority to sign checks only, he does not have authority to indorse the name of the corporation on a note.[370]

---

[361]Raftis v. McCloud River Lumber Co., (1917) 35 Cal. App. 397, 170 P. 176.

[362]Italo-Petroleum Corp. v. Hannigan, (1940) 40 Del. 534, 14 A. 2d 401; Rosenthal v. Thirty-fourth St. Shop, (1927) 129 N.Y. Misc. 822, 222 N.Y. Supp. 733; Victoria Gravel Co. v. Neyland, (1938) Tex. Civ. App. 114 S.W. 2d 415. See also Vincennes Sav. & Loan Ass'n v. Robinson, (1939) 107 Ind. App. 558, 23 N.E. 2d 431, in which it was held that the president has power to execute negotiable instruments only where the board of directors expressly delegates such power or clothes the president with apparent authority by a continuity of acts and practices.

[363]Hasenfratz v. Berger Apartments, Inc., (1946) 61 N.Y.S. 2d 12.

[364]Hufstedler v. Sides, (1942) Tex. Civ. App. 165 S.W. 2d 1006.

[365]Raftis v. McCloud River Lumber Co., (1917) 35 Cal. App. 397, 170 P. 176.

[366]Morgan v. Cedar Grove Ice Co., (1949) 215 La. 741, 41 So. 2d 521.

[367]Miller v. Wick Bldg. Co., (1950) 154 Ohio St. 93, 93 N.E. 2d 467.

[368]Emmerglick v. Philip Wolf, Inc., (1943) 138 F.2d 661.

[369]Catholic Foreign Mission Soc'y v. Oussani, (1915) 215 N.Y. 1, 109 N.E. 80.

[370]Bennett v. Corporation Finance Co., (1927) 258 Mass. 306, 154 N.E. 835. In the absence of evidence to the contrary, the president and treasurer of a corporation are the proper officials to execute notes of a corporation. Downey v. People's State Bank, (1935) 101 Ind. App. 121, 194 N.E. 793.

Effect of improper execution of corporate instruments. Failure to comply with the provisions of the statute, charter, by-laws, or resolutions concerning execution of corporate instruments may render the instrument or contract invalid, and, consequently, not binding on the corporation.[371] However, under the following conditions, the corporation's failure to comply will not constitute a defense against liability: (1) if the provision in the statute or charter is directory, not mandatory;[372] (2) if the improper execution violates a by-law not required by statute or charter and persons dealing with the corporation had no notice of that by-law;[373] (3) if the execution was made in the regular course of business, and in the manner in which the corporation usually executes its instruments or contracts;[374] (4) if the person dealing with the corporation entered into the agreement in good faith, with no knowledge that the requirement had been violated, and was justified in assuming that it had been complied with;[375] (5) if the corporation has received the benefits of the contract;[376] (6) if the corporation has ratified the contract;[377] or (7) if the contract has been carried out on both sides.[378]

RESIGNATION AND REMOVAL OF
DIRECTORS AND OFFICERS

Right of directors and officers to resign. A director or officer may resign at any time, even though he has been elected or appointed for a definite period, unless some limitation is placed upon his right to resign by statute, charter, or by-laws of the corporation, or by the officer's contract with the company.[379]

---

[371]Rothberg v. Manhattan Coil Co., (1951) 84 Ga. App. 528, 66 S.E. 2d 390; Pring v. Benevolent and Protective Order of Keglers, (1949) 34 Wash. 2d 510, 209 P.2d 284.

[372]Rubottom v. Pioneer Life Ins. Co., (1921) 207 Mo. App. 616, 227 S.W. 835. What is directory and what mandatory is not definitely fixed, but is to be determined by the intention of the legislature, and the language, nature, and object of the provision.

[373]Doehler v. Lansdon, (1931) 135 Ore. 687, 298 P. 200.

[374]Blanc v. Germania Nat'l Bank, (1905) 114 La. 739, 38 So. 537.

[375]Where the corporation's secretary, on signing and delivering an order for a broker's commission, stated that the president's signature was also necessary, failure of the president to sign rendered the order ineffective. Harrop v. Coffman-Dobson Bank & Trust Co., (1931) 160 Wash. 449, 295 P.165.

[376]Big Creek Gap Coal & Iron Co. v. American Loan & Trust Co., (1904) 127 F. 625; Harlan Pub. Serv. Co. v. Eastern Constr. Co., (1934) 254 Ky. 135, 71 S.W. 2d 24; Webb v. Duvall, (1940) 177 Md. 592, 11 A. 2d 446; East Texas Title Co. v. Parchman, (1938) Tex. Civ. App. 116 S.W. 2d 497; Magruder v. Hagen-Ratcliff & Co., (1948) 131 W. Va. 679, 50 S.E. 2d 488.

[377]Bank of America Nat'l Trust & Sav. Ass'n v. Cryer, (1935) Cal. App. 49 P. 2d 864, aff'd, (1936) 6 Cal. 2d 485, 58 P. 2d 643; Ryan v. Charles E. Reed & Co., (1929) 266 Mass. 293, 165 N.E. 396.

[378]Alabama Consol. Coal & Iron Co. v. Baltimore Trust Co., (1912) 197 F. 347.

[379]Briggs v. Spaulding, (1891) 141 U.S. 132, 11 S. Ct. 924; Schuckman v. Rubenstein, (1947) 164 F.2d 952, cert. denied, 333 U.S. 875, 68 S. Ct. 905; Fearing v. Glenn, (1896) 73 F. 116; Gerdes v. Reynolds, (1941) 28 N.Y.S. 2d 622.

A provision in the statute, charter, or by-laws that an officer shall hold office until his successor is elected, or appointed, and qualified, does not limit the right of the officer or director to resign.[380] Nor will such a provision prevent a vacancy in office upon the filing of a resignation by one who is an incumbent of such office.[381] The law differs in the various jurisdictions as to whether an officer's resignation is effective, for the purpose of service of process, before his successor is appointed.[382]

If a director or officer resigns without fulfilling obligations placed upon him either by his contract or by the statute, charter, or by-laws, he may become liable to the corporation for the damages caused by his breach.[383]

Directors or officers cannot resign, of course, for fraudulent reasons,[384] as, for example, for the express purpose of instituting an action to procure the appointment of a receiver on the ground that the corporation is without officers.[385] Nor can they resign if the immediate effect would be to leave the interests of the corporation without proper care and protection.[386]

An agreement to resign for pecuniary gain is void, for it is deemed to be against public policy,[387] but, if the corporation is not insolvent, an agreement made in good faith, whereby the president is to resign in consideration of the purchase of his stock by the corporation, the payment to him of a reasonable salary allowance for the loss of his position, and the giving of a note for the amount owed to him by the company, is not a breach of trust.[388]

---

[380]Modern Heat & Power Co. v. Bishop Steamotor Corp., (1949) 239 Iowa 1257, 34 N.W. 2d 581. See also In re McNaughton's Will, (1909) 138 Wis. 179, 118 N.W. 997, 120 N.W. 288, where it was added that if the charter also specifically required acceptance of a resignation, resignation without such an acceptance would be ineffective.

[381]Western Pattern & Mfg. Co. v. American Metal Shoe Co., (1921) 175 Wis. 493, 185 N.W. 535.

[382]A resignation by a secretary and director, mailed to the corporation and the president thereof, was complete and effective, notwithstanding a by-law provision that "each director shall serve for the term for which he shall have been elected and until his successor shall have been duly elected and have qualified. . . ," and service had upon an officer who had thus resigned was the same as if made upon a stranger. Security Investors' Realty Co. v. Superior Court, (1929) 101 Cal. App. 450, 281 P. 709. But see Ross v. Western Land & Irrigation Co. et al., (1915) 223 F. 680, in which it was held that an officer elected under a by-law similar to the one mentioned in the preceding case, remains an officer on whom service of process against the corporation may be had, even if the officer has tendered his resignation, where the resignation has not been acted upon by the corporation, directors, or stockholders. See also Liken v. Shaffer, (1946) 64 F. Supp. 432.

The rule in New York is that, for the purpose of service of process, an officer's resignation is not effective until a successor has been appointed. Timolate v. S.J. Held Co., (1896) 17 N.Y. Misc. 556, 40 N.Y. Supp. 692.

[383]Bosworth v. Allen, (1901) 168 N.Y. 157, 61 N.E. 163.

[384]Inventions Corp. v. Hobbs, (1917) 244 F. 430.

[385]Zeltner v. Henry Zeltner Brewing Co., (1903) 174 N.Y. 247, 66 N.E. 810.

[386]Gerdes v. Reynolds, (1941) 28 N.Y.S. 2d 622.

[387]Forbes v. McDonald, (1880) 54 Cal. 98; Noel v. Drake, (1881) 28 Kan. 265; Elliott v. Chamberlain, (1884) 38 N.J. Eq. 604; Gerdes v. Reynolds, (1941 28 N.Y.S. 2d 622.

[388]Joseph v. Raff, (1903) 82 App. Div. 47, 81 N.Y. Supp. 546.

Acceptance of resignation; revocation before acceptance. The general rule is that acceptance of a resignation is not necessary in order to terminate the directorship or office, unless it is required by the statute, charter, by-laws, or contract.[389] However, if in resigning, the director or officer has stated that the resignation is to take effect upon acceptance, he will remain a director or continue to hold office until the resignation is accepted, or his successor is appointed.[390] Where a written resignation is tendered but never acted upon, and the director continues to attend meetings, the resignation is ineffective.[391] The resigning director must cease to act as a director at the time his resignation is to take effect,[392] but he can continue to act until that time.[393]

A director can revoke his resignation at any time before it is accepted.[394] Participation in a directors' meeting is sufficient to revoke a resignation.[395] On the other hand, if a resignation is to take effect at once, it is effective when tendered, and no subsequent act of the officer may revoke that resignation.[396]

Notice of resignation of directors and officers. In order that a resignation may be effective, notice must be given to the corporation. The proper person or body to receive the resignation is the one having the power to fill the vacancy.[397] It has been held, however, that notice served on the president is sufficient in the absence of a contrary provision.[398]

No notice need be given to creditors or to the general public.[399]

Form of resignation. The resignation may be either in writing or oral;[400] it need not be in any particular form,[401] and it may even be

---

[389]Briggs v. Spaulding, (1891) 141 U.S. 132, 11 S. Ct. 924; (1896) 73 F. 116; Du Bois v. Century Cement Products Co., (1936) 119 N.J. Eq. 472, 183 A. 188; President, etc., of Manhattan Co. v. Kaldenberg, (1900) 165 N.Y. 1, 58 N.E. 790; Bell v. Texas Employers' Ins. Ass'n, (1931) Tex. Civ. App. 43 S.W. 2d 290; State ex rel. Northwestern Development Corp. v. Gehrz, (1939) 230 Wis. 412, 283 N.W. 827. But see Young v. Janas, (1954) Del. Ch. 103 A. 2d 299, where the court held that director's resignation was not effective until accepted.

[390]Clark v. Oceano Beach Resort Co., (1930) 106 Cal. App. 574, 289 P. 946; Lincoln Court Realty Co. v. Kentucky Title Sav. Bank & Trust Co., (1916) 169 Ky. 840, 185 S.W. 156.

[391]Venner v. Denver Union Water Co., (1907) 40 Colo. 212, 90 P. 623.

[392]J.L. Mott Iron Works v. West Coast Plumbing Supply Co., (1896) 113 Cal. 341, 45 P. 683; Chemical Nat'l Bank v. Colwell, (1892) 132 N.Y. 250, 30 N.E. 644; Union Nat'l Bank v. Scott, (1900) 53 App. Div. 65, 66 N.Y.S. 145.

[393]Mayo v. Interment Properties, (1942) 53 Cal. App. 2d 654, 128 P. 2d 417.

[394]In re Fidelity Assurance Ass'n, (1941) 42 F. Supp. 973, reversed on other grounds, (1942) 129 F. 2d 442, aff'd, (1943) 318 U.S. 608, 63 S. Ct. 807.

[395]Ibid.

[396]Harry Levi & Co. v. Feldman, (1946) 61 N.Y.S. 2d 639.

[397]Movius v. Lee, (1887) 30 F. 298.

[398]International Bank v. Faber, (1898) 86 F. 443; Goodrich Rubber Co. v. Helena Motor Co., (1917) 53 Mont. 526, 165 P. 454.

[399]Bruce v. Platt, (1880) 80 N.Y. 379.

[400]Briggs v. Spaulding, (1891) 141 U.S. 132, 11 S. Ct. 924; Fearing v. Glenn, (1896) 73 F. 116.

[401]Briggs v. Spaulding, (1891) 141 U.S. 132, 11 S. Ct. 924.

implied.[402] It is advisable that the resignation be in writing,[403] in order that a record may be available for future use in case of controversy, and that it indicate when the resignation is to take effect. In the absence of such a statement, a resignation takes effect immediately.

Power to remove directors and officers. Directors and officers are generally elected for a definite term. They are entitled to hold their positions for the term for which they are elected.[404] In most states, there is no statutory provision for removal of directors or officers; the subject is usually covered by the corporate charter or by-laws.[405] Whether or not there is a charter or by-law provisions, a corporation has the inherent right to remove a director or officer at any time for cause.[406] Under some circumstances it may even remove a director or officer without cause. (See page 272.)

Acts that constitute cause for removal. The following illustrate acts that have been held to constitute cause for removal:

1. Conversion of corporate funds.[407]
2. Making an unwarranted attack on the character of the president and refusing to work with him.[408]
3. Careless management by the president that resulted in embezzlement of funds by the bookkeeper.[409]
4. Attempting to divert company business.[410]
5. Impairing the efficient administration of the company's business by

---

[402]In Dodge v. Kenwood Ice Co., (1913) 204 F. 577, a resignation was held to be implied from acts of the directors, without either oral or written statement.

[403]See Union Nat'l Bank of Troy v. Scott, (1900) 53 App. Div. 65, 66 N.Y.S. 145, in which certain declarations of a director were held not to constitute a resignation.

[404]Toledo Traction, Light & Power Co. v. Smith, (1913) 205 F. 643; Walsh v. State ex rel. Cook, (1917) 199 Ala 123, 74 So. 45.

[405]Templeman v. Grant, (1924) 75 Colo. 519, 227 P. 555; Walker v. Maas, (1926) 4 N.J. Misc. 230, 132 A. 322.

[406]Templeman v. Grant, (1924) 75 Colo. 519, 227 P. 555; Fox v. Cody, (1931) 141 N.Y. Misc. 552, 252 N.Y. Supp. 395.

Several states have statutes regulating the removal of directors elected under cumulative voting. Generally these laws prohibit the removal of such directors if the number of shares voted against their removal would have been sufficient to elect them if voted cumulatively. See Prentice-Hall *Corporation*. These statutes are designed to prevent the circumvention of the purpose behind cumulative voting which could occur if a simple majority of the stockholders could dismiss any director. (See "Cumulative Voting" on page 40, Chapter 1.)

In the absence of a statute governing the removal of directors elected by cumulative voting, a director so elected may nevertheless be removed *for cause*. Campbell v. Loew's, Inc., (1957) Del. Ch. 134 A.2d 852. But a director elected under a charter calling for cumultive voting may not be removed *without cause*, even though there is a by-law provision providing for such removal. In re Rogers Imports, Inc., (1952) 202 N.Y. Misc. 761, 116 N.Y.S. 2d 106.

[407]Smock v. Buchanan & Smock Lumber Co., (1924) 96 N.J. Eq. 308, 125 A. 115; Green Bay Fish Co. v. Jorgensen, (1917) 165 Wis. 548, 163 N.W. 142.

[408]Gutmann Silks Corp. v. Reilly, (1919) 189 App. Div. 258, 178 N.Y. Supp. 457.

[409]Boulicault v. Oriel Glass Co., (1920) 283 Mo. 237, 223 S.W. 423.

[410]McClayton v. W.B. Cassell Co., (1946) 66 F. Supp. 165.

speaking disparagingly of fellow officers and openly defying the board of directors.[411]

Acts that do not constitute cause for removal. The following illustrate acts that have been held insufficient grounds for removal:

1. Mere friction between two officers.[412]
2. Mere failure to use care—it must be a willful or negligent failure.[413]
3. Acts causing financial loss to the corporation, where the acts were done in good faith and the methods used were known and approved by the board of directors.[414]

Removal without cause. A director or officer may be removed without cause: (1) if he has not been elected for a definite term, and removal for cause is not expressly required,[415] or (2) if express provision is made in the statute, charter, or by-laws that he may be removed without cause.[416] If the person to be removed has been elected or appointed to his office for a definite term, he cannot be removed without cause,[417] unless some statute or provision of the charter or by-laws authorizes such removal.[418] However, some courts hold that a ministerial officer has no franchise in his office and may be removed from office at the pleasure of the board of directors.[419] It has been held that a board of directors that has the right to create an office and appoint the officer has the right to remove him at pleasure.[420]

Who may remove directors and officers. The removal of an officer

[411]Holmes v. United Mut. Life Ins. Co., (1955) 286 App. Div. 500, 145 N.Y.S. 2d 26, aff'd, (1956) 1 N.Y. 2d 828, 135 N.E. 2d 718.

[412]Mortimer v. D.T. McKeithan Lumber Corp., (1923) 127 S.C. 266, 120 S.E. 723.

[413]W.F. Boardman Co. v. Petch, (1921) 186 Cal. 476, 199 P. 1047.

[414]Roberts v. J.A. Masquere Co., (1925) 158 La. 642, 104 So. 484

[415]In re A.A. Griffing Iron Co., (1898) 63 N.J.L. 168, 41 A. 931, aff'd, (1899) 63 N.J.L. 357, 46 A. 1097.

[416]Walker v. Maas, (1926) 4 N.J. Misc. 230, 132 A. 322; In re Schwartz, (1922) 119 N.Y. Misc. 387, 196 N.Y. Supp. 679.

[417]Under the Washington statute such removal does not prejudice contractual rights between the discharged officer and the corporation. Jansen v. Columbia Breweries, Inc., (1942) 12 Wash. 2d 554, 122 P. 2d 489.

[418]Barker v. National Life Ass'n, (1918) 183 Iowa 966, 166 N.W. 597; Cohen v. Camden Refrigerating & Terminals Co., (1943) 129 N.J.L. 519, 30 A. 2d 428; Costello v. Thomas Cusack Co., (1922) 96 N.J. Eq. 83, 90, 124, A. 615; In re Schwartz, (1922) 119 N.Y. Misc. 387, 196 N.Y. Supp. 697.

But see Realty Acceptance Corp. v. Montgomery, (1930) 51 F. 2d 636, in which it was held that a contract authorized by directors employing the president of the corporation for a five-year period prevailed over an inconsistent by-law empowering a majority of the board to remove the president.

[419]Brindley v. Walker, (1908) 221 Pa. 287, 70 A. 794.

See Bussing v. Lowell Film Productions, Inc., (1931) 233 N.Y. App. Div. 493, 253 N.Y. Supp. 719, in which it was held that under the statute the directors had full authority to remove an officer "at pleasure." See also Schepp v. Evansville Television, Inc., (1957) Ind. 141 N.E. 2d 400, holding that the corporation can enjoin its former officers from purporting to act as officers after their removal.

[420]Christy v. Laclede-Christy Clay Products Co., (1923) Mo. App. 253 S.W. 106.

or a director must be undertaken by the body or person vested with the power to remove.[421] Where authority to remove is not specifically granted to a particular body or person, the removal must be by the body or person who had the authority to elect or appoint the person to be removed.[422] A director cannot be removed by his fellow directors in the absence of express power in the board of directors to do so;[423] he is an officer chosen by the stockholders and must be removed by the stockholders.[424] The question whether a director should be removed for misconduct is not arbitrable.[425]

A person who is about to be removed cannot vote upon the question of his own removal, on the principle that a man cannot act as a judge in his own case.[426]

See page 274 for removal of directors and officers by the courts.

Unlawful removal. If an officer is unlawfully removed, he may apply to the court for reinstatement.[427] Mandamus and quo warranto are legal remedies that have been resorted to for this purpose.[428] The courts limit themselves, in cases concerning removal, to inquiring whether the person or body assuming the authority to remove acted within their power

---

[421]Ginter v. Heco Envelope Co., (1925) 316 Ill. 183, 147 N.E. 42, holding that, where the power to remove an officer is vested in the directors, action by them is necessary to constitute a removal.

[422]Feldman v. Pennroad Corp., (1945) 60 F. Supp. 716, aff'd, (1946) 155 F. 2d 773; Stott v. Stott Realty Co., (1929) 246 Mich. 267, 224 N.W. 623; Kiel v. Fred Medart Mfg. Co., (1932) Mo. App. 46 S.W. 2d 934; In re A.A. Griffing Iron Co., (1898) 63 N.J.L. 168, 41 A. 931, aff'd (1899) 63 N.J.L. 357, 46 A. 1097.

If the statute gives the directors power to elect a treasurer, the directors may remove him, even though the by-laws provide that the stockholders shall elect the treasurer. A by-law that is inconsistent with a statute is invalid. Bechtold v. Stillwagon, (1922) 119 N.Y. Misc. 177, 195 N.Y. Supp. 66. Ordinarily the selection of the secretary and treasurer is committed to the board of directors; but, when the stockholders have elected these officers, only the stockholders can remove them. Brindley holders have elected these officers, only the stockholders can remove them. Brindley v. Walker, (1908) 221 Pa. 287, 70 A. 794. See also Birmingham Realty Co. v. Hale, (1918) 16 Ala. App. 460, 78 So. 723; Fensterer v. Pressure Lighting Co., (1914) 85 N.Y. Misc. 621, 149 N.Y. Supp. 49; Spahn & Bielefeld v. Spahn Co., (1917 256 Pa. 543, 100 A. 987.

[423]But see Lloyd v. Decca Records, Inc., (1954) 131 N.Y.L.J. No. 56, p. 6, 3-24-54, holding that a by-law delegating to the board of directors the power to remove a director is valid and binding. Its adoption or employment does not, in any way, offend any statute, decisional law or public policy.

[424]Bruch v. National Guarantee Credit Corp., (1922) 13 Del. Ch. 180, 116 A. 738; Matter of Auer, (1954) 306 N.Y. 427, 118 N.E. 2d 590. In Leviton v. North Jersey Holding Co., (1930) 106 N.J. Eq. 517, 151 A. 389, it was held that concerted action by stockholders controlling a majority of the stock, to oust a director owning a minority of the stock, was not an unlawful conspiracy warranting the appointment of a receiver and a termination of the affairs of the corporation.

[425]Matter of Burkin, (1956) 1 N.Y. 2d 570, 154 N.Y.S. 2d 898, 136 N.E. 2d 862.

[426]Hinkley v. Sagemiller, (1926) 191 Wis. 512, 210 N.W. 839.

[427]Walsh v. State ex rel. Cook, (1917) 199 Ala. 123, 74 So. 45.

[428]Fuller v. Plainfield Academic School, (1827) 6 Conn. 532; State ex rel. G.T. Welch v. Passaic Hospital, (1904) 59 N.J.L. 142, 36 A. 702; People ex rel. Manice v. Powell, (1911) 201 N.Y. 194, 94 N.E. 634; State ex rel. Weingart v. Board of Officers of Gegenseitige Unterstuetzungs Gesellschaft Germania. (1911) 144 Wis. 516 129 N.W. 630.

fairly and in good faith, after giving notice to the accused and affording him an opportunity to prepare and make his defense.[429]

Officers continuing to act after removal and pending determination of litigation over their removal, are de facto officers,[430] and contracts made by them bind the corporation, especially where the corporation acquiesced in their making and received their benefits.[431]

Removal of directors and officers by the courts. In the absence of fraud, the courts may remove officers only when they are given express power to do so by statutory provision.[432] Removal of an officer is unwarranted interference with internal corporate affairs, unless the deposed officer is guilty of fraud of such a nature that directors or stockholders should have removed him and did not do so.[433] The misconduct must be current—mere apprehension of future misconduct based upon prior mismanagement does not warrant removal.[434] In one case, a court removed for a two-year period a director who continually and irresponsibly harassed officers and employees in the conduct of the business.[435]

Notice of removal of directors and officers. Where the removal of a director or an officer is being made for cause, notice of the proposed removal must be given the accused. He must have opportunity to be heard in his own defense and a reasonable time in which to prepare his defense.[436] A corporation, however, is not required to act with the strict regularity that obtains in judicial proceedings.

FILLING VACANCIES AMONG DIRECTORS AND OFFICERS

Power to fill vacancies. Unless a vacancy in the board of directors causes the number of directors to fall below the number required to

---

[429]State ex rel. Blackwood v. Brast, (1925) 98 W. Va. 596 127 S.E. 507. Where business was always transacted with the acquiescence of the plaintiff (a member of the board), without any formal meeting, the corporation had the right to discharge the plaintiff without a formal meeting. Kahn v. Colonial Fuel Corp., (1923) 198 N.Y. Supp. 596.

[430]Cohen v. Miller, (1949) 5 N.J. Super. 451, 68 A. 2d 421, comment, 23 TEMP. L.Q. 420.

[431]American Concrete Units Co. v. National Stone-Tile Corp., (1931) 115 Cal. App. 501, 1 P. 2d 1084.

[432]Feldman v. Pennroad Corp., (1945) 60 F. Supp. 716, aff'd, (1946) 155 F. 2d 773; Whyte v. Faust, (1924) 281 Pa. 444, 127 A. 234.

[433]Nahikian v. Mattingly, (1933) 265 Mich. 128, 251 N.W. 421.

[434]Feldman v. Pennroad Corp., (1945) 60 F. Supp. 716, aff'd. (1946) 155 F. 2d 773.

[435]Markovitz v. Markovitz, (1939) 336 Pa. 145, 8 A.2d 46.

[436]Bruch v. National Guarantee Credit Corp., (1922) 13 Del. Ch. 180, 116 A. 738; Alliance Co-op Ins. Co. v. Gasche, (1914) 93 Kan. 147, 142 P. 882; Costello v. Thomas Cusack Co., (1922) 96 N.J. Eq. 83, 90, 124 A. 615. An attempted removal of a director was held void where no notice was given to the director of the meeting at which his removal was voted upon. Piedmont Press Ass'n v. Record Publishing Co., (1930) 156 S.C. 43, 152 S.E. 721. See also Teperman v. Atcos Batts, Inc., (1956) 4 N.Y. Misc. 2d 738, 158 N.Y.S. 2d 391, calling for service of specific charges, adequate notice, and a hearing.

constitute a quorum, a vacancy does not interfere with the transaction of business.[437] In the absence of express statutory, charter, or by-law provision on the subject, the power of filling vacancies in the board of directors rests with the stockholders.[438] If a statute gives the directors permission to fill vacancies for an unexpired term, a resigning director can vote upon his successor before the resignation becomes effective.[439] Under such a statute, the directors do not have the same right to appoint newly created directors;[440] the stockholders must therefore elect directors to fill vacancies arising through an increase in the number of directors on the board.[441] The stockholders need not wait for an annual meeting to fill vacancies created by an increase in the number of directors, but may fill the vacancies at once.[442]

The statute, of course, may give the directors power to fill vacancies caused by an increase in the number of directors. The statutory provision giving directors the power to fill vacancies should be read carefully to see if there is any limitation on the right of the directors to fill vacancies when the number remaining falls below a quorum.[443] (See page 134 in Chapter 3 for quorum requirements when the board has vacancies.)

Vacancies occurring among the officers should be filled according to the by-laws. Where no provision whatever is made in the statute, charter, or by-laws, vacancies may be filled by those who had the power to appoint or to elect the officers in the first instance. When the office of president becomes vacant, the vice-president has authority to act in the place of the president until the office of president is filled as provided in the by-laws.[444]

Conduct of meeting to fill vacancies. A meeting of stockholders, called to fill vacancies among directors, is conducted in the same manner as any meeting for the election of directors. In states where directors are permitted to fill vacancies only when they have a quorum, it is advisable

---

[437]Dodge v. Kenwood Ice. Co., (1913) 204 F. 577; A.E. Touchet, Inc. v. Touchet, (1928) 264 Mass. 499, 163 N.W. 184.

See Porter v. Lassen County Land & Cattle Co., (1899) 127 Cal. 261, 59 P. 563, holding that a mortgage executed by the board of directors when its members were below the minimum required may subsequently be ratified by a board with the required number of directors.

[438]Sylvania & G. Ry. v. Hoge, (1907) 129 Ga. 734, 59 S.E. 806.

[439]Mayo v. Interment Properties, (1942) 53 Cal. App. 2d 654, 128 P. 2d 417.

[440]Belle Isle v. MacBean, (1948) 30 Del. Ch. 373, 61 A. 2d 699; Automatic Steel Products, Inc. v. Johnson, (1949) 31 Del. Ch. 241, 64 A. 2d 416, aff'g Del Ch. 60 A. 2d 455.

[441]Gold Bluff Mining & Lumber Corp. v. Whitlock, (1903) 75 Conn. 669, 55 A. 175; In re A.A. Griffing Iron Co., (1898) 63 N.J.L. 168, 41 A. 931, aff'd, (1899) 63 N.J.L. 357, 46 A. 1097.

[442]Moon v. Moon Motor Car Co., (1930) 17 Del. Ch. 176, 151 A. 298.

[443]In re Chelsea Exchange Corp., (1932) 18 Del. 442, 159 A. 432, held that under the statute a majority of the remaining directors may elect directors to fill vacancies regardless of whether or not a quorum of the board is then in office. But see Moses v. Thompkins, (1887) 84 Ala. 613, 4 So. 763, in which the filling of vacancies by directors when the board had fallen below a majority was held invalid. See Harris v. Brown, (1925) 6 F.2d 922; also People ex rel. Weber v. Cohn, (1930) 339 Ill. 121, 171 N.E. 159 interpreting statutes relating to filling of vacancies.

[444]Hufstedler v. Sides, (1942) Tex. Civ. App. 165 S.W. 2d 1006.

that the vacancies be filled promptly before further vacancies in the board reduce the number to less than a quorum.[445]

If, at a meeting of the board, several directors are to be elected to fill vacancies caused by resignations to be tendered at the same meeting, it is advisable not to accept all the resignations at one time and then proceed to fill the vacancies; if this procedure is followed, it is likely that a quorum will not be present when the vacancies are being filled. Each resignation should therefore be accepted separately, and, immediately after acceptance, the successor to the resigning director should be elected and should, upon election, assume his duties as a director. He then becomes qualified to act in the election of the director to fill the vacancy caused by the acceptance of the next resignation. The secretary should be assured in advance that the directors who are to replace the resigning directors will be present at the meeting.

If the statute provides that where a resignation is tendered, to be effective at a future date, the board shall have the power to fill the vacancy caused by the resignation, such vacancy to take effect when the resignation becomes effective, the above procedure is, of course, unnecessary.[446] The resignations may be accepted together, the minutes indicating that they are to take effect at the close of the meeting, or at some future time, and the directors may proceed immediately to elect directors to fill the vacancies which will occur upon the effective date of the resignations.

---

[445]See Freidus v. Kaufman, (1955) 36 N.J. Super. 321, 114 A. 2d 751.
[446]In re Vicksburg Bridge & Terminal Co., (1937) 22 F. Supp. 490.

Chapter 10

FORMS OF RESOLUTIONS CONCERNING MANAGEMENT OF THE CORPORATION

Contents—Chapter 10

277

Committees, Assistant Officers, Agents

CONTENTS

CONTENTS

MEETINGS OF DIRECTORS
AND STOCKHOLDERS

DIRECTORS' RESOLUTION FIXING DATE OF REGULAR MEETING OF BOARD, AND DISPENSING WITH FURTHER NOTICE

RESOLVED, That the regular .... *(insert monthly or weekly)* meeting of the Board of Directors of the .... Corporation, other than the regular annual meeting of the Board of Directors, be held at the principal office of the Corporation, at .... *(Street)*, ... *(City)*, ... *(State)*, on the .. day of each .... *(month or week)*, at ..... A.M., and that no further notice of such regular meetings need be given.

DIRECTORS' RESOLUTION FIXING DATE OF MEETING OF BOARD AND EXECUTIVE COMMITTEE WHEN REGULAR MEETING DATE FALLS ON HOLIDAY

RESOLVED, That whenever the date for a regular meeting of the Board of Directors or the Executive Committee falls upon a holiday, or upon a day on which business is generally suspended by request or direction of any Federal, State, or municipal authority, whether declared to be a holiday or not, such meeting shall be held on the next succeeding business day at the usual hour and place, or at such other hour and place as the Chairman of the Board may designate.

DIRECTORS' RESOLUTION CHANGING DATE OF REGULAR MEETING OF BOARD

RESOLVED, That until otherwise provided by resolution of the Board of Directors, regular meetings of the Board shall be held at the office of the Corporation, ... *(Street)*, ... *(City)*, ... *(State)*, on the .. day of each month, at ..... P.M., instead of on the .. day thereof at .... o'clock .. M., and that the Secretary of this Corporation is hereby directed to serve notice of this resolution on each director not present at this meeting.

DIRECTORS' RESOLUTION ADJOURNING MEETING TO A SPECIFIED DATE

RESOLVED, That this meeting adjourn to ...., 19.., at ..... A.M., the said adjourned meeting to be held at the office of this Corporation, ...*(Street)*, ... *(City)*, ... *(State)*.

DIRECTORS' RESOLUTION EXTENDING INVITATION TO BOARD MEETING

WHEREAS, this Board of Directors has under advisement the purchase of property located at ....*(Street)*, ...*(City)*, ...*(State)*, and

WHEREAS, ... has expressed his willingness to advise, assist, and co-operate with this Corporation in financing this purchase, be it

RESOLVED, That .... be invited to attend a .... *(insert regular or special)* meeting of the Board of Directors, to be held at the office of the Corporation at .... *(Street)*, ... *(City)*, ... *(State)*, ..., 19.., at ..... P.M., to discuss with the members of the Board the matter of financing the purchase, and the Secretary of this Corporation is hereby directed to transmit to .... a written invitation to the meeting.

DIRECTORS' RESOLUTION AUTHORIZING HOLDING OF DIRECTORS' MEETINGS OUTSIDE OF STATE

RESOLVED, That until otherwise ordered by resolution of the Board of Directors, meetings of the Board of Directors may be held either at the principal office of this Corporation in the state, at .... *(Street)*, ... *(City)*, ... *(State)*, or at the office established and maintained by this Corporation at .... *(Street)*, ... *(City)*, ... *(State)*.

DIRECTORS' RESOLUTION CALLING STOCKHOLDERS' MEETING TO ELECT DIRECTORS UPON FAILURE TO HOLD ANNUAL MEETING

WHEREAS, the annual meeting of stockholders for the election of directors was not held at the time designated by Article ....., Section ..... of the By-laws, and no Board of Directors has been elected for the year 19.., be it

RESOLVED, That the Secretary of this Corporation is hereby authorized and directed to serve notice of a meeting of the stockholders for the election of directors for the ensuing year, to be held at the office of the Corporation .... *(Street)*, ... *(City)*, ... *(State)*, on ...., 19.., at ..... P.M.

DIRECTORS' RESOLUTION AUTHORIZING PRESIDENT TO ADDRESS EXPLANATORY LETTER ACCOMPANYING NOTICE OF SPECIAL MEETING OF STOCKHOLDERS

RESOLVED, That ...., President of the Company, address a letter to the stockholders, to accompany the notice of stockholders' meeting to be held on ...., 19.., setting forth the reasons underlying the calling of the special meeting of the stockholders.

DIRECTORS' RESOLUTION AUTHORIZING CALLING OF MEETINGS OF EXECUTIVE COMMITTEE

RESOLVED, That meetings of the Executive Committee be called from time to time by the Secretary of this Corporation at the request of the Chairman of the Board of Directors, the President, or any two members of the Executive Committee, upon notice to each member of the Committee (either at his last-known business address in the City of ...., or at any address which he may have filed with the Secretary), at least ..... hours *(or days)* before the time set for any such meeting. Such notice may be either written or oral, and may be delivered personally, or transmitted by mail, telegraph, or telephone to either address.

RESOLUTION OF EXECUTIVE COMMITTEE FIXING TIME AND PLACE OF ITS REGULAR MEETINGS

RESOLVED, That until otherwise provided by the Executive Committee, the regular meetings of the Committee shall be held at the office of the Corporation, ... *(Street)*, ... *(City)*, ... *(State)*, on the .... of each ...., at ..... A.M., or at such other time and place as the Chairman of the Committee or the Board of Directors may designate.

DIRECTORS' RESOLUTION FIXING RECORD DATE TO DETERMINE STOCKHOLDERS ENTITLED TO NOTICE OF AND TO VOTE AT ANNUAL MEETING

RESOLVED, That pursuant to Article ..... of the By-laws and Section ..... of the Corporation Laws of the State of ...., the Board of Directors hereby declares that stockholders of record at the close of business on ...., 19.., shall be entitled to notice of and to vote at the annual meeting of stockholders to be held ...., 19...

STOCKHOLDERS' RESOLUTION APPROVING AFFIDAVIT OF NOTICE OF MEETING AND OTHER FORMS

RESOLVED, That the affidavit of notice of the time, place, and purpose of this meeting, together with the attached form of notice are hereby approved, and that copies thereof be attached to the minutes of this meeting and marked "Exhibit A."

STOCKHOLDERS' RESOLUTION DISPENSING WITH REGULAR ORDER OF BUSINESS

RESOLVED, That the regular order of business, as prescribed in Section ..... of Article ..... of the By-laws of this Corporation, be dispensed with, and that the meeting proceed to a consideration of the matters contained in the notice of this meeting.

ELECTION, RESIGNATION, AND REMOVAL

STOCKHOLDERS' RESOLUTION AUTHORIZING A VOTE UPON A PROPOSED RESOLUTION AND ELECTION OF DIRECTORS BY THE SAME BALLOT

RESOLVED, That to avoid delay, the stockholders shall vote by ballot at the same time upon the resolution offered by Mr. .... to .... *(insert subject matter of resolution)*, and for the election of directors, and that action upon the resolution and for the election of directors shall be by stock vote.

STOCKHOLDERS' RESOLUTION CLASSIFYING DIRECTORS

WHEREAS, under the laws of the State of ....., the state in which this corporation is organized, the stockholders have the power to divide the Board of Directors into three (3) classes when the Board of Directors consists of ..... (.....) or more members, and

WHEREAS, the Board of Directors of this corporation consists of ..... (.....) members, and

WHEREAS, the stockholders of this corporation deem it advisable to divide the Board of Directors into three (3) classes so that the term of office of one class shall expire in each year, be it

RESOLVED, That the directors shall be divided into three (3) classes, each of which shall consist of ..... (.....) directors. The term of office of the first class shall expire on the day of the next annual election of this corporation; the term of office of the second class shall expire one year thereafter; and that of the third class two (2) years thereafter. At each annual election after such classification, the number of directors equal to the number of the class whose term expires on the day of such election shall be elected for a term of three (3) years.

DIRECTORS' RESOLUTION REQUESTING RESIGNATION
OF OFFICER

RESOLVED, That ...., President of this Corporation, is hereby requested to resign as President of the Corporation, and the Secretary of the Corporation is hereby authorized and directed to send a copy of this resolution to the said ....

DIRECTORS' RESOLUTION ACCEPTING RESIGNATION OF A
MEMBER OF BOARD

RESOLVED, That the resignation of .... as a member of the Board of Directors of the .... Corporation, as evidenced by his letter to the Corporation, dated ...., 19.., is hereby accepted, and the Secretary of this Corporation is hereby instructed to notify .... of the acceptance of his resignation.

DIRECTORS' RESOLUTION ACCEPTING
RESIGNATION OF OFFICER

RESOLVED, That the resignation of Mr. .... as .... *(insert office)* be and it hereby is accepted to take effect on ...., 19...

RESOLUTION OF DIRECTORS EXPRESSING GRATITUDE FOR SERVICES OF RESIGNING OFFICER

WHEREAS, ... has, for the past ..... (.....) years, been President of the Company, and WHEREAS, ... declines to be a candidate for re-election, this Board of Directors desires to spread the following resolution upon the minutes:

RESOLVED, That we recognize the excellent, energetic, and intelligent service which .... has rendered the Company during his incumbency. We feel that the high position which the Company has attained has been in large measure due to his earnest efforts and untiring devotion.

RESOLVED FURTHER, That in recognition of his services to the Company, ... be elected Chairman to preside at the meetings of the Board for the ensuing year.

DIRECTORS' RESOLUTION RECORDING DISQUALIFICATION OF DIRECTOR AND FILLING VACANCY

RESOLVED, That .... ceased to be a director of this corporation on ...., 19.., by reason of his ceasing on that day to be a stockholder of the corporation *(or insert any other reason for disqualification)*.

RESOLVED FURTHER, That the Secretary of this corporation is hereby directed to send written notice to .... of his disqualification as director.

RESOLVED FURTHER, That the office of .... as director of this corporation is hereby declared vacant, and that .... is hereby appointed director of this corporation to fill this vacancy.

STOCKHOLDERS' RESOLUTION REMOVING ENTIRE BOARD OF DIRECTORS

RESOLVED, That the entire Board of Directors of this Corporation, consisting of ...., ..., and ...., is hereby removed, and the office of each member of the Board is hereby declared vacant.

RESOLVED FURTHER, That an election of a new Board of Directors, to fill the vacancies caused by the removal of the Board, be held immediately.

DIRECTORS' RESOLUTION REMOVING DIRECTOR FOR CAUSE

WHEREAS, ... has participated in the organization of the .... Company, a competitor of this Corporation, and is now an officer and director of, and is otherwise interested in, said Company, and

WHEREAS, the conduct of .... has not, in the judgment of this Board of Directors, been for the best interests of this Corporation, be it

Resolved, That sufficient cause exists for the removal of .... from the office of director, and that his removal from such office is desirable and for the best interests of this Corporation.

Resolved further, That pursuant to Article ....., Section ..... of the By-laws of this Corporation, ... is hereby removed from the office of director of this Corporation, and the Secretary of the Corporation is hereby directed to send him written notice of his removal.

DIRECTORS' RESOLUTION REMOVING OFFICER ON CHARGES

Whereas, The Board of Directors has read and considered the charges of "A," "B," and "C" against ...., President of this Company, and the reply by ...., and

Whereas, ... has absented himself from this meeting and given the Board no opportunity to examine into the points made controversial, and

Whereas, there is disclosed, in the judgment of the Board, a sufficient number of undisputed facts to warrant the removal of .... as President of this Company, and

Whereas, ... has advised the officers of this Company, through his attorney, of his willingness to retire from the Company upon the disposal of his stock, be it

Resolved, That this Board finds that the above charges are sustained, and the office of President is hereby declared vacant by the removal of ....

DIRECTORS' RESOLUTION REMOVING OFFICER WITHOUT SPECIFYING CAUSE

Resolved, That pursuant to Article ....., Section ..... of the By-laws of this Corporation, ... is hereby removed from his office as .... of this Corporation, and

Resolved further, That the Secretary of this Corporation is hereby authorized and directed to give notice of such removal to ....

DIRECTORS' RESOLUTION SUSPENDING OFFICER PENDING DETERMINATION OF CHARGES

Whereas, ... and .... did, on ...., 19.., cause to be filed with the Secretary of this Corporation specifications in writing of certain charges preferred by them against .... as .... *(insert title of officer)* of this Corporation, and

Whereas, a copy of the charges against him was duly served upon

.... on ...., 19.., together with a notice that the charges would be heard at a regular meeting of the Board of Directors, to be held on ...., 19.., and

Whereas, ... has asked for further time within which to prepare himself to meet these charges, be it

Resolved, That the hearing of the charges against .... is hereby adjourned to a special meeting of the Board of Directors of this Corporation, to be held on ...., 19.., at ..... A.M., at the office of the Corporation, ... *(Street)*, ... *(City)*, ... *(State)*, and

Resolved further, That, pending the hearing and determination of the charges, any and all powers of .... as .... *(insert title of officer)* of this Corporation shall be suspended, and the .... *(insert title of officer next in rank)* of this Corporation shall, during such time, exercise all the powers and perform all the duties of ....

STOCKHOLDERS' RESOLUTION REMOVING OFFICER AND DIRECTOR

Whereas, it appears that ...., Vice-president and director of the .... Corporation, has been remiss in his duties as such officer, and has shown himself to be inefficient, untrustworthy, and generally unfit to discharge the duties of his office, be it

Resolved, That .... is hereby removed as Vice-president and director of the .... Corporation, and these offices are hereby declared vacant.

DIRECTORS' RESOLUTION DISMISSING CHARGES AGAINST OFFICER

Whereas, the Board of Directors has read and considered the written specifications of charges preferred by .... and .... as .... *(insert titles of officers)* of this Corporation, and filed with the Secretary of this Corporation on ...., 19.., and

Whereas, the members of this Board are unanimously agreed that the charges are unwarranted, unjustified, and entirely without foundation, be it

Resolved, That the charges of .... and .... against .... are hereby dismissed.

DIRECTORS' RESOLUTION FILLING VACANCY IN BOARD UNTIL NEXT ANNUAL STOCKHOLDERS' MEETING

Resolved, That .... is hereby appointed a director of the .... Corporation until the next annual stockholders' meeting, to fill the vacancy caused by the resignation of ....

COMMITTEES, ASSISTANT OFFICERS, AGENTS

DIRECTORS' RESOLUTION APPOINTING EXECUTIVE COMMITTEE, DEFINING ITS POWERS, AND PROVIDING FOR ITS MEETINGS

RESOLVED, That pursuant to Article ....., Section ..... of the By-laws of this Corporation, Messrs. ...., ..., and ...., are hereby appointed an Executive Committee, to hold office for a period of ...., commencing ...., 19.., and until their respective successors are appointed, and

RESOLVED FURTHER, That the said Executive Committee shall have the following powers while the Board of Directors is not in session:

1. To appoint officers of the Corporation and determine their salaries;
2. To appoint agents of the Corporation and determine their salaries;
3. To borrow money, and issue bonds, notes, or other obligations and evidences of indebtedness therefor;
4. To authorize the corporate seal to be affixed to documents of the Corporation;
5. To determine questions of general policy with regard to the business of the Corporation;
6. To make recommendations as to declaration of dividends, and

RESOLVED FURTHER, That the Executive Committee shall have such other powers as may lawfully be delegated to it by the Board of Directors, not in conflict with specific powers conferred by the Board of Directors upon any other committee appointed by it, and

RESOLVED FURTHER, That the Executive Committee shall report all its actions to the Board of Directors, and

RESOLVED FURTHER, That meetings of the Executive Committee shall be called by the Secretary of the Corporation, from time to time, at the direction and upon the request of the President or any two members of the Executive Committee; that notice of such meetings shall in each instance be given to each member of the Committee at his last-known business address, at least ..... (.....) *(insert hours or days)* before the meeting, either orally or in writing, delivered personally or by mail, telegraph, telephone, or radio.

DIRECTORS' RESOLUTION GRANTING POWERS TO EXECUTIVE COMMITTEE BETWEEN BOARD MEETINGS

RESOLVED, That beginning with ...., 19.., and until otherwise provided by resolution of this Board of Directors, the Executive Committee, between the meetings of the Board and while the Board is not in session, shall have all the powers and exercise all the duties of the Board of Directors in the management of the business of the Corporation which may lawfully be delegated to it by the said Board.

RESOLUTION OF EXECUTIVE COMMITTEE DELEGATING ITS POWERS TO CHAIRMAN, BETWEEN MEETINGS

WHEREAS, Article ....., Section ..... of the By-laws of this Corporation provides that the Executive Committee may, from time to time, confer upon the Chairman of the Committee any or all of the powers vested in the said Committee, during the intervals between meetings of the Committee, and

WHEREAS, during the months of .... and ...., 19.., the various members of the Committee will be absent from the State of ...., and will therefore be unable to attend meetings without great inconvenience, be it

RESOLVED, That the Executive Committee hereby confer upon the Chairman of said Committee all the powers of said Committee, these powers to be vested in and exercised by the Chairman during the intervals between the meetings of the committee, and until this resolution and the authority hereby conferred are rescinded and withdrawn by resolution of the Executive Committee or of the Board of Directors.

DIRECTORS' RESOLUTION AUTHORIZING EXECUTIVE COMMITTEE TO SUGGEST NOMINATIONS FOR NEW MEMBERS OF BOARD OF DIRECTORS FOR SUBSIDIARIES

RESOLVED, That the Executive Committee is hereby authorized to nominate new members of the Board of Directors for the various subsidiaries of this Corporation, such nominations to be approved later by the Board of Directors.

DIRECTORS' RESOLUTIONS FIXING QUORUM FOR COMMITTEE MEETINGS

RESOLVED, That the presence in person of ..... (.....) members of any committee appointed by the Board of Directors shall be necessary to constitute a quorum of the committee at any meeting for the purpose of passing upon any matter that may come before it or of taking any action thereon, unless the Board of Directors shall otherwise provide by resolution with regard to any particular committee.

DIRECTORS' RESOLUTION APPOINTING FINANCE COMMITEE

RESOLVED, That a Finance Committee is hereby appointed to consist of Messrs. .... and ...., with power in such Commitee to increase its number by naming another member who shall be a director or officer of this company, and

RESOLVED FURTHER, That such Committee shall have power to supervise the financial affairs of this company, and that it shall report to the Board of Directors from time to time, or whenever it shall be called upon to do so.

DIRECTORS' RESOLUTION APPOINTING
INVESTMENT COMMITTEE

RESOLVED, That ...., ..., and ...., are hereby appointed to act as an Investment Committee, to invest the funds of this Corporation in the purchase and acquisition of stocks, bonds, and other securities, in the name and in behalf of this Corporation, and to sell and dispose of the stocks, bonds, and other securities owned by this Corporation, at such times and upon such terms as it may deem wise and advantageous to this Corporation, and

RESOLVED FURTHER, That except where the investment of such funds in stocks, bonds, or other securities involves the active participation of the Corporation in the management of the business represented by such securities, the said Investment Committee may make investments without consulting with or obtaining the approval of the directors, the officers, or any other committee of this Corporation.

DIRECTORS' RESOLUTION APPOINTING INSURANCE COMMITTEE

WHEREAS, to protect the property and assets of this Corporation, it is necessary that they be adequately insured, and

WHEREAS, to protect this Corporation from loss of earnings in case of certain events, it is necessary that adequate insurance be purchased, be it

RESOLVED, That ...., and .... *(names of officers)* are appointed a Committee on Insurance with .... to act as Chairman, and

RESOLVED FURTHER, That this Committee on Insurance is to review the Company's insurance program by surveying all the properties of the company and all the risks involved in the operations of the business and to recommend a policy on insurance and to report to this Board on or before ...., 19.., on the risks that should be insured, the amount of insurance needed to cover such risks, and the costs of such coverage, and

RESOLVED FURTHER, That the Committee shall report to the Board of Directors from time to time, or whenever it shall be called upon to do so.

STOCKHOLDERS' RESOLUTION RECOMMENDING THAT THE
MANAGEMENT FORM A COMMITTEE TO WORK WITH IT ON
CERTAIN MATTERS

RESOLVED, That it is the sense of the stockholders voting in person at this Annual Meeting that a committee including small and large stockholders should be formed by the Management of this Company to work with Management on labor and government matters in order to emphasize the fact that both Management and labor employment is made possible by the stockholders' investments, and

Further, Resolved That in this manner the stockholders' interest may at all times be prominently set forth and their investments and reasonable income assured and safeguarded.

DIRECTORS' RESOLUTION ABOLISHING COMMITTEE

Whereas, the purpose for which the .... Committee was appointed has not been fulfilled, and it is the judgment of the Board of Directors that this Committee is no longer required by this Corporation, be it

Resolved, That the .... Committee is hereby abolished, and the members thereof are hereby relieved of all the duties imposed, and divested of all the powers conferred upon them as members of such Committee

DIRECTORS' RESOLUTION APPOINTING SPECIAL
INVESTIGATING COMMITTEE

Resolved, That........, ..., and ...., are hereby appointed a Committee for the purpose of investigating, inquiring into, and considering .... *(state purpose of Committee)*, and

Resolved further, That the said Committee shall have all the powers of the Board of Directors necessary to carry on the investigation and inquiry, subject to any qualification, limitations, or restrictions that may be imposed upon it from time to time by the Board of Directors, and

Resolved further, That this Committee is hereby directed to report to the President from time to time, and at his request, as to the progress and result of its investigation and inquiry.

DIRECTORS' RESOLUTION ADOPTING REPORT OF COMMITTEE
AND SENDING COPY TO STOCKHOLDERS

Resolved, That the report dated ...., 19.., submitted to the Board of directors by the .... Committee, with regard to .... *(insert nature of report)*, is hereby adopted and confirmed, and the Secretary of this Corporation is hereby directed to send a copy of the said report to every stockholder of record ...., 19.., with notice of the adoption of this resolution.

DIRECTORS' RESOLUTION ADOPTING REPORT OF AND
DISCHARGING SPECIAL COMMITTEE

Resolved, That the report of the .... Committee, appointed by the Board of Directors on ...., 19.., to .... *(insert purpose of Committee)*, and submitted to this meeting, is hereby adopted and accepted, and that the Committee is hereby discharged and relieved from further service.

DIRECTORS' RESOLUTION APPOINTING ASSISTANT SECRETARY

RESOLVED, That .... is hereby appointed Assistant Secretary of this Corporation, to hold office during the pleasure of the Board of Directors, and to receive such compensation as shall be fixed by the Board, and

RESOLVED FURTHER, That the said Assistant Secretary shall perform the duties and have the powers of the Secretary during his absence, and shall perform such other duties as the Secretary may designate from time to time.

DIRECTORS' RESOLUTION AUTHORIZING OFFICER TO APPOINT ASSISTANTS

RESOLVED, That the .... *(insert title of officer)* of this Corporation is hereby authorized to appoint one or more assistants to the .... *(insert title of officer)* from time to time as he may deem advisable, the assistant or assistants to hold office during the pleasure of the .... *(insert title of officer)*, and to perform such duties as may be delegated by, and to receive such compensation as may be fixed by, the officer.

DIRECTORS' RESOLUTION RATIFYING APPOINTMENT OF OFFICER'S ASSISTANTS

RESOLVED, That the action of the .... *(insert title of officer)* in appointing .... as assistant to the .... *(insert title of officer)* is hereby ratified, confirmed, and approved.

DIRECTORS' RESOLUTION APPOINTING GENERAL MANAGER

RESOLVED, That .... is hereby appointed General Manager of this Corporation for a period of ..... (.....) years, to commence on ...., 19.., and the proper officers of this Corporation are hereby authorized and directed to make and execute, for and in behalf of this Corporation, an agreement with ...., in the form of the proposed agreement presented to and approved by this meeting, employing him as General Manager for the said period.

DIRECTORS' RESOLUTION APPOINTING BRANCH MANAGER

WHEREAS, this corporation has duly qualified to do business as a foreign corporation in the State of ...., be it

RESOLVED, That the officers of this Corporation establish a branch office in said state, in the City of ...., and that .... is hereby appointed Manager of the branch office, for a period of ...., at a salary of ..... ($.....) Dollars per year, and

Resolved further, That the proper officers of this Corporation are hereby authorized to enter into a formal contract with the ...., employing him to act as branch manager for the period and at the salary aforesaid.

STOCKHOLDERS' RESOLUTION APPOINTING AUDITOR

Resolved, That the firm of ...., of .... *(City)*, ... *(State)*, is hereby appointed to made an audit of the books and accounts of this Company and its subsidiary companies for the calendar year 19.. and to make a report as of the last day of such calendar year, at a remuneration to be fixed by the Board of Directors, and such audit to be of the scope as shall be fixed and determined by the Board of Directors of the Company.

DIRECTORS' RESOUTION ENGAGING AUDITOR

Resolved, That .... be engaged to make the annual audit of the books of this Corporation for the year ending ...., 19.., and that .... be paid the sum of ..... ($.....) Dollars for such services; and that the proper officers of this Corporation are hereby authorized and directed to execute a written retainer for the aforesaid services of ....

DIRECTORS' RESOLUTION AUTHORIZING EMPLOYMENT OF NEW AUDITOR

Resolved, That, upon expiration of the contract of employment, dated ...., 19.., with ...., Auditors for this Corporation, the said contract of employment shall not be renewed, and

Resolved further, That the President of this Corporation is hereby authorized to enter into a contract with ...., employing the said .... to act as Auditors for this Corporation for a period of ...., commencing on ...., 19.., at a yearly compensation of ..... ($.....) Dollars.

DIRECTORS' RESOLUTION REMOVING ONE AUDITOR AND INCREASING SALARY OF REMAINING AUDITOR

Resolved, that .... is hereby removed as Auditor of this Corporation, and that .... shall hereafter take complete and sole charge of the auditing of the accounts of this Corporation, the compensation to be increased from ..... ($.....) Dollars per annum to ..... ($.....) Dollars per annum.

Resolved further, That the Secretary of this Corporation is hereby directed to send written notice to .... of his removal as Auditor for this Corporation, and to .... of his appointment as sole Auditor, and of the increase in his compensation.

DIRECTORS' RESOLUTION APPOINTING A SPECIAL AGENT

RESOLVED, That .... is hereby appointed as agent for this corporation for the sole purpose of entering into a contract, in the name and in behalf of this corporation, with the .... Company for the construction of all the fixtures and equipment required by this corporation in its store to be located at ..... *(Street)*, ... *(City)*, ... *(State)*, the price and terms of payment of said fixtures and equipment to be in accordance with the written statement submitted by the .... Company on ...., 19...

DIRECTORS' RESOLUTION APPOINTING PURCHASING AGENT

RESOLVED, That .... is hereby appointed Purchasing Agent of this Corporation with power to make purchases in an amount not exceeding in the aggregate ..... ($.....) Dollars, for and in behalf of this Corporation, in his own name and in the name of this Corporation, of .... *(enumerate articles which he may purchase)*, and such other furniture, fixtures, machinery, and other materials and supplies as may be required for the branch of this Corporation at .... *(Street)*, ... *(City)*, ... *(State)*.

DIRECTORS' RESOLUTION RATIFYING RESOLUTION OF EXECUTIVE COMMITTEE APPOINTING AGENT PLENIPOTENTIARY TO NEGOTIATE CONTRACT

RESOLVED, That the resolution of the Executive Committee adopted on ...., 19.., to the effect that Mr. .... be appointed Agent Plenipotentiary of the .... Corporation in Mexico, for the purpose of negotiating a contract to provide for the construction of a railroad from ...., or from a point on the line running between .... and ...., to ...., Mexico, and for an option to construct a railroad from ...., Mexico, to theAmerican border at or near the town of ...., and the same is hereby ratified and confirmed.

DIRECTORS' RESOLUTION APPOINTING FISCAL AGENT

WHEREAS, this Corporation desires to employ .... Company, of the City of ...., State of ...., as its fiscal agent, to arrange with .... & Company a permanent plan of financing for this Corporation, in connection with the proposed authorized issue of ..... ($.....) Dollars of its 5 Per Cent Bonds secured by a first mortgage on all of its property, and

WHEREAS, the said .... Company has agreed to act as such agent on the terms presently set forth, and to assist this Corporation from time to time in any other financing that may be necessary, both in regard to advances of further funds and in using its information and facilities in obtaining such funds, be it

RESOLVED, That this Corporation hereby employs .... Company to act as fiscal agent during the pleasure of this Corporation, and

FURTHER RESOLVED, That, in consideration of such services, this Corporation agrees to pay .... Company, while it acts as such agent, a sum equal to one half of one per cent of the par value of bonds which may be issued under said proposed mortgage, and sold to and purchased by .... & Company.

DIRECTORS' RESOLUTION AUTHORIZING OFFICER TO EXECUTE AGREEMENT EMPLOYING SELLING AGENT

RESOLVED, That the President of this Company is hereby authorized to enter into an agreement with the .... Corporation, a corporation of the State of ...., appointing the said Corporation to act as exclusive agent of this Company, for a term of ..... (.....) years, beginning ...., 19.., and any extension of said term, for the sale and distribution in the State of .... of the .... *(insert nature of product)* manufactured by this Company, upon the terms and conditions set forth in said agreement, a copy of which was submitted to this meeting and is hereby approved.

DIRECTORS' RESOLUTION EMPLOYING RENTING AGENT

RESOLVED, That .... be employed as the renting agent for this Corporation of the building owned by it and located at .... *(Street)*, ... *(City)*, ... *(State)*, and to perform all the usual duties of a renting agent, including the following:

1. Collection of rents from month to month.
2. Rental of vacant apartments to responsible tenants.
3. Signing of leases of apartments in the name and in behalf of this Corporation.
4. Supervision of repairs necessary to maintain the building in good and tenantable condition, and

RESOLVED FURTHER, That the said .... shall receive as compensation for his services as renting agent, a commission of ..... per cent (.....%) of the gross rents received from this building, and

RESOLVED FURTHER, That .... shall be under a duty and obligation to render to this Corporation on the .. day of each month, an itemized account of all rents received from, and all expenditures made in connection with, said building, and to transmit to this Corporation on the said day the full amount so received, less the expenditures made, and less the commissions to which he is entitled as aforesaid.

DIRECTORS' RESOLUTION APPOINTING AGENT FOR SERVICE OF PROCESS

RESOLVED, That .... is hereby appointed agent of this Corporation in charge of its registered office, upon whom process against the Corporation may be served in accordance with the laws of the State of ....

DIRECTORS' RESOLUTION CHANGING RESIDENT AGENT

WHEREAS, the principal office in the State of .... of .... Corporation is now located at .... *(Street)*, ... *(City)*, ... *(State)*, and the authorized registered agent in charge thereof is ...., be it

RESOLVED, That the authorization of .... as registered agent is hereby withdrawn, and the .... Company, a corporation of the State of ....., is hereby constituted and appointed the agent of said .... Corporation in charge of its principal office located at .... *(Street)*, ... *(City)*, ... *(State)*, where service of process against this Corporation may be made, and

RESOLVED FURTHER, That the .... Company is hereby authorized to do all the things required by the statutes of the State of .... to be performed by the resident agent of a corporation created by the laws of the State of ...., and

RESOLVED FURTHER, That the President or a Vice President and the Secretary or an Assistant Secretary of this Corporation are hereby authorized and instructed to file a copy of this preamble and resolution, duly signed by them and sealed with the seal of this Corporation, with the Secretary of State of the State of ...., and a copy thereof, certified by the Secretary of State, recorded in the office of the Recorder of .... County.

RESOLUTION APPROVING POWER OF ATTORNEY GRANTED BY OFFICERS AND EMPOWERING AGENT TO REPRESENT CORPORATION IN FOREIGN TERRITORY

WHEREAS, ... Corporation has entered into a contract with ...., Ltd., dated the ...., 19.., for the development and drilling of certain acreage in .... Field in the Island of Trinidad, in which this Corporation has undertaken to drill certain wells, and for which purpose it is necessary to appoint a general agent in the Island of Trinidad to conduct the business of this Corporation there and particularly under the aforesaid contract, and

WHEREAS, a general power of attorney was executed and delivered to

.... on ...., 19.., in the name of this Corporation by
..............., President, and ...., Secretary, which power of attorney is
presented to this meeting, be it

RESOLVED, That the said power of attorney executed and delivered to
.... is hereby ratified and approved, and the said .... is hereby
authorized and empowered to represent .... Corporation in all its business
in the Island of Trinidad, before any and all political, administrative, and judicial
authorities of Trinidad, and before all private persons and companies, with all the
powers which this Corporation might have if actually present in Trinidad.

DIRECTORS' RESOLUTION EMPOWERING PRESIDENT TO GRANT POWERS OF ATTORNEY FOR PURPOSES INDICATED

RESOLVED, That the President of this Corporation is hereby authorized to grant,
sign, and deliver, in the name and under the seal of the Corporation, such power or
powers of attorney, either general or special, to such person or persons as the
President may, from time to time, deem advisable and convenient, such power or
powers of attorney to include any or all the following powers and attributes: To
appear and represent the Corporation before all governmental departments, tribun-
als, and officials; to make and enter into agreements for the purchase, sale, and
transfer of real and personal property, and to execute and accept conveyances and
transfers thereof; to buy, sell, trade, exchange, deal in, import, and export any and
all kinds of goods, wares, and merchandise; to draw, sign, indorse, accept, and
negotiate checks, drafts, bills of exchange, bills of lading, or other commercial
documents (except promissory notes); to demand, collect, and receive any and all
sums of money, securities, documents, and property of every kind which may be
due or belonging to the Corporation; to adjust, settle, and compromise debts,
accounts, and claims pertaining to the business of the Corporation, and to give
receipt and acquittances therefor; together with such other general and special
powers and subject to such limitations as the President may, in his discretion, deem
necessary or expedient to prescribe.

DIRECTORS' RESOLUTION AUTHORIZING OFFICERS TO EXECUTE POWER OF ATTORNEY

RESOLVED, That the officers of the Corporation are hereby authorized and
directed to execute and deliver a power of attorney, substantially in form as that
presented to the meeting, to Mr. ...., to represent the Corporation in the
Republic of ....

DIRECTORS' RESOLUTION REVOKING POWER OF ATTORNEY

RESOLVED, That all powers of attorney heretofore executed and delivered by
the Company to Mr. .... are hereby revoked.

DIRECTORS' RESOLUTION REVOKING POWER OF ATTORNEY AND AUTHORIZING EXECUTION OF NEW ONE

The President presented to the Board of Directors a form of power of attorney proposed to be given by the Company to ...., of the City of .. .., State of ....., and stated that this power was intended to revoke and supersede a prior power of attorney given to Mr. ....

Upon motion duly made and seconded, it was:

RESOLVED, That the President be authorized to execute such power of attorney to Mr. ...., of the City of ..... State of ....., in behalf of the Company, and

FURTHER RESOLVED, That the power of attorney heretofore given to Mr. .... to act for and in behalf of the Company in ...., and his authority to manage the funds of the Company deposited in the .... Trust Company of the City of ...., State of ...., are hereby revoked and rescinded, and that the account now standing in the name of ...., Agent, be transferred to an account in the name of ....

RESOLUTION OF DIRECTORS EXTENDING POWER OF ATTORNEY

RESOLVED, That the power of attorney heretofore granted to Mr. .... to represent the corporation in .... *(insert name of foreign country)*, executed on ...., 19.., is hereby extended from ...., 19.., and continued in full force and effect to and including ...., 19...

DIRECTORS' RESOLUTION AUTHORIZING OFFICER TO PURCHASE MATERIALS

RESOLVED, That, until further order of the Board of Directors, ... is hereby authorized to purchase, for and in behalf of this Company, spelter, copper, and lead, in such amounts, and at such prices, and from such person or persons, firms or corporations, as he in his discretion may determine.

SIGNATURES ON CHECKS AND DOCUMENTS

DIRECTORS' RESOLUTION AUTHORIZING OFFICERS TO SIGN CHECKS AND DOCUMENTS

RESOLVED, That the following officers are authorized to sign and execute all legal documents, contracts, and checks on the Company's depositaries—to wit, any President or Vice President with any Assistant Secretary or Assistant Treasurer—but in no case shall any one officer sign in the capacity of two officers.

RESOLUTION AUTHORIZING SPECIFIC INDIVIDUAL TO SIGN CHECKS, BILLS OF LADING, AND OTHER DOCUMENTS

RESOLVED, That .... is hereby authorized to sign and endorse checks, drafts, and orders for the payment of money upon the active accounts of the Company in the .... Bank in conjunction with any other authorized signatory, and he is hereby authorized to sign bills of lading, receipts for money paid to the Company, and other documents necessary and incidental to the routine conduct of the Company's business.

DIRECTORS' RESOLUTION ELIMINATING COUNTERSIGNATURE DURING ABSENCE OF OFFICER

WHEREAS, under Article ....., Section ..... of the By-laws of this Corporation, all checks, notes, and other evidences of obligation of this Corporation are required to be signed by its President and countersigned by its Treasurer, and

WHEREAS, ..., the Treasurer of this Corporation, will be absent from the City of .... for several weeks beginning ...., 19.., be it

RESOLVED, That from ...., 19.., until otherwise provided by resolution of the Board of Directors, the countersignature of the Treasurer on all checks, notes, and other evidences of obligation of this Corporation is hereby dispensed with, and all such checks, notes, and other evidences of obligations shall be signed only by the President, and need not be countersigned, and

RESOLVED FURTHER, That the Secretary of this Corporation is hereby directed to transmit to the .... Bank, depositary of the funds of this Corporation, a certified copy of the foregoing resolution.

DIRECTORS' RESOLUTION REINSTATING COUNTERSIGNATURE UPON RETURN OF OFFICER

WHEREAS, a resolution was adopted by this Board of Directors on ...., 19.., dispensing with the countersignature of ...., Treasurer of this Corporation, on all checks, notes, and other evidences of obligation of this Corporation, beginning ...., 19.., because of his protracted absence from the City of ...., and

WHEREAS, the said .... has now returned to the City of ...., be it

RESOLVED, That the said resolution of the Board, adopted ...., 19.., is hereby rescinded and set aside, and, beginning on ...., 19.., all checks, notes, and other evidences of obligation shall require the countersignature of the Treasurer of this Corporation in addition to the signature of the President, and

RESOLVED FURTHER, That the Secretary of this Corporation is hereby directed to transmit to the .... Bank, depositary of the funds of this Corporation, a certified copy of the foregoing resolution.

DIRECTORS' RESOLUTION REDUCING SURETY BONDS ON OFFICERS SIGNING CHECKS

RESOLVED, That the surety bonds held by this Corporation on officers authorized to sign checks be reduced in each instance to the sum of ..... ($.....) Dollars.

RESOLUTION OF DIRECTORS AUTHORIZING OFFICERS TO SIGN AND SEAL CERTIFICATES OF STOCK MANUALLY, PENDING PREPARATION OF PERMANENT CERTIFICATES

RESOLVED, That prior to the preparation of permanent certificates for common stock bearing the facsimile signatures of the President and the Secretary of the Corporation and the facsimile seal of the Corporation, the proper officers of the Corporation are hereby authorized to sign and seal certificates for common stock of the Corporation manually.

DIRECTORS' RESOLUTION AUTHORIZING OFFICERS TO SIGN WAREHOUSE BONDS

RESOLVED, That the President, Vice President, Secretary, Treasurer, or Assistant Treasurer, each, is hereby authorized to sign the name of this Company as principal to any and all bonds required by the United States Government for the bonding of all of the floors or warehouses owned or controlled by this Company.

DIRECTORS' RESOLUTION AUTHORIZING PERSONS TO EXECUTE BONDS OF SURETY COMPANY

RESOLVED, That "A," or "B," or "C," *(insert as many as are desired)*, attorneys in fact for this Company in the State of .... are hereby, and each of them is, authorized to execute and deliver and to attach the seal of the Company to any and all bonds and undertakings for or in behalf of the Company in its business of guaranteeing the fidelity of persons holding places of public or private trust and the performance of contracts other than insurance policies, and in executing or guaranteeing bonds and other undertakings required or permitted in all actions or proceedings or required by law, including co-suretyship and reinsurance agreements, and all other bonds, undertakings, or guaranties of whatsoever nature not specifically covered by the foregoing authority; such bonds, undertakings, and agreements, however, to be attested in every instance by one other of the persons above named, as occasion may require, provided that, if such bonds, undertakings, and agreements are not executed by either "A," or "B," or "C," then, in such event, said bonds, undertakings, and agreements shall be attested by either the said "A," or "B," or "C"; and the aforesaid attorneys in fact are, and each of them is, hereby authorized to certify a copy of this resolution under the seal of this Company.

BANK ACCOUNTS AND SAFE DEPOSIT BOXES

DIRECTORS' RESOLUTION AUTHORIZING OPENING OF BANK ACCOUNTS

RESOLVED, That the Treasurer of this Corporation, with the approval of the President, is hereby authorized to open such bank accounts in the name and in behalf of this Corporation as he may deem necessary, payments from said bank accounts to be made upon and according to the check of this Corporation, signed by the Treasurer and countersigned by the President.

DIRECTORS' RESOLUTION AUTHORIZING OPENING OF BANK ACCOUNT IN SPECIFIC BANK

RESOLVED, That the funds of this Corporation be deposited in the .... Bank, subject to checks made in the corporate name and signed by its President and Treasurer, who are hereby authorized to make, collect, discount, negotiate, indorse, assign, and deposit in the corporate name all checks, drafts, notes, and other negotiable paper; and all such checks, drafts, notes, and other negotiable paper, payable to or by this Corporation, signed as aforesaid (including checks drawn to cash or bearer, or to the individual order of the officer signing the checks), shall be honored and paid by said bank, and charged to the Corporation's account.

RESOLUTION OF DIRECTORS AUTHORIZING DEPOSIT OF FUNDS IN A CERTAIN BANK

RESOLVED, That any and all checks, drafts, notes, bills of exchange, and orders for the payment of money payable to or belonging to this Corporation may be indorsed by any of its officers, employees, or agents, and deposited with the .... Trust Company of .... for the credit and use of ...., and that said indorsements may be made in writing or by a stamp, and without designation of the person so indorsing, and

FURTHER RESOLVED, That any officer, employee, or agent authorized to act for this Corporation as aforesaid, shall be and he hereby is further authorized to waive presentment, demand, protest, and/or notice of dishonor or protest with respect to any negotiable paper involved in any of said transactions, and

FURTHER RESOLVED, That the Secretary or any other officer of this Corporation is hereby authorized to certify to said Bank a copy of these resolutions, and the Bank is hereby authorized to rely upon such certificate until formally advised by a like certificate of any changes therein, and is authorized to rely on any such additional certificates.

DIRECTORS' RESOLUTION AUTHORIZING OPENING OF SPECIAL ACCOUNT FOR PAYROLL AND PETTY CASH

RESOLVED, That the President of this Corporation is hereby authorized to open a Special Account with the .... Bank & Trust Company for payrolls and petty cash payments, and that checks on this account may be signed in behalf of the Corporation by the President, Vice President, or Treasurer, without countersignature.

RESOLUTION AUTHORIZING DEPOSIT OF CASH ON CALL

RESOLVED, That the officers of the Company are hereby authorized to deposit up to $..... of the Company's cash in the .... Bank, on ..... days' call, at an interest rate of not less than .....% per annum.

RESOLUTION AUTHORIZING CREATION OF MANAGER'S FUND

RESOLVED, That the officers of this Corporation are hereby authorized, in their discretion, and until further order of the Board of Directors of this Corporation, to set aside a fund, not to exceed at any one time ..... ($.....) Dollars, in any depository of their selection in the City of ...., State of ...., to be known as "manager's fund," and that the fund so set aside shall be subject to checks, drafts, or orders when signed in the name of the Corporation by .... or ....

DIRECTORS' RESOLUTION AUTHORIZING BRANCH BANK ACCOUNTS

RESOLVED, That the Treasurer of this Corporation, with the approval of the President, may from time to time open a bank account in the name of this Corporation, in a bank or trust company located at or near any branch office established by this Corporation outside of the State of ...., to establish a local account necessary and convenient for the carrying on of the business of said branch office, and

RESOLVED FURTHER, That until otherwise provided by resolution of this Board, such local banks or trust companies are hereby authorized to make payments from the funds of this Corporation on deposit with them, upon and according to the check of this Corporation, signed by the local branch manager and countersigned by the local branch cashier, or signed by the President and countersigned by the Treasurer of this Corporation, and

RESOLVED FURTHER, That the Treasurer, with the approval of the President, is hereby authorized to deposit in such bank accounts, in the name of this Corporation, such amounts as may be necessary for the needs of any such branch office.

DIRECTORS' RESOLUTION TRANSFERRING BANK ACCOUNT

RESOLVED, That the account of this Corporation now carried with the .... Bank be discontinued and closed, and that the Treasurer of this Corporation is hereby authorized and directed to take all steps necessary to withdraw all the funds of this Corporation in the account, and

RESOLVED FURTHER, That the Treasurer of this Corporation is hereby authorized and directed to open a new account in the name of this Corporation with the .... Banking Company, transferring to the new account all funds withdrawn from the account with the .... Bank; and that the funds in said account may be drawn against, in behalf of the Corporation, by checks bearing the signature of the President and the Treasurer.

RESOLUTION OF DIRECTORS AUTHORIZING RENTING OF SAFE DEPOSIT BOX

RESOLVED, That the President is hereby authorized and directed to rent a safe deposit box of suitable size, in the name of the Corporation, in the vaults of .... *(insert name of bank or trust company)*, and that the Executive Committee, in its discretion, may deposit therein any securities, books, records, and other property of the Corporation, and

RESOLVED FURTHER, That, subject to the rules and regulations of the .... *(insert name of bank or trust company)*, any one or more of the following-named persons, ..., ..., or ...., shall have access to such safe deposit box standing in the name of this Corporation in the vaults of .... *(insert name of bank or trust company)*.

DIRECTORS' RESOLUTION FOR RENTAL OF SAFE DEPOSIT BOX AND THE DEPOSIT THEREIN OF DOCUMENTS RELATING TO SECRET PROCESS

RESOLVED, That this Corporation rent a safe deposit box in the vaults of the .... Safe Deposit Vaults, Inc., and that ...., President of this Corporation, and Mr. ...., are hereby directed to deposit in this safe deposit box all the documentary evidence, history, and instructions relating to the .... secret process, and

RESOLVED FURTHER, That ...., President of this Corporation, together with Mr. ...., or either of them, accompanied by a voting trustee of this Corporation, shall have access to and control of said safe deposit box and its contents, and

RESOLVED FURTHER, That ...., President of this Corporation, and Mr. ...., or either of them, accompanied by a voting trustee, be authorized to enter into such contract or agreement with the .... Safe Deposit Vaults, Inc., as may be necessary to carry this resolution into effect.

RESOLUTION OF EXECUTIVE COMMITTEE (OR DIRECTORS) AUTHORIZING DEPOSIT OF COMPANY'S SECURITIES WITH CUSTODIAN

Resolved, That all securities owned by this Company shall be deposited with the .... Trust Company as custodian, and that they be withdrawn only on the order of the Executive Committee or Board of Directors, such order to be evidenced to the .... Trust Company by certified copies of the resolution authorizing the withdrawal.

RESOLUTION OF DIRECTORS AUTHORIZING CUSTODIAN TO PLACE STOCK PURCHASED OR HELD FOR THE CORPORATION IN THE NAME OF AGENTS

Resolved, That stock or other registered securities for the account of the .... Corporation may be placed in the names of either .... or ...., and that the custodian, the .... Trust Company of ...., is authorized to place stock or other registered securities purchased or held for the account of the corporation in said names; and to place such securities in the Trust Company's custody for the .... Corporation, after having procured indorsement of such securities by the nominees thereof.

EXCERPT OF MINUTES OF DIRECTORS RATIFYING CONTRACT WITH CUSTODIAN OF SECURITIES AND AUTHORIZING ANY TWO OFFICERS TO WITHDRAW SECURITIES

Upon motion duly made, seconded, and unanimously carried, a contract between this corporation and the .... Trust Company of ...., dated ...., 19.., providing for the deposit of securities owned by this corporation with said trust company was ratified, and a copy of this contract follows the waiver of notice of this meeting.

Upon motion duly made, seconded, and unanimously carried, it was

Resolved, That any two of the following officers, the President, the Vice President, the Secretary, and the Treasurer of the .... Corporation, are authorized to withdraw any or all securities deposited with the .... Trust Company of ..... in accordance with agreement between the .... Corporation and the .... Trust Company of ....

RESOLUTION AUTHORIZING PERSONS TO HAVE ACCESS TO SAFE DEPOSIT BOX

Resolved, That any two of the following named persons, ..., ... or ...., one accompanying the other, be and they are hereby authorized to have access to the Company's safe deposit box located in the vault of the .... Bank.

RESOLUTIONS RELATING TO CONTRACTS

DIRECTORS' RESOLUTION APPROVING PROPOSED CONTRACT

RESOLVED, That the proposed contract between this Corporation and .... Company submitted to this meeting, be and it hereby is accepted, and that ...., President, and ...., Vice President, be and they hereby are authorized to execute, in the name and in behalf of this Corporation, a contract substantially in the form submitted to this meeting.

DIRECTORS' RESOLUTION AUTHORIZING PRESIDENT TO ENTER INTO A CONTRACT UPON TERMS FIXED BY PRESIDENT

RESOLVED, That the President of this Corporation be and he hereby is authorized and empowered to enter into a contract for .... *(set forth the nature of the contract)* with the .... Company, in the name and in behalf of this Corporation, upon such terms and conditions as may be agreed upon between him and said .... Company.

DIRECTORS' RESOLUTION CONCERNING AUTHORITY FOR MAKING ESTIMATES FOR PROPOSED CONTRACTS

RESOLVED, That estimates of the cost of all work on which propositions by this Corporation may be submitted shall be prepared by the President or the Secretary, or by some person specifically appointed by either of them, and, when completed, shall be entered by the Secretary in a book kept expressly for that purpose, and no proposition shall be submitted by this Corporation until such estimate has been prepared and checked by or submitted to the President or the Secretary, and

RESOLVED FURTHER, That all orders for material shall be given in writing, by the President and the Secretary, or by either one of them acting with the consent of the other, and that no order shall be valid except when signed by the President or the Secretary. Copies of all orders for material shall be preserved in a book kept expressly for that purpose, and

RESOLVED FURTHER, That all contracts for the performance of work shall be valid and binding on the Corporation only when signed by the President or the Vice President, and by the Treasurer or the Secretary.

DIRECTORS' RESOLUTION PROPOSING TO TERMINATE CONTRACT

WHEREAS, the .... Construction Corporation, by resolution of its Board of Directors, made a proposition to this Company for the construction of the telephone lines and systems of this Company in ...., for which this Company has received a concession from the government of ...., which proposition this Company duly accepted by resolution of its Board of Directors passed on ...., 19.., and which thereby became a contract between this Company and said Construction Corporation, and

WHEREAS, the said Construction Corporation has completed a large portion of the construction work which it was obligated to do under its contract, and has received a portion of the total consideration for such work provided for in said contract, and

WHEREAS, it is now considered more economical for this Company, and to the mutual advantage and best interests of the Construction Corporation and this Company, that said contract be terminated, and that this Company take over at once all telephone material and supplies belonging to said Construction Corporation, and that this Company undertake the further work of construction under its own management and control, be it

RESOLVED, That this Company make to the Construction Corporation the following proposition:

(Here follows the proposition.)

EXCERPT OF DIRECTORS' MINUTES SHOWING REPORT OF TERMINATION OF CONTRACT AND APPROVAL THEREOF

The President reported that the contract between the Corporation and .... Corporation, dated ...., 19.., had been terminated by mutual agreement.

Upon motion duly made, seconded, and unanimously carried, it was

RESOLVED, That the termination of the aforesaid contract is hereby approved and ratified.

DIRECTORS' RESOLUTION ACCEPTING ASSIGNMENT OF CONTRACT AND AUTHORIZING PAYMENT IN CAPITAL STOCK AND A NOTE

RESOLVED, That this Company accept the offer of "A" to assign, transfer, and set over the contract and the claim of "A" against "B," doing business as "B" & Co., described in the agreement presented at this meeting, a copy of which agreement is in words and figures as follows—to wit:

(Here insert copy of agreement.)

and that the Board of Directors does hereby declare that the contract and claim of "A" against "B," doing business as "B" & Co., is of the fair value of ..... ($.....) Dollars, and that the same is necessary for the business of this Company, and

FURTHER RESOLVED, That the President and the Treasurer are hereby authorized and directed to execute said agreement in behalf of the Company and issue certificates of the fully paid capital stock of this Company to the aggregate amount of ..... ($.....) Dollars to "A," as provided in the agreement; and to execute the promissory note of this Company for the sum of ..... ($.....) Dollars, payable to the order of ...., ... (.....) months after ...., 19.., with interest at ..... per cent (.....%) per annum, as provided by the agreement.

DIRECTORS' RESOLUTION AUTHORIZING OFFICER TO ENTER INTO AGREEMENT WITH COMMISSIONER OF INTERNAL REVENUE FOR DETERMINATION OF INCOME TAXES

WHEREAS, this Company has requested the Commissioner of Internal Revenue to enter into an agreement relative to the final determination of its income taxes, and it is necessary as a condition to making such an agreement that the President be duly authorized to execute same, be it

RESOLVED, That the President of this Company is hereby authorized to enter into an agreement with the Commissioner of Internal Revenue, in accordance with the applicable provisions of law, with respect to any income taxes paid by this Company.

DIRECTORS' RESOLUTION AUTHORIZING OFFICERS TO NEGOTIATE FOR THE ERECTION OF A GARAGE, WITHOUT POWER TO BIND

RESOLVED, That ...., President, and ...., Vice President, of this Corporation are hereby authorized to negotiate with the .... Company for the purpose of making a contract for the erection of a garage on property owned by this Corporation at .... *(Street)*, ... *(City)*, ... *(State)*, in accordance with plans and specifications on file in the office of the Corporation, submitted by .... on ...., 19.., and to report to the Board of Directors the price at which and the terms under which the .... Company will undertake the aforesaid construction, and the date of completion. ....
and .... shall not have power to execute any contract with the .... Company until a proposed form of contract has been submitted by the .... Company to the Board of Directors and has been approved by at least ..... (.....) members of the Board, and until authority to execute such contract with the .... Company has been expressly given to .... and ....

RESOLUTION OF DIRECTORS AUTHORIZING THE PURCHASE OF LAND AND BUILDING

WHEREAS, this corporation has entered upon a policy of expansion and requires additional land for that purpose, and

WHEREAS, ..., owner of the land and building immediately adjoining the property of this corporation at .... Street, City of ....,
State of ...., has offered to sell his land and building to this corporation

for the sum of ..... Dollars ($.....), upon the terms hereinafter set forth, and

Whereas, the Board of Directors deems it advisable that the corporation acquire said land and building from .... for the price aforementioned, be it

Resolved, That this corporation purchase from .... the land and building more specifically described as follows:

(Here insert description.)

Resolved further, That the President and Secretary of this corporation are hereby authorized to enter into an agreement on behalf of this corporation with .... to purchase the above described property for the sum of ..... Dollars ($.....), upon the following terms: ..... Dollars ($.....) to be paid upon the execution of the contract of sale, ... Dollars ($.....) to be paid upon the closing of title and the delivery of a warranty deed conveying a good and marketable title to the premises free from all encumbrances, except a first mortgage in the sum of .... Dollars ($.....) now a lien upon the premises and held by the .... Trust Co., the balance to be paid by the execution of a purchase money mortgage in the sum of .... Dollars ($.....) payable in semiannual installments of .... Dollars ($.....), with interest at ..... per cent (..%), and

Resolved Further, That the President and Secretary of this corporation are hereby authorized to execute all instruments and make all payments necessary to carry the foregoing resolution into effect, and to accept all documents, duly executed, which may be necessary for the transfer and conveyance of the land and building to this corporation.

RESOLUTION OF DIRECTORS AUTHORIZING CONTRACT WITH ADVERTISING AGENCY; COMPLIANCE WITH FEDERAL AND STATE LAWS REQUIRED

Resolved, That ...., Vice-President of this Corporation, is hereby authorized to execute a contract with .... Advertising Agency, employing them for the period of one year beginning ...., 19.., to handle all the advertising of this Corporation relating to drug products; and

Resolved further, That such contract shall specify that all advertisements prepared thereunder shall be in accordance with the requirements of all applicable Federal and State laws.

RESOLUTION OF DIRECTORS ADOPTING CONTRACT OF PROMOTERS FOR SERVICES IN ORGANIZATION OF CORPORATION

Resolved, That the contract of the promoters of this corporation with ...., Esq., of ...., to organize this corporation under the laws of the State of ...., and to that end to prepare and file all certificates, reports, and other instruments required by law and to do everything necessary to obtain a charter from the State of .... for this corporation, in consideration of the payment of ..... Dollars ($.....) to ...., Esq., for such services, is hereby adopted as a contract of this corporation.

STOCKHOLDERS' RESOLUTION PERMITTING CORPORATION TO ENTER INTO CONTRACTS IN WHICH DIRECTORS ARE INTERESTED

RESOLVED, That no contract between this Corporation and any other corporation shall be affected by the fact that directors of this Corporation are interested in, or are directors or oficers of, such other corporation, if, at the meeting of the Board of Directors or of the Executive Committee, making, authorizing, or affirming such contract or transaction, there shall be present a quorum of directors, or of the Executive Committee, as the case may be, not so interested; and any director, nevertheless, may be a party to or may be interested in any contract or transaction of this Corporation, provided that at least a majority of the directors of the Corporation are not so interested, and that such contract or transaction shall be approved or ratified by the affirmative vote of at least a majority of the directors not so interested.

[*Note.* This is often provided for in the charter.]

EXCERPT OF MINUTES SHOWING RESOLUTION OF DIRECTORS AUTHORIZING PURCHASE TO BE MADE FROM A MEMBER OF THE BOARD

RESOLVED, That this corporation purchase from B all of his right, title, and interest in the coal lease between A, of the first part, and the said B, of the second part, dated the .. day of ...., 19.., covering certain property in the Township of ...., in the County of ...., in the State of ...., and give in payment therefore the sum of .... Dollars ($.....) upon receipt of all documents, properly executed, necessary to transfer all right, title, and interest in said lease to this corporation, and

RESOLVED FURTHER, That this authority is hereby given notwithstanding the fact that said B is a member of the Board of Directors of this corporation.

All the members of the Board of Directors voted in favor of the above resolution, except Mr. B, who did not vote upon the resolution.

RESOLUTIONS RELATING TO EMPLOYEES

DIRECTORS' RESOLUTION AUTHORIZING EXECUTION OF EMPLOYMENT AGREEMENT

RESOLVED, That the employment agreement with ...., dated ...., 19.., submitted to this meeting, is hereby authorized and approved, and

RESOLVED FURTHER, That the Vice President and the Secretary of this Corpora-

tion are hereby authorized and directed to execute the employment agreement with
.... in substantially the form submitted to this meeting, and

RESOLVED FURTHER, That a copy of the said employment agreement be inserted
in the minute book following the minutes of this meeting.

DIRECTORS' RESOLUTION AUTHORIZING TERMINATION OF EMPLOYMENT CONTRACT UPON NOTICE TO EMPLOYEE

WHEREAS, this Corporation entered into an agreement dated ....., 19.., with
..............., whereby it employed .... as .... for a period of
..... (.....) years, and

WHEREAS, under the terms of the said contract, it was provided that the
agreement could be terminated by either party at any time by giving ....
(.....) weeks' notice to the other party, and

WHEREAS, this Board of Directors believes that the best interests of this
Corporation require a termination of the contract, it is

RESOLVED, That this Corporation elects to terminate the said contract as of
...., 19.., and

RESOLVED FURTHER, That the proper officers of this Corporation are hereby
authorized and directed to serve upon .... a notice of termination of the
contract as therein provided.

DIRECTORS' RESOLUTION AUTHORIZING TERMINATION OF EMPLOYMENT CONTRACT PURSUANT TO AGREEMENT OF TERMINATION

WHEREAS, an agreement was entered into between this Corporation and
.... on ...., 19.., under the terms of which .... was
employed by this Corporation as ...., for a period of ..... (.....) years
from the said date, and

WHEREAS, the said .... has expressed his desire and willingess to
terminate the contract, and

WHEREAS, it is deemed advisable in behalf of this Corporation to terminate the
contract, be it

RESOLVED, That the agreement of employment be terminated and canceled,
and

RESOLVED FURTHER, That the proper officers of this Corporation are hereby
authorized and directed to enter into an agreement with .... terminating

the aforesaid contract of employment, and releasing each of the parties from all claims and demands against the other arising out of or under the contract.

DIRECTORS' RESOLUTION APPOINTING COMMITTEE TO DEVELOP TRAINING PROGRAM

WHEREAS, the Board of Directors believes that it is essential to the continued welfare and progress of the Corporation that it have a program for the development of managerial and executive employees, be it

RESOLVED, That ...., Vice-President, and ...., Personnel Manager, are hereby appointed a Committee for the purpose of investigating, inquiring into, and considering any methods for the training, teaching, and development of the Corporation's employees.

RESOLVED FURTHER, That the said Committee is hereby directed to report and recommend such a training program to the Board of Directors on or before ...., 19.., or at such times as the Board may request.

DIRECTORS' RESOLUTION GIVING OFFICER AUTHORIZATION TO ENTER INTO INDEMNITY AGREEMENTS

WHEREAS, it is desirable that certain officers and employees use their motor vehicles in furtherance of the business of this Corporation, and

WHEREAS, it is the intention of the Corporation to indemnify such officers and employees as far as practical from any loss resulting from the operation of their motor vehicles while in furtherance of the business of the Corporation, be it

RESOLVED, That the President of this Corporation is hereby authorized, in his discretion, to enter into agreements with officers and employees providing for such usage and indemnifying them from all loss, expenses, damages, costs and attorneys' fees incurred by the officers or employees, in excess of any amounts otherwise reimbursed by insurance, from the operation of their motor vehicles by themselves or by others while in furtherance of the business of the Corporation, but in no event shall liability under any such agreement exceed ..... Dollars ($.....) in the aggregate, including costs, expenses and attorneys' fees.

RESOLUTION OF DIRECTORS AUTHORIZING CONTRACT WITH A LABOR UNION

WHEREAS, it appears that the .... Union represents a majority of the employees of this Corporation, be it

RESOLVED, That the President of this Corporation is hereby directed to enter into a contract with .... Union covering the wages, hours, and working conditions of the employees of this Corporation; and that such contract, and the execution thereof, shall be in accordance with all applicable Federal and State laws.

RESOLUTION OF DIRECTORS AUTHORIZING THE PAYMENT OF EXPENSES OF AN EMPLOYEES' RELIEF ASSOCIATION

WHEREAS, the .... Relief Association is composed of employees late of the .... Company, who will, until further notice, be continued in the service of the .... Company, and

WHEREAS, the operation of the said association has been to the mutual advantage of the Company and of the employees, and therefore, in the opinion of this Board, the association as now constituted should be continued, be it

RESOLVED, That the .... Company will assume all expenses of clerk hire, office room, and all charges for stationery, etc., required in the conduct and management of the .... Relief Association, leaving the fund liable only to legitimate demands to be made upon it, and will facilitate in every way, without charge, the investment and handling of the fund from time to time, for the benefit of the Relief Association, and will contribute to said fund to the amount of five per cent, of all sums paid by the employees, such contributions to be made by the .... Company from time to time in accordance with the regulations of said Relief Association, and

RESOLVED FURTHER, That the President be authorized to make such payments from time to time as may be necessary to carry into effect this resolution.

DIRECTORS' RESOLUTION AUTHORIZING OFFICERS TO ARRANGE FOR MEDICAL EXAMINATIONS

WHEREAS, the Board of Directors believes that illness of executive employees and officers considerably increases the cost of operations and causes loss of business, be it

RESOLVED, That the officers of this Corporation are hereby authorized to allocate and set aside a proper amount for the purpose of obtaining medical examinations by competent physicians designated by the officers, and that such examination shall be offered once a year to each employee of this Corporation above the age of ..... whose salary is $..... or more per annum, the amount to be expended by the Corporation for each such medical examination not to exceed $................

DIRECTORS' RESOLUTION AUTHORIZING REIMBURSEMENT OF EMPLOYEES FOR MOVING EXPENSES WHEN COMPANY RELOCATES

WHEREAS, the Company is presently constructing a new building in .... (City), ... (State), and

WHEREAS, this new building will be completed and ready for occupancy by ...., 19.., and

WHEREAS, it is the intention of the Company that upon completion of the building all company business will be conducted from the new building, and

WHEREAS, it is desired that all present employees remain in the employ of the company after its relocation, and

WHEREAS, it is the intention of the Company to assist all employees who, in order to remain in the company's employ, will have to move their residences and household furnishings to .... *(City)*, ... *(State)*, and

WHEREAS, a committee was appointed by the Board of Directors on ...., 19.., to make recommendations with regard to the reimbursement of all officers and employees for the following expenses incurred by them in connection with moving to .... *(City)*, ... *(State)* in order to remain in the employ of the Company, and the committee has presented to this meeting recommendations that the Company reimburse officers and employees for moving expenses up to but not exceeding the following amounts for the following classifications:

Executive	$1,500
Technical	$1,000
Supervisory	$ 700
Clerical	$ 300

be it

RESOLVED, That the above described recommendations are hereby approved and adopted, and the Treasurer is hereby authorized and directed to make payments to the respective officers and employees in accordance with this resolution, and

RESOLVED FURTHER, That all problems in connection with employee relocation be handled by the Personnel Department of this Company, and

RESOLVED FURTHER, That the Personnel Department is hereby authorized and directed to engage the services of a real estate broker in .... *(City)*, ... *(State)* for the purpose of advising and assisting employees in the purchase or rental of housing in that area.

RESOLUTION OF STOCKHOLDERS APPROVING RETIREMENT PLAN

RESOLVED, That it is advisable and to the best interests of .... Corporation that a Retirement Plan be adopted and made effective, and

RESOLVED FURTHER, That the Retirement Plan considered at this meeting, which was approved and adopted by the Board of Directors of .... Corporation at its meeting held on ...., 19.., and recommended for adoption to the Stockholders (a copy thereof having been sent to each stockholder of record at the close of business on ...., 19.., with the Notice of a Special Meeting of

Stockholders, to be held on ...., 19.., to consider such Plan) is hereby in all respects duly approved, adopted and directed to be made effective, subject to its terms, as of ...., 19..; and that the adoption thereof by the Board of Directors is ratified, approved, and confirmed; and

RESOLVED FURTHER, That the Board of Directors and the officers of .... Corporation and the Retirement Committee are hereby authorized and directed to do all things to make the Retirement Plan effective as of ...., 19.., and to take any action necessary to carry out said Plan, including the execution of papers and documents that may seem proper, advisable, or convenient.

RESOLUTIONS—CLAIMS, SUITS, AND SETTLEMENTS

DIRECTORS' RESOLUTION REQUIRING OFFICER TO REIMBURSE CORPORATION FOR LOSS SUSTAINED THROUGH HIS ACTS

WHEREAS, ... Corporation, in the year 19.., suffered a loss of ..... ($.....) Dollars by reason of failure on the part of ...., its President, to secure promptly contracts for English exchange in connection with sales of merchandise made by the Corporation, thus injecting into the business of this Corporation a speculative element which this Board of Directors, at a previous meeting, decided was contrary to the policy of the business, and

WHEREAS, in previous years, the Corporation has given to the said President and other officers of the Corporation bonuses in addition to their salary for the extraordinary value of their services in such years, and

WHEREAS, by reason of the loss in English exchange above mentioned, caused as aforesaid, the Corporation has lost a considerable part of the value of the services of the said President, and has, perhaps, a cause of action against the said President, personally, and

WHEREAS, said President has stated his willingness to abide by the resolution of this Board, and to do the things and acts herein mentioned in consideration of the satisfaction of this claim against him and of his continued employment by the Corporation, it is

RESOLVED, That the said ...., President of the Corporation, be required to pay to this Corporation the sum of ..... ($.....) Dollars in reimbursement of the said loss, and that the same be charged to his account and be and remain an indebtedness to the Corporation until paid.

DIRECTORS' RESOLUTION RETAINING GENERAL COUNSEL

RESOLVED, That ...., of the City of ...., State of ...., be retained as General Counsel for this Corporation for a period of ...., and that the proper officers of this Corporation are hereby authorized and directed to execute a written retainer of the said .... for the said period, at an annual compensation of ..... ($.....) Dollars, the said amount to cover all compensation for all services to be rendered by .... for the said period.

> [*Note.* The following may be added to the above resolution: "except compensation for litigation, for which counsel is to bill the Corporation at its usual rates." If the directors desire to leave the compensation arrangements entirely to the officers, the resolution would stop at the word "period" in the sixth line. Or, the following clause may be added after the word "Dollars" in the fifth line: "It is understood that all services rendered by counsel shall be billed to the Corporation at its usual rates, and if the total amount so billed is in excess of the amount of the retainer, the Corporation will pay the excess at the end of the aforesaid period."]

DIRECTORS' RESOLUTION RATIFYING SUBSTITUTION OF ATTORNEY

RESOLVED, That the action of the President in substituting .... in place of .... as attorney for this Corporation in the action pending in the .... Court, entitled ".............. v. ....," and in paying to the said .... the sum of ..... ($.....) Dollars in full settlement of all services rendered by him to this Corporation, be and the same hereby is ratified, confirmed, and approved.

DIRECTORS' RESOLUTION REPUDIATING ACTS OF ATTORNEY

RESOLVED, That the action of .... in .... *(insert act repudiated)* is hereby repudiated as being contrary to the best interests of this Corporation, and as having been taken without authority, and

RESOLVED FURTHER, That the President of this Corporation is hereby authorized to engage .... as attorney for this Corporation, to take all legal steps necessary to rescind and withdraw the action so taken, and to substitute .... as attorney for this Corporation in the place of ....

DIRECTORS' RESOLUTION AUTHORIZING COUNSEL TO DEFEND CLAIM AGAINST CORPORATION

WHEREAS, a claim has been presented by .... against this Corporation for .... *(insert nature of claim)*, and

WHEREAS, it appears that this claim is without foundation and unjustified, be it

RESOLVED, That ...., attorneys of this Corporation, are hereby authorized to resist and defend said claim in behalf of this Corporation, and to take any and all steps which they may deem advisable in furtherance thereof, under the advice and direction of the President of this Corporation.

DIRECTORS' RESOLUTION AUTHORIZING EMPLOYMENT OF SPECIAL COUNSEL TO PROSECUTE CLAIM AGAINST DIRECTOR

WHEREAS, the Board of Directors of this Company is of the belief and opinion that Messrs. .... and ...., directors of this Company, have fraudulently benefited themselves at the expense of this Company and are indebted to the Company in various amounts, and

WHEREAS, the general counsel for the Company, ..., is also counsel for Messrs. .... and ...., and, in the opinion of the Board, should not be requested to represent the Company in any proceedings had against Messrs. .... and ...., be it

RESOLVED, That the President of the Company be and he hereby is authorized and directed to employ special counsel with whom to consult and advise in the matter of any claim or claims had by the Company against Messrs. .... and ...., or any other person, firm, or corporation growing out of the organization, management, and operation of the Company; and that special counsel be authorized and directed, in behalf of the Company, to proceed against Messrs. .... and ...., and any person, firm, or corporation, by such legal proceedings as in his opinion are deemed advisable, for the purpose of procuring for the Company a full and complete accounting and the return to this Company of all money or other property due the Company by Messrs. .... and ...., or any other person, firm, or corporation, and for the prosecution of such suit or proceeding to its conclusion.

DIRECTORS' RESOLUTION DENYING DEMAND OF STOCKHOLDERS THAT SUIT BE BROUGHT AGAINST FORMER DIRECTORS

WHEREAS, The Board of Directors, having examined the report of the committee appointed to consider the application of A, having heard the statements made by the committee, and having examined documents, accounts, and statements showing the history and affairs of the Company in the years 19.. and 19..; and the Board being satisfied, from its examination, that the dividends declared in those years were reasonably made in the light of what was known and believed at that time, that the said dividends were declared fairly and in good faith, and that it is not for the best interests of the Company that suit should be brought against the directors to recover said dividends; and the advice of counsel having been taken regarding the power and duty of this Board; be it

RESOLVED, That the demand of A that suit be brought against the former directors of the Company to recover the dividends declared by them in the years 19.. and 19.. is hereby denied, until such suit shall be ordered by a majority in interest of the stockholders, other than former directors, and that, unless so ordered, no suit shall bc brought by the Company, or in its behalf, to recover from the former directors any of the dividends declared.

RESOLVED, That, on the written demand of A, or of any other stockholder, the President shall call a meeting of stockholders to consider the application of said A, or of such other stockholders, for the bringing of such suit.

STOCKHOLDERS' RESOLUTION RATIFYING ACTION OF DIRECTORS IN REFUSING TO BRING SUIT AGAINST FORMER DIRECTORS

WHEREAS, it appears that no just ground exists for a suit against the former directors of the Company on account of the declaration by them of the dividends in the years 19.. and 19..; and it further appears that it is neither expedient nor for the best interests of the Company that a suit on that account should be brought against the said former directors, be it

RESOLVED, That the action of the Board of Directors in refusing to bring suit against the former directors of the Company to recover dividends declared by them in the years 19.. and 19.. be approved and ratified.

RESOLVED, That no suit shall be brought by the Company, or in its behalf, to recover from the former directors of the Company any of the dividends declared by them, or to recover any damages or penalties on account of such declaration of dividends.

EXTRACT FROM MINUTES OF DIRECTORS' MEETING DECLINING STOCKHOLDERS' REQUEST THAT CORPORATION BRING SUIT

The President, Mr. ''A,'' in behalf of the Committee appointed at the last meeting for the purpose of submitting to competent, disinterested counsel the matter of the demand of ''B'' that suit be instituted in the name of this Corporation against .... & Company, reported that said Committee had, on ...., 19.., engaged the law firm of ...., of the City of ...., State of ...., to render such opinion, having submitted to said firm all papers and correspondence relating thereto, as well as the minute book of the Corporation. He further reported that the Committee had received from said firm its opinion in writing, which the Committee recommended should be received as its report, and should be adopted by this Board of Directors. The opinion thereupon was read, and upon motion of Mr. ''C,'' seconded by Mr. ''D,'' it was ordered that the opinion be spread upon the minutes and be accepted as the report of said Committee. Said opinion is as follows:

(Here insert copy of opinion.)

After discussion of said report by Mr. ''E,'' and by Mr. ''F'' of the firm of ...., who was present at the meeting by invitation, it was moved by Mr. ''E'' that a Committee be appointed to confer with Mr. ''B'' and his attorneys in an effort to avoid the litigation threatened by them, and that no further action in the matter be taken by this Board until after such effort shall have been made by such Committee.

Upon such motion, Messrs. "E," "G," and "H" voted "aye," and Messrs. "A," "C," "D," "I," and "J" voted "no." The motion thereupon was declared lost.

It was then moved by Mr. "C" that the recommendation of said special Committee be adopted; that this Board decline to institute the suit against .... & Company for the reasons given in said opinion of counsel; and that this action of the Board be reported to the meeting of the stockholders to be held this date. Said motion was declared duly adopted upon the affirmative vote of Messrs. "A," "C," "D," "I," and "J." Messrs. "E" and "H" voted in the negative, and Messrs. "K" and "G" did not vote.

DIRECTORS' RESOLUTION RATIFYING SETTLEMENT OF BREACH OF CONTRACT CLAIM

RESOLVED, That the settlement of the claim of this Company against the .... Corporation, arising through the alleged breach by the corporation of its contract with this Company dated ...., 19.., by the allowance to this Company by the corporation of the sum of ..... ($.....) Dollars, be and it hereby is accepted, ratified, and approved, and that the officers of this Company be, and they hereby are, empowered to make settlement on such basis, and to take such steps and to execute such papers in behalf of this Company as may be necessary to carry this resolution into effect.

RESOLUTION OF DIRECTORS APPROVING ACTION OF ATTORNEYS IN SETTLING CONTROVERSY

RESOLVED, That the action of ...., attorney for this Corporation, in settling the controversy between the .... Company and this Corporation by a cancellation of the present contract and the execution of a new contract between this Corporation and the .... Company, on exactly the same basis as the present contract, except that the term is for ..... (.....) years, commencing with the year 19.., be and the same hereby is ratified, approved, and confirmed, and

RESOLVED FURTHER, That the President be, and he hereby is, authorized to enter into a new contract with the .... Company in accordance with the foregoing resolution.

DIRECTORS' RESOLUTION SETTLING PERSONAL INJURY CLAIM

WHEREAS, ..., of the City of ...., State of ...., has presented to this Corporation a claim against it for personal injuries alleged to have been sustained by him on ...., 19.., through the negligence of an agent of this Corporation in the operation of one of the Corporation's trucks, and

WHEREAS, ..., attorneys for this Corporation, recommend the acceptance of an offer to settle the said claim for the sum of ..... ($.....) Dollars, be it

RESOLVED, That the said offer of settlement is hereby accepted, and the Treasurer is hereby authorized and directed to pay to .... the sum of ..... ($.....) Dollars, upon his signing and delivering to the Treasurer a release of all claims which he now has or may have against this Corporation, in form approved by the attorneys for this Corporation.

DIRECTORS' RESOLUTION APPROVING ATTORNEY'S BILL FOR SERVICES

RESOLVED, That the bill rendered this Corporation by .... on ...., 19.., as attorney for this Corporation during the year ending ...., 19.., is hereby accepted and approved, and the Treasurer is hereby authorized and directed to make payment of the said bill forthwith and to obtain a proper receipt therefor.

DIRECTORS' RESOLUTION AUTHORIZING PAYMENT OF SPECIAL COMPENSATION TO GENERAL COUNSEL

WHEREAS, subsequent to the death of Mr. "A" on ...., 19.., and up to ...., 19.., Mr. "B," General Counsel for the Company, gave valuable services to the Company in directing its affairs until such time as the Company could be reorganized, for which services no compensation was heretofore fixed, be it

RESOLVED, That for his services rendered in directing and managing the Company from the period ...., 19.., to ...., 19.., the compensation of Mr. "B" is hereby fixed at the sum of ..... ($.....) Dollars, in addition to any amounts paid him as General Counsel for the Company during such period.

DIRECTORS' RESOLUTION AUTHORIZING ISSUANCE OF TREASURY STOCK IN PAYMENT FOR SERVICES RENDERED IN SETTLING LITIGATION

RESOLVED, That .... Company issue to ...., of the City of ...., State of ...., ... (.....) shares of the stock of said Company held in its treasury, which shares of stock shall constitute full payment for the services rendered by .... in effecting a settlement of the litigation between the Company and its stockholders.

STOCKHOLDERS' RESOLUTION AUTHORIZING OFFICERS TO PAY COST OF SUIT BROUGHT AGAINST DIRECTORS PERSONALLY

WHEREAS, an action against the directors of this Corporation personally was instituted in the .... Court, on ...., 19.., by .... and others, for .... *(insert nature of suit)*, be it

RESOLVED, That the said directors are hereby authorized to defray the expense of defending said action out of the funds of this Corporation.

RESOLUTION AUTHORIZING INDEMNIFICATION OF DIRECTORS, OFFICERS, AND EMPLOYEES AGAINST EXPENSE IN SUITS INVOLVING OFFICIAL ACTS

RESOLVED, That .... Corporation indemnify its Directors, Officers, and Employees against all expense, including attorneys' fees, or liability for such expense sustained by them or any of them in connection with any suit or suits which may be brought against such Directors, Officers, or Employees, involving or pertaining to any of their official acts or duties and in which suit no personal liability is finally established or which may be compromised.

DIRECTORS' RESOLUTION ADOPTING INDEMNIFICATION POLICY AND RECOMMENDING AMENDMENT OF BY-LAWS TO SO PROVIDE

WHEREAS, it is the belief of the Board of Directors of this Corporation that its directors and officers will be encouraged to remain with the firm and that they will become more secure in their decisions with the knowledge that the Corporation will back them up in time of litigation, and

WHEREAS, the laws of this state permit the adoption, by corporations formed under its laws, of by-law provisions authorizing the corporation to reimburse its officers and directors for litigation expenses arising out of the performance of their duties, be it

RESOLVED, That the Board of Directors does hereby approve the policy of indemnifying the directors and officers of this Corporation for such litigation expenses as are designated in the attached proposed amendment to the by-laws, subject to the approval of the stockholders and,

RESOLVED FURTHER, That the Board of Directors of this Corporation does hereby recommend to the stockholders that they approve and adopt the attached proposed amendment to the by-laws of this Corporation.

RESOLUTION OF STOCKHOLDERS INSTRUCTING DIRECTORS AND OFFICERS TO BRING SUIT IN NAME OF CORPORATION UPON REQUEST OF STOCKHOLDER

WHEREAS, on or about ...., 19.., ..., a stockholder of .... Corporation, made demand upon the Board of Directors of such Corporation that it cause an action or actions to be instituted by the Corporation against .... & Company, and the members thereof, seeking .... *(insert nature of action)*, and

WHEREAS, said stockholder has explained in detail to the Board of Directors of .... Corporation the basis for such an action, and has furnished thereto a form of petition by .... Corporation against .... & Company, and the members thereof, setting forth said cause of action in detail, and

WHEREAS, the agent and proxy of .... has explained to this meeting the grounds upon which said action should be instituted and the facts upon which it would be based, and it is the sense of the stockholders that such an action should be instituted by .... Corporation and vigorously prosecuted, be it

RESOLVED, That the directors and officers of .... Corporation are hereby instructed to cause an action or actions to be instituted forthwith in the proper jurisdiction by .... Corporation against .... & Company, and the members thereof, of the character specified in said demand and set forth in said petition, and to cause said actions to be prosecuted vigorously to judgment.

RATIFICATION OR RESCISSION OF ACTION

DIRECTORS' RESOLUTION RATIFYING ALL ACTS OF OFFICERS DURING THE YEAR

Mr. ...., President of the Corporation, then made an oral report, at length, concerning all the acts performed by him as such officer during the year ending ...., 19... A similar report concerning their respective activities was then made by Mr. ...., Vice-President, Mr. ...., Secretary, and Mr. ...., Treasurer of the Corporation.

On motion duly made and seconded, it was

RESOLVED, That all acts of the officers of this Corporation in the general conduct of the business during the year ending ...., .., 19.., are hereby approved, ratified, and adopted.

DIRECTORS' RESOLUTION RATIFYING SPECIFIC ACT OF AN OFFICER

RESOLVED, That the contract entered into by ...., as President of this Corporation, in the name and in behalf of the Corporation, on ...., .., 19.., with the .... Company, for the .... (set forth nature of contract), is hereby adopted, confirmed, and ratified.

DIRECTORS' RESOLUTION RESCINDING ACTS AND RESOLUTIONS OF EXECUTIVE COMMITTEE

RESOLVED, That all acts and resolutions passed by Messrs. .... and .... as an Executive Committee, as shown by the minutes of the meetings of the committee dated ...., 19.., and ...., .., 19.., and submitted to this meeting, are hereby rescinded, and the attempted confirmation of the same by the Board of Directors at the regular meeting of the Board held on ...., 19.., is hereby also rescinded, and

RESOLVED FURTHER, That the Secretary notify Mr. .... of the rescission of the contract purported to be made with him at the meeting of the Executive Committee held on ...., 19...

DIRECTORS' RESOLUTION RESCINDING PREVIOUS RESOLUTION

RESOLVED, That the following resolution, adopted by the Board of Directors of this Corporation at a .... meeting held on ...., 19.., is hereby rescinded, annulled, and set aside, and

(Here insert previous resolution in full.)

RESOLVED FURTHER, That any and all authority given to .... by and under the aforesaid resolution is hereby revoked and canceled.

DIRECTORS' RESOLUTION DISAVOWING CONTRACT ENTERED INTO BY OFFICER

RESOLVED, That the agreement made on ...., 19.., between ...., as President of this Corporation, and ...., of the City of ...., State of ...., in which .... agreed, in the name and in behalf of this Corporation, to convey by general warranty deed to .... or to any person, persons, or corporations designated by the latter, title to the property known as .... *(insert description of property)*, on or before the .. day of ...., 19.., for the sum of ..... ($.....) Dollars, is hereby disavowed, and

FURTHER RESOLVED, That any action taken or to be taken by .... in behalf of this Corporation in connection with the aforesaid property is hereby disavowed and disapproved, unless such action was or is taken in compliance with instructions of ...., attorneys for this Corporation, and

FURTHER RESOLVED, That the Secretary of this Corporation is hereby authorized and directed to send a copy of this resolution to .... forthwith.

STOCKHOLDERS' RESOLUTION RATIFYING ACTS OF DIRECTORS SINCE LAST ANNUAL STOCKHOLDERS' MEETING

RESOLVED, That all of the resolutions, acts, and proceedings of the Board of Directors of the Corporation heretofore adopted and taken at the several meetings of the Board held since the last stockholders' meeting of this Corporation, as shown by its records in the minute book of this Corporation, all of the acts of the officers of this Corporation in carrying out and promoting the purposes, objects, and interests of this Corporation since the last stockholders' meeting, are hereby approved, ratified, and made the acts and deeds of this Corporation.

[*Note.* It would be proper for the Secretary to add in the minutes accompanying this resolution a statement as follows: "As this resolution was proposed, the Secretary brought to the table a minute book containing pages ..... to ....., the same being the records of directors' meetings from ....,

19.., to ...., 19.., the book, for a period of ....., having previously been on a table at the ..... of the room in which this meeting was held, where it was open to inspection, as required by the by-laws, after announcement had been made by the President that the stockholders were invited to make the inspection.'']

STOCKHOLDERS' RESOLUTION REVOKING AUTHORITY PREVIOUSLY GIVEN

Resolved, That the authority given to .... and .... by the following resolution passed by the stockholders at a special meeting held on ...., 19..—to wit:

(Here insert resolution.)

is hereby revoked, and the resolution aforementioned is hereby canceled, annulled, and set aside.

[*Note*. For directors' resolution rescinding previous resolution, see page 323.]

MISCELLANEOUS MANAGEMENT RESOLUTIONS

DIRECTORS' RESOLUTION AUTHORIZING INSURANCE ON LIFE OF OFFICER FOR BENEFIT OF CORPORATION

Resolved, That, in order to compensate this Corporation for financial losses which it may suffer in the event of the death of ...., Chairman of the Board of Directors of this Corporation, the .... is hereby authorized and requested to apply to the .... Insurance Company for a straight life insurance policy upon his life, in the principal sum of ..... ($.....) Dollars, irrevocably naming this Corporation as beneficiary of said policy, and

Resolved Further, That all premiums on the policy shall be paid by this Corporation as they become due and payable, and that all dividends, accumulations, and other benefits and rights accruing from the policy shall belong and be payable to this Corporation, including the right, when so authorized by resolution of the Board of Directors, to surrender the policy and receive the cash surrender or other value thereof.

[*Note*. A corporation may insure the life of a corporate officer for its own benefit and pay the premiums. Harris v. H.C. Talton Wholesale Grocery Co., (1929) 11 La. App. 331, 123 So. 480. See also Venters, ''Right of Corporation to Insure Life of Officer,'' 35 *Law Notes* 46.]

DIRECTORS' RESOLUTION AUTHORIZING OFFICER TO PROCURE INSURANCE ON OFFICER'S LIFE FOR BENEFIT OF HIS WIFE

Resolved, That the officers of this Corporation are hereby duly authorized to procure insurance in the amount of ..... ($.....) Dollars on the life of ...., President of this Corporation. The policy or policies procured shall designate ...., wife of ...., beneficiary of such insurance, and shall deny to the insured any and all legal incidents of ownership in the policies, as, for example, a power to change the beneficiary, to surrender or cancel the policies, to assign them, to revoke an assignment of them, to pledge them for loans, or otherwise to dispose of them and their proceeds for his own benefit. All legal incidents of ownership in such policy or policies shall reside in the named beneficiary. The Corporation is hereby authorized to pay the premiums on said insurance policy or policies, and to charge all amounts so paid as ordinary and necessary business expenses on the books of the Corporation.

DIRECTORS' RESOLUTION ATUHORIZING RELEASE OF INSurance ON LIFE OF OFFICER

WHEREAS, the .... Insurance Company has insured the life of ...., President of this Corporation, under Policy No. ....., in the principal sum of ..... ($.....) Dollars, and

WHEREAS, this Corporation is named as beneficiary under the policy, with the right to receive all benefits accruing from said policy and to surrender the policy and receive the cash or other value, be it

RESOLVED, That the Vice President and the Treasurer of this Corporation are hereby authorized to assign or release the interest of this Corporation in said policy designated above to the .... Insurance Company, for any cash, loan, paid-up, or other value which the .... Insurance Company may grant.

DIRECTORS' RESOLUTION AUTHORIZING THE SALE OF A POLICY UPON THE LIFE OF AN OFFICER TO THE INSURED

RESOLVED, That in consideration of the payment to the Corporation of the cash surrender value of Policy No. ....., issued by the .... Insurance Company, in the principal sum of ..... ($.....) Dollars, on ...., 19.., upon the life of ...., President of the Corporation, in which the Corporation is named as beneficiary, the Corporation is hereby authorized to sell, assign, and transfer all its interest in and to said life insurance policy to ...., the insured, and

RESOLVED FURTHER, That the proper officers are hereby authorized to execute such assignments or other documents as may be necessary to effect said transfer of ownership of said policy to ...., upon receipt by the Corporation of the consideration.

DIRECTORS' RESOLUTION AUTHORIZING QUALIFICATION FOR BUSINESS IN ANOTHER STATE

WHEREAS, this Corporation is desirous of doing business in the State of ...., and

WHEREAS, under the laws of the State of ...., no business may be transacted in such state until this Corporation has fully complied with all legal requirements for qualification by foreign corporations, be it

RESOLVED, That the proper officers of this Corporation are hereby authorized and directed to do all acts, and to make, file, and record all documents required by law to qualify this Corporation to do business in the State of ....

DIRECTORS' RESOLUTION ESTABLISHING OFFICE FOR BUSINESS IN FOREIGN COUNTRY

WHEREAS, this Corporation has previously expressed its desire to transact business in the City of ...., ..., and has allocated to and set aside for that purpose the sum of ..... ($.....) Dollars, be it

RESOLVED, That the President of this Corporation is hereby authorized and directed to perform all acts and to do all things necessary for the establishment of an office of this Corporation in the City of ...., ..., and to execute and file all certificate and other instruments necessary or expedient to authorize the Corporation to transact business in the City of ....,
....

DIRECTORS' RESOLUTION ATUHORIZING REMOVAL OF MANUFACTURING PLANT TO ANOTHER STATE

WHEREAS, the .... Company has been engaged in business since ...., 19.., in the manufacture of ...., and

WHEREAS, it appears that the sources from which the .... Company draws its raw material have gradually centered in the Middle West, and that the market in which it sells its product is not located in .... *(State)*, and

WHEREAS, the cost of freight on receiving raw materials, and the cost of freight on delivering the finished product to market, amount each year to approximately ..... ($.....) Dollars more than said item of freight would cost the Company if it had a plant situated in .... *(State)*, and

WHEREAS, after making a careful study of the situation, and receiving from competent sources advice with respect to the same, it appears that the Company could produce its product at a much larger profit if it established a plant somewhere in .... *(State)*, be it

RESOLVED, That the Company proceed at once to make plans and preparations to establish a manufacturing plant at such place or location in .... *(State)*, and to do all things necessary, desirable, or incidental to the establishment of a manufacturing plant in that State; and for that purpose, ..., as Treasurer of the Company, and ...., as Secretary of the Company, are hereby authorized and directed to proceed immediately, subject to the approval of the Board of Directors, to choose a location in said State for a manufacturing plant; to purchase or to build and construct an adequate manufacturing plant, including the proper purchase or lease of land therefor, on such terms and conditions as may seem proper; to purchase, lease, or construct all necessary equipment for said plant; and, from time to time, to remove from the manufacturing plant in the City of .... as much of the equipment as, in their opinion, may be desirable to install in said proposed new plant; and, from time to time, to transfer from said plant in the City of .... to said new plant as much of the business or manufacturing operations of the Company as, in their judgment, shall be advisable; and to do all things necessary or incidental to establish a manufacturing plant in .... *(State)*, and

RESOLVED FURTHER, That the said officers of the Company, from time to time, shall report the progress of their negotiations to the Board of Directors, in order that the Board of Directors may, from time to time, give or withhold its assent or approval, and further direct the officers of the Company with respect to establishing the said manufacturing plant.

RESOLUTION OF DIRECTORS REIMBURSING PROMOTER FOR EXPENSES INCURRED IN PROMOTING COMPANY

RESOLVED, That the Treasurer of this Corporation is hereby authorized and directed to pay to .... the sum of ..... ($.....) Dollars, representing all moneys advanced and expenses incurred by .... in promoting, organizing, and incorporating this Corporation.

RESOLUTION OF DIRECTORS (OR STOCKHOLDERS) EXTENDING SYMPATHY UPON DEATH OF ASSOCIATE

WHEREAS, the directors of the .... Corporation desire to record their deep sorrow at the death of ...., 19.., of their esteemed associate ...., who since ...., 19.., had served as director of this Corporation, be it

RESOLVED, That the Board of Directors of this Corporation hereby gives formal expression of its grievous loss in the death of ...., and does hereby note in its records the passing from this life of a man who was esteemed by his associates, loved by his friends, and respected by all, and

RESOLVED FURTHER, That a copy of this resolution be tendered to his family as a humble expression of the Board's heartfelt sympathy in its bereavement.

DIRECTORS' RESOLUTION MAKING APPROPRIATION FOR RADIO AND TELEVISION ADVERTISING

RESOLVED, That the sum of ..... ($.....) Dollars be allocated to and set aside for advertising the products of this Corporation over the radio and television, for a period of ...., beginning with ...., 19.., the said appropriation to be additional to all other appropriations heretofore made for advertising the products of this Corporation during the period.

RESOLUTION OF STOCKHOLDERS ACCEPTING A PROPOSITION

RESOLVED, first, that the proposition of the .... Company to this company this day presented to the stockholders, is hereby accepted; second, that the President and Secretary of the company are hereby authorized and directed to execute all papers and to do all things necessary to carry out said proposition on the part of this company, including the issuance of the bonds of this company through the .... Company.

RESOLUTION OF DIRECTORS AUTHORIZING SUBSCRIPTION TO GOVERNMENT BONDS

RESOLVED, That the officers of this corporation are hereby authorized to subscribe, on behalf of this corporation, for ..... Government Bonds, known as the *(insert full description of the issue)*, to the amount of ..... ($.....) Dollars.

Chapter 11

COMPENSATION OF DIRECTORS, OFFICERS, AND EMPLOYEES

Contents—Chapter 11

THE RIGHT TO COMPENSATION

Right of employees to compensation. The right of an ordinary
employee or agent of a corporation to compensation for his services is well
established. In the absence of an express employment contract or an
agreement that the services are to be gratuitous, the employee is entitled to
the reasonable worth of his services.[1] In many commercially important
states, there are statutes that impose personal liability on the largest
stockholders for compensation due employees.[2] If there is an express
contract of employment; the employee is entitled to the agreed compensation.

Directors and officers, as such, however, are not considered as
employees under these rules and their right to compensation is governed by
the rules set forth in the following paragraphs.

Right of directors to compensation, in general. A corporate
director's usual duties consist largely of giving the corporation the benefit
of sound business experience and judgment, advising, formulating business policy, and giving broad direction to the affairs of the business. While
the responsibility for putting these policies into effect also rests upon the
directors under the law, it may be, and usually is, delegated to officers,
employees, or agents.

The director himself, however, may be such an officer, employee, or
agent, and may be entitled to compensation for the services he renders in
this latter capacity. Hence, in determining his right to receive compensation, the nature of the services rendered by the director, and the capacity in
which they were performed, are controlling, rather than the individual
performing them.

Bad faith or other breach of trust by the directors in fixing their
compensation is grounds for redress in a suit by a dissenting stockholders.[3]
Thus, the president of a corporation who controlled 60 percent of its stock
and dominated its board had to repay the amount of salary he received
above what his services were reasonably worth, together with all the profits
he made from options on company stock.[4] The Court will set aside salaries
the directors voted themselves as officers, unless the directors can show
that the salaries were justified by the work they did.[5] Directors of an

---

[1] Brown v. Crown Gold Milling Co., (1907) 150 Cal. 376, 89 P. 86; Norelli v. Mutual Savings
Fund Harmonia, (1938) 121 N.J.L. 60, 1 A. 2d 440.

[2] Joncas v. Krueger, (1973) Wis. S. Ct., 213 N.W. 2d 1; Miller v. Presti, (1971) N.Y. S. Ct.,
N.Y.L.J., 11-26-71, p. 19.

[3] Holmes v. Republic Steel Corp., (1946) Ohio S. Ct., 69 N.E. 2d 396.

[4] Teren v. Howard, (1963) CA-2, 322 F. 2d 949.

[5] Binz v. St. Louis Hide and Tallow Co., (1964) Mo. Ct. of App., 378 S.W. 2d 228.

insolvent corporation are personally liable to the corporation's judgment creditor when they pay themselves excessive salaries that deplete the corporation's assets; the corporation's pending counterclaim against the same judgment creditor is not a corporate asset in determining when the claim is inchoate, uncertain and contested.[6]

In accordance with the general principle that a director may not vote upon a matter of personal interest, it is generally held that where the compensation of a director is voted upon, the action is illegal if the vote of the interested director was necessary to the passage of the resolution.[7] If the directors have acted in good faith but in excess of their authority, and fixed a salary that is reasonable, their act is voidable merely, and may be ratified by the stockholders.[8] Thus, a corporation trustee in bankruptcy cannot recover directors' salaries and legal fees paid by the corporation, when both the stockholders and the directors approved them.[9] However, if the directors are guilty of any fraud in voting compensation to themselves, their acts are absolutely void as being a violation of the duty they owe to the stockholders. A resolution, illegal because of the vote of an interested director, can be ratified by the stockholders.[10]

Right of directors to compensation for services within the scope of their duties. Directors have no right to compensation for services rendered *within the scope of their duties as directors*.[11] They can be compensated for such services only if the payment is authorized in one of the following ways: (1) by the articles of incorporation; (2) by the by-laws;[12] (3) by express contract between the director and the corporation;[13] (4) by resolution of the stockholders;[14] (5) in some cases, by a prior resolution of the directors, if the directors have specific authority to fix their own compensation.[15]

The rule that services of a director, as such, are gratuitous is based upon the debatable presumption[16] that directors have a direct personal

[6]Glenomore Distilleries Company v. Seideman, (1967) DC E.D.N.Y., 267 F. Supp. 915.
[7]Pece v. Tama Trading Co., (1937) Calif. App. Ct., 22 Cal. App. 2d 219, 70 P. 2d 652.
[8]Booth v. Beattie, (1922) N.J. Eq. Ct., 95 N.J. Eq. 776, 118 A. 257.
[9]Cunningham v. Jaffee, (1966) DC D.S.C., 251 F. Supp. 143.
[10]Tefft v. Chaefer, (1925) Wash. S. Ct., 136 Wash. 302, 239 P. 837, 1119.
[11]Pindell v. Conlon Corp., (1940) 303 Ill. App. 232, 24 N.E. 2d 882; Fox v. Arctic Placer Mining & Milling Co., (1920) 229 N.Y. 124, 128 N.E. 154; Herman v. Gutman, (1935) 244 App. Div. 694, 280 N.Y. Supp. 410; Dowdle v. Texas American Oil Corporation, (1973) Texas Ct. of Civ. App., 503 S.W. 2d 647.
[12]Finch v. Warrior Cement Corp., (1928) 16 Del. Ch. 44, 141 A. 54.
[13]Baltimore & Jamaica Trading Co. v. Dinning, (1922) 141 Md. 318, 118 A. 801.
[14]Cahall v. Lofland, (1921) 12 Del. Ch. 299, 114 A. 224, aff'd, (1922) 13 Del. Ch. 384, 118 A. 1.
[15]Moon Motor Car Co. v. Moon, (1932) 58 F. 2d 90; Taussig v. St. Louis & K. Ry., (1901) 166 Mo. 28, 65 S.W. 969; Gaines v. Gaines Bros. Co., (1936) 176 Okla. 583, 56 P. 2d 863; Nashville Breeko Block & Tile Co. v. Hopton, (1946) 29 Tenn. App. 394, 196 S.W. 2d 1010.
[16]See, for example, STEVENS, CORPORATIONS, 753-54 (2d ed. 1949).

interest in the welfare of the corporation which is a sufficient motive for them to serve without pay. This presumption stands even though the director may have expected compensation for his services, or even though there may have been an informal agreement among the directors themselves that the services would be compensated.[17] This rule applies whether the services as directors are rendered singly or as members of a committee.[18] It also applies to compensation for attending directors' meetings.[19]

Right of directors to compensation for services beyond the scope of regular duties. When directors perform services *beyond the scope of their regular duties* they may be entitled to compensation for such services. There are some states that follow a strict rule under which, in the absence of an express contract, a director or officer-director may not recover payment for his services, regardless of their extraordinary nature or their value.[20] In most states, however, the courts have followed a more liberal rule, and will, under certain circumstances, imply a contract to pay for services rendered outside the ordinary duties of a director or officer, even if there has been no prior express agreement for payment.[21] This liberal rule is applied only if such services have been performed at the instance of the corporation and not merely volunteered, or if the services have been ratified and accepted by the corporation.[22] or if they have been rendered under circumstances tending to show the parties understood (or ought to have understood) that payment was to have been made for them.[23]

---

[17]Moon Motor Car Co.,v. Moon, (1932) 58 F. 2d 90; Alabama Lime & Stone Co. v. Adams, (1929) 218 Ala. 647, 119 So. 853; Lofland v. Cahall, (1922) 13 Del. Ch. 384, 118 A. 1; Green v. Felton, (1908) 42 Ind. App. 675, 84 N.E. 166; Alexander v. Equitable Life Assurance Soc. of U.S., (1922) 233 N.Y. 300, 135 N.E. 509; First Nat'l Bank v. Daugherty, (1926) 122 Okla. 47 250 P. 796.

[18]Taussig v. St. Louis & K. Ry., (1901) 166 Mo. 28, 65 S.W. 969.

[19]Norway-Pleasant Tel. Co. v. Tuntland, (1942) 68 S.C. 441, 3 N.W. 2d 882.

[20]Savage v. The Lorraine Co., (1954) 217 F. 2d 378; Moon Motor Car Co. v. Moon, (1932) 58 F. 2d 90; Lofland v. Cahall, (1922) 13 Del. Ch. 384, 118-A. 1; Dixmoor Golf Club, Inc. v. Evans, (1927) 325 Ill. 612, 156 N.E. 785; Kirk Oil Co. v. Bristow, (1932) 154 Okla. 188, 7 P. 2d 682; Althouse v. Cobaugh Colliery Co., (1910) 227 Pa. 580, 76 A. 316.

[21]Jablow v. Baller, (1966) N.Y.S. Ct., 4-29-66; Western Properties, Inc. v. Barksdale, (1965) Wash. S. Ct. 1st Dept., 65 Wash. 592; Alexander v. Lindsay, (1963) La. Ct. of App., 152 So. 2d 262; Trust No. 5522 v. Commissioner, (1936) 83 F. 2d 801; Wright v. McLaury, (1936) 81 F. 2d 96; Navco Hardwood Co. v. Bass, (1925) 214 Ala. 553, 108 So. 452; Finch v. Warrior Cement Corp., (1928) 16 Del. Ch. 44. 141 A. 54.; Joy v. Ditto, Inc., (1934) 356 Ill. 348, 190 N.E. 671; Johnson v. Tri-union Oil & Gas Co., (1939) 278 Ky. 633, 129 S.W. 2d 111; Kinsella v. Marquette Finance Corp., (1929) Mo. App. 16 S.W. 2d 619; Enders v. Northwestern Trust Co., (1928) 125 Ore. 673, 268 P. 49.

[22]Air Traffic & Service Corp. v. Fay, (1952) 196 F. 2d 40 Del. law; Morris v. North Evanston Manor Building Corp., (1943) 319 Ill. App., 298, 49 N.E. 2d 646; Nashville Breeko Block & Tile Co., (1946) 29 Tenn. App. 394, 196 S.W. 2d 1010.

[23]In re A.F. Brown Packing Corp., (1927) 22 F. 2d 419; Gettinger v. Heaney, (1930) 220 Ala. 613, 127 So. 195; Lofland v. Cahall, (1921) 12 Del. Ch. 299, 114 A. 224, aff'd, (1922) 13 Del. Ch. 384, 118 A. 1; Baltimore & Jamaica Trading Co. v. Dinning, (1922) 141 Md. 318, 118 A. 801.; Alexander v. Equitable Assurance Society of U.S., (1922) 233 N.Y. 300, 135 N.E. 509; N.C. Agricultural Credit Corp. v. Boushall, (1927) 193 N.C. 605, 137 S.E. 721; Security Savings & Trust Co. v. Coos Bay Lumber & Coal Co., (1935) 219 Wis. 647, 263 N.W. 187.

In states applying these liberal rules, the claim for payment will always be scanned critically for indications that those in control of the corporation are infringing on the rights of stockholders by diverting corporate funds or assets to themselves.[24] In determining whether there was an implication that the services were to be compensated, the courts will look to the nature of the corporation and its business, the character and extent of the services, the value thereof, and whether it was understood by both the proper officials and the one rendering the services that payment was to be made.[25]

The fact that a person is an officer or director of a corporation does not prevent his employment, at a contracted salary, to perform duties outside the ordinary duties of such office.[26] But a court will set aside salaries the directors voted themselves as officers, unless the directors can show that the salaries were justified by the work they did.[27]

Right of officers to compensation, in general. The term "officer" is frequently broadly used to include three classes of employees. There are executive officers whose duty it is to manage and control the activities and property of the corporation, exemplified in most corporations by the president and treasurer.[28] They may or may not be directors. There are also administrative officers,[29] sometimes called ministerial officers.[30] Such officers, for the most part, carry out orders and instructions from their superiors, with little or no area for the exercise of independent judgment. They do not formulate company policy or carry out broad corporate functions.[31] They, too, may or may not be directors. Finally, there are employees who may bear an "official" title, and are sometimes called officers, based on the corporate organization, rather than its legal structure. Typical of these are superintendents, department heads, sales managers, and the like.

---

[24]Teren v. Howard, (1963) CA-9, 322 F. 2d 949; McQuillan v. National Cash Register Co., (1940) 112 F. 2d 879 Md. law, cert. denied, (1940) 311 U.S. 695, 61 S. Ct. 140, 316; Backus v. Finkelstein, (1924) 163 Minn. 165, 203 N.W. 978; Talbot v. Nevada Fire Ins. Co., (1930) 52 Nev. 145, 283 P. 404.

[25]Jones v. Foster, (1934) 70 F. 2d 200; Clifford v. Walker, (1929) 180 Ark. 592, 22 S.W. 2d 36; Bartlett v. Mystic River Corp., (1890) 151 Mass. 433, 24 N.E. 780. See also In re Curran's Will, (1953) 203 Misc. 956, 120 N.Y.S. 2d 207.

[26]Mortenson v. Ballard, (1945) 209 Ark. 1, 188 S.W. 2d 749; Riddle v. Mary A. Riddle Co., (1948) 142 N.J. Eq. 147, 59 A. 2d 599.

[27]Binz v. St. Louis Hide and Tallow Co., (1964) Mo. Ct. of App., 378 S.W. 2d 228.

[28]State ex rel. McNamara v. Civil Serv. Comm'n, (1942) 128 Conn. 585, 24 A. 2d 846; Powers v. Rutland R.R., (1914) 88 Vt. 376, 92 A. 463; Diederich v. Wisconsin Wood Products, Inc., (1945) 247 Wis. 212, 19 N.W. 2d 268. See 15A WORDS AND PHRASES 277 (perm. ed. 1940).

[29]WORDS AND PHRASES 264 (perm. ed. 1940).

[30]In re Gold, (1937) 93 F. 2d 676 N.J. law; State v. Quinn, (1930) 35 N.M. 62, 290 P. 786. See 27 WORDS AND PHRASES 250-69 (perm. ed. 1940).

[31]State v. Lundquist, (1927) 171 Minn. 334, 214 N.W. 260; Chesterfield County v. State Highway Dept., (1936) 181 S.C. 323, 187 S.E. 548; People v. Hinkle, (1924) 130 Wash. 419, 227 P. 419.

The right of an "officer" to compensation will, in part, depend upon the class into which the individual falls. The rights of executive officers are very similar to those of directors and are described on page 333. The rules pertaining to the compensation of administrative or ministerial officers are not as strict and are also discussed on page 333. Finally the rights of those who are "officers" in name only are identical to the rights of ordinary employees as illustrated at page 330.

Since there is little uniformity among companies in the use of titles or in the duties and authority assigned to holders of a particular title, an inquiry into the facts and circumstances of each case and each company is necessary before it can be determined into what class of "officer" any particular individual falls.

For example, in the typical small, closely held corporation, the same persons constitute the principal stockholders, the directors, the officers, and the actual managers and operators of the business. In the larger corporate "giants," on the other hand, the stockholding is very diffuse. The directors control the policies of the business with little actual check by the stockholders. The officers may or may not be directors. They may not even be stockholders. They are employees, and to them the board of directors delegates broad powers and responsibility to manage the corporation under the policies adopted by the directors.

Rights of executive officers to compensation for services within the scope of their duties. In most cases executive officers are also likely to be directors. In general the courts, therefore, apply the same rules to such officers as in the case of directors, even though the officer may not also be a director.[32] Officers are not entitled to compensation for services rendered in an official capacity or which are incidental to their offices, in the absence of a charter or by-law provision, or a prior express agreement, or a prior resolution of the board of directors.[33] Indeed the board of directors may provide, by by-law, that no salary or compensation be paid to a director or officer without the board's prior formal resolution, regardless of how extraordinary or valuable the services of the officer or director may be.[34]

Right of executive officers to compensation for services outside the scope of their normal duties. Although the services of an executive

---

[32]In re A. F. Brown Packing Corp., (1927) 22 F. 2d 419; Navco Hardwood Co., v. Bass, (1925) 214 Ala. 553, 108 So. 452; Baltimore & Jamaica Trading Co. v. Dinning, (1922) 141 Md. 318, 118 A. 801; Alexander v. Equitable Life Assurance Soc'y of U.S., (1922) 233 N.Y. 300, 135 N.E. 509; Alderton Dock Yards Ltd., (1928) 225 App. Div. 675, 231 N.Y. Supp. 215.

[33]Upright v. Brown, (1938) 98 F. 2d 802; Gettinger v. Heaney, (1930) 220 Ala. 613, 127 So. 195; Winfield Mortgage & Trust Co. v. Robinson, (1913) 89 Kan. 842, 132 P. 979; N.C. Agricultural Credit Corp. v. Boushall, (1927) 193 N.C. 605, 137 S.E. 721; McCulloch v. Perry, (1931) 150 Okla. 203, 1 P. 2d 170; Felsenheld v. Bloch Bros. Tobacco Co., (1937) 119 W. Va. 167, 192 S.E. 545.

[34]Enders v. Northwestern Trust Co., (1928) 125 Ore. 673, 268 P. 49.

officer, as such, impose no obligation on the part of the corporation to pay for them in the absence of a contract,[35] by-law, or charter provision, a contract may be implied with regard to services outside the ordinary scope of the duties of the office. Thus a presumption that such services will be paid for may arise from the circumstances under which the duty is accepted,[36] or from the value and burdensomeness of the work.[37] No formal vote of the directors is necessary to raise such a presumption.[38] For example, the directors of a corporation passed a resolution establishing a salary for one of their members serving as "secretary and general manager." This director later became the president, but still served as general manager. No resolution was passed covering his service while president. The court held he could not recover the same salary voted to him while in the earlier position but that he was entitled to the reasonable value of his services as "general manager."[39] In the absence of contrary circumstances, the presumption may also arise from the fact that a salary was paid the same officer for the same duties in several previous years.[40] On the other hand, a vice-president serving as president during the latter's disability, is not entitled to extra compensation in the absence of express provision to that effect.[41]

It is a question of fact rather than law as to what circumstances will give rise to an implied contract.[42] As in the case of directors, the nature of the business, and the extent and value of the services will be considered in determining whether there was a mutual understanding that payment was to be made for the services.[43] The following cases are illustrative of situations in which an implied contract has been found:

1. A director who was vice-president and manager of a corporation received the reasonable value of the services he rendered beyond those usually rendered by a director and officer.[44]

---

[35]Shaw v. Harding, (1940) 306 Mass. 441, 28 N.E. 2d 469.

[36]Jones v. Foster (1934) 70 F. 2d 200; Clifford v. Walker, (1929) 180 Ark. 592, 22 S.W. 2d 36; Calkins v. Wire Hardware Co., (1929) 267 Mass. 52, 165 N.E. 889; Kinsella v. Marquette Finance Corp., (1929) Mo. App. 16 S.W. 2d 619.

[37]Trust No. 5522 v. Commissioner, (1936) 83 F. 2d 801; Navco Hardware Co. v. Bass, (1925) 214 Ala. 553, 108 So. 452; Kenton v. Woods, (1940) 56 Ariz. 325, 107 P. 2d 380; Stout v. Oates, (1950) 217 Ark. 938, 234 S.W. 2d 506; Rowland v. Demming Exploration Co. (1927) 45 Idaho 99, 260 P. 1032; Barrows v. J.N. Fauver Co., (1937) 280 Mich. 553, 274 N.W. 325; Hunter v. Conrad, (1928) 132 N.Y. Misc. 579, 230 N.Y. Supp. 202.

[38]Calkins v. Wire Hardware Co., (1929) 267 Mass. 52, 165 N.E. 889.

[39]Caminetti v. Prudence Mut. Life Ins. Ass'n, (1944) 62 Cal. App. 2d 945, 146 P. 2d 15.

[40]Gillespie Land & Irrigation Co. v. Jones, (1945) 63 Ariz. 535, 164 P. 2d 456.

[41]Brown v. Galveston Wharf Co., (1899) 92 Tex. 520, 50 S.W. 126.

[42]Red Bud Realty Co. v. South, (1910) 96 Ark. 281, 131 S.W. 340; Joy v. Ditto, Inc., (1934) 356 Ill. 348, 190 N.E. 671; Security Savings & Trust Co. v. Coos Bay Lumber & Coal Co., (1935) 219 Wis. 647, 263 N.W. 187.

[43]Red Bud Realty Co. v. South, (1910) 96 Ark. 281, 131 S.W. 340.

[44]Bassett v. Fairchild, (1901) 132 Cal. 637, 64 P. 1082; Pence v. West Side Hospital, (1932) 265 Ill. App. 560; Hewson v. Charles P. Gillen & Co., (1928) N.J. Eq. 142 A. 250.

2. A secretary and general manager was held entitled to compensation for his services as general manager.[45]
3. Directors devoting almost all of their time to corporate affairs in the capacity of manager or superintendent were held entitled to the reasonable value of the service they rendered as manager or superintendent.[46]
4. Directors acting as land commissioner,[47] consulting engineer,[48] and company arbitrator and auditor[49] were held entitled to compensation for services beyond those usually rendered as director.

Presidents or other executive officers serving in similar capacities may also recover the value of their extraordinary services.[50]

In the following situations, compensation was held not due for special services, without an express contract:

1. Director, who had agreement calling for finding of purchaser, secured manufacturing contract.[51]
2. Director made damage settlement favorable to corporation.[52]

Time of fixing executive officer's compensation. If an officer is entitled to compensation either by statutory or by-law provision or by a mutual understanding between the parties, it is not necessary that the amount of such compensation be fixed before the service is rendered, since the officer may recover the reasonable worth of his services.[53] It has been held that a by-law providing that the compensation of officers shall be fixed before their election, is directory and not mandatory, and that the act of the board in fixing the amount of an officer's salary after his election is valid.[54] The fact that an officer's salary is not fixed until a month after his election does not deprive him of his right to his salary for the full time, in the absence of a claim that the salary is excessive.[55]

Further, an organizers' agreement to equally share profits bound the subsequently formed corporation to honor such agreement, since no out-

---

[45]Lammerding v. Lammerding Lumber & Supply Co., (1931) 107 N.J. Eq. 551, 153 A. 380; Engler v. Ipswich Printing Co., (1934) 63 S.D. 1,256 N.W. 132.

[46]Navco Hardwood Co. v. Bass, (1925) 214 Ala. 553, 108 So. 452; Nashville Breeko Block & Tile Co. v. Hopton, (1946) 29 Tenn. App. 394, 196 S.W. 2d 1010.

[47]Rogers v. Hastings, etc. Ry., (1875) 22 Minn. 25.

[48]Bogart v. New York & L.I.R.R., (1907) 118 App. Div. 50, 102 N.Y. Supp. 1093.

[49]Paine v. Kentucky Refining Co., (1914) 159 Ky. 270, 167 S.W. 375.

[50]Red Bud Realty Corp. v. South, (1910) 96 Ark 281, 131 S.W. 340; Gumaer v. Cripple Creek Tunnel, Transportation & Mining Co., (1907) 40 Colo. 1, 90 P. 81; Barrows v. J.N. Fauver Co., (1937) 280 Mich. 553, 274 N.W. 325.

[51]Pindell v. Conlon Corp., (1940) 303 Ill. App. 232, 24 N.E. 2d 882.

[52]Norway-Pleasant Tel. Co. v. Tuntland, (1942) 68 S.D. 441, 3 N.W. 2d 882.

[53]Jezeski v. Northeast Investment Co., (1925) 163 Minn. 165, 203 N.W. 978; Bogart v. New York & L.I.R.R. (1907) 118 App. Div. 50, 102 N.Y. Supp. 1093. Contra: Air Traffic & Service Corp. v. Fay, (1952) 196 F. 2d 40 (Del. law).

[54]Francis v. Brigham-Hopkins Co., (1908) 108 Md. 233, 70 A. 95.

[55]Robson v. Fenniman Co., (1912) 83 N.J.L. 453, 85 A. 356.

side parties were involved and under the corporation's by-laws the board could fix its own compensation.[56]

Continuation of compensation. Once a salary is attached to an office, there is a presumption that is continues. Thus, where an officer, entitled by resolution to a certain annual salary, was re-elected, but no mention was made of his salary, it was held that he was to receive the same salary.[57] The presumption that re-election without a new compensatory agreement is a renewal of the original contract is not necessarily affected by the fact that the duties of the officer are lessened.[58] If a by-law provision requires the directors to agree annually upon the amount of salary that each officer and director shall receive, the directors are powerless to fix salaries for more than a year.[59]

Officers receiving a salary and bonus under contract are not entitled to compensation after the contract expires, when they continue to manage the business in defiance of the corporation's legal action in discharging them.[60] After a director who is an officer is voted out of the office, he has no claim to the salary that went with the office.[61]

Further, a discharged officer cannot claim salary for other services rendered the corporation pending outcome of a disputed discharge, when he had no employment agreement with the corporation, and, as a result of the discharge, he was not rendering services for which he could be paid; it did not matter that summary dismissal might be wrongful under a provision in the merger instrument requiring unanimous consent of the board of directors before discharging the officer.[62] Also, a product manager whose regular employment ended when his product line was discontinued was not entitled to exercise a stock option issued to him under a stock option plan, even though he was a consultant to the company until orders for products of the discontinued line were completed, since an option plan was set up for those employed on a regular basis, not for one who was a casual consultant at the company's discretion.[63]

A board of directors may pay an officer during temporary illness, just as they do other employees. This is a matter of policy and the honest judgment of the board of directors.[64]

[56]Petruzzi v. Feduka Construction, Inc., (1972) Mass. S. Jud. Ct., 285 N.E. 2d 103.
[57]Eicks v. Whitteman Co., (1913) 157 App. Div. 412, 142 N.Y. Supp. 190. See also Gillespie Land & Irrigation Co. v. Jones, (1945) 63 Ariz. 535, 164 P. 2d 456; Jezeski v. Northeast Investment Co., (1925) 163 Minn. 165, 203 N.W. 978; Yeager v. Phillips, (1953) 128 N.Y.S. 2d 376.
[58]Metropolitan Rubber Co. v. Place, (1906) 147 F. 90.
[59]Hurricane Gold Mining Co. v. Bright, (1912) 193 F. 46.
[60]Saltz Bros., Inc. v. Saltz, (1941) 122 F. 2d 79.
[61]Murray v. Requardt, (1942) 180 Md. 245, 23 A. 2d 697.
[62]Vogal v. Herlinger-Bristol, Ltd., (1972) N.Y.S. Ct., N.Y.L.J., 12-21-72, p. 18.
[63]Sparks v. Microwave Associates, Inc., (1971) Mass. S. Jud. Ct., 270 N.E. 2d 909.
[64]Solimine v. Hollander, (1940) 128 N.J. Eq. 228, 16 A. 2d 203.

Right to compensation for past services. Directors and officers are not entitled to back pay for services rendered voluntarily.[65] Payment for past services must be based upon on agreement, express or implied.[66] It was held that there was no agreement upon which to base pay for past services where a claimant had offered to work voluntarily until the corporation was on a paying basis, and had failed to charge a salary to himself, although he had charge of the corporation's books.[67] Also, a discharged officer could not claim salary for other services rendered to the corporation pending the outcome of a disputed discharge, when he had no employment agreement with the corporation and, as a result of the discharge, he was not rendering those services for which he could be paid.[68] Further, a corporation was not obligated to pay severance and vacation pay to the former president and chairman of the board when he resigned, even though management had informally adopted a policy of making such payments, since his contract of employment did not provide for those benefits.[69]

Forfeiture of compensation. Generally an officer forfeits all right to compensation if he is guilty of fraud, dishonesty, misconduct, or gross negligence in the performance of his duties.[70] For example, a president of a corporation who actively opposed its interests and tried to put it out of business was held to be entitled to no salary even though he had a contract.[71] Also, corporations subject to the federal laws as to the registration of stock issues and securities that have bonus and profit-sharing arrangements with directors, officers, or employees have a duty to make full disclosure of all such arrangements to the Securities and Exchange Commission. Accordingly, officers cannot recover salaries allegedly due them from the corporation under an oral agreement when they have signed and filed with the Commission an offering circular for the sale of debentures which contained a statement that they were not aware of any other claims, and they did not list their claim for salaries as a corporate liability.[72]

Further, use of corporate profits to cover costs of unreasonable salary and living expenses of a majority stockholder-director was a breach of

[65]National Loan & Inv. Co. v. Rockland Co., (1899) 94 F. 335.
[66]Stafford's Estate v. Progressive Nat'l Farm Loan Ass'n, (1945) 207 La. 1097, 22 So. 2d 662; Landstreet v. Meyer, (1947) 201 Miss. 826, 29 So. 2d 653. See also Talbot v. Nevada Fire Ins. Co., (1930) 52 Nev. 145, 283 P. 404; Felsenheld v. Bloch Bros. Tobacco Co., (1937) 119 W. Va. 167, 192 S.E. 545.
[67]Clifford v. Walker, (1929) 180 Ark. 592, 22 S.W. 2d 36.
[68]Vogel v. Herlinger-Bristol, Ltd., (1972) N.Y.L.J. 12-21-72.
[69]Dowdle v. Texas American Oil Corporation, (1973) Tex. Ct. of Civ. App. 503 S.W. 2d 647.
[70]Kassat v. Ragnar Benson, Inc., (1966) DC W.D. Pa., 254 F. Supp. 830; Toy v. Lapeer Farmers Mut. Fire Ins. Ass'n., (1941) 297 Mich. 188, 297 N.W. 230, citing 5 Fletcher, Corporations §2145.
[71]Slosberg v. Callahan Oil Co., (1939) 125 Conn. 651, 7 A 2d 853.
[72]Stillman v. Kinsman Mfg. Co., Inc., (1968) N.H. S. Ct., 244 A. 2d 191.

fiduciary obligation owed by him to the corporation, and so he forfeited such salary.[73]

Under the general rule that a director may not vote upon a matter of personal interest, if a director-officer induces his co-directors to vote him an excessive salary, he is not entitled to such salary.[74] The rule is not inflexible, however.[75] Thus officers who breached their fiduciary duty towards their corporation were permitted to recover the reasonable value of their services outside their regular duties as officers, when it was shown that the success of the corporation was largely due to their diligence and ability and that the stockholders had acquiesced in, and benefited by, the services.[76]

Right of administrative or ministerial officers to compensation. Since, as we shall see, the rules for compensation of administrative or ministerial officers are not as strict as in the case of executive officers, the first inquiry must be into the nature and scope of the duties of the officer concerned, and the degree of discretion and freedom of decision and action allowed him, remembering that the administrative or ministerial officer is one whose duty it is to execute orders and administer policies lawfully issued by his superiors. The title of the office alone is not a dependable guide. For example, the offices of secretary,[77] assistant secretary,[78] manager,[79] superintendent[80] and treasurer[81] have all been held, in particular circumstances, to be administrative, while, under other circumstances, the offices of manager,[82] cashier,[83] and assistant secretary[84] were held to be executive.

The general rule is that, in the absence of an understanding that the services were to be gratuitous, administrative or ministerial officers are entitled to the reasonable value of their services, whether within or without the ordinary scope of the duties of their office.[85] This rule is based on the theory that since ministerial officers do not control the affairs or property of

---

[73]Cole Real Estate Corp. v. Peoples Bank and Trust Co., (1974) Ind. Ct. of App. 310 N.E. 2d 275.

[74]Sarner v. Fox Hill, Inc., (1963) Conn. S. Ct. of Errors 199 A.2d 6.

[75]Richardson v. Blue Grass Mining Co., (1939) 29 F. Supp. 658.

[76]Ibid.

[77]Leader Holding Corp. v. McLintock, (1937) 121 N.J. Eq. 542, 191 A. 768.

[78]Goodin v. Dixie-Portland Cement Co., (1916) 79 W. Va. 83, 90 S.E. 544.

[79]Freeport Journal-Standard Publishing Co. v. Frederic W. Ziv Co., (1952) 345 Ill. App. 337, 103 N.E. 2d 153.

[80]Gettinger v. Heaney, (1930) 220 Ala. 613, 127 So. 195.

[81]In re Gold, (1937) 93 F. 2d 676 (N.J. law).

[82]Bay City Lumber Co. v. Anderson, (1941) 8 Wash. 2d 191, 111 P. 2d 771.

[83]Cox v. First Nat'l Bank, (1935) 10 Cal. App. 2d 302, 52 P. 2d 524.

[84]Seaman v. Bighorn Canal Ass'n, (1923) 29 Wyo. 391, 213 P. 938.

[85]King v. Grass Valley Gold Mines, Inc., (1928) 205 Cal. 698, 272 P. 290; Sirbeck v. Sunbeam Divide Mining Co., (1926) 50 Nev. 46, 249 P. 865.

the company, they do not have the same fiduciary relationship to the stockholders as do the directors and executive officers. Hence their right to compensation is governed by the same rules that apply to ordinary employees.[86]

In a case in which the same individual was secretary for two corporations, he was permitted to recover the reasonable value of his services for the first company when it was shown that the duties of the two positions were not in conflict and did not involve the doing of any act prejudicial to either corporation.[87]

Compensation of ministerial officers who are also directors or stockholders. A person is not necessarily deprived of all compensation merely because he is a director. If the duties of a ministerial officer are clearly outside the scope of his duties as a director, the duties as an officer are compensable.

Similarly, a ministerial officer will not necessarily lose his right to salary or other compensation just because he is, at the same time, a stockholder.[88] Small stockholdings will be ignored. Thus a secretary who was required to buy one share of stock to qualify for his position was held entitled to payment for his services.[89] And even if the officer is a major stockholder, the law will imply a contract to pay the reasonable value of the services in the absence of circumstances refuting such an implication.[90]

AUTHORITY TO FIX COMPENSATION OF DIRECTORS AND OFFICERS

Source of authority to fix compensation. Compensation of directors and officers is a subject rarely regulated by state corporation laws. In the few jurisdictions where some statutory provision is found, the law merely states (1) that the corporation shall have power to prescribe compensation of directors and officers; (2) that the directors shall have power to fix the

---

[86]Sirbeck v. Sunbeam Divide Mining Co., (1926) 50 Nev. 46, 249 P. 865; Goodin v. Dixie-Portland Cement Co., (1916) 79 W. Va. 83, 90 S.E. 544.

[87]Mobile, J. & K, C, Ry. v. Owen, (1899) 121 Ala. 505, 25 So. 612.

[88]Huntington Fuel Co. v. McIlwaine, (1907) 41 Ind. App. 328, 82 N.E. 1001; Sirbeck v. Sunbeam Divide Mining Co., (1926) 50 Nev. 46, 249 P. 865; Goodin v. Dixie-Portland Cement Co., (1916) 79 W. Va. 83, 90 S.E. 544.

[89]Pease, Kolbert & Co. v. Bates, (1927) 85 Cal. App. 786, 260 P. 399.

[90]Huntington Fuel Co. v. McIlwaine, (1907) 41 Ind. App. 328, 82 N.E. 1001. See Eisenberg v. Central Zone Property Corp., (1956) 1 App. Div. 353, 149 N.Y.S. 2d 840, aff'd, memo dec., 3 N.Y. 2d 729, 143 N.E. 2d 516, cert. den., (1957) 78 S. Ct. 151, where the court ruled that a successful stockholder-attorney could not recover counsel fees for the legal services he rendered in a stockholder derivative action. It was reasoned that to allow such recovery might encourage the institution of such litigation for the purpose of obtaining a fee.

salaries of officers; or (3) that the by-laws may provide for the compensation of directors and officers.

A corporation has the right to enter into an express contract to pay a salary or other compensation to its directors or officers for services performed within or without the scope of their duties. Payment must be fixed without fraud and by the proper authority.[91] The method of fixing the compensation of directors and officers is usually covered in a by-law. This by-law can make practically any provision so long as it does not conflict with the charter of the corporation.

By-law provisions authorizing compensation. Some of the most common by-law provisions on the subject of compensation are as follows: (1) The directors shall receive no compensation for their services as directors, but this provision shall not preclude a director from serving the corporation in another capacity and receiving compensation for his services. (2) The salaries of officers shall be fixed by resolution of the board of directors. (3) The directors shall be entitled to a fixed fee and expenses for attendance at each meeting and to no other compensation for their services as directors. (4) The salaries of the directors and officers shall be recommended by a committee subject to approval by the board of directors.

A by-law provision which provided that no salary should be allowed to any officer, director, agent, or employee without the consent of holders of three-fourths of the stock was held to be inconsistent with the statutory provision vesting care and management of the corporate property in the directors, and hence void.[92]

Compliance with fixed authority to authorize compensation. A charter or by-law provision delegating authority to vote compensation or regulating the amount thereof must be strictly complied with. Payment to directors and officers for services must be authorized by those to whom the authority to fix compensation has been delegated by statute, or by the charter or by-laws of the corporation. Thus, where the statute provides that salaries shall be fixed by the by-laws, a resolution of the board of directors fixing salaries is insufficient.[93]

All persons dealing with the corporation are bound by the limitations and restrictions contained in the statute, charter, or by-laws.[94] For exam-

---

[91]Finch v. Warrior Cement Corp., (1928) 16 Del. Ch., 44, 141 A. 54; Green v. Felton, (1908) 42 Ind. App. 675, 84 N.E. 166.

[92]Security Savings & Trust Co. v. Coos Bay Lumber & Coal Co., (1935) 219 Wis. 647, 263 N.W. 187.

[93]Hayes v. Canada, Atlantic and Plant S.S. Co., (1910) 181 F. 829; Sirbeck v. Sunbeam Divide Mining Co., (1926) 50 Nev. 46, 249 P. 865; Enders v. Northwestern Trust Co., (1928) 125 Ore. 673, 268 P.49; Engler v. Ipswich Printing Co., (1934) 63 S.D. 1, 256 N.W. 132; Shannon v. Early Foundry Co. (1929) 296 Pa. 141, 145 A. 708.

[94]Colpe v. Jubilee Mining Co., (1905) 2 Cal. App. 393, 84 P. 324.

ple, the by-laws provided that the board of directors should fix the salary of officers and agents of the corporation. The president promised additional compensation to a person in a position similar to that of an officer. As the additional compensation was not agreed to by the board, and as the board did not know of the president's promise, the corporation was not required to pay it.[95] Also, where absolute power to fix officers' salaries was vested in the board of directors, an officer's informal agreement with stockholders to take less than the salary fixed by the directors was invalid and not binding on the officer.[96]

The president or managing officer of a corporation is usually authorized to hire and fix the salaries of employees other than officers. He may have authority to hire ministerial officers. A valid express contract for services in these circumstances will be upheld by the courts. As noted earlier, employees, who are not officers, are entitled to the reasonable value of their services even in the absence of an express contract.

A corporation can waive a by-law delegating authority to fix compensation in the same way that it can waive other by-laws. It can change or waive a by-law by custom, usage, acquiescence, or by unanimous consent and continuous action. Such waiver may be express or implied. But a corporation cannot waive a charter provision, nor can a charter provision be changed by a by-law. It was held that in a case in which the corporation allowed its president to fix salaries and pay bonuses to officers over a period of many years, it had waived a by-law requiring that the board of directors fix the salaries of its officers.[97]

Authority of directors and officers to fix their own compensation. The power to fix salaries or other compensation of directors, as such, lies with the stockholders. The authority to fix such compensation may be delegated by the stockholders to the directors. Directors cannot legally vote themselves compensation of any kind, for performing their duties as directors or as officer-directors, unless they are specifically and expressly authorized to do so, by statute, charter or by-law.[98] However, in the absence of fraud or bad faith, directors may vote compensation to themselves for services rendered as employees, or for unusual services outside

---

[95]Vredenburg v. International Trade Exhibition, Inc., (1928) 166 La. 390, 117 So. 437.

[96]Superior Brewing Co. v. Curtis, (1938) Tex. Civ. App. 116 S.W. 2d 853.

[97]Upright v. Brown, (1938) 98 F. 2d 802; Joy v. Ditto, Inc., (1934) 356 Ill. 348, 190 N.E. 671; Bay City Lumber Co. v. Anderson, (1941) 8 Wash. 2d 191, 111 P.2d 771. See also U. PITT . L. REV. 295; 30 CALIF. L. REV. 195 (1942).

[98]Redstone v. Redstone Lumber & Supply Co., (1931) 101 Fla. 226, 133 So. 882; Schulte v. Ideal Food Products Co., (1929) 208 Iowa 767, 226 N.W. 174; Bates Street Shirt Co. v. Waite, (1931) 130 Me. 352, 156 A. 293; Jones v. Van Heusen Charles Co., (1930) 230 App. Div. 694, 246 N.Y. Supp. 204.

the scope of their duties as directors.[99] But here, as we have seen, the provision for payment must come before the services are rendered. Even if there is a by-law provision authorizing directors to vote themselves compensation, they cannot pay themselves salary or a bonus for already rendered service in the absence of authorization by the stockholders, and a showing that the amount of the compensation has a proper relationship to the value of the services rendered.[100]

Directors are not generally considered to be officers within the meaning of a by-law provision giving the board of directors power to vote compensation to officers and employees.[101]

Corporate officers are under a similar disability to fix their own compensation.[102] Thus, it has been held that officers cannot agree among themselves that they shall each have a salary for a term of years and that the profits of the business shall be distributed in a certain way. Such an agreement is void as against public policy and is a violation of their duty owing to the stockholders.[103]

Authority of directors to fix officers' salaries. In the absence of any prohibitory statutory or by-law provision, directors may fix the salary of officers as an incident of their power to appoint such officers.[104] Undoubtedly the board of directors may fix the salaries of officers who are not directors,[105] but excessive salaries of officers, voted by the directors, can be repudiated by the stockholders.[106] Where the directors have power to fix the salaries of officers, the court will not interfere with the discretion of the board, even if their action seems ill advised, in the absence of fraud.[107]

In the absence of an express provision giving the board of directors power to fix the salaries of officers or prohibiting them from doing so, the board has the power to fix the salary, as an officer, of one of its members who occupies one of the corporate offices and performs services which are beyond the scope of his duties as a director. For instance, it can fix the

[99]Plotsky v. Plotsky Egg Co., (1934) 154 N.Y. Misc. 297, 273 N.Y. Supp. 214.

[100]Sarner v. Fox Hill, Inc., (1963) Conn. S. Ct. of Errors 199 A. 2d 6; Richardson v. Blue Grass Mining Co., (1939) 29 F. Supp. 658. See also Seitz v. Union Brass & Metal Mfg. Co., (1922) 157 Minn. 460, 189 N.W. 586.

[101]Bennett v. Klipto Loose Leaf Co., (1926) 201 Iowa 236, 207 N.W. 228.

[102]Chabot & Richard Co. v. Chabot, (1912) 109 Me. 403, 84 A. 892; Stevenson v. Sicklesteel Lumber Co., (1922) 219 Mich. 18, 188 N.W. 449. See also Taylor v. Citizens' Oil Co., (1918) 182 Ky 350, 206 S.W. 644; Bloom v. Nathan Vehon (1930) 341 Ill. 200, 173 N.E. 270.

[103]Abbott v. Harbeson Textile Co., 1914) 162 App. Div. 405, 147 N.Y. Supp. 1031.

[104]Harris v. Harris, (1930) 137 N.Y. Misc. 73, 241 N.Y. Supp. 474.

[105]Godley v. Crandall & Godley Co., (1914) 212 N.Y. 121, 105 N.E. 818; Tilton v. Gans, (1915) 90 N.Y. Misc. 84, 152 N.Y. Supp. 981.

[106]Monterey Water Co. v. Voorhees, (1935) 45 Ariz. 338, 43 P. 2d 196.

[107]Cron v. Tanner, (1951) 171 Kan. 57, 229 P. 2d 1008; Beacon Wool Corp. v. Johnson, (1954) 331 Mass. 274, 119 N.E. 2d 195; Nahikian v. Mattingly, (1933) 265 Mich. 128, 251 N.W. 421.

salary, as general manager, of a director who is the general manager of the corporation.[108] However, such agreements are subject to careful scrutiny by the courts because of the interest of the director, and will be set aside if they are fraudulent or if the salary is grossly excessive.[109]

Amount of compensation. The amount of compensation which a director or officer may claim is fixed in one of the following ways: (1) by the corporate by-laws; (2) by resolution of the stockholders; (3) by resolution of the board of directors; (4) by a contract between the corporation and the director or officer, executed by the proper authority; or (5) by implication arising from circumstances indicating an understanding that payment was to be made for the services. The third method is applicable to the salaries of directors only when they have authority to fix their own salaries. The fifth method does not apply to directors' salaries for their services as directors, because directors cannot decide among themselves what their salaries shall be.

The board of directors may not grant a salary higher than that permitted in the by-laws,[110] and an officer who accepts such a salary must account to the stockholders of the excess.[111]

Factors in determining reasonableness of compensation. Corporate directors, in fixing their own salaries as officers or agents, must have some regard for the financial condition of the corporation, and the amounts so fixed must be reasonable and not excessive.[112] To be reasonable, the compensation must be in proportion to the executive's ability, his services, and the time which he devoted to such services.[113] In addition, cognizance must be taken of such factors as the difficulties involved, responsibilities assumed, success achieved, corporate earnings, profits, and prosperity, increase in volume or quality of business or both, and all relevant facts and circumstances.[114] Thus, utilization of corporate profits to cover costs of unreasonable salary and living expenses of a majority

[108]Ransome Concrete Machinery Co. v. Moody, (1922) 282 F. 29. But see Redstone v. Redstone Lumber & Supply Co., (1931) 101 Fla. 226, 133 So. 882 which held that directors cannot fix their own compensation for services to be rendered as officers, unless expressly authorized by charter or by the stockholders.

[109]McQuillen v. National Cash Register Co., (1940) 112 F. 2d 879 (Md. law), cert. denied, (1940) 311 U.S. 695, 61 S. Ct. 140, 316; Barrett v. Smith, (1932) 185 Minn. 596, 242 N.W. 392; Worley v. Dunkle, (1948) (N.J.) 62 A. 2d 699; Wellington Bull & Co. v. Morris, (1928) 132 N.Y. Misc. 509, 230 N.Y. Supp. 122; Sotter v. Coatsville Boiler Works, (1917) 257 Pa. 411, 101 A. 744.

[110]Hingston v. Montgomery, (1906) 121 Mo. App. 451, 97 S.W. 202.

[111]Hall v. Woods, (1927) 325 Ill. 114, 156, N.E. 258.

[112]Backus v. Finkelstein, (1924) 23 F. 2d 531; Presidio-Mining Co. v. Overton, (1919) 261 F. 933; Barrett v. Smith, (1932) 185 Minn. 596, 242 N.W. 392; Jezeski v. Northeast Investment Co., (1925) 163 Minn. 165, 203 N.W. 978.

[113]Boyum v. Johnson, (1942) 127 F. 2d. 491; Winkelman v. General Motors Corp., (1942) 44 F. Supp. 960; Keough v. St. Paul Milk Co., (1939) 205 Minn. 96, 285 N.W. 809; Heller v. Boylan, (1941) 29 N.Y.S. 2d 653; Wineburgh v. Seeman Bros., Inc., (1940) 21 N.Y.S. 2d 180.

[114]Koplar v. Warner Bros. Pictures, (1937) 19 F. Supp. 173; Black v. Parker Mfg. Co., (1952) 329 Mass. 105, 106 N.E. 2d 544.

stockholder-director is a breach of a fiduciary obligation owed by such shareholder- director to the corporation, and is the basis for a cause of action by a minority shareholder, but the burden of proving unreasonableness lies with the minority stockholder.[115] The compensation should not unduly diminish dividends properly payable to stockholders.[116] Where salaries have remained on the same level for many years, they are presumptively reasonable.[117] Compensation paid to officers by other businesses connected with the corporation should be considered in fixing salaries.[118]

Examination of compensation by courts. The reasonableness of a salary voted by the directors to one of their members may be examined in a court of equity for the benefit of the corporation, and if the salary is found to be excessive, wasteful, or illegal, it may be recovered.[119] For example, a board of directors has no right to forgive or authorize retention of short-swing profits by the president, and so the president remains liable for the note he made to the corporation after the board rescinded an extra bonus in the president's employment agreement that was meant to cancel out the short-swing profits, even though it was understood that the board would reconsider the rescission; this is so, since any such agreement would siphon corporate funds to the president with which to return illegal profits, and the court will not accept such a compensation arrangement.[120] Further, a stockholder who voted to authorize officers and directors who owned 80 percent of the corporation's stock, to fix their own salaries, was not estopped from challenging the directors' salaries and fringe benefits as excessive, since authority did not imply fixing unreasonable compensation; the stockholder could sue derivatively in court to recover the excess compensation for the corporation.[121]

The courts, however, do not interfere with the activities of either directors or stockholders in fixing compensation unless there is an injustice amounting to fraud or clear abuse of power.[122] The dissenting stockholders

---

[115]Cole Real Estate Corp. v. Peoples Bank and Trust Co., (1974) Ind. Ct. of App., 310 N.E. 2d 275.

[116]Keough v. St. Paul Milk Co., (1939) 205 Minn. 96, 285 N.W. 809; Gallin v. National City Bank, (1934) 152 N.Y. Misc. 679, 273 N.Y. Supp. 87.

[117]Wineburgh v. Seeman Bros., Inc., (1940) 21 N.Y.S. 2d 180.

[118]Richardson v. Blue Grass Mining Co., (1939) 29 F. Supp. 658.

[119]McQuillen v. National Cash Register Co., (1940) 112 F. 2d 879 (Md.law), cert. denied, (1940) 311 U.S. 695, 61 S. Ct. 140, 316; Albers v. Villa Moret, (1941) 46 Cal. App. 2d 54, 115 P. 2d 238; Calkins v. Wire Hardware Co., (1929) 267 Mass. 52, 165 N.E. 889; Worley v. Dunkle, (1948) N.J. 62 A. 2d 699; Von Herberg v. Von Herberg, (1940) 6 Wash. 2d 100, 106 P. 2d 737; Gauger v. Hintz, (1952) 262 Wis. 333, 55 N.W. 2d 426.

[120]Seilon v. Hickman, (1972) N.Y.S. Ct., N.Y.L.J., 5-30-72, p. 19.

[121]Goldman v. Jameson, (1973) Ala. S. Ct., 275 S. 2d 108.

[122]Perrott v. U.S. Banking Corp. ,(1944) 53 F. Supp. 953; Cron v. Tanner, (1951) 171 Kan. 57, 229 P.2d 1008; Nahikian v. Mattingly, (1933) 265 Mich. 128, 251 N.W. 421; Schmitt v. Eagle Roller Mill Co., (1937) 199 Minn. 382, 272 N.W. 277; Gottfried v. Gottfried, (1952) 112 N.Y.S. 2d 431; Shannon v. Early Foundry Co. (1929) 296 Pa. 141, 145 A. 708.

who seek redress on the ground that compensation is excessive must show bad faith or other breach of trust by the directors in fixing compensation.[123]

Increase in salaries, voted by directors. The same rules apply to the voting, by directors, of salary increases for themselves as apply to the voting of the original salaries (pp. 342-343). Hence the directors' action in voting themselves additional compensation for services already rendered is voidable.[124] And if the additional compensation bears no relationship to the services actually rendered, the action is fraudulent and cannot be cured by ratification by the majority stockholders.[125]

Extra compensation may be authorized by directors for work done by officers beyond the scope of their duties,[126] unless the statute, charter or by-laws require that the stockholders fix all compensation paid to officers.[127] Directors cannot vote additional compensation to an officer for services completed in the past, and for which he has already been paid a salary.[128] There is no consideration for such additional payment, hence it is a gift of corporate property.

If the passage of a resolution granting an increase in salary is dependent upon or effected by the vote of an interested director, it is prima facie voidable at the election of a stockholder.[129] However, a director-officer's act in increasing his own salary was held valid under the following circumstances: there was no fraud and no attempt to appropriate the corporate funds unlawfully under the pretense of salary; the salary was not excessive; the objecting stockholders knew of the increase at the time and did not object. In this case, the board of directors had informally agreed to and approved the increase and, after it had been put into effect by the manager-director, had ratified it in a blanket resolution ratifying all of the acts of the officers.[130]

The fact that the passage of a resolution, increasing the compensation of a director for services not connected with his office, depended upon the vote of the interested director did not mean that he could not recover the reasonable value of his services.[131]

---

[123]Gallin v. National City Bank, (1934) 152 N.Y. Misc. 679, 273 N.Y. Supp. 87.

[124]Godley v. Crandall & Godley Co., (1914) 212 N.Y. 121, 105 N.E. 818

[125]Ibid; see also Sarner v. Fox Hill, Inc., (1963) Conn. S. Ct. of Errors 199 A. 2d 6.

[126]Francis v. Brigham-Hopkins Co., (1908) 108 Md. 233, 70 A. 95.

[127]Ontjes v. MacNider, (1942) 232 Iowa 562, 5 N.W. 2d 860.

[128]Fidanque v. American Maracaibo Co., (1952) 33 Del. Ch. 262, 92 A 2d 311; Beacon Wool Corp. v. Johnson, (1954) 331 Mass. 274, 119 N.E. 2d 195.

[129]Davis v. Pearce, (1928) 30 F. 2d 85; Backus v. Finkelstein, (1924) 23 F. 2d 531; Barrett v. Smith, (1932) 185 Minn. 596, 242 N.W. 392.

[130]Cook v. Cook, (1930) 270 Mass. 534, 170 N.E. 455. See also Lowman v. Harvey R. Pierce Co., (1923) 276 Pa. 382, 120 A. 404.

[131]Gauger v. Hintz, (1952) 262 Wis. 333, 55 N.W. 2d 426.

Increase in salaries, voted by stockholders. A stockholders' resolution providing for extra compensation for managing directors is not voidable at the election of a minority stockholder merely because it was passed by the votes of the stockholder-directors benefited thereby. Such a resolution will be set aside only if it is found to be disadvantageous to the minority stockholders.[132] Nor will a stockholders' resolution that authorizes payment to the president of additional salary for additional services be set aside, if the additional services are worth the amount specified. The legality of such a resolution is not affected by the fact that the president owns practically all of the stock.[133]

Necessity for formal contract to fix compensation. A formal contract is not necessary to establish the right of an officer or employee to compensation for services. Nor need there be a formal resolution of the board of directors or the stockholders, except where the compensation is to be paid to a director or corporate officer for the performance of duties incidental to his office.[134] It is not absolutely necessary that the directors exercise their power to fix compensation of officers at a formal meeting or by a formal vote, or that a record be shown of the directors' exercise of their power, if the person to be paid can show that there was a mutual understanding between him and all the directors.[135] Thus, if an officer is called before the board of directors, or a duly authorized committee, and promised a stated increase in salary as inducement to continue in the service of the corporation, he is entitled to the increase if he assents to the proposition and acts upon it. The agreement does not have to be reduced to writing or included in a formal resolution.[136]

As a general rule, however, where the board is given the power to determine salaries, it must act as a board, and an agreement regarding compensation, made between an officer and one or two of the directors, is not binding on the corporation.[137]

A resolution to pay an officer a salary for extraordinary services has been held to be a valid contract, subject, however, to review by the courts as to amount.[138]

---

[132]Booth v. Beattie, (1922) 95 N.J. Eq. 776, 118 A. 257.

[133]Wiseman v. Musgrave, (1944) 309 Mich. 523, 16 N.W. 2d 60.

[134]In re Gouverneur Publishing Co., (1909) 168 F. 113; Jezeski v. Northeast Investment Co., (1925) 163 Minn. 165, 203 N.W. 978; Sotter v. Coatesville Boiler Works, (1917) 257 Pa. 411, 101 A. 744.

[135]Chabot & Richard Co. v. Chabot, (1912) 109 Me. 403, 84A. 892; Cook v. Cook, (1930) 270 Mass, 534, 170 N.E. 455.

[136]Young v. U.S. Mortgage & Trust Co., (1915) 214 N.Y. 279, 108 N.E. 418.

[137]Shannon v. Early Foundry Co., (1929) 296 Pa. 141, 145A 708; Dubbs v. Kramer, (1931) 302 Pa. 455, 153 A. 733.

[138]McMahon v. Burdette, (1930) 106 N.J. Eq. 79, 150 A. 12.

Resolutions fixing compensation. While it is not always absolutely essential, from a legal standpoint, that a resolution be passed fixing the compensation of directors and officers, the corporation that would avoid misunderstandings, disputes, and lawsuits would do well to fix the compensation of directors and officers by resolution and to keep a careful record of the action taken. The utmost care should be exercised in drawing the resolutions. The cases that have come before the courts for construction as to the meaning of resolutions authorizing compensation show the necessity for clear and unambiguous language.

Rules for framing compensation resolutions. A study of the decisions shows that the rules given below should be followed by those who are called upon to frame compensation resolutions.

1. Name the person to whom compensation is to be paid.
2. Indicate the service for which the compensation is to be paid.[139]
3. State the period of the service to be covered by the compensation.[140]
4. Show when payment is to be made.
5. Indicate clearly the amount to be paid. (See page 451 for a discussion of payment for services with stock of the corporation.)
6. State exactly the formula for determining any amount to be paid in addition to a specific salary.[141]
7. State clearly the basis upon which payment is to be made.
8. If payment is to be made on a percentage basis, define clearly the basis upon which the percentage is to be calculated.
9. If payment of compensation is to be made contingent upon the profits of the corporation, define clearly what is meant by profit.[142]
10. If compensation is to be paid in any event, do not limit the resolution by saying that "salaries shall be paid out of earnings," since it has been held that such a clause refers to "net earnings," and consequently, where there are no net earnings, salaries cannot be paid.[143]
11. Guard against unnecessary implications in the wording of the resolution.
12. Consider each resolution concerning compensation to be a contract of employment, and give it the same care and thought that you would give such a contract.

---

[139]Tietsort v. Irwin, (1925) 9 F. 2d 65. A resolution will not be invalid because it does not define the duties for which extra compensation was paid. Booth v. Beattie, (1922) 95 N.J. Eq. 776, 118 A. 257.

[140]The phrase "for ensuing year" means that salary is to be paid for that year only. Heubner v. Advance Refrigerator Co., (1920) 200 Wis. 233, 227 N.W. 868.

[141]Church v. Harnit, (1929) 35 F. 2d 499; National Loan & Inv. Co. v. Rockland Co., (1899) 94 F. 335; Holmes v. Republic Steel Corp., (1948) 84 Ohio App. 442, 84 N.E. 2d 508.

[142]See Witt v. McNeil & Bros. Co., (1929) 296 Pa. 386, 146 A. 27, construing the meaning of "divided profits." See also Harvey v. Missouri Valley Elec. Co., (1954) (Mo.) 268 S.W. 2d 820.

[143]Harlan-Kellioka Coal Co. v. Kelly, (1924) 203 Ky. 260, 262 S.W. 259; Heller v. Boylan, (1941) 29 N.Y.S. 2d 653, aff'd, memo dec., (1941) 32 N.Y.S. 2d 131. See Baker, "Executive Salaries and Bonus Plans," (McGraw-Hill, 1938).

13. In recording the vote on the resolution, state whether the interested director voted. If he absented himself at the time of the vote, or if he refrained from voting, be sure to show the fact on the record.[144]
14. If the intention is to establish a definite salary structure for the executive and management positions and offices of the company, be sure that the resolution indicates the duties assigned to each office, and that the salary is regarded as an incident of the office, to be paid to whatever person is the incumbent.

Right of interested directors and officers to vote on compensation. The general principle that prohibits a director from voting upon a matter in which he has a personal interest is enforced with great vigor against directors voting upon the question of their own salaries. It is well settled that, when a salary or compensation is voted to a director, the vote is void or voidable if it is carried only by including the vote of the director who is to receive the pay or salary, or if the vote is induced by the influence of the interested director.[145] The same rule would apply if the salary were being voted by the directors for themselves as officers. The resolution should be passed without the vote of anyone pecuniarily interested in the resolution.[146]

Effect of vote by interested directors and officers. Voting by directors and officers on resolutions fixing their own salaries does not necessarily take from them their right to compensation. Even if a contract under which a director or officer draws a salary for special services, over and beyond what his ordinary duties require, is void or voidable because he voted for it, and because his vote was necessary to the passage of the resolution, he might be allowed to keep the salary on the theory that he is entitled to the reasonable value of his services.[147] When yearly salaries are fixed by the stockholders, any subsequent action by the board is unnecessary; the fact that a director votes in favor of his own salary is then immaterial.[148]

A resolution fixing a director's salary will not be invalid just because the interested director voted in favor of it, provided that a sufficient number

---

[144]Onties v. MacNider, (1942) 232 Iowa 562, 5 N.W. 2d 860.

[145]Sarner v. Fox Hill, Inc., (1963) Conn. S. Ct. of Errors 199 A. 2d 6; Kenton v. Wood, (1940) 56 Ariz. 325, 107 P. 2d 380; Connors v. Swards Co., (1934) 276 Ill. App. 318; Bennett v. Klipto Loose Leaf Co., (1926) 201 Iowa 236, 207 N.W. 228; State v. Miller, (1939) 62 Ohio App. 43, 23 N.E. 2d 321. See also Savage v. The Lorraine Co., (1954) 217 F. 2d 378. Compare Elward v. Peabody Coal Co., (1956) 9 Ill. App. 2d 234, 132 N.E. 2d 549.

[146]Angelus Securities Corp. v. Ball, (1937) 20 Cal. App. 2d 423, 67 P. 2d 152; Wonderful Group Mining Co. v. Rand, (1920) 111 Wash. 557, 191 P. 631. But see Caminetti v. Prudence Mut. Life Ins. Ass'n, (1944) 62 Cal. App. 2d 945, 146 P. 2d 15.

[147]Kenton v. Wood, (1940) 56 Ariz. 325, 107 P. 2d 380.

[148]Kimball v. Kimball Bros., (1944) 143 Ohio St. 500, 56 N.E. 2d 60.

of disinterested directors also vote in favor of the resolution.[149] Similarly the presence of the interested director at the meeting will not invalidate a resolution fixing his salary, if he did not vote for the resolution.[150]

It is the settled rule that an action of the board of directors which is fraudulent or ultra vires is void.Subsequent ratification by the stockholders is ineffective. Generally, however, a resolution providing for compensation for a director, and which is passed only by counting his vote, is voidable rather than void. In such cases, the burden is on the director to show that the compensation is reasonable and fair. If such a reslution is ratified by the holders of a majority stock interest, it can still be questioned by an objecting minority stockholder, but then the burden is on him to show that the compensation was excessive or otherwise oppressive.[151]

A by-law adopted by the directors, authorizing payment of attendance fees to directors, was held to be valid, although directors who voted in favor of the by-law subsequently benefited from it.[152]

Counting an interested director to make a quorum. As a general rule, interested directors cannot be counted in determining whether a quorum is present to pass upon the question of their own salaries.[153] However, a resolution was considered valid where it was passed by a majority of the board of directors and a majority of the quorum, the interested director not voting on the resolution, but his presence being counted to make up the quorum.[154]

As in the case of voting, the tendency is to look upon the counting of an interested director to make up a quorum as making the action of the board voidable, rather than void. If a stockholder questions the board's action, the burden of proof is on the board to show that the action was fair and reasonable, and was entered into in the best interests of the corporation.[155]

---

[149]Rinn v. Asbestos Mfg. Co., (1938) 101 F. 2d 344; Anderson v. Calaveras Central Mining Corp., (1936) 13 Cal. App. 2d 338, 57 P.2d 560; Barrett v. Smith, (1932) 185 Minn. 596, 242 N.W. 392; Standard Furniture Co. v. Hotel Butler Co., (1931) 161 Wash. 109, 296 P. 153.

[150]Mathews v. Fort Valley Cotton Mills, (1934) 179 Ga. 580, 176 S.E. 505; Hax v. R.T. Davis Mill Co., (1890) 39 Mo. App. 353.

[151]Kenton v. Wood, (1940) 56 Ariz. 325, 107 P.2d 380; Anderson v. Calaveras Central Mining Corp., (1936) 13 Cal. App. 2d 338, 57 P.2d 560; Kaufman v. Schoenberg, (1952) 33 Del. Ch. 211, 91 A. 2d 786; Kerbs v. California Eastern Airways, Inc., (1952) 33 Del. Ch. 69, 90 A. 2d 652. aff'd, 33 Del. Ch. 174, 91 A. 2d 62; Francis v. Brigham-Hopkins Co., (1908) 108 Md. 233, 70 A. 95; State v. Miller, (1939) 62 Ohio App. 43, 23 N.E. 2d 321; 3 FLETCHER , CORPORATIONS , §921.

[152]Carter v. Louisville R.R., (1931) 238 Ky. 42, 36 S.W. 2d 836.

[153]See page 000. See also Holcomb v. Forsyth, (1927) 216 Ala. 486, 113 So. 586; Mortensen v. Ballard, (1951) 218 Ark. 459, 236 S.W. 2d 1006; Bassett v. Fairchild, (1901) 132 Cal. 637, 64 P. 1082; Angelus Securities Corp. v. Ball, (1937) 20 Cal. App. 2d 423, 67 P. 2d 152; Carter v. Louisville R.R., (1931) 238 Ky. 42, 36 S.W. 2d 836; McKey v. Swenson, (1925) 232 Mich. 505, 205 N.W. 583. In some states, statutory provisions permit directors to be counted or to vote under certain conditions. See, for example, Illinois Business Corporation Act, §33.

[154]Gumaer v. Cripple Creek Tunnel, Transp. & Mining Co., (1907) 40 Colo. 1, 90 P. 81.

[155]Fountain v. Oreck's Inc., (1955) 245 Minn. 202, 71 N.W. 2d 646; Landstreet v. Meyer, (1947) 201 Miss. 826, 29 So. 2d 653; Gauger v. Hintz, (1952) 262 Wis. 333 55 N.W. 2d 426.

Voting of salaries of officers by officer-directors. The rule that interested directors should not vote on the question of the payment of salaries to themselves may mean that the salaries of the directors or officers must be fixed by the stockholders even in cases where the power to fix salaries has been given to the board of directors.

Salaries for officers cannot validly be voted by a single resolution if the majority of the directors voting on the resolution are also the officers whose salaries are being fixed. In such a case the court will regard each director as having voted for his own salary, and that it had not been fixed by the votes of the others.[156]

Nor will it help to break the proposition up into a series of resolutions, even though each officer-director, in turn, refrains from voting on the resolution fixing his particular salary. Such a series of resolutions has been held to be a part of the same general purpose to get a salary for each director-officer.[157] However, in some instances, this procedure has been upheld when it appeared that there was no fraud practiced upon the stockholders.[158]

Nor can directors, even though they have authority to adopt by-laws, pass a by-law which gives them authority to fix salaries of director-officers, and then under the authority of such by-law, vote salaries to themselves.[159]

Hence if the directors fill all or most of the offices, to fix their compensation as officers with absolute certainty, they should have their action ratified by the stockholders, or have the stockholders fix the salaries of the officers at the stockholders' meeting.

Ratification of compensation of directors and officers. If the directors have exceeded their authority in fixing compensation for themselves or the officers, whether their acts can be validated by ratification depends upon the facts in each case and the circumstances under which the action was taken.[160] If the directors have acted honestly and have fixed a reasonable compensation, their acts will be considered voidable only,[161]

---

[156]Beha v. Martin, (1914) 161 Ky. 838, 171 S.W. 393.

[157]Angelus Securities Corp. v. Ball, (1937) 20 Cal. App. 2d 423, 67 P.2d 152; Mallory v. Mallory Wheeler Co., (1891) 61 Conn. 131, 23 A. 708; Davids v. Davids, (1909) 135 App. Div. 206, 120 N.Y. Supp. 350; Wonderful Group Mining Co. v. Rand, (1920) 111 Wash. 557, 191 P. 631; Stoiber v. Miller Brewing Co., (1950) 257 Wis. 13, 42 N.W. 2d 144.

[158]Funsten v. Funsten Com. Co., (1896) 67 Mo. App. 559; McNab v. McNab & Harlem Mfg. Co., (1892) 133 N.Y. 687.

[159]Savage v. The Lorraine Corp., (1954) 217 F. 2d 378; Holcomb v. Forsyth, (1927) 216 Ala. 486, 113 So. 586. Compare Carter v. Louisville R.R., (1931) 238 Ky. 42. 36 S.W. 2d 836.

[160]Rinn v. Asbestos Mfg. Co., (1938) 101 F.2d 344; Bates St. Shirt Co. v. Waite, supra (1931) 130 Me. 352, 156 A. 293; Chamberlain v. Chamberlain, Care & Boyce, Inc., (1925) 124 N.Y. Misc. 480, 209 N.Y. Supp. 258; Collins v. Hite. (1909) 109 W. Va. 79, 153 S.E. 240; Gauger v. Hintz, (1952) 262 Wis. 333, 55 N.W. 2d 426.

[161]Godley v. Crandall & Godley, Co., (1914) 212 N.Y. 121, 105 N.E. 818; Sotter v. Coatesville Boiler Works, (1917) 257 Pa. 411, 101 A. 744.

i.e., subject to ratification by the stockholders, or to attack by minority stockholders.[162] If the directors have perpetrated a fraud upon the stockholders or have voted themselves excessive salaries, their act will be absolutely void and it cannot be ratified by the stockholders.[163]

A resolution that is voidable because the vote of an interested director was necessary to its passage can be ratified subsequently by complying with the general rules for ratification given at page 263. If a statutory method is prescribed it must be strictly followed. In some cases ratification may be made by a competent board of directors.[164] In other cases, it may be made by a majority of the stockholders,[165] while in still others a unanimous vote of the stockholders may be required.[166]

At a stockholders' meeting to ratify such a resolution, interested director-stockholders have the right to vote.[167]

Effect of excessive salaries. Even though the contract has been ratified, a court of equity may scrutinize it carefully to hold the directors to a high standard of conduct.[168] Hence, salaries of corporate officers, fixed by corporate resolution at the time such officers were in control of the corporation, are open to investigation, whether or not the resolution providing for them was void.[169] If it is found that the salaries were exorbitant, the court will permit a recovery of the excess that has been paid, or will grant any other relief that the circumstances require.[170] Officers have been held liable for all salaries received by them when no justification was offered for the salaries, and the reasonable worth of the services was not shown.[171]

Employee benefits as salary supplements. About 20 percent of today's payroll costs are not represented by wages and salaries, but by the so-called "fringe benefits" plans. Increasingly, corporations have been

---

[162]Rosenthal v. Burry Biscuit Corp., (1948) 30 Del. Ch. 299, 60 A. 2d 106; United States Steel Corp. v. Hodge, (1903) 64 N.J. Eq. 807, 54 A.1.

[163]Bassett v. Fairchild, (1901) 132 Cal. 637, 64 P. 1082; McKey v. Swenson, (1925) 232 Mich. 505, 205, N.W. 583; Miner v. Belle Isle Ice. Co., (1892) 93 Mich. 97, 53 N.W. 218.

[164]Pece v. Tama Trading Co., (1937) 22 Cal. App. 2d 219, 70 P. 2d 652 (California statute provides for ratification by disinterested board).

[165]United States Steel Corp. v. Hodge, (1903) 64 N.J. Eq. 807, 54 A.1.; Godley v. Crandall & Godley Co., (1914) 212 N.Y. 121, 105 N.E. 818; Sotter v. Coatesville Boiler Works, (1917) 257 Pa. 411, 101 A. 744.

[166]Massoth v. Central Bus Corp., (1926) 104 Conn. 683, 134 A. 236; Rosenthal v. Burry Biscuit Corp. (1948) 30 Del. Ch. 299, 60 A.2d 106.

In Collins v. Hite, (1909) 109 W. Va. 79, 153 S.E. 240 it was suggested that payments in excess of authorized amounts could also be ratified by a unanimous vote of the stockholders.

[167]United States Steel Corp. v. Hodge, (1903) 64 N.J. Eq. 807, 54 A.1; Russell v. Henry G. Patterson Co., (1911) 232 P. 113, 81 A.136.

[168]Rinn v. Asbestos Mfg. Co., (1938) 101 F. 2d 344; Booth v. Beattie, (1922) 262 Wis. 333, 55 N.W. 2nd 246.

[169]Backus v. Finkelstein, (1924) 23 F. 2d 531.

[170]Beha v. Martin, (1914) 161 Ky. 838, 171 S.W. 393; Worley v. Dunkle, (1948) N.J. 62 A. 2d 699; Sotter v. Coatesville Boiler Works, (1917) 257 Pa. 411, 101 A. 744.

[171]McKey v. Swenson, (1925) 232 Mich. 505, 205 N.W. 583.

adopting such benefits for their employees as pension and profit-sharing plans, wage continuation plans, medical and surgical insurance, split-dollar life insurance, bonus plans, educational loan plans and the like. The steady growth of benefits of this kind has been spurred by the following facts: (1) a large part of the cost of these benefits is deductible as a business expense in arriving at the company's net taxable income; (2) these benefits attract a better class of employees, increase employee efficiency, and reduce labor turnover; (3) they offer a means of providing economic security for employees that could not be achieved by straight salary increases because of the personal income tax structure.

Authorization and administration of employee benefit plans. Unless prohibited by statute, charter or by-law, the board of directors has authority to establish an employee benefit plan.[172] Any plan adopted by a corporation must, of course, conform to the requirements of the applicable laws. Furthermore, the benefits under the plan must bear a reasonable relation to salaries or wage.

Even though neither statute, charter, nor by-law requires stockholder approval of a benefit plan, the usual practice is to obtain such approval. Such plans involve not only a considerable corporate expenditure but also the establishment of a fundamental corporate policy. Consequently, it is appropriate that the question have stockholder approval. Such approval is particularly desirable if directors are to participate in the plan so that there is not a disinterested quorum of directors available to adopt the plan. Furthermore, if an employee benefit plan is adopted or ratified by a majority of the stockholders, after a full and frank explanation, it will usually be binding on the minority.[173] However, if the minority is able to prove that the plan is unfair, or amounts to waste of corporate assets, they will not always be foreclosed by such ratification.[174]

The rule that a corporation is without power to pay compensation for past services does not prevent a corporation from making lump-sum payments for pension annuities for employees near retirement age when a pension plan is established.[175]

Plans must be administered in strict accordance with their terms. Non-officer directors and general counsel cannot be included in a bonus plan providing for payment of bonuses to ''officers and employees,'' even

---

[172]Nemser v. Aviation Corp., (1942) 47 F. Supp. 515; Holmes v. Republic Steel Corp. (1948) 84 Ohio App. 442, 84 N.E. 2d 508.
[173]Diamond v. Davis, (1945) 62 N.Y.S. 2d 181.
[174]Fogelson v. American Woolen Co., (1948) 170 F. 2d 660.
[175]Osborne v. United Gas Improvement Co., (1944) 51 Pa. D. & C. 383, aff'd, (1946) 354 Pa. 57, 46 A. 2d 208. But compare Fogelson v. American Woolen Co.,(1948) 170 F.2d 660.

though specified officers are authorized to distribute the bonuses in such proportions as they see fit.[176]

Additional compensation plans for directors and officers. Just as has been the case with employee benefits, it has become increasingly common practice for corporations to set up formal plans providing compensation in addition to their regular salary for directors and officers.[177] Typical of these plans are stock option plans, deferred (post-retirement) compensation plans, bonus plans and death benefit plans. Some plans may even provide for combinations of these forms of compensation.[178]

There must be some consideration flowing to the company if the plan is to be upheld. Sometimes this may be found in the fact that the plan induces desirable executives to associate with the company.[179] Other times, it may be found in the individual's agreement to an express or implied contract of employment which requires him to stay with the company to enjoy the full benefits of the plan.[180] Again, consideration for the plan benefits may be found in the services rendered.[181]

In the absence of consideration, the benefits are merely a gift, and the plan is invalid,[182] unless the stockholders unanimously waive the absence of consideration.[183] Among the factors courts have found to indicate lack of consideration are: where the benefits under the plan were to go to the directors setting it up;[184] when the circumstances indicated a gift of corporate assets under the guise of a bonus or option plan;[185] where the beneficiaries of the plan were already employees of the company;[186] and when no consideration was reasonably assured to the company by the granting of the options under a stock option plan.[187]

Although the courts will hold the directors to a high standard of

---

[176]Mann v. Luke, (1943) 44 N.Y.S. 2d 202.

[177]Of course officers and directors may be, and usually are, eligible for participation in employee benefit plans, such as pensions and profit-sharing. The following discussion, however, is principally concerned with those plans restricted primarily to directors, officers and key employees.

[178]Read Mullan Motor Co. v. McAtee, (1954) 77 Ariz. 188, 268 P.2d 1108; Black v. Parker Mfg. Co., (1952) 329 Mass. 105, 106 N.E.2d 544.

[179]Sandler v. Schenley Industries, Inc., (1951) 32 Del. Ch. 46, 79 A.2d 606.

[180]Wyles v. Campbell, (1948) 77 F. Supp. 343; Kerbs v. California Eastern Airways, (1952) 33 Del. Ch. 69, 90 A.2d 652; aff'd, 33 Del. Ch. 174, 91 A.2d 62.

[181]Wyles v. Campbell, (1948) 77 F. Supp. 343; Gottfried v. Gottfried, (1952) 112 N.Y.S. 2d 431.

[182]Fidanque v. American Maracaibo, (1952) 33 Del. Ch. 262, 92 A. 2d 311.

[183]Rosenthal v. Burry Biscuit Corp., (1948) 30 Del. Ch. 299, 60 A. 2d 106.

[184]Beacon Wool Corp. v. Johnson, (1954) 331 Mass. 274, 119 N.E. 2d 195.

[185]Auer v. Wm. Meyer Co., (1944) 322 Ill. App. 244, 54 N.E.2d 394.

[186]Frankel v. Donovan, (1956) Del. Ch. 120 A. 2d 311.

[187]Frankel v. Donovan, (1956) Del. Ch. 120 A. 2d 311; Kaufman v. Schoenberg, (1952) 33 Del. Ch. 211, 91 A.2d 786; Kerbs v. California Eastern Airways, Inc., (1952) 33 Del. Ch. 69, 90 A. 2d 652, aff'd. 33 Del. Ch. 174, 92 A.2d 62; Eliasberg v. Standard Oil Co., (1952) 23 N.J. Super. 431, 92 A. 2d 862, aff'd. 12 N.J. 467, 97.

conduct and the utmost good faith in setting up a plan for directors, officers and key employees,[188] they will not upset a plan which represents the best judgment of the directors unless there is evidence of fraud, overreaching or disregard of the rights of minority stockholders.[189] And, unless the board's action is ultra vires, illegal or fraudulent, ratification of the plan by the stockholders will cure any defects in such action.[190]

In determining the reasonableness of a plan, courts will look at the effect of taxes upon the executive's compensation and on the corporation's income[191] as well as the purchasing power of the dollar.[192]

For right of directors to vote on plan in which they are interested see page 353.

Executive compensation plans have been the subject of numerous legal articles.[193]

Bonuses not given under a plan. The payment of bonuses without a plan, after services have been rendered, to persons whose salaries have been fixed, has been recognized by the courts as a common practice among large corporations.[194] The danger here is that the bonus may be looked upon as being without consideration and, therefore, an invalid gift. A corporation ordinarily cannot make bonus payments to officers, for example, after the services have been performed, expecially over the protest of any stockholder.[195] This can be avoided, however, if the bonus is given under an express contract or agreement.[196] recognizing that the bonus is designed

---

[188]Rinn v. Asbestos Mfg. Co., (1938) 101 F. 2d 344.

[189]McQuillen v. National Cash Register Co., (1940) 112 F. 2d 879 Md. law, cert. denied, (1940) 311 U.S. 695, 61 S. Ct. 140, 316; Kerbs v. California Eastern Airways, Inc., (1952) 33 Del. Ch. 69, 90A. 2d 652, aff'd, 33 Del. Ch. 174, 91 A. 2d 62; Cron v. Tanner, (1951) 171 Kan. 57, 229 P.2d 1008; Beacon Wool Corp. v. Johnson, (1954) 331 Mass. 274, 119 N.E. 2d 195; Gauger v. Hintz, (1952) 262 Wis. 333, 55 N.W. 2d 426.

[190]Beacon Wool Co. v. Johnson, (1954) 331 Mass. 274, 119 N.E. 2d 195; Fidanque v. American Maracaibo Co., (1952) 33 Del. Ch. 262, 92 A. 2d 311; Eliasberg v. Standard Oil Co., (1952) 23 N.Y. Super, 431, 92 A.2d 862, aff'd 12 N.J. 467, 97 A.2d 437.

[191]Black v. Parker Mfg. Co., (1952) 329 Mass. 105, 106 N.E. 2d 544.

[192]Riddle v. Mary A. Riddle Co., (1948) 142 N.J. Eq. 147, 59 A.2d 599.

[193]See, for example, "Stock Option Plans for Executives," 41 CALIF. L. REV. 535; "Stock Option Plans," 34 CHI. BUS. REC. 391; "Computation of Net Profits in Contingent Compensation Arrangements," 51 COLUM. L. REV. 867; "Stock Option Plans and the Business Judgment Rule in Delaware," 53 COLUM. L. REV. 283; J.L. King, "Deferred Compensation and Other Fringe Benefits," 35 MICH. ST. BUS. J. 69; J.C. Bruton, "Profit Sharing Plans," 5 S.C.L.Q. 201; T. B. Rhodes, "Unrestricted Stock Options," 11 SW. L.J. 39; "Executive Stock Options," 11 SW. L.J. 70; W.L. Sabin, "Non-restricted Employee Stock Options—An Executive's Delight," 11 TAX L. REV. 179; "Restricted Stock Option Plans—A Windfall to Corporate Officers," 8 WESTERN RES. L. REV. 206. See also, generally, Prentice-Hall *Pension and Profit-Sharing*.

[194]Neff v. Gas & Elec. Shop, (1929) 232 Ky. 66, 22 S.W. 2d 265; Putnam v. Juvenile Shoe Co., (1925) 307 Mo. 74, 269 S.W. 593. For general discussions of this subject, see 17 MINN. L. REV. 433, 54 HARV. L. REV. 733; 41 MICH. L. REV. 501.

[195]In re Fergus Falls Woolen Mills Co., (1941) 41 F. Supp. 355.

[196]Boyum v. Johnson, (1942) 127 F. 2d 491; Holmes v. Republic Steel Corp., (1948) 84 Ohio App. 442, 84 N.E. 2d 508; Security Savings & Trust Co. v. Coos Bay Lumber & Coal Co., (1935) 219 Wis. 647, 263 N.W. 187. See Also 60 HARV. L. REV. 650, and authorities cited.

to encourage executives and employees to work diligently, become less wasteful, remain with the company, and become more skillful.[197] This is justified on the ground that such bonuses are, in fact, additional compensation and not payments for past services rendered.[198] The bonuses must be reasonable in amount considered in relation to the payee's services and salary.[199] Thus, for example, stockholders cannot set aside the directors' award of a bonus for the president merely on the ground that the president voted for it as director, when it is shown the bonus was compensation for the low salary paid the president during the previous years.[200] On the other hand, a shipping corporation could not give its directors, their families and servants free or reduced rate trips which could not be justified as relating to the directors' services for the company.[201]

It is neither illegal nor against public policy to contract to pay a bonus if (1) the services are valuable and are rendered with the understanding they are to be so rewarded, or (2) they are rendered under circumstances raising a presumption of the intent to pay.[202] The contract should result from formal board actions, rather than an informal agreement.[203] If the bonus is to be paid to directors and officers, the general rule that directors should not fix their own compensation applies. Hence, in the absence of special authority, directors and officers working under a fixed salary should not vote themselves bonuses.[204] A resolution to pay a bonus to a director, adopted only by counting his vote, would be voidable.[205]

---

[197]Wyles v. Campbell, (1948) 77 F. Supp. 343; Gottlieb v. Heyden Chemical Corp., (1952) 33 Del. Ch. 177, 91 A.2d 57. See G.D. Miller, "Requirements for Consideration for Employee Options," 51 MICH. L. REV. 559.

In Kerbs v. California Eastern Airways, Inc., (1952) 33 Del. Ch. 69, 90 A. 2d 652, aff'd 33 Del. Ch. 174, 91 A.2d 62, it was said "[s]ufficient consideration to the corporation may be, inter alia, the retention of the services of an employee, or the gaining of the services of a new employee, provided there is a reasonable relationship between the value of the services to be rendered and the value of the option granted. . . ." However, the plan was enjoined in this case because it was "not reasonably calculated to insure that defendant [corporation] will receive the contemplated benefits."

[198]Wineburgh v. Seeman Bros., Inc., (1940) N.Y.S. Ct. 21 N.Y.S. 2d 180.

[199]Menser v. Aviation Corp., (1942) 47 F. Supp. 515; Neff. v. Gas & Elec. Shop, (1929) 232 Ky. 66, 22 S.W. 2d 265. If bonuses are not reasonable, they may be considered a misappropriation of funds, even though provided by proper formalities. Shera v. Carbon Steel Co., (1917) 245 F. 589; Kaufman v. Schoenberg, (1952) 33 Del. Ch. 211, 91 A.2d 786.

[200]Western Properties, Inc. v. Barksdale, (1965) Wash. S. Ct. 1st Dept., 65 Wash. 592.

[201]Spirt v. Bechtel, (1956) CA-2, 232 F. 2d 241.

[202]Church v. Harnet, (1929) 35 F. 2d 499. In this case four of the five directors were the corporate officers. Bonuses were paid to the officers under an agreement among the directors. It was held that the bonuses were not nullified because the directors had agreed among themselves as to the amount of the bonuses since no fraud or lack of good faith was shown, and since the bonuses appeared to be fair and reasonable. See also In re Wood's Estate, (1941) 299 Mich. 635, 1 N.W. 2d 19; Wineburgh v. Seeman Bros., Inc., (1940) 21 N.Y.S. 2d 180.

[203]Nemser v. Aviation Corp., (1942) 47 F. Supp. 515.

[204]Stevenson v. Sicklesteel Lumber Co., (1922) 219 Mich. 18, 188 N.W. 419; Schall v. Althouse, (1924) 208 App. Div. 103, 203 N.Y. Supp. 36; A.J. Anderson Co. v. Kinsolving 1924, (Tex. Civ. App.) 262 S.W. 150; Thauer v. Gaebler, (1930) 202 Wis. 296, 232 N.W. 561.

[205]A.J. Anderson Co. v. Kinsolving, (1924) (Tex. Civ. App.) 262 S.W. 150.

It has been held that, in the absence of an established bonus plan, directors must have a formal authorization from the stockholders in order to give bonuses for past services.[206] But the better rule seems to be that stockholders, including interested director-stockholders, may ratify the act of directors in granting such a bonus if no fraud is involved.[207] Ratification may occur by formal vote, by acquiescence, or by failure to take contrary action upon learning the facts.[208]

Even though properly authorized, a bonus is not necessarily valid. The circumstances under which it was given are subject to scrutiny by the courts to determine whether the action is free of fraud and bad faith and whether it imposes on the rights of the minority.[209] Thus it is illegal for directors to donate to themselves property of the corporation in the guise of additional compensation even though it is approved by the stockholders.[210] And while stockholders may validly adopt a by-law providing for payment of a percentage of the net profits to officers as a bonus, this by-law cannot, against the protest of a stockholder, be used to justify payments so large as to amount to waste of corporate property.[211]

---

[206]Richardson v. Blue Grass Mining Co., (1939) 29 F. Supp. 658.

[207]Sotter v. Coatesville Boiler Works, (1917) 257 P.A. 411, 101 A. 744; Schmidt v. Paper Box Co., (1936) 185 Pittsburgh Leg. J. 541.

[208]Parrott v. Noel, (1925) 8 F. 2d 368.

[209]Kassab v. Ragnar Benson, Inc., (1966) D.C.W.D. Pa. 254, F. Supp. 830; Rinn v. Asbestos Mfg. (1938) 101 F. 2d 344; Fountan v. Oreck's, Inc., (1955) 245 Minn. 202, 71 N.W. 2d 646; Putnam v. Juvenile Shoe Co., (1925) 307 Mo. 74, 269 S.W. 593.

[210]Auer v. Wm. Meyer Co., (1944) 322 Ill. App. 244, 54 N.E. 2d 394; Schall v. Althaus, (1924) 208 App. Div. 103, 203 N.Y. Supp. 36. See also Moore v. Keystone Macaroni Mfg. Co., (1952) 370 Pa. 172, 87 A.2d 295, holding payment of annual sum to employee's widow was invalid gift.

[211]Rogers v. Hill, (1933) 289 U.S. 582, 53 S. Ct. 731. It was stated the court could determine whether or not, and to what extent, such payments constituted a waste. See also, "The American Tobacco Co. Bonus Plans, Legal Control of Executive Remuneration," 46 HARV. L. REV. 828; "Profit-Sharing for Executives and Employees—American Tobacco Co., a Case in Point," 42 YALE L.J. 419; "Legal Problems of Corporate Executive Bonus Plans," 41 YALE L.J. 109.

Chapter 12

FORMS OF RESOLUTIONS CONCERNING COMPENSATION OF DIRECTORS, OFFICERS, AND EMPLOYEES

Contents—Chapter 12

DIRECTORS' RESOLUTION
FIXING SALARY OF DIRECTOR

Resolved, That, pursuant to Article ....., Section ..... of the By-laws of this Corporation, the salary of ...., as a director of this Corporation, is hereby fixed at the sum of ..... ($.....) Dollars per year, to be paid to the said .... during his incumbency in said office, and until otherwise provided by resolution of the Board of Directors, in monthly installments of ..... ($.....) Dollars each, on the last day of each month.

RESOLUTION OF DIRECTORS FIXING SALARY OF
VICE-PRESIDENT AND GENERAL MANAGER

Whereas, ... was duly elected by this Board of Directors on the .. day of ...., 19.., to the office of Vice-President and General Manager of this company, and the salary to be paid to .... as compensation for services rendered in the capacity of Vice-President and General Manager of this company was not fixed, be it

Resolved, That the salary of .... as Vice-President and General Manager of this company is hereby fixed at ..... Dollars ($.....) per month from ...., 19.., to ...., 19.., to be paid on the .. day of each month.

RESOLUTION OF DIRECTORS AUTHORIZING COMPENSATION
OF MEMBERS OF EXECUTIVE COMMITTEE,
BASED UPON NET PROFIT

Resolved, That the Executive Committee, composed of five members, shall receive as compensation ten per cent (10%) per annum of the net profits of the .... Corporation, and that ten per cent (10%) shall be paid to the five members of the Executive Committee in equal amounts, that is, one-fifth (1/5) of ten per cent (10%) per annum of the net profits to each member of said Committee, and that the amount paid to each member of said Committee shall not exceed ten thousand dollars ($10,000) per annum. For the purpose of fixing such compensation it is understood that net profits shall be the amount available for dividends on the common stock and for surplus and reserves, that is, net income after deductions have been made for interest on the indebtedness, expenses, all accrued taxes, and preferred dividends.

DIRECTORS' RESOLUTION FIXING ATTENDANCE FEES OF
NONSALARIED DIRECTORS

Resolved, That beginning with the next regular meeting of the board of Directors, to be held on ...., 19.., the fee of nonsalaried members of the Board for attending any regular or special meeting of said Board shall be the sum of ..... ($.....) Dollars per meeting.

DIRECTORS' RESOLUTION ALLOTTING LUMP SUM AS FEE FOR ATTENDING DIRECTORS' MEETINGS

RESOLVED, That at every meeting of the Board of Directors of this Corporation, whether general or special, the aggregate sum of ..... ($.....) Dollars shall be paid as attendance fees to the Board of Directors, this sum to be divided equally among those directors who are present at the roll call and are still present at the adjournment of the meeting, or have been properly excused during the meeting.

DIRECTORS' RESOLUTION FIXING ATTENDANCE FEES FOR DIRECTORS AND MEMBERS OF EXECUTIVE COMMITTEE

RESOLVED, That a fee of ..... ($.....) Dollars be paid to each member of the Board of Directors for attendance at meetings of directors, adjourned meetings on the same day counting as one meeting only, and adjourned meetings to a subsequent date counting as two meetings. Members of the Board of Directors, however, residing out of town, shall be paid ..... ($.....) Dollars each for attendance at such meetings; and

RESOLVED FURTHER, That a fee of ..... ($.....) Dollars be paid to each member of the Executive Committee for attendance at meetings of the Executive Committee, adjourned meetings on the same day counting as one meeting only, and adjourned meetings to a subsequent day counting as two meetings.

DIRECTORS' RESOLUTION FIXING OFFICERS' SALARIES AT STATED SUMS

RESOLVED, That commencing with ...., 19.., and until changed by resolution of the Board of Directors of the .... Corporation, the salaries of the officers of this Corporation, payable in monthly installments on the last day of each month, shall be as follows:

President .... $.....
Vice President .... $.....
Secretary .... $.....
Treasurer .... $.....

DIRECTORS' RESOLUTION FIXING OFFICERS' SALARIES AT FIXED AMOUNT MONTHLY, PLUS PROPORTION OF NET PROFITS AT END OF YEAR; DEDUCTION FOR INACTIVITY

WHEREAS, the earnings of the Corporation are due largely to the engineering knowledge and training of ...., ..., and ...., President and Secretary, respectively, and it is necessary to fix their compensation for services during the time each shall be actively engaged in the business of the Corporation during the year 19.., be it

RESOLVED, That the salaries of ...., President, and ....,
Secretary for the year 19.., are hereby fixed at the sum of ..... ($.....) Dollars per
month to each of them, payable to each at the end of each month, and that at the end
of the year, each of them shall receive as salary the further sum of an amount equal
to one third of the net profits of the Corporation, it being understood that the term
"net profits" means earnings made in the operation of the business of the
Corporation after: (1) all expenses incident to the operation of the business have
been paid; (2) five 5%) per cent on the capital employed has been set aside; and (3)
depreciation of ten (10%) per cent on fixtures, equipment, and small tools, and six
(6%) per cent depreciation on buildings, have been set aside; provided, however,
that if either of said officers shall not be active in the affairs of the Corporation for
any period exceeding one week at any one time, a proportionate deduction shall be
made from such salary.

DIRECTORS' RESOLUTION AUTHORIZING PAYMENT OF
PERCENTAGE OF NET PROFITS AS COMPENSATION TO OFFICER
FOR SPECIAL SERVICE DURING YEAR

RESOLVED, That as special compensation for the services rendered by
..............., President of this Corporation, in effecting the consummation of
numerous contracts for the sale of the products of this Corporation during the year
19.., ... shall receive ..... (.....%) per cent of the net profits of this
Corporation during the year 19.., as shown by the books of the Corporation, but
not to exceed the sum of ..... ($.....) Dollars, the said special compensation to be
paid to .... at the end of the year 19.., and

RESOLVED FURTHER, That for the purpose of fixing such compensation, net
profits shall comprise the amount available for dividends on the common stock and
for surplus and reserves—that is, net income after deductions have been made for
interest on the indebtedness, expenses, all accrued taxes, and preferred dividends.

[*Note*. The definition of "net profits" is a matter that requires careful consideration from
persons skilled in accounting practice. See also the following two forms and the Resolution of
Executive Committee for special compensation to an officer (page 369).]

DIRECTORS' RESOLUTION AUTHORIZING PARTICIPATION OF
OFFICERS IN NET EARNINGS OF CORPORATION

RESOLVED, That in addition to their present salaries, the officers of the
corporation, comprising ...., ..., and ...., holding, respectively,
the offices of ...., ..., and ...., shall participate from year to year
in the net earnings, as shown by the books at the close of each business year, to the
extent of ..... (.....%) per cent of the net gain after the regular ..... (.....%) per cent
dividend to the stockholders has been set aside, to be equally divided among them.
The remaining ..... (.....%) per cent of the net gain shall be proportioned to "wear
and tear of plant and machinery," and to a surplus or undivided profit account, as
may be determined by the Board of Directors.

[*Note*. See note to preceding resolution.]

RESOLUTION OF DIRECTORS AUTHORIZING PAYMENT OF PERCENTAGE OF NET EARNINGS TO CHIEF EXECUTIVES IN PROPORTIONS RECOMMENDED BY PRESIDENT

RESOLVED, That the Treasurer is hereby authorized to make payments to the President and certain other officers and employees of the Company of additional compensation for services rendered during the year 19... The total so to be paid shall be ten (10%) per cent of net earnings in excess of ..... ($.....) Dollars.

For the above purpose, net earnings for the year shall mean the consolidated net earnings of the Company and all its subsidiaries, after provision has been made for depreciation and all other reserves, and after all interest charges and all taxes, except United States corporation income taxes and British income taxes, have been deducted, but before any deduction for sinking fund requirements has been made.

The amount so computed shall be divided among such officers and employees of the Company and in such proportions as the President may recommend, subject to the approval of a committee of three (3) directors appointed by the President from those directors not actively engaged in the business.

[*Note.* See note to resolution authorizing payment of percentage of net profits on page 363.]

DIRECTORS' RESOLUTION AUTHORIZING PAYMENT OF BONUS TO OFFICERS

WHEREAS, a Committee was appointed by this Board of Directors on ...., 19.., to make recommendations with regard to the payment of bonuses to the various officers of this Corporation for the year ending ...., 19.., and

WHEREAS, the said Committee has presented to this meeting its memorandum of recommendations for bonuses to officers, as follows:

<pre>
        To ...., President, $.....
           ...., Vice-Pres., $.....
           ...., Secretary, $.....
           ...., Treasurer, $.....
</pre>

RESOLVED, That the said recommendations are hereby approved and adopted, and that the Treasurer of this Corporation is hereby authorized and directed to make payments ot the respective officers, in accordance with the recommendations hereinabove set forth.

DIRECTORS' RESOLUTION AUTHORIZING PAYMENT OF HONORARIUM TO OFFICER

WHEREAS, ..., ... *(insert title of office)* of this Corporation, has rendered valuable services in behalf of this Corporation apart from his usual duties as such officer and in connection with the .... *(insert matter in which services were rendered)*, be it

RESOLVED, That an honorarium of ..... ($.....) Dollars be voted to ....
in recognition and appreciation of the additional services so rendered by him, and
the Treasurer of this Corporation is hereby authorized and directed to pay the said
sum to .... forthwith.

DIRECTORS' RESOLUTION AUTHORIZING PAYMENT FOR PAST SERVICES OF OFFICER AND FIXING FUTURE SALARY

WHEREAS, ... was duly elected by this Board of Directors on
...., 19.., to the office of .... *(insert title of office)*,

WHEREAS, the salary to be paid to .... as such .... was not
fixed by this Board, and no compensation has been paid to .... to date for
his services to this Corporation as such ...., and

WHEREAS, Article ....., Section ....., of the By-laws of this Corporation
authorizes the Board of Directors to fix the compensation of officers of the
Corporation for their services as such officers, be it

RESOLVED, That this Corporation pay to .... the sum of ..... ($.....)
Dollars, as reasonable compensation and in full payment for services rendered by
him to the Corporation up to and including ...., 19.., and that commencing
with ...., 19.., the salary of .... as .... of this Corporation is hereby fixed at the sum of ..... ($.....) Dollars per year, payable monthly on
the .. day of each month.

Mr. ...., although present, took no part in the vote upon this
resolution.

DIRECTORS' RESOLUTION GIVING OFFICER TREASURY STOCK AS COMPENSATION FOR SERVICES RENDERED

RESOLVED, That the Board of Directors, recognizing the valuable services
rendered by .... as Secretary and Factory Manager of, and as purchaser
for, the .... Corporation for the past ..... (.....) years, does hereby grant
to .... the same compensation as the President of this Corporation
received during the said ..... (.....) years, and

RESOLVED FURTHER, That the amount so granted to .... shall be the
difference between the amount received by .... as compensation for his
services for the period between ...., 19.., and ...., 19.., and the
amount received by ...., President of this Corporation, during the said
period for his services as such officer, and that, in lieu of payment thereof in cash,
the officers of the .... Corporation are hereby authorized to issue to
.... the balance of the unsold treasury stock—to wit ..... (.....) shares of
the common stock of the Corporation—in full settlement of the compensation due
him for services rendered.

DIRECTORS' RESOLUTION AUTHORIZING ADDITIONAL COMPENSATION TO OFFICERS

WHEREAS, the earnings of the Corporation are due largely to the knowledge and training of ...., and ...., President and Secretary respectively, and

WHEREAS, in addition to their ordinary executive duties the said .... and .... did perform valuable services to this Corporation by taking charge of all large purchases and sales, and by directing the general policies and management of the Corporation, thereby increasing the net earnings of this Corporation during the past fiscal year.

THEREFORE, in recognition of the skill and fidelity of .... and ...., be it

RESOLVED, That this Corporation do pay to .... the sum of ..... ($.....) Dollars, and to .... the sum of ..... ($.....) Dollars, as extra compensation for their respective past services to this Corporation as officers thereof, the extra compensation to be paid immediately.

DIRECTORS' RESOLUTION AUTHORIZING ISSUANCE OF STOCK TO OFFICERS AS EXTRA COMPENSATION FOR SERVICES

RESOLVED, That as extra compensation for their services to ...., 19.., there shall be issued to the following officers of the company the number of shares of common stock of this company set opposite their respective names—to wit:

Name of Officer	Title of Office	Number of Shares
....	....	....
....	....	....
....	....	....

STOCKHOLDERS' RESOLUTION RESERVING STOCK FOR ALLOTMENT TO OFFICERS AND KEY MEN

RESOLVED, That ..... (.....) shares of the common stock of this Corporation, of the par value of ..... ($.....) Dollars each, be reserved for the purpose of allotment by the Board of Directors to such officers and key men of the Corporation as it may determine, and that such reserved stock be allotted to and purchased by those designated by the Board of Directors at ..... ($.....) Dollars per share, to and including ...., 19..; ..... ($.....) Dollars per share from ...., 19.., to and including ...., 19.., at which time the reservation of said shares, for the purpose of allotment as herein provided, shall terminate.

DIRECTORS' RESOLUTION CHANGING OFFICERS' SALARIES

RESOLVED, That the salary of the President of the .... Corporation be increased *(or decreased)* from the sum of ..... ($.....) Dollars per year to the sum of ..... ($.....) Dollars per year, and that the salary of the Vice-President of the Corporation be increased *(or decreased)* from the sum of ..... ($.....) Dollars per year to the sum of ..... ($.....) Dollars per year.

DIRECTORS' RESOLUTION ELIMINATING OFFICERS' SALARIES

RESOLVED, That, beginning with ...., 19.., the salaries of the President, Vice-President, Secretary, and Treasurer of this Corporation, fixed by resolution of the Board of Directors adopted on ....,19.., shall cease, and that, until otherwise provided by resolution of the Board of Directors, the said officers shall render their services to the Corporation as such officers without compensation.

DIRECTORS' RESOLUTION DISCONTINUING OFFICER'S EXPENSE ALLOWANCE

RESOLVED, That the expense allowance of ..... ($.....) Dollars per year, voted by resolution of this Board of Directors on ...., 19.., to ....,
.... *(insert title of office)* of this Corporation, is hereby withdrawn, canceled, and discontinued as of ...., 19...

[*Note*. A corporation may discriminate among its employees in allowing expense accounts, in the absence of any agreement to the contrary. Renauld v. Marine Specialty & Mill Supply Co., (1931) 172 La. 835, 135 So. 374.]

DIRECTORS' RESOLUTION APPOINTING COMMITTEE TO RECOMMEND SALARIES FOR EXECUTIVE OFFICERS

RESOLVED, That ...., ..., and ...., are hereby appointed a committee to recommend to this Board of Directors the amount of salaries to be paid to the executive officers of this Company, the Committee to take into account any preliminary or tentative arrangements that may have been made prior to the incorporation of the Company.

DIRECTORS' RESOLUTION RATIFYING OFFICER'S COMPENSATION

WHEREAS, ... was duly elected by this Board of Directors on
...., 19.., to the office of Vice-President of this Corporation, and

WHEREAS, the salary to be paid to .... as such Vice-President was not fixed by this Board, and

WHEREAS, at the direction of the President of this Corporation, ...
has been paid a salary at the rate of ..... ($.....) Dollars per month for his services

as such Vice-President, and said compensation appears to be reasonable for the services rendered, be it

RESOLVED, That the salary of the said .... as Vice-President of this Corporation is hereby fixed at the sum of ..... ($.....) Dollars per month, payable on the last day of each month, and that the payments heretofore made to ...., under the direction of the President are hereby ratified, confirmed, and approved.

STOCKHOLDERS' RESOLUTION FIXING SALARIES OF DIRECTORS

RESOLVED, That beginning with ...., 19.., and until otherwise provided by resolution of the stockholders of this Corporation, every person who shall have been duly elected to and shall hold the office of director of this Corporation, shall be entitled to receive as compensation for his services as such director, the sum of ..... ($.....) Dollars per year, to be paid in monthly installments of ..... ($.....) Dollars on the last day of each month.

STOCKHOLDERS' RESOLUTION FIXING EXTRA COMPENSATION OF DIRECTOR

WHEREAS, at the request of this Corporation, ... has rendered valuable services to the Corporation outside of the scope of his duties as a director of the Corporation, in making a complete audit of the books of the Corporation for the year ending ...., 19.., be it

RESOLVED, That this Corporation pay to ...., as compensation for the services rendered by him, the sum of ..... ($.....) Dollars, and

RESOLVED FURTHER, That the Treasurer is hereby authorized and directed to make payment to ...., as provided, and to take a receipt therefor.

STOCKHOLDERS' RESOLUTION RATIFYING ACT OF BOARD OF DIRECTORS IN VOTING SALARY TO A DIRECTOR

RESOLVED, That the action of the Board of Directors in voting to .... a salary of ..... ($.....) Dollars per annum, to be paid to .... in monthly installments of ..... ($.....) Dollars during his term of office, in accordance with the resolution of the Board of Directors adopted at the meeting of ...., 19.., is hereby ratified and approved.

STOCKHOLDERS' RESOLUTION RATIFYING INCREASE IN SALARIES OF DIRECTORS

RESOLVED, That the increase in the salaries of directors of this Corporation, voted by the Board of Directors at a meeting of the Board held on ...., 19.., is hereby ratified and approved.

STOCKHOLDERS' RESOLUTION ALLOWING DIRECTORS TRAVELING AND OTHER EXPENSES TO ATTEND BOARD MEETINGS

RESOLVED, That the members of the Board of Directors of this Corporation be allowed their actual traveling expenses to and from the City of ...., State of ...., and the sum of ..... ($.....) Dollars per day for their expenses while in the City of .... to attend meetings of the Board of Directors.

STOCKHOLDERS' RESOLUTION RATIFYING INCREASE IN SALARY OF OFFICER

WHEREAS, prior to ...., 19.., ..., President of this Corporation, received the sum of ..... ($.....) Dollars per month as compensation for his services as such officer, and

WHEREAS, on the said ...., 19.., the salary of ...., as President of the Corporation, was increased to the sum of ..... ($.....) Dollars per month, and since that date the Treasurer of this Corporation has paid to .... the sum of ..... ($.....) Dollars each month as compensation for his services as President of this Corporation, be it

RESOLVED, That the aforesaid increase in the salary of ...., as President of this Corporation, and the payments made to him by the Treasurer as aforesaid, are hereby ratified, and

RESOLVED FURTHER, That the Treasurer of this Corporation is hereby authorized to continue to pay to .... such increased salary of ..... ($.....) Dollars per month, as compensation for his services as President of this Corporation.

STOCKHOLDERS' RESOLUTION RATIFYING PAYMENT OF ADDITIONAL COMPENSATION TO MANAGERS

RESOLVED, That the action of the Board of Directors in paying to ...., ..., and ...., as managers of this company, a share of the profits of the business at the end of each year from ...., 19.., to ...., 19.., inclusive, in accordance with the resolution of the Board of Directors, adopted at the meeting of ...., 19.., which reads as follows:

(Here insert directors' resolution.)

is hereby ratified, and that the method employed by the Board in arriving at the amount of net profits at the end of each year is hereby approved.

RESOLUTION OF EXECUTIVE COMMITTEE RECOMMENDING SPECIAL COMPENSATION TO OFFICER BASED ON NET PROFITS

RESOLVED, That the Executive Committee recommend to the Board of Directors that the Committee be authorized to award to the President, as compensation for his services during the year ending ...., 19.., and in addition to his regular salary for that year, a participation in the net profits of the Company to the extent of ..... per cent (.....%) of such profits as shown on the books of the Company.

[*Note.* For other resolutions providing for compensation based on net profits, see pages 363-364.]

RESOLUTION OF DIRECTORS AUTHORIZING OFFICER'S COMPENSATION FOR SECURING LEASE, AND PROVIDING CONDITIONAL PAYMENT

WHEREAS, at the request of this corporation .... has expended large sums of money and has rendered valuable services to this corporation outside the lines of his employment, in negotiating and securing for this corporation that certain lease from the .... Company to this corporation dated ...., 19.., and set forth in these minutes on pages ....., ..., and ....., and will render further valuable services to this corporation by securing to this corporation a continuation of said lease, thereby securing large profits to this corporation, be it

RESOLVED, That this corporation do pay said ...., as compensation for said services heretofore rendered and hereafter to be rendered, the sum of forty-five thousand ($45,000) dollars in the manner following, to wit: eleven thousand ($11,000) dollars forthwith, the further sum of ten thousand ($10,000) dollars ninety days from this date, the further sum of twelve thousand ($12,000) dollars five months from this date, and the further sum of twelve thousand ($12,000) dollars six months from date: Provided that, if the earnings of this corporation shall not be sufficient to make said deferred payments at the respective times above provided, then said deferred payments shall be made to .... as fast as the earnings of this company permit. The President and Secretary are hereby authorized and directed to make the payments herein provided and to take receipts therefor as made.

[*Note.* See Presidio Mining Co. v. Overton, (1919) 261 F. 993, in which a similar resolution appears.]

DIRECTORS' RESOLUTION AUTHORIZING REIMBURSEMENT TO OFFICER FOR MONEY ADVANCED

RESOLVED, That the Treasurer of this Corporation is hereby authorized and directed to pay to ...., President *(or insert other officer)* of the Corporation, the sum of ..... ($.....) Dollars, in full reimbursement for moneys advanced and expenses incurred and paid for by .... in connection with .... *(insert subject matter of advancement)*.

[*Note.* Where an officer advances funds for the corporation, official authorization by the directors is required for reimbursement. Fischer v. Streeter Milling Co., (1931) 60 N.D. 362, 234 N.W. 392. Unless the corporation expressly or impliedly requested the officer to make the advances or ratified them by acquiescence, the officer has no right to reimbursement. See In re Gouverneur Pub. Co., (1909) 168 F. 113.]

DIRECTORS' RESOLUTION AUTHORIZING PRESIDENT TO PAY ADDITIONAL COMPENSATION TO EMPLOYEES

RESOLVED, That the President is hereby authorized to make payments to all employees of this Company in an amount that seems to him to be equitable as additional compensation for services rendered during the period ...., 19.., to ...., 19.., the total amount to be expended by him in carrying this out not to exceed ..... per cent (.....%) of the Company's payroll for the period above mentioned.

DIRECTORS' RESOLUTION AWARDING BONUSES RECOMMENDED BY EXECUTIVE COMMITTEE

There was presented to the meeting a memorandum of recommendations regarding additional compensations to be paid to the various officers and employees for the year 19.., amounting to approximately ..... ($.....) Dollars, and salary increases to the amount of approximately ..... ($.....) Dollars for the year 19.., and after a consideration of the matter, upon motion duly made and seconded, it was

RESOLVED, That the recommendations are hereby adopted, and the Treasurer is hereby authorized to make payments accordingly.

DIRECTORS' RESOLUTION AUTHORIZING APPROPRIATION FOR DISTRIBUTION TO OFFICERS AND EMPLOYEES

RESOLVED, That an appropriation equal in amount to ..... ($.....) Dollars per share on the outstanding stock of the Company be set aside out of the assets for distribution to certain officers and employees of the Company, and that the Executive Committee be authorized to make such distribution as it may deem wise and proper.

DIRECTORS' RESOLUTION DISTRIBUTING BONUS PREVIOUSLY APPROPRIATED

WHEREAS, at a special meeting of the Board of Directors of ...., Inc., held at the office of the company on ...., 19.., at ..... P.M., a resolution to set aside the sum of ..... ($.....) Dollars for extra compensation for the calendar year ending ...., 19.., for distribution among the employees at the discretion of the Board of Directors, was unanimously passed, be it

RESOLVED, That the above-mentioned sum of ..... ($.....) Dollars be distributed as follows:

$..... to ....
$..... to ....

and to the other employees in the service of this company in the City of ......,............, on ...., 19.., ... (.....%) per cent of their respective salaries at that time, provided that, on the aforementioned date, they shall have been in the service of this company for at least one year, and

RESOLVED FURTHER, That the Treasurer is hereby authorized to pay such extra compensation in four (4) installments, as follows: April 1, July 1, October 1, and December 1, 19.., to each of the employees entitled to compensation under this resolution, provided such employee is in the service of this company on the date payment becomes due, unless otherwise specified by the Board of Directors.

DIRECTORS' RESOLUTION AUTHORIZING PAYMENT OF CHRISTMAS BONUS TO EMPLOYEES

RESOLVED, That the Treasurer is hereby authorized and directed to pay to each officer and employee of this Corporation who has been in its employ for a period of six (6) months or more, a sum equal to ..... per cent (.....%) of his or her annual salary, and to each employee who has been in the employ of the Corporation for a period of less than six (6) months, the sum of ..... ($.....) Dollars, as additional compensation, the total sum thus expended to be charged by the Treasurer to the salary account.

DIRECTORS' RESOLUTION AUTHORIZING PURCHASE OF COUNTRY CLUB MEMBERSHIP FOR COMPANY VICE-PRESIDENT

WHEREAS, the Board of Directors has carefully considered the advisability of purchasing a membership in .... Country Club, for Vice-President ...., and

WHEREAS, it was determined that such membership would be desirable and beneficial to this Company in that it would provide a place for entertaining visitors, customers, members of the press, and the like, thereby increasing the Company's goodwill, improving its public relations, and increasing its business, and

WHEREAS, ..., as Vice-President in charge of public relations, will have the primary responsibility and duty of seeing to the accommodations and entertainment of such visitors, customers and the like, and

WHEREAS, the expenses involved in such entertainment, etc., are properly those of the Company and not of a private individual, be it

RESOLVED, That as a step to maintain and increase the Company's business, Vice-President .... is hereby authorized to apply for membership in .... Country Club for the year .... and to obtain reimbursement from the Company for any dues or initiation fees thereby incurred, and

RESOLVED FURTHER, That Vice-President .... is hereby authorized to obtain reimbursement from the Company for all expenses incurred at .... Country Club during the year in connection with the entertainment, accommodations, meals, etc., of the Company's guests, including, but not limited to, expenses for lodging and meals, bar bills, greens fees, caddy fees, rental or purchase of sporting equipment, locker fees, and tips, and including Mr. ....'s own such expenses.

DIRECTORS' RESOLUTION AUTHORIZING THE MAKING OF A DEATH-BENEFIT CONTRACT

WHEREAS, the Board of Directors realizes that ...., a junior executive of this Corporation, has performed valuable services for this Corporation during the past several years apart from the usual duties and responsibilities of his position, be it

RESOLVED, That the President of the Corporation is hereby authorized to make a contract with ...., under which, if he is still in the Corporation's employ at the time of his death, or has previously retired in accord with the Corporation's retirement policy, the Corporation shall on his death, pay to his beneficiary or beneficiaries, as named in said contract, the sum of $5,000.

[*Note*. Under the 1954 Internal Revenue Code, payments of up to $5,000 made to a deceased employee's beneficiary may be excluded from his or her income.]

DIRECTORS' RESOLUTION TO ESTABLISH SCHOLARSHIP AID PROGRAM

WHEREAS, this Corporation desires to provide scholarship aid to children of its employees, and to contribute in this way toward the educational expenses of its employees' children, and

WHEREAS, it will improve management and employee relationships if the Corporation puts into effect a tangible, definite and specific plan to award scholarships to the children of employees to enable those most deserving of them to be educated properly, be it

RESOLVED, That the Board of Directors hereby adopts the ...., Inc. Scholarship Plan as set forth in the annexed copy, and

FURTHER RESOLVED, That the officers of the Corporation are hereby authorized to take such action as may be necessary to carry the plan into execution.

DIRECTORS' RESOLUTION ESTABLISHING AN EDUCATIONAL LOAN PLAN

WHEREAS, this Corporation desires to make loans to its employees to enable them to educate their children, and

WHEREAS, it will improve management and employee relationships if the Corporation puts into effect a tangible, definite and specific plan to give financial assistance to its employees to enable them to educate their children, be it

RESOLVED, That the Board of Directors hereby adopts the employees' Children Educational Loan Plan as set forth in an annexed copy, and

FURTHER RESOLVED, That the officers of the Corporation are hereby authorized to take such action as may be necessary to carry the Plan into execution.

DIRECTORS' RESOLUTION ADOPTING WAGE CONTINUATION PLAN

WHEREAS, the officers of this Corporation, after careful study, have prepared a plan providing for wage payments to sick and injured employees, and

WHEREAS, the officers have presented to this meeting their recommendation for the adoption of a Wage Continuation Plan substantially in the form, a copy of which is attached to and made a part of this Resolution, be it

RESOLVED, That the Board of Directors hereby adopts the attached Wage Continuation Plan, and that the Treasurer of this Corporation is hereby authorized and directed to make payments to eligible employees in accord with said Plan.

DIRECTORS' RESOLUTION AUTHORIZING SPLIT-DOLLAR INSURANCE PLAN

WHEREAS, it is the considered judgment of the Board of Directors of this Corporation that the institution of a split-dollar insurance program is desirable to promote better company-employee relations by enabling employees to take out a sufficient amount of insurance to protect their families, be it

RESOLVED, That the Treasurer is hereby authorized to negotiate with the .... Insurance Company of ...., for the setting up of a split-dollar insurance program which shall provide that:

(1) All employees, other than officers and directors, may be issued policies, subject to the approval of the Board of Directors of this Corporation;

(2) Such policies shall be issued for not less than $7,500 nor more than five times the employee's annual compensation at the time he applies for insurance under the program;

(3) The Corporation shall pay the annual increase in the cash surrender value of all policies and shall on the death of any insured receive the cash surrender value of such policy;

(4) Any insured party may purchase the Corporation's interest on any anniversary of the policy by paying the Corporation the then cash value of the policy;

(5) Upon termination of employment for any reason, the insured may purchase the Corporation's interest as described in (4), and if he fails to do so, the Corporation shall surrender the policy to the Insurance Company for the cash value of such policy; and

(6) Such further provisions as the Treasurer may deem advisable; and

RESOLVED FURTHER, That the Treasurer submit the Agreement between the .... Insurance Company and this Corporation to the Board of Directors for approval.

DIRECTORS' RESOLUTION ADOPTING EMPLOYEES' WELFARE PLAN

WHEREAS, this Corporation on numerous occasions has extended financial aid and assistance to its employees and members of their immediate families in financial distress because of illness, injury or other disability when the employee involved did not have the necessary financial reserves to meet the situation, and

WHEREAS, it will improve management and labor relationship if the Corporation puts into effect a tangible, definite and specific plan to give financial assistance to needy employees, and

WHEREAS, in furtherance of this purpose, the officers of the Corporation have prepared and submitted to the Board of Directors an Employees' Welfare Plan calling for the creation of a charitable foundation to perpetuate the Corporation's policy of rendering financial assistance to needy employees, a copy of which is hereto annexed, be it

RESOLVED, That the Board of Directors hereby adopts the Employees' Welfare Plan as set forth in the annexed copy, subject to the approval of the stockholders at their next regular meeting, and

RESOLVED FURTHER, That the officers of the Corporation are hereby authorized to take such action as may be necessary to carry the Plan into execution.

STOCKHOLDERS' RESOLUTION APPROVING EMPLOYEES' WELFARE PLAN

RESOLVED, That it is advisable and to the best interest of .... Corporation that an Employees' Welfare Plan be adopted and made effective, and

RESOLVED FURTHER, That the Employees' Welfare Plan considered at this meeting which was approved and adopted by the Board of Directors of .... Corporation at its meeting held on ...., 19.., and recommended for adoption to the stockholders, is hereby in all respects duly adopted and directed to be made effective, subject to its terms, as of ...., 19.., and that the adoption thereof by the Board of Directors is ratified, and

RESOLVED FURTHER, That the Board of Directors and the officers of ....
Corporation are hereby authorized and directed to do all things to make the Plan
effective, and to take all action to carry out said Plan, including the execution of all
papers and documents that may seem proper, advisable, or convenient.

DIRECTORS' RESOLUTION ADOPTING PROFIT-SHARING PLAN

WHEREAS, the Board of Directors of this Corporation deems it advisable to
reward employee loyalty, to encourage long-term service with this Corporation,
and to encourage greater productivity and efficiency on the part of said employees,
and

WHEREAS, said Board of Directors believes that a profit-sharing plan will
accomplish the aforesaid objectives, be it

RESOLVED, That the .... Corporation Employee Profit-Sharing Plan,
heretofore considered and discussed and a copy of which is hereby ordered
annexed to and made a part of the minutes of this meeting, is hereby adopted,
subject to the approval of the stockholders at their special meeting to be called after
a favorable ruling under Secs. 401(a) and 404 of the Internal Revenue Code of
1954 has been secured from the Internal Revenue Service,

RESOLVED FURTHER, That ...., Secretary of this Corporation, is hereby
authorized and directed on behalf of this Corporation, to execute, seal, and deliver
the Trust Agreement between the ....Corporation and ....,
Trustee, pursuant to the .... Corporation Profit-Sharing Plan, a copy of
which Agreement is hereby ordered annexed to and made part of the minutes of this
meeting, and

RESOLVED FURTHER, That ...., ..., and ...., are appointed
members of, and shall constitute, the Profit-Sharing Committee provided for in the
.... Corporation Profit-Sharing Plan, the members of said Committee to
hold office until the next annual meeting of the Board of Directors or until their
successors are duly appointed, and

RESOLVED FURTHER, That the President and the several officers of this Corporation and each of them are authorized to retain ...., as counsel, to give him
an appropriate power of attorney, and to instruct him to take such action as shall be
necessary to secure a ruling from the Internal Revenue Service that the
.... Corporation Employee Profit-Sharing Plan is qualified under Secs.
401(a) and 404 of the Internal Revenue Code of 1954 and to take other action as
said officers or any of them shall deem appropriate and necessary to put the
.... Corporation Profit-Sharing Plan into operation.

RESOLUTION OF STOCKHOLDERS APPROVING PROFIT-SHARING PLAN AND AUTHORIZING SECRETARY TO EXECUTE TRUST AGREEMENT

RESOLVED, That the .... Corporation Employee Profit-Sharing Plan, a copy of which is appended to this resolution, is hereby approved, and

FURTHER RESOLVED, That the Secretary is hereby authorized to execute the Trust Agreement with the .... Trust Company as provided in the Plan.

[For resolutions on stock option plan, see Chapter 18.]

STOCKHOLDERS' RESOLUTION AUTHORIZING DIRECTORS TO SET ASIDE PART OF PROFITS FOR PENSION FUND AND PROFIT-SHARING PURPOSES

RESOLVED, That the Board of Directors of the .... Bank in .... City, is hereby empowered to set aside from the net earnings of the bank annually, after first deducting losses and a sum equal to six per cent of the capital, surplus, and undivided profits, as the latter appear at the beginning of the year, such a sum as they may deem proper, not to exceed one tenth (1/10) of the remainder of said net profits, for the purpose of creating an officers' and employees' pension fund and an officers' and employees' profit participation fund, under such rules and regulations as may from time to time be enacted by said Board.

Chapter 13

SUBSCRIPTIONS
TO CAPITAL STOCK

Contents—Chapter 13

Subscription to stock distinguished from purchase and sale of stock. A subscription to stock is an agreement by which the subscriber agrees to take and pay for a fixed number of shares of the stock of a corporation which is organized or is about to be organized.[1] A contract for the purchase and sale of stock, on the other hand, is an agreement by the corporation or other seller to sell a certain number of shares for a fixed consideration and by the purchaser to take the stock and pay the consideration fixed. For example, in one case the instrument read "Application for Stock; I subscribe to 5 shares of stock in ABC Corp., and agree to pay $800; Paid on the above bond, $72. (Signature)." The parties also agreed that the price of $800 would be paid in yearly installments of $72 and that the corporation would credit the payor with interest. When the trustee in bankruptcy brought an action to enforce the subscription, the court denied relief on the ground that this was not a subscription, but rather a contract of sale. *Reasons:* (1) No stockholder rights were granted; (2) instead of the corporation receiving interest, as would be the case in a subscription, the payor was credited with interest; (3) in a subscription, receipts are generally intended to be credited to capital immediately or within a very short period, not, as here, over an 11-year period.[2]

An agreement to purchase stock "when issued" is not a subscription to stock to be issued, but a contract to purchase.[3]

Before a corporation has been organized, its stock can be acquired only by subscription; after incorporation, it can be acquired either by subscription or by purchase from the corporation or from individual owners. Whether a particular transaction constitutes a subscription or a purchase and sale generally depends upon the terms of the contract and the intention of the parties.[4]

Difference in legal effect of subscription to stock and contract for purchase and sale of stock. The importance of the distinction between a subscription and a contract for purchase and sale lies in the difference in the legal effect of the two types of contracts:

1. A subscriber is a member of the corporation even though he is not fully paid up and has not been issued the stock certificates. He has the liabilities of a stockholder as well as the privileges.[5] He can, for example,

---

[1] Putnam v. U.S., (CA-1, 1945) 149 F. 2d 721; McDowell v. Lindsay, (1906) 213 Pa. 591, 63 A. 130.

[2] Stern v. Mayer, (1926) 166 Minn. 346, 207 N.W. 737; Crichfield-Loeffler, Inc. v. Taverna, (1926) N.J. 132 A. 494.

[3] Clucas v. Bank of Montclair, (1933) 110 N.J.L. 394, 166 A. 311.

[4] Burke v. Walker, (1938) 124 N.J. Eq. 141, 200 A. 546. See also Frey, "Post-Incorporation Subscriptions," 77 U. PA. L. REV. 750-783.

[5] Shiffer v. Akenbrook (1921) 75 Ind. App. 149, 130 N.E. 241; Stull v. Terry & Tench, Inc., (1948) 81 N.Y.S. 2d 43.

vote. He can remove directors and hold them personally liable.[6] A purchaser is not a member of the corporation and is not subject to liabilities until the contract is executed, that is, until he has been issued a stock certificate.[7]

2. If the corporation becomes *insolvent* its trustee in liquidation can sue the subscriber to recover the unpaid *balance* of the subscription.[8] The trustee cannot get a purchaser to pay the balance of the contract price because the corporation cannot perform. That is, it cannot make good delivery on stock.[9] There is failure of consideration.

3. If a subscriber defaults in paying to a *solvent* corporation, that is, one that can perform, the measure of damages is the unpaid balance of the subscription price or the amount of the call.[10] On the other hand, if a purchaser defaults, the damages are the difference between market and contract price. However, if the stock has no ready market value the contract may be specifically enforced.[11]

4. In some states, under the sale of goods provision of the statute of frauds, a subscription does not have to be in writing, while a contract for sale must be.[12] But if the subscription contract is not to be performed within a year, it should under the statute of frauds be in writing to be enforceable. Special statutes in some states require a subscription to be in writing in all cases.

Subscriptions to stock before incorporation. Formerly, most states required that all or a substantial part of the authorized stock be subscribed to before the corporation could be organized. This was for the protection of creditors. Some few states still adhere to this rule, but many now require only that incorporators be subscribers, without specifying the dollar value of the stock to be subscribed. Many others require that a stated minimum amount of capital be paid in, usually one or two thousand dollars, before the organized corporation can commence business. Thus, the minimum initial capital imposed by statute is less a protection for creditors today than it once was. However, subscribers for their own protection can require by the subscription contract that a larger amount of capital be subscribed to

---

[6]Brown v. North Ventura Road Dev. Co. 216 (1963), 30 Cal. Reptr. 568.

[7]Bigelow v. Bicek (1938) 298 Ill. App. 73, 18 N.E. 2d 398; Schmitz v. 75 and Exchange Drug Co., Inc., (1940) 303 Ill. App. 192, 24 N.E. 2d 889.

[8]Mills v. Friedman, (1922) 181 N.Y.S. 285, affd. 184 N.Y.S. 613, affd. 135 N.E. 899; Shiffer v. Akenbrook, 75 Ind. App. 149; 130 N.E. 241; Buckman v. Gordon, (1942) 312 Mass. 6, 42 N.E. 2d 811; Strong v. Turner (1938) Mo. App., 122 S.W. 2d 71.

[9]Bigelow v. Bicek, (1938) 289 Ill. App. 73, 18 N.E. 2d 398.

[10]Haglin v. Ashley, (1942) 212 Minn. 445, 4 N.W. 2d 109.

[11]Spencer v. McGuffin, (1921) 190 Ind. 380, 130 N.E. 407. See also Mills v. Friedman, (1922) 181 N.Y.S. 285, affd. 184 N.Y.S. 613, affd. 135 N.E. 899.

[12]Louisiana Oil Exploration Co., Inc. v. Raskob, (1925) 32 Del. 564, 127 A. 713; Boroseptic Chemical Co. v. Nelson, (1928) 53 S.D. 546, 221 N.W. 264.

before each can be bound on his subscription, or that the corporation will not be organized unless a certain sum of money is committed to it. Courts honor this condition among the contracting parties, and apparently also against the corporation's suing creditors. Since the corporation is not in existence and not a party to the contract, the agreement must be drawn with care. If precautions are not taken a subscriber may be able to withdraw his subscription before the corporation is formed or before it adopts the contracts.

Generally, if two or more persons mutually agree to organize a corporation and each subscribes for stock to be paid for after the corporation comes into existence, such an agreement is valid and enforceable by the parties or the corporation, as their agent, *after its formation*.[13] The corporation may maintain the action even if it is not named in the subscription agreement.[14] Whether or not the contract of subscription is dated before or after organization it is enforceable by the corporation if the corporation accepts the subscription and enters the business for which it was created.[15] But a subscriber is not liable unless the specifically contemplated corporation is formed.[16] Even though the contemplated corporation is formed the subscription must be accepted by the corporation according to its terms, otherwise the subscriber will be released.[17] To be valid this agreement must have all the essentials of an ordinary contract.

Formalities in subscribing to stock. Unless the statute under which the corporation is organized, or the charter, prescribes a certain form of agreement, no formal agreement, in writing or otherwise, is required to make one a subscriber.[18] Where the statute or charter contains provisions as to the form of the subscription agreement, substantial compliance therewith will be sufficient.[19] Where the statute prescribes the use of subscription books, the use of subscription paper instead has been upheld.[20] But such a statute has been held to require the subscription contract to be in writing, proof of an oral contract being excluded.[21] Statutes in some states

---

[13]Positype Corp. v. Flowers, (CA-7, 1930) 36 F.2d 617; Perry Hotel Co. v. Courtney, (1931) 102 Fla. 1041, 136 So. 691; U.S. Grant Hotel Co. v. Keheas, (1929) 255 Ill. App. 101; Jermyn v. Searing, (1919) 225 N.Y. 525, 122 N.E. 706; Martin v. Cushwa, (1920) 86 W. Va. 615, 104 S.E. 97.

[14]Ocala Community Hotel Co. v. Holloway, (1931) 103 Fla. 521, 137 So. 882; Perry Hotel Co. v. Courtney, (1931) 102 Fla. 1041, 136 So. 691.

[15]Hatcher-Powers Shoe Co. v. Hitchins, (1929) 232 Ky. 87, 22 S.W. 2d 444.

[16]Harlie R. Norris Co. v. Lovett, (1932) 123 Cal. App. 640, 12 P.2d 141.

[17]Wallace v. Duel, (1935) 18 Tenn. App. 483, 79 S.W. 2d 595.

[18]Dickinson County Hospital Co. v. Kessinger, (1929) 128 Kan. 576, 279 P. 7; Dingle v. Shaab, (1941) 179 Md. 589, 20 A. 2d 149. Gibson v. Oswalt, (1934) 269 Mich. 300, 257 N.W. 825; Froug v. Miami Savings & Loan Co., (1953) Ohio App. 128 N.E. 2d 449; Farrell v. Simons, (1937) 180 Okla. 600, 71 P.2d 688.

[19]See Windsor Hotel Co. v. Schenck, (1915) 76 W. Va. 1, 84 S.E. 911.

[20]Nebraska Chicory Co. v. Lednicky, (1907) 79 Neb. 587, 113 N.W. 245.

[21]Vreeland v. N.J. Stone Co., (1878) 29 N.J. Eq. 188.

expressly require that a subscription be in writing.[22] Unless the statute or charter provides otherwise, actual signing of a formal subscription paper or stock book is not essential to a binding contract.[23] The intention of the parties controls. If it is clear that the purpose of the parties was to create the relationship of stockholder in the corporation, the court will find a valid subscription.[24] If the statute requires the subscribers to sign the articles of incorporation, such signatures with the number of shares placed opposite each signature have been held a sufficient subscription to bind both subscriber and corporation.[25] However, to be valid, the subscription must be for a definite number of shares,[26] and the amount to be paid therefor must be ascertainable. In actions on subscription agreements made before incorporation, the courts will generally apply the law of the place where the contract was made, in preference to the law of the state in which the corporation was organized.[27]

Conditions for liability of subscriber on preorganization subscription. An agreement to subscribe for shares in a corporation to be formed is an executory contract. One of the conditions of such a contract is the formation of the corporation contemplated by the parties. The subscriber will be released from his obligation under the subscription contract: (1) if there is a material change in the charter of the corporation without his consent;[28] or (2) if the corporation is not validly organized.[29] These conditions are discussed in the following paragraphs.

Change in proposed charter sufficient to release subscriber. In determining whether or not an alteration or change in the charter of the corporation is material and sufficient to release the subscriber, the facts in

---

[22]See, for example, New York B.C.L.S. 503; Beck v. Motler (1973) 348 N.Y.S. 2d 397.

[23]Butler University v. Scoonover, (1897) 114 Ind. 381, 16 N.E. 642.

[24]Nulton v. Clayton, (1880) 54 Iowa 425, 6 N.W. 685; Rensselaer & W. Plank Road Co. v. Barston, (1854) 16 N.Y. 460.

[25]Dupee v. Chicago Horse Shoe Co., (CA-7, 1902) 117 F. 40; Zander v. Schuneman, (1927) 170 Minn. 353, 212 N.W. 587.

[26]Wheeler v. Ocker & Ford Mfg. Co., (1910) 162 Mich. 204, 127 N.W. 332.

[27]Community Hotel Corp. v. Gilbert, (1930) 135 Misc. 676, 241 N.Y.S. 352.

[28]The reason for the general rule is given in Nugent v. The Supervisors of Putnam Co., (1873) 86 U.S. 83, as follows: "A subscription is always presumed to have been made in view of the main design of the corporation, and of the arrangements for its accomplishment. A radical change in the organization or purposes of the company may, therefore, take away the motive which induced the subscription, as well as affect injuriously the consideration of the contract. For this reason it is held that such a change exonerates a subscriber from liability for his subscription; or, if the contract has been executed, justifies the stockholder in resorting to a court of equity to restrain the company from applying the funds of the original organization to another project not contemplated by it." The general rule was not at issue in the case itself.

[29]Capps v. Hastings Prospecting Co., (1894) 40 Neb. 470, 58 N.W. 956; Tonge v. Item Publishing Co., (1914) 244 Pa. 417, 91 A. 229.

each case must be considered.[30] In general, so long as the provisions of the charter conform to the main objects or purposes of the corporation contemplated at the time the subscription contract was made, the subscriber is not released by the alteration.[31] But if the main objects or purposes of the corporation formed are different from those of the corporation proposed, then the subscriber will be released.[32] A mere enlargement of corporate powers that does not actually change the purpose for which the corporation was formed is not material, and will not release the subscriber.[33]

If the amount of capital stock of the corporation formed is greater than the amount originally proposed, the change is material, and the subscriber is discharged.[34] A change in the capital stock structure has been held to be material so as to release the subscriber.[35] A decrease in the amount of stock which could be legally issued and outstanding at any given time was held not to be such an alteration as would release the stockholder from liability on the subscription.[36]

Release of subscriber when corporation is not validly organized. A subscriber to stock before organization may insist upon the organization of a regular and legal corporation.[37] The statutory requirements for the organization of a corporation must be met. Thus, failure to record the certificate of incorporation, where recording is a condition precedent to corporate existence, is defective incorporation, and sufficient to release the subscriber.[38] If the promoters fail to organize the corporation, they are personally liable to return to preincorporation subscribers money paid on their subscriptions.[39] However, aggrieved subscribers to an unregistered pre-organization subscription agreement for a proposed corporation which

---

[30]National Bank of Union Point v. Amoss, (1915) 144 Ga. 425, 87 S.W. 406; Kingston v. Nichols, (1923) 221 Mich. 677, 192 N.W. 768; Ginter v. Blaine, (1913) 2 Ohio App. 482; Mann v. Mitchell (1923) Tex. Com. App., 255 S.W. 980.

[31]Menominee Community Bldg. Co. v. Rueckert, (1929) 245 Mich. 37, 222 N.W. 162. See also Crawford v. Coleman Hotel Co., (1929) Tex. Civ. App. 16 S.W. 2d 307.

[32]Bunn v. Farmers' Warehouse Co., (1916) 18 Ga. App. 567, 90 S.E. 78; Owensboro Seating & Cabinet Co. v. Miller, (1908) 130 Ky. 310, 113 S.W. 423; Macon Union Co-op Ass'n. v. Chance, (1924) 31 Ga. App. 363, 122 S.E. 66.

[33]Watters & Martin v. Homes Corp., (1923) 136 Va. 114, 116 S.E. 366.

[34]Atlanta Steel Co. v. Maynahan, (1912) 138 Ga. 668, 75 S.E. 980.

[35]Lane v. Coin Mach. Mfg. Co., (1918) 69 Super. 373; Wallace v. Duel, (1934) 18 Tenn. App. 483, 79 S.W. 2d 595.

[36]In re Gillham's Estate, (1936) 286 Ill. App. 370, 3 N.E. 2d 524, discussed in 25 GEO. L.J. 184 (1936). See also Country Club Real Estate Improvement Co. v. Gillham's Estate, (1938) 294 Ill. App. 184, 13 N.E. 2d 631.

[37]In an action on a subscription agreement made before incorporation, the plaintiff generally must show the existence of a corporation de jure, and not merely de facto. Community Hotel Corp. v. Gilbert, (1930) 135 N.Y. Misc. 676, 241 N.Y. Supp. 352; Wright Bros. v. Merchants' & Planters' Packet Co., (1913) 104 Miss. 507, 61 So. 550. See, however, A.H. Frey, "Modern Development in the Law of Preincorporation Subscriptions," 79 U. PA. L. REV. 1005.

[38]See Tonge v. Item Pub. Co., (1914) 244 Pa. 417, 91 A. 229.

[39]Smith v. Secor, (1938) 225 Iowa 650, 281 N.W. 178.

was never formed were not entitled to avoid the agreement and recover their money where they had acquiesced in cancellation and accepted in lieu of their rights in it another corporation's stock; the agreement qualified for registration exemption under securities law even though proposed corporation was never formed.[40]

Withdrawal by a subscriber prior to corporation's acceptance. The right of a subscriber to withdraw depends on whether or not there is a binding contract prior to acceptance by the corporation. Before it comes into existence the corporation, of course, cannot accept the contract.

There is no such contract when an individual, acting alone and not in concert with others, offers to take stock in a corporation to be formed. Reason: that is an offer looking toward a unilateral contract which can be withdrawn at any time before the contract is brought into existence by the formation of the corporation and its acceptance of the offer.[41]

The cases are in conflict as to whether there is such a contract when two or more persons mutually agree to organize a corporation and each subscribes for stock therein. Some courts hold there is a contract between the subscribers themselves and a continuing offer to the corporation to be formed, upon the acceptance of which there is a contract constituting each subscriber a stockholder.[42] Under this holding there can be no withdrawal by one or more subscribers without the consent of all the subscribers.[43] When the subscriber was party to pre-incorporative argument and made no effort to withdraw his subscription, even becoming a director, the corporation could affect his indebtedness to it against debts owed him by the corporation.[44]

Other courts hold that there is no contract between the subscribers;[45] hence, until the corporation is organized, the subscriptions are mere offers which must be accepted by the corporation before they become contracts constituting the subscribers-stockholders and the subscribers may withdraw at any time prior to acceptance by the corporation.[46]

Subscribers who desire to withdraw must give notice of their withdrawal. Such notice need not be in any particular form, nor need it be in writing or given at a meeting of the subscribers. If it is given to the person

[40]Greenberg v. Wolf, (1974) 19 Ill. App. 3d 905.

[41]Collins v. Morgan Grain Co., Inc., (CA-9 1926) 16 F. 2d 253.

[42]Marysville Elec. Light & Power Co. v. Johnson, (1892) 93 Cal. 538, 29 P. 126.

[43]Cravens v. Eagle Cotton Mills Co., (1889) 120 Ind. 6, 21 N.E. 981. See, also, Crawford v. Coleman Hotel Co., (1929) Tex. 16 S.W. 2d 307.

[44]Duncan v. Brookview House, Inc., (S.C., 1974) 205 S.E. 2d 707.

[45]Macon-Union Co-op. Ass'n v. Chance, (1924) 31 Ga. App. 636, 122 S.E. 66. Compare Gillespie v. Camacho, (1926) 28 Hawaii 32.

[46]Glass Coating Co. v. Clark, (1928) 118 Ohio St. 10, 160 N.E. 10 (held its attempted exercise of right of withdrawal came too late); Coleman Hotel Co. v. Crawford, (1927) Tex. Civ. App., 290 S.W. 810.

who obtained the subscription or to the person who has charge of the subscription list it is sufficient.[47]

Acceptance of preorganization subscription by corporation. The final act that gives complete validity to a subscription procured prior to corporate organization is the acceptance of the subscription by the corporation after its formation. Acceptance of the subscription after incorporation is necessary to make the subscriber a shareholder, and to fix his liability to pay for the stock.[48]

No particular form of acceptance is required: it may be express or implied, oral or written, and may depend upon acts as well as words. Recognition of the subscriber as a stockholder is sufficient to imply acceptance.[49] However, the statute or the charter may require acceptance in a particular way.

When the corporation accepts the charter granted in conformity with the purpose and powers as described in the subscription agreement,[50] the subscription becomes binding, and the subscriber becomes a stockholder.[51]

Some states, by statute, give the corporation a specified period from the time the subscription is signed, to accept the subscription. In the meantime the subscriber's offer is irrevocable. The purpose of these statutes is to afford some stability to the fund raising process. However this type of statute leaves the option entirely with the corporation and it can be used to pressure or "freeze out" minority subscribers who must then resort to the courts for relief. To prevent this some statutes make acceptance automatic upon incorporation. Decisional law to the same effect also exists.[52] However, automatic acceptance also creates a problem in that it forces the corporation to accept the subscriptions.

Subscriptions to stock after incorporation. Some courts have held that there is a distinction, so far as the status of the subscriber is concerned,

---

[47]Planters & Merchants Independent Packing Co. v. Webb, (1908) 156 Ala. 551, 46 So. 977; Hudson Real Estate Co. v. Tower, (1894) 161 Mass. 10, 36 N.E. 680; Palais Du Costume v. Beach, (1910) 144 Mo. App. 456, 129 S.W. 270.

[48]Cornhusker Development and Investment Group, Inc. v. Knecht (Neb. 1966) 49 SCJ 873. Cramer v. Burnham, (1928) 107 Conn. 216, 140 A. 477; Glass Coating Co. v. Clark, (1928) 118 Ohio St. 10, 160 N.E. 460.

For a discussion of what constitutes acceptance by the corporation, see A.H. Frey, "Modern Development in the Law of Preincorporation Subscriptions," 79 U. Pa. L. Rev. 1005.

[49]Nebraska Chicory Co. v. Lednicky, (1907) 79 Neb. 587, 113 N.W. 245.

[50]Crawford v. Coleman Hotel Co., (1929) Tex. Civ. App. 16 S.W. 2d 307; Menominee Community Bldg. Co. v. Rueckert, (1929) 245 Mich. 37, 222 N.W. 162.

[51]Baltimore City Passenger Ry. v. Hambleton, (1893) 77 Md. 341, 26 A. 279.

[52]Utah Hotel Co. v. Madsen, (1943) 43 Utah 285, 134 P. 577; Crawford v. Coleman Hotel Co. (1929) Tex. Civ. App. 16 S.W. 2d 307; Watters & Martin, Inc. v. Homes Corp., (1923) 136 Va. 114, 116 S.E. 366. See also Moser v. Western Harness Racing Ass'n, (Dist. Ct. App., Gal., 1948) 200 P.2d 7.

between a subscription for stock in a corporation to be formed and a subscription for stock in an existing corporation.[53] In the former case, the subscriber becomes a stockholder when the corporation is organized; in the latter case, the subscription is considered a mere contract of purchase and sale between the subscriber and the corporation.[54] The general view, however, is that there is no distinction between a subscription to the stock of a corporation already organized and a subscription made prior to and for the purpose of organization.[55]

So far as the subscription agreement is concerned, the general rule is that whereas a subscription before incorporation is governed by the law of the state in which the contract was made,[56] a subscription agreement after incorporation is governed by the laws of the state in which the corporation was organized.[57]

Validity and enforceability of a subscription. A corporation which has accepted subscriptions to its capital stock may enforce each subscription agreement, provided the agreement is a valid and enforceable contract[58] under the laws of the state of incorporation.[59] Pertinent provisions of the state constitution,[60] applicable statutory provisions,[61] and the charter of the corporation[62] become part of the stock subscription contract.

Elements essential for validity of stock subscription. To be valid and enforceable, a capital stock subscription must contain the following elements:

---

[53]Schwartz v. Manufacturers Cas. Ins. Co. (1939) 385 Pa. 130, 6 A. 2d 299; Baltimore City Pass. Ry. Co. v. Hambleton (1893) 77 Md. 341, 26 A. 279.

[54]Reagan v. Midland Packing Co., (1924) 298 F. 500; Stern v. Mayer, (1926) 166 Minn. 346, 207 N.W. 737; Crichfield-Loeffler, Inc. v. Taverna, (1926) N.J. 132 A. 494.

[55]"All those who join in the enterprise of accumulating the capital of the corporation, represented by subscriptions to the original issue of capital stock, should be regarded as subscribers, rather than as purchasers, whether the agreement is made before or after the articles are filed." Reagan v. Midland Packing Co., (1924) 298 F. 500; Louisiana Oil Ex. Co. v. Raskob, (1925) 32 Del. 564, 127 A. 713; First Caldwell Oil Co. v. Hunt (1925) 101 N.J. Law 240, 127 A. 209.

[56]See page 383.

[57]May v. Roberts, (1930) 133 Ore. 643, 286 P. 546; McAlister v. Eclipse Oil Co., (1935) Tex. Civ. App. 79 S.W. 2d 895. See also Thomas v. Kalbfus, (1918) 97 Ohio St. 232, 119 N.E. 412.

[58]Where the subscription to the capital stock of a corporation was unexecuted by payment and delivery of the certificate of stock, the court held that it was an executory contract. Steele v. Singletary, (1922) 120 S.C. 132, 110 S.E. 833. To the same effect, see Kappers v. Cast Stone Constr. Co., (1924) 184 Wis. 627, 200 N.W. 376. However, in Jackson v. Sabie, (1917) 36 N.D. 49, 161 N.W. 722, the court said: "In the absence of regulations to the contrary, the principles which govern the formation of an ordinary contract apply with full force to a contract of subscription to corporate stock." See Farm Lands Development Co. v. Taft, (1922) 194 Iowa 481, 186 N.W. 431; Thomas v. Scoutt, (1927) 115 Neb. 848, 215 N.W. 140.

[59]Collins v. Morgan Grain Co., (1926) 16 F. 2d 253.

[60]Thomas v. Scoutt, (1927) 115 Neb. 848, 215 N.W. 140; Guaranty Trust Co. v. Scoon (1927) 144 Wash. 33, 256 P. 74.

[61]Thomas v. Kalbfus, (1918) 97 Ohio St. 232, 119 N.E. 412.

[62]Bryan v. St. Andrews Bay Community Hotel Corp., (1930) 99 Fla. 132, 126 So. 142; Geiger v. American Seeding Mach. Co., (1931) 124 Ohio St. 222, 177 N.E. 594.

1. *Competency of parties.* The parties to the agreement must be competent. Any individual who is competent to enter into a contract may make a valid subscription to stock, unless the charter of the corporation offering the stock, or the statute under which the corporation is organized, expressly or impliedly contains some contrary provision.[63]

    A corporation has no power to subscribe for or to purchase and hold shares of stock in another corporation, unless clearly authorized to do so by statute or by the provisions of its charter. Many states do have that kind of provision. The reason for the rule is that the stockholders are entitled to assume, in the absence of notice to the contrary in the charter of statute, that the directors will use the capital and assets in the business authorized by the charter and not share the capital with others.[64]

2. *Consideration.* The subscription must be supported by a valid consideration. The promise of the subscriber to take the stock and pay for it, and the promise of the corporation to issue the stock upon payment, constitute a sufficient consideration.[65] It is not necessary that the corporation be named as promisee in the agreement to subscribe.[66]

3. *Offer and acceptance.* This element of a valid contract is supplied by the subscriber's offer to take the shares and the corporation's acceptance of the subscription. A capital stock subscription before incorporation must be accepted by the corporation according to its terms, otherwise the subscriber will be released.[67] Non-acceptance by the corporation or refusal to receive tendered payment will exonerate the subscriber from his obligation.[68] If the subscriber revokes or rescinds his offer before acceptance by the corporation, his obligation is at an end. A corporation was held to have accepted a subscriber's offer when it deposited his check for initial payment in its bank.[69]

4. *Meeting of minds.* The minds of the parties must meet upon the subject matter of the agreement. A mutual mistake about some material fact connected with the subscription may entitle the subscriber to rescind his subscription.[70]

5. *Legality of contract.* The contract must not be illegal. The contract will be illegal, for example, if the purpose for which the corporation is formed is illegal;[71] or the subscription may be illegal if the agreement violates

---

[63]Cattlemen's Trust Co. v. Turner, (1916) Tex. Civ. App. 182 S.W. 438.

[64]City Coal & Ice Co. v. Union Trust Co., (1924) 140 Va. 600, 125 S.E. 697; Kappers v. Cast Stone Constr. Co., (1924) 184 Wis. 627, 200 N.W. 376.

[65]Scranton Axle & Spring Co. v. Scranton Board of Trade, (1921) 271 Pa. 6, 113 A. 838.

[66]Ocala Community Hotel Co. v. Holloway, (1931) 103 Fla. 521, 137 So. 882; Perry Hotel Co. v. Courtney, (1931) 102 Fla. 1041, 136 So. 691.

[67]Wallace v. Duel, (1935) 18 Tenn. App. 483, 79 S.W. 2d 595.

[68]Potts v. Wallace, (1892) 146 U.S. 689.

[69]Becker v. Tower National Life Inv. Co. (Mo. S. Ct., 1966) 406 S.W. 2d 553; Penn-Allen Broadcasting Co. v. Trayor (1957) 389 Pa. 490, 133 A. 2d 528.

[70]Moseley v. Red River Oil Mill, (1927) 6 La. App. 725; Hill v. International Products Co., (1925) 129 N.Y. Misc. 25, 220 N.Y. Supp. 711.

[71]Le Werne v. Meyer, (1889) 38 Fed. 191; Clemshire v. Boone County Bank, (1890) 53 Ark. 512, 14 S.W. 901.

some statute.[72] Thus, a subscription was held invalid, where the subscription price was fixed at less than par in violation of a statute requiring the par value to be paid for all shares.[73] Contracts also have been held to be illegal when they called for the issue of stock in excess of the amount authorized by the corporation's charter.[74]

6. *Freedom from fraud.* The contract must be free from fraud. Subscriptions obtained by fraudulent misrepresentations, under duress, or through the use of undue influence, can be avoided by the subscriber.[75] (See pages 426-428 as to liability under the Federal Securities Act of 1933 for fraud and misrepresentation in the sale of securities.)

Subscriptions obtained through fraud. The courts have not laid down any definite rules as to what does and what does not constitute fraud sufficient to invalidate a subscription to stock; each case must be determined by its own facts. In general, however, the following elements must be present to constitute actionable fraud:[76]

1. The representation must be made as to a past or present material fact. The court made a distinction between statements about the prospects of the enterprise and statements representing facts that do not exist. The former are merely matters of opinion and not grounds for annulling the contract; the latter are material representations that are fraudulent and hence are grounds for annulment. For example, a statement made by a representative of a corporation that the company was actually engaged in manufacturing the product that it was organized to manufacture, when it was not so engaged, was a misrepresentation of a material fact. On the other hand, a statement that the stock would pay an annual dividend of 9 per cent was merely a promise and not a misrepresentation of a material fact.[77]

2. The representation must be made by an authorized agent of the corporation to the subscriber.[78] A notation printed in the margin of a subscription blank furnished by the corporation, to the effect that the company is not responsible for representations made by its agent, does not relieve the corporation from liability for false representations made by him.[79]

[72]Castle v. Acme Ice Cream Co., (1929) 101 Cal. App. 94, 281 P. 396.

[73]Rudolph Christy Casket Co. v. Taneto (1928) 24 Ill. App. 314; Tramp v. Marquesen, (1920) 188 Iowa 968, 176 N.W. 977.

[74]Crawford v. Twin City Oil Co., (1927) 216 Ala. 216, 113 So. 61; World Oil Co. v. Hicks (1929) Tex. Civ. App. 19 S.W. 2d 605.

[75]Schnuth v. Harrison (Wis. 1969) 171 N.W. 2d 370.

[76]Bohn v. Burton-Lingo Co., (Tex., 1915). 175 S.W. 173. See also Kentucky Elec. Development Co's Receiver v. Head, (1934) 252 Ky. 656, 68 S.W. 2d 1; Berwick Hotel Co. v. Vaughan, (1930) 300 Pa. 389, 150 A. 613; Goodin v. Palace Store Co., (1931) 164 Wash. 625, 4 P. 2d 493.

[77]Steele v. Singletary, (1922) 120 S.C. 132, 110 S.E. 833. See also Fuhrman v. American Nat'l Bldg. & Loan Ass'n, (1932) 126 Cal. App. 202, 14 P. 2d 601.

[78]Seacoast Packing Co. v. Long, (1921) 116 S.C. 406, 108 S.E. 159. See also Fuhrman v. American Nat'l Bldg. & Loan Ass'n, (1932) 126 Cal. App. 202, 14 P. 2d 601.

[79]Edge v. Alertox, Inc., (1933) 47 Ga. App. 598, 171 S.E. 181.

3. The statement must be false.[80]

4. The party making the statement must know that it is false,[81] or must have made it recklessly with no knowledge of its truth and as a positive assertion.[82]

5. The misrepresentation must be intended to induce the subscriber to act upon it.[83]

6. The acts of the subscriber must show that he relied upon the representations. The signature of the subscriber to the subscription agreement, in the absence of evidence to the contrary, is proof that he relied upon the representations and acted on the faith of them.[84] Not only must the subscriber rely on the representations, but he must be justified in relying on them.[85] He must also exercise a reasonable degree of care to avoid being misled.[86] He is not bound, however, to investigate the truth of the statements that induced him to subscribe to the stock.[87]

7. The subscriber must have suffered injury.[88] Thus a stockholder suffered no damage from alleged illegal acts by a corporation and individual defendants, when acts occured after acquisition of stock and so could not have induced it; also, a sudden rise and fall in stock prices allegedly due to illegal acts did not prove damage to stockholder.

Remedies of subscriber in case of fraud. A contract procured by fraud is not void but it is voidable only at the option of the party defrauded. This means that it is valid until disaffirmed.[89] In most states, several remedies are open to a subscriber induced by fraud to subscribe for stock of a corporation. (1) He may rescind the subscription by notification to the corporate authorities without taking legal proceedings.[90] If he rescinds the contract, he must surrender or at least tender, what he received under the

---

[80]Denis v. Nu-Way Puncture-Cure Co., (1919) 170 Wis. 333, 175 N.W. 95.

[81]Peake v. Thomas, (1927) 222 Ky. 405, 300 S.W. 885; Guynn v. Shulters, (1955) 223 Miss. 232, 78 So. 2d 114.

[82]Kentucky Elec. Development Co.'s Receiver v. Head, (1934) 252 Ky. 656, 68 S.W. 2d1. See West Text Utilities Co. v. Ellis, (1937) (Tex. Civ. App.) 102 S.W. 2d 234. This case holds that it is immaterial whether the false representations were made in good faith or not.

[83]Equity Co-op Ass'n v. Equity Co-op Milling Co., (1922) 63 Mont. 26, 206 P. 349.

[84]American Alkali Co. v. Salom, (1904) 131 F. 46.

[85]See Chandler v. McKerral, (1934) 68 F. 2d 343; Fuhrman v. American Nat'l Bldg. & Loan Ass'n, (1932) 126 Cal. App. 202, 14 P. 2d 601.

[86]Hines v. Saart Bros. Co., (1931) 51 R.I. 436, 155 A. 533.

[87]American Alkali Co. v. Salom, (1904) 131 F. 46; Griffin v. Burrus, (1927) Tex. Civ. App. 292 S.W. 561.

[88]Corporate Finders & Consultants, Inc. v. Universal Container Corp. (N.Y. 1972) 39 A.D. 2d 533.

[89]Upton v. Englehart, (1874) 3 Dill. (U.S.) 496; Akers v. Radford State Bank, (1929) 153 Va. 1, 149 S.E. 528.

[90]Kentucky Elec. Development Co.'s Receiver v. Head, (1934) 252 Ky. 656, 68 S.W. 2d1; McGrath v. C.T. Sherer Co., (1935) 291 Mass. 35, 195 N.E. 913; Bohn v. Burton-Lingo Co., (Tex., 1915) 175 S.W. 173.

contract,[91] unless it was wholly executory on the part of the fraud doer.[92] (2) He may repudiate the subscription and bring an action in equity to have the subscription canceled, thus assuring himself of relief from all liability as a stockholder.[93] (3) If the corporation brings an action against the subscriber to enforce payment of the subscription price, or an assessment on the shares, the subscriber may defend the action brought against him, setting forth fraud as a defense.[94] (4) If he has paid any money to the corporation on the subscription, he may bring an action to recover what he has paid.[95] (5) He may affirm the contract and sue for damages.[96]

When rescission must be made. Rescission of a subscription contract because of fraud must be made promptly upon discovery of the fraud.[97] Whether or not a subscriber has been guilty of undue delay depends on the facts in each case.[98] The subscriber's refusal to make payments on the subscription as soon as he learns of the fraud is equivalent to prompt rescission, although a bill for rescission is not filed until some time later.[99] Moreover, the subscriber must exercise due diligence in discovering the fraud.[100]

Remedies of subscriber after insolvency of the corporation. The remedies mentioned above may be invoked while the corporation is solvent. If the corporation becomes insolvent, and the rights of creditors are involved, the opportunity to rescind the subscription, even though it has been procured through fraud, may be denied.[101] No definite rule applicable to every jurisdiction in this country can be stated regarding the effect of corporate insolvency upon the right of a subscriber to rescind his contract on the ground of fraud. However, in a leading case the court said:

---

[91]Kentucky Elec. Development Co.'s Receiver v. Head, (1934) 252 Ky. 656, 68 S.W. 2d1.

[92]Roberts v. James, (1912) 83 N.J.L. 492, 85 A. 244; Gould v. Bester, (1928) 127 Ore. 308, 271 P. 988.

[93]Tyler v. Savage, (1892) 143 U.S. 79, 12 S. Ct. 340.

[94]American Alkali Co. v. Salom, (1904) 131 F. 46; Davis v. Gifford, (1918) 182 App. Div. 99, 169 N.Y. Supp. 492.

[95]Davis v. Gifford, (1918) 182 App. Div. 99, 169 N.Y. Supp. 492; Hunsicker v. Gilham, (1927) 163 La. 651, 112 So. 518.

[96]Fulmele v. Los Angeles Inv. Co., (1921) 51 Cal. App. 417, 196 P. 923; Davis v. Gifford, (1918) 182 App. Div 99, 169 N.Y. Supp. 492; (1918) 182 App. Div. 99, 169 N.Y. Supp. 492.

[97]Fulmele v. Los Angeles Inv. Co., (1921) 51 Cal. App. 417, 196P. 923; Davis v. Gifford; Wilson v. Empire Holding Corp., (1934) 145 Ore. 598, 28 P. 2d 843; Coyle v. Franklin State Bank, (1934) 213 Wis. 601. 252 N.W. 361.

[98]Depositors Bond Co. v. Christensen, (1936) 185 Wash. 161, 53 P. 2d 312.

[99]Mitschele v. Pyramid Bond & Mortgage Corp., (1938) 124 N.J. Eq. 190, 1 A. 2d 59.

[100]Upton v. Tribilcock, (1875) 91 U.S. 203, 23 S. Ct. Rep. 45; Gannon v. Grayson Water Co., (1934) 254 Ky. 251, 71 S.W. 2d 433. See also Trinity Universal Ins. Co. v. Maxwell, (1937) Tex. Civ. App. 101 S.W. 2d 606.

[101]Willentz v. Hickox Finance Corp., (1939) 125 N.J. Eq. 28, 4 A. 2d 43; Forman v. Irby, (1938) Tex. Civ. App. 115 S.W. 2d 1229.

> The decisions of the courts, we think, sustain the doctrine laid down in the textbooks, that a person who has to all external appearances become a stockholder cannot, as to creditors who may have trusted the company upon the faith of his membership, have his contract of subscription rescinded upon the ground of fraud, where he did not repudiate the contract, and take steps to have it rescinded, before the company stopped payments and became actually insolvent.....[102]

The attempt to lay aside the garb of stockholder after a corporation has become bankrupt is looked upon with suspicion. A Federal court has held that the right to rescind should be denied under any of the following circumstances:[103] (1) if a considerable period of time has elapsed since the subscription was made; (2) if the subscriber has actively participated in the management of the corporation; (3) if there has been any want of diligence on the part of the stockholder either in discovering the alleged fraud or in taking steps to rescind when the fraud was discovered; or (4) above all, if any considerable amount of corporate indebtedness has been created since the subscription was made.

Insolvency alone does not take from the subscriber his right to rescind the contract, unless insolvency proceedings have been instituted or an act of insolvency committed. For example, it has been held that if the subscriber is diligent in discovering fraud and repudiating the contract, he does not lose his right to rescind.[104] If the creditors had knowledge of the fraud, insolvency does not bar the defrauded subscriber's right to rescind the subscription agreement.[105]

Corporation's power to release subscribers. Officers and directors cannot release subscribers without the consent of all the stockholders unless they are empowered to do so by statute, charter or by-laws.[106] The consent of the stockholders may be implied from their acquiescence.[107] The subscriber-directors to the corporation's stock are released from their stock subscriptions, when they have entered into an agreement under which the other subscriber-directors assumed liability for the subscriptions, and the corporation consented to such agreement.[108]

On the other hand, subscribers to stock of a corporation who signed

---

[102]Martin v. South Salem Land Co., (1896) 94 Va. 28, 26 S.E. 591.

[103]In re Marcella Cotton Mills, (1925) 8 F. 2d 522; Newton Nat'l Bank v. Newbegin, (1896) 74 F. 135.

[104]Gordon v. Ralston, (1936) 155 Ore. 310, 62 P. 2d 1328.

[105]Jagels v. Cox, (1930) 50 Idaho 67, 294 P. 515.

[106]E.M.T. Coal Co. v. Rogers, (1926) 216 Ky. 440, 288 S.W. 342; Haebler v. Crawford, (1931) 232 A.D. 122, 249 N.Y.S. 184.

[107]Silica Brick Co. v. Winsor, (1915) 171 Cal. 18, 151 P. 425.

[108]Sobol v. Avila (Colo. App., 1970) 480 P. 2d 116.

noninterest, nonobligatory notes in payment are liable on these notes, even though the board of directors has canceled them, since (1) securities commissioner had approved OTC trading on basis of these shares being counted, (2) agreements themselves had said stock was to be paid for when bought, and (3) subscribers were themselves directors.[109]

To be valid the release must be supported by a valuable consideration as in the case of other contracts,[110] but no particular formalities are required.[111] However, assent to the release should be obtained at a properly called meeting of the stockholders or directors and a resolution authorizing the release duly entered in the minutes. If release or rescission is allowed pursuant to a by-law requiring the corporation to return the price of stock to any stockholder who fulfills a business condition, the stockholder's compliance must fairly come within the terms of the by-law.[112]

When release and rescission of subscriptions come before the courts a frequently litigated question is the effect they have on creditors. Some validate the release if existing creditors are not injured.[113] Under this holding future creditors cannot set aside the release. Some courts however refuse to recognize the release of subscriptions either as to present or future creditors.[114]

At the basis of the rules respecting the effect upon present and subsequent creditors of the release of the subscriber's liability by the corporation is the "trust fund" theory of capital stock. Under this theory the subscribed capital stock, both paid and unpaid, is considered a trust fund, which the stockholders and creditors have the right to insist shall not be impaired without their consent.[115] The creditor "is presumed to have given credit upon the faith that the working capital of the corporation, whether actually paid in or promised to be paid, will be kept available to satisfy his debt. The corporation, then, cannot, without committing a fraud against such creditor, wipe out the fund, either by returning the money paid by subscribers or releasing the obligors on their unpaid subscription contracts.[116]

---

[109]Little Switzerland Brewing Co. v. Oxley, (1973) 197 W. Wa. S.E. 2d 301.

[110]In re Eureka Furniture Co., (ED Pa. 1909) 170 F. 485; Zirkel v. Joliet Opera house Co., (1875) 79 Ill. 334; United Growers Co. v. Eisner, (1879) 22 A.D. 1, 47 N.Y.S. 906.

[111]Inter-Mountain Ass'n v. Davies, (1923) 61 Utah 461, 214 P. 307; Elliott v. Ashby, (1905) 104 Va. 716, 52 S.E. 383.

[112]Fillmore v. Farmers' Union Co-op Ass'n. (1929) 139 Okla. 38, 280 P. 1072.

[113]Farnsworth v. Robbins, (1887) 36 Minn. 369, 31 N.W. 349; Cartwright v. Dickinson, (1890) 88 Tenn. 476, 12 S.W. 1030; Shoemaker v. Washburn Lumber Co., (1897) 97 Wis. 585, 73 N.W. 333.

[114]In Christmam-Sawyer Banking Co. v. Independence Wool Mfg. Co., (1902) 168 Mo. 634, 68 S.W. 1026.

[115]Thomas v. Wentworth Hotel Co.,(1911) 16 Cal. App. 403, 117 P. 1041.

[116]Putnam v. N.A. & S.C.J.R. Co., (1873) 83 U.S. 390; Silica Brick Co. v. Winsor, (1915) 171 Cal. 18, 151 P. 425.

Payment of capital stock subscription. In the absence of charter or statutory requirements, neither all nor any particular part of the subscription price of stock need be paid in at the time of the subscription but payment may be called for by the directors as the money is needed.[117]

At one time, corporation laws of many states provided that subscriptions must be accompanied by a cash payment of at least a specified percentage of the face amount of the subscription. Many of these statutes in recent years have been repealed.

However, many states require a minimum of paid in capital, e.g. $500 or $1000 before the corporation can commence business. Therefore the directors at the first meeting should call in at least sufficient capital, committed by subscription or otherwise, to cover the statutory requirement. In some states an affidavit of compliance must also be filed. If these steps are not taken organizers can be liable.[118] In several states a percentage of total authorized capital stock must be paid in before the corporation can commence business.

Some states prohibit forfeiture of the subscription unless the amount due has been demanded in writing and remains unpaid for a specific time.[119]

A subscription contract, under which the subscriber gives the corporation only an unsecured note but is not to get stock or stockholder rights until he pays the note, is a valid subscription. The corporation must pay a note it gives that subscriber in settlement of his rights when it cancels the subscription.[120] The mere fact that a subscriber has not paid for his stock in full does not mean that he is not the owner of the stock.[121] If other stockholders agree, a subscriber may pay for his stock by lending the corporation his credit.[122]

Discharge from liability on subscription by payment. By full payment of the amount due on his capital stock subscription, the subscriber is discharged from further liability to the corporation. But the subscriber, by statute or charter provision, may be subject to assessment on his stock for the benefit of the corporation or its creditors.

It is a fundamental principle of corporation law that a subscriber must pay for his stock.[123] Depositing subscription payments in a bank to the

---

[117]Peoria Inv. Corp. v. Hoagland, (1939) 300 Ill. App. 54, 20 N.E. 2d 627, distinguishing Rockford Metal Specialty Co. v. Wester, (1924) 234 Ill. App. 260; Ross v. Bank of Gold Hill, (1888) 20 Nev. 191, 19 P. 243, Dysart v. Flemister, (1940) Tex. Civ. App., 140 S.W. 2d 350.

[118]Tri-State Developments Inc. v. Moore (Ct. of App., Ky., 1961) 343 S.W. 2d 812.

[119]Sweeney v. Bridal Fair, Inc., (1976) Neb., 237 N.W. 2d 138.

[120]Don Johnson Drilling Co. v. Howard, (S. Ct., 1959) 30 Okl. B.A.J. 1506.

[121]Marshal v. Wittig, (1933) 213 Wis. 374, 251 N.W. 439.

[122]Town and Country Trailer Sales v. Godwin, (S.Ct., 1961) 344 S.W. 2d 338.

[123]Amick v. Elliott, (1928) 222 Ky. 753, 2 S.W. 2d 367.

credit of a corporation has been held a payment.[124] Nonpayment, by the terms of the contract of subscription, may give the corporation the right to cancel the shares and sue at law for damages.[125] The subscription contract need not contain an express promise to pay. In the absence of an express promise, the courts will imply a promise on the part of the subscriber to pay in full.[126] The inability of the subscriber to pay a balance on his subscription on the due day may not affect the validity of the subscription.[127] If, thereafter, the subscriber discharges his liability to pay by performance and the corporation fails to deliver the stock certificate, the subscriber can maintain an action to recover the amount already paid,[128] although delayed payment by the subscriber may affect his right to an immediate delivery of the stock certificate.[129]

Liabilities on subscriptions. Unless the corporation law provides otherwise, a subscriber becomes a stockholder as soon as a binding contract of subscription is made, and he is subject to all the liabilities of a stockholder.[130] The primary liability of a stockholder is to take and pay for his stock.[131] This liability is contractual[132] and may be enforced as such by the company. Since the liability is a debt due the corporation from the stockholder, appropriate legal and equitable remedies for enforcing it are available to the corporation, as in cases of all other valid debts.[133] The corporation may sue the stockholder in equity for an accounting to determine the balance due.[134] Only the corporation, not the stockholders, can bring an action to recover moneys owing on stock subscriptions.[135] In a suit on a post-incorporation subscription, the corporation recovers the full contract price not, as formerly, the difference between the contract price and market value.[136]

The liability of a stockholder to pay to the corporation the purchase price of his stock, or any unpaid balance thereof, must be carefully

---

[124]Dysart v. Flemister, Tex. Civ. App., 1940) 140 S.W. 2d 350.

[125]Levy v. Doherty, (1930) 136 Misc. 34, 239 N.Y.S. 239.

[126]In re Hannevig, (CCA-2, 1926) 10 F. 2d 941; Hodde v. Hahn, (1920) 283 Mo. 320, 222 S.W. 799.

[127]Farmers' Lumber Co. v. Luikart, (1927) 37 Wyo. 201, 259 P. 1053.

[128]Texla Oil Co. v. Calhoun, (1927) 36 Ga. App. 536, 137 S.E. 84; Beaumont Hotel Co. v. Caswell, (1929) Tex. Civ. App., 14 S.W. 2d 292.

[129]Harris v. La Salle Fire Ins. Co. (1928) 6 La. App. 407.

[130]Ellis v. Capps, (1928) 46 Idaho 606, 269 P. 597; Walter A. Wood Harvester Co. v. Robbins, (1893) 56 Minn. 48, 57 N.W. 317; Stull v. Terry & Tench, Inc., (1948) 81 N.Y.S. 2d 43.

[131]Amick v. Elliot, (1928) 222 Ky. 753, 2 S.W. 2d 367; Strong v. Turner, (1938) Mo. App., 122 S.W. 2d 71; Harr v. Wright, (1937) 298 N.Y.S. 270, aff'd. 250 A.D. 830, 296 N.Y.S. 463.

[132]Dickinson County Hospital Co. v. Kessinger, (1929) 128 Kan. 576, 279 P. 7; Lamphere v. Lang, (1915) 213 N.Y. 585, 108 N.E. 82.

[133]Stoddard v. Lum, (1899) 159 N.Y. 265, 53 N.E. 1108.

[134]Kirchner v. Grover, (1938) 343 Mo. 448, 121 S.W. 2d 796.

[135]Shingledecker v. Spencer (La. App., 1967) 193 So. 2d 340.

[136]Penn-Allen Broadcasting Co. v. Traylor, (1957) 389 Pa. 490, 133 A.2d 528.

distinguished from his liability to make similar payment to creditors of an insolvent corporation.[137] Recovery of the purchase price by the corporation does not depend upon the existence of corporate creditors, but may be enforced according to the terms of the contract of subscription.[138] Unless the statute provides otherwise, the stockholders' liability to the corporation for the purchase price of his stock, or for the unpaid portion thereof, is several and not joint,[139] and extends only to the purchase price, or the unpaid part thereof, of the stock subscribed for by the stockholder individually.[140]

The corporation or its trustee in bankruptcy can recover unpaid subscriptions.[141] In case of insolvency a hearing on notice to subscriber is required before the assessment of the unpaid balance or its enforcement.[142] A creditor of an insolvent corporation cannot hold the incorporators liable for the unpaid stock subscriptions, unless and until he obtains a judgment against the corporation and it is returned unsatisfied.[143]

At one time there was an implied condition that all or an agreed percentage of stock must be subscribed to before the subscribers could be held liable. This grew out of the theory that organizers agreed beforehand how much capital was needed for the business and could not get started until they had it all.[144] Some few states still require that a certain percentage of authorized stock be subscribed to before the corporation can commence business. But the prevailing rule today is to allow the parties themselves to express minimum capital requirements for starting business. The law will not imply the condition.[145] Because all stock does not have to be subscribed to, organizers usually allow for an authorized capital in excess of present needs, with an eye to future financing. Though the state may not require all or a portion of the authorized stock to be paid in before the corporation is organized, still it may require a minimum paid-in capital, e.g., $500 or $1000, before the corporation can commence business.

---

[137]Philips v. Slocomb, (1933) 35 Del. 462, 167 A. 698, and Harr v. Mikalarias, (1937) 328 Pa. 49, 195 A. 86.

[138]Geary St. P. & O. R. Co. v. Rolph, (1922) 189 Cal. 59, 207 P. 539; Philips v. Slocomb, (1933) 35 Del. 462, 167 A. 698; Preston v. Jeffers, (1918) 179 Ky. 384 200 S.W. 654; Basting v. Ankeny, (1896) 64 Minn. 133, 66 N.W. 266; Commerce Trust Co. v. Hettinger, (1914) 181 Mo. App. 338, 168 S.W. 911.

[139]Terry v. Little, (1880) 101 U.S. 864; Turner v. Fidelity Loan Concern, (1905) 2 Cal. App. 122, 83 P. 62; Edwards v. Schillinger, (1910) 245 Ill. 231, 91 N.E. 1048; Williams v. Chamberlain, (1906) 29 Ky. 606, 94 S.W. 29.

[140]Shipman v. Portland Const. Co., (1913) 64 Or. 1, 128 P. 989.

[141]Kersoec v. Yirga (Ill. App. Ct., 1967) 230 N.E. 2d 487; Buckman v. Gordon, (1942) 312 Mass. 6, 42 N.E. 2d 811; Strong v. Turner, (1938) Mo. App., 122 S.W.2d 71.

[142]Merola v. Fairlawn Newspaper Printing Corp., (1944) 135 N.J. Eq. 152, 36 A.2d 290.

[143]Frosh v. Sportman's Showcase, Inc. (1966) 4 Mich. App. 408, 145 N.W. 2d 241.

[144]Enterprise Sheet Metal Works v. Schendel, (1918) 55 Mont. 42, 173 P. 1059; Whalen v. Hudson Hotel Co., (1918) 183 A.D. 316, 170 N.Y.S. 855.

[145]Tyler v. Receivers of the Cambridge Co., (1931) 160 Md. 333, 152 A. 896.

Included in the liability to pay for the stock is the liability to pay interest, at the legal rate, on the unpaid balance of the purchase price, unless provided otherwise in the contract of subscription.[146] Interest generally runs from the date of default to the date of payment.[147] In the absence of a provision for call for payment in the contract of subscription, interest runs from the due date of the subscription.[148]

In the case of stock subscriptions payable on call, interest runs from the date of the call, when no notice or demand is required.[149] If notice or demand is required, interest runs from the date notice is given or demand made.[150]

In addition to their liability to suit for failure to take and pay for stock subscribed, stockholders may also be liable to forfeiture of their shares of stock to the corporation at the latter's instance.

Grounds for release of subscription. Being an executory contract, the agreement to subscribe for shares in a corporation to be formed is governed by the same rules as are applicable to contracts in general. Hence, the subscriber will be released if a material alteration or change is made in the charter without his consent,[151] provided he has not waived his rights.[152] If the subscriber pays any installments on his stock or participates in any meeting of the stockholders after the charter is obtained he will be estopped to deny knowledge of changes in the charter and he will be held to have waived his right to release from his subscription.[153]

While the rule itself is clear, difficulties often arise in applying it, that is, in determining what is a material alteration or change sufficient to release the subscriber. In general, so long as the provisions of the charter conform to the main objects or purposes of the corporation contemplated at the time the subscription contract was made, it will be sufficient to prevent a release of the subscriber on this ground. But if the main objects or purposes of the corporation formed are different from those of the corporation proposed, then the subscriber will be released.[154] If the amount of capital stock of the corporation formed is greater than the amount proposed

---

[146]Eastern, etc. Exposition v. Vail's Estate, (1923) 96 Vt. 517, 121 A. 415.

[147]Bergman v. Evans, (1916) 92 Wash. 158, 158 P. 961.

[148]Mountain Timber Co. v. Case, (1913) 65 Or. 417, 133 P. 92.

[149]Seattle Trust Co. v. Pitner, (1898) 51 P. 1048; Jackson Fire & Marine Ins. Co. v. Walle, (1900) 105 La. 89, 29 So. 503.

[150]American Pastoral Co. v. Gurney, (WD Mo. 1894) 61 F. 41; Bergman v. Evans, (1916) 92 Wash. 158, 158 P. 961.

[151]Nugent v. The Supervisors of Putnam Co., (1873) 86 U.S. 241. See In re Gillham, (1936) 286 Ill. App. 370, 3 N.E. 2d 524.

[152]Watters & Martin v. Homes Corp., (1923) 136 Va. 114, 116 S.E. 366.

[153]Macon Union Co-op Ass'n v. Chance, (1924) 31 Ga. App. 363, 122 S.E. 66; Owensboro Seating & Cabinet Co. v. Miller, (1908) 130 Ky. 310, 113 S.W. 423.

[154]Ibid.

the change is material and the subscriber is discharged.[155] A change in the physical location of the corporation's property may be material and discharge the subscriber.[156] A change in the capital stock structure is also material and will discharge the subscriber.[157]

While the facts in each case must be considered in determining what will or will not constitute a material alteration or change,[158] a mere enlargement of corporate powers, not amounting to a change of purpose, is not material and will not release the subscriber.[159]

Inasmuch as the liability of a subscriber for stock in a corporation to be formed is contingent upon the valid incorporation of the contemplated company, he is not liable on his subscription, in the absence of waiver or estoppel,[160] if the corporation is defectively incorporated.[161] This rule does not apply in the case of subscriptions after incorporation. There the subscriber may not set up defective incorporation to defeat liability on his subscription contract because by contracting with it he has recognized the existence of the corporation.[162]

Where blue-sky laws specifically render void contracts entered into in violation of them, subscribers may be released from their subscriptions,[163] but where they do not make void and unenforceable contracts entered into in violation of them, subscribers will not be released.[164]

As in the case of other contracts, a willful and material change in the subscription contract after execution thereof, made by the corporation without the subscriber's consent, will render the subscription void and release the subscriber.[165]

A contract of subscription for shares beyond authorized capital stock of the corporation is void, since a corporation cannot issue shares in excess of the amount of capital stock authorized by its charter and the subscriber will be released from liability to the corporation and its creditors.[166]

---

[155]Bank v. Amoss, (1915) 144 Ga. 425, 87 S.E. 406.

[156]Texas City Hotel Corp. v. Wilkenfeld, (Tex. Ct. of Civ. App., 1966) 410 S.W. 2d 860; Bank v. Amoss, (1915) 144 Ga. 425, 87 S.E. 406.

[157]Lane v. Coin Mach. Mfg. Co., (1918) 69 Pa. Super. Ct. 373.

[158]Bank v. Amoss, (1915) 144 Ga. 425, 87 S.E. 406; Kingston v. Nichols, (1923) 221 Mich. 677, 192 N.W. 768; Ginter v. Blain, (1913) 20 Ohio App. 482; Mann v. Mitchell, (1923) Tex. Civ. App., 255 S.W. 980.

[159]Watters & Martin v. Homes Corp., (1923) 136 Va. 114, 116 S.E. 366.

[160]Indianapolis Furnace, etc., Co. v. Herkimer, (1874) 46 Ind. 142; Capps v. Hastings Prospecting Co., (1894) 40 Neb. 470, 58 N.W. 956; Dorris v. Sweeney, (1875) 60 N.Y. 463.

[161]See Tonge v. Item Pub. Co., (1914) 244 Pa. 417, 91 A. 229.

[162]Dorris v. Sweeney, (1875) 60 N.Y. 463.

[163]Maner v. Mydland, (1967) 250 Cal. App. 2d 526, 58 Cal. Rptr. 740; Witt v. Trustees Loan & Savings Co., (1925) 33 Ga. App. 802, 127 S.E. 810; Burlington Hotel Corp. v. Bell, (1926) 192 N.C. 620, 135 S.E. 616.

[164]Watters & Martin v. Homes Corp., (1923) 136 Va. 114, 116 S.E. 366.

[165]Bohn v. Burton-Lingo Co., (1915) Tex. Civ. App., 175 S.W. 173.

[166]Scovill v. Thayer, (1881) 105 U.S. 143.

If a subscriber is discharged in bankruptcy, he is released from existing liability on his stock subscription contract. But where the subscription is payable in installments, since the discharge operates as a release from debts existing prior to the discharge, the subscriber will not be released from liability for calls made after the discharge.[167]

Generally, an *ultra vires* transaction on the part of the corporation, that is, a transaction beyond the powers of the corporation, will not be sufficient to release a subscriber from his subscription contract.[168]

A subscriber cannot claim a release from his subscription by reason of negligent or fraudulent corporate management.[169] Nor do acts of mismanagement on the part of syndicate managers constitute a defense to an action against a subscriber for failure to pay his subscription, although they do constitute a cause of action against the managers individually.[170]

Failure on the part of a corporation to use its franchise, although such failure may be grounds for a proceeding by the state to revoke the corporate charter,[171] will not release a subscriber from his subscription contract. Cessation of corporate business does not imply corporate dissolution so as to deprive the company of the right to maintain an action to recover on an unpaid subscription.[172]

---

[167]Sayre v. Glenn, (1888) 87 Ala. 631, 6 So. 45; Glenn v. Howard, (1885) 85 Md. 40.

[168]Cartwright v. Dickinson, (1890) 88 Tenn. 476, 12 S.W. 1030.

[169]Cravens v. Eagle Cotton Mills, (1889) 120 Ind. 6, 21 N.E. 981.

[170]First Bank & Trust Co. v. Ogden (1932) 109 N.J. Law 492, 162 A. 635; Farmers Union Co-operative Royalty Co. v. Cook, (1944) 195 Okl. 53, 154 P. 2d 957.

[171]Crump v. U.S. Min. Co., (1851) 7 Gratt. (Va.) 352.

[172]Brookline Canning & Packing Co. v. Evans, (1912) 163 Mo. App. 564, 146 S.W. 828.

Chapter 14

FORMS RELATING TO

SUBSCRIPTIONS TO STOCK

Contents—Chapter 14

INDIVIDUAL SUBSCRIPTION AGREEMENT BETWEEN A SUBSCRIBER AND A PROPOSED CORPORATION, SHOWING PAYMENT TO BE MADE IN PROPERTY, CASH, OR SERVICES

WHEREAS, it is proposed by certain interested parties to organize a corporation under the laws of the State of ...., to be known as ...., with its principal office and place of business at .... *(Street)*, ... *(City)*, ... *(State)*, said corporation to have an authorized capital stock of ..... (.....) shares of Class A stock having a par value of ..... ($.....) Dollars per share, and ..... (.....) shares of Class B stock without par value:

NOW, THEREFORE, I, ..., do hereby subscribe to ..... (.....) shares of the Class B stock of the said corporation, on the following terms and conditions:

1. Payment for said subscription shall be made at the rate of ..... ($.....) Dollars per share.

2. There shall be credited to the amount due on said subscription the sum of ..... ($.....) Dollars, representing advances made by me in behalf of the corporation up to the time of incorporation.

3. The said subscription shall be payable in cash, in property, or in services rendered to the corporation by me before or after incorporation, and accepted by the Board of Directors, at such reasonable valuation as the Board shall determine.

4. Payment for said subscription shall be made within ..... (.....) years from the date of incorporation of said corporation, in such amounts and at such time or times within said period as shall be determined by me.

5. The said corporation shall issue to me a certificate for the full amount of said subscription as soon as possible after the organization of said corporation is completed, and shall note thereon the amount paid on said subscription by me up to the time of incorporation, and all sums thereafter paid by me on account of said subscription.

6. The said corporation, at any time, at my request, shall transfer as fully paid and nonassessable, any or all shares of stock that shall be fully paid for by me at the rate of ..... ($.....) Dollars per share up to the time of transfer, and the proper officers shall issue a new certificate or certificates for such shares so transferred to whomsoever I may direct. In the event that less than all of the shares hereby subscribed for by me are transferred, the proper officers shall issue to me a new certificate, representing the difference between the number of shares hereby subscribed for and the aggregate number of shares so transferred, and shall note thereon the amount paid for said subscription, including moneys advanced before incorporation, and the sum represented by the stock transferred—that is, ... ($.....) Dollars times the number of shares transferred.

Dated ...., 19...

INDIVIDUAL SUBSCRIPTION AGREEMENT BETWEEN A SUBSCRIBER AND A PROPOSED CORPORATION, SHOWING PAYMENTS ON DEMAND

I, the undersigned, hereby agree to take the number of shares of the capital stock of .... Company, set opposite my name, and I agree to pay for any part or all of the same to the Treasurer of the Company on demand and at such time or times and in such amounts as the Company, by its Board of Directors, may direct.

Dated ...., 19..

Name	Number of Shares	Amount
....	....	....
(Signature)		

INDIVIDUAL SUBSCRIPTION AGREEMENT BETWEEN A SUBSCRIBER AND A PROPOSED CORPORATION, SHOWING PAYMENTS IN INSTALLMENTS

I, ..., the undersigned, hereby subscribe for ..... (.....) shares of the ..... (.....%) per cent cumulative preferred stock of ...., a corporation to be organized under the laws of the State of ....., with an authorized capitalization of ..... (.....) shares of ..... (.....%) per cent cumulative preferred stock of a par value of ..... ($.....) Dollars, and ..... (.....) shares of common stock without par value, for the purpose of ...., and do hereby agree to pay for said preferred stock the sum of ..... ($.....) Dollars, in such installments from time to time as shall be determined by the Board of Directors of said corporation.

Dated ...., 19..

SUBSCRIPTION BY SEVERAL INDIVIDUALS TO STOCK OF CORPORATION IN PROCESS OF ORGANIZATION, EXPRESSED TO SHOW SEPARATE SUBSCRIPTION BY EACH SUBSCRIBER

We, the undersigned, do each for himself, separately and severally, subscribe for and agree to purchase the number of shares set opposite our respective names, of the capital stock of the .... Company, a corporation now being organized under and pursuant to the laws of the State of ...., with an authorized capital of ...... ($.....) Dollars, divided into ..... (.....) shares of the par value of ...... ($.....) Dollars each, and we do severally agree to pay the par value of our respective subscriptions at such time or times and in such manner as called for by the Board of Directors.

Dated ...., 19..

Name	Number of Shares	Amount
....	....	....
....	....	....
....	....	....

SUBSCRIPTION AGREEMENT PRIOR TO ORGANIZATION IN WHICH THE SUBSCRIBERS CONTRACT WITH EACH OTHER AND WITH THE PROMOTERS

WHEREAS, it is proposed to organize under the laws of the State of ...., a corporation, to be known as ...., or by such other name as the parties in interest may determine, and

WHEREAS, it is proposed that said Corporation shall transact the business of ...., and

WHEREAS, it is proposed that the said Corporation shall have an authorized capital stock of ..... ($.....) Dollars, divided into ..... (.....) shares of the par value of ..... ($.....) Dollars each,

Now, THEREFORE, The signers hereto, in consideration of their mutual promises, do severally agree with one another, and with ...., the promoter and founder of said Corporation, that they will take and pay for, and they do hereby severally subscribe to, the number of shares of the capital stock of said Corporation set opposite their respective names; and they do further severally agree to pay for said shares at their par value, in the following manner: ..... (.....%) per cent of their subscriptions immediately upon organization of the Corporation and upon notice to that effect from ....; ..... (.....%) per cent within ..... (.....) months thereafter; and the remaining ..... (.....%) per cent on demand and when called for by the Board of Directors of the Corporation, but not later than ..... (.....) months after incorporation of said Corporation.

Dated ...., 19..

Name	Residence	Number of Shares	Amount
....	....	....	....
....	....	....	....
....	....	....	....

SUBSCRIPTION AGREEMENT PRIOR TO INCORPORATION, IN WHICH THE SUBSCRIBERS PURPORT TO CONTRACT WITH EACH OTHER AND WITH THE PROPOSED CORPORATION

We, the undersigned, in consideration of the mutual covenants and agreements herein contained, do hereby agree with one another and with ...., a corporation to be hereafter organized under the laws of the State of ...., for the purpose of ...., with an authorized capital stock of ..... ($.....) Dollars, to consist of ..... (.....) shares, each having a par value of ..... ($.....) Dollars, that we and each of us does hereby subscribe to the capital stock of said corporation to the amount hereinbelow set opposite our respective signatures, and we do further hereby severally agree to pay the par value of the number of shares set opposite our respective names, in such installments from time to time as shall be determined by the Board of Directors of said corporation.

Name	Residence	Number of Shares	Amount
....	....	....	....
....	....	....	....
....	....	....	....

Dated ...., 19..

SUBSCRIPTION TO STOCK, TO BE PAID FOR BY CASH AND NOTE; ISSUANCE OF STOCK UPON PAYMENT OF NOTE; EFFECT OF DEFAULT IN PAYMENT; POWER OF CORPORATION TO REJECT APPLICATION; OBLIGATION TO OFFER STOCK TO CORPORATION BEFORE TRANSFER

I hereby subscribe for ..... (.....) shares of the preferred stock of the .... Corporation, ... *(City)*, ... *(State)*, and agree to pay therefor one hundred ($100) Dollars per share, on the following terms: Not less than one fourth in cash, accompanying this application, and the balance thereof, as evidenced by my promissory note of this date, with interest at six (6%) per cent per annum, payable ..... days after date.

It is expressly agreed that no stock is to be issued until the amount of this subscription and note given therefor are paid in full in cash, and any payment becoming due on the stock hereby subscribed for, or any note given therefor, not paid within sixty (60) days after its due date, shall, at the option of the Corporation, cause this subscription and any note or notes given therefor to become null and void, and all payments made on this subscription by the subscriber shall become the property of the Corporation absolutely as liquidated damages for the failure of the subscriber to carry out this contract.

The Corporation may reject this application by refunding all moneys paid thereon.

This subscription contract contains the entire contract between the subscriber and the Corporation and no agent or representative of the Corporation or any other person has any power to change or alter the terms of this subscription.

I hereby agree that, before selling or agreeing to sell the stock hereby subscribed for, I will first offer same to the .... Corporation.

All payments will be made to the .... Corporation, at .... *(City)*, ... *(State)*.
Dated this .. day of ...., 19...

....
(Name of subscriber)

....
(Address)

[*Note*. See Hedman v. Security Title & Guaranty Co., (1935) 245 App. Div. 224, 281 N.Y. Supp. 565, in which it was held that the provision on a printed agreement for the sale of guaranteed mortgage certificates, that no agent or other person had permission to change or in any way alter the terms of the agreement or bind the company by any representations, oral or written, not contained therein, applied only to the negotiations leading up to the execution of the agreement. Where the agreement was executed in accordance with the printed form, the provision did not prevent modification of the agreement by a district manager after its execution.]

SUBSCRIPTION TO STOCK; PART PAYMENT AT TIME OF SUBSCRIPTION, BALANCE BEFORE FIXED DATE; APPLICATION OF SUBSCRIPTION PRICE; RESERVATION OF RIGHT TO REJECT OR ALLOT SUBSCRIPTIONS; ISSUANCE OF RECEIPTS

SUBSCRIPTION AGREEMENT

New Issue

..... Shares
.... Company of the City of .....
Authorized Capital ..... Shares Par Value $.....
Present Offering ..... Shares at $..... per Share
Payable $..... per Share with Subscription,
Balance ...., 19..
Company's Treasury Will Receive Entire Proceeds of This
Stock, Fully Paid and Nonassessable. No Personal Liability
Attaches to Stockholders

The undersigned hereby subscribes at one hundred ($100) Dollars per share for ..... (.....) shares of the capital stock of .... Company of the par value of ..... ($.....) Dollars each, and agrees to pay ..... ($.....) Dollars therefor, as follows: ..... ($.....) Dollars (at least $..... per share) herewith: Balance on or before ...., 19...

TERMS AND CONDITIONS OF SUBSCRIPTION

..... ($.....) Dollars per share shall be applied to the capital of the Company, and ..... ($.....) Dollars per share shall be applied to the surplus and reserve funds of the Company.

It is understood and agreed that the Company reserves the right to accept subscriptions in excess of the present offering and to issue stock therefor, including the right to increase, to the extent of an additional ..... (.....) shares, the authorized capital stock of the Company, if necessary, to provide for subscriptions accepted. The Company also reserves the right to reject, reduce, and/or allot all subscriptions received.

Receipts will be issued in respect of payments received on account of subscriptions, the amount represented thereby to be applied toward payment for the number of shares finally allotted.

Checks for payments on account of subscriptions shall be drawn to the order of .... Company, and may be forwarded to the following firms, banks, or trust companies or their branches:

....	....
(Name of bank)	(Name of bank)
....	....
(Address)	(Address)

Subscription books will close at ..... P.M., ..., 19...

IN WITNESS WHEREOF, I (we) have hereunto set my (our) hand(s) and seal(s), this .. day of ...., 19..

....
(Signature)
....
(Address)

....
(Witness)

LETTER CONTAINING OFFER TO SUBSCRIBE TO STOCK

.... Co.
.... CITY, ... STATE

...., 19..

Gentlemen:

We hereby subscribe to ..... (.....) shares of your common stock without nominal or par value at the subscription price of ..... ($.....) Dollars per share, and hand you herewith ..... ($.....) Dollars representing ..... (.....%) per cent payment on account of such subscription, the balance of the subscription to be payable on call of the board of directors of your company, provided not less than ..... (.....) days' notice of such call shall be given.

Will you kindly indicate your acceptance of this offer by signing in the space below, and thereby constitute this an agreement between us.

Very truly yours,

Accepted, ..., 19..
.... Co.
By ....
Vice-President

.... Co.
By ....
President

APPLICATION FOR STOCK ON CASH PLAN OR MONTHLY
PAYMENT PLAN, IN ACCORDANCE WITH CIRCULAR;
RIGHT TO REJECT OR REDUCE APPLICATION;
ADJUSTMENT OF ACCRUED
DIVIDENDS AND INTEREST ALLOWANCES*

Dated ...., 19..

To .... Company, Inc.

....
(Address)

I hereby apply for shares of Class A stock of the .... Company, in accordance with the terms of your circular of ...., 19.., as follows:

.....
No. of Shares

CASH PLAN—Approximate payment in full to accompany the application; difference between this payment and cost of stocks to be refunded or collected before delivery of certificate.

.....
No. of Shares

MONTHLY PAYMENT PLAN—Payment to be made in total monthly installments of $............... (first payment $..... per share, subsequent monthly payments $....., or multiple thereof per share), first payment to accompany application; an adjustment for accrued dividends and interest allowances to be made in connection with final payment.

Total amount of payment made on account of this application, $..... *Please make remittances payable to the .... Company, Inc.*

....
(Signature of applicant—give first or middle name in full; if a woman, indicate whether "Miss" or "Mrs.")

Applicant will please also PRINT name in this space ....
Applicant's address to which stock certificates and notices should be mailed:

....
(Street and Number)   (City or Town)   (State)

It is understood that you may reject ths application or accept if for a lesser number of shares.

(see reverse side of application)

*For right to allow interest on installments paid, see Hardin County v. Louisville & N. R.R., (1891) 92 Ky. 412, 17 S.W. 860; Stone v. Young, (1924) 210 App. Div. 303, 206 N.Y. Supp. 95.

PRICE

The price per share is the price at which the last sale is made on the American Stock Exchange on the day on which the application is received by the ....
Company, plus an amount equal to brokerage charges, which at present are .....
(.....¢) cents a share. The applicant will be notified of the price at which the application is accepted.

PAYMENT IN FULL PLAN

Stock may be paid for in full by a single payment to accompany the application.

MONTHLY PAYMENT PLAN

Monthly payments shall be ..... ($.....) Dollars or any multiple thereof per share. A first payment of ..... ($.....) Dollars per share must accompany the application.

Interest will be allowed on each monthly payment, at the rate of ..... (.....%) per cent per annum, from the first of the month on payments received on or before the ..... day of such month; otherwise from the ..... day of the following month. An adjustment on account of accrued dividends will be made in connection with the final payment.

The applicant will be granted, upon request, one extension of monthly payments for not exceeding ..... months. The applicant, at any time, may take up any or all of the shares applied for by payment of the balance due.

At any time prior to the final payment, the applicant may elect, by written notice, to have his contract canceled as to any or all of the shares applied for, in which case he will be refunded the amount paid in, with interest at the rate of .....
(.....%) per cent per annum; or, he may take up the number of shares which the amount paid in, plus interest at the rate of ..... (.....%) per cent per annum, will pay for in full, any balance to be refunded in cash. However, if, on the day of such cancellation, the last sale of the stock is made on the American Stock Exchange at a price less than the price ot be paid for the shares (including adjustment for accrued dividends), the applicant will be charged with the difference. The ....
Company reserves the right to reject any application under either option, or to accept it for a lesser number of shares, and to withdraw this offer at any time without notice, and to cancel the application, with refund under the above terms, in case of an unadjusted difference with the applicant, or if a monthly payment is not received within ..... months after it is due.

.... Company

By ....

President

Dated ...., 19..

NOTICE OF ALLOTMENT OF SHARES

.... Company
.... City, ... State

Dear ....:

Respecting your recent subscription to ..... (.....) shares of the capital stock of .... Company, you have been allotted ..... (.....) shares, and your subscription has been accepted to this extent. The following is a statement of your account:

1. Number of shares allotted (...) at $30 per share .... $.....
2. Paid at time of subscription .... $.....
   Paid since filing of subscription .... $..... $.....
   Balance due or (if item No. 2 exceeds item No. 1) amount
   of overpayment .... $.....

Payment of balance due on allotted shares is due and payable by ...., 19.., at the office of the undersigned bank.

Check for overpayment, if any, will be sent on or about ...., 19...

The undersigned will be prepared to deliver on ...., 19.., definitive or temporary stock certificate for the number of shares allotted.

Yours very truly,

....
(Insert name of bank)
Depository for ....Company

RECEIPT FOR NOTE AND CASH PAYMENT ON SUBSCRIPTION

No. .....   Amount $ .....
                                       Dated ...., 19..

RECEIVED, of ...., of .... *(City)*, ... *(State)*, the sum of ..... ($.....) Dollars and note(s) for ..... ($.....) Dollars of even date, all payable to the order of the .... Company, in payment for ..... (.....) shares of the Capital Stock of the .... Company.

....

(see reverse side)

(The reverse side of the receipt contains a duplicate of the subscription contract.)

[*Note*. See Long v. Mayo, (1931) 156 Va. 185, 157 S.E. 767, in which it was held that a receipt for cash and note given in payment of stock may be construed as forming part of the contract of subscription.]

RECEIPT FOR FULL PAYMENT OF SUBSCRIPTION PRICE

.... *(City)*, ... *(State)*,.............. .., 19..

RECEIVED, of ...., ... ($.....) Dollars in full payment for ..... (.....) shares of stock of .... Corporation.

This receipt will be exchangeable, on surrender, for an engraved certificate when said certificate is completed and ready for delivery.

.... Corporation

By ....

President

TRANSFER OF SUBSCRIPTION; ASSUMPTION OF LIABILITY BY TRANSFEREE; CONSENT OF CORPORATION AND OTHER SUBSCRIBERS

KNOW ALL MEN BY THESE PRESENTS, That I, ..., in consideration of ..... ($.....) Dollars, to me paid before the ensealing and delivery of these presents, the receipt of which is hereby acknowledged, and for other good and valuable considerations, have sold, assigned, transferred, and set over, and by these presents do sell, assign, transfer, and set over unto ...., my right, title, and interest as a subscriber to and an incorporator of ...., a corporation organized under the laws of the State of ....., to the extent of ..... (.....) shares, and I do hereby request and direct the said Corporation to issue the certificate for said ..... (.....) shares to and in the name of said ...., or such other person as he may name.

IN WITNESS WHEREOF, I have hereunto set my hand and seal, this .. day of ...., 19...

.... (L.S.)

Sealed and delivered in the presence of:

....

IN CONSIDERATION of the above transfer of subscription, I hereby assume all liabilities, obligations, and duties attached to said subscription for said ..... (.....) shares of the Capital Stock of the Corporation, or devolving upon me by reason thereof.

.... (L.S.)

Witness:

....

The undersigned hereby consent to the foregoing Transfer of Subscription.

Witness: .... Corporation

....   By ....

Witness: President

.... (L.S.)

.... (L.S.)

.... (L.S.)

Original Subscribers to

Capital Stock of

....

Corporation

[*Note*. See also Transfer of Subscription on page 216 in Chapter 8.]

TRANSFER OF SUBSCRIPTIONS BY SEVERAL SUBSCRIBERS

For and in consideration of the sum of one dollar and other valuable consideration, the receipt of which is hereby acknowledged, we, the undersigned subscribers to the capital stock of ...., a corporation organized under the laws of the State of ...., do hereby jointly and severally sell, transfer and assign unto .... all our right, title and interest in and to our subscriptions for stock in said corporation in the amounts set opposite the name of each, as follows:

From	To	Number of Shares
....	....	....
....	....	....
....	....	....

We do also hereby authorize, request and direct said corporation to issue a certificate for said stock to the said .... or such other persons as they may order, upon payment by them or their assigns of the amounts due on said subscriptions, and compliance with the other terms and conditions of said subscriptions.

This instrument is executed upon the express condition that the said transferees, by the acceptance of this assignment, agree to pay the balance due on said subscriptions, and to comply with, all and singular, the terms and conditions of said subscriptions and hold and save the undersigned harmless from any and all claims of any kind or nature on account of said subscriptions.

IN WITNESS WHEREOF, the undersigned have hereunto set their hands and seals on this .. day of ...., 19...

.... (L.S.)
.... (L.S.)
.... (L.S.)

RESOLUTION OF DIRECTORS OPENING SUBSCRIPTIONS TO CAPITAL STOCK

RESOLVED, That subscriptions to the capital stock be opened.

RESOLUTION OF DIRECTORS AUTHORIZING SUBSCRIPTIONS TO BE TAKEN FOR REMAINING UNISSUED STOCK, AND REQUIRING PART PAYMENT WITH SUBSCRIPTIONS

RESOLVED, That subscriptions for the remainder of the authorized capital stock at par, amounting to .... (...............) shares of unissued common stock, be opened forthwith at the office of the company, and that each subscriber shall be required to pay to the Treasurer at least ..... (.....%) per cent of the amount of his subscription in cash at the time of subscribing, the balance to be paid upon call made pursuant to the statutory and by-law requirements.

RESOLUTION OF DIRECTORS APPOINTING AGENT TO RECEIVE SUBSCRIPTIONS TO CAPITAL STOCK

RESOLVED, That the .... Trust Company is hereby appointed the agent of this Company for the purpose of receiving subscriptions to its capital stock and is hereby authorized to countersign any subscriptions, warrants, or receipts in the form approved by this Board, which shall have been signed by the Company's Treasurer, or by its Assistant Treasurer, and

RESOLVED FURTHER, That all moneys received by the .... Trust Company on such subscriptions be held subject to the order of this Company, to be paid out only upon checks signed by any two of the following officers: ...., President; ...., Vice-President; ...., Treasurer; and ...., Assistant Treasurer.

RESOLUTION OF DIRECTORS APPROVING SUBSCRIPTION AGREEMENT

RESOLVED, That the subscription agreement now presented to this meeting, which is appended to the minutes hereof, be approved, and that the subscriptions to the capital stock of this corporation, as evidenced by this agreement, be hereby accepted.

RESOLUTION OF DIRECTORS ADOPTING TERMS OF ORIGINAL SUBSCRIPTION

RESOLVED, That the terms of the original subscription to the capital stock of this Corporation as shown by the Statement of Incorporation are hereby adopted, and the President and Secretary are authorized and directed to deliver certificates to each subscriber for the amount of his respective subscription upon receipt of the consideration therefor.

RESOLUTION DIRECTING EXECUTION OF AFFIDAVIT OF SUBSCRIPTION TO CAPITAL STOCK

RESOLVED, That the Treasurer be directed to report to the Board of Directors as soon as payment of .....% of the authorized capital stock has been made, and that immediately upon receipt of such report the Board of Directors shall execute and file the affidavit of subscription to capital stock as required by law, so that this Corporation may be authorized to commence business.

RESOLUTION AUTHORIZING DIRECTORS TO ACCEPT SUBSCRIPTIONS TO CAPITAL STOCK

RESOLVED, That the Board of Directors of this Company is hereby authorized, on behalf of this Company, to accept subscriptions to the common capital stock of this Company to be issued upon the payment to the Company in cash of the par value thereof.

RESOLUTION AUTHORIZING ISSUANCE OF STOCK
TO SUBSCRIBERS

RESOLVED, That the corporation issue its Preferred Stock to the persons who have already subscribed for such stock for a consideration of ..... ($.....) Dollars per share, and that the corporation issue its Common Stock to the persons who have already subscribed for such stock for a consideration of ..... ($.....) Dollars per share.

RESOLUTION RATIFYING ACCEPTANCE BY DIRECTORS OF
PAYMENT IN CASH AND PROPERTY IN DISCHARGE OF
SUBSCRIBERS' CONTRACTS TO PURCHASE CAPITAL STOCK

RESOLVED, That the acceptance by the board of directors of the payment in cash, or the conveyance and delivery of property, as the case may be, in discharge of the several contracts of the several subscribers to the capital stock, is hereby ratified; and said board may issue the shares of capital stock of the company therefor.

RESOLUTIONS DIRECTING ISSUANCE OF CERTIFICATES
OF STOCK

RESOLVED, That certificates of stock be issued to the subscribers, or their assignees, when the regular stock certificate book is prepared, and that until then all subscriptions, with the rights and liabilities pertaining thereto, may be transferred or assigned by said subscribers by any suitable instrument filed with the Clerk of the corporation.

RESOLUTION OF DIRECTORS REFUSING TO
ACCEPT SUBSCRIPTIONS

RESOLVED, That the following subscriptions to the common stock of this corporation be refused, and that the Secretary is hereby directed to notify the persons concerned of this action of the Board.

Name of Subscriber	Address	Shares
....	....	......
....	....	......
....	....	......

RESOLUTION OF DIRECTORS AUTHORIZING PARTIAL
RELEASE OF SUBSCRIBERS

RESOLVED, That all subscribers who subscribed to the common stock of this corporation prior to ...., 19.., are hereby authorized to surrender one half of the amount of stock subscribed for, or as much less as they may prefer, and the installments paid heretofore by said persons on account of the subscription price shall be applied as if they had been made upon the amount of the subscription retained, and shall be credited to them accordingly; provided that, if any subscribers to the stock of this corporation who surrender one half or other part of their subscription shall omit to pay any installment that may be hereafter called for, on the amount retained, such subscribers shall be considered as having waived this offer, and shall be bound for the amount of common stock originally subscribed for.

RESOLUTION OF STOCKHOLDERS RATIFYING RELEASE OF SUBSCRIBERS BY THE CORPORATION

RESOLVED, That the action of the Board of Directors of this corporation, releasing subscribers from their subscriptions to stock of this corporation, as expressed in a resolution adopted by the Board of Directors on ...., 19.., which resolution reads as follows:

(Here insert the previous resolution, authorizing partial release.)

and the same hereby is approved.

RESOLUTION OF STOCKHOLDERS RELEASING CONDITIONAL SUBSCRIBER UPON INABILITY OF CORPORATION TO MEET CONDITION

WHEREAS, at and before the organization of this company, the following parties agreed to subscribe for the common stock of this company, in the amounts set opposite their names—to wit:

"A" .... shares
"B" .... shares
"C" .... shares
"D" .... shares

and

WHEREAS, *"A"* and *"B"* subscribed for the number of shares of stock set opposite their respective names as above, upon the condition that the same should be paid for in services to be rendered this corporation in the construction of a fourteen-story building to be located at the corner of .... and .... Streets in the City of ...., State of ...., and *"C"* and *"D"* subscribed for the number of shares of stock set opposite their respective names as above, upon the condition that the company would proceed forthwith to erect the said building upon said lot, and the said "C" and "D" have paid in upon said stock subscriptions the following amounts—to wit:

> "C" .... $.....
> "D" .... $.....

and

WHEREAS, it has been decided by the stockholders and officers of this corporation that it is not expedient at this time to proceed with the erection of said building, in view of the fact that a sufficient amount of stock has not been subscribed to enable the corporation to proceed therewith, and

WHEREAS, it has become unnecessary for "A" and "B" to render the services with which they were to pay for their respective subscriptions, be it

RESOLVED, That each of the subscribers to the common stock of this corporation is hereby released from any and all liabilities on his subscription to the stock of this corporation, it being recognized by the stockholders of this corporation that the corporation is unable to fulfill the conditions upon which said subscriptions were made, and

RESOLVED FURTHER, That the Treasurer is hereby authorized and directed to remit to "C" the sum of ..... ($.....) Dollars and to "D" the sum of ..... ($.....) Dollars, being the amounts paid in upon said stock subscriptions by "C" and "D" respectively.

Chapter 15

ISSUANCE AND SALE
OF CAPITAL STOCK

Contents—Chapter 15

ISSUANCE OF STOCK AND STOCK CERTIFICATES

Power of corporation to issue stock. The power to issue capital stock must be conferred upon the corporation either by the law of the state in which it is organized, or by its articles of incorporation.[1] The articles also fix the maximum amount of stock which the corporation may issue.[2]

A corporation that has issued the full amount of its authorized capital stock can make no further issues unless it increases the amount of capital stock in the manner prescribed by statute.[3] (See methods of increasing stock, on page 787.) After an additional issue is authorized, the laws that apply to the original issue generally apply to the additional issue.[4] For example, if a state law requires that the corporation must get permission from a state committee to issue stock for any consideration other than money, the permission must be obtained whether the issue is of new stock or the original stock.

Issuance of authorized stock. Action in regard to the issuance of authorized stock should be taken by the directors at a valid meeting, regularly called.[5] However, if all the stockholders and directors are present and concur in the authorization of an issue of stock, formal action by the board of directors is unnecessary.[6] In such a case the board will be presumed to have ratified the action of the stockholders, though in fact it did not go formally into the matter. The kind of stock to be issued, the consideration for which the stock is to be issued, and the manner of issuing the stock are governed by the laws of the state in which the corporation is organized,[7] by the certificate of incorporation, and by the provisions of the by-laws of the corporation. The requirements set forth therein must be met by those authorizing the issuance of stock.

---

[1]Savie v. Kramlich, (1932) 52 Ida. 156, 12 P.2d 260; Rice & Hutchins v. Triplex Shoe Co., (1929) 16 Del. Ch. 298, 147 A. 317, aff'd, (1930) 17 Del. Ch. 356, 152 A. 342; Reno Oil Co. v. Culver, (1901) 60 App. Div. 129, 69 N.Y. Supp. 969; Cooke v. Marshall, (1899) 191 Pa. 315, 43 A. 314, aff'd on rehearing, (1900) 196 Pa. 200, 46 A 447.

[2]Mitchell v. Mitchell Woodbury Co., (1928) 263 Mass. 160, 160 N.E. 539.

[3]Commissioner of Banks v. Tremont Trust Co., (1927) 259 Mass. 162, 156 N.E. 7; Bahr v. Breeze Corp., (1939) 126 N.J. Eq. 124, 8 A.2d 185, aff'd in memo dec., (1940)) 127 N.J. Eq. 257, 12 A.2d 678.

[4]State ex rel. Weede v. Iowa Southern Utilities Co., (1942) 231 Iowa 784, 2 N.W.2d 372.

[5]Belle Island Corp. v. MacBean, (1946) 27 Del. Ch. 261, 49 A.2d 5.

[6]Fitzpatrick v. O'Neill, (1911) 43 Mont. 552, 118 P. 273. In East Lake Lumber Co. v. Van Gorder, (1919) 105 N.Y. Misc. 704, 174 N.Y. Supp. 38, it was held that no formal resolution was necessary for the issuance of stock, where the stock was in fact issued as a result of corporate action, acquiesced in by the stockholders, and was part of the very plan and purpose which underlay the formation and organization of the corporation; see also Topkis v. Delaware Hardware (Del Ch. Ct., 1938) 2A.2d 114.

[7]Rogers v. Guaranty Trust Co., (1933) 288 U.S. 123, 53 S. Ct. 295.

The resolution adopted by the directors authorizing the issuance of stock should contain the following information: (1) the kind of stock to be issued; (2) the amount to be issued; (3) the price at which the stock is to be sold; (4) the consideration to be received for the stock; (5) the terms of the sale; and (6) authority for the proper officers to issue and deliver the certificates of stock upon payment.

Every state, and the District of Columbia, has some form of "Blue Sky" law governing the issue, registration, and sale of securities. Many have adopted, in substantial form, the Uniform Securities Act.[8] In several states too, it is necessary for the corporation to file a certificate with the secretary of state or some other designated official, showing that the directors have authorized the issuance of stock and giving other required information.[9] The authorities differ as to whether an issue of stock is illegal[10] or merely irregular,[11] when the required certificate of issue is not filed.

As to registration of stock under Federal law, see pages 425-426.

Void or irregularly issued stock. Any issue of stock in excess of the amount prescribed or limited by the charter, or any amendment of the charter, is void.[12] Stock issued for a consideration that does not meet constitutional and statutory requirements is also void.[13] (See consideration for stock on page 449, et seq.) No one can be the owner of stock that the corporation is not authorized to issue.[14] Therefore, a void issue is void even in the hands of a bona fide purchaser for value,[15] or a bona fide pledgee.[16] A bona fide holder, however, is entitled to damages;[17] the corporation cannot claim the defense of fraud in the issuance of the stock against a bona fide holder.[18]

Stock which the corporation has power to issue, but which it issues irregularly, is valid so far as the holder of the stock is concerned. In a suit

---

[8]For a complete digest of the "Blue Sky" laws, see Prentice-Hall, *Securities Regulation.*

[9]Ibid

[10]Black v. Taft, (1933) 284 Mass. 77, 187 N.E. 96, criticized in 82 U. PA. L. REV. 284.

[11]Chicago Title & Trust Co. v. Central Republic Trust Co., (1939) 299 Ill. App. 483, 20 N.E.2d 351.

[12]Scovill v. Thayer, (1881) 105 U.S. 143; Crawford v. Twin City Oil Co., (1927) 216 Ala. 216, 113 So. 61; Taylor v. Lounsbury-Soule Co., (1927) 106 Conn. 41, 137 A 159; Pruitt v. Oklahoma Steam Baking Co., (1913) 39 Okla. 509, 135 P. 730; Com. v. Tremont Trust Co., (1927) 259 Mass. 162, 156 N.E. 7; Bahr v. Breeze Corp., (1939) 126 N.J. Eq. 124, 8 A.2d 185, aff'd (1940) 127 N.J. Eq. 257, 12 A.2d 278.

[13]Rochell v. Oates, (1941) 241 Ala. 372, 2 So. 2d 749; Oklahoma Gas & Elec. Co. v. Hathaway, (1943) 192 Okla. 626, 138 P.2d 832.

[14]Bahr v. Breeze Corp., (1939) 126 N.J. Eq. 124, 8 A.2d, 185; Oklahoma Gas & Elec. Co. v. Hathaway, (1943) 192 Okla. 626, 138 P.2d.

[15]Oklahoma Gas & Elec. Co. v. Hathaway, (1943) 192 Okla. 626, 138 P.2d; East River Bottom Water Co. v. Dunford, (1946) 109 Utah 510, 167 P.2d 693.

[16]Commercial Bank v. Spanish Fork South Irrigation Co., (1944) 107 Utah 279, 153 P.2d 547.

[17]East River Bottom Water Co. v. Dunford, (1946) 109 Utah 510, 167 P.2d 693.

[18]First Nat'l Bank v. Alaska Airmotive, (1941) 119 F.2d 267 (Alaska law).

for the payment of the stock the stockholder may not avoid his obligation on the ground that the stock was irregularly issued.[19] The state alone may raise the question of irregularity.[20]

Issuance of certificates of stock. The issuance of a certificate of stock is not necessary to establish the existence of the shares or their ownership.[21] Thus, for example, a gift of corporate shares conferring ownership rights was held complete upon registration in the names of the donees, thereby divesting the donor of all such rights, even though certificates had not yet been issued; further, the donor was precluded from challenging existence of that corporation after issuance of a certificate of incorporation.[22]

A certificate of stock is not the stock itself, but merely the tangible evidence of a stockholder's interest in the corporation[23] —evidence that the person named is the owner of the number of shares stated in the certificate.[24] A person may be a full-fledged stockholder even if no certificate of stock is issued;[25] title to shares may pass without delivery of the certificates.[26] For example, a person accepted stock from the corporation in payment of a debt, with the understanding that the corporation would buy back the stock at a certain time. No certificate was delivered. In the meantime, the corporation became bankrupt and could not buy back the stock. (See agreement by corporation to repurchase stock, on page 472.) The stockholder could not claim that he was a creditor instead of a stockholder, on the ground that no certificate was ever delivered to him.[27] However, a purchaser who had not received his shares was considered only a subscriber, not yet entitled to inspect corporate records.[28]

Every stockholder who has fully paid for his stock has a right to a

---

[19]Benedict v. Anderson, (1934) 70 F.2d 227. See also Gill v. Wading River Realty Co., (1931) 10 N.J. Misc. 65, 157 A. 840.

[20]Upton v. Tribilcock, (1875) 91 U.S. 203, 23 S. Ct. Rep. 45; In re Rombach & Co., (CA-3, 1926) 9 F. 2d 359; Randall v. Mickle, (1931) 103 Fla. 1229, 138 So. 14, 141 So. 317.

[21]Curtis v. Prudential Ins. Co., (1932) 55 F.2d 97; Mau v. Montana Pac. Oil Co., (1928) 16 Del. Ch. 114, 141 A. 828; Savic v. Kramlich, (1932) 52 Idaho 156, 12 P.2d 260; Illinois-Indiana Fair Ass'n v. Phillips, (1926) 328 Ill. 368, 159 N.E. 815; Harlan Nat'l Bank v. Carbon Glow Coal Co., (1956) (Ky.) 289 S.W.2d 200; Gibson v. Oswalt, (1934) 269 Mich. 300, 257 N.W. 825; Greenspun v. Greenspun, (1946) (Tex. Civ. App.) 194 S.W.2d 134.

[22]Wagner v. Wagner, (Pa. S. Ct, 1976) 353 A.2d 819.

[23]Kansas, O. & G. Ry. v. Helvering, (1941) 124 F.2d 460; Mindenberg v. Carmel Film Productions, Inc., (1955) 132 Cal. App.2d 598, 282 P.2d 1024; Millar v. Mountcastle, (1954) 161 Ohio St. 409, 119 N.E.2d 626.

[24]Laden v. Baader, (1943) 134 N.J. Eq. 24, 34 A.2d 82.

[25]Conover v. Hasselman, (1928) 206 Iowa 100, 220 N.W. 42; Burchett v. Louisa Light & Power Co., (1930) 235 Ky. 296, 31 S.W.2d 373.

[26]Helvering v. Kaufman, (1943) 136 F.2d 356; In re Penfield Distilling Co., (1942) 131 F.2d 694; Commonwealth v. Nixon, (1928) 94 Pa. Super. 333.

[27]In re Penfield Distilling Co., (1942) 131 F.2d 694.

[28]Redemer v. Hollis (La., 1977) 347 So. 2d 48.

certificate as evidence of his title to the stock.[29] However, a buyer of stock could not compel an employee of an issuing corporation to issue stock certificates under a sales agreement that provided delivery of individual stock certificates would be made when either (1) two weeks after a public stock offering, or (2) after permission from corporate directors; neither of these conditions occurred prior to the corporation's dissolution.[30] Also, a stock transfer agent was entitled to refuse to register transfer of stock certificates, when it was shown that the purchaser knew that certificates had been canceled before accepting delivery; that was not a rightful transfer, and the purchaser was not a bona fide purchaser for value.[31]

A stockholder can compel a corporation to issue new stock certificates to him, when he had never authorized their sale, even though the corporation had transferred them to an innocent purchaser for value.[32] And when a corporation has received adequate notice of the loss of stock certificates from a stockholder, it must reissue certificates even though they had been fraudulently endorsed and subsequently transferred.[33]

The statutes generally confirm this right to a certificate. In addition, provision for issuance of the stock certificate is often included in the by-laws. Refusal by the corporation to accept tender for payment, or refusal to issue the shares, does not deprive the stockholder of his privileges.[34]

Where stock is only partly paid for, the corporation generally withholds the certificate[35] or it may cancel the stock.[36] It may, however, issue the certificate immediately, marking it "part paid," provided the charter or statute does not prohibit issuance of stock certificates before full payment has been made.

The provision found in the constitutions and statutes of many states that no corporation shall issue stock, except for money paid, labor done, or property actually acquired by the corporation (see page 449), does not prohibit the corporation from issuing stock as partly paid for; the provision is considered violated only if shares are issued as fully paid, when in fact they are totally or partly unpaid.[37] Subscribers have no right to require the

---

[29]Williams v. Everett, (1917) (Mo.) 200 S.W. 1045; Gallatin County Farmers' Alliance v. Flannery, (1921) 59 Mont. 534, 197 P. 996; Southwestern Slate Co. v. Stephens, (1909) 139 Wis. 616, 120 N.W. 408; see also Jacobson v. The Five Ivy Corp., (N.Y.S. Ct., 1973) N.Y.L.J., 2-8-73, p.16.
[30]Molinaro v. Frezza, (N.Y. App. Div., 1975) 49 A.D. 2d 148.
[31]Folsom v. Security National Bank, (Colo. Ct. of App., 1973) 507 P. 2d 1114.
[32]Scott v. Ametek, Inc. (Del. Ct. of Ch., 1971) No. 3469, 4-29-71.
[33]Arizona Public Service Company v. Gammons, (Ariz. Ct. of App., 1974) 519 P. 2d 1165.
[34]Beck v. Beck Inv. Co., (1946) 249 Wis. 5, 23 N.W.2d 454. See also Mellen v. Berg, (1944) 316 Mass. 252, 55 N.E.2d 463.
[35]California Southern Hotel Co. v. Callender, (1892) 94 Cal. 120, 29 P. 859.
[36]State ex. rel. Wede v. Bechtel, (Iowa, 1948) 31 N.W.2d 853.
[37]Scully v. Automobile Finance Co., (1920) 12 Del. Ch. 174, 109 A. 49.

corporation to issue to them paid-up stock certificates to the amount of cash paid in on their entire subscription.[38]

Generally, the board of directors, acting under authority given to it in the by-laws, decides the units in which certificates representing the shares owned by a single stockholder shall be drawn. A stockholder, however, may specify the manner in which the certificates are to be issued, provided his demands are reasonable and there is no regulatory provision on the subject.[39]

Form of certificates of stock. There is no required form for a certificate of stock. The statutes in most of the states, however, specify the contents of the certificate. These usually include:[40]

1. The name of the record holder.
2. The number of shares represented by the certificate.
3. The class of shares represented by the certificate.
4. The par value of the shares, or a statement that they are without par value.
5. The rights and restrictions of the respective classes of stock.
6. The number of shares constituting each class of stock.

There should be no ambiguity on the face of the certificate. For example, a certificate should not be made out to "A and/or B."[41]

Registration of stock under Securities Act of 1933, as amended. Before any action is taken on the disposition of stock, it is important to determine whether or not the sale of the securities is subject to the federal Securities Act of 1933, as amended.[42] The purposes of this Act are (1) to provide full and fair disclosure to prospective investors of the character of the securities, and (2) to prevent fraud and misrepresentation in the sale of the securities.

To effect the first purpose, the Act requires that, before new offerings of securities may be made to the public[43] through the mails or through the channels of interstate commerce, the securities must, with certain exceptions, be registered with the Securities and Exchange Commission by the filing of a registration statement. This statement must contain certain

---

[38]Cisco & N.E. R.R. v. Ricks, (1931) (Tex. Civ. App.) 33 S.W.2d 878.

[39]See Schell v. Alston Mfg. Co., (1906) 149 F. 439, in which the court held the demand of a shareholder who owned 25 shares to have 25 one-share certificates issued unreasonable.

[40]See Watson v. Santa Carmelita Mut. Water Co., (1943) 58 Cal. App. 2d 709, 137 P.2d 757.

[41]Ward v. Jersey Central Power & Light Co., (1945) 136 N.J. Eq. 181, 41 A. 2d 22. In this case, the certificate was issued to "A and B as joint tenants with right of survivorship." The court refused to reform the certificate and have it issued to "A and/or B."

[42]For complete information regarding the Securities Act of 1933, as amended, see Prentice-Hall *Securities Regulation.*

[43]For a discussion of the meaning of the phrase "to the public," see Securities and Exchange Commission v. Ralston Purina Co., (1953) 346 U.S. 119, 735 Ct. 981; Mary Pickford Co. v. Bayly Bros., (1939) 12 Cal.2d 501, 86 P.2d 102, discussed in 12 So. Calif. L. Rev. 473.

specified details regarding the securities, calculated to enable the buying public to judge the value of the security offered. The registration statement must be signed by the issuer, certain of its principal officers, and a majority of its board of directors. The Act also requires the use of prospectuses containing information similar to that contained in the registration statement.

Liability under Securities Act of 1933. Civil and criminal liabilities are imposed for failure to comply with the registration law, and so it is important, before any action is taken toward disposition of stock, (1) to determine whether or not registration is required in the particular case, and (2) if registration is required, to file a proper registration statement with SEC. It may also be necessary to comply with state "Blue-Sky" laws before securities are offered for sale.[44]

The primary duty of registering the securities rests with the issuer of the securities. However, any person who sells an unregistered security that should have been registered may incur liability. Penalties are also imposed on anyone who sells securities in interstate transactions or through the use of the mails unless a required registration statement is in effect. This is broad enough to include the use of a telephone in intrastate conversations; that is enough to let a federal court hear an action alleging sale of stock in violation of the registration requirements of the 1933 Act and the antifraud rule of the Exchange Act of 1934.[45]

The Securities Act imposes civil liability for material defects in the registration statement (including omissions of material facts) upon the issuer, the directors, officers and certain other persons. Any person who innocently acquired the security may sue to recover damages for such defects or omissions. Such a person may recover as damages the difference between the amount paid for the security (not exceeding the price at which the security was offered to the public) and (1) the value at the time of suit, or (2) the price at which the security was disposed of in the market before suit, or (3) the price at which the security was disposed of after suit but before judgment, if the damages are less than under (1).

Although only a majority of the directors need sign the registration statement, every person who, at the time of filing of the registration statement, was a director of the issuing corporation or performed functions similar to those of a director or who, with his consent, is named in the

---

[44]For example, a buyer can recover from a seller the purchase price of stock the seller sold without a permit from the California Blue-Sky law commissioner and also can get punitive damages when the seller's fraudulent misrepresentations induced the purchase [Walton v. Anderson, (1970) 6 Cal. App. 3d 1003, 86 Cal. Rptr. 345]. But an out-of-state corporation need not get a permit in California to negotiate sale of its stock to a California resident where actual sale takes place outside California [Sandor v. Ruffer, Ballan & Co., (DC, SDNY, 1970) 309 F. Supp. 849].

[45]Ingraffia v. Belle Meade Hospital, Inc., (DC, ED, La., 1097) 319 F. Supp. 537.

registration statement as being or about to become a director, is also civilly liable for material defects or omissions in the registration statement.

However, directors, and persons other than the issuing corporation are given certain specific defenses, whereby they may avoid liability for defects in the registration statement. These defenses are:

(1) Resignation prior to the effective date of the registration statement and filing of a notice of such resignation and disclaimer of liability with SEC and the issuing corporation; a registration statement and filing of a notice of such resignation and disclaimer of liability with the SEC and the issuing corporation;

(2) Lack of knowledge that the registration statement became effective, and giving notice thereof to the S.E.C. and the public;

(3) Reasonable ground of belief and actual belief in the truth and accuracy of the statements contained in the registration statement. This is known as the "due diligence" defense. "Due diligence" means that if you are connected with a public offering, you *must make your own independent investigation* of the accuracy of the statements contained in the registration statement. You cannot rely on management assurances. And this liability attaches to everyone—officers, inside directors, outside directors, underwriters (both the principal underwriter and all participating underwriters), accountants and lawyers.[46]

It is unlawful (1) to make any untrue statement of a material fact in a registration statement or to omit to state any material fact required to be stated therein or necessary to make the statements therein not misleading, (2) to affix a signature on a registration statement without the authority of the purported signer, or (3) to make or cause to be made to any prospective purchaser, any representation that the filing or effectiveness of a registration statement indicates a finding by the S.E.C. that the registration statement is true and accurate or that the S.E.C. has given its approval to the security.

Furthermore, liability is not dependent on showing the technical elements of common law deceit.[47] An underwriter guilty of not thoroughly checking into the issuer's offering circular under Regulation A exemption from registration is liable for its misconduct and cannot enforce its indem-

---

[46]Escott v. Bar Chris Construction Corporation, (DC, SDNY, 1968) 283 F. Supp. 643. This decision was the first to test the "due diligence" defense. However, prior cases have said that those connected with a registration statement or company reports may be liable if they do not check their accuracy. See, for example, SEC v. Frank, (CA-2, 1968) 388 F.2d 486; Fischer v. Kletz, (DC, SDNY, 1967) 266 F. Supp. 180.

[47]Globus v. Law Research Service, Inc., (CA-2, 1969) 418 F.2d 1276, cert. denied, (U.S.S.Ct., 1970) 397 U.S. 913, 90 S. Ct. 913; later phase, (CA-2, 1971) 442 F.2d 1346, cert. denied, (U.S. S.Ct., 1971) 92 S.Ct. 286. See also, Herzfeld v. Laventhal, Krekstein, Horwath & Horwath, (CA-2, 1976) Nos. 74-2405, 74-2505, 7-15-76.

nification agreement against the issuer.[48] For example, many cases have held that proof of intent to deceive (scienter) is unnecessary in actions for fraud brought under the Securities Act of 1933.[49]

Therefore, anyone who has anything to do with a registration statement—whether as an officer or director (both inside and outside), lawyer, accountant, or underwriter—cannot rely on others when it comes to checking the accuracy of the information in these statements. He must make a thorough independent check and verification of all the facts to avoid personal liability.

Registration of stock under Securities Exchange Act of 1934.[50] In addition to registration of stock under the Securities Act of 1933 as amended, it must also be determined whether or not registration is required under the Securities Exchange Act of 1934, as amended.

So that investors will have adequate information about securities owned and held by them, the Exchange Act provides for (1) registration of securities traded on a stock exchange, (2) registration of securities of certain unlisted companies, (3) furnishing of periodical and other reports, (4) controlling unfair use of information by corporate insiders, (5) regulating securities exchanges and markets and (6) preventing unfair practices on such exchanges and markets by imposing civil liability and criminal penalty sanctions.

Registration of securities traded on a stock exchange. The Securities Exchange Act of 1934 requires the registration under the Act of securities listed on an exchange. Registration is effected by filing, with the exchange on which the security is listed, an application for registration containing certain information and accompanied by certain documents listed in the Act. Duplicates of the registration statement are filed by the exchange with the Securities and Exchange Commission. Ordinarily only issued securities may be registered. Unissued securities may be registered only when necessary in the public interest or for the protection of investors. An issuer of a registered security must file with the exchange information and documents necessary to keep current the information and documents filed in registering the securities. Duplicate originals are to be filed with the Commission as required. The issuer must also file annual and other reports as prescribed by the Commission. The Act makes it unlawful for a member of an exchange, or for a broker or dealer, to effect a transaction in any security on

---

[48]Ibid. But the indemnities can recover from the issuer and its president their proportionate part of the total damages the underwriter pays for the antifraud violations on which they are jointly liable; this has nothing to do with the inability of the underwriting agreement. Globus v. Law Research Service, Inc., (DC SDNY, 1970) 318 F. Supp. 956, aff'd., (CA-2, 1971) 442 F.2d 1346.

[49]SEC v. World Radio Mission, Inc., (CA-1, 1976), No. 76-1285, 11-4-76; University Hill Foundation v. Goldman, Sacks & Co., (DC SDNY, 1976) 71 Cu.1116, 11-8-76. But in antifraud actions brought under the Securities Exchanges Act of 1934, proof of scienter is required. See Notes 50 and 51 below.

[50]For complete information regarding the Securities Exchange Act of 1934, see Prentice-Hall *Securities Regulation.*

a registered exchange unless the security is registered under the Securities Exchange Act.

The Act also provides that a registered security may be withdrawn from an exchange listing in accordance with the rules of the exchange and upon terms that the Commission imposes to protect the investors.

Registration of securities of certain over-the-counter companies. Since July 1, 1966, every issuer that is engaged in interstate commerce or whose securities are traded by use of the mails or channels of interstate commerce, must file a registration statement with the Commission, if (a) it has more than $1 million in total assets *and* (b) any class of its equity securities is held of record by 500 or more persons. The issuer must file the registration statement within 120 days after the last day of its fiscal year, and such statement must contain information similar to that required in an application for registration with an exchange. The registration terminates 90 days after the issuer files a certification with the Commission that the number of stockholders of record for the class of equity security is less than 300 persons.

Note that failure to register a security will not bar brokers and dealers from trading in the security, since the provision is aimed at the issuer. But, if the issuer fails to register, the Commission may order it to do so. If the issuer refuses to comply the Commission may then ask the federal courts to enforce the order.

Furnishing of periodical and other reports. Every issuer of a registered security must file with the Commission (duplicate originals to be filed with the exchange, if the security is listed on an exchange) such information and documents as the Commission may require to keep current the information in the registration statement. The issuer must also file such annual and other reports (and copies thereof) as the Commission may prescribe. The form in which the information must be presented and the method of preparing the reports are prescribed by the Commission.

As a result of the 1964 amendments to the Securities Exchange Act, an issuer may have to file periodic and other reports with the Commission, even though it has not filed a registration statement for a security with the Commission. Specifically, every issuer that registers an offering of securities with the Commission under the Securities Act of 1933 must file such supplementary and periodic reports as the Commission may prescribe for the fiscal year in which its registration under the Securities Act became effective, regardless of the kind of securities registered or the number of stockholders. The duty to file reports for any later fiscal year is automatically suspended if, at the beginning of such fiscal year, the securities to which the registration relates are held by less than 300 persons. The duty to file such reports is also suspended while the issuer has a security registered under the Securities Exchange Act.

Any issuer that filed an undertaking with the Commission, before August 20, 1964 (the effective date of the 1964 Amendments to the Securities Exchange Act), to keep up-to-date the information in a registration filed under the Securities Act of 1933, must continue to file its reports in accordance with the terms of such undertaking. However, the duty to file the reports is suspended if, at the beginning of any fiscal year, the registered security is held by less than 300 persons.

Control of acts of insiders. Corporate "insiders" whose acts and transactions are controlled by the Securities Exchange Act of 1934 include beneficial owners of more than 10 percent of any class of registered equity securities,[51] and all directors[52] and officers[53] of a corporation having registered equity securities. Control is exercised by requiring such insiders to file periodic statements with the exchange and with the Commission, showing the amount of securities owned by them and any changes in ownership.[54] Profits realized from the purchase and sale of such securities by corporate insiders within any period of less than six months are recoverable by the corporation. These are known as "short-swing" profits.[55] The

---

[51]The expression "equity security" is primarily intended to mean "stock." It also includes (1) bonds convertible into stock, (2) bonds carrying warrant or right to subscribe to stock, (3) any warrant or right to subscribe to stock, and (4) any other similar security which the Commission may, by rules and regulations, treat as an equity security.

[52]A director need not be expressly designated as such. A person will be considered a "director" if he occupies a position equivalent to that of a director [Securities Exchange Act, § 3 (a) (7)]. The trustee of a Massachusetts trust, for example, is considered a director [Investment Company Act of 1940, (a) (12)]. In a far-reaching decision, the U.S. Court of Appeals for the Second Circuit held that a corporation is an "insider" and so is liable for short-swing profits from transactions in the stock of another corporation when its chief executive officer was a director of that other corporation [Feder v. Martin Marietta Corporation, (CA-2, 1969) No. 32159, 1-4-69.

[53]"Officer" means a president, vice-president, secretary, treasurer, comptroller and any other person who performs for an issuing corporation the functions of those officers [SEC Rule X-3b-2, Exchange Act Release No.1, 8-13-34]. *It does not include, however, an officer of the issuing corporation's subsidiary* [National Corp. v. Segur, (DC, ED, Pa., 1968) 281 F. Supp. 851]. An assistant secretary, or assistant treasurer, for example, is usually not an officer. However, an assistant is an officer if his chief is so inactive that the assistant is really performing his chief's functions. Temporary absence, or a brief vacation, of an officer during which the assistant performs the officer's duties does not make the assistant an officer [Exchange Act Release No. 2687, 11-16-40].

[54]If the company has stock listed on more than one exchange, it may designate which one of those exchanges the reports should be filed with, and thereafter, the insiders need file them with that exchange only [SEC Rule X-16a-1; Amended Exchange Act Release No. 8697, 11-20-69]. Insiders must include in their reports all holdings and transactions in transferable options, puts, calls, spreads, and straddles. If stock was acquired through the exercise of options, the insider must give the exercise price per share. If stock was acquired in a private transaction or by gift, stock dividend, etc., the insider must so state. An insider who is a member of a partnership that owns securities of his company must report the partnership's holding (and changes in its holdings); he may also, but need not, report the extent of his interest in the partnership and its transactions. *Exception for small transactions:* An insider need not report acquisitions of stock if (a) he makes no sales of stock of the same class within six months thereafter, and (b) the total of his other transactions in stock of the same class during that six month period is under $3,000. Also, securities acquired or disposed of by gift need not be reported if the gifts are less than $3,000 during any six month period. But in the next report that the insider files, He must show his acquisitions and dispositions for each six month period since his last filing [SEC Rule, X-16a-9; Exchange Act Release No. 4801, 3-30-53].

[55]If an insider makes a profit from any "purchase and sale" or "sale and purchase" of stock of the same class in his company within any period of less than six months, he can be compelled to turn over these "short swing" profits to his company. If the company fails or refuses to sue the insider to recover the profit, then any stockholder of the company can sue. (NOTE: SEC summarizes the information insiders file with it monthly in its "Official Summary of Security Transactions and

Act further regulates the acts of insiders by prohibiting them from selling stock of their company "short" or "against the box,"[56] and by making solicitation of proxies in respect to registered securities subject to rules and regulations of the Commission.[57]

SEC has made several exceptions to the rule that insiders can be compelled to turn over their short-swing profits:

(1) Good faith underwriting transactions by insiders under certain conditions are excepted.[58]

(2) Insiders' acquisition of stock under a bonus, profit sharing or similar plan that meets certain SEC conditions (for example, stockholder approval) is not a "purchase."[59]

(3) "Small transactions."[60]

(4) Certain transactions in which an insider acquires one security through the redemption of another security are excepted.[61]

(5) Profits realized by an insider from the sale of optioned stock (if the option was more than 6 months old when exercised), are limited to the difference between the sale price and the lowest market price of the stock within 6 months before or after the sale.[62]

(6) Certain acquisitions pursuant to mergers or consolidations.[63]

(7) Certain transactions involving the deposit of equity securities under a voting trust,[64] conversion of equity securities,[65] mergers approved by Interstate Commerce Commission,[66] and sale of subscription rights.[67]

Regulations of securities exchanges and markets. All exchanges must be registered with the Commission as national securities exchanges, except small exchanges exempt by the Commission on application. The Act makes it unlawful for a broker, a dealer, or an exchange to use the mails or the channels of interstate commerce for the purpose of using a facility of an exchange to effect or report a transaction in a security unless the exchange

---

Holdings", available from the Superintendent of Documents, Government Printing Office, Washington, D.C. 20549). It is not necessary in a suit against an insider to prove that he had used any inside information. Nor need he have sold the identical shares that he purchased. All that is necessary is to prove a "purchase and sale" or "sale and purchase" within a period of less than six months, and that the insider made a profit from the transaction.

[56]Securities Exchange Act, § 16(c). A "sale against the box" is similar to a short sale. In both, a sale is made of a security with the expectation that a subsequent drop in the market price of the stock will enable the seller to realize a profit. However, in the "short sale" the seller sells a security which he does not own. In a "sale against the box," the seller already is the owner of the security sold, but prefers to retain possession of the security and to have his broker borrow equivalent stock with which to make delivery. In the event the market prices does not drop, the seller, in case of a sale against the box, makes good on the stock loan by delivering the shares he owns.

[57]Securities Exchange Act, §814 (a)-14(c).

[58]SEC Rule X-16b-2; Exchange Act Release No. 6131, 12-4-56.

[59]SEC Rule X-16b-3; Exchange Act Release No. 8592, 5-1-69.

[60]See Note 46.

[61]SEC Rule X-16b-5; Exchange Act Release No. 4754, 9-24-52, eff. 11-1-52.

[62]SEC Rule X-16b-6; Amended Exchange Act Release No. 7717, 10-1-65.

[63]SEC Rule X-16b-7; Exchange Act Release No. 8177, 10-10-67.

[64]SEC Rule X-16b-8; Amended Exchange Act Release No. 7826, 2-17-66.

[65]SEC Rule X-16b-9; Amended Exchange Act Release No. 7826, 2-17-66.

[66]SEC Rule X-16b-10; Exchange Act Release No. 7551, 3-10-65.

[67]SEC Rule X-16b-11; Exchange Act Release No. 8229, 1-17-68.

is registered. The Act also regulates brokers and dealers trading in over-the-counter markets. No broker or dealer may use the mails or the channels of interstate commerce to effect a transaction in any security otherwise than on a registered exchange unless such broker or dealer is registered with the Securities and Exchange Commission in accordance with its rules.

Liability under Securities Exchange Act of 1934. In addition to the specific liability of insiders for ''short-swing'' profits discussed above, the Securities Exchange Act of 1934 imposes civil or criminal liabilities or both on directors and officers. These are in connection with: (1) applications, reports or documents that are filed or must be filed by the corporation;[68] (2) manipulation of security prices;[69] (3) use of manipulative

---

[68]*Section 18* of the Exchange Act provides that any person who makes or causes to be made any statement in any application, report or document filed uner the Act or under any rule or regulation or in any undertaking contained in a registration statement which is false or misleading as to a material fact shall be liable to any person who (1) did not know that the statement was false or misleading, and (2) relied on the false or misleading statement in purchasing or selling the security at a price affected by the statement, unless the person sued shall prove that he acted in good faith and had no knowledge that such statement was false or misleading. In this connection, it is important to note that not only may the corporation's stockholders sue their directors, but also stockholders of affiliated corporations can hold those same directors liable if these stockholders can show injury. For example, a minority stockholder can hold directors of a parent corporation liable for damages, when the parent allegedly used false and misleading statements to buy up enough shares to enable it to effect a merger with the subsidiary, since the state's merger statue would obligate the stockholder to sell her shares at their appraised value. Voege v. American Sumatra Tobacco Corp., (D.C., D. Del., 1965) 241 F. Supp. 369. See also Marsh v. Armada Corporation, (CA-6, 1976) 533 F. 2d 978, cert. den. (U.S. S. Ct., 1977) 97 S. Ct. 1598; Holdsworth v. Strong, (CA-10, 1976) 545 F. 2d 687, cert. den.(U.S. S. Ct.,1977) 97 S. Ct. 1600.

Section 20(c) of the Act makes it unlawful for any director, officer or stockholder without just cause to hinder, delay or obstruct the making or filing of any document, report or information required to be filed under the Act or under any rule or regulation of any undertaking contained in a registration statement.

Section 32(a) of the Exchange Act imposes a criminal liability on any person who willfully violates any provision of the Act or any rule or regulation thereunder, or who willfully and knowingly makes or causes to be made a false or misleading statement in any application, report or document filed under the Act or any rule or regulation thereunder.

[69]*Section 9* of the Exchange Act makes it unlawful for any person, directly or indirectly, by the use of the mails or the channels of interstate commerce, or any facility of a registered exchange, to participate in the following practices for manipulation of security prices:

(1) Fictitious transactions, including wash sales and matched orders.

(2) Transaction to raise or depress prices, including pool activities and rigging or jiggling of prices.

(3) Inducing purchase or sale of a registed security by circulation of information that the market price may change.

(4) Inducing purchase or sale of registered security through false or misleading statements.

(5) Inducing purchase or sale of a registered security by circulation of information that the price will change, for a consideration received from a dealer or broker or other person selling or purchasing the security.

(6) Pegging, fixing or stabilizing security prices in contravention of SEC rules and regulations.

(7) Puts, calls, straddles or other options to buy or sell a security without being bound to do so, in contravention of SEC rules and regulations. (Puts and calls are options to buy or sell a certain number of securities at a stipulated price within a stipulated time, usually 30, 60, or 90 days. A call gives its owner the right to demand delivery of a stock at a certain price within the period. A put gives the owner the right to deliver a certain number of shares at a certain price within the period to the person selling the put. A straddle is the purchase of a put and call on the same stock at the same price.)

Violations involve civil liability as well as criminal penalties.

devices;[70] (4) solicitation of proxies;[71] and (5) unlawful representations.[72]

The section and rule under the Exchange Act that have been subject to most litigation are the antifraud provisions. These are Section 10b of the Act and SEC Rule 10b-5.[73] This section and this rule have wide application.

Their purpose is to give to all investors trading on exchanges equal access to material information. This means that "insiders" and "tippees" cannot take advantage of any information they have over the general investing public, without first publicly disclosing that information. Until they do that, they cannot deal in the stock about which they have such information.

For example, insiders (defined here as employees as well as officers, directors and more-than-10 percent stockholders) violate the Rule when they buy their corporation's stock without first revealing to the public material information they have about the corporation's probable mineral strike, which if publicly revealed would have caused the price of the stock to rise. Also, officers who did not disclose that information to the corporation's stock option committee before accepting options must have those options rescinded. Further, the company's press release violates the Rule when it contains statements that are misleading and are made in a manner reasonably calculated to influence the public.[74] The court also said

---

[70]*Section 10a* of the Exchange Act makes it unlawful for any person to use the mails or channels of interstate commerce or any facility of an exchange to effect a short sale, or to use a stop-loss order, or to use any other manipulative or deceptive device, in contravention of rules and regulations of the Securities and Exchange Commission.

[71]*Section 14* of the Exchange Act makes it unlawful for any person, by use of the mails or channels of interstate commerce or of any facility of a registered exchange or otherwise, to solicit or permit the use of his name to solicit any proxy or consent or authorization in respect of any security (other than an exempted security) registered under Section 12 of the Act, in contravention of rules and regulations of the SEC.

Example: Court will enjoin solicitation of proxies by an insurgent group, when the corporation claims that insurgents' solicitations violated section 14(a) of the Exchange Act, and that the insurgents failed to disclose that they planned to acquire the corporation's assets and earnings for speculation and manipulation to their personal advantage. Studebaker v. Allied Products Corp., (DC, WD, Mich., 1966) 256 F. Supp. 173. But see Marsh v. Armada Corporation, see Note 68.

[72]*Section 26* of the Exchange Act makes it illegal to represent, to any prospective purchaser or seller of a security, that action or failure to act by SEC or by the Federal Reserve Board indicates a passing by SEC or the Board on the merits of any transaction or the truth of any report.

[73]*Section 10b* of the Exchange Act and *SEC Rule 10b-5* provide in part that "it is unlawful for any person to use the mails or channels of interstate commerce or any facility of a national securities exchange ... to make any untrue statement of a material fact or to omit to state a material fact necessary in order to make the statements made, in light of the circumstances under which they were made, not misleading ... in connection with the purchase or sale of any security."

[74]SEC v. Texas Gulf Suphur Co., (CA-2, 1968) 401 F.2d 833, cert. denied, (U.S.S. Ct., 1969) 394 U.S. 976. Although this decision is under the federal securities law, state courts have also held that under their law coporate officers can not use information they get because of their position in the corporation for their own gain, and must account to the corporation and return any profits they made in their dealing with the corporation's stock. This is so, even though their acts actually did not cause the corporation any harm. Diamond v. Oreamuno, (N.Y App. Div., 1968) 287 N.Y.S. 2d 300.

that "tipping" of outsiders violates the Rule, but since the "tippees" were not defendants, the court did not have to decide if they also violated, though their conduct was equally reprehensible.

But when "tippees' are actually named as defendants, and it is shown that they are close friends of corporate insiders, or members of their families, courts will not hesitate to hold such "tippees" liable as insiders.[75] Further, a "tippee" has no standing in court to claim that he himself was defrauded because the insider gave him what was purportedly secret confidential information that later turned out to be false. The court will dismiss any such action by the "tippee" against the insider, since Rule 10b-5 is intended to protect the ordinary person who buys and sells securities based upon information generally available to the investing public, and not one who has access to, or believes he has access to, secret corporate information.[76]

The SEC takes the definitive position that all "tippees" are liable. It says, if a broker knows that a company's earning power is low, and may fall to nothing, although previous public statements did not reveal this fact, the broker violates the Rule when he does not make public disclosure, but instead informs his institutional investors who sell the stock before the public is told. Further, the SEC claims, the institutional investors are equally liable,[77] as well as any corporation that reveals to a favored broker-dealer its plan to take over another company weeks before it reveals this to the public.[78]

Landmark cases under the antifraud section and Rule have focused on three important issues: (1) whether there must be a showing of an intent to deceive (scienter) on defendant's part for the action to be successful; (2) when misrepresentation or concealment of information is "material"; and (3) whether a showing of a valid "corporate purpose" is required in a "going private" or "freeze-out" merger?

Intent to deceive. The U.S. Supreme Court has ruled that in a private suit for damages under the Exchange Act antifraud rule, a showing of mere negligence alone is not enough. Thus, auditors cannot be held personally

---

[75]Ross v. Licht, (DC SDNY, 1967) 263 F. Supp. 395; see also SEC v. Geon Industries. Inc., (CA-2, 1976) 531 F. 2d 39.

[76]Kuehnert v. Texstar Corporation, (DC, SD Texas, 1968) 286 F. Supp. 340.

[77]In re Merrill Lynch, Pierce, Fenner & Smith, Inc., SEC Administrative Proceeding File No. 3-1680, 8-26-68.

[78]SEC v. Glen Alden Corporation, (DC, SDNY, 1968) 68 Civ. 3203, 8-7-68.

unless it is also shown that they had a knowing intent to deceive, manipulate, defraud or "scienter."[79] But the Court specifically left open the questions whether (1) reckless behavior is sufficient intentional conduct to amount to scienter so as to impose liability under the antifraud rule[80] and whether such scienter is also a necessary element in an action by SEC for injunctive relief.[81]

Materiality. The U.S. Supreme Court has set what it calls an objective standard for "materiality." It held that when a corporation solicits proxies the information it must reveal to its stockholders is only that which a reasonable shareholder *would* consider important in deciding how to vote. It need not include all facts that a reasonable shareholder *might* consider important.[82] This means that "materiality" will now have to be decided in each instance on a case-by-case basis. It is no longer a rule or question of law, but one of fact to be determined at a trial by the triers of fact—whether it be a jury or judge.[83]

Valid corporate purpose. When a company is planning to "go private," the usual merger rout is no longer as simple as it used to be. It is not enough that the controlling stockholder complies in all respects with the states corporate merger statutes. "Freezing-out" the minority cannot be the *sole* objective. It must be shown that the contemplated merger is for a

---

[79]Ernst v. Ernst v. Hochfelder (U.S.S. Ct., 1976) 96 S. Ct. 1375. As a result of this decision, the U.S. Supreme Court vacated some Appeals Court judgments and remanded them for reconsideration. For example, the court held that, in the absence of a showing of an intent to deceive, an underwriter of short-term commercial paper in the mistaken belief that a CPA's financial statements regarding an issue were correct does not necessarily make the auditor liable for damages resulting from the issuer's default, John Nuveen & Co., Inc. v. Sanders (U.S.S. Ct., 1976) 425 U.S. 929, vacating judgment against the auditor in Sanders v. John Nuveen & Co., Inc., (CA-7, 1975) 524 F. 2d 1066. See also Adams v. Standard Knitting Mills, Inc., (DC ED Tenn., 1976) No. 8052, 5-19-76.

[80]However, some lower courts have already considered this issue and have held that reckless behavior is sufficient to spell out liability under the scienter requirement 7 Hochfelder [McLean v. Alexander, (DC Del., 1976) 420 F. Supp. 1057.] In this case an accountant was held liable for knowing misconduct in failing to check issuer's accounts receivables and sales. But see University Hill Foundation v. Goldman, Sachs & Co., (DC SDNY, 1976) 422 F. Supp. 879, where the court held there could be no liability under the 1934 Act for misconduct, but liability could attach under the 1933 Act. However, in SEC v. World Radio Mission, Inc., (CA-1, 1976) 544 F. 2d 535, the Appeals Court said by way of dictum that it could find liability for "careless or reckless" conduct under the 1934 Act—such conduct would satisfy the scienter requirement.

[81]A federal district court applied the "scienter" test in an injunction action by SEC. It said there is no difference whether the action is by a private litigant or by SEC. However, it found no intent to deceive in the particular case before it, saying that the officer of the corporation released material information on estimated earnings to an analyst inadvertently without any evil intent, SEC v. Bausch & Loomb, Inc., (DC, SDNY, 1976) 420 F. Supp. 1226, aff. (CA-2, 1977).

[82]TSC Industries, Inc., v. Northway, Inc., (U.S.S. Ct., 1976) 96 S. Ct. 2126.

[83]In the light of TSC Industries, the U.S. Supreme Court vacated the judgment in S.D. Cohn & Co. v. Woolf, (CA-5, 1975) 515 F. 2d 591.

valid or justifiable corporate purpose.[84] Even so-called "short-form" mergers may be effective.[85]

However, in the area statute law is decisive. The United States Supreme Court has said that the federal anti-fraud law and rules do not apply to these "freeze-out" situations.[86]

Listing stock on an exchange. Whether or not stock should be listed on an exchange is a question to be determined by the board of directors. Details of the listing are generally attended to by the secretary of the corporation, often with the aid of bankers or attorneys familiar with listing procedure. These details include conferences with the Stock Exchange Committee on Listing of the particular exchange, and the preparation and filing of the formal application for listing.

Underwriting the issuance of stock. The general purpose of underwriting an issue of stock is to guarantee through bankers the successful flotation of the securities.[87] A new issue of stock may also be underwritten by the stockholders themselves.[88] An issue of stock may be underwritten whether or not the new securities are first offered to existing stockholders. One of two methods may be used to effect distribution of the stock with the aid of bankers: (1) distribution of the securities to the public after the banker or a group of bankers has purchased the issue of stock outright from the corporation, or has received an option thereon, or has been authorized to act as selling agent; or (2) an agreement between the corporation and the

---

[84]Tanzer Economic Associates, Inc. Profit Sharing Plan v. Universal Food Specialties, Inc., (N.Y.S. Ct., 1976) 383 N.Y.S. 2d, 472.

[85]A "short-form" merger allows a parent corporation owning at least 90 percent (in some states 95 percent of a subsidiary corporation's stock) to merge with the latter simply by vote of the parent's directors and stockholders. In most states, neither the parent nor the subsidiary needs to give any prior notice, or send a proxy statement relating to the proposed merger, to the subsidiary's minority stockholders, nor is their consent necessary. All that is required is that the merged corporation offer them cash in an amount determined by it, or, if they refuse, to give them the alternatives to seek appraisal of their stock. People v. Concord Fabrics, Inc., (N.Y.S. Ct., 1975) 271 N.Y.S. 2d 550, aff'd. (N.Y. App. Div. 1975) 377 N.Y.S. 2d 85; Schulwolf v. Cerro Corp., (N.Y.S. Ct., 1976).

[86]Santa Fe Industries, Inc. v. Green (U.S.S. Ct., 1976) 97 S. Ct. 1292.

[87]See Marine Nat'l Exchange Bank v. Kalt-Zimmers Mfg. Co., (1934) 293 U.S. 540, 55 S.Ct. 85; Bone v. Hayes, (1908) 154 Cal. 759, 99 P. 172; Stewart v. G.L. Miller & Co., (1926) 161 Ga. 919, 132 S.E. 535; International Products Co. v. Vail's Estate, (1924) 97 Vt. 318, 123 A. 194; Fraser v. Home Tel. & Tel. Co., (1916) 91 Wash. 253, 157 P. 692; 28 COLUM. L. REV. 634; Masslich, "Financing a New Corporate Enterprise," 5 ILL. L. REV. 70-78.

An underwriting agreement must be distinguished from a subscription agreement. In a subscription agreement, the signer unqualifiedly obligates himself to take the amount of securities designated. In the underwriting agreement, the obligation is to take only what is unsold. See Positype Corp. v. Flowers, (1930) 36 F.2d 617, in which an agreement designated as an "underwriting syndicate agreement" was held to be a subscription contract. See also In re Danville Hotel Co., (1930; 38F.2d 10; Positype Corp. v. Mahin, (1929) 32 F.2d 202; Bush v Stromberg-Carlson Tel. Mfg. Co., (1914) 217 F. 328.

For a discussion of the difference between the relation of a corporation to an underwriter and to a subscriber, see "The Nature and Function of Underwriting Agreements," 79 U. PA. L. REV. 941.

[88]See Weishsel v. Jones, (1937) (Tex. Civ. App.) 109 S.W.2d 332, involving such an underwriting agreement.

bankers, before the securities are offered to the corporation's stockholders, that in the event all the stock offered is not taken up, the bankers or underwriters will purchase the remaining stock from the corporation.[89]

The arrangement between the corporation and the bankers is reduced to a written contract, usually in the form of a letter. The contract may be signed by each of the bankers in the group that is underwriting the security issue, or by one banker as agent and representative of the rest of the purchasing group. Each of the bankers assumes a definite contractual liability to take a fixed proportion of the security issue.

The contract entered into by the corporation with the bankers must be duly authorized by proper corporate action. Whether the stockholders or the directors must approve the underwriting arrangement depends upon the nature of the financing and upon the provisions of the statute, charter, or by-laws governing the corporation. For example, if a corporation desires to increase its stock and to have the offering of such stock to its old stockholders underwritten by bankers, it will generally be necessary for the directors to obtain the consent of the stockholders to the increase of stock. The matter of entering into a contract for the sale of a security issue, on the other hand, may be a detail of corporate management that the directors of a particular corporation may have the power to determine.

When offering an issue of stock through investment bankers, a corporation enters into a contract with the investment bankers called an underwriting agreement. It is generally prepared in the form of a letter agreement and usually includes these points:

1. Designation and amount of issue.
2. Agreement by the underwriters to buy the stock at the price specified.
3. Agreement to make the public offering as soon as possible after the registration statement becomes effective.
4. Warranties by the corporation that a registration statement and prospectus has been filed and meets the requirements of the Securities Act of 1933.
5. Agreement that the corporation will pay the expenses of preparing the registration statement and prospectus, of qualifying the issue under the Blue Sky laws of various states, and of issuing and delivering the stock, and that the corporation will furnish sufficient copies of the prospectus to the underwriters.
6. Agreements by the corporation and by the underwriters that each will indemnify the other for claims arising out of alleged untrue statements or

---

[89]For a discussion of underwriting agreements under Securities Act of 1933, see Lockwood and Anderson, ''Underwriting Contracts Within Purview of Securities Act of 1933, with Certain Suggested Provisions,'' 8 GEO. WASH. L. REV. 33.

omissions of a material fact in the registration statement and prospectus on the authority of each.[90]

7. Statement of place and date for delivery of and payment for the stock.

8. Conditions for the underwriters' obligation to become effective: That the registration, must become effective, that legal opinions as to the legality of the issue have been received, and that the affirmation has been made that the representations of the issuer are true and correct.

9. A "market out" clause relieving the underwriters of their obligation when unforeseen changes in market conditions make the offering impractical in the opinion of the underwriters.

CLASSIFICATION OF STOCK

Right to classify stock. In the absence of charter regulation or prohibition by the law of the state under which it is organized, the corporation may, at its organization, classify its stock and provide for a preference of one class over another.[91] The statutes of many states provide express authority for the issuance of two or more kinds of stock. Ordinarily, the certificate of incorporation sets forth the classes of stock which the corporation may issue, and, if a change in classification is desired, the certificate is amended. Unless a statute or charter provision forbids it, additional classes of stock can be created with priority over preexisting classes.[92] (See reclassification of stock on pages 783-786 in Chapter 25.)

But a corporation's attempt to remove former employees as shareholders by recapitalizing so that their shares were reduced to fractional shares subject to repurchase by the corporation was barred when fraud was alleged and no proof of legitimate business purpose was shown; existence of an appraisal rights remedy did not mandate its application exclusively.[93] On the other hand, a corporation that used a reverse stock split to reclassify remaining stock and eliminate fractional shares did not violate a dissenting minority shareholder's rights; reclassification was proper since it reduced corporate expenses and the dissenting shareholder got fair cash value.[94]

The various kinds of stock that may be provided for in the articles of incorporation or by an amendment thereto are discussed in the following paragraphs.

---

[90]But if the underwriter is found quilty of an antifraud violation he may not be able to recover against the issuer under the indemnity agreement [Globus v. Law Research Service, Inc. (see footnotes 47 and 48)].

[91]Barson v. The Pioneer Savings & Loan Co., (S.Ct. Ohio, 1955) 163 O.S. 424; Hamlin v. Toledo, St. L. & K. C. R.R., (1897) 78 F. 644; People ex rel. Recess Exporting & Importing Corp. v. Hugo, (1920) 191 App. Div. 628, 182 N.Y. Supp. 9. See also Breslav v. New York & Queens Elec. Light & Power Co., (1936) 249 App. Div. 181, 291 N.Y. Supp. 932, aff'd, 273 N.Y. 593, 7 N.E.2d 708.

[92]Shanik v. White Sewing Mach. Co., (1941) 25 Del. 371, 19 A.2d 831.

[93]Clark v. Pattern Analysis and Recognition Corp., (N.Y.S. Ct., 1976) 184 N.Y.S. 2d 660.

[94]Teschner v. Chicago Title & Trust Co., (1974) 59 Ill. 2d 452, 322 N.E.2d 54, aff'd., (U.S. S.Ct., 1975) 95 S.Ct. 2673.

Common and preferred stock. Stock may be broadly divided into two kinds:

1. Common stock.
2. Preferred stock.

The universal attribute of common stock is that owners are entitled to a pro rata division of profits and participation in the management of the corporation.[95] Preferred stock, as its name implies, entitles its holders to some preference over another class of stock.[96] This preference may relate to a right to dividends, a right to vote, a right to assets of the corporation upon dissolution, or any other preference. The most usual preference which preferred stock bears is the right to receive dividends from the earnings of the corporation before the holders of the common stock can participate in the profits.[97] (See the attributes of preferred stock on page 440.)

In recent years many corporations have issued stock designated as Class A, Class B, etc. These are, in effect, classes of preferred and common stock. Both common and preferred stock may be subdivided into various classes with distinguishing designations, each class having different attributes. A corporation's board of directors may issue preferred shares in series without prior approval of shareholders when articles of incorporation grant the board such authority.[98] Stock may be further classified into par value and no par value stock.

Stock with or without par value. Par value stock has a definite value, fixed by the certificate of incorporation.[99] The value is stated in terms of dollars, but usually the stock may be issued for money, property, or services. (See consideration for stock, page 449, ct seq.)

No par value stock may be defined roughly as stock without any nominal or designated money value. Such stock may be either common or preferred. No par stock can be issued only by authority of the statutes.[100] However, of all the states, only Nebraska now lacks a statute permitting corporations to issue stock without any face or par value. Most of the statutes require that provision must be made for its issuance in the certificate of incorporation or in an amended certificate.

---

[95]Elko Lamoille Power Co. v. Commissioner, (1931) 50 F.2d 595; General Inv. Co. v. Bethlehem Steel Corp., (1917) 87 N.J. Eq. 234, 100 A. 347.

[96]Storrow v. Texas Consol. Compress & Mfg. Ass'n, (1898) 87 F. 612; Starring v. American Hair & Felt Co., (1937) 21 Del. Ch. 380, 191 A. 887, aff'd, memo dec., (Del.) 2 A.2d 249.

[97]James F. Powers Foundry Co. v. Miller, (1934) 166 Md. 590, 171 A. 842.

[98]S.C. Op. Atty. Gen. No. 3018, 11-2-70.

[99]G. Loewus & Co. v. Highland Queen Packing Co., (1939) 125 N.J. Eq. 534, 6 A.2d 545.

[100]West Texas Utilities Co. v. Ellis, (1939) 133 Tex. 104, 126 S.W.2d 13, discussed in 18 TEXAS L. REV. 67.

Constitutional provisions prohibiting the issuance of stock except for money, services, or property do not prohibit the issuance of stock without par value.[101]

The statutes authorizing the issuance of no par stock generally provide that (1) no individual liability shall attach to any holder of such stock beyond his obligation to comply with the terms of subscription, and (2) stock for which the agreed consideration shall have been paid shall be nonassessable.

Change of par stock into no par stock. Stock that has been issued with a par value may not subsequently be changed to stock without a par value, against a stockholder's objection, in the absence of statutory authority. Statutes in some states specifically authorize such a change, and, conversely, allow the exchange of no par shares for shares with par value. The exchange is usually brought about by an amendment to the articles of incorporation. In some states, it is effective by the filing of a certificate by the directors with the designated state authorities, after the adoption of a resolution by the stockholders. The procedure prescribed by the statute must be strictly followed.

Attributes of preferred stock. Calling stock ''preferred stock'' does not of itself determine the rights of the holders. If no description of the preference is indicated, calling the stock ''preferred'' is useless, and the shares are treated exactly like common stock.[102] The extent of the preference is determined by the terms of the contract between the corporation and the stockholders.[103] Preferred stock has only those preferences that are specifically defined; in all other respects, preferred stock has no rights that are not shared equally with common stock.[104] The preferences must be clearly expressed, either by direct statement or by necessary implication.[105]

The statutes vary considerably as to the terms upon which preferred stock may be issued. Some of them leave the details to the corporation. When no restriction or limitation is placed upon the authorized issuance of preferred stock, the company is free to attach such considerations as it sees fit, provided only that the conditions do not violate any law and are not

---

[101]Lewis v. Oscar C. Wright Co., (1930) 234 Ky. 814, 29 S.W.2d 566. See also Israels, ''Problems of Par and No-Par Shares: A Reappraisal,'' 47 COLUM. L. REV. 1279.

[102]Rice & Hutchins, Inc. v. Triplex Shoe Co., (1929) 16 Del. Ch. 298, 147 A. 317, aff'd, (1930) 17 Del. Ch. 356, 152 A. 342.

[103]Lloyd v. Pennsylvania Elec. Vehicle Co., (1909) 75 N.J. Eq. 263, 72 A. 16; Lyman v. Southern Ry., (1928) 149 Va. 274, 141 S.E. 240. Contract includes certificate of incorporation and pertinent statutes. Windhurst v. Central Leather Co., (1931) 107 N.J. Eq. 528, 153 A. 402.

[104]Penington v. Commonwealth Hotel Constr. Corp., (1930) 17 Del. Ch 188, 151 A. 228; Grover v. Cavanagh, (1907) 40 Ind. App. 340, 82 N.E. 104.

[105]Holland v. National Automotive Fibres, (1937) 22 Del. Ch. 99, 194 A. 124.

contrary to public policy.[106] In many states, the statutes specifically provide that stock may be issued:[107]

1. With preferences as to dividends.
2. With preferences as to assets upon liquidation of the corporation.
3. With full, limited, or no voting powers.
4. With or without the right to convert the stock into stock of another class or bonds. This is called a conversion right.
5. Subject to redemption.
6. With right to render the stock assessable.

Stock with preference as to dividends. The statutes of many states permit a corporation to issue various classes of stock with preferences. The most common privilege granted under this provision is a preference as to dividends. Usually this means that a class of stock may be given the right to receive a fixed percentage of the profits of the company before any dividend is declared on another class of stock. (See Chapter 23, page 703, for a discussion of the rights of stockholders to dividends; page 683, for the rights of preferred stockholders to cumulative dividends.

Stock with preference as to assets on liquidation. Holders of stock preferred as to assets have the right to be paid back the par value of their stock, or, if stock is without par value, a certain fixed amount, before any other class of stockholders receives anything.[108] Of course, creditors must first be satisfied,[109] and there may not be enough funds left to pay the full par value. Sometimes the preference is designated as nonparticipating. This means that the holders of the nonparticipating preferred stock will receive the full par value of their stock if there are sufficient funds, but that they cannot participate in the profits which may be left after all the stockholders receive the amount of their shares.

Nature of voting rights attached to stock. A stockholder has the power to vote as an incident of his holding stock in the corporation.[110] This applies to preferred stock as well as to common stock.[111] Although a

---

[106]Vanden Bosch v. Michigan Trust Co., (1929) 35 F. 2d 643; Coggeshall v. Georgia Land & Inv. Co., (1914) 14 Ga. App. 637, 82 S.E. 156.

[107]For a discussion of the various attributes of preferred stock, see I. Grossman, "Corporate Securities—Especially Common and Preferred Stock," 17 A.B.A.J. 123.

[108]Hull v. Pfister & Vogel Leather Co., (1940) 235 Wis. 653, 294 N.W. 18.

[109]In distribution upon dissolution, creditors' rights are ordinarily superior to those of stockholders. Armstrong v. Union Trust & Sav. Bank, (1918) 248 F. 268; Guaranty Trust Co. v. Galveston City R.R., (1901) 107 F. 311; O'Neal v. Automobile Piton & Parts Co., (1939) 188 Ga. 380, 4 S.E. 2d 40; Hoyt v. Hampe, (1927) 206 Iowa 206, 214 N.W. 718, 220 N.W. 45; Koeppler v. Crocker Chair Co., (1930) 200 Wis. 476, 228 N.W. 130.

[110]Talbot J. Taylor & Co. v. Southern Pac. Co., (1903) 122 F. 147; Reimer v. Smith, (1932) 105 Fla. 671, 142 So. 603; Hall v. Woods, (1927) 325 Ill. 114, 156 N.E. 258; In re Wallace's Estate, (1929) 131 Ore. 597, 282 P. 760.

[111]Williams v. Davis, (1944) 297 Ky. 626, 180 S.W. 2d 874; Millspaugh v. Cassedy, (1920) 191 App. Div. 221, 181 N.Y. Supp. 276.

stockholder has not fully paid for his shares, he may vote them,[112] in the absence of an agreement to the contrary. The right to vote is a contractual one; the stockholder may not subsequently be deprived of it without his consent.[113] However, the statutes and the articles of incorporation are part of that contract. The right to vote, therefore, is not necessarily exempt from the corporation's general power to amend its charter in any way permitted by law.[114] Amendments of the charter that transfer the voting power from one class of stock to another, or that change the capital structure with the same result, have been upheld.[115] It must be remembered, however, that some of the statutes that permit a reclassifiction of stock through amendment of the charter with consent of a fixed proportion of the stockholders (under which voting rights may be transferred from one class of stock to another), provide that a dissenting stockholder is entitled to appraisal of his shares and payment for them.

Stock with voting restrictions. The right to vote may be relinquished by the stockholder. A corporation has the right to restrict the voting power of the stock and make a contract with a stockholder whereby he will have no voice in the management of the business, unless the state statute makes equal voting rights for all classes of stock mandatory. There is no rule of public policy which forbids a corporation and its stockholders to make any contract they please in regard to restrictions on the voting power.[116] For example, failure to note voting restriction on Class B common stock did not nullify this restriction, but rendered the subscription voidable, nor did the non-voting restriction violate the stockholders' right to vote outstanding stock in the election of directors, when, pursuant to statute, the corporation provided in its articles of incorporation for issuance of classes of shares with different rights of participation.[117] But provisions of certificate of incorporation restricting the number of votes a shareholder could cast to less than the number of shares he held and varying application of the rule according to the number of shares held were illegal, since they did not

---

[112]Price v. Holcomb, (1893) 89 Iowa 123, 56 N.W. 407.

[113]Lord v. Equitable Life Assurance Soc'y, (1909) 194 N.Y. 212, 87 N.E. 443; Stokes v. Continental Trust Co., (1906) 186 N.Y. 285, 78 N.E. 1090. (These cases were decided before amendment of New York statute permitting reclassification of stock to make changes in voting rights.)

[114]Topkis v. Delaware Hardware Co., (1938) 23 Del. Ch. 125, 2 A. 2d 114; Lord v. Equitable Life Assurance Soc'y, (1909) 194 N.Y. 212, 87 N.E. 443. See also Brown v. McLanahan, (1944) 58 F. Supp. 345. But see Faunce v. Boost Co., (1951) 15 N.J. Super. 534, 83 A 2d 649.

[115]Heller Inv. Co. v. Southern Title & Trust Co., (1936) 17 Cal. App. 2d 202, 61 P.2d 807; Aldridge v. Franco-Wyoming Oil Co., (1939) 24 Del. Ch. 126, 7 A.2d 153, aff'd, (1940) 24 Del. Ch. 349, 14 A.2d 380. See also "Corporate Charter Amendments and the Impairment of Voting Rights," 54 HARV. L. REV. 1368.

[116]Orme v. Salt River Valley Water Users' Ass'n, (1923) 25 Ariz. 324, 217 P. 935; Millspaugh v. Cassedy, (1920) 191 App. Div. 221, 181 N.Y.Supp. 276.

[117]Hampton v. Tri-State Finance Corp., (Colo. Ct. of App., 1972) 495 P.2d 566.

apply to distinct classes of stock but discriminated among shareholders of a single class of stock.[118]

The statutes in some of the states expressly provide that a corporation may create classes of stock with restrictions on the power to vote.[119] For a complete discussion of the methods of voting, see page 19 in Chapter 1.

Ordinarily, restrictions on voting power are attached to preferred rather than to common stock,[120] although some statutes authorize the creation of non-voting common shares.[121] Common stock frequently carries with it the exclusive right to vote.[122]

Non-voting stock is often given certain voting rights upon the occurrence of designated defaults in the payment of dividends,[123] sinking fund payments or other obligations. Provision is also made in many instances that the consent of a specified portion of stockholders is required to do certain acts, whether or not such stockholders are otherwise entitled to voting rights. Some of these acts are: increase of stock, creation of stock with prior rights, issuance of bonds, and so forth.

Convertible stock. Stock which may be converted into some other form of security, for example, another class of stock or bonds, is called convertible stock. Ordinarily, preferred stock rather than common stock is made convertible, and the conversion is at the option of the preferred stockholder rather than at the election of the corporation. Provision is also generally made for the exercise of the option within a specified time. The right to convert is usually suspended while the transfer books are closed.

Some doubt exists as to whether statutory authority is necessary to enable a corporation to issue convertible stock. The statutes in some states expressly authorize the issuance of stock convertible into bonds or some other class of stock, under terms and conditions set forth in the certificate of incorporation or in an amendment thereto, or in the resolution providing for the issue of such stock. But states will not interfere with the conversion problem as it affects unqualified corporations. Thus, for example, shareholders of preferred stock seeking extension of conversion rights to

---

[118]Baker v. Providence and Worcester Co., (Del. Ch. Ct., 1976) No. 4127, 7-30-76.

[119]See Heller Inv. Co. v. Southern Title & Trust Co., (1936) 17 Cal. App. 2d, 202, 61 P.2d 807.

[120]Rice & Hutchins v. Triplex Shoe Co., (1929) 16 Del. Ch. 298, 147 A. 317, aff'd, (1930) 17 Del. Ch. 356, 152 A. 342; Morris v. American Pub. Utilities Co., (1923) 14 Del. Ch. 136, 122 A. 696; People ex rel. Browne v. Koenig, (1909) 133 App. Div. 756, 118 N.Y. Supp. 136; Miller v. Ratterman, (1890) 47 Ohio St. 141, 24 N.E. 496.

[121]See General Inv. Co. v. Bethlehem Steel Corp., (1917) 87 N.J. Eq. 234, 100 A. 347.

[122]See Starring v. American Hair & Felt Co., (1937) 21 Del. Ch. 380, 191 A. 887, aff'd. memo dec., (Del.) 2 A.2d 249.

[123]See Pierce Oil Corp. v. Voran, (1923) 136 Va. 416, 118 S.E. 247. When preferred stock is given power to vote if dividends are unpaid for two or more periods, it is assumed the reference is to lawful dividends. Vogtman v. Merchants' Mortgage & Credit Co., (1935) 20 Del. Ch. 364, 178, A. 99.

include their shares were prevented from bringing their suit against a corporation because the corporation was unqualified in New Jersey and had no contracts there, most shareholders did not reside in New Jersey or have any contacts with that state, and the state itself had no special interest in the suit.[124]

However, even in the absence of statutory authority, it has been held that such stock could be issued.[125] Under some statutes stock cannot be made convertible into bonds except at the option of the corporation; otherwise stockholders would convert their stock when the company became insolvent and thus would get an advantage over creditors.

Where convertible stock is issued, the corporation usually makes provision to carry the conversion into effect by having available sufficient shares of the stock or bonds into which the change is to be made. A sufficient number of shares of common stock may be reserved to make the conversion. The converted stock is not reissued, but the total authorized capital stock is reduced by the number of shares so converted. Or a financial plan may be necessary to take care of the conversion. For example, if the stock is convertible into stock of another class, it may be necessary to increase the latter class in accordance with the statutory provisions.

Redeemable stock. Stock is redeemable if the corporation may require the stockholder to surrender his shares and accept in lieu of them a certain sum of money. A corporation cannot compel a stockholder to give up his stock in redemption, unless the right to redeem has been granted to the corporation by statute, by the certificate of incorporation, or by agreement with the stockholder.[126] The statutes of many states authorize the issuance of stock subject to redemption. These statutes generally refer only to preferred stock.[127]

Corporation's rights and obligations attached to redeemable stock. The right and the obligation of a corporation to redeem a class of

---

[124]Feldman v. Bases Mfg. Co., Inc., (N.J. Super Ct., 1976) No. A-1939-75, 7-13-76.

[125]General Inv. Co. v. Bethlehem Steel Corp., (1917) 87 N.J. Eq. 234, 100 A. 347. In this case, the right of the corporation to issue convertible stock was based on its right to issue preferred stock, to retire it, and to issue common stock purchased with the proceeds of the preferred stock. The court permitted the corporation to take the short cut of issuing preferred shares convertible into common shares. See also Berger v. U.S. Steel Corp., (1902) 63 N.J. Eq. 809, 53 A. 68, which holds that if the corporation may purchase its own shares, it may do so by the device of issuing the shares convertible into bonds and then buying them back with its bonds upon exercise of the conversion right.

[126]Star Publishing Co. v. Ball, (1922) 192 Ind. 158, 134 N.E. 285; Empire Trust Co. v. Panola Cotton Mills, (1929) 149 S.C. 8, 146 S.E. 612.

[127]Corporation may not redeem common stock. Starring v. American Hair & Felt Co., (1937) 21 Del. Ch. 380, 191 A. 887, aff'd, memo dec., (Del.) 2 A.2d 249. Redeemable common stock legal. Lewis v. H.P. Hood & Sons, Inc., (1954) 331 Mass. 670, 121 N.E. 2d 850, noted in 54 MICH. L. REV. 132. Maryland statute makes any class redeemable.

stock are contractual.[128] The contract terms—the terms upon which the stock is to be redeemed—and the time when the redemption may be effected, must usually be set forth in the articles of incorporation or in an amendment thereto.[129] These terms must include any statutory conditions that are imposed on the privilege of redeeming stock.[130] In some states, the terms may be fixed by resolution of the directors providing for the issuance of the stock, pursuant to authority vested in the board by the articles, or by an amendment granting such authority. The terms of the statute, articles of incorporation, or resolution relating to the redemption must be strictly observed.[131] Thus, if the stock is to be redeemed at a fixed date, the corporation cannot make it payable only at the call of the corporation, unless the stockholders consent.[132] Nor can the corporation redeem stock before the redemption date.[133] A corporation cannot reclassify preferred stock, not subject to redemption, so as to make it subject to redemption at a price below its real value.[134]

Also, a corporation cannot selectively redeem preferred stock, before the expiration of a voting trust agreement giving control to certain directors and officers, when it appears that such redemption would assure continued control of the corporation by those directors and officers; it does not matter that the corporate charter allows selective redemption of preferred shares.[135] Nor can a corporation redeem its stock and hold it as treasury stock when no right of redemption is provided for in the articles of incorporation.[136]

In some situations, the holder of stock with an unconditional promise

---

[128]Crimmins & Peirce Co. v. Kidder Peabody Acceptance Corp., (1933) 282 Mass. 367, 185 N.E. 383; Ammon v. Cushman Motor Works, (1935) 128 Neb. 357, 258 N.W. 649.

[129]But preferred shareholders can, by mutual arrangement with the corporation, provide for redemption of their shares on any fair basis which is not prejudicial to the corporation or to the other shareholders. Hay v. Big Ben Land Co., (1949) 32 Wash. 2d 887, 204 P.2d 488.

[130]In re Culbertson's, (1932) 54 F.2d 753; In re Greenebaum Bros. & Co., (1945) 62 F. Supp. 769.

[131]State ex rel. Waldman v. Miller-Wohl Co., (1942) 42 Del. 73, 28 A. 2d 148; People ex rel. Colby v. Imbrie & Co., (1926) N.Y. Misc. 457, 214 N.Y. Supp. 53, aff'd, memo dec., 214 N.Y. Supp. 819. See Allied Magnet Wire Corp. v. Tuttle, (1926) 199 Ind. 166, 154 N.E. 480. See also Corbett v. McClintic Marshall Corp., (1930) 17 Del. Ch. 165, 151 A. 218. In this case, the stock was redeemable at the corporation's option at $100 per share or at book value, if the book value, as shown by the last annual statement, exceeded $100. The directors voted to redeem the stock at the book value. A stockholder refused to surrender her shares on the ground that the price fixed did not truly reflect the book value. It was held that the directors could not be compelled to redeem at the higher and true value. The stockholder was entitled to no more relief than a decree continuing her in her status as a stockholder, if she could establish that the directors were not justified in approving the values at which the assets were carried on the books.

[132]Koeppler v. Crocker Chair Co., (1930) 200 Wis. 476, 228 N.W. 130.

[133]People ex rel. Colby v. Imbrie & Co., (1926) 126 N.Y. Misc. 457, 214 N.Y. Supp. 53.

[134]Breslav v. New York & Queens Elec. Light & Power Co., (1936) 249 App. Div. 181, 291 N.Y. 465, Supp. 932, aff'd, 273 N.Y. 593, 7 N.E. 2d 708.

[135]Petty v. Penntech Papers, Inc., (Del. Ch. Ct., 1975) 347 A. 2d 140.

[136]Ky. Op. Atty. Gen. No. 74-326, 4-30-74.

of redemption may be treated as a creditor and may be able to force the corporation to redeem the stock.[137]

When redemption contract cannot be enforced. An agreement to redeem stock is at all times conditional upon the solvency of the corporation at the time the stockholder attempts to exercise his right to have the stock redeemed.[138] When the stock matures, the stockholder is entitled to have it redeemed in accordance with the terms of the agreement, unless the redemption will prejudice the rights of the creditors of the corporation.[139] Stock cannot be redeemed even though permitted by a valid contract, or by statute or charter, if the retirement of the stock will be detrimental to the interests of the corporation's creditors,[140] or will freeze the minority out of profits.[141] The corporation's contractual obligations will not be enforced if the corporation has become insolvent and its capital stock depleted.[142] Its refusal, in such a situation, is not a breach of its agreement to redeem, though the corporation is not in liquidation and though no creditor is asking relief.[143] Usually shares cannot be redeemed if there is reasonable ground for believing that the redemption would leave the corporation with less assets than liabilities.[144] If a corporation has actually canceled shares under circumstances that do not prejudice existing creditors, a subsequent creditor cannot complain.[145]

Status and liability of stockholder when stock is redeemed. After the redemption date, the holder of redeemable stock has no further rights as a stockholder, except to receive the redemption price of the stock.[146] If a corporation illegally redeems stock by a method not authorized, the

---

[137]Oklahoma Wheat Pool Elevator Corp. v. Bouquet, (1937) 180 Okla. 159, 68 P.2d 97.

[138]Campbell v. Grant Trust & Sav. Co., (1932) 97 Ind. App. 169, 182 N.E. 267; Kraft v. Rochambeau Holding Co., (1956) 210 Md. 325, 123 A.2d 287.

[139]Cring v. Sheller Wood Rim Mfg. Co., (1932) 98 Ind. App. 310, 183 N.E. 674. See also Koeppler v. Crocker Chair Co., (1930) 200 Wis. 476, 228 N.W. 130.

[140]Vanden Bosch v. Michigan Trust Co., (1929) 35 F.2d 643; In re Fechheimer Fishel Co., (1914) 212 F. 357; Campbell v. Grant Trust & Sav. Co.; Westerfield-Bonte Co. v. Burnett, (1917) 176 Ky. 188, 195 S.W. 477; Kraft v. Rochambeau Holding Co., (1956) 210 Md. 325, 123 A. 2d 287; Miller v. M.E. Smith Bldg. Co., (1929) 118 Neb. 5, 223 N.W. 277; Koeppler v. Crocker Chair Co., (1930) 200 Wis 476, 228 N.W. 130.

[141]Zahn v. Transamerica Corp., (1951) 99 F. Supp. 808, subsequent opinion, 100 F. Supp. 461. (This case had a long history in the courts.)

[142]In re Greenebaum Bros. & Co., (1945) 62 F. Supp. 769. While the corporation may redeem only if it has the funds with which to do so, a person who guarantees redemption may be called upon to pay if the corporation does not do so, regardless of whether or not the corporation could be compelled to redeem. Hamilton v. Meiks, (1936) 210 Ind. 610, 4 N.E. 2d 536.

[143]Booth v. Union Fibre Co., (1919) 142 Minn. 127, 171 N.W. 307.

[144]Wildermuth v. Lorain Coal & Dock Co., (1941) 138 Ohio St. 1, 32 N.E. 2d 413.

[145]Peoples-Pittsburgh Trust Co. v. Pittsburgh United Corp., (1940) 338 Pa. 328, 12 A.2d 430.

[146]In re Greenebaum Bros. & Co. (1945) 62 F. Supp. 769.

owner's status as a stockholder is not changed.[147] Of course, if the corporation fails to redeem the stock, the stockholder does not lose any of his rights. Provision for redemption of preferred stock does not ordinarily make the stockholder a creditor of the corporation.[148] The board cannot change a mandatory call for the redemption of stock to an optional call, if the change is detrimental to another class of stock.[149]

The statutes of many of the states provide that, if capital stock is refunded to the stockholders before payment of the corporation's debts, the stockholders shall be liable to creditors of the corporation. They are liable to the amount of the sum refunded to them.[150] A stockholder who accepts the redemption price of stock offered in violation of the redemption provisions of the stock may subject himself to subsequent liability to repay the money received.[151]

Procedure in redeeming stock. The usual practice, in effecting a redemption of stock, is to have the board of directors vote upon a resolution to redeem the shares in accordance with the terms of the contract.[152] After the board calls certain stock for redemption, it cannot rescind or modify its action.[153] The stock is usually made redeemable on a dividend date, in order to avoid any question as to accrued dividends. Notice is generally required; from ten days to several months is not unusual.

Effect of redemption of stock. When a corporation redeems stock, it is in effect purchasing its own shares.[154] The mere fact that it has purchased shares does not mean that the shares are retired.[155] As in the case of an

---

[147]State ex rel. Waldman v. Miller-Wohl Co.; (1942) 42 Del. 73, 28 A. 2d 148. In this case, a clause in the certificate of incorporation provided for redeeming stock "by lot or pro rata, or otherwise." The court held that the method designated by "or otherwise" had to conform in principle with the method designated by "by lot or pro rata." Therefore, selection for redemption of shares belonging to stockholders who were not company officers or employees was an attempt at an illegal redemption.

[148]Kraft v. Rochambeau Holding Company, Inc., (1956) 210 Md. 325, 123 A. 2d 287; In re Culbertson's (1932) 54 F.2d 753; But see Oklahoma Wheat Pool Elevator Corp. v. Bouquet, (1937) 180 Okla. 159, 68 P.2d 97.

[149]Taylor v. Axton-Fisher Tobacco Co., (1943) 295 Ky. 226, 173 S.W.2d 377, discussed in 42 MICH. L. REV. 530.

[150]First Nat'l Bank v. A. Heller Sawdust Co., (1927) 240 Mich. 688, 216 N.W. 464.

[151]In re Fechheimer Fishel Co., (1914) 212 F. 357. See also A.B. Leach & Co. v. Grant, (1932) 54 F.2d 731.

[152]See Hacket v. Northern Pac. R.R., (1901) 36 N.Y. Misc. 583, 73 N.Y. Supp. 1087. In this case, a resolution of the board of directors authorizing the retirement of preferred stock was held to be a valid exercise of the option by the corporation to redeem the preferred stock. The charter of the corporation provided for the management of its affairs by the directors. They were vested with all the powers of the corporation, with certain exceptions. The charter also provided for the retirement of the preferred stock.

[153]Taylor v. Axton-Fisher Tobacco Co., (1943) 295 Ky. 226, 173 S.W. 2d 377.

[154]Mannington v. Hocking Valley Ry., (1910) 183 F. 133.

[155]Borg v. International Silver Co., (1926) 11 F. 2d 143.

ordinary purchase, the corporation may either retire and cancel the redeemed stock or hold it to be reissued. However, if the statute or charter under which the redeemable stock has been issued provides that stock redeemed must be retired and may not be reissued, the corporation has no alternative; it must cancel the shares.

In the case of a redemption, just as in the ordinary repurchase of stock, the capital stock is not reduced where the corporation does not retire the stock but sells and transfers it to others or holds the stock ready for such sale and transfer.[156] When the stock is retired, and a reduction in the capital stock is made, the provisions of the statute with regard to a decrease in the capital stock must be complied with. In a case where the corporation failed to comply with the statute, the retired stock was considered "outstanding capital stock" for franchise tax purposes.[157]

See the corporation's power to purchase its own stock, on page 471.

Assessable stock. Assessable stock is stock upon which the corporation is given the privilege of demanding additional payment after the full consideration has been paid. The corporation has the right to issue such stock in the absence of statutory or charter prohibition. The stockholder is free to make a contract with the corporation waiving certain rights and submitting to certain restrictions,[158] and, having accepted the assessable provision as part of his subscription agreement, he is bound by it.[159]

Difficulty arises where the corporation issues stock without indicating that it is subject to future assessments and then attempts to make such additional assessments. In such cases, as later indicated,[160] assessments upon fully paid stock may be made only if (1) the statute authorizes the assessment, or (2) an express agreement for the assessment, supported by a valid consideration, is made with the stockholder.[161]

A second difficulty arises where an attempt is made to amend the articles so as to permit either the issuance of assessable stock in the future or an assessment to be made upon stock already issued and fully paid. If the statute permits an assessment to be levied, and the articles of incorporation do not contain any provision for such an assessment, the articles may subsequently be amended so as to authorize the issuance in the future of

---

[156]Ruffner v. Sophie Mae Candy Corp., (1925) 35 Ga. App. 114, 132 S.E. 396. See also Porter v. Plymouth Gold Mine Co., (1904) 29 Mont. 347, 74 P. 938, holding that, whether the stock is extinguished or is held as an asset for sale is much a matter of intention on the part of the corporation.

[157]A.B. Frank Co. v. Latham, (1946) 145 Tex. 30, 193 S.W. 2d 671.

[158]Blue Mt. Forest Ass'n v. Borrowe, (1901) 71 N.H. 69, 51 A. 671; Child v. Idaho Hewer Mine (1930) 155 Wash. 280, 284 P. 80.

[160]Stson v. Hoggan, (1914) 44 Utah 295, 140 P. 128.

[161]See Hnter 19, p. 000.

Bergstrom, (1916) v. Northern Blue Grass Land Co., (W.D. Wis., 1911) 185 F. 192; Milton v. A. 788. 197, 70 So. 1008; Johnson v. Tennessee Oil Co., (1908) 74 N.J. Eq. 32, 69

stock that will be subject to assessment.[162] However, as to stock already issued and fully paid, the courts are not in agreement as to whether an amendment making nonassessable fully paid stock assessable affects the contractual relations of the stockholders among themselves, and is an impairment of the obligation of a contract.[163]

Preferred stock issued in series. In some states the certificate of incorporation may authorize the issuance of preferred stock in series. Instead of designating the preferences and other attributes of the authorized stock in the certificate of incorporation, the board of directors is given authority to determine the details of any series issued by resolution adopted upon the issuance of the stock. Under such a statute, if the corporation desires to issue stock with preferences other than those already authorized, no amendment of the certificate of incorporation is necessary, the board of directors having the broad power to determine the particular qualification of the stock by resolution. If the certificate fails to provide for the issuance of stock in series, it may subsequently be amended in the manner prescribed by statute so as to authorize it.

If not prohibited by statute, preferred stock issued in series may be subject to redemption, or it may be converted into another class of stock, or from one series to another. The conversion is made at prices and with such adjustments as are set forth in the articles of incorporation, or in an amendment, or in the resolution adopted by the board of directors for the issuance of the stock.

CONSIDERATION FOR STOCK

Nature of consideration to be paid for stock. The corporation must receive a consideration for the issuance of stock.[164] The nature of this consideration is indicated by the statutes in most of the states. When the

---

[162]La Plante v. Hopper, (1932) 127 Cal. App. 146, 15 P.2d 525; Nelson v. Keith-O'Brien Co., (1907) 32 Utah 396, 91 P. 30.

[163]Amendment held invalid in Garey v. St. Joe Mining Co., (1907) 32 Utah 497, 91 P. 369. Compare Evans v. Nellis, (1900) 101 F. 920, in which an act doubling the liability of stockholders was held invalid. Amendment held valid in South Bay Meadow Dam Co. v. Gray, (1849) 30 Me. 547; Gardner v. Hope Ins. Co., (1869) 9 R.I. 194; Fenton v. Peery Land & Livestock Co., (1955) 3 Utah 2d 156, 280 P. 2d 452. (The court in the Fenton case distinguished the Garey case, above, on the basis of a change in the Utah statute.) See also Wilson v. Cherokee Drift Mining Co., (1939) 14 Cal. 2d 56, 92 P. 2d 802, in which it was held that a corporation could amend its articles to provide for a power of assessment and could assess its stockholders for debts existing prior to the amendment.

[164]Stock issued without consideration was held void in Kahle v. Stephens, (1931) 214 Cal. 89, 4 P.2d 145. See also Rice & Hutchins v. Triplex Shoe Co., (1929) 16 Del. Ch. 298, 147 A. 317, aff'd, (1930) 17 Del. Ch. 356, 152 A. 342; Bryan v. Northwest Beverages, (1939) 69 N.D. 274, 285 N.W. 689. But stock issued without consideration may nevertheless confer rights as stockholders on bona fide holders for value. B. & C. Elec. Constr. Co. v. Owen, (1917) 176 App. Div. 399, 163 N.Y.S. 31, aff'd, (1919) 227 N.Y. 569, 126 N.E. 927.

nature of the consideration is indicated, stock issued for anything else is void.[165] If no special provision is made as to the kind and quality of consideration for which no par stock may be issued, and the laws of the state indicate the nature of consideration for which stock shall be issued, the provision would apply to no par stock as well as to stock with par value.[166]

The usual statutory provision is that stock may be issued for money, labor done, or property actually received.[167] The corporation, in the absence of a statutory or other express provision to the contrary, may issue stock for property or services.[168] This power is subject to the following provisions: (1) the corporation must have the express or implied power under its charter to acquire the property taken or contracted to be taken in payment for the stock, and to contract for the labor;[169] and (2) the action of the corporation in issuing the stock for such consideration must be taken in good faith and not as a fraud upon other stockholders or creditors.[170] The agreement of a stockholder with the corporation to purchase its stock for property or labor, or to accept the stock in payment of a claim against the corporation, is an agreement to take the stock at its par value, in the absence of any special agreement for a different price.[171]

The stock need not be issued to the person who puts up the consideration. For example, two men formed a corporation. One supplied all the property that made up the assets of the corporation. Half the stock was issued to each of them. All the stock was legally issued because the corporation received full value for it.[172]

Notwithstanding the usual prohibition against issuing stock except for

---

[165]Thoms v. Sutherland, (1931) 52 F.2d 592, citing Tooker v. National Sugar Refining Co., (1912) 80 N.J. Eq. 305, 84 A. 10.

[166]Atlantic Refining Co. v. Hodgman, (1926) 13 F. 2d 781; Cohen v. Beneficial Industrial Loan Corp., (1946) 69 F. Supp. 297; Bodell v. General Gas & Elec. Corp., (1926) 15 Del. Ch. 119, 132 A. 442, aff'd, (1927) 15 Del. Ch. 420, 140 A. 264.

[167]Rice & Hutchins v. Triplex Shoe Co., (1929) 16 Del. Ch. 298, 147 A. 317. In some states there are constitutional provisions. See Grafton v. Masteller, (CA-3, 1956) 232 F. 2d 773.

[168]Parrish v. American Ry. etc. Corp., (1927) 83 Cal. App. 298, 256 P. 590; G. Loewus & Co. v. Highland Queen Packing Co., (1939) 125 N.J. Eq. 54, 6A.2d 545.

[169]Stemple v. Bruin, (1909) 57 Fla. 173, 49 So. 151; Kimball v. New England Roller-Grate Co., (1899) 69 N.H. 485, 45 A. 253.

[170]Coffin v. Ransdell, (1887) 110 Ind. 417, 11 N.E. 20; Reed & Fibre Products Corp. v. Rosenthal, (1927) 153 Md. 501, 138 A. 665; Thomas v. Scoutt, (1927) 115 Neb. 848, 215 N.W. 140; New Bern Tire Co. v. Kirkman & Cobb, (1927) 193 N.C. 534, 137 S.E. 585; Crumley v. Crumley Business College, (1927) 120 Ore. 306, 252 P. 85.

[171]San Bernadino County Sav. Bank v. Denman, (1921) 186 Cal. 710, 200 P. 606; Hoffman v. Bloomsburg & S.R. Co., (1893) 157 Pa. St. 174, 27 A. 564. Agreement to pay for stock in services, void under statute, does not make subscriber liable for payment in money. Terrell v. Warten, (1921) 206 Ala. 90, 89 So. 297.

[172]Winston v. Saugerties Farms, Inc., (1941) 262 App. Div. 435, 29 N.Y.S. 2d 292, aff'd, (1942) 287 N.Y. 718, 39 N.E. 2d 934.

money, labor done, or property actually received, a corporation may issue stock as a dividend out of surplus.[173] (See payment of dividends in stock, pages 689-693.) The issuance of a new stock in exchange for outstanding stock also meets the usual requirement for consideration.[174] But a stock option plan, permitting employees to purchase stock at a fixed price, requires some consideraiton,[175] which may be found in the fact that the employee, to exercise his rights in the plan, must continue in the employ of the company.[176] (See also pages 535-536 in Chapter 17.)

Stock issued in satisfaction of a judgment in a consent decree does not meet the requirement, where the judgment satisfied was without adequate consideration of the sort required by the constitution or statute.[177] Also, a court will enjoin a corporation from issuing stock to its president to discharge the corporation's debt allegedly owed to the president, when it is shown (1) the validity and amount of the debt are in dispute, (2) the debt has been outstanding and unclaimed for many years, and (3) the directors issued the stock to insure the president's control of the corporation then being challenged by other stockholders.[178]

Payment for stock in services. In most of the states the statutes provide that stock may be issued for "labor done." But the majority rule is that promotional services cannot be paid for in stock if the statute calls for consideration in the form of money paid, work done, or property actually received.[179] Nevertheless these states frequently recognize the fact that pre-incorporation services may actually be valuable to the corporation. For example, a data processing corporation could not recover shares it issued to an incorporator on the grounds that such issue was without consideration, when it was shown the incorporator expended time and money assessing

---

[173]Gearhart v. Lee-Clay Products Co., (1941) 287 Ky. 316, 152 S.W. 2d 1003; Whetsel v. Forgey, (1929) 323 Mo. 681, 20 S.W. 2d 523.

[174]Shanik v. White Sewing Machine Co., (1941) 25 Del. 371, 19 A.2d 831; Francke v. Axton-Fisher Tobacco Co., (1942) 289 Ky. 687, 160 S.W. 2d 23; Johnson v. Lamprecht, (1938) 133 Ohio St. 567, 15 N.E. 2d 127. But if original stock was void for lack of consideration, the shares for which it is exchanged are likewise void. Rice & Hutchins v. Triplex Shoe Co., (1929) 16 Del. Ch. 298, 147 A. 317, aff'd, (1930) 17 Del. Ch. 356, 152 A. 342.

[175]Holthusen v. Budd Mfg. Co., (1943) 52 F. Supp. 125; Gottlieb v. Heyden Chemical Corp., (1952) 33 Del. Ch. 82, 90 A. 2d 660, limited reargument permitted, 33 Del. Ch. 177, 91 A.2d 57; Kerbs v. California Eastern Airways, (1952) 33 Del. Ch. 69, 90 A.2d 652, reargument denied, 33 Del. Ch. 174, 91 A.2d 62; Note, "Stock Option Plans for Executives," 41 CALIF. L. REV. 535.

[176]Holthusen v. Budd Mfg. Co., (1943) 53 F. Supp. 488; Frankel v. Donovan, (1956) Del. Ch. 120 A.2d 311; Meschel v. Phoenix Hosiery, (1957) 137 N.Y.L.J. No. 94, p. 6; Diamond v. Davis, (1942) 38 N.Y.S. 2d 103 (N.J. law).

[177]Mudd v. Lanier, (1945) 247 Ala. 363, 24 So. 2d 550.

[178]Chicago Stadium Corporaiton v. Scallen, (CA-8, 1976) Nos. 75-1825, 75-1857, 2-10-76.

[179]Cooney v. Arlington Hotel Co., (1917) 11 Del. Ch. 286, 101 A. 879, mod. on other grounds, Du Pont v. Ball, (1918) 11 Del. Ch. 430, 106 A. 39; Kimmel Sales Corp. v. Lauster, (1938) 167 N.Y. Misc. 514, 4 N.Y.S. 2d 88, and cases cited therein.

market prospects, and financed consultations with experts in the field and organized and trained personnel.[180] Also, they may permit stock to be issued for non-promotional services,[181] such as legal services in preparing the charter and by-laws,[182] or for monies expended on its behalf,[183] before the creation of the corporation. In other states, the effect of the statute is to make stock issued for promotional services voidable rather than void, and the defect can be cured if the stockholders consent to the issue.[184] Agreements to render future services are not, however, recognizable consideration for the issuance of stock to promoters.[185] And any issue of stock to promoters must be free from fraud and concealment to be valid.[186]

A corporation cannot legally issue stock to a person upon the sole consideration that that person's name may be used in the corporation,[187] nor can it legally issue stock upon the sole consideration that the corporation shall have the benefit of a certain person's business and financial standing.[188] But the power of a corporation to compensate its agents and officers for services rendered by the issuance of stock is implied from its power to allow suitable compensation to its agents and officers.[189]

Issuance of stock for future services. There is some difference of opinion as to whether stock may be issued for services to be rendered in the future. Some cases have held that, under a statute which prohibits the issuance of stock except for money paid, labor done, or property actually received, services to be rendered in the future cannot be a valid consideration for the issuance of fully paid nonassessable shares.[190] Shares of stock

---

[180]Prickett v. Allen, (Tax Ct. of Civ. App., 1971) 475 S.W. 2d 308; this has been given statutory recognition in some states. See STEVENS, CORPORATION, (2nd ed., 1949) p. 200—201 (footnote 42).

[181]Shore v. Union Drug Co., (1931) 18 Del. Ch. 74, 156 A. 204.

[182]Hackney v. York, (1929) (Tex. Civ. App.) 18 S.W. 2d 923.

[183]Shore v. Union Drug Co., (1931) 18 Del. Ch. 74, 156 A. 204; Geneva Mineral Spring Co. v. Coursey, (1899) 45 App. Div. 268, 61 N.Y. Supp. 98.

[184]Blish v. Thompson Automatic Arms Corp., (1948) 30 Del. Ch. 538, 64 A. 2d 581, Bryan v. Northwest Beverages, Inc., (1939) 69 N.D. 274, 285 N.W. 689; Denis v. Nu-Way Puncture Cure Co., (1919) 170 Wis. 333, 175 N.W. 95. But all stockholders must be informed by notice that they will be called on to ratify action. Blair v. F.H. Smith Co., (1931) 18 Del. Ch. 150, 156 A. 207.

[185]Sarasohn v. Andrew Jergens Co., (1943) 45 N.Y.S. 2d 888. Compare Bryan v. Northwest Beverages, Inc., (1939) 69 N.D. 274, 285 N.W. 689.

[186]State v. Bellin, (1935) 55 R.I. 374, 181 A. 804.

[187]Bowen v. Imperial Theatres, (1922) 13 Del. Ch. 120, 115 A. 918.

[188]B. & C. Elec. Constr. Co. v. Owen, (1917) 176 App. Div. 399, 163 N.Y.S. 31, aff'd. (1919) 227 N.Y. 569, 126 N.E. 927. See also Brown v. Watson, (1955) 285 App. Div. 587, 139 N.Y.S. 2d 628.

[189]Rogers v. Guaranty Trust Co., (1932) 60 F. 2d 114. See, however, Morgan v. Bon Bon Co., (1917) 222 N.Y. 22, 118 N.E. 205.

[190]Blair v. F.H. Smith Co., (1931) 18 Del. Ch. 150, 156 A. 207; Scully v. Automobile Finance Co., (1920) 12 Del. Ch. 174, 109 A. 49; Mas Patent Bottle Corp. v. Cox, (1932) 163 Md. 176, 161 A. 243; B. & C. Elec. Constr. Co. v. Owen, (1917) 176 App. Div. 399, 163 N.Y.S. 31, aff'd. (1919) 227 N.Y. 569, 126 N.E. 927; Stevens v. Episcopal Church History Co., (1910) 140 App. Div. 570, 125 N.Y. Supp. 573. But constitutional prohibition, without implementing statute, will not make such stock void. Grafton v. Masteller, (CA-3, 1956) 232 F. 2d 773. Compare, however, Gearhart v. Standard Steel Car Co., (1909) 233 Pa. 385, 72 A. 699.

may be issued, however, for services to be rendered as long as they are not marked "fully paid" until the services have been rendered.[191] A contract providing for the future delivery of stock if and when certain services are performed has been upheld.[192] There is some authority which supports the issuance of stock for services to be performed in the future if the transaction is bona fide.[193]

Valuation of services accepted in payment of stock. Services accepted in payment for stock must be reasonably worth the face value of the stock given therefor. The principles concerning the issuance of stock for overvalued property, discussed on pages 460-466, are equally applicable to the issuance of stock for overvalued services.[194]

The statutes of some of the states require that, where stock is issued for a consideration other than money, the board of directors shall by resolution state its opinion of the actual value of any consideration other than money for which it authorizes such stock to be issued.[195] In some states a statement must be filed with a designated official showing the valuation of services or property received for stock issued. Where such statutes exist, a resolution should be passed by the directors, or by those having authority to authorize the issuance of stock, showing the price paid or to be paid for the labor for which the stock is to be issued. As a matter of good practice, such a resolution should be presented, adopted, and recorded in the minutes of the corporation, even where no formal resolution valuing the labor done is required by statute.[196]

Payment for stock in notes. In a few states, the statutes specifically provide that a promissory note shall not be accepted in payment for stock.[197] These statutes apply to stock issued after the corporation is a going concern, as well as to subscriptions before organization.[198] However, they

---

[191]Scully v. Automobile Finance Co., (1920) 12 El. Ch. 174, 109 A. 49. Stock issued for future services is voidable, not void. Sarasohn v. Andrew Jergens Co., (1943) 45 N.Y.S. 2d 888.

[192]McQuillen v. National Cash Register Co., (1939) 27 F. Supp. 639, aff'd, (1940) 112 F. 2d 877, cert. denied, (1940) 311 U.S. 695, 61 S. Ct. 140.

[193]Irwin v. Prestressed Structures, Inc., (Tex. Ct. of Civ. App., 1969) 442 S.W. 2d 406; Shannon v. Stevenson, (1896) 173 Pa. St. 419, 34 A. 218, in which it was said that a proviso that no stock shall be issued "except for money, labor done, or money or property actually received" does not prevent either payment for bona fide labor or services to be thereafter rendered, or contracts to pay in advance for property to be furnished. (However, in this case, the services had apparently already been performed.) See also Vogeler v. Punch, (1907) 205 Mo. 558, 103 S.W. 1001; Vineland Grape Juice Co. v. Shandler, (1912) 80 N.J. Eq. 437, 85 A. 213.

[194]Chouteau, Harrison & Valle v. Dan, (1879) 7 Mo. App. 210.

[195]But directors cannot evaluate their own services and determine the amount of stock to be issued therefore. Maclary v. Pleasant Hills, Inc., (1954) Del. Ch. 109 A. 2d 830.

[196]See Bowen v. Imperial Theatres, (1922) 13 Del. Ch., 120, 115 A. 918.

[197]See, for example, State v. Stookey, (1953) 95 Ohio App. 97, 113 N.E. 2d 254.

[198]Graves v. Commissioner of Int. Rev., (1953) 202 F. 2d 286, cert. denied, 346 U.S. 812, 74 S. Ct. 21; Merchants Bank & Trust Co. v. Walker, (1942) 192 Miss. 737, 6 So. 2d 107.

do not usually forbid the substitution of a note for a subscription contract as evidence of indebtedness.[199]

In states where there is no such express prohibition against the acceptance of notes but where the statute provides that stock may be issued only for money, labor done, or property actually received, the courts have differed in their decisions as to whether or not a promissory note can be included in the term "property actually received."[200] Decisions fall, generally, into two groups. In the first group are those cases that regard a note as personal property and hence a valid consideration for the issuance of stock.[201] In the second group are those that ordinarily regard the note merely as a promise to pay and not as property.[202] This is the majority position. However, if something in addition is given with the note, such as the indorsement of a financially responsible person or a valid first mortgage on real estate, the note is considered as property and sufficient consideration to support the issue of stock.[203] In jurisdictions following the majority position, if the stock is not actually issued and the purchaser is not recognized as a stockholder until after the note has been paid, there is no violation of the provision prohibiting the issuance of stock other than for money, labor done, or property actually received.[204] For example, a corporation cannot issue stock when payment for it is made by a promissory note, but such issue becomes valid when the note is paid in full, since payment by note is only a voidable transaction, not void.[205]

In many jurisdictions, a note accepted in payment for stock and the stock issued therefore are not necessarily void, even though the note may

---

[199]Thomas v. Arkansas State Fair Ass'n, (1930) 181 Ark. 748, 27 S.W. 2d 515; In re Gillham's Estate, (1936) 286 Ill. App. 370, 3 N.E. 2d 524.

[200]See Paskus, "The 'Illegal' Creation of Shares in Return for Notes," 39 YALE L.J. 706; Waterman, "The Creation of Corporate Shares in Return for Promissory Notes," 7 TEXAS L. REV. 215.

[201]See Pacific Trust Co. v. Dorsey, (1886) 72 Cal. 55, 12 P. 49; Meholin v. Carlson, (1910) 17 Idaho 742, 107 P. 755; German Mercantile Co. v. Wanner, (1913) 25 N.D. 479, 142 N.W. 463; Empire Holding Corp. v. Coshow, (1935) 150 Ore. 252, 41 P. 2d 426; Schiller Piano Co. v. Hyde, (1917) 39 S.D. 74, 162 N.W. 937.

[202]Teehan v. United States, (1928) 25 F. 2d 884, states the rule applying in these cases: "It is settled law that, where a statute or a constitutional provision permits a corporation to issue stock only for money paid, services rendered, or property actually received, stock issued for notes of the shareholder is not stock legally issued." See Graves v. Commissioner of Int. Rev., (1953) 202 F.2d 286, Cert. denied, 346 U.S. 812, 745 Ct. 21; Lepanto Gin Co. v. Barnes, (1930) 182 Ark, 422, 31 S.W. 2d 746; Sohland v. Baker, (1927) 15 Del. Ch. 431, 141 A. 277. See also Bank of Commerce v. Goolsby, (1917) 129 Ark. 416, 196 S.W. 803; Lofland v. Cahall, (1922) 13 Del. Ch. 384, 118 A. 1; Arndt v. Abbott, (1941) 308 Ill. App. 633, 32 N.E. 2d 342; Shafer v. Home Trading Co., (1932) 227 Mo. App. 347, 52 S.W. 2d 462; Southwestern Tank Co. v. Morrow, (1925) 115 Okla. 97, 241 P. 1097; Dunagan v. Bushey, (1953) 152 Tex. 630, 263 S.W. 2d 148.

[203]Harn v. Smith, (1922) 85 Okla. 137, 204 P. 642; General Bonding & Cas. Ins. Co. v. Moseley, (1920) 110 Tex. 529, 222 S.W. 961; Opinion, Attorney General, Texas, to Secretary of State, 4-25-47, No. V-163, Contra: Graves v. Commissioner of Int. Rev., (1953) 202 F.2d 286, cert. denied, 346 U.S. 812, 745 Ct. 21.

[204]Smith v. McAdams, (1918) (Tex. Civ. App.) 206 S.W. 955.

[205]Area, Inc. v. Stetenfeld, (Alaska, S. Ct., 1975) 541 P.2d 755.

not be a valid payment.[206] The note may be enforced against the maker in a suit by the corporation or its trustee in bankruptcy.[207] The provisions of the statute that stock shall be issued only for money paid, for labor done, or for property actually received are intended for the protection of the corporation, its creditors and other stockholders, and not for the relief of the offending stockholder.[208] At least in one jurisdiction, however, the note is not enforceable by the corporation or holders who knew that the note was given for stock.[209]

Payment for stock in property. In each state the constitution or the statute, directly or indirectly, sanctions the issuance of capital stock for property. These provisions differ in their requirements regarding: (1) the kinds of property which the corporation may accept in payment for stock; (2) the procedure to be followed in authorizing the issuance of stock for property; (3) the method of valuing the property; and (4) the liability resulting from the issuance of stock for overvalued property.

Kinds of property acceptable in payment of stock. In a few states the statutes indicate that real and personal property may be received in payment for stock; in others, in addition to real and personal property, such property as mining rights, patent rights, rights of way, goodwill, and contracts are specifically made acceptable. If the statutes do not expressly enumerate the kinds of property that the corporation may accept for its stock, it is generally held that the corporation may accept real or personal property. Such property, however, must be of the kind that the corporation has the power to acquire and hold in carrying out the objects and purposes for which it was organized. Or it must be of the kind in which the corporation is authorized by statute to invest its funds.[210] Patents,[211]

---

[206]Joy v. Godchaux, (1929) 35 F.2d 649; Teehan v. United States, (1928) 25 F. 2d 884; Lofland v. Cahall, (1922) 13 Del. Ch. 384, 118 A. 1; Washer v. Smyer, (1909) 109 Tex. 398, 211 S.W. 985. But see General Beverages Inc. v. Rogers, (1954) 216 F.2d 413 (Ala. law); Lepanto v. Barnes, (1930) 182 Ark. 442, 31 S.W. 2d 746; Aldridge v. Rice, (1932) 161 Miss. 879, 138 So. 570; Shafer v. Home Trading Co., (1932) 227 Mo. App. 347, 52 S.W. 2d 426; Southwestern Tank Co. v. Morrow, (1925) 115 Okla. 97, 241 P. 1097.

[207]Backus v. Hutson, (1930) 136 N.Y. Misc. 290, 240 N.Y. Supp. 610.

[208]Theunissen v. Continental Trust Co., (1926) 15 F.2d 894; Bell v. Aubel, (1943) 151 Pa. Super. 569, 30 A.2d 617; Washer v. Smyer, (1909) 109 Tex. 398, 211 S.W. 985.

[209]Western Nat'l Bank v. Spencer, (1922) 112 Tex. 49, 244 S.W. 123.

[210]Harn v. Smith, (1922) 85 Okla. 137, 204 P. 642.

[211]West v. Sirian Lamp Co., (1944) 28 Del. Ch. 90, 37 A.2d 835, s.c., (1945) 28 Del. Ch. 328, 42 A.2d 883, 28 Del. Ch. 398, 44 A.2d 658; Atlas Trailers and Water Mufflers v. McCallum, (1929) 118 Tex. 173, 12 S.W.2d 957. But worthless patents are not considered "property." Edgerton v. Electric Improvement & Constr. Co., (1892) 50 N.J. Eq. 354, 24 A. 540. However, a board of directors' failure to set the value of a patent received as consideration for corporate stock did not nullify the stock issue, since the requirement that the board determine the value of property received for stock is not mandatory, and so absent bad faith, court can set relative value of property as of the date received. Crowder v. Electro-Kinetics Corp., (Ga. S. Ct., 1972) 187 S.E. 2d 249.

trade-marks,[212] formulas,[213] applications for patents,[214] mines, leases,[215] and the assignments of contracts[216] are a few kinds of property which may be received. Extension of the due date of a mortgage has been held to be sufficient consideration for the issuance of stock;[217] also conveyance of the equity in mortgaged property, to avoid expense of litigation,[218] and the release of a valid claim against the corporation.[219] A license to use certain trade-marks that is considerably broader than a prior license is good consideration for stock.[220]

A corporation may accept stock in another corporation, in payment for its stock, if the corporation has the power to hold stock in other corporations.[221] The corporation may not issue its stock, however, for the worthless stock of some other corporation.[222]

A corporation may discharge its indebtedness to a subscriber to whom it has issued its stock by writing off the indebtedness on its books, and crediting the amount to the subscriber in payment for his stock. To effect this result it is not necessary to go through the formality of having the subscriber pay for his stock and the corporation return to him a sum sufficient to discharge the indebtedness.[223]

What constitutes value in property acceptable in payment for stock. While property accepted in payment for stock need not have a market value, nevertheless, in order to constitute a satisfactory consideration for the issuance of stock, it must have a commercial value.[224] For example, the anticipated profits of an executory contract may give commercial value to a contract, so that an assignment of it may be accepted in

---

[212]Brown v. Weeks, (1917) 195 Mich. 27, 161 N.W. 945.

[213]Murray v. Murray Laboratories, (1954) 223 Ark. 907, 270 S.W.2d 927. But unpatentable formulas, and formulas and processes with no substantial value, are not sufficient consideration. Trotta v. Metalmold, (1953) 139 Conn. 668, 96 A.2d 798; Webster v. Okmulgee Webster Refining Co., (1912) 36 Okla. 168, 128 P.261; O'Bear-Nester Glass Co. v. Antiexplo Co., (1908) 101 Tex. 431, 109 S.W. 931.

[214]Hills v. Skagit Steel & Iron Works, (1922) 122 Wash. 22, 210 P. 17.

[215]Seches v. Bard, (1931) 67 Cal. App. 374, 4 P.2d 167; McAlister v. Eclipse Oil Co., (1936) 128 Tex. 449, 98 S.W.2d 171.

[216]Ainscow v. Potter, (1937) 22 Del. Ch. 138, 193 A. 926; Miller v. Youmans-Burke Oil & Gas Co., (1937) 278 Mich. 647, 270 N.W. 819.

[217]Burge v. Midway Pacific Oil Co., (1929) 99 Cal. App. 714, 279 P. 181; 28 MICH. L. REV. 1048.

[218]Morris v. North Evanston Manor Building Corp., (1943) 319 Ill. App. 298, 49 N.E. 2d 646.

[219]United States v. Cole, (1950) 90 F. Supp. 147; Blish v. Thompson Automatic Arms Corp., (1948) 30 Del. Ch. 538, 64 A.2d 581. See also Reed v. Norman, (1953) 41 Cal. 2d 17, 256 P.2d 930.

[220]Sarasohn v. Andrew Jergens Co., (1943) 45 N.Y.S. 2d 888.

[221]Southern Trust & Deposit Co. v. Yeatman, (1905) 134 F. 810; Shanik v. White Sewing Mach. Co., (1941) 25 Del. 371, 19 A.2d 831; Mitchell v. Mitchell Woodbury Co., (1928) 263 Mass. 160, 160 N.E. 539.

[222]Loring v. Lamson & Hubbard Corp., (1924) 249 Mass. 272, 143 N.E. 916.

[223]Rogers v. H.S. Kerbaugh, Inc., (1921) 190 N.Y. Supp. 245.

[224]Kunkle v. Soule, (1920) 68 Colo. 524, 190 P. 536.

payment for stock.[225] The mere pretended exercise of judgment by the directors cannot give value to that which has no value.[226] Thus, a business idea which is not salable or transferable, that is, an idea which others have used and which anyone can use freely, has no commercial value and does not constitute a consideration for stock.[227] Equal value in property, dollar for dollar, need not be received for stock. It is sufficient if the amount received reasonably approximates the amount of stock issued.[228]

The goodwill of a business may be accepted in payment of stock,[229] but the goodwill must have value.[230] There is no value in the goodwill of a business which has never been profitable, even though the business when taken over is a going concern.[231]

But the "going concern value" can be considered in evaluating the property.[232] The goodwill, prestige, and influence of subscribers in assisting in selling stock is not sufficient consideration.[233]

Procedure in authorizing issuance of stock for property. The procedure to be followed in authorizing the issuance of stock for property depends upon the requirements of the statutes of the state in which the corporation is organized, and upon the provisions of the charter and by-laws of the corporation. In many states, the statutes require the corporation to keep a record showing the nature of property accepted in payment of stock, as well as the value of the property. Some of the states require that upon issuance of stock for a consideration other than cash, a certificate be filed with the Secretary of State, or some other designated official. Substantial compliance with these statutory provisions is required.

Ordinarily authority to value property and issue stock for it is vested under the statute or charter in the board of directors. In this case only the board can act in the matter. The minutes of the directors' meeting should contain an entry of the valuation of the property. However, failure to

---

[225]Ewing v. Swenson, (1926) 167 Minn. 113, 208 N.W. 645.

[226]Scully v. Automobile Finance Co., (1920) 12 Del. 174, 109 A. 49; Ellis v. Penn Beef Co., (1911) 9 Del. Ch. 213, 80 A. 666.

[227]Scully v. Automobile Finance Co., (1920) 12 Del. 174, 109 A. 49.

[228]Park v. Compton, (1932) 55 F. 2d 80.

[229]Randall v. Bailey, (1940) 23 N.Y.S. 2d 173; Bryan v. Northwest Beverages, Inc., (1939) 69 N.D. 274, 285 N.W. 689. A contract under which stock was issued in consideration of an agreement not to sell certain photographic paper in designated countries was upheld where the restrictive covenant was incidental to the sale of the business. Thoms v. Sutherland, (1931) 52 F.2d 592, citing Tooker v. National Sugar Refining Co., (1912) 80 N.J. Eq. 305, 84A. 10, discussed in 30 MICH. L. REV. 971.

[230]Linden Bros. v. Practical Electricity & Engineering Publishing Co., (1923) 309 Ill. 132, 140 N.E. 874; Hodde v. Hahn, (1920) 283 Mo. 320, 222 S.W. 799.

[231]Linden Bros. v. Practical Electricity & Engineering Publishing Co., (1923) 309 Ill. 132, 140 N.E. 874; William E. Dee Co. v. Proviso Coal Co., (1919) 290 Ill. 252, 125 N.E. 24.

[232]Randall v. Bailey, (1940) 23 N.Y.S. 2d 173.

[233]Laing v. Hutton, (1932) 138 Ore. 307, 6 P.2d 884.

include such a record of the transaction will not invalidate it if appropriate corporate action was taken.[234]

Offers to exchange property for stock of a corporation to be organized may be considered at the first meeting of incorporators, directors, or stockholders. However, if the meeting is being held by dummy incorporators or directors, it is not advisable to pass upon such matters as contracts concerning the purchase of property by the corporation. Consideration and vote upon such contracts should be postponed until a meeting in which the actual incorporators, directors, or stockholders participate.

Usually, authority to value property and issue stock therefor is vested in the board of directors, under the statute or charter, in which case only the board of directors can act in the matter. The board must consider and accept the offer, value the property, authorize the issuance of the stock and comply with any additional applicable statutory provisions, such as provisions requiring the approval of a commission under Blue-Sky laws or the filing of a certificate in a designated state office or with a designated state official, before the stock is actually issued.

The directors' minutes should contain an entry of the valuation of the property accepted in payment for stock, whether required by statute or not. However, the failure to include in the minutes a record of the transaction concerning the authorization of the issuance of stock and the valuation of property, will not invalidate the transaction if appropriate corporate action was taken.[235]

For special minutes to be kept by corporations subject to statutes imposing a personal liability upon directors who participate in issuance of stock for overvalued property, see pages 162-163 in Chapter 5.

Method of valuing property received in payment for stock. The issuance of stock for property always involves a valuation of the property to be acquired in exchange for the stock. The corporation laws or constitution of most of the states indicate the method of valuing property for the purpose of issuing stock therefor. The most usual statutory provision is that the corporation may issue stock to the amount of the value of the property taken in payment; the judgment of the directors as to the value of the property purchased is conclusive, in the absence of fraud.[236] Other statutory provi-

---

[234]Whitlock v. Alexander, (1912) 160 N.C. 465, 76 S.E. 538. See also East Lake Lumber Co. v. Van Gorder, (1919) 105 N.Y. Misc. 704, 174 N.Y. Supp. 38. But see Bowen v. Imperial Theatres, Inc., (1922) 13 Del. Ch. 120, 115 A. 918.

[235]Whitlock v. Alexander, (1912) 160 N.C. 465, 76 S.E. 538. See also East Lake Lumber Co. v. Gorder, (1919) 105 Misc. 704, 174 N.Y.S. 38, leave to appeal denied, 189 App. Div. 884, 177 N.Y.S. 914.

[236]See Miller v. Youmans-Burke Oil & Gas Co., (1937) 278 Mich. 647; 270 N.W. 819; Compton v. Perkins, (1933) 144 Ore. 346, 24 P.2d 670. In many cases the discretion of the board may be limited or curtailed as a result of statutes such as public service regulations or blue-sky laws. See, for example, Moore v. Moffat, (1922) 188 Cal. 1, 204 P. 220; Peden Iron & Steel Co. v. Jenkins, (1918) (Tex. Civ. App.) 203 S.W. 180.

sions permit the acquisition of property at (1) its reasonable value, (2) its actual value, (3) a bona fide and fair value, (4) its actual cash value, or (5) its true money value.

Under the usual statutory provision that the judgment of the directors as to the value of the property is conclusive, in the absence of fraud, a stockholder is protected from demands for further payment on account of stock acquired by him in exchange from property. He must, however, show that his property was accepted by the corporation in payment for his stock at a valuation determined by the board of directors. This protection is lost only when actual fraud in the transaction is shown by one who alleges that the stockholder has not paid for his stock in money or money's worth.[237]

If the statute makes the directors' judgment conclusive, they must make an honest attempt to determine the value of property taken in exchange for stock.[238] They must act in the interests of the corporation and secure for it all that it is justly entitled to. Anything less than that is dishonest and fraudulent.[239] Thus a conscious overvaluation by the directors constitutes fraud.[240] The directors may exercise very poor judgment, or may make a mistake, in the valuation of the property. If, in doing so, they act fairly and honestly and not in furtherance of their own interests, the valuation they arrive at is conclusive.[241] Property is not considered overvalued merely because it subsequently turns out to be so, if the valuation has been made in good faith.[242] Nor does the fact that the corporation may have to spend money to protect its property rights in the future necessarily make the consideration invalid.[243]

"Good faith" and "true value" rules of valuation of property received for stock. The valuation fixed by the board of directors for property received by the corporation in payment for stock must meet the tests applied by the courts in passing upon the value fixed. Two rules have been developed to test such valuation, the "true value" rule and the "good faith" rule. Which of these rules shall be applied in a given case depends

---

[237]Lamprecht v. Swiss Oil Corp., (1929) 32 F.2d 646; New Bern Tire Co. v. Kirkman & Cobb (1927) 193 N.C. 534, 137 S.E. 585. See also Sokoloff v. Wildwood Pier & Realty Co., (1931) 108 N.J. Eq. 362, 155 A. 125.

[238]Bowen v. Imperial Theatres, Inc., (1922) 13 Del. Ch. 120, 115 A. 918. Directors cannot delegate this statutory duty to an independent appraiser but they can employ assistance in their appraisal. Field v. Carlisle Corp., (1949) 31 Del. Ch. 227, 68 A. 2d 817.

[239]Rugger v. Mt. Hood Elec. Co., (1933) 143 Ore. 193, 20 P.2d 412.

[240]Scully v. Automobile Finance Co., (1920) 12 Del. Ch. 174, 109 A. 49.

[241]Alpha Portland Cement Co. v. Schratweiser, (1915) 221 F. 258. Judgment not conclusive when majority of directors have personal interest in property being valued. Compton v. Perkins, (1933) 144 Ore. 346, 24 P.2d 670. See also Bennett v. Breuil Petroleum Corp., (1953) Del. Ch. 99 A.2d 236.

[242]Smith v. Schmitt, (1924) 112 Ore. 687, 231 P. 176. See also H.B. Humphrey Co. v. Pollack Roller Runner Sled Co., (1932) 378 Mass. 350, 180 N.E. 164; Tintic Indian Chief Mining & Milling Co. v. Clyde, (1932) 79 Utah 337, 10 P.2d 932.

[243]West v. Sirian Lamp Co., (1944) 28 Del. Ch. 90, 37 A.2d 835, S.C., (1945) 28 Del. Ch. 328, 42 A. 2d 883, 28 Del. Ch. 398, 44 A.2d 658.

upon the decisions of the state in which the corporation issuing the stock is organized. In states in which the "true value" rule is followed, the motive, intent, or good faith of those valuing the property is disregarded. The subscriber must show that the property given for the stock was worth in dollars, at the time of the transaction, the face value of the shares, or the value that was authorized to be received for the issue.[244] In most states the "good faith" rule is followed. It is the presence or absence of good faith on the part of the directors, or others making the valuation, which determines the sufficiency or insufficiency of the value fixed. The only difficulty encountered in applying the good faith rule is in determining what constitutes good faith.[245] Some of the decisions hold that, in the absence of an affirmative showing of fraud, mere overvaluation of the property given in exchange for stock will not render the stockholder liable for the difference between the amount paid and the value of the stock received. Of course, an affirmative showing of fraud will render the stockholder liable for the difference between the amount paid and the value of the stock received.[246] Others hold that gross overvaluation itself constitutes, or at least raises a strong presumption of, fraud.[247]

Liability of directors upon issuance of stock for overvalued property. In some states, the statutes impose a personal liability upon directors who participate in the issuance of stock for overvalued property. Where these laws are in force, the corporate minutes should record the names of the directors voting for the issuance of stock for property at the value fixed. Where the law also provides that directors, in order to escape personal liability for the acts of their fellow directors in authorizing the issuance of stock for overvalued property, must enter their dissent from the valuation in writing, the dissents should appear in the minutes.

Liability for payment of stock issued for overvalued property or for property not legal payment. Stock issued for overvalued property is

---

[244]See, for example, Detroit-Kentucky Coal Co. v. Bickett, (1918) 251 F. 542; Tramp v. Marquesen, (1920) 188 Iowa 968, 176 N.W. 977; Lavell v. Bullock, (1919) 43 N.D. 135, 174 N.W. 764. The true value rule was largely applied only in cases involving claims of creditors, and has now been abandoned in most states formerly following it. See, for example, Strickland v. Washington Bldg. Corp., (1936) 287 Ill. App. 340, 4 N.E. 2d 973.

[245]Following are some cases in which the "good faith" rule has been followed: Coit v. Gold Amalgamating Co., (1886) 119 U.S. 343; Clinton Mining & Mineral Co. v. Jamison, (1919) 256 F. 577; Winters v. Lindsay, (1921) 52 Cal. App. 93, 198 P. 43; West v. Sirian Lamp Co., (1944) 28 Del. Ch. 90, 37 A. 2d 835, S.C. (1945) 28 Del. Ch. 328, 42 A. 2d 883, 28 Del. Ch. 398, 44 A. 2d 658; Diamond State Brewery, Inc. v. De La Rigaudiere, (1941) 25 Del. Ch. 257, 17 A.2d 313; Miller v. Youmans-Burke Oil & Gas Co., (1937) 278 Mich. 647, 270 N.W. 819; Johansen v. St. Louis Union Trust Co., (1939) 345 Mo. 135, 131 S.W. 2d 599 (Fla. law); Caldwell v. Robinson, (1920) 179 N.C. 518, 103 S.E. 75.

[246]Johansen v. St. Louis Union Trust Co., (1939) 345 Mo. 135, 131 S.W. 2d 599 (Fla. law).

[247]Tapanga Corp. v. Gentile, (1967) 1 Cal. App. 3d 572, 81 Cal. Rptr. 863; Kennedy, Jr. v. Emerald Coal & Coke Co., (Del. Ch. Ct., 1942) 28A. 2d 433, aff'd., (Del. S. Ct., 1944) 42A. 2d 398, cert den., (U.S.S. Ct., 1945) 324 U.S. 872, 65 S. Ct. 1017; Scully v. Automobile Finance Co., (1920) 12 Del. Ch. 174, 109 A. 49; State Trust Co. v. Turner, (1900) 111 Iowa 664, 82 N.W. 1029.

commonly called "watered" stock.[248] Since the corporation may not issue watered stock, questions arise as to the rights and liabilities of parties involved in case the corporation does issue stock for overvalued property. Similar questions arise: (1) when stock is issued at less than par value in violation of a provision prohibiting the issue of stock at less than par value; (2) when stock is issued for an illegal consideration; (3) when, in violation of a statute, fully paid certificates are issued before full payment has been received; and (4) when any fraudulent issue of stock has been made. The parties involved in such transactions are the corporation, the stockholders, subsequent transferees, and creditors. Their rights and liabilities depend upon the nature of the transaction, that is, whether it is fraudulent, illegal, or ultra vires. If the corporation's action in issuing watered stock is a fraud upon the public, the state may institute proceedings to forfeit the corporation's charter for misusing or abusing its franchise.[249]

A contract to issue stock is illegal if it is made in violation of some statutory, constitutional, or charter provision. Illegal contracts are generally not enforceable either by or against the corporation. Thus, under a statute requiring that par value shares shall be issued only for a consideration equal to the par value, an executory stock subscription agreement for the issuance of stock for money less than the par value is not enforceable and, if the illegal contract has been executed, neither the corporation nor the person with whom the contract was made may bring a suit for relief from the effects of the contract.[250]

The rights and liabilities of parties involved in an ultra vires contract to issue stock for an inadequate payment—that is, a contract beyond the powers of the corporation—are governed by the same principles that apply to ultra vires contracts in general. Thus, if an ultra vires contract to issue stock for overvalued property is still to be performed, the contract is void and will not be enforced.[251] If an ultra vires contract to issue watered stock has been executed, the transaction cannot be questioned by the corporation, or by stockholders who have consented to the transaction. Stockholders who dissent, however, have the right to enjoin the issuance of watered stock under an executory ultra vires contract.[252]

---

[248]The term "watered stock" embraces a variety of transactions, classified as follows in Thomason v. Miller, (1928) (Tex. Civ. App.) 4 S.W. 2d 668:
   "1. Where stock is issued as a bonus or otherwise without consideration.
   "2. Where it is issued for a less sum of money than par value.
   "3. Where it is issued for labor, services, or property which at a fair valuation is less than par."
   A distinction is sometimes made between bonus stock and watered stock. See 17 PHIL. L.J. 85.
[249]State v. New Orleans Debenture Redemption Co., (1899) 51 La. Ann. 1827, 26 So. 586.
[250]Stone v. Young, (1924) 210 App. Div. 303, 206 N.Y. Supp. 95; Pacific American Gasoline Co. v. Miller, (1934) (Tex. Civ. App.) 76 S.W. 2d 833.
[251]Garret v. Kansas City Coal Mining Co., (1892) 113 Mo. 330, 20 S.W. 965; Zelaya Mining Co. v. Meyer, (1890) 8 N.Y. Supp. 487.
[252]Fisk v. Chicago, R.I. & P. R.R., (1868) 53 Barb. (N.Y.) 513.

Position of the corporation upon issuance of stock for overvalued property. A corporation that has issued stock as fully paid, without getting full value for it, cannot afterward repudiate the transaction, if there is no express statutory or charter provision declaring such a transaction void, and if the stockholders have unanimously consented to the issue.[253] It cannot exclude the holders of the stock from participating in the company's affairs. Nor can it compel them to pay the difference between the face value of the stock and what has been paid or agreed upon as full payment. As between the corporation and the stockholders, the corporation has no claim after taking property in full payment for stock.[254] (See stockholders' liability to creditors, on page 464.)

Many of the statutes that provide that no corporation shall issue stock except for money, for labor done, or for property actually received also declare that all fictitious increases of stock shall be void. Under such a constitutional or statutory provision, stock issued purely as a gratuity, nothing having been received in payment, has been held to be void; the person to whom such stock was issued obtained no rights as against the corporation.[255] But, under such a statute, where some value had been given for the stock, only the part of the stock which was in excess of the payment received was held to be fictitious and voidable at the suit of the corporation.[256]

The position of subscribers and stockholders upon issuance of stock for overvalued property. A stockholder who has paid full value for his shares, or a subscriber who undertakes to pay for his shares in full, has the right to assume that every other stockholder or subscriber has paid or will pay full consideration for his stock. However, a stockholder who assents to an issue of stock for payment not equal to the value of the shares issued therefor cannot complain against the issue of the fictitiously paid-up stock.[257] Nor can he complain, if, with knowledge of the facts, he does not

---

[253]Scovill v. Thayer, (1881) 105 U.S. 143; In re Associated Oil Co., (1923) 289 F. 963 (S.D. law); Ackerman Tool & Constr. Co. v. McArthur, (1954) (La. App.) 73 So. 2d 507; Grants Pass Hardware Co. v. Calvert, (1914) 71 Ore. 103, 142 P. 569; Vasey v. New Export Coal Co., (1921) 89 W. Va. 491, 109 S.E. 619. Compare Cooney v. Arlington Hotel Co., (1917) 11 Del. Ch. 286, 101 A. 879.

[254]Martin v. Heymann, (1929) 251 Ill. App. 89; Heidler v. Werner & Co., (1924) 95 N.J. Eq. 374, 124 A. 49.

[255]Clark v. Milsap, (1926) 197 Cal. 765, 242 P. 918; L.J. Mueller Furnace Co. v. Holmes, (1921) 175 Wis. 518, 185 N.W. 641. See also Wells v. Comstock, (1956) 46 Cal. 2d 528, 297 P. 2d 961.

[256]Belle Isle Corp. v. MacBean, (Del. Ch. Ct., 1946) 49 A.2d 5; Rice v. Thomas, (1919) 184 Ky. 168, 211 S.W. 428; Taylor v. Citizens' Oil Co., (1918) 182 Ky. 350, 206 S.W. 644.

[257]In re Charles Town Light & Power Co., (1912) 199 F. 846; Topkis v. Delaware Hardware Co., (1938) 23 Del. Ch. 125, 2A 2d 114; Vasey v. New Export Coal Co., (1921) 89 W.Va. 491, 109 S.E. 619.

object to the transaction within a reasonable time.[258] If a stockholder has not voluntarily assented to or acquiesced in an issuance of fully paid shares for a consideration less than par, or for property not equal in value to the stock issued for it, he may file a bill to annul the entire transaction.[259] Directors have been known to vote themselves unissued stock at a reduced price, in consideration of "a large amount of labor and weighty responsibilities." Dissenting stockholders can compel them to pay the full price for the stock and certificates.[260]

In some jurisdictions, if the issue has been made in violation of the constitution or statute, the dissenting stockholder can compel the surrender for cancellation of all stock in excess of the value paid.[261] A stockholder who dissents to a proposal to issue stock for less than its full value may enjoin the corporation from issuing the stock, if the proposed transaction violates the rights of existing stockholders, or the provisions of the constitution, the statute, or the corporation's charter.[262]

According to the weight of authority, if fraud has been committed against creditors or stockholders who have paid for their stock in full, the holders of the watered stock, or fictitiously paid up stock, can be compelled to pay the difference between the amount actually paid for the stock and the par value, or value authorized to be received in return for the stock.[263] Only persons defrauded can obtain relief on the ground of fraud.

Position of the transferee of overvalued or watered stock. The rights of those who have become owners of watered or fictitiously paid up stock by purchase or transfer from a previous stockholder or subscriber generally depend upon whether the transferee acquired the stock with or without knowledge of the true state of the original transaction. An innocent purchaser of a certificate marked "fully paid and nonassessable," but not in fact fully paid, has the right to maintain an action for damages against those who defrauded him, or against the corporation if it is guilty of deception.[264] On the other hand, a transferee with knowledge, or one to whom know-

---

[258]Taylor v. S. & N. Alabama R.R., (1882) 13 F. 152; Keeney v. Converse, (1894) 99 Mich. 316, 58 N.W. 325.

[259]Voorhees v. Mason, (1910) 245 Ill. 256, 91 N.E. 1056; Perry v. Tuscaloosa Cotton Seed Oil-Mill Co., (1891) 93 Ala. 364, 9 So. 217; Fisk v. Chicago, R.I. & P.R.R., (1868) 53 Barb. (N.Y.) 513.

[260]Voorhees v. Mason, (1910) 245 Ill. 256, 91 N.E. 1056.

[261]State ex rel. Wede v. Bechtel, (Iowa S. Ct., 1948) 31 N.W. 2d 853; Diamond State Brewery, Inc. v. De La Rigaudiere, (Del. Ch. Ct., 1941) 17 A.2d 213; Rice v. Thomas, (1919) 184 Ky. 168, 211 S.W. 428; Taylor v. Citizens' Oil Co., (1918) 182 Ky. 350, 206 S.W. 644.

[262]American Alkali Co. v. Campbell, (1902) 113 F. 398; Donald v. American Smelting & Refining Co., (1901) 62 N.J. Eq. 729, 48 A. 771, 1116.

[263]Camden v. Stuart, (1892) 144 U.S. 104, 12 S. Ct. 585. But see Wells v. Comstock, (1956) 46 Cal. 2d 528, 297 P.2d 961.

[264]Fosdick v. Sturges, (1858) 1 Biss. (U.S.) 255.

ledge could be attributed, that stock issued as fully paid was in fact illegally issued cannot compel a corporation to issue a new certificate to him which would state that the stock is fully paid and nonassessable.[265] A transferee in whose name shares were registered without his knowledge or assent is not liable to creditors if the shares are watered.[266]

The liability of a purchaser of watered stock to the corporation also depends upon whether the transferee had knowledge of the facts concerning the fictitious issue. If the certificate states that the stock is fully paid and nonassessable, and the transferee has no knowledge that full value has not been given for the stock by the original holder, the corporation will be estopped from claiming that the stock has not been fully paid for.[267] On the other hand, a purchaser with knowledge that the stock has been issued for overvalued property may be liable to the corporation for the difference between the value of the property conveyed to the corporation for the stock and the amount of stock issued therefor.[268] Under a statute which declares illegally issued stock void, a bona fide purchaser of such stock has been held to have acquired the stock subject to the corporation's right to cancel it.[269] In another state, a constitutional provision that declared all fictitious increases of stock void was held not to apply to one who had in good faith for value purchased stock from a third person, without knowledge that full payment had not been made for the stock.[270] The liability of transferees to creditors is discussed below.

Liability of holder of watered stock to creditors. The liability of stockholders for watered stock is governed by the laws of the state in which the corporation is organized.[271] Creditors generally have a right to compel stockholders who have not paid for their stock in full, in money, property, or other good consideration, to make up the deficiency.[272] They have this right even in cases where the contract is valid and binding as between the corporation and the stockholder or the transferee of the stockholder.[273] A

---

[265]Bowen v. Imperial Theatres, Inc., (1922) 13 Del. Ch. 120, 115 A. 918.

[266]Williams v. Vreeland, (1919) 250 U.S. 295, 39 S.Ct. 438.

[267]Bowen v. Imperial Theatres, Inc., (1922) 13 Del. Ch. 120, 115 A. 918.

[268]Jose v. Utley, (1921) 185 Cal. 656, 199 P. 1037.

[269]Walton v. Standard Drilling Co., (1921) 43 S.D. 576, 181 N.W. 96. See, however, Maclary v. Pleasant Hills, Inc., (1954) Del. Ch. 109 A 2d 830, holding that where stock has been issued without consideration but the equities favor the stockholder, the stockholder will be given the election of retaining the stock on payment of a fair price.

[270]Taylor v. Citizens' Oil Co., (1918) 182 Ky. 350, 206 S.W. 644.

[271]Speakman v. Bernstein, (1932) 59 F.2d 520.

[272]Scovil v. Thayer, (1881) 105 U.S. 143; Bing Crosby Minute Maid Corp. v. Eaton, (1956) 46 Cal.2d 484, 297 P.2d 5; Trotta v. Metalmold Corp., 2d 798; G. Loewus & Co. v. Highland Queen Packing Co., (1939) 12; Jeffrey v. Selwyn, (1917) 220 N.Y. 77, 115 N.W. 275. But see Stone v. Hudgens, (1955) 129 F. Supp. 273.

[273]Camden v. Stuart, (1892) 144 U.S. 104, 12 S. Ct., 585; Handley v. Stutz, (1890) 139 U.S. 417, 11 S.Ct. 530; Fogg v. Blair, (1890) 139 U.S. 118, 11 S.Ct. 476; Scovill v. Thayer, (1881) 105 U.S. 143; J. F. Lucey Co. v. McMullen, (1918) 178 Cal. 425, 173 P. 1000. See also Mudd v. Lanier, 363, 24 So. Absence of knowledge of the fraud is no defense against the creditor for a stockholder who was not vigilant in uncovering the fraud. Smith v. Schmitt, (1924) 112 Ore. 687, 231 P. 176.

creditor, however, in order to be entitled to this right, must have given credit on the faith that the stock was fully paid.[274] Thus, one who became a creditor before the watered or fictitiously paid up stock was issued could not compel the holders of such stock to pay for their shares in full.[275] Such an antecedent creditor could not have given credit on the faith that the stock had been paid for in full. Likewise, a creditor who knew that stock had been issued for overvalued property, or for less than par, generally cannot require the holders of watered stock to pay the full value of the shares.[276] Thus, a creditor, who has participated as a stockholder or officer in the issuance of stock as fully paid for which the corporation did not receive full payment, cannot recover from the holders of the fictitiously issued shares.[277] In some jurisdictions, however, creditors may recover for unpaid stock, even though they had knowledge of the circumstances under which the unapid stock was issued as fully paid.[278]

A creditor can hold a transferee liable if the transferee had knowledge that the stock issued as fully paid was not so in fact;[279] but a creditor cannot compel a stockholder who is a transferee of watered stock to make good the overvaluation, if the transferee took his stock unaware of the fact that the corporation did not originally receive full payment.[280] The transferor in such cases remains liable.[281]

When liability is found, recovery is based on the difference between what the stockholders paid or the value of what they gave for the stock and its par value.[282] If they did not pay or give anything for the stock, then they are liable to pay its par value, but only in an amount sufficient to satisfy the claims of such creditors.[283] The theory of this liability seems to be based by

---

[274]Liability here is based upon the so-called "misrepresentation" theory. Reliance is generally presumed, but the presumption is rebuttable. Handley v. Stutz, 417, 11 S.Ct.; Hospes v. Northwestern Mfg. & Car. Co., (1892) 48 Minn. 174, 50 N.W. 1117. Compare R. H. Herron Co. v. Shaw, (1913) 165 Cal. 668, 133 P. 488. See however, Vermont Marble Co. v. Declez Granite Co., (1902) 135 Cal. 579, 67 P. 1057.

[275]Handley v. Stutz, (1890) 139 U.S. 417, 11 S.Ct. 530.

[276]Frank v. Carman Distributing Co., (1935) 97 Colo. 211, 48 P.2d 805; Townley Metal & Hardware Co. Cramer, (1934) 169 Okl. 525, 37 P.2d 915; Coit v. Gold Amalgamating Co., (1886) 119 U.S. 343. See also 25 COLUM. L. REV. 421.

[277]Coit v. Gold Amalgamating Co., (1886) 119 U.S. 343.

[278]Du Pont v. Ball, (1918) 11 Del. Ch. 430, 106 A. 39; Easton Nat'l Bank v. American Brick & Tile Co., (1906) 70 N.J. Eq. 732, 62 A. 917; Atwell v. Schmitt, (1924) 111 Ore. 96, 225 P. 325. See also 44 CALIF. L. REV. 941, criticizing failure of California Supreme Court to follow this "Statutory obligation" theory in Bing Crosby Minute Maid Co. v. Eaton, (1956) 46 Cal. 2d 484, 297 P.2d 5. The Bing Crosby case is also discussed in 55 MICH. L. REV. 719 and 9 STAN. L. REV. 191

[279]But the transferee with knowledge is not liable if there has been an intervening innocent purchaser. Graham v. Fleissner's Ex'rs, (1931) 170 N.J.L. 278, 153 A. 526.

[280]Enright v. Heckscher, (1917) 240 F. 863; Rhode v. Dock-Hop Co., (1920) 184 Cl. 367, 194 P. 11; Gray Constr. Co. v. Fantle, (1934) 62 S.D. 345, 253 N.W. 464.

[281]Palmer v. Scheftel, (1921) 194 App. Div. 682, 186 N.Y. Supp. 84, aff'd, memo dec., 236 N.Y. 511, 142 N.E. 263.

[282]Camden v. Stuart, (1892) 144 U.S. 104, 12 S.Ct., 585; Handley v. Stutz, (1890) 139 U.S. 417, 11 S.Ct. 530; Fogg v. Blair, (1890) 139 U.S. 118, 11 S.Ct. 476; Scovill v. Thayer, (1881) 105 U.S. 143; J.F. Lucey Co. v. McMullen, (1918) 187 Cal. 425, 173 P. 1000.

[283]Scovill v. Thayer, (1881) 105 U.S. 143; Compare, Smith v. Miss. Livestock Producers Ass'n., (Miss. S.Ct., 1966) 188 So. 2d 758.

some courts on tort.[284] Other grounds of liability are statutory added or double liability, and contract liability, that is liability for the subscription price.[285]

Amount of consideration for stock with par value. A corporation, in offering to sell its stock to a subscriber or purchaser, must set the price at which it is to be sold. If the stock has a par value fixed by the charter, by the general law, or by the articles of association, the price at which the stock is to be sold must be at least equal to the par value of the stock.[286] In some states, the statutes authorize the board of directors or the stockholders to fix a price for the stock at less than its par value. In other states, the constitution or the statutes specifically require that the consideration paid for stock shall be equal to its par value. Stock issued for less is void. Its status is similar to that of an overissue and is generally void even in the hands of a bona fide purchaser for value.[287] (See overissuance of stock, on page 421.) A requirement that the full par value of stock shall be paid does not keep the corporation from spending money to promote the sale of stock, although the expense brings the amount paid in below par.[288]

A subscription made at a price above the par value of the stock is not ultra vires. A subscriber may be compelled to pay both the par value of the stock and the premium agreed to be paid before becoming entitled to a fully paid nonassessable certificate for the shares purchased.[289]

Agreement to sell stock below par. In the absence of an express statutory, constitutional, or charter provision calling for the payment of stock at par value, a corporation may make a valid agreement with its subscribers for the sale of stock at less than par value. For example, in Idaho the issuance of a par value stock pursuant to an option agreement was held void, when the option provided for a consideration that was less than par; that violated Idaho's B.C.A. § 30-120.[290] Also, in New York, par value stock cannot be purchased at less than par value; cancellation of a debt from a corporation was held to be cash payment for shares equal to the amount of the debt; that is required by N.Y.B.C.L. § 504 (c).[291]

---

[284]Gray Const. Co. v. Fantle, (1934) 62 S.D. 345, 253 N.W. 464; Blair v. Patterson, (1934) 62 S.D. 407, 253 N.W. 478.

[285]Ibid.

[286]Okla. Gas & Electric Co. v. Hathaway, (1943) 192 Okl. 626, 138 P. 2d 832; Dicker v. Italo-American Oil Corp., (1932) 119 Cal. App. 451, 6 P. 2d 550; Wark Co. v. Beach Hotel Corp., (1931) 113 Conn. 119, 154 A. 252.

[287]Oklahoma Gas & Elec. Co. v. Hathaway, (1943) 192 Okla. 626, 138 P.2d 832.

[288]Restlawn Memorial Park Ass'n v. Solie, (1940) 233 Wis. 425, 289 N.W. 615.

[289]Grone v. Economic Life Ins. Co., (1911) Del. Ch. 80 A. 809; Esgen v. Smith, (1901) 113 Iowa 25, 84 N.W. 954.

[290]Yreka United, Inc. v. Harrison, (Ida. S.Ct., 1973) 20 I.C.R. 311, No. 11057, 5-15-73.

[291]Frankowski v. Palermo (N.Y. App. Div., 1975) 363 N.Y.S. 2d 159. See also Okla. Gas & Electric Co. v. Hathaway, (1943) 192 Okl. 626, 138 P.2d 832; Dicker v. Italo-American Oil Corp., (1932) 119 Cal. App. 451, 6 P. 2d 550; Wark Co. v. Beach Hotel Corp., (1931) 113 Conn. 119, 154 A. 252.

The corporation can then issue fully paid stock upon the payment of the agreed-upon price. This can be done, however, only if the rights of the other stockholders are not violated and there is no fraud against creditors. As between the corporation and the subscriber, the agreement is valid; the corporation cannot maintain a suit to collect the difference between the par value and the amount paid upon the stock for which the fully paid certificates have been issued.[292] But such a contract, while binding on the corporation, will not be binding on creditors; when the rights of creditors are to be satisfied, the stockholders who have paid less than par for their shares may be required to pay for their stock in full.[293]

A going concern in need of capital, whose stock has fallen below par value, will of course find difficulty in selling its unissued stock at par value. In practice, the corporation will market its shares for the best price that can be obtained. So long as the transaction is bona fide, and the consideration obtained represents the actual value of the stock, the courts generally will not disturb the transaction. In the absence of fraud, the purchaser will be liable only for the contract price.[294] Creditors cannot recover the difference between the contract price and the par value of the stock without proof of bad faith on the part of those entering into such a transaction. They must also show that the stock of the corporation, when issued under such circumstances, had in fact a higher actual value at the time of its issuance than that at which the stock was sold.[295]

Amount of consideration for no-par shares. The statutes of all but a few of the states that provide for issuance of no-par value shares indicate the manner of fixing the consideration for which such stock shall be issued.[296] The statutory provisions on the subject of determining consideration for which no-par shares may be issued vary throughout the states. The most usual provision is that no-par shares may be issued for such consideration as may be prescribed in the charter or an amendment, or, if there is no provision in this respect, then for such consideration (1) as may be fixed by the stockholders at a meeting duly called for that purpose; or (2) as may be

---

[292]Scovill v. Thayer, (1881) 105 U.S. 143; Bacich v. Northland Transp. Co., (1932) 185 Minn. 544, 242 N.W. 379.

[293]See page 464.

[294]Handley v. Stutz, (1890) 139 U.S. 417, 11 S.Ct. 530; Morrow v. Nashville Iron & Steel Co., (1889) 87 Tenn. 262, 10 S.W. 495. See also Fogg v. Blair, (1890) 139 U.S. 118, 11 S.Ct. 476; J.F. Lucey Co. v. McMullen (1918) 778 Cal. 425, 173 P. 1000.

[295]Ibid.

A stockholder who dissents to the issue of additional stock by an undercapitalized corporation cannot enjoin such issue on the grounds that the price, set at par value, is grossly inadequate, if the offer is made in good faith, and the price, under the circumstances, is fair. The directors "should not be subject to the peril of having a court . . . merely differ as to its value . . . " The stockholder's case was not aided by the fact that she was financially unable to exercise her pre-emptive rights since a higher price would not help her. Maguire v. Osborn, (1957) 388 Pa. 121, 130 A.2d 157, comment in 19 PITT. L. REV. 283.

[296]See Masterson, "Consideration for Non-par Shares and Liability of Subscribers and Stockholders," 17 TEXAS L. REV. 247.

fixed by the directors acting under general or special authority granted by the stockholders or conferred by the certificate of incorporation.[297] The practice generally followed in the organization of corporations having no-par shares is to have the charter provide that the directors shall have the power to determine from time to time the consideration to be received for stock without par value.[298] When this method is followed, the decision of the directors is conclusive, in the absence of fraud or clear abuse of discretion.[299]

The action of directors or stockholders in fixing the price at which no-par value shares shall be sold may be subject to the approval of public service commissions, Blue-Sky commissions, or other regulatory bodies. In some states an affidavit must be filed with a designated state authority showing the financial plan under which stocks are to be issued before the corporation may issue its stock. Such a provision may apply to issues of par value stock as well as no-par value stock.

Fixing the price of no-par stock. In determining the price at which no-par value shares shall be sold, the directors or stockholders who have authority to fix the consideration are furnished with no yardstick for measuring the amount that is to be paid for the stock. They are given practically unlimited latitude. Within the authority conferred by the articles of incorporation, the board of directors may fix the price at its real, market, or book value,[300] or at a minute or arbitrary figure, subject to review by a court of equity.[301] If the board accepts an offer to transfer property for a certain number of shares of no-par stock, the board thereby fixes the amount of consideration for the stock.[302] Even if no-par value shares are given a nominal value, it is no indication of their actual value, any more than the par value of shares is an indication of their actual value.[303]

The sale price of no-par shares should be fixed in the light of all legitimate considerations. These include appraisal and sale value of assets, book values, market values of outstanding shares, present and probable earning power, market conditions, size of the issue, and reputation of the

[297]Cohen v. Beneficial Industrial Loan Corp., (D.N.J.; 1946 69 F. Supp. 297; Millberg v. Baum, (N.Y.S. Ct., 1941) 25 N.Y.S. 2d 451; Topkis v. Delaware Hardware Co., (Del. Ch. Ct., 1938) 2 A 2d 114.

[298]Lewis v. Oscar C. Wright Co., (1930) 234 Ky. 814, 29 S.W. 2d 566.

[299]Alexander v. Phillips Petroleum Co., (1942) 130 F. 2d 593.

[300]Wilhelm v. Doubleday, Doran & Co., (N.Y. S.Ct., 1940) N.Y.L.J., 6-1-40, P. 2500.

[301]Cohen v. Beneficial Industrial Loan Corp., (D.N.J., 1946) 69 F. Supp. 297; Rice & Hutchins v. Triplex Shoe Co., (1929) 16 Del. Ch. 298, 147 A. 317; Bodell v. General Gas & Elec. Co., (1926) 15 Del. Ch. 119, 132 A. 442, aff'd. (1927) 15 Del. Ch. 420, 140 A. 264.

[302]Rose Theater, Inc. v. Jones, (1955) 224 Ark. 951, 278 S.W. 2d 105; G. Loewus & Co. v. Highland Queen Packing Co., (1939) 125 N.J.Eq. 534, 6 A.2d 545, discussed in 4 U. NEWARK L. REV. 448.

[303]Chadwick v. McClurg, (1928) 103 N.J. Eq. 55, 142 A. 173.

corporation. The particular conditions surrounding the transaction, and such other considerations as honest and fair-minded men might properly take into account, are also weighed in fixing the sale price.[304]

The decision of the board of directors as to the sale price of no-par shares will also depend upon whether the stock is issued by a corporation recently formed or by an old established corporation. If the corporation has just been formed, it makes little difference how much or how little is received in consideration of its original no-par stock.[305] If assets of $1,000 are received, let us say, it is of no consequence whether five, ten, or one thousand shares are given for it. Each share is worth one-fifth, one-tenth, or one-thousandth part of the $1,000, as the case may be.[306] However, if the corporation is a going concern, it makes considerable difference to the existing stockholders at what price the stock is sold. The new no-par stockholders and the existing no-par stockholders will share equally in the total net assets of the corporation. Therefore, if the new shares are sold for less than the actual value of the existing shares, the interest of the old shareholders in the total net assets of the corporation after the new stock has been sold will be less than it was before the new stock was sold. Equity will interfere to protect existing stockholders where the consideration fixed for no-par shares impairs the values underlying the holdings of existing stockholders.[307]

The directors authorized to fix the price of no-par shares cannot ordinarily sell the same issue of no-par stock at different prices to different persons. However, if such differential sales are justified by a showing of fairness in the light of all circumstances, and are made for the beneficial interest of the corporation, the sales will be sustained.[308]

When the corporation must, by statute, state the total amount of capital with which it will commence business, and this amount is stated at $5,000, holders of no-par shares who bought all authorized shares for $325 are liable to creditors for the balance.[309] Further, even though a seller to the corporation of its only asset, for no-par stock, said the asset was worth more than it was, a later stockholder could not complain since the corporation was not injured. The value of the stock at the time of conveyance was

[304]Bodell v. General Gas & Elec. Co., (1926) 15 Del. Ch. 119, 132 A. 443, aff'd. (1927) 15 Del. Ch. 420, 140 A. 264.

[305]Finch v. Warrior Cement Corp., (1928) 16 Del. Ch. 44, 141 A. 54. See also State v. Pierce Petroleum Corp., (1928) 318 Mo. 1020, 2 S.W. 2d 790.

[306]Cohen v. Beneficial Industrial Loan Corp., (D.N.J., 1946) 69 F. Supp. 297; West v. Sirian Lamp Co., (Del. Ch. Ct., 1944) 37 A. 2d 835; cc., (Del. Ch. Ct., 1945) 42 A. 2d 883, 44 A. 2d 658.

[307]Bodell v. General Gas & Elec. Co., (1926) 15 Del. Ch. 119, 132 A. 442, aff'd., (1927) 15 Del. Ch. 420, 140 A. 264.

[308]Atlantic Refining Co. v. Hodgman, (1926) 13 F. 2d 781; Bodell v. General Gas & Elec. Co., (1926) 15 Del. Ch. 119, 132A. 442, aff'd., (1927) Del. Ch. 420, 140 A. 264.

[309]Livingston v. Adams, (Mo. S. Ct., 1931) 43 S.W. 2d 836.

the value of the land whatever it was.[310] A minority stockholder cannot have set aside the sale of stock to the controlling stockholder on the ground the latter paid inadequate consideration, when the book value and the valuation by a former prospective purchaser showed the price was fair.[311]

It should be remembered that the price for which no-par shares are sold is entirely distinct from the question of how much of this price should be allocated to capital and how much should be allocated to paid-in surplus. The latter is frequently controlled by statute and further limited by the rights of existent shareholders and creditors.[312]

Amount of consideration for treasury stock. Treasury stock is capital stock that has been legally issued, fully paid for, and then returned to the treasury of the corporation, by purchase or otherwise, to be disposed of for the benefit of the corporation.[313]

In the disposition of treasury stock, the corporation is not controlled by the provisions of the constitution, statute, or charter regulating the kind or amount of consideration for which stock of an original issue must be sold.[314] The corporation may sell treasury stock at whatever price it can procure for it,[315] even though this price is less than par[316] or less than market price.[317] Purchasers do not become liable to corporate creditors for the difference between the par value of the stock and the amount that they paid for it.[318] Similarly, the corporation may give away treasury stock as a bonus to stimulate the sale of original issues of stock.

But the sale of treasury stock must be bona fide. For example, directors cannot buy treasury stock either to gain corporate control or to resell it at a profit even if they paid an adequate price. If the directors sell on the open market they should try to get the best possible price. A non-director's purchase of treasury stock is valid unless the price is so low that he should have known it was inadequate.[319]

---

[310]Rose Theater v. Jones, (Ark. S.Ct., 1955) 278 S.W. 2d 105.

[311]Robinson v. Malheur Publishing Co., (D.C. Ore., 1967) 272 F. Supp. 57.

[312]Israels, "Problems of Par and No Par Shares: A Reappraisal," 47 COLUM. L. REV. 1279.

[313]State ex rel. Weede v. Bechtel, (1953) 244 Iowa 785, 56 N.W. 2d 173; Miners Nat. Bank of Pottsville v. Frackville Sewerage Co., (1945) 157 Pa. Super. 167, 42 A.2d 177; Vanderlip v. Los Molinos Land Co., (1945) 56 Cal. App. 2d 747, 133 P. 2d 467; State v. Stewart Bros. Cotton Co., (1939) 193 La. 16, 190 So. 317.

[314]See Borg. v. International Silver Co., (1925) 11 F. 2d 147; Mudd v. Lanier., (1945) 247 Ala. 363, 24 So. 2nd 550.

[315]Mudd v. Lanier, (1945) 247 Ala. 363, 24 So. 2d 550; Furlong v. Johnston, (1924) 209 App. Div. 198, 204 N.Y. Supp. 710, aff'd, 237, N.Y. 141, 145 N.E. 910. See, however, State v. Stewart Bros. Cotton Co., (1939) 193 La. 16, 190 So. 317, involving a statute prohibiting officers from disposing of treasury stock at a price less than they paid for it.

[316]Belle Island Corp. v. MacBean, (1948) 30 Del. Ch. 373, 61 A.2d 699.

[317]Sandler v. Schenley Industries, Inc., (1951) 32 Del. Ch. 46, 79 A.2d 606.

[318]Enright v. Heckscher, (1917) 240 F. 863; Pullman v. Railway Equipment Co., (1897) 73 Ill. App. 313; Simonds v. Noland, (1927) 142 Wash. 423, 253 P. 638.

[319]Johnson v. Duensing, (Mo. S.Ct., 1967) 340 S.W. 2d 758, Mod., 351 S.W. 2d 27.

Stockholders do not have preemptive rights in treasury stock.[320]

Treasury stock does not pass under a contract of sale of all the corporation's assets and the buyer cannot get a liquidating dividend when such stock is redeemed.[321]

The same rule applies to stock that has once been fully paid for and subsequently purchased by the corporation. On purchase by the corporation it becomes treasury stock. If the stock is resold by the corporation at less than its par value, the purchasers do not become liable to corporate creditors for the difference between its par value and what they paid for it.[322] Treasury shares are issued, but not outstanding. However, for some tax purposes, for example, a state franchise tax, treasury shares may be regarded as outstanding.

ACQUIRING OWN STOCK

Power of corporation to purchase its own stock. The general corporation laws of all states now permit the corporation to acquire its own stock under certain circumstances.[323]

When a corporation purchases its own stock, it becomes treasury stock, and the general rule is that it may reissue the stock, that is resell it, for any price it can get.[324] The treasury stock may be sold to officers with the consent of majority shareholders and the directors.[325] Treasury stock has the status of issued and outstanding shares for franchise tax and other purposes. That is to say, purchase by a corporation of shares of its own capital stock does not itself effect a reduction or retirement of the capital stock. Ordinarily, reduction of capital stock can be effected only by following the statutory procedure. But such treasury stock may be retired, and a capital stock reduction thereby effected, unless the right to retire the stock is restricted by the certificate of incorporation.[326]

Ordinarily when a corporation wants to reduce capital by buying stock from its stockholders, it selects the stock by lot or on a pro rata basis for the

---

[320]Ibid.

[321]Fultz v. Anzac Oil Corp., (Ca-5,1957) 240 F.2d 21.

[322]Pullman v. Railway Equipment Co., (1897) 73 Ill. App. 313.

[323]See, for example, Midenberg v. Carmel Film Productions, Inc., (1955) 132 Cal. App. 2d 598, 282 P. 2d 1024; Brown v. Eastern States Corp., (1949) 86 F. Supp. 887, aff'd., (1950) 181 F.2d 26, cert. denied, (U.S.S.Ct., 1950) 340 U.S. 864, 71 S.Ct. 88. For state statutes, see Prentice-Hall *Corporation.*

[324]Furlong v. Johnson, (1924) 209 N.Y. App. Div. 198, 204 N.Y.S. 710, aff'd, 239 N.Y. 141, 145 N.E. 910.

[325]Provident Trust Co. of Philadelphia v. Couse, (1941) (Pa. Ct. Common Pleas) No. 7, Phila. Co.) 40 D.& C. 628. See also, Bank v. Frackville Sewerage Co., (1945) 157 Pa. Super. 167, 42 A.2d 177.

[326]State v. Stewart Bros. Cotton Co., Inc., (1939) 193 La. 16, 190 So. 317. See also Vanderlip v. Los Morinos Land Co., (1943) 56 Cal. App. 2d 747, 133 P.2d 467.

class to be retired. The obvious reason is to assure equal treatment for all stockholders of the class.

Agreement with stockholders to repurchase stock. The power of a corporation to purchase its own stock carries with it, as an inseparable incident, the right to enter into agreements or contracts with stockholders or prospective stockholders for the purchase of their shares. Such agreements generally are valid provided the corporation has an available surplus out of which to pay the purchase price.[327] Otherwise the rights of creditors and other stockholders would be jeopardized.[328] If there was a surplus when the contract to repurchase was entered into, the contract won't be enforced when the surplus turns to a deficit.[329] A corporation cannot redeem stock under a repurchase agreement, when to do so would render it unable to meet its debts as they mature in the usual course of business.[330]

A corporation, to induce the purchase of stock, may agree to take the stock back within a certain time if the purchaser is not satisfied with the investment. Such contracts are valid and enforceable provided the purchaser has performed his part of the agreement and the corporation has available a surplus at the time of performance,[331] out of which to pay the purchase price. If the contract is unenforceable because the corporation has no surplus available out of which to pay the repurchase price, the stockholder cannot, collect damages for breach of contract, recover the purchase price in a suit to rescind for failure of consideration,[332] or file a claim in bankruptcy against an insolvent corporation based on the contract.[333] If in spite of its insolvency the corporation repurchases under its agreement, the money must be restored to the corporation's trustee in bankruptcy.[334]

However, there is a considerable trend in the other direction, when the contract to repurchase is a negotiable note promising to pay for the share at

---

[327]Wright v. Iowa Power & Light Co., (1937) 223 Iowa, 1192, 274 S.W. 892.

[328]In Re Belmetals Mfg. Co. (DC, N.D. Calif., 1969) 299 F. Supp. 1290. Dustin v. Randall Faichney Corp., (1921) 263 Mass. 99, 160 N.E. 528; Model Clothing House v. Dickinson, (1920) 146 Minn. 367, 178 N.W. 957; Smith v. Citizens' Ins. & Mortg. Co., (1925) 284 Pa. 380, 131 A. 191.

[329]Cross v. Beguelin, (1929) 252 N.Y. 262, 169 N.E. 378. See also Tracy v. Perkins-Tracy Printing Company (S.Ct. Minn. 1967) 153 N.W. 2d 241.

[330]McConnell v. Estate of Butler (Ca-9, 1968) 402 F.2d 362. Kraft v. Rochambeau Holding Company, Inc., (Ct. of App., 1956) 123 A.2d 287.

[331]Bates v. Daley's Inc., (1935) 5 Cal. App. 2d 95, 42 P.2d 706; Bishop v. Middle States Utilities Co. of Delaware, (1928) 225 Ia. 941, 282 N.W. 305; Peterson v. New England Furniture & Carpet Co., (1941) 210 Minn. 449, 299 N.W. 208; Steinbugler v. William C. Atwater & Co., Inc., (1942) 264 App. Div. 864, 35 N.Y.S. 2d 349. See also In re Fechheimer Fishel Co., (CCA-2, 1914) 212 F. 357; Hesse Envelope Co. v. Addison, (1914) 166 S.W. 898; Hoops v. Leddy, (1936) 119 N.J. Eq. 296, 182 A. 271.

[332]Allen v. Bank, (CA-6, 1911) 191 F. 97; In re Tichenor-Grand Co., (1913) (DC, N.Y.) 203 F. 720; Hoover Steel Ball Co. v. Schaefer Co., (1919) 90 N.J. Eq. 164, 106 A. 471; Quinn-Marshall Co. v. McDaniels Co., (1934) (DC, N.C.) 5 F. Supp. 937.

[333]Quinn-Marshall Co. v. McDaniels Co., (1934) (MD, N.C.) 5 F. Supp, 937.

[334]Jackson v. Colagrossi (S. Ct., 1957) 150 Wash. Dec. 540.

some future date. The rule in some states now is that if the corporation was solvent and in a sufficient earned surplus position when the note was delivered, it is an enforceable contract to repurchase even though the corporation becomes insolvent or bankrupt at the time when the note becomes due.[335] This rule has been incorporated in the statutory law of some states.[336] As an extension of this principle, one court has held that former directors of a defunct corporation were not liable to a creditor for unearned rent even though the corporation had no earned surplus at the time (after execution of the lease) that it purchased its own shares, since accrued rent claims must be excluded from the calculation of earned surplus and become due only on default, not on signing of the lease.[337]

If, after subscribing, the subscriber's name is not entered on the books of the corporation as a stockholder and no certificates are issued[338] to him, he never becomes a stockholder, hence there can be no promise by the corporation to ''repurchase'' the shares from him.[339] He may be treated as a creditor of the corporation for money loaned and allowed to recover on the refund agreement even when the corporation has no surplus.[340] Directors can be personally liable to a judgment debtor of the corporation for repurchasing stock when the corporation had no surplus.[341] Though a corporation has power to repurchase, the officer who undertakes to do so must be properly authorized to bind the corporation.[342]

Contracts to repurchase from existing stockholders do not require general stockholder consent. If it is not unfair to other stockholders it may be specifically enforced.[343] However, if the purchase is made at a time

---

[335]In re National Tile & Terrazzo Co., Inc., Bankrupt; Paterna v. Walsh, Trustee (CA-9, 1975) No. 74-1549, 11-7-75.

[336]For example: (a) California, in revamping its entire corporation law in 1976, provides that if a negotiable debt security (note) is given in exchange for the repurchase of shares, the date when the corporation acquires the shares determines the time when the corporation must have the required earnings or assets to make the purchase and such requirement doesn't extend to any other later date [Calif. G.C. L. §§ 166;500, effective 1-1-77], (b) Connecticut, in a 1975 amendment, specifically provides that statutory restrictions on a corporation's purchase of its own shares do not invalidate a note debenture or obligation given as consideration for such shares when the corporation had the proper funds to make the purchase at the time of the delivery of such note, debenture or obligation and was not made insolvent by such delivery [Conn. S.C.A. § 33-3587] (c) Delaware also in 1974 changed its law on repurchase of stock to provide that "nothing . . . shall invalidate or otherwise affect a note, debenture or other obligation of a corporation given by it as consideration for its acquisition by purchase, redemption or exchange of its shares of stock if at the time such note, debenture or obligation was delivered by the corporation its capital was not then impaired or did not thereby become impaired," [Del. G.C.L. § 160 (1)].

[337]UMF Systems, Inc., v. Eltra Corporation (Calif. Dist. Ct. of App., 1976) 56 C.A. 3d 151.

[338]In re Tichenor-Grand Co., (1913) (DC, N.Y.) 203 F. 720..

[339]Mulford v. Torrey Co., (1909) 45 Colo. 81; Vent v. Duluth Coffee Co., (1896) 64 Minn. 307, 67 N.W. 70; Hyman v. Real Estate Co., (1913) 79 Misc. 439, 140 N.Y. Supp. 138.

[340]Hyman v. Real Estate Co., (1913) 79 Misc. 439, 140 N.Y.S. 138.

[341]David McDonough, Inc. v. Berger, (S.Ct., N.Y. 1959) 22 Misc.2d 646.

[342]Hack v. Elevator Supplies Co., (1935) 118 N.J. Eq. 90, 117 A. 458.

[343]Gate v. Pagel-Clikeman Co. (App. Ct. Ill., 1967) 230 N.E.2d 387. Winchell v. Plywood Corp., (1949) Mass. 85 N.E. 2d 313.

when the company is insolvent, and not for legitimate corporate purposes, it is invalid and a claim predicated thereon cannot be sustained against the corporation after it has gone into bankruptcy.[344] A corporation cannot purchase its own stock when its only purpose is to perpetuate control by a dominant stockholder.[345] For example, selective redemption of preferred stock before the expiration of a voting trust agreement giving control to certain directors and officers was barred, since it appeared that the redemption would assure continued control of the corporation by such directors and officers; it did not matter that the corporate charter allowed selective redemption.[346] Directors who approve of the corporations' purchase, when the motive is to retain control, are individually liable in a derivative suit.[347] But a subsequent creditor of a corporation who voluntarily becomes such with knowledge of the company's purchase of its own stock cannot enjoin the carrying out of the purchase contract.[348] Also, a corporation cannot purchase its own stock when its own purpose is to resolve disputes among stockholders.[349]

A by-law has been held valid that gave the corporation an option to buy its deceased stockholder's stock at the price he paid for it though the price was well below current value, and there were many stockholders.[350]

Close corporations. Stockholders of close corporations may agree that, if they desire to dispose of their stock, they will make the first offer of it to the corporation or the other stockholders or both. Such contracts have been held binding.[351]

Employment contracts. An option to repurchase stock is often found in employment contracts. A corporation, for example, can, under an agreement, repurchase shares at a fraction of value, from officers discharged for cause, though the cause be failure to achieve good results.[352] Also a corporation's forbearance from dismissing an employee is good

---

[344]In re Morrisville Concrete Products Co., (D N.J. 1934) 6 F. Supp. 465.

[345]Propp v. Sadacca, (Ch. Ct., Del., 1961) 175 A.2d 33.

[346]Petty v. Penntech Papers, Inc., (Del. Ch. Ct., 1975) 347 A. 2d 140.

[347]Mathes v. Cheff, (Del. Ch. Ct., 1963) Civ. No. 943, 4-23-63.

[348]Loveland & Co. v. Doernbecher Mfg. Co., (1934) 149 Ore. 58, 39 P.2d 668.

[349]England v. Christensen, (Calif. Dist. Ct. of App., 1966) 52 Cal. Rptr. 402, 243 Cal. App. 2d 413.

[350]Allen v. Biltmore Tissue Corp. (Ct. of App. 1957) 14 N.E. 2d 812; 2 N.Y. 2d 534.

[351]Model Clothing House v. Dickinson, (1920) 146 Minn. 367, 178 N.W. 957; Wright v. Iredell Tel. Co., (1921) 182 N.C. 308, 108 S.E. 744. See also Lawson v. Household Finance Corp., (1929) 17 Del. Ch. 1, 147 A. 312.

[352]Georesearch, Inc. v. Morriss, (DC, W.D. La., 1961) 193 F. Supp. 163.

consideration for termination of its agreement to buy back his stock and substituting in its stead an option on the part of the corporation to repurchase.[353]

But a corporation cannot risk insolvency to buy its stock for sale to employees, when the corporation has no definite stock purchase plan.[354] And a corporation's trustee in bankruptcy can recover payments to directors under a stock redemption agreement, when the redemption impaired capital.[355]

---

[353]Kready v. Bechtel, Lutz & Jost (Com. Pls., (1962) Berks County L.J., 8-9-62, p. 231.

[354]Lowry v. Sunday Creek Coal Co. (1965) 2 Ohio App.2d 260, 207 N.E. 2d 678.

[355]Cunningham v. Jaffee (DC, D.S.C.M. 1966) 251 F. Supp. 143.

Chapter 16

RESOLUTIONS RELATING TO ISSUANCE AND SALE OF STOCK

Contents—Chapter 16

RESOLUTION OF STOCKHOLDERS AUTHORIZING DIRECTORS TO ISSUE STOCK, AND INSTRUCTING THEM TO COMPLY WITH BLUE-SKY LAWS

RESOLVED, That the Board of Directors of this Corporation is hereby authorized and instructed to sell and issue the entire unsubscribed and unissued authorized capital stock of this Corporation, amounting to ..... (.....) shares of common stock with a par value of ..... ($.....) Dollars per share, at par, and that the President and the Secretary are hereby authorized and directed to take all steps necessary to comply with the blue-sky laws of the State of .... and the Federal laws governing the issuance and sale of securities, before offering any of the authorized capital stock for sale.

RESOLUTION OF DIRECTORS AUTHORIZING CORPORATION TO MAKE APPLICATION UNDER BLUE-SKY LAWS TO SELL AND ISSUE STOCK TO ORIGINAL SUBSCRIBERS FOR CASH OR PROPERTY

RESOLVED, That the President and the Secretary of this Corporation are hereby directed to make an application to the ....*(insert department or officer)* of the State of .... for leave to sell and issue capital stock of this Corporation as follows:

If stock is to be issued to original subscribers for cash:

..... (.....) shares of the common stock of this Corporation having a par value of ..... ($.....) Dollars per share, to each of the ..... *(insert number)* original subscribers therefor, upon payment to the Corporation of the full par value of each share in cash.

If stock is to be issued to original subscribers in exchange for property:

..... (.....) shares of the common stock of this Corporation having a par value of ..... ($.....) Dollars per share, fully paid and non-assessable, to each of the ..... *(insert number)* original subscribers therefor, in exchange for property described in the written proposal of ...., submitted to this meeting, and

RESOLVED FURTHER, That the form of application to be made to the .... *(insert department or officer)* of the State of ...., submitted to this meeting by the Secretary, is hereby approved, and the President and Secretary are hereby authorized to execute the same for and in behalf of this Corporation, and to take all steps necessary to present said application to the .... *(insert department or officer)*, and

If stock is to be issued to original subscribers for cash:

RESOLVED FURTHER, That the President and the Secretary are hereby directed, after they have obtained a permit from the .... *(insert department or*

officer) of the State of ...., to issue to each of the ..... original subscribers, ... (.....) shares of the common stock of this Corporation having a par value
of ..... ($.....) Dollars per share, upon payment therefor in cash, and

If stock is to be issued to original subscribers in exchange for property:

RESOLVED FURTHER, That the President and the Secretary are hereby directed,
after they have obtained a permit from the .... *(insert department or
officer)* of the State of ...., to issue to each of the ..... original subscribers, ... (.....) shares of the common stock of this Corporation having a par value
of ..... ($.....) Dollars per share, upon payment therefor, and to accept as payment
for said shares the property described in the proposal of ...., submitted to
this meeting.

RESOLUTION OF DIRECTORS AUTHORIZING APPLICATION
FOR THE SALE AND ISSUANCE OF AUTHORIZED STOCK

RESOLVED, That, subject to the approval of the .... *(insert department
or officer)* of the State of ...., this Corporation issue and sell at the par
value of ..... ($.....) Dollars per share, for cash, ... (.....) shares of the
authorized capital stock of this Corporation, and

RESOLVED FURTHER, That the President and the Secretary of this Corporation are
hereby authorized and directed to make an application to the .... *(insert
department or officer)* of the State of .... for leave to issue and sell ..... (.....)
shares of the authorized capital stock of this Corporation, or such part thereof as the
Board of Directors may hereafter deem advisable, at the par value of ..... ($.....)
Dollars per share for cash, and

RESOLVED FURTHER, That, subject to the approval of the .... *(insert
department or officer)*, this Corporation pay as brokerage for the sale of stock of
this Corporation, a commission not to exceed ..... (.....%) per cent of the selling
price.

RESOLUTION OF DIRECTORS AUTHORIZING BONUS OF
COMMON STOCK TO PURCHASERS OF PREFERRED STOCK

WHEREAS, it is deemed advisable by the Board of Directors that this Corporation offer for sale ..... (.....) shares of unissued preferred stock, having a par value
of ..... ($.....) Dollars per share, and

WHEREAS, this Corporation holds in its treasury ..... (.....) shares of fully paid
common stock, having a par value of ..... ($.....) Dollars each, and

WHEREAS, it is the opinion of the Board of Directors that, in order to facilitate
the sale of the preferred stock at par, it is advisable that the Corporation offer a
bonus of one share of common stock with each share of preferred stock purchased,
be it

RESOLVED, That the President, or such other officer or officers as he may designate, is hereby authorized to sell ..... (.....) shares of the preferred stock having a par value of ..... ($.....) Dollars each, at par for cash, and to offer as a bonus with each share of the preferred stock purchased, one share of common stock having a par value of ..... ($.....) Dollars, fully paid and nonassessable, and that the said shares of prefered and common stock be delivered upon receipt of full payment of the par value of each share of preferred stock purchased.

RESOLUTION OF DIRECTORS CREATING A SERIES OF PREFERRED STOCK AND FIXING DESIGNATIONS, PREFERENCES, AND OTHER RIGHTS OF INITIAL SERIES

RESOLVED, That, pursuant to authority expressly granted to and vested in the Board of Directors of the Corporation (hereinafter called the "Board of Directors") by the provisions of the Certificate of Incorporation of the Corporation as amended (hereinafter called the "Certificate of Incorporation"), the Board of Directors hereby creates a series of the Preferred Stock of the Corporation to consist initially of 50,000 shares, and hereby fixes the designations, powers, conversion privileges, preferences and other special rights, and the qualifications, limitations or restrictions thereof, of the shares of such series (in addition to the designations, powers, preferences and other special rights, and the qualifications, limitations or restrictions thereof, set forth in the Certificate of Incorporation, as amended, which are applicable to the Preferred Stock of all series) as follows:

(a) The designation of the series of Preferred stock created by this resolution shall be "$6.75 Cumulative Convertible Preferred Stock" (hereinafter in this resolution referred to as "This Series");

(b) The dividend rate of This Series shall be $6.75 per share in cash per annum, and no more, payable quarterly on the 15th days of January, April, July and October in each year, and the date from which dividends on all shares of such series issued prior to January 15, 19.. shall be cumulative beginning October 15, 19..;

(c) The redemption price which the holders of any shares of This Series shall be entitled to receive upon the redemption of such shares shall be

$110 per share if redeemed on or before December 31, 19..;

$109 per share if redeemed after December 31, 19.. and on or before December 31, 19..;

$108 per share if redeemed after December 31, 199.. and on or before December 31, 19..;

$107 per share if redeemed after December 31, 19.. and on or before December 31, 19..;

$106 per share if redeemed after December 31, 19.. and on or before December 31, 19..;

$105 per share if redeemed after December 31, 19..;

in each case plus an amount equal to all dividends accrued and unpaid to the redemption date;

(d) The shares of This Series shall be convertible at the option of the respective owners of record thereof upon surrender of the certificates representing the shares to be converted at the office of any transfer agent for the shares of This Series, at any time after December 15, 19.., or as to any shares of This Series called for redemption at any time up to, but not after the close of business on the day prior to the date fixed for such redemption, into fully paid and nonassessable shares (calculated to the nearest one one-hundredth [1/100] of a share) of Common Stock of the corporation in the ratio of one and three-sevenths (1-3/7) shares of Common Stock for each one (1) share of This Series; subject, however, to the terms and conditions hereinafter stated with respect to the adjustment of such ratio and otherwise.

1. The basic conversion price per share of the Common Stock for the purpose of such conversion shall be deemed to be $70; provided, however, that the conversion price per share of the Common Stock shall be subject to adjustment from time to time as hereinafter in this subdivision (d) provided; and in the event of the adjustment of the conversion price per share of the Common Stock as hereinafter in this subdivision (d) provided, the ratio in which shares of Common Stock shall thereafter be delivered upon conversion of each share of This Series shall be determined by dividing $100 by such adjusted conversion price per share of the Common Stock.

The term "Additional Shares of Common Stock" as used in this subdivision (d) shall mean and include any and all shares of Common Stock of the corporation in excess of the shares of Common Stock now outstanding, which may at any time be issued and sold for cash at a price to net the corporation less than the conversion price then in effect, including all shares of Common Stock which may be deliverable in connection with any options or convertible securities issued by the corporation after December 1, 19.., and irrespective of whether or not such shares of stock are issued, sold or offered to officers, employees and stockholders of the corporation; provided, however, that the term "Additional Shares of Common Stock" shall not include the issue of all or any part of the following: 200,026 shares reserved as of October 1, 19.. for conversion of the corporation's Five Years 4½% Debentures due July 1, 19..; 13,196 shares reserved for exercise of options by officers and supervisory personnel of the corporation as of October 1, 19..; and 25,000 shares which may from time to time be reserved for future disposition by the Board of Directors.

In case, and whenever the corporation shall issue or sell any Additional Shares of Common Stock and such Additional Shares of Common Stock shall be issued and sold for cash at a price to net the corporation less than the conversion price then in effect, then the conversion price per share of the Common Stock shall be immediately adjusted, and, if more than one such issue and sale shall occur, shall successively be adjusted as hereinafter in this subdivision (d) provided.

2. The adjusted conversion price per share of the Common Stock shall be determined by multiplying 600,000 by $70 and adding thereto the aggregate amount in cash (determined as provided in this subdivision (d)) received by the corporation from the issue and sale of all Additional Shares of Common Stock then and theretofore issued and sold and the resulting total shall be divided by 600,000 increased by the number of Additional Shares of Common Stock then issued and sold, if any, and the quotient resulting from such division shall be the conversion price per share of the Common Stock after such adjustment, until a further adjustment, if any, of the conversion price of the Common Stock shall be required to be made by reason of the issue and sale of Additional Shares of Common Stock; provided, however, that, subject to the provisions of paragraph 13 of this subdivision (d), in no event shall the conversion price per share of the Common Stock ever be increased.

3. In case the corporation shall issue any shares of Common Stock for property or services instead of for cash, the net fair value to the corporation of such property or services shall be conclusively determined by resolution adopted by the Board of Directors of the corporation, and such stock shall be deemed to have been sold for cash within the meaning of paragraph 1 of this subdivision (d), and the amount of cash that the corporation shall be deemed to have received from the issue of such shares shall be the net fair value to the corporation of such property or services as so determined.

4. In case the corporation shall issue any shares of Common Stock (i) by the way of split-up of outstanding shares of Common Stock, or (ii) by way of dividends payable in Common Stock, such shares shall be deemed to have been sold for cash within the meaning of paragraph 1 of this subdivision (d) for the price of zero dollars and zero dollars shall be deemed the aggregate amount of cash received by the corporation from the issue of such shares.

5. In case the corporation after the date of filing of this resolution shall issue any securities other than the shares of This Series authorized by this resolution which may be convertible into Common Stock of the corporation, it shall be deemed to have issued shares of Common Stock, simultaneously with the issuance of such convertible securities, in an amount equal to the maximum number of shares of Common Stock deliverable upon the conversion of such convertible securities so issued, and such shares of Common Stock shall be deemed to have been sold for cash within the meaning of paragraph 1 of this subdivision (d) and the corporation shall be deemed to have received for such shares of Common Stock a price determined by dividing the aggregate par value or principal amount (or in the case of stock without par value, the amount of money or the value in money of any property, labor or services for which such stock without par value shall have been issued and sold) of the convertible securities so issued by the maximum number of shares of Common Stock issuable upon the conversion of such convertible securities so issued.

6. In case the corporation, after the date of filing of this resolution shall issue any options, rights or warrants to purchase or subscribe for shares of Common Stock of the corporation, other than 25,000 shares reserved as provided in paragraph 1 hereof, it shall be deemed to have issued shares of Common Stock, simultaneously with the issuance of such options, rights or warrants, in an amount equal to the maximum number of shares of Common Stock deliverable upon the exercise of such options, rights or warrants so issued, and such shares of Common Stock shall be deemed to have been sold for cash within the meaning of paragraph 1 of this subdivision (d) and the corporation shall be deemed to have received for such shares the minimum price at which such shares may be purchased by the holders of such options, rights or warrants.

7. In determining the aggregate amount of cash received by the corporation from the sale of Additional Shares of Common Stock, such determination shall be made without deducting the amount of any commissions or expenses which may have been paid or incurred by the corporation for any underwriting of such stock or securities in connection with the sale thereof.

8. No reorganization of the corporation and no consolidation or merger thereof with or into any other corporation or corporations and no conveyance of all or substantially all of the assets of the corporation to any other corporation shall be made unless, as a part of such reorganization, consolidation or merger or conveyance, arrangements shall be made whereby the holders of the shares of This Series then outstanding shall thereafter be entitled to convert the same into any stock, securities or other assets given in exchange for the Common Stock of the corporation on such reorganization or in connection with such consolidation, merger or conveyance, in such amounts as would, at the time, have been given in exchange for the Common Stock then issuable upon conversion of such shares of This Series under the foregoing provisions hereof. Every right of the holder of such shares of This Series shall be continuous and preserved with respect to any stock and other securities and assets which such holder may so become entitled to receive upon conversion.

9. In lieu of issuing fractions of shares of Common Stock upon conversion of shares of This Series, the corporation shall issue fractional scrip certificates in such form calculated to the nearest 1/100th of a share as shall be approved by the Board of Directors, not entitling the holder to vote or receive dividends, but exchangeable for certificates of Common Stock when surrendered prior to the last day of the following calendar year, or such later time as may be specified by the Board of Directors, with other similar fractional scrip certificates in sufficient aggregate amount to equal one or more full shares, fractions of less than 1/100th being disregarded. The corporation, within a reasonable time after the end of each calendar year, shall cause to be sold in such manner as the Board of Directors may determine, the number of full shares of Common Stock represented by such fractional scrip certificates at the time outstanding which expired at the end of such calendar year, and thereafter the proceeds of such sale shall be held for the pro rata benefit of such outstanding and expired fractional scrip certificates.

10. Anything herein contained to the contrary notwithstanding, an adjustment of the conversion price of the Common Stock shall be required to be made

from time to time only when and as often as the issue and sale of Additional Shares of Common Stock would change the conversion price per share of Common Stock previously in effect by at least one dollar.

11. In each case where the corporation shall issue any Additional Shares of its Common Stock while any of the shares of This Series are outstanding (except shares issued upon the conversion of the shares of This Series, but including all shares of Common Stock which may be deliverable upon conversion of any convertible securities issued by the corporation after December 1, 19.., or upon the exercise of any options, rights or warrants issued by the corporation after December 1, 19..), it shall immediately file with the registrar and transfer agent for the shares of This Series written notice of the number of shares so issued and, as soon as may be and in no event later than thirty days after such issue, shall also file with such registrar and transfer agent a certificate showing:

(i)　the number of shares so issued and the date of issue;

(ii)　the price or prices at which such shares shall have been sold or be deemed to have been sold and the cash received or deemed to have been received by the corporation from the sale of such shares determined as hereinbefore provided;

(iii)　the adjusted conversion price per share which the Common Stock of the corporation shall therefter be deemed to have for the purposes of this subdivision (d);

(iv)　the ratio in which the shares of Common Stock shall thereafter, and until a further adjustment is made, be issuable upon the conversion of each share of This Series.

In the event that any Additional Shares shall have been issued for property or services the corporation, at he same time that it files the certificate hereinabove provided for, shall file with the registrar and transfer agent a certified copy of the resolution of the Board of Directors with respect to the net value to the corporation of such property or services as determined in the manner provided in paragraph 4 hereof.

12. The corporation shall give notice to the holders of record of the shares of This Series by mail, postage prepaid, at their respective addresses as the same appear on the stock transfer records of the corporation at least twenty (20) days before consummation of any transaction provided for or contemplated by paragraphs 4, 8, or 13 of this subdivision (d) or the issuance of rights to holders of the Common Stock by the corporation. The stock transfer books of the Common Stock and shares of this Series shall not be closed at any time so long as any of the shares of This Series shall remain outstanding, unless required by law and then only provided ten days' prior notice thereof shall have been given by publication in a daily newspaper published and of general circulation in the City of ....,
State of ....

In no event shall any allowance or adjustment be made on account of dividends accrued and unpaid on the shares of This Series surrendered for conversion or on account of any dividends on the Common Stock issued in exchange therefor; provided, however, that dividends declared on the shares of This Series payable to holders of record of such shares on a date prior to the surrender of the certificates for such shares for conversion shall be payable to the party or parties who were the record holders of such shares on said record date; and dividends declared on the Common Stock payable to holders of record of Common Stock on a date co-incident with or subsequent to the surrender of such shares for conversion shall be payable to the person who is the holder of record of such shares of Common Stock at the date of issue thereof.

Any holder of shares of This Series desiring to convert the same into Common Stock shall surrender the certificates representing the shares of This Series so to be converted at the office of any transfer agent of the corporation duly endorsed in blank or accompanied by proper instruments of transfer in such form as the corporation may require, and shall give written notice to the corporation at the office of such transfer agent that he elects to convert the said shares of This Series and set forth in such notice the name or names in which the certificate or certificates of Common Stock are to be issued. Shares of This Series surrendered for conversion shall be cancelled and shall not be reissued.

The corporation, as soon as practicable after such surrender of certificates for shares of This Series, accompanied by the notice above prescribed, will deliver, at the office of said transfer agent to the person by whom or for whose account such certificates for shares of This Series were so surrendered, certificates for the number of full shares of Common Stock deliverable upon such conversion accompanied by a scrip certificate for the excess fractional share, if any. Such conversion shall be deemed to have been made as of the date of such surrender of the certificates for the shares of This Series to be converted and the person or persons entitled to receive the Common Stock upon such conversion shall be treated for all purposes as the record holder or holders of such Common Stock as of the close of business on such date.

13. In case the corporation, by reclassification of its Common Stock by amendment to its Certificate of Incorporation, shall reduce the number of shares of such Common Stock outstanding, the conversion price per share of the Common Stock thereafter shall be immediately adjusted, and the adjusted conversion price per share of the Common Stock shall be determined by multiplying the number of shares of Common Stock outstanding immediately before such reduction by the then conversion price per share and the resulting product shall be divided by the reduced number of shares of Common Stock outstanding, and the quotient resulting from such division shall be the conversion price per share of the Common Stock after such adjustment, until a further adjustment of the conversion price of the Common Stock shall be required to be made by reason of a further reduction of the number of shares of such Common Stock outstanding or the issue and sale of Additional Shares of Common Stock. If, after any such reduction in the number of shares of Common Stock of the Corporation issued and outstanding by such

reclassification, there shall be issued and sold any Additional Shares of Common Stock over and above the number of shares of Common Stock issued and outstanding as reduced by such reclassification, then the conversion price per share of the Common Stock shall be immediately adjusted in the manner hereinbefore provided, except that, in place of the multiplication figure of 600,000 used in paragraph 2 of this subdivision (d), there shall be used a figure equal to the number of shares of Common Stock to which 600,000 shares would have been reduced if outstanding and in place of the basic conversion price of $70 per share used in said paragraph 2 of the subdivision (d) there shall be used the adjusted conversion price resulting from such reclassification, and in place of the divisor provided in said paragraph 2 of this subdivision (d) the divisor shall be the sum of (a) a figure equal to the number of shares of Common Stock to which the 600,000 shares would have been reduced if outstanding plus (b) the number of Additional Shares of Common Stock outstanding as reduced by such reclassification and (c) the number of Additional Shares of Common Stock issued subsequent to such reclassification.

14. The corporation shall at all times keep available out of its authorized but unissued and unreserved Common Stock for the purpose of effecting the conversion of shares of This Series and the exchange of such scrip certificates, if any, which may be issued as aforesaid, such number of shares of its Common Stock as shall from time to time be sufficient to effect the conversion of all outstanding shares of This Series and to effect the exchange of any such scrip certificates which shall not have expired. All shares of Common Stock issued or delivered upon conversion of the shares of This Series shall be duly and validly issued and fully paid and nonassessable. The corporation shall pay the amount of any and all taxes imposed in respect of the issue or delivery of shares of the Common Stock upon conversion of any of the shares of This Series in the name or names of the respective owners of record of the shares of This Series surrendered for conversion.

RESOLUTION OF DIRECTORS AUTHORIZING ISSUANCE OF A NEW SERIES OF STOCK, AND FIXING THE PREFERENCES AND OTHER ATTRIBUTES THEREOF

WHEREAS, under Section ..... of the Certificate of Incorporation of .... Corporation, this Corporation is permitted to issue its Class A Stock, having a par value of ..... ($.....) Dollars per share, in series, with such designations, preferences, and relative participating, optional, or other rights and qualifications, limitations, or restrictions as may be fixed by the Board of Directors, and

WHEREAS, the Board of Directors has authorized, under said provision of the Certificate of Incorporation, the issuance of Series A and B, with variations among the series as to the rate of dividends, premium on redemption, and conversion price, such variations having been adapted to the condition of the Corporation and the market situation at the time of issuance, and

WHEREAS, the directors deem it advisable to issue a new series of Class A Stock at this time, and have carefully investigated the relation of the condition of the Corporation to the condition of the security market, and have determined that it is for the best interests of the Corporation to give the new series, to be denominated Series C, the attributes set forth in this resolution, be it

RESOLVED, That the Corporation issue forthwith ..... (.....) shares of Series C, Class A Stock. The holders of series C, Class A Stock shall be entitled to receive, out of the net earnings, a cumulative dividend at the rate of ..... (.....%) per cent per annum, when declared by the Board of Directors, payable quarterly, half-yearly, or yearly, as the directors may from time to time determine, when and after a dividend of ..... (.....%) per cent per annum and all accumulated dividends, if any, shall have been paid to the holders of Series A and B, Class A Stock, but before any dividends shall be set apart for or paid in any year on Class B Stock; and the holders of Series C, Class A Stock shall not participate in any additional earnings or profits.

In case of liquidation, dissolution, or winding up of the affairs of the Corporation, whether voluntary or involuntary, holders of Series C, Class A Stock shall be preferred, equally with holders of Series A and B, Class A Stock, over all other holders of stock of the Corporation, to the amount of ..... ($.....) Dollars per share and accumulated or accrued and unpaid dividends thereon, and

RESOLVED FURTHER, That the President and Secretary are hereby authorized and directed to cause to be filed, under corporate seal such certificates as shall be requisite, to the end that the stock shall be issued as aforesaid, and

RESOLVED FURTHER, That the Secretary is hereby authorized and directed to instruct Messrs. .... and ...., counsel for this Corporation, to prepare a form of stock certificate for Series C, Class A Stock, in accordance with the above resolution.

DIRECTORS' RESOLUTION AUTHORIZING ISSUANCE OF ADDITIONAL VOTING TRUST CERTIFICATES

WHEREAS, this corporation is in need of working capital, and

WHEREAS, from time to time, opportunity is offered to sell additional voting trust certificates for common stock of this Corporation upon advantageous terms, be it

RESOLVED, That this Corporation issue voting trust certificates for not exceeding ..... (.....) additional shares of common stock from time to time, upon such terms and conditions as the Executive Committee of this Corporation may determine, and

RESOLVED FURTHER, That any transfer agent and the appropriate registrar for voting trust certificates for the common stock of this Corporation are hereby authorized and directed from time to time to countersign and register voting trust certificates for not exceeding ..... additional shares of the common stock of this Corporation, as may be provided by resolution of the Executive Committee of this Corporation, and

RESOLVED FURTHER, That the proper officers are hereby authorized and directed from time to time to issue common stock of this Corporation to an amount not exceeding ..... (.....) shares, to provide for the issuance of an equal amount of voting trust certificates for said common stock, as hereinbefore set forth, and to deliver the same to the depository for the voting trustees under the Voting Trust Agreement.

RESOLUTION OF DIRECTORS AUTHORIZING ISSUANCE OF STOCK FOR CASH

WHEREAS, ... Corporation has offered to turn over to this Company the sum of ..... ($.....) Dollars, in consideration that this Company issue to the order of .... Corporation ..... (.....) shares of capital stock of this Company, fully paid and nonassessable, including the shares subscribed by the incorporators, be it

RESOLVED, That the offer of .... Corporation is hereby accepted; that the proper officers are hereby authorized and directed to execute, issue, and deliver, in the name and in behalf of this Company, and under its corporate seal, certificates of stock for ..... (.....) shares to the order of .... Corporation.

RESOLUTION OF DIRECTORS AUTHORIZING ISSUANCE OF STOCK AT LESS THAN PAR BECAUSE OF FINANCIAL CONDITION OF THE COMPANY

WHEREAS, this corporation has been engaged in the business of .... since the year 19.., and

WHEREAS, the common stock of this corporation, having a par value of ..... ($.....) Dollars per share, has declined in value to ..... ($.....) Dollars per share, owing to a decline in earnings during the past ..... (.....) years, and

WHEREAS, it is necessary for this corporation, in order to meet its obligations, to sell and issue ..... (.....) shares of the common stock of this corporation, and

WHEREAS, on account of the financial condition of the corporation, it will be impossible for this corporation to sell such shares of unissued common stock at par, be it

RESOLVED, That ..... (.....) shares of unissued common stock, having a par value of ..... ($.....) Dollars per share, be sold and issued for the consideration or price of ..... ($.....) Dollars per share, which is the fair market value thereof.

[*Note.* For legal principles governing power of corporation to issue shares of stock with par value for less than par, see pages 466-467 in Chapter 15.]

RESOLUTION OF DIRECTORS ADVISING STOCKHOLDERS TO AUTHORIZE ISSUANCE OF STOCK AT LESS THAN PAR AND/OR STOCK WITHOUT PAR VALUE FOR MONEY

Resolved, That the stockholders of the Corporation are hereby advised to authorize the issuance of not exceeding ..... (.....) fully paid and nonassessable shares of the par value of ..... ($.....) Dollars each of the preferred stock of the Corporation, for money, at not less than ..... ($.....) Dollars for each share thereof (and/or not exceeding ..... (.....) fully paid and nonassessable shares without par value of the common stock of the Corporation, for money, at not less than ..... ($.....) Dollars for each share thereof).

DIRECTORS' RESOLUTION AUTHORIZING ISSUANCE OF STOCK FOR SERVICES AND ADVANCES

Whereas, ... and .... have rendered services and paid expenses for this Corporation in its organization, of the reasonable value of ..... ($.....) Dollars, be it

Resolved, That the President and Secretary issue to each of said persons one share of the common stock of this Corporation, fully paid and non-assessable, in full payment of said indebtedness.

DIRECTORS' RESOLUTION AUTHORIZING ISSUANCE OF STOCK FOR SERVICES RENDERED BY AN INDIVIDUAL

Whereas, ..., as attorney for the Company, has purchased land for this Company, has represented the Company in numerous financial transactions, tax matters and other litigation and business, and is presently rendering services in connection with the erection of the Company's new building at .... *(Street)*, ... *(City)*, ... *(State)*, and

Whereas, ... has been paid no compensation during the past ..... years for any of the above mentioned services, be it

Resolved, That there be issued to .... the sum of ..... (.....%) per cent of the common capital stock of the Company—to wit, ... (.....) shares of the said stock—which stock will be issued to him fully paid and nonassessable in consideration for his release of the Company from all liability to him in connection with the above-mentioned services as well as from all liability to him in connection with any services that he may perform in the future in connection with the completion of the above-mentioned new building.

RESOLUTION OF DIRECTORS AUTHORIZING ISSUANCE OF STOCK FOR SERVICES RENDERED BY A CORPORATION

WHEREAS, this Company was organized, promoted, and developed into a going concern and placed on a firm and profitable basis by the capital supplied by the .... Corporation, and

WHEREAS, the said Corporation, since the organization of this Company and until the present date, has supplied the bulk of the labor and office organization necessary to carry on its business, and has permitted its officers to manage and direct the affairs of this Company without making any charge, which work, labor, and services so rendered by the said Corporation have been of inestimable value and assistance to this Company and necessary to a businesslike and profitable conduct of its business, be it

RESOLVED, That this Company issue to the .... Corporation, or its assignees or nominees, in consideration of the foregoing, ... (.....) shares of the common stock of this Company having a total par value of ..... ($.....) Dollars, fully paid and nonassessable, and

RESOLVED FURTHER, That the President and the Secretary are hereby authorized and directed to execute and deliver certificates of stock to the .... Corporation, or its nominees, as aforesaid.

RESOLUTION OF DIRECTORS AUTHORIZING ISSUANCE OF STOCK AS COMPENSATION FOR SERVICES IN ORGANIZING CORPORATION

WHEREAS, ..., of .... *(City)*, ... *(State)*, and .... of .... *(City)*, ... *(State)*, have heretofore rendered valuable services to this Corporation in organizing, incorporating, and placing it upon a sound financial basis, and

WHEREAS, the said .... and .... have expressed their willingness to accept, as compensation for such services, shares of common stock of this Corporation, be it

RESOLVED, That the Board of Directors of this Corporation does hereby determine that the services so rendered are worth to the Corporation the sum of ..... ($.....) Dollars, and

RESOLVED FURTHER, That the President and the Secretary of this Corporation are hereby authorized and directed to issue to ...., ... (.....) shares of fully paid capital stock of this Corporation, and to ...., ... (.....) shares of fully paid capital stock of this Corporation, as compensation for services rendered by .... and .... as aforesaid.

RESOLUTION OF DIRECTORS AUTHORIZING ISSUANCE OF STOCK FOR CONSIDERATION OTHER THAN MONEY

Resolved, That the issuance of ..... (.....) fully paid and nonassessable shares of the par value of ..... ($.....) Dollars each of the preferred stock of the Corporation (and/or ..... (.....) fully paid and nonassessable shares without par value of the common stock of the Corporation), for the following consideration, be and the same hereby is authorized:

(Here insert particular description of consideration, showing its nature and character.)

EXCERPT FROM MINUTES OF DIRECTORS' MEETING INCLUDING RESOLUTION AUTHORIZING ISSUANCE OF STOCK FOR PROPERTY

The Secretary laid before the meeting a written proposal submitted by ...., to sell and transfer to the Corporation in consideration of the issuance to him of ..... fully paid and non-assessable shares of the common stock of this Corporation having an aggregate par value of ..... ($.....) Dollars, real property valued at ..... ($.....) Dollars, as set forth in said communication.

The communication was ordered spread upon the minutes and is as follows: *(Insert written offer as indicated above.)*

Said proposal was discussed in detail, after which, upon motion duly made and seconded, the following resolution was unanimously adopted:

Whereas, an offer has been made by .... to sell and transfer to this Corporation certain real property described as follows *(insert description)*, and to accept in full payment thereof, ... (.....) fully paid and non-assessable shares of the common stock of this Corporation having an aggregate par value of ..... ($.....) Dollars, as provided in a certain written proposal dated ...., 19.., signed by said ...., which has been submitted to and entered upon the minutes of this meeting, and is hereby referred to and made part of this resolution, be it

Resolved, That said property mentioned in said offer is suitable for the purpose of this Corporation, and that it is advisable for this Corporation to purchase said property, and to issue in payment therefor ..... (.....) shares of common stock having an aggregate par value of ..... ($.....) Dollars, and that said offer is accordingly accepted in its entirety, and

Resolved Further, That the issuance of ..... (.....) fully paid and non-assessable shares of common stock having an aggregate par value of ..... ($.....) Dollars, to ...., is hereby authorized for the following consideration; viz.: the transfer to this Corporation of a good title to the real property hereinbefore mentioned and described, and

RESOLVED FURTHER, That, in the opinion of the Board of Directors, the actual value of said property is not less than ..... ($.....) Dollars (*or*, "is at least worth the par value of such shares"), and

RESOLVED FURTHER, That on the execution and delivery of a good and sufficient deed conveying to this Corporation the fee simple title to said property in accordance with the terms of said proposal, the officers of this Corporation are hereby authorized and directed to execute and deliver to ...., a certificate for ..... (.....) shares of the common stock of this Corporation, fully paid and nonassessable, in full payment for said property.

RESOLUTION OF DIRECTORS AUTHORIZING ISSUANCE OF STOCK FOR PATENTS

WHEREAS, ... has offered to assign to this Corporation, for and in consideration of the issuance to him of ..... (.....) shares of the capital stock of this Corporation having a par value of ..... (.....) Dollars each, fully paid and nonassessable, certain patents covering inventions relating to .... *(state nature of invention)*, which are more particularly described as follows: United States Patent No. ....., dated ...., 19.., and United Stated Patent No. ....., dated ...., 19.., both issued to ...., and

WHEREAS, in the judgment of this Board of Directors, said patents are necessary for the business of this Corporation, and the fair value thereof is ..... ($.....) Dollars, be it

RESOLVED, That this Corporation issue to ...., ... (.....) shares of its capital stock having a par value of ..... ($.....) Dollars each, fully paid and nonassessable, in consideration of the assignment of said patents to this Corporation; and the President and the Treasurer are hereby authorized and directed to deliver ..... (.....) shares of capital stock to .... upon the execution and delivery of the proper legal instruments necessary to transfer said patents to this Corporation.

RESOLUTION OF DIRECTORS AUTHORIZING ISSUANCE OF STOCK FOR PATENTS, DRAWINGS, AND SIMILAR ASSETS

WHEREAS, this Company has been organized for the purpose of manufacturing, selling, and dealing in traction engines and all types and styles of internal combustion engines and other machinery and implements, and

WHEREAS, for the conduct and establishment of said business, it is necessary to secure certain patents, patent rights, blueprints, etc., and

WHEREAS, "A" of .... *(City)*, ... *(State)*, has represented himself as being the owner of the following patents and various serial applications for patents, as follows:

(Here insert number, date of issuance, and nature of patents.)

WHEREAS, said "A" is also the owner of certain full and complete detailed drawings or blueprints of a certain traction engine which the said "A" has developed and constructed, and

WHEREAS, the said "A" has offered to convey to this Corporation all his rights, title, and interest in and to all of the said patents, patent rights, blueprints, and any patents or serial applications or improvements upon tractors not yet protected by application, other than those specifically herein mentioned, in or to which "A" may have any right, title, or interest whatsoever, all in consideration of the transfer to "A" by this Corporation of ..... (.....) shares of the common stock of this Corporation and ..... (.....) shares of the preferred stock of this Corporation, as shown by the offer of "A" in writing herewith filed, and

WHEREAS, the use of said patents and patent rights is necessary for the commencement and carrying on of the business of this Corporation, be it

RESOLVED, That the offer of "A" is hereby accepted, and the officers of this Corporation are hereby duly authorized and directed, upon the receipt from "A" of the transfers of the patents, patent rights, and the delivery of the blueprints, to receive the same in full payment of ..... (.....) shares of the common stock of this Corporation and ..... (.....) shares of the preferred stock of this Corporation, and to issue and deliver said stock to "A."

RESOLUTION OF DIRECTORS AUTHORIZING ISSUANCE OF STOCK IN SETTLEMENT OF INDEBTEDNESS

WHEREAS, this corporation, under an agreement with the .... Company, dated ...., 19.., has borrowed from .... Company the sum of ..... ($.....) Dollars for the purchase of properties for this corporation, and is now indebted to .... Company for such amount plus interest accrued thereon from the .. day of ...., 19.., at ..... (.....%) per cent per annum, and

WHEREAS, the .... Company has agreed to accept ..... (.....) shares of stock of this corporation, fully paid and nonassessable, in full payment of the principal sum of the indebtedness of this corporation to said .... Company, including interest accrued thereon from ...., 19.., at .... (.....%) per cent per annum, be it

RESOLVED, That the proper officers are hereby authorized and directed to execute and deliver to the .... Company, or their nominee, ... (.....) shares of the common stock of this corporation, in full payment of the aforementioned indebtedness of this corporation to the .... Company, and to obtain from the .... Company evidence of such indebtedness.

RESOLUTION OF DIRECTORS ACCEPTING NOTE IN PAYMENT FOR STOCK.

RESOLVED, That the proper officers of this Corporation are hereby authorized to sell and issue ..... (.....) shares of common stock of this Corporation, at par, to ...., upon payment to this Corporation of ..... ($.....) Dollars in cash, the

balance of the price of said stock to be evidenced by a promissory note of said
................, secured by the pledge of the stock so purchased, said note to be due
and payable in ..... (.....) days, with interest at ..... (.....%) per cent per annum.

DIRECTORS' RESOLUTION ACCEPTING ASSIGNMENT OF CONTRACT AND AUTHORIZING PAYMENT IN STOCK AND A NOTE

RESOLVED, That this Company accept the offer of A to assign, transfer, and set
over the contract and the claim of A, against B, doing business as B & Co.,
described in the agreement presented at this meeting, a copy of which agreement is
in words and figures as follows *(insert copy of agreement)*; and that the Board of
Directors does hereby declare that the contract and claim of A against the said B,
doing business as B & Co., is of the fair value of ..... ($.....) Dollars, and that the
same is necessary for the business of this Company, and

RESOLVED FURTHER, That the President and the Treasurer are hereby authorized
and directed to execute said agreement on behalf of the Company, and to issue
certificates of fully paid capital stock of this Company to the aggregate amount of
..... ($.....) Dollars, to A, as provided in said agreement; and to execute the
promissory note of this Company for the sum of ..... ($.....) Dollars, payable to
the order of ...., four (4) months after ...., 19.., with interest at six
(6%) per cent per annum as provided by said agreement.

RESOLUTION OF DIRECTORS FIXING VALUE OF NO-PAR SHARES

RESOLVED, That, in the judgment of the Board of Directors, the fair market
value of the shares of stock which this Corporation is authorized to issue without
par value is ..... ($.....) Dollars per share; and the proper officers of the Corpora-
tion are hereby authorized to issue and sell the unissued shares of stock without par
value at said price of ..... ($.....) Dollars per share.

RESOLUTION OF DIRECTORS FIXING THE PRICE OR CONSIDERATION TO BE RECEIVED FOR REMAINING NO-PAR UNISSUED STOCK

RESOLVED, That the remaining unsubscribed and unissued shares of
preferred/common stock without nominal or par value, of this Corporation,
amounting to ..... (.....) shares, be sold for the consideration or price of .....
($.....) Dollars per share, which is the fair value thereof, and

RESOLVED FURTHER, That the directors are hereby authorized to sell the remaining unissued shares of preferred/common stock without par value at the price
above fixed, and to offer subscribers thereto the option of paying for their
subscriptions in full at the time of making the subscription, or of paying in two
installments as follows: ..... ($.....) Dollars to be paid at the time of making the

subscription, and the balance of ..... ($.....) Dollars to be paid within ..... (.....) months from the date of subscription.

RESOLUTION OF DIRECTORS FIXING THE PRICE OF NO-PAR STOCK AND AUTHORIZING ISSUE OF STOCK

RESOLVED, That the Board of Directors of this Corporation does hereby place a value of ..... ($.....) Dollars per share upon the common stock without par value of this Corporation, for the purpose of sale for cash or other authorized consideration, and

RESOLVED FURTHER, That an issue of the common stock without par value of this Corporation to the extent of ..... (.....) shares is hereby authorized, and that the President and the Treasurer of the Corporation are hereby authorized to accept subscriptions to the common stock of the Corporation at the price above stated.

DIRECTORS' RESOLUTION FIXING MINIMUM CASH CONSIDERATION FOR A DESIGNATED PORTION OF NO-PAR STOCK TO BE ISSUED AND SOLD

RESOLVED, That the officers of this Company are hereby authorized to issue and sell, from time to time, not exceeding ..... (.....) shares of the $6 no-par preferred stock of this Company, with the understanding, however, that until further order of this Board of Directors, there shall be issued, from time to time, in the discretion of such officers, not exceeding ..... (.....) shares of such stock, which shall be sold for a cash consideration of not less than ..... ($.....) Dollars per share, and the accrued unpaid dividends thereon, and that the cash consideration received from such stock (less any amounts representing accrued dividends) is hereby fixed and determined as the consideration for which such shares of the $6 preferred stock shall, from time to time, be issued.

RESOLUTION OF DIRECTORS STATING PART OF THE CONSIDERATION FOR NO-PAR STOCK TO BE REGARDED AS CAPITAL

RESOLVED, That ..... ($.....) Dollars of the consideration received by the Corporation for any of the shares of its capital stock without par value which it shall from time to time issue shall be capital.

RESOLUTION OF DIRECTORS STATING PART OF THE CONSIDERATION RECEIVED FOR NO-PAR STOCK TO BE REGARDED AS CAPITAL (ANOTHER FORM)

RESOLVED, That .... Dollars ($...............) of the consideration received for the ..... (.....) shares of stock without par value, authorized to be issued under (this or the foregoing) resolution, shall be considered capital.

[*Note*. This resolution may be added to any resolution authorizing the issuance of stock without par value. In states that have a statute requiring allocation of the consideration paid for stock without par value to be made by the directors at the time of issuance of the stock where the consideration is cash, it is important that this resolution be coupled with the resolution authorizing the issue of stock without par value; otherwise, all the consideration will be treated as capital and none as paid-in surplus.]

RESOLUTION OF DIRECTORS APPROVING FORM OF REGISTRATION STATEMENT AND PROSPECTUS

RESOLVED, That the forms of registration statement and related prospectus submitted to the meeting are hereby approved for initial filing of the registration statement, and that only such changes shall be made therein as shall be approved by the Chairman of the Board of Directors of the Company and by counsel for the Company.

RESOLUTION OF DIRECTORS AUTHORIZING FILING OF REGISTRATION STATEMENT AND PROSPECTUS, AND AMENDMENTS THEREOF

RESOLVED, That the officers of this Corporation are hereby authorized to execute in the name of the Corporation and to file with the Securities and Exchange Commission, Washington, D.C., registration statement on Form ....., substantially in the form of such registration statement submitted to and considered at this meeting, with such changes therein as the officers executing the same may consider advisable or necessary; and that the officers of the Corporation are hereby similarly authorized to sign and file a prospectus in the form of the proposed prospectus submitted to and considered at this meeting, with such changes therein as they may consider advisable and necessary, with power to the officers of the Corporation to file such amended registration statement and/or such amended prospectus as they in their discretion deem necessary or advisable in order to effect the registration with the Securities and Exchange Commission of the securities referred to in the said registration statement, Form ....., in accordance with the requirements of the Securities Act of 1933, as amended.

EXCERPT OF MINUTES OF DIRECTORS' MEETING AUTHORIZING AMENDMENT OF REGISTRATION STATEMENT AND PROSPECTUS

There was submitted to the meeting a proposed form of amendment to the registration statement, and a proposed amendment of prospectus appertaining to the registration of 150,000 shares of the 200,000 authorized shares of the 5% Cumulative Preferred Stock of the Corporation. Explanations with respect thereto were made by certain officers of the Corporation. Representatives of .... & Co., auditors for the Corporation, and Mr. ...., Vice-President of .... Corporation, were requested to attend the meeting ,and questions were asked of them with respect to matters appertaining to such amendment of the registration statement and prospectus. After consideration thereof, upon motion duly made and seconded, it was unanimously

RESOLVED, That the proper officers of this Corporation are hereby authorized and directed in behalf of this Corporation to cause such amendment of the registration statement and the prospectus, in the respective forms thereof presented to the meeting, to be executed and to be duly filed with the Securities and Exchange Commission at Washington, D.C., and to do such acts and execute such documents as may be necessary and proper to effect due registration of such shares of stock.

DIRECTORS' RESOLUTION AUTHORIZING APPLICATION FOR LISTING STOCK ON STOCK EXCHANGE

RESOLVED, That application be made to the .... Stock Exchange for the listing of ...., of this Corporation and that .... be designated by the Corporation to appear before the Department of Stock List of said Exchange, with authority to make such changes in said application, or in any agreements relative thereto, as may be necessary to conform with requirements for listing.

DIRECTORS' RESOLUTION AUTHORIZING FILING WITH SECURITIES AND EXCHANGE COMMISSION FOR REGISTRATION OF SHARES RESULTING FROM SPLIT-UP

RESOLVED, That the proper officers of this Corporation are authorized and directed to prepare and file with the Securities and Exchange Commission, and with the .... Stock Exchange, an application, on the proper form, for the registration of the additional shares of common stock without par value of this Corporation resulting from the split-up of the shares of common stock of the Corporation now outstanding.

DIRECTORS' RESOLUTION AUTHORIZING ISSUANCE OF PROSPECTUS ADVERTISING THE SALE OF STOCK

RESOLVED, That the officers of this Corporation are hereby authorized to issue a prospectus advertising the offer to sell ..... (.....) shares of the common stock of this Corporation, in substantially the form presented at this meeting and set forth in the minutes below, after the approval of the *(insert department or officer)* of the State of .... has been obtained, as required by the laws of the State of ...., and after all federal requirements relating to the issuance and sale of securities have been met.

RESOLUTION OF STOCKHOLDERS AUTHORIZING SALE AND ISSUE OF STOCK TO PERSONS DETERMINED BY BOARD OF DIRECTORS

RESOLVED, That the Board of Directors is hereby authorized and empowered to issue such additional shares of the company's presently authorized but unissued ..... ($.....) par value common stock to such persons and at such time and price as the Board of Directors in its sole discretion shall determine to be in the best interests of the Corporation.

RESOLUTION OF DIRECTORS AUTHORIZING OFFICERS
TO ISSUE STOCK TO A DESIGNATED INDIVIDUAL

Resolved, That the proper officers of this company are hereby authorized and instructed to issue in the name of ...., certificates for ..... (.....) shares of the preferred stock of this company, and to deliver the same to .... Trust Co., as Transfer Agent of said stock, for countersignature, and to .... Bank & Trust Co., as Registrar of said stock, for registration.

RESOLUTION OF DIRECTORS AUTHORIZING SALE AND
ISSUE OF STOCK TO PERSONS DETERMINED BY
EXECUTIVE COMMITTEE

Resolved, That this corporation sell and issue ..... (.....) shares of the Preferred Stock of this corporation at par, and ..... (.....) shares of Common Stock have no par value at .... dollars ($.....) per share, payable in cash at the time of purchase, to such persons, firms, or corporations as the Executive Committee shall determine, and the President and the Secretary of this corporation are hereby authorized to execute and deliver certificates of stock to purchasers upon receipt of full payment for shares purchased.

RESOLUTION OF DIRECTORS RECOMMENDING
THAT STOCKHOLDERS AUTHORIZE THE ISSUANCE
OF STOCK TO EMPLOYEES

Whereas, by the recent increase of capital stock of this corporation, there has become available for further subscriptions a total of ..... (.....) shares of the common stock without par value, of this corporation, and

Whereas, it is the belief of the Board of Directors of this corporation that its employees would be interested in acquiring a part of the capital stock, and that ownership of stock of this corporation by employees would be to the advantage of this corporation, be it

Resolved, That the Board of Directors of this corporation does hereby recommend to the stockholders that they authorize the Board of Directors to set aside a total of ..... (.....) shares of the common stock of this corporation, for sale to the employees and officers upon the following terms:

Subscriptions to said stock shall be received from any employee of the corporation from ...., 19.., up to and including ...., 19... Subscriptions to the common stock shall be on the basis of the book value of said stock as of ...., 19.., namely, ... dollars ($.....). Payment for such stock shall be made as follows:

..... per cent (...%) of the subscription shall be payable simultaneously with the execution and delivery of such subscription, and the balance shall be payable in installments of ..... per cent (...%) per month until the amount of the subscription shall have been fully paid in. The stock subscribed for shall not be actually issued until the full amount of such subscription shall have been paid in, and, pending the full payment of such subscription, no dividend shall be declared and paid upon the stock so subscribed for. The company, however, shall credit and pay to each subscriber interest on installments paid in at the rate of ..... per cent (...%) per annum. Subscriptions for stock as herein provided for shall contain an agreement that, in the event that any installment shall not be paid on its due date, the corporation shall have the right to return to such subscriber any installment or installments standing to his credit, without interest, and cancel the balance of such subscription. Subscribers shall further agree that, in the event that the subscriber shall leave the employ of the corporation, whether voluntarily or involuntarily, he or she shall resell to the corporation any stock actually issued at the book value of such stock at the time when the stock is to be resold to the company.

Subscribers shall further agree that any payment standing to his or her credit at the time when he or she shall leave the employ of the corporation, whether voluntarily or involuntarily, not represented by certificates of stock actually issued, shall be repaid to him or her without interest, and that the subscription shall be canceled.

Subscribers shall further agree that, upon the death of such subscriber, if his or her heirs or legal representatives shall not wish to retain ownership of such stock or continue to pay the installments, any stock issued or installments paid shall be subject to the same conditions that apply in the case of a subscriber who leaves the employ of the corporation.

RESOLUTION OF STOCKHOLDERS AUTHORIZING BOARD OF DIRECTORS TO SET ASIDE UNISSUED STOCK FOR SALE TO EMPLOYEES

RESOLVED, That the Board of Directors is hereby authorized to set aside ..... (.....) shares of the common stock without par value of this Corporation, provided for by the increase in the capital stock duly authorized by the stockholders of this Corporation on the .. day of ...., 19.., for sale and issuance to the employees of this Corporation and of its subsidiaries, upon the following terms:

(Here insert terms as given in preceding resolution.)

RESOLUTION OF STOCKHOLDERS OR DIRECTORS AUTHORIZING THE CORPORATION TO SELL STOCK TO AN EMPLOYEE, RESERVING THE RIGHT TO REPURCHASE

WHEREAS, it is the desire of this Corporation that ...., an employee of this Corporation, shall own stock of this Corporation, be it

RESOLVED, That the Board of Directors of this Corporation is hereby authorized to enter into an agreement with ...., to sell ..... (.....) shares of the common stock of this Corporation for ..... ($.....) Dollars, said agreement to provide that in event of the death of ...., the Corporation, or its assigns, shall for 90 days thereafter have the right to repurchase the said stock, at its election, for the sum of ..... ($.....) Dollars per share, plus interest upon the amount from the date of the last dividend paid upon the stock to the date of such purchase, at the rate of ..... (.....%) per cent per annum. Said agreement shall provide further that, in order to effectuate the purposes of the agreement, the stock so purchased by .... shall be issued to the .... Bank, as Trustee, and shall be held by it in trust for the parties to the agreement, pursuant to the terms of the agreement, until such time, if any, as this Corporation, or its assigns, shall elect to repurchase the said stock, subject to the terms of the agreement. All dividends upon the said stock during said period shall be paid to .... as they become due, and .... shall have the right during the period to vote the stock at all meetings of this Corporation, but he shall not pledge or transfer said stock, or otherwise prevent the carrying out of the agreement. The agreement shall provide further that, in the event this Corporation, or its assigns, shall elect under the agreement to repurchase the stock, it shall pay the purchase price therefor to the bank, as trustee, and the bank shall thereupon transfer the stock to this Corporation, or its assigns, and pay over the purchase price to the executors or administrators of .... If, having the right to repurchase said stock, this Corporation, or its assigns, shall elect not to do so, said bank shall thereupon, and after 90 days after the death of said ...., transfer the same to his executors or administrators, whose title thereto shall thereupon become absolute.

RESOLUTION OF DIRECTORS ALLOTTING SHARES
OF STOCK TO EMPLOYEES

WHEREAS, the ..... (.....) shares of common stock of this corporation, reserved for sale to the employees of this corporation at ..... dollars ($.....) per share have been oversubscribed, be it

RESOLVED, That the President is hereby authorized to allot the ..... (.....) shares of common stock reserved for employees, to subscribers in the proportion that the subscription of each employee bears to the total amount of common stock subscribed for by all employees, and that the President is authorized to make such allotment, among employeee subscribers, of shares not allotted because of fractional subscriptions resulting from this method of allotment, as in his discretion seems most beneficial to this corporation.

RESOLUTION OF DIRECTORS APPOINTING COMMITTEE TO
ALLOT SHARES TO EMPLOYEES AS THEY DEEM BEST

WHEREAS, the ..... (.....) shares of common stock of this corporation, reserved for sale to the employees of this corporation at ..... dollars ($.....) per share have been oversubscribed, be it

RESOLVED, That ...., ..., and ...., are hereby appointed members of a committee to make such allotment of the shares of common stock reserved for employees of this corporation as they shall deem to be for the best interests of the corporation.

RESOLUTION OF DIRECTORS AUTHORIZING SALE OF TREASURY STOCK AT AUCTION

WHEREAS, in the judgment of this Board, it is necessary and desirable for this Company to raise money for additional working capital and to meet the costs of improving the company's property, and to that end to sell shares of common stock of the Company now held in the treasury, be it

RESOLVED, That this Company offer to sell at public auction, as soon as possible, ... (.....) shares of said common stock, giving to the general public the opportunity of making bids for all or any part of such stock, and

RESOLVED FURTHER, That all persons desiring to make bids for such stock be required to deliver the same in writing to .... Bank, Transfer Agent of this Company, specifying the number of shares desired and the price offered, and to deposit therewith ..... (.....%) per cent of such price in lawful money of the United States, and that this Company reserves the right to accept or to reject all or any of such bids, and

RESOLVED FURTHER, That the Secretary of this Company is hereby authorized and directed to prepare a form of circular containing the terms and conditions of said offer, and a form of bid, and to submit the same for approval at the next meeting of this Board.

RESOLUTION OF DIRECTORS ADOPTING FORM OF INVITATION FOR BIDS FOR TREASURY STOCK, AND FORM OF BID

RESOLVED, That the form of invitation for bids for ..... shares of the common stock of this Company, now held in the treasury, and the form of bid submitted at this meeting, and the terms and conditions stated therein, are hereby approved and adopted, and,

RESOLVED FURTHER, That the Secretary of this Company is hereby authorized and directed to cause said invitation for bids and said form of bid to be printed and mailed to the stockholders of this Company and also to such other persons, firms, and corporations as the officers of the Company may deem desirable, including bankers and brokers in the Cities of ...., ..., and ...., and to cause appropriate notices of said invitation for bids to be published in such newspapers as the President and the Secretary may select in the Cities of ...., ..., and ....

RESOLUTION OF DIRECTORS APPROVING FORM AND TERMS OF PROPOSED UNDERWRITING AGREEMENT

RESOLVED, That the form and terms of the proposed underwriting agreement with Messrs. .... & Co., ... Brothers, ... & Company, Incorporated, and .... & Co., covering the issuance and sale of 250,000 shares of Convertible Preferred Stock, $6.25 Series of 19.., as set forth in the draft submitted to this meeting, directed to be marked for identification by the Secretary and filed with the records of the Corporation, is in all respects approved, and the officers of the Corporation are authorized at such time as shall be acceptable to such officers to enter into such agreement, with such changes therein as may be approved by said officers and by counsel, and to fix such terms as are omitted in the draft approved at this meeting, with the privilege to such officers, in their discretion, to permit additions or substitutions in the members of such underwriting group.

MINUTES OF DIRECTORS RATIFYING, BY RESOLUTION, OFFICERS' ACTION IN CLOSING UNDER UNDERWRITING AGREEMENT

The Chairman reported that the closing under the agreement with .... & Co., ... & Co., Inc., and .... & Co., Inc., as underwriters, relating to the Ten-Year 7% Sinking Fund Debentures due ...., 19.., (with common stock purchase warrants attached), had taken place that morning at the office of .... & Co., and that the Company had received a certified check for the proceeds of the debentures and warrants, and had deposited with the .... Bank and Trust Company an amount sufficient to pay on ...., 19.., all of the presently outstanding 6% Sinking Fund Debentures of the Company with accrued interest.

On motion duly made, seconded, and unanimously adopted, it was

RESOLVED, That all actions of the officers of the Company in connection with the consummation of the sale to .... & Co., ... & Co., Inc., and .... & Co., Inc. of $..... principal amount of Ten-Year 7% Sinking fund Debentures of the Company, due ...., 19.. (with common stock purchase warrants attached), be and the same hereby are in all respects ratified and approved.

RESOLUTION OF STOCKHOLDERS AUTHORIZING OFFICERS TO ENTER INTO UNDERWRITING AGREEMENT AS SUBMITTED TO MEETING

RESOLVED, That the President of the Company is hereby authorized and directed, in behalf of the Company, to enter into an underwriting agreement covering the sale by the Company to .... & Co. and associates of $32,000,000 in principal amount of First Mortgage Bonds, Series A, 7%, due ...., 19.., of the Company, and that said underwriting agreement in the form submitted to this meeting and all the terms and provisions thereof, are hereby approved and adopted and that a copy thereof be spread of record in or following the minutes of this meeting, and

RESOLVED FURTHER, That the officers of the Company are authorized, empowered, and directed to sell and deliver said $32,000,000 in principal amount of First

Mortgage Bonds, Series A, 7%, due ...., 19.., of the Company upon the terms and conditions stated in said agreement, and to do all things by them deemed necessary or appropriate to carry out the terms and provisions of said underwriting agreement.

RESOLUTION OF DIRECTORS AUTHORIZING CALL FOR REDEMPTION OF ALL OUTSTANDING PREFERRED STOCK

WHEREAS, under Article ..... of the Certificate of Incorporation of this Corporation, this Corporation, through its Board of Directors, from time to time upon ..... days' notice, may redeem, on any dividend date, the whole or any part of the preferred stock from surplus at ..... (.....%) per cent of the par value thereof, plus any accrued and unpaid dividends, and

WHEREAS, this Board of Directors deems it advisable to redeem the entire outstanding preferred stock out of surplus, be it

RESOLVED, That pursuant to Article ..... of the Certificate of Incorporation, all the outstanding preferred stock of this Corporation—namely, ... (.....) shares, having a par value of ..... ($.....) Dollars, amounting in the aggregate to ..... ($.....) Dollars is hereby called for redemption on ...., 19.., and

RESOLVED FURTHER, That said stock shall be redeemed at the office of this Corporation .... *(Street)*, ... *(City)*, ... *(State)*, by the payment of ..... ($.....) Dollars per share, plus accumulated, accrued, and unpaid dividends to the date of redemption thereof, upon surrender of certificates representing such shares, properly indorsed or accompanied by other proper assignment in blank, and

RESOLVED FURTHER, That if any stockholder shall fail to surrender his certificate or certificates of preferred stock on ...., 19.., such stockholder shall not in any event be entitled to receive further dividends thereon, or to exercise any rights with respect thereto, except to receive from this Corporation the amount set aside for the redemption thereof without interest, and

RESOLVED FURTHER, That the Secretary is hereby authorized and directed to send to each stockholder of record on ...., 19.., a written notice of the redemption of the outstanding preferred stock on ...., 19.., and to publish notice of such redemption as required by statute and the By-laws of this Corporation.

DIRECTORS' RESOLUTION AUTHORIZING CALL FOR REDEMPTION OF ALL OUTSTANDING PREFERRED STOCK, RETIREMENT OF SUCH REDEEMED STOCK AND OF PREFERRED STOCK HELD IN TREASURY, AND APPOINTMENT OF AGENT TO REDEEM

WHEREAS, the Board of Directors of this Corporation, at a special meeting held on ...., 19.., by resolution duly adopted by said Board, declared it advisable that there be a reclassification of the stock of this Corporation by the redemption of its 7% Cumulative Preferred Stock of the par value of ..... ($.....) Dollars each, ... (.....) shares of which Preferred Stock are outstanding in the hands of the public, ... (.....) shares of which are owned by the Corporation and held in the Treasury thereof and cannot be reissued, and ..... (.....) shares of which stock have been cancelled, be it

RESOLVED, That this Corporation call for redemption on ...., 19.., at the office of .... Trust Company, No. .... *(Street)*, ... *(City)*, ..., all of the 7% Cumulative Preferred Stock of the Corporation, consisting ..... (.....) shares of Preferred Stock, held by the public, at the price of ..... ($.....) Dollars for each share of stock, together with a sum of money equivalent to dividends thereon at the rate of ..... (.....%) per cent per annum on the par vlaue thereof from ...., 19.., to the date fixed for such redemption, less the amount of dividends theretofore paid thereon, and

RESOLVED FURTHER, That the proper officers of this Corporation hereby are authorized and directed to mail to each holder of record of said stock as his name appears on the books of the Corporation, not less than ..... days nor more than ..... days previous to ...., 19.., notice of the redemption of said stock, which notice is to be in such form as said officers and counsel for the Corporation shall approve, and to publish notice of the redemption in a newspaper of general circulation in the City of ...., ..., on the ..... day of ...., 19.., and

RESOLVED FURTHER, That the .... Trust Company is hereby appointed agent of this Corporation, to redeem said Preferred Stock in accordance with the terms and provisions of these resolutions and notice, when the same are presented to it for such redemption, and that this Corporation, on or prior to said redemption date, deposit with the .... Trust Company cash equivalent to ..... ($.....) Dollars, for each share of stock so to be redeemed, together with cash equivalent to dividends at the rate of ..... (.....%) per cent per annum on the par value thereof from ...., 19.., to the date fixed for such redemption, less the amount of dividends paid thereon, and that after certificates for said Preferred Stock have been surrendered to it for redemption, and the redemption price paid thereon as herein provided, the .... Trust Company is hereby authorized and directed to cancel said certificates for said Preferred Stock, and to deliver the same to the Corporation so cancelled, and

RESOLVED FURTHER, That the proper officers of this Corporation are hereby authorized and directed to turn in to .... Trust Company, stock certificates for .... (......) shares of said Preferred Stock, now held in the Treasury of the Corporation for cancellation, and .... Trust Company is hereby authorized and directed to cancel the certificates for said ...... (.....) shares of said stock presented to it for cancellation by said officers, and to deliver the same to the Corporation so cancelled, and

RESOLVED FURTHER, That the proper officers of this Corporation are hereby authorized and directed to pay all fees and expenses of .... Trust Company in connection with such redemption, and all other fees and expenses incurred by this Corporation or its counsel in the redemption of said stock, and

RESOLVED FURTHER, That upon the redemption of the 7% Preferred Stock of the corporation as aforesaid, the proper officers of this Corporation are hereby authorized and directed to execute and acknowledge on behalf of this Corporation, all papers, documents, and certificates made necessary by the retirement of said Preferred Stock, and to file the same in the proper office in the State of ...., all in accordance with the statutes of the State of ...., and to take all steps required by the State of .... to amend the Certificate of Incorporation of the Corporation so as to eliminate all reference to the shares of 7% Cumulative Preferred Stock of the Corporation, and

RESOLVED FURTHER, That a quarterly dividend of ..... ($.....) Dollars per share upon the outstanding shares of Preferred Sock of the Corporation is hereby declared payable for the quarter ending ...., 19.., as part of the redemption price of the Preferred Stock of this Corporation outstanding on said ...., 19.., to stockholders presenting their Preferred Stock for redemption on said date.

RESOLUTION OF DIRECTORS AUTHORIZING CALL FOR REDEMPTION OF ONE-HALF OF EACH STOCKHOLDER'S HOLDINGS; WHOLE SHARE TO BE REDEEMED IF DIVISION WOULD RESULT IN FRACTIONAL SHARES; PRIVILEGE OF STOCKHOLDERS TO OFFER SHARES FOR EARLIER REDEMPTION IF PRESENTED ON DESIGNATED DAYS IN VARIOUS MONTHS

RESOLVED:

1. That in accordance with the option accorded to the Corporation by Article ....., Section ..... of the Certificate of Incorporation of this Corporation, the Board of Directors does hereby declare that fifty thousand (50,000) shares of the one hundred thousand (100,000) shares of preferred stock of this Company at present outstanding are hereby called for redemption on ...., 19.., together with as many additional shares as shall result from the redemption of fractional shares because of holdings of shares in odd numbers as hereinafter provided;

2. That the holders of said preferred stock to be redeemed be paid for at the rate of One Hundred Five ($105) Dollars per share, together with all accrued and unpaid dividends, and no more;

3. That the shares to be redeemed shall be redeemed ratably from the holdings of the holders of the preferred stock—that is to say, one-half of the holdings of each stockholder as the same shall appear of record at the close of

business on ...., 19.., shall be redeemed; that in the case of any holding of an odd number of shares, where the redemption of one half of the holding will result in a fractional one-half share, the whole share so affected shall be redeemed;

4. That One Hundred ($100) Dollars of the redemption price shall be charged against the Preferred Capital account and Five ($5) Dollars against the earned Surplus account;

5. That in accordance with Section ..... of Article ..... of the Certificate of Incorporation, the specified notice be given to each and every holder of the preferred stock as shall be shown by the stock records of the Corporation as of ...., 19.., and that due publication of the proposed redemption be made, as provided in said Section.....;

6. That said preferred stock be redeemed at the offices of the Corporation, ... (Street), ... (City), ... (State), on ...., 19.., and when offered within a reasonable time thereafter; provided that, at the option of the holder of such stock to be redeemed, such stock may be offered for earlier redemption and will be redeemed by the Corporation at One Hundred Five ($105) Dollars per share if presented for redemption at the offices of the Corporation during the first fourteen days of either of the months of ...., ..., or ...., 19..;

7. That from and after ...., 19.., or in case of earlier redemption from the date of such earlier redemption, all dividends on the said preferred stock called for redemption or redeemed shall cease to accrue, and all rights of the holders thereof as stockholders of the Corporation, except the right to receive the redemption price, shall cease and determine;

8. That the proper officers are hereby authorized and directed to make and file such certificate or certificates concerning such shares as may be required by law.

DIRECTORS' RESOLUTION AUTHORIZING CALL FOR REDEMPTION OF SHARES OF PREFERRED STOCK OF A FIXED AGGREGATE PAR VALUE, TO BE SELECTED BY LOT

RESOLVED, That the officers of this Corporation are hereby severally authorized and directed to take all proper and necessary steps to call and redeem on ...., 19.., pursuant to the charter of this Corporation, at the rate of ..... ($.....) Dollars per share, plus any dividend accrued and unpaid to said date, the shares of preferred stock of the aggregate par value of ..... ($.....) Dollars, of this Corporation, represented by the certificates bearing the numbers to be selected by lot by the committee appointed by the Chairman this day.

RESOLUTION OF DIRECTORS AUTHORIZING CALL FOR REDEMPTION OF PART OF OUTSTANDING PREFERRED STOCK, TO BE CHOSEN BY LOT BY TRANSFER AGENT; CERTIFICATES TO BE DIVIDED INTO THREE CLASSES ACCORDING TO DENOMINATION, AND PROPORTIONATE NUMBER OF EACH CLASS TO BE DRAWN FOR REDEMPTION

[*Note*. The headings in boldface do not ordinarily appear in the resolution; they have been inserted here merely to facilitate use of the form.]

[Number of shares to be redeemed; time and price]

RESOLVED, That this Corporation call for redemption 25,000 shares of its Cumulative Preferred Stock, Series A, on ...., 19.., at the redemption price of ..... ($.....) Dollars per share, plus the sum of ..... ($.....) Dollars per share, being an amount equal to the dividends accrued thereon to said date, and

[Manner of choosing by lot]

RESOLVED FURTHER, That the 25,000 shares of such Series A Preferred Stock to be redeemed shall be chosen by lot by "T" Trust Company, Transfer Agent of such Preferred Stock, in the following manner:

1. There shall be ascertained the total number of shares of such stock outstanding at the close of business on ...., 19.., represented, respectively, by: (1) certificates for 100 shares each; (2) certificates for 50 to 99 shares each, both inclusive; and (3) certificates for 1 to 49 shares each, both inclusive;

2. The number of shares to be redeemed, 25,000, shall be divided among and allotted to the three classes of certificates above specified in the proportion, as nearly as may be practicable, which the number of shares in each class bears to the total number of shares outstanding at the close of business on ...., 19.., and there shall be drawn separately from the certificate numbers of each such class certificates representing the number of shares allotted to it, subject to the following provisions:

If the resultant figure for the class composed of certificates for 100 shares each shall not be a multiple of 100, there shall be drawn certificates for 100 shares each for an aggregate number equal to the highest multiple of 100 contained in such resultant figure, and the excess number of shares shall be added to the number of shares to be drawn from the class represented by certificates for 50 to 99 shares each. Certificates representing 50 to 99 shares each shall be drawn by lot without consideration of the exact number of shares represented by the particular certificate drawn, until there shall have been drawn certificates for the total number of shares allotted to such class, and if the last certificate drawn represents such number of shares that the total drawn exceeds the total allotted to such class, then the number of shares available for drawing from the class represented by certificates from 1 to 49 shares each shall be reduced to the extent of such excess. Certificates for 1 to 49 shares each shall be drawn by lot without consideration of the exact number of shares represented by the particular certificate drawn, until certificates for the total number of shares allotted to such class have been drawn, and if the last certificate drawn represents such number of shares that the total drawn exceeds the amount so allotted, that number of the shares represented by such last certificate shall be redeemed as is sufficient to exhaust the total number of shares to be redeemed.

All details in connection with the drawing by lot of said 25,000 shares shall be determined, subject to the principles hereinbefore set forth, by said Transfer Agent in its uncontrolled discretion.

[Closing of transfer books]

RESOLVED FURTHER, That the stock transfer books of the Preferred Stock of this Corporation be closed at the close of business on ...., 19.., and remain closed until the opening of business on ...., 19.., in the case of Preferred Stock not drawn for redemption, and permanently in the case of all Preferred Stock drawn for redemption, provided, however, that if the drawing shall result in the calling for redemption of less than all the shares represented by any certificate, the shares represented thereby not called for redemption may be transferred, and

[Approval of notice of redemption]

RESOLVED FURTHER, That the form of notice of redemption, to be mailed to each of the holders of shares of Preferred Stock, Series A, called for redemption, presented to this meeting, is hereby approved, and the Secretary is hereby authorized and directed to cause a notice of redemption in substantially such form to be mailed on or before ...., 19.., to each such holder of record of the Preferred Stock to be redeemed, and

[Place of payment of redemption price; cancellation of certificates]

RESOLVED FURTHER, That payment of the redemption price shall be made to the registered holders of the Preferred Stock called for redemption, or their assigns, upon presentation and surrender, on or after ...., 19.., of the certificates therefor, at the office of the Transfer Agent of such stock, "T" Trust Company, ... (Street), ... (City), ... (State),and that upon such payment the certificates shall be canceled, and

[Deposit of redemption funds with agent]

RESOLVED FURTHER, That the proper officers of the Corporation are hereby authorized and directed to deposit funds equal to the aggregate redemption price with "T" Trust Company for the payment of the redemption price to the holders of the shares to be redeemed upon surrender of the certificates for such shares, on or before said redemption date; and upon the deposit of said money, or in any event upon said redemption date, the holders of the stock so called for redemption shall cease to be stockholders with respect to said shares and shall have no interest in or claim with respect to said shares, except only to receive the redemption price on and after ...., 19.., from "T" Trust Company, without interest thereon, upon surrender of the respective certificates for such stock, and

[Reduction of capital]

RESOLVED FURTHER, That upon the redemption of the 25,000 shares of Cumulative Preferred Stock, Series A, the capital of the Corporation shall be reduced by the amount of ..... ($.....) Dollars, being ..... ($.....) Dollars for each share called for redemption, and the proper officers of the Corporation are hereby authorized to execute, file, and record a certificate in respect of such reduction pursuant to the provisions of the law of the State of ...., and

[Cancellation of redeemed stock by Registrar]

RESOLVED FURTHER, That the "R" Trust Company, as Registrar of the Cumulative Preferred Stock, Series A, of this Corporation, is hereby authorized and instructed to cancel upon its books the registration of the 25,000 shares of Cumulative Preferred Stock, Series A, to be redeemed on ...., 19.., such cancellation to be effective on that date, and the maximum number of shares which said Registrar has heretofore been authorized to register is hereby reduced by 25,000, effective ...., 19...

DIRECTORS' RESOLUTION AUTHORIZING CALL FOR REDEMPTION OF FIXED PROPORTION OF SHARES HELD BY EACH STOCKHOLDER; NO FRACTIONAL SHARES TO BE REDEEMED

RESOLVED, That there be called for redemption on ...., 19.., at ..... ($.....) Dollars per share and accrued dividends, one share of each seven shares held by each holder of the preferred stock of this Corporation as shown on the books of the Corporation on ...., 19.., and that no fractions of shares shall be so redeemed.

DIRECTORS' RESOLUTION AUTHORIZING REDEMPTION OF PREFERRED STOCK STANDING IN THE NAME OF A TRUSTEE

RESOLVED, That the following certificates of preferred stock of this Corporation now standing in the name of ...., trustee, be redeemed on ...., 19.., at ..... ($.....) Dollars per share, plus dividends accrued and unpaid thereon, and that dividends shall cease to accrue upon said preferred stock from and after ...., 19..,

Certificate Number	Number of Shares
....	....
....	....
....	....

RESOLVED FURTHER, That the Treasurer of this Corporation give due notice by mail to ...., Trustee, at his address on the books of .... Corporation, of the election by the Corporation so to redeem said preferred stock.

Resolved Further, That at the election of the holders of the preferred stock so called for redemption, the Treasurer of this Corporation is hereby authorized to accept delivery of such stock prior to the redemption date, and to make payment of the redemption price and dividends accrued and unpaid thereon to and including the date of such delivery.

EXCERPT FROM MINUTES OF EXECUTIVE COMMITTEE ADOPTING RESOLUTION RECOMMENDING TO BOARD OF DIRECTORS CALL FOR REDEMPTION OF STOCK

Mr. .... stated to the meeting that it was desirable that the .... Corporation call all of its outstanding first preferred stock for redemption on ...., 19... After a full discussion, upon motion duly made and seconded, it was unanimously

Resolved, That it be recommended to the Board of Directors of the .... Corporation that they call all of the outstanding first preferred stock for redemption on ...., 19...

RESOLUTION OF DIRECTORS CREATING SINKING FUND TO REDEEM PREFERRED STOCK

Whereas, this Corporation has heretofore issued preferred stock of the aggregate par value of ..... ($.....) Dollars, with the right in this Corporation to redeem the said preferred stock should it so desire, by paying the par value thereof with accrued dividends at the rate of ..... (.....%) per cent, and

Whereas, this Corporation deems it expedient and advisable to create a sinking fund for the purpose of redeeming and retiring the said stock, be it

Resolved, That, commencing with ...., 19.., ... (.....%) per cent of the gross earnings of the Corporation be set aside and formed into a sinking fund, to be known as the Preferred Stock Sinking Fund, to be established, kept, and maintained for the purpose of redeeming the preferred stock as aforesaid; that when there has accumulated in said fund an amount equal to ..... (.....%) per cent of the entire amount due on the preferred stock as aforesaid, the said amount so accumulated shall be apportioned equally among the preferred stockholders, and a proportionate number of shares of preferred stock shall be redeemed and retired; and that this process of accumulation, distribution, and redemption shall continue until the entire amount of the preferred stock and accrued dividends shall have been paid in full.

RESOLUTION OF DIRECTORS REDEEMING PART OF PREFERRED STOCK OUT OF SINKING FUND

Whereas, under Article ..... of the Certificate of Incorporation of this Corporation, this Corporation may, through its Board of Directors, from time to time upon ..... days' notice, redeem, on any dividend date, the whole or any part of the preferred stock from surplus at ..... (.....%) per cent of the par value thereof, plus any accrued and unpaid dividends, and

WHEREAS, a sinking fund has been created and maintained for the purpose of providing funds to redeem outstanding preferred stock from time to time, and

WHEREAS, there has accumulated in said sinking fund the sum of ..... ($.....) Dollars, be it

RESOLVED, That the Treasurer of this Corporation is hereby authorized to apply the sum of ..... ($.....) Dollars of said sinking fund to the purchase and retirement of ..... (.....) shares of preferred stock having a par value of ..... ($.....) Dollars per share, amounting in the aggregate to ..... ($.....) Dollars;

RESOLVED FURTHER, That said redemption shall be made at the office of the Corporation, ... *(Street)*, ... *(City)*, ... *(State)*, on ...., 19.., by the payment of ..... ($.....) Dollars per share, plus accumulated, accrued, and unpaid dividends to the date of redemption thereof, upon the surrender of certificates representing shares to be redeemed, properly indorsed or accompanied by other proper assignment in blank, and

RESOLVED FURTHER, That each preferred stockholder shall be given an equal opportunity to offer for redemption a proportionate share of the stock held by him, and if any preferred stockholder shall fail to notify the Treasurer of this Corporation on or before ...., 19.., of his desire to have his proportionate number of shares redeemed, the right of such stockholder to have his stock redeemed shall be lost, and the Treasurer shall thereupon purchase from any stockholder or stockholders an additional amount of stock for redemption to make up the full amount to be redeemed under this resolution, at the price hereinabove set forth, and no stockholder shall have the right to demand that his stock be purchased, and

RESOLVED FURTHER, That the Secretary is hereby authorized and directed to mail forthwith to each stockholder of record on ...., 19.., a notice of said redemption, and to publish notice of said redemption as required by statute and by the By-laws of this Corporation.

ARTICLE OF INCORPORATION AUTHORIZING CORPORATION TO PURCHASE ITS OWN STOCK BY CASH, PROMISSORY NOTE OR DEBENTURE OR BOTH

The Corporation may purchase its own shares and pay for them with cash, promissory notes or debentures, or both, provided that at the time of such payment (1) stockholder transfers ownership of such shares to the Corporation, (2) the Corporation is not then insolvent nor made insolvent by such payment and (3) the notes or debentures are secured by property recorded liens or the property of the Corporation.

[*Note.* This clause can be adapted for use only in those states that permit payment by note or debenture when sufficient required surplus exists at the time of execution of the note or debenture, even though it does not have such surplus at the time when the Corporation has to make actual payment on the note or debenture.]

RESOLUTION OF STOCKHOLDERS AUTHORIZING BOARD OF DIRECTORS TO PURCHASE, HOLD, OR TRANSFER SHARES OF CORPORATION'S OWN STOCK

RESOLVED, That the Board of Directors is hereby authorized to purchase, acquire, hold, or transfer shares of the capital stock of this Corporation, from time to time, in such amounts and for such consideration as the Board shall determine, provided that no purchase shall be made which might favor any shareholder over any other, and provided further that the Board shall not purchase any shares of the capital stock of this Corporation unless, after such purchase, there shall remain an excess of assets over all the debts and liabilities of the Corporation, plus the par value of the capital stock outstanding, after the amount of the par value of the shares to be purchased has been deducted. *(If stock is without par value, substitute the following for last proviso:* provided, further, that the Board of Directors shall not purchase any shares of this Corporation unless, after such purchase, there shall remain an excess of assets over all the debts and liabilities of the Corporation, plus stated capital, after the amount of stated capital in respect of the shares to be purchased has been deducted.)

RESOLUTION OF DIRECTORS PROHIBITING CORPORATION FROM PURCHASING ITS OWN STOCK EXCEPT UPON CONSENT OF STOCKHOLDERS

RESOLVED, That the Corporation shall be prohibited (except for retirement and for the purpose of decreasing the capital stock as authorized by law) from buying, holding, or transferring shares of its own stock, except upon the consent in writing of stockholders of the Corporation owning at least two-thirds of the voting rights of the capital stock, or except upon the consent of stockholders of record owning not less than two-thirds of the voting rights of the capital stock of the Corporation, given in person or by proxy at an annual meeting, or at a special meeting of the stockholders called for the purpose.

RESOLUTION OF DIRECTORS AUTHORIZING CORPORATION TO ACQUIRE ITS OWN STOCK ACCORDING TO AGREEMENT

WHEREAS, under an agreement between ...., owner of record of ..... (.....) shares of common stock without par value of this Corporation, and this Corporation, dated ...., 19.., this Corporation has the option to purchase the aforesaid shares of stock held by .... upon his withdrawal from the active management of the Corporation's affairs, at the book value of the shares at the close of the fiscal year preceding the withdrawal of said ...., and

WHEREAS, ... withdrew from the active management of the affairs of this Corporation on ...., 19.., and this Corporation, under its agreement with ...., now has the right to purchase the shares of stock held by ...., and

WHEREAS, the surplus of this Corporation is larger than the sum required to purchase the shares, and, in the opinion of the Board of Directors of this Corporation, it is to the best interests of the Corporation that the shares above mentioned be purchased by the Corporation, be it

RESOLVED, That this Corporation purchase the ..... (.....) shares of common stock without par value of this Corporation, standing in the name of ...., at a price of ..... ($.....) Dollars per share, which was the book value of each share of stock of this Corporation on ...., 19.., as shown by the certified balance sheet of the Corporation prepared at the close of the fiscal year 19...

RESOLUTION OF DIRECTORS AUTHORIZING CORPORATION TO ACCEPT ITS OWN STOCK IN PAYMENT OF DEBT DUE CORPORATION

WHEREAS, ..., owner of record of ..... (.....) shares of fully paid common stock of this Corporation having a par value of ..... ($.....) Dollars each is indebted to this Corporation in the amount of ..... ($.....) Dollars, for merchandise purchased from this Corporation on ...., 19.., and

WHEREAS, ... is unable to make payment and has offered to give this Corporation, in full settlement of his debt, ... (.....) shares of the common stock of this corporation owned by him, having an aggregate par value of ..... ($.....) Dollars, be it

RESOLVED, That this Corporation accept the offer of ...., and the President is hereby authorized upon receipt of the certificates of capital stock for ..... (.....) shares of the capital stock of this Corporation, properly indorsed by ...., to deliver to .... a receipt in full discharge of all claims which this Corporation has against him on account of the purchase mentioned in the preamble of this resolution.

RESOLUTION OF STOCKHOLDERS AUTHORIZING PURCHASE OF STOCK OF UNDESIRABLE ASSOCIATE IN ACCORDANCE WITH AGREEMENT

WHEREAS, an agreement was entered into on ...., 19.., empowering a majority of the holders of the common stock of this Corporation to declare that a stockholder had ceased to be a desirable associate, and thereupon to appraise and purchase his stock at its cash value, and

WHEREAS, a majority of the holders of the common stock of this Corporation are agreed that .... has ceased to be a desirable associate because of his personal conduct and because of his incompetency (*or insert other reasons for undesirability*), and

WHEREAS, ... is now the holder of ..... (.....) shares of the common stock of this Corporation, of the value of ..... ($.....) Dollars per share, as shown by the books of the Corporation, be it

RESOLVED, That the said ..... (.....) shares of common stock held by .... be redeemed, in accordance with the aforesaid agreement, at ..... ($.....) Dollars per share, and that the proper officers of this Corporation are hereby authorized and directed to do all things necessary and proper to carry out this resolution.

DIRECTORS' RESOLUTION AUTHORIZING OFFER TO PURCHASE FROM STOCKHOLDERS UP TO CERTAIN PERCENTAGE OF THEIR HOLDINGS, DETAILS TO BE ATTENDED TO BY SPECIAL COMMITTEE

RESOLVED, That without intending or proposing in any way to impair, enlarge, restrict, or otherwise affect the priorities, preferences, or voting rights of any class of stock of this Corporation, but for the purpose of investment, the proper officers of this Corporation are hereby fully authorized and directed to expend from the funds of this Corporation, ... ($.....) Dollars in the purchase of its Prior Preference Stock at the price of ..... ($.....) Dollars per share, said purchase to be made in the following manner; to wit: by mailing to each Prior Preference stockholder of record on ...., 19.., both a notice of this resolution and an offer to purchase from such stockholders, at ..... ($.....) Dollars per share, ... (.....%) per cent of the Prior Preference Stock standing on the records of this corporation in his name at the close of business on ...., 19.., and

RESOLVED FURTHER, That the details, preparation of the written notice and offer, and other matters incidental to the purchase of said stock in substantial conformity with this resolution, be attended to by a committee of three members of this Board, to be by it appointed.

RESOLUTION OF DIRECTORS AUTHORIZING RETIREMENT OF STOCK PURCHASED BY CORPORATION

WHEREAS, this Corporation holds in its treasury ..... (.....) shares of the 6% Preferred Stock of this Corporation, of the par value of ..... ($.....) Dollars, acquired by purchase from time to time out of surplus funds of the Corporation, and

WHEREAS, under the laws of the State of ...., shares of stock so acquired may be retired by resolution of the Board of Directors, and no procedure for the reduction of the issued capital stock of the Corporation is necessary to effect such retirement, be it

RESOLVED, That this Corporation does hereby retire the ..... (.....) shares of the 6% Preferred Stock of this Corporation, of the par value of ..... ($.....) Dollars, heretofore acquired by purchase and held in the treasury of the Corporation, and

RESOLVED FURTHER, That said retired shares shall, in conformity with the statute, have the status of authorized but unissued stock of the Corporation, and shall retain the classification obtaining before such retirement, and shall be subject to sale in the same manner and upon the same terms as other authorized but unissued 6% Preferred Stock.

NOTICE THAT TEMPORARY CERTIFICATES WILL BE EXCHANGED FOR PERMANENT CERTIFICATES ON AND AFTER FIXED DATE

...., 19..

To the Holders of Temporary Certificates Representing Class A Common Stock:

You are hereby notified that on and after ...., 19.., holders of Temporary Certificates representing Class A Common Stock will be entitled to receive, upon surrender of their Temporary Certificates at the principal office of .... Trust Company in the City of ...., State of ...., Permanent Certificates for the number of shares of Class A Common Stock represented by the Temporary Certificates so surrendered.

The certificates of stock will be issued in the name of and to the person appearing on the books of the Corporation as the holder of the Temporary Certificates surrendered, unless the Temporary Certificates are indorsed in blank, accompanied by instructions to issue the stock certificates to and in the name of someone other than the record holder, and by the necessary State and Federal transfer stamps.

PUBLISHED NOTICE THAT PERMANENT STOCK CERTIFICATES WILL BE ISSUED UPON SURRENDER OF TEMPORARY CERTIFICATES

.... & Co.

6½% CUMULATIVE PREFERRED STOCK

Permanent engraved stock certificates for 6½% Cumulative Preferred Stock of this Company are now ready for delivery in exchange for the outstanding temporary certificates. Stockholders should send their temporary certificates for exchange to the Transfer Agents, the .... Bank of ...., ... (Street), ... (City), ... (State),or the .... Company of ...., (Street), ... (City), ... (State).

Temporary certificates surrendered for exchange need not be indorsed unless it is desired that the permanent certificates be issued in a name other than that in which the temporary certificate is registered. In such case the temporary certificates should be presented in duly transferable form, together with funds to cover stamp taxes, and the signature to the indorsement or assignment must be guaranteed by a bank or trust company with a correspondent in New York City, or by a New York Stock Exchange firm.

...., 19..   .... & Co.

                                                              ....
                                                              Secretary

EXCERPT FROM MINUTES OF STOCKHOLDERS' MEETING ADOPTING RESOLUTIONS APPROVING FORM OF TEMPORARY STOCK CERTIFICATE

The Secretary then submitted to the meeting forms of temporary certificates to represent the 6% Cumulative Preferred Stock and the Common Stock of this corporation which would be required in lieu of the present certificates as a result of the amendment of the Certificate of Incorporation. Copies of such temporary certificates are attached to the minutes of this meeting, marked "Exhibit B" and "Exhibit C."

On motion duly made and seconded, the following resolutions were unanimously adopted:

RESOLVED, That the proposed forms of temporary certificates to represent the 6% Cumulative Preferred Stock and the Common Stock of this corporation, presented to this meeting, are hereby approved and adopted as the certificates to represent the 6% Cumulative Preferred Stock and the Common Stock of this corporation, and that specimens be attached to the minutes of this meeting marked "Exhibit B" and "Exhibit C."

RESOLVED, That the Secretary of this corporation is hereby authorized and directed to obtain definitive engraved certificates to represent the 6% Cumulative Preferred Stock and the Common Stock of this corporation, substantially in the form of the temporary certificates approved at this meeting.

RESOLVED, That the proper officers of this corporation are hereby authorized and directed to notify the stockholders of this corporation when such definitive engraved certificates are ready for delivery, and to request the stockholders of this corporation to surrender the then outstanding certificates representing the capital stock of this corporation for exchange, share for share of the same class respectively, for such definitive engraved certificates.

RESOLVED, That pending the preparation of such definitive engraved certificates, the Secretary of this corporation is hereby authorized and directed to procure a suitable supply of temporary certificates, and that the proper officers of this corporation are hereby authorized to execute and to issue such temporary certificates, share for share, for the presently outstanding certificates representing the capital stock of this corporation, if and when presented to this corporation for such exchange.

RESOLUTION AUTHORIZING AUTHENTICATION AND ISSUANCE OF STOCK CERTIFICATES SIGNED BY AN OFFICER WHO HAS RESIGNED

WHEREAS, ... has signed, as Secretary of this corporation, together with the President, stock certificates of this corporation, Nos. ..... to ....., inclusive, for one hundred (100) shares each, which certificates are now lodged with the .... Trust Company, Transfer Agent, and are unissued at this date, and

WHEREAS, the resignation of the said ...., as Secretary, has been this day accepted to take effect immediately, be it

RESOLVED, That stock certificates of this corporation, Nos. ..... to ..... inclusive, for one hundred (100) shares each, signed by ...., as Secretary, may be hereafter authenticated and issued by the .... Trust Company, Transfer Agent, and .... Company, as Registrar, as though .... were the Secretary of this corporation at the time said certificates may be hereafter authenticated, issued, and registered.

Chapter 17

RIGHTS TO SUBSCRIBE TO STOCK, STOCK PURCHASE WARRANTS, AND OPTIONS TO PURCHASE STOCK

Contents—Chapter 17

Stockholders' preëmptive right to subscribe for new shares.
Stockholders of a corporation generally have the right to subscribe for new
shares of an issue of the capital stock of the company—what is generally
known as their preëmptive right.[1] The general corporation laws in many
states contain provisions concerning this right. If there are no controlling
statutory provisions, the preëmptive right may be limited, modified, or
abrogated by the articles or certificate of incorporation, or by agreement
with the incorporations.[2] The rights may or may not be exercised and may
be bought and sold. See below as to meaning of preëmptive right.

In the absence of statutory or charter provisions governing preëmptive
rights, common law principles determine the existence, definition, extent,
protection and enforcement of this very important right, incident to stock
ownership in private business corporations. Almost without exception the
cases say that stockholders who presently hold stock have a right to
subscribe for and take new stock in proportion to their respective shares.[3]

This right is a property right, of which the stockholders cannot be
deprived by the directors or other stockholders without their consent.[4] As
such, it is entitled to the same recognition and protection accorded other
rights of property by the law. It is a right based on the stockholder's right to
control corporate affairs by the exercise of his voting power and to share in
the surplus of the corporations, and is incident to an increase of stock.

"As the right to increase the stock belonged to them [the
stockholders], the stock when increased belonged to them also, * * *
By the increase of stock the voting power * * * was reduced * * *.
They (a majority of the stockholders) cannot, however, dispose of it
(the increased stock) to strangers against the protest of any stockholder
who insists that he has a right to his proportion. Otherwise the majority
could deprive the minority of their proportionate power in the election
of directors and their proportionate right to share in the surplus. Each
of which is an inherent, preëmptive, and vested right of property. ***

We are thus led to lay down the rule that a stockholder has an
inherent right to a proportionate share of new stock issued for money
only and not to purchase property for the purposes of the corporation

---

[1]Miles v. Safe Deposit & Trust Co., (1922) 259 U.S. 247, 42 S.Ct. 483; Yoakam v. Providence
Biltmore Hotel Co., (D R.I. 1929) 34 F.2d 533; Kingston v. Home Life Insurance Co., (1917) 11 Del.
Ch. 258, 101 A. 898.

[2]Heller Inv. v. So. Title & Trust Co., (1936) 17 Cal. App.2d 202, 61 P.2d 807; Burkan v.
Ex-Lax, Inc., (1938) 168 Misc. 735, 6 N.Y.S.2d 740; Milwaukee Sanatorium v. Swift, (1941) 238
Wis. 628, 300 N.W. 760, following Johnson v. Bradley Knitting Co., (1938) 28 Wis. 566, 280 N.W.
688 (leading case).

[3]Gray v. Portland Bank, (1807) 3 Mass. 364 is the leading case.

[4]Albrecht, Maguire & Co. v. Gen. Plastics, Inc., (1939) 256 A.D. 134, 9 N.Y.S.2d 415, aff'd.
(1939) 280 N.Y. 840, 21 N.E.2d 887.

or to effect a consolidation, and while he can waive that right, he cannot be deprived of it without his consent except when the stock is issued at a fixed price not less than par, and he is given the right to take at that price in proportion to his holding, or in some other equitable way that will enable him to protect his interest by acting on his own judgment and using his own resources.[5]

Statutes of some states permit the charter to deny preëmptive rights;[6] other states prohibit this.[7]

Meaning of preëmptive right. This is the right of a stockholder, upon the issuance by the corporation of additional shares of stock, to subscribe for and demand from the corporation such a proportion of the new stock as the number of shares already owned by him bears to the total number of shares previously issued. This right is based upon two principles: (1) present stockholders must be given an opportunity to keep proportionate control,[8] and (2) the equities of the stockholders in the surplus of the corporation must be preserved. For example, a corporation which increases its capital stock 25 per cent must allow each stockholder the right to subscribe to the new issue up to 25 per cent of his holdings. A, owning $5,000, par value, of an authorized issue of $50,000, par value, of common stock, will, upon a 50 per cent increase in the common stock, be entitled to subscribe to $2,500, par value, of the new stock at the price fixed, before the stock may be offered to any outsider.

Each stockholder having a preëmptive right must be given reasonable notice of his right to subscribe and an opportunity to obtain his proportionate share in the increase of the capital stock upon the same terms as the other stockholders.[9] Further, any stock not taken by the old stockholders can't be offered to outsiders on terms more favorable than those on which the stock was previously offered to the stockholders. Stockholders who are not in a position to take and pay for the stock to which they are entitled can sell the rights to anyone who is able to take and pay for the stock.[10]

Stock to which preëmptive right applies. Corporations offer stock either from their original authorized capital stock or from an authorized increased in their capital stock. Some states have statutes governing the preëmptive right of stockholders and making it clear to which issue or class of stock preëmptive rights attach. Some states provide that the certificate of

[5]Vann, J., in Stokes v. Continental Tr. Co., (1906) 186 N.Y. 285, 78 N.E. 1090.

[6]Mobile Press Register v. McGowan, (S.Ct., Ala., 1960) 124 So.2d 812.

[7]Op. of Atty. Gen. to Sec. of State, S.C. 4-8-57.

[8]Canada Southern Oils Ltd. v. Manabe Exploration Co., Inc. (Ch. Ct. Del., 1953) 96 A.2d 810; Rowland v. Times Pub. Co. (S. Ct. Fla., 1948) 35 So.2d 399.

[9]Hoyt v. Great American Ins. Co., (1922) 201 App. Div. 352, 194 N.Y.S. 449.

[10]Stokes v. Continental Tr. Co., (1906) 186 N.Y. 285, 78 N.E. 1090.

incorporation may limit and deny the preëmptive right to any issue or to any class of stock. Under such a statute, the Oregon Supreme Court said that a one-third stockholder of a close corporation could not complain when his preëmptive rights were abolished by vote of two-thirds of the stockholders amending the articles of incorporation, even though a pre-incorporation agreement provided for filing articles that contain a clause protesting preëmptive rights.[11] If there are no statutory provisions, however, reference must be made to the various decisions which have developed the doctrine of preëmptive rights, to determine whether or not such rights exist. Note, however, that these decisions are often conflicting and confused.

Where a statute applies, its provision are, of course, controlling. Where no statute applies, the cases generally hold that preëmptive rights exist only as to an increased issue of voting, participating common or preferred stock.[12] Preëmptive rights do *not* attach to an issue of nonvoting, non-participating preferred stock. Reason: The holders of shares of the original issue of such stock have no control and no interest in the corporate surplus so they cannot be affected by a failure to give them the right to subscribe to shares of a new issue of the same class in proportion to their holdings in the original issue.[13]

Generally, of course, no preëmptive rights exist in connection with an original issue of stock. But if the corporation does not fully dispose of the entire issue of original stock after it is organized, and instead retains the remaining authorized original but unissued stock for sale at a later date when it needs additional capital, the question of the stockholders' preëmptive rights in this delayed issuance of original stock arises. In dealing with this question different courts have reached different results. Some have held that there can be no preëmptive rights in capital stock of an original issue, preëmptive rights existing only as to an increase of authorized capital stock,[14] while others have held that, in the absence of a statute to the contrary, each stockholder has a preëmptive right to purchase shares upon a delayed issuance of original stock, when the shares are offered for sale.[15] Existing stockholders, one court said, had preëmptive rights to subscribe to the original authorized capital stock issued long after business was commenced by the corporation, when the proceeds of the issue were to be used for the purpose of business expansion.[16] Another court saw that stockholders had preëmptive rights to unissued part of the original authorized stock when it was being issued 40 years after the

---

[11]McCallum v. Gray (Ore. S.Ct., 1975) 542 P.2d 1025.
[12]Stokes v. Continental Tr. Co., (1906) 186 N.Y. 285, 78 N.E. 1090.
[13]Gen. Invest. Co. v. Bethlehem Steel Corp., (1917) 88 N.J.E. 237, 102 A. 252.
[14]Yasik v. Wachtel and Diamond State Brewery, Inc., (1941) Del. Ch., 17 A.2d 309, Archer v. Hesse, (1914) 164 App. Div 493, 150 N.Y.S. 296; Curry v. Scott, (1867) 54 Pa. St. 270.
[15]Titus v. Paul State Bank (1919) 32 Idaho 23, 179 P. 514.
[16]Dunlay v. Ave. M. Garage & Repair Co., (1930) 253 N.Y. 274, 170 N.E. 917.

original issue and the motive of directors in making the later issue was to continue their control.[17]

In the absence of an agreement to the contrary, stockholders do not have so called "residual preëmptive rights," that is, they do not have a proportionate right to buy stock not bought by the other stockholders.[18]

Statutes in some states say that no preëmptive rights shall exist as to stock issued and sold, with the written or voted consent of a certain percentage of the stockholders entitled to preëmptive rights, to employees pursuant to employee stock purchase plans. Where such statutes exist, provision is sometimes made in the statute for meeting the demands of dissenting stockholders by buying out their stock after appraisal, or other remedy.

Stockholders do not have preëmptive rights to reissued treasury shares; that's because their original proportionate interest is not affected by reissuance.[19] In fact the status quo is maintained.[20] However, if treasury shares are retired or held indefinitely, they may, like delayed issuance of original stock in some states, be subject to preëmptive rights.[21]

Stockholders of close corporations can also have preëmptive rights in treasury stock, when directors deal in that stock for their private advantage.[22]

No preëmptive rights exist in stock issued for services or property instead of cash.[23] On the principle that all sales of stock are to be made for the benefit of the corporation, property may be acquired for stock without first offering the stock to the stockholders, since otherwise it would be difficult for the corporation to get specially needed property or services. However, the vendor of the property must take the stock at its book value, if the latter is greater than its par value. The rule denying preëmptive rights in stock issued for property has been criticized by leading authorities, but is defended on the ground of practical necessity. The issuance of stock for property must, of course, be made at a fair value, and cannot be employed as a way for a particular stockholder[24] to get voting control. However,

---

[17]Carlson v. Ringgold County Mut. Tel. Co. (S. Ct. Iowa 1961) 108 N.W. 2d 478.

[18]Dyer v. Sec, (CA-8, 1961) 290 F.2d 534, following Maynard v. Doe Run Lead Co. (1924) 305 Mo. 356, 265 S.W. 94.

[19]Johnson v. Duensing, (Mo., 1960) 340 S.W.2d 758, aff'd, 351 S.W.2d 27; Fuller v. Krogh (S. Ct., 1962) 15 Wis. 2d 412, 113 N.W.2d 25. *Contra:* Dunn v. Acme Auto & Garage Co., (1918) 168 Wis. 128, 169 N.W. 297.

[20]Borg. v. International Silver Co., (SD N.Y. 1926) 11 F. 2d 143, aff'd, (CA-3, 1926) 11 F. 2d 147.

[21]Hammer v. Werner, (1933) 265 N.Y.S. 172.

[22]Borg v. International Silver Co., (SD N.Y. 1926) 11 F. 2d 143, aff'd, (CA-3, 1926) 11 F. 2d 147.

[23]Thom v. Baltimore Trust Co., (1930) 158 Md. 352, 148 A. 234; Bingham v. Savings Inv. & Trust Co., (1927) 101 N.J. Eq. 413, 138 A. 659, 140 A. 321.

[24]Witherbee v. Bowles, (1911) 201 N.Y. 427, 95 N.E. 27.

some courts recognize the existence of preëmptive rights when stock is issued for property of common character and there is nothing urgent or extraordinary about the transaction.[25]

Preëmptive rights have been denied on the grounds of necessity when stock is issued to purchase land to settle a dispute,[26] effectuate a merger or consolidation,[27] pay a debt,[28] secure a loan[29] and pay for services rendered.[30] Further, issuance of stock to an employee for *past* services have been set aside though the corporation could have issued the stock for *future* services pursuant to an approved statutory plan for employee stock compensation.[31]

Statutes in some states specifically deny preëmptive rights when stock is issued for a consideration other than cash.

Persons in whom preëmptive rights vest. Generally the persons in whom preëmptive rights in a new issue of capital stock vest are stock holders who were such when the increase was made and whose interests in the right of corporate control and the right to share in corporate surplus will be affected by the issue.[32] In other words, to be entitled to exercise preëmptive rights upon an increase in capital stock, the stockholders must be holders of voting, participating shares. In determining who are stockholders entitled to subscribe to shares of a new issue of stock, you look at the time when the charter amendment authorizing the increase became effective.[33]

Holders of convertible scrip or bonds must exercise their conversion privilege before the time of the increase in order to be entitled to exercise preëmptive rights in the new stock.[34]

Generally, preëmptive rights are vested in stockholders of record. In some states statutes provide for the directors to close the corporate books a certain number of days prior to the date of allotment of preëmptive rights. Other statutes provide that the by-laws may fix or authorize the directors to

---

[25]Fuller v. Krogh, (S. Ct., 1962) 15 Wis. 2d 412, 113 N.W. 2d 25.

[26]Meredith v. Zinc & Iron Co., (1897) 55 N.J. Eq. 211, 37 Atl. 539, aff'd, 56 N.J. Eq. 454, 41 Atl. 1116.

[27]Bonnet v. First Nat. Bank, (1900) 24 Tex. Civ. App. 613, 60 S.W. 325. And see Bingham v. Savings Investment & Trust Co., (1928) 101 N.J.E. 413, 140 A. 321 and Thom. v. The Baltimore Trust Co., (1930) 158 Md. 352, 148 A. 234.

[28]Musson v. New York & Queens El. L. & P. Co., (1931) 138 Misc. 881,247 N.Y.S. 406.

[29]Todd v. Maryland Casualty Co. (CA-7, 1946) 155 F. 2d 29.

[30]Milwaukee Sanitarium v. Lynch, 238 Wis. 628, 300 N.W. 760 (1941).

[31]Hyman v. Behar, (S. Ct., 1963) 39 Misc.2d 617, 241 N.Y.S.2d 625.

[32]Stockholders, as used here, include common and preferred. Jones v. Concord, etc., Co., (1892) 67 N.H. 234, 30 A. 614; Howell v. Chicago, etc., Co., (1868) 51 Barb. (N.Y.) 378; Hammer v. Cash, (1920) 172 Wis. 185, 178 N.W. 465.

[33]Real Estate Trust Co. v. Bird, (1899) 90 Md. 229, 44 A. 1048.

[34]Pratt v. American Bell Tel. Co., (1886) 141 Mass. 225, 5 N.E. 307; Van Slyke v. Norris, (1924) 159 Minn. 63 198 N.W. 409; Wall v. Utah Copper Co., (1905) 70 N.J. Eq. 17, 62 A. 533.

fix a day not more than a certain number of days before the rights are to be allotted, known as the record date, after which persons registered as stockholders will not be entitled to participate in the allotment. The object of these statutes is to determine who are entitled, as stockholders of record, to be allotted preëmptive rights on the date the allotment is made. After the date fixed and before the allotment is made, transfers of the shares cannot affect, so far as the corporation is concerned, the determination of who are entitled to the rights as stockholders of record.

Assignees and transferees of stock are entitled to exercise the preëmptive rights of original owners, unless the rights have been reserved by the assignors.[35] Unless the corporation has notice of the assignment, the warrant may be issued to the assignor as stockholder of record.

As between the pledgor and pledgee of stock, the right to exercise preëmptive rights[36] generally is in the pledgor.

If between the time a contract for the sale of stock is entered into and the time it is executed, an increase in the authorized capital stock is made, the preëmptive right vests in the vendee but the vendor is not obligated to advance his own money to exercise the right; if the right is lost by his failure to do so, he incurs no liability to his vendee.[37] If he desires to prevent the right from becoming lost the vendee must supply his vendor with the funds necessary to exercise it.

Sometimes shares of stock are owned by stockholders whose ownership is not absolute but may be for life only. Such stockholders are called tenants for life of the shares thus, in whom the absolute ownership of the shares will vest upon the termination of the life tenancy are called remaindermen of the shares. It is generally held that the entire value of the preëmptive rights attached to the shares inures to the benefit of the remaindermen,[38] though this rule is not always followed.[39]

Even though shareholders have not paid in full for their shares, or are in default for nonpayment of calls, they nevertheless are entitled to exercise the preëmptive rights attached to their stock.[40]

Preëmptive rights and equitable considerations. In large corporations with many classes of stock it is often difficult strictly to adhere to

---

[35]See Schmidt v. Pritchard, (1907) 135 Iowa 240, 112 N.W. 801; Baltimore etc., Co. v. Hambleton, (1893) 77 Md. 341, 26 A. 279. See Machen, § 606; Cook § 286.

[36]Murdock v. Murdock, (1931) 304 Pa. 565, 156 A. 303.

[37]Currie v. White, (1871) 45 N.Y. 822.

[38]In re Merill's Estate, (1928) 196 Wis. 351, 220 N.W. 215. See Hayes v. St. Louis Union Trust Co., (1927) 317 Mo. 1028, 298 S.W. 91 and Plainfield Trust Co. v. Bowlby, (1930) 107 N.J. Eq. 68, 151 A. 545.

[39]See Holbrook v. Holbrook, (1907) 74 N.H. 201, 66 A. 124.

[40]Reese v. Bank of Montgomery County, (1855) 31 Pa. St. 78. See also Elec. Co. v. Edison,

existing rights of preëmption. The courts are relegated to the adoption of rules of fairness and reasonableness on the part of directors in issuing the stock. Otherwise, the financing of corporations with a complex capital stock structure might be hamstrung.

But in the close corporation more reason exists to follow preëmptive rules literally. The stock structure is not complicated and the relative positions of the stockholders should be maintained when possible. Often, however, even though a shareholder in a small corporation is given preëmptive rights he can be "frozen out" by amendment of the articles or[41] by the issuance of stock he can't afford to buy. Sometimes the courts will afford relief,[42] other times not.[43] But whether or not preëmptive rights exist minority shareholders will be protected against arbitrary action of directors in transferring stock to themselves to gain control.[44] This rule applies to large and small corporations alike.[45]

Time when preëmptive rights must be exercised. Generally the right of a stockholder to subscribe for his proportionate amount of the shares of a new issue of the authorized capital stock of a corporation must be exercised within the time fixed by the resolution authorizing the increase, or, if no time is specified, within a reasonable time.[46] The time within which stockholder must exercise his preëmptive right is generally fixed in the resolution authorizing the increase of capital stock. A majority of the stockholders have a right to fix the time to suit themselves and the interests of the corporation; the only limitation upon the exercise of that prerogative is that every stockholder "must" be treated alike and be afforded a reasonable opportunity to subscribe.[47] Sometimes, rules of a stock exchange prescribe a limit within which holders of stock listed on the exchange must exercise preëmptive rights. If a stockholder fails to exercise his right within the time fixed, he is deemed to have waived his right, provided that the time was reasonable.[48] However, a stockholder who was told to pay on a day certain, did not lose his preëmptive rights thereafter, when the notice to pay did not specifically say that forfeiture would be the

---

etc., Co., (1901) 200 Pa. 516, 50 A. 164.

[41]McCallum v. Gray, (Ore. S. Ct., 1975) 542 P. 2d 1025.

[42]Browning v. C & C Plywood Corp. (1967) 248 Ord. 574, 434 P.2d 339.

[43]Pohl v. H.J. Manchester & Co., Inc., (S. Ct., 1970) NYLJ 10-8-70, p. 2; Bellows v. Porter, (W.D. Mo., 1952) 104 F. Supp. 648.

[44]Schwab v. Schwab-Wilson Machine Corp., (1936) 13 Cal. App. 2d 1, 55 P.2d 1268.

[45]Rowland v. The Times Publishing Co., (1948) 160 Fla. 465, 35 So. 2d 399 (1948); Ross Transport v. Crothers, (1946) 185 Md. 573, 45 A.2d 567; Greenbaum v. American Metal Climax, Inc., (1967) 27 A.D. 2d 225, 278 N.Y.S. 123.

[46]Crosby v. Stratton, (1902) 17 Colo. App. 212, 68 P. 130.

[47]Hoyt v. Great Am. Ins. Co., (1922) 201 App. Div. 352, 194 N.Y.S. 449.

[48]Noble v. Great Am. Ins. Co., (1922) 200 App. Div. 773, 194 N.Y.S. 60.

consequence of failure to pay on the stated day. If the stock is still undisposed of the stockholder can exercise his preëmptive right. The cut-off date merely prevented the stockholder from contesting a disposition if made to someone else.[49] If no time is fixed, the stockholder must assert his right to subscribe within a reasonable time; otherwise it is forfeited.[50] What is a reasonable length of time is a question of fact.[51] A stockholder who, by absenting himself from the state or otherwise, places himself in such a position that notice which ordinarily would be reasonable cannot reach him in time for him to act thereon, must bear the consequences of his own acts, and cannot complain that he was not given reasonable opportunity to subscribe.[52]

Of course, a stockholder cannot exercise preëmptive rights based on stock illegally issued to him. Nor can he exercise the rights after the expiration of the allowable time even though a court later validates the issuance on independent grounds, namely paying off a debt owed the stockholder by the corporation.[53]

While the preëmptive right cannot be exercised prior to the time the increase of the authorized capital stock is made by the corporation, a stockholder can, by a valid contract, agree in advance to exercise the right when it accrues, which contract would bind him (and probably any transferee with notice of the agreement) to take the shares when issued.[54]

After the time fixed by the corporation in the resolution authorizing the increase for exercising the rights has expired, or, when no time is fixed, after a reasonable time, the stockholder cannot exercise his preëmptive rights as a matter of right,[55] unless the company by its own fault, such as failing to notify him of his right, prevents him from exercising his right in time. In such case the stockholder will be allowed to exercise his right within a reasonable time after the expiration of the original time.[56]

Example: A resolution passed January 3rd, giving stockholders the right to subscribe on written application on or before January 14th, is a mere mockery as to a stockholder who was in Europe at the time.[57]

On the other hand a stockholder in Japan is bound when a new

---

[49]Sommer v. Armor Gas & Oil Co., (1911) 71 Misc. 211, 128 N.Y.S. 382.

[50]Crosby v. Stratton, (1902) 17 Colo. App. 212, 68 P. 130.

[51]Jones v. Morrison, (1883) 31 Minn. 140, 16 N.W. 854; Hoyt v. Great Am. Ins. Co., (1922) 201 A.D. 352, 194 N.Y.S. 449.

[52]Hoyt v. Great Am. Ins. Co., (1922) 201 App. Div. 352, 194 N.Y.S. 449.

[53]National Oil Co. v. Reeves (S. Ct., Ark., 1958) 310 S.W.2d 242.

[54]See Real Estate Trust Co. v. Bird, (1899) 90 Md. 229, 44 A. 1048.

[55]Hart v. St. Charles St., etc., Co., (1878) 30 La. Ann. 758; Hoyt v. Great Am. Ins. Co., (1922) 201 App. Div. 352, 194 N.Y.S. 449. But see Sommer v. Armor Gas & Oil Co., (1911) 71 Misc. 211, 128 N.Y.S. 382.

[56]Mason v. Davol Mills, (1882) 132 Mass. 76.

[57]Jones v. Morrison, (1883) 31 Minn. 140, 16 N.W. 854.

issue was authorized on October 24th, an offer was made on November 4th to subscribe and pay for stock on or before December 16th, and the stockholder's agent in the state was notified.[58]

If the corporation requires the stockholder to pay a deposit on the new stock at the time of subscribing, failure to make the payment in time will result in a loss of the right to subscribe. When the corporation's notice says that preëmptive rights must be exercised by a certain day, acceptance of the offer is sufficient and tender of payment is not necessary to preserve preëmptive rights, particularly when the stock is still available.[59]

Price at which shares subject to preëmptive right must be offered. Generally, the corporation does not have to offer shares of a new issue of capital stock to its stockholders, pursuant to their preëmptive rights, at par, if the stock is worth more than par.[60] But the company cannot dispose of the stock to outsiders at a price lower than the price at which it was offered to the stockholders.[61] However, a few cases hold that the corporation must offer the shares at par although they may be worth more than par.[62]

Waiver of preëmptive right. The stockholder who has a right to subscribe for shares of an issue of the increased capital stock of a corporation, may waive his preëmptive right, either in the certificate of incorporation, or by agreement with the corporation.[63]

No waiver of the preëmptive rights attached to shares of stock is effective against a transferee of the shares who has not had notice of it.[64]

Note: a good way to assure this notice is for the corporation to note the waiver in the stock certificate issued to the transferee to replace the certificate held by the transferor. A stockholder director waives preëmptive rights when, knowing of the issuance of stock, he fails to exercise the rights within a reasonable time.[65]

Stockholder's remedies against corporation for violation of preëmptive rights. If a corporation violates the preëmptive rights of the stockholder, he has an action in equity for specific performance,[66] or at law

---

[58]Hoyt v. Great Am. Ins. Co., (1922) 201 App. Div. 352, 194 N.Y.S. 449.

[59]Oppenheimer v. Wm. F. Chimiquy Co., (1948) 335 Ill. App. 190, 81 N.E.2d 260.

[60]McClanhan v. Heidelberg Brewing Co., (1947) Ky., 199 S.W.2d 127.

[61]Stokes v. Continental Trust Co., (1906) 186 N.Y. 285, 78 N.E. 1090.

By-law leaving it to directors to determine price at which new stock was to be offered to old stockholders ruled invalid as deprivation of preëmptive right. Op. Atty. Gen., Wis., to Banking Commission, 9-20-46, 35 Ops. Atty. Gen. 340.

[62]Hammond v. Edison Illuminating Co., (1902) 131 Mich. 79, 90 N.W. 1040.

[63]See Public Bancorporation v. Atlantic City Wimsett Thrift Co., (1932) 110 N.J. Eq. 23, 158 A. 729; Hoyt v. Shenango Valley Steel Co., (1903) 207 Pa. 208, 56 A. 422; Heylandt Sales Co. v. Welding Gas Products Co., (1943) 180 Tenn. 437, 175 S.W.2d 557.

[64]Real Estate Trust Co. v. Bird, (1899) 90 Md. 229, 44 A. 1048.

[65]Fuller v. Krogh, (S. Ct., 1962) 15 Wis. 2d 412, 113 N.W.2d 25.

[66]Schmidt v. Pritchard, (1907) 135 Iowa 240, 112 N.W. 801; Electric Co. v. Edison, etc., Co. (1901) 200 Pa. 516, 50 A. 164; Thomas Branch & Co., (1927) 147 Va. 522, 137 S.E. 614.

for damages, as his remedies.[67] Another possible remedy is a mandamus to compel the corporation to issue the shares to which the stockholder is entitled by virtue of his preëmptive rights.[68]

The courts will not award a decree for specific performance if the company has already issued the shares to a bona fide holder.[69] In that case the stockholder is relegated to an action "at law" to recover his damages.[70] That kind of action, though, calls for a demand for the shares and a tender of the price as conditions precedent.[71] The measure of damages is the difference between what the stockholder would have had to pay the company for the shares and the value of the shares at the time the company wrongfully refused to issue them.[72]

To exercise a remedy against the company for its failure to recognize preëmptive rights, the stockholder must show that his own rights have been violated, not merely those of other stockholders. Thus, a common stockholder has no standing in court to complain because preferred shareholders have not been permitted to subscribe to an issue of new shares.[73]

A stockholder who has waived, or failed to exercise, his preëmptive rights cannot recover from the corporation a premium, or excess over the par value, which it has received upon a sale of the shares, unless a statute specifically so provides.[74]

Stockholder's right against person taking shares in violation of preëmptive rights. Stockholders whose preëmptive rights in a new issue of capital stock have been violated may sue to cancel the issue so long as the shares remain in the hands of persons who took them with knowledge of the circumstances under which they were sold.[75] The corporation itself may sue to reacquire the stock but cannot cancel the issue unless it can be shown that there was some fraud involved.[76] After the shares have come into the hands of bona fide holders for value they cannot be canceled. If one of the original stockholders purchases new stock and transfers some of the new shares, he may be enjoined from voting or selling a corresponding number of his old shares until the validity of the new sale is finally determined.[77]

---

[67]Meredith v. New Jersey Zinc & Iron Co., (1897) 55 N.J. Eq. 211, 37 A. 539, aff'd 56 N.J. Eq. 454, 41 A. 1116; Reading Trust Co. v. Reading Iron Works, (1890) 137 Pa. St. 282, 21 A. 169; Thomas Branch & Co. v. Riverside & Dan River Cotton Mills, (1927) 147 Va. 522, 137 S.E. 614.

[68]Hammond v. Edison Mfg. Co., (1902) 131 Mich. 79, 90 N.W. 1040.

[69]Morris v. Stevens, (1897) 178 Pa. St. 563, 36 A. 151.

[70]Real Estate Trust Co. v. Bird, (1899) 90 Md. 229, 44 A. 1048.

[71]Bonnet v. First Nat. Bank, (1900) 24 Tex. Civ. App. 613, 60 S.W. 325.

[72]Gray v. Portland Bank, (1807) 3 Mass. 364; Reading Trust Co. v. Reading Iron Works, (1890) 137 Pa. St. 282, 21 A. 169.

[73]Weidenfeld v. Northern Pac. Ry. Co., (CA-8, 1904) 129 F. 305.

[74]Mason v. Davol Mills, (1882) 132 Mass. 76.

[75]Rowland v. Times Publ. Co., (1948) Fla., 35 So.2d 399; Schmidt v. Pritchard, (1907) 135 Iowa 240, 112 N.W. 801; Whitaker v. Kilby, (1907) 55 Misc. 337, 106 N.Y.S. 511.

[76]Barson v. The Pioneer Savings & Loan Co., (S.Ct., Ohio, 1955) 163 O.S. 424.

[77]Morris v. Stevens, (1897) 178 Pa. St. 563, 36 A. 151.

STOCK PURCHASE WARRANTS

Nature of stock purchase warrants. A stock purchase warrant is an instrument granting to the owner the right to purchase a fixed number of shares of stock of the issuing corporation at a fixed price in the *future*. These warrants are usually created and issued in connection with the sale of stock, or other corporate securities, such as bonds or debentures. They may also be issued independently.[78] Warrants issued in connection with the security may be detachable, non-detachable, or attached but detachable after a fixed date. A detachable warrant may be exercised merely by presentation and payment of the price.[79] The corporate obligation must accompany non-detachable warrants. Warrants generally call for the issuance of common stock.

The purchase rights under a warrant should be distinguished from the stockholders' subscription rights (preëmptive rights) to *presently* purchase shares of the corporation.[80] They must also be distinguished from the right of conversion granted with some stock and some bonds. The conversion right is exercised by exchanging shares of one class of stock for shares of another class, or by exchanging bonds for stock. Note an important distinction: ordinary conversions shift one form of capital into another, but provide no *new* capital; the exercise of warrants, however, does bring in new capital.[81]

Purpose of stock purchase warrants. These warrants may be a simple financing device when they are issued independently. Their primary purpose is to enhance the value and marketability of the corporate securities with which they are issued. They offer an element of speculation in the sale of securities usually considered non-speculative. Stock purchase warrants have been used to assure corporate control by the existing management.[82] They also may be used as a protection against losses in short sales, if the price of the stock that has been sold short goes up.

Authority for issuance of stock purchase warrants. Generally, the power to issue stock purchase warrants is vested by statute solely in the

---

[78]See Tripp v. North Butte Mining Co., (1938) 100 F.2d 188.

[79]In Garner and Forsythe, "Stock Purchase Warrants and 'Rights' " 4 So. CALIF. L. REV. 375, it was stated that, although a stock purchase warrant is not a negotiable instrument, some of the qualities of a negotiable instrument may be secured by the insertion of a provision in the warrant making title transferable.

[80]Preëmptive rights are discussed at pp. 522 et seq. The relation of preëmptive rights to stock purchase warrants is discussed in 4 So. CALIF. L. REV. 269-292, 375-395. See also 36 Yale L.J. 649 on "Convertible Bonds and Stock Purchase Warrants."

[81]Dewing: "Financial Policy of Corporations," 265 (5th Ed., 1853).

[82]See Hechler v. Emery, (1928) 131 N.Y. Misc. 393, 226 N.Y. Supp. 599, 133 N.Y. Misc. 689, 234 N.Y. Supp. 46, for a comparable option contract situation.

board of directors, and consent of the stockholders is not required unless the corporation charter so provides. If there is no provision in the statute or in the charter authorizing issuance of stock purchase warrants, authority for their creation and issuance would seem to rest with the body having power to authorize creation and issuance of the stock purchasable upon exercise of the warrant.

Procedure when stock purchase warrants are issued with other securities. When the stock purchase warrants are issued in connection with some other security, issuance of the warrants is usually authorized at the same time and in the same manner as is the issuance of the underlying security. The resolution authorizing the issuance of the securities with the warrants generally empowers the officers of the corporation to execute an indenture, setting forth the form of the warrants and the terms and conditions upon which they are to be issued and exercised. The indenture is in the form of an agreement between the corporation and some bank or trust company as trustee for the warrant holders, and sets forth all the rights and obligations of the warrant holders, the corporation, and the trustee. While it is customary to have a warrant agreement, such an agreement is not necessary. In some instances, the terms and conditions under which the warrants are issued are set forth in the warrant itself.

Protection of holders of stock purchase warrants. To protect holders of stock purchase warrants against possible dilution, change, or destruction of their privilege of purchasing stock at a fixed price through acts of the corporation, the warrant or the agreement under which it is issued ordinarily includes co-provision for adjustment of the terms of the warrant in the event of such dilution, change, or destruction. These protective provisions generally cover the following acts of the corporation that may affect the privilege of the stock purchase warrant holder: (1) the sale of the stock purchasable upon exercise of the warrant at a price lower than that fixed in the warrant; (2) the grant of options to acquire the stock purchasable upon exercise of the warrant at a price lower than that fixed in the warrant; (3) the issuance of stock convertible into shares purchasable upon exercise of the warrant at a price lower than that fixed in the warrant; (4) the issuance of stock with the right to participate in dividends with the stock purchasable upon exercise of the warrant; (5) a split-up or combination of shares of stock purchasable upon exercise of the warrant; (6) the payment of stock dividends in stock purchasable upon exercise of the warrant; (7) an offer of rights to subscribe to the stock purchasable upon exercise of the warrant; (8) redemption of stock to which the warrant is attached; and (9) reclassification of stock, sale of assets, merger, consolidation, reorganization, or dissolution.

OPTIONS TO PURCHASE STOCK

Nature of options to purchase stock. The same legal principles of contract law apply to stock purchase options as apply to options on the other property.[83] An option is a contract, by the terms of which the owner of property, the optionor, agrees that another, the optionee, shall have the right to buy property at a fixed price within a certain time.[84] The option contract may provide a method of computing the price instead of stating the sum.[85] An option at a stated price "on terms to be agreed upon" was held valid when the optionee offered all cash within the time limit.[86] If no time is fixed in the contract, the option may be exercised within a reasonable time.[87] The distinguishing feature of a valid option is that the optionee assumes no obligation,[88] but the optionor cannot withdraw from the contract until the time limit expires.[89] The optionor cannot compel the optionee to proceed even if the latter has made some payment on the option.[90]

In effect, a valid option is an offer to sell,[91] *and* a contract to keep the offer open for a specified time.[92]

The necessity for consideration. An option,supported by a consideration, is an enforceable contract.[93] An option agreement that is not

[83]Frissell v. Nichols, (1927) 94 Fla. 403, 114 So. 431; Jones v. Vereen, (1935) 52 Ga. App. 157, 182 S.E. 627; Monahan v. Allen, (1913) 47 Mont. 75, 130 P. 768.

[84]For definitions of options, see Jones v. Vereen, (1935) 52 Ga. App. 157, 182 S.E. 627. Mitzlaff v. Midland Lumber Co., (1930) 338 Ill. 575, 170 N.E. 695; Axe v. Tolbert, (1914) 179 Mich. 556, 146 N.W. 418; Anthis v. Sandin, (1931) 149 Okla. 126, 299 P. 458; Northside Lumber & Bldg. Co. v. Neal, (1929) (Tex. Civ. App.) 23 S.W. 2d 858.

[85]R.F. Robinson Co. v. Drew, (1928) 83 N.H. 459, 144 A. 67; In re Galewitz' Estate, (1955) 3 N.Y. Misc. 2d 197, 148 N.Y.S. 2d 823; In re Sherman's Will (1956) 2 App. Div. 2d 662, 152 N.Y.S. 2d 250; Morrison v. St. Anthony Hotel, (1955) (Tex. Civ. App.) 274 S.W. 2d 556. See also Allen v. Biltmore Tissue Corp., (1957) 2 N.Y. 2d 534, 141 N.E. 2d 812; Comment, 31 N.Y.U.L. REV. 1429.

[86]Morris V. Ballard, (1926) 16 F.2d 175.

[87]West Texas Utilities Co. v. Ellis, (1937) (Tex. Civ. App.) 102 S.W.2d 234, rev'd on other grounds, 126 S.W.2d 13. But see Kingston v. Home Life Ins. Co., (1917) 11 Del. Ch. 258, 101 A. 898, aff'd, 11 Del. Ch. 428, 104 A. 25.

[88]Suburban Improvement Co. v. Scott Lumber Co., (1932) 59 F.2d 711, cert. denied, 53 S.Ct. 123; Oleson v. Bergwell, (1939) 204 Minn. 450, 283 N.W. 770; McHenry v. Mitchell, (1908) 219 Pa. 297, 68 A. 729. Whether a particular agreement is an option or a sale depends upon the document and intent of the parties. Thompson v. Sweet, (1932) 91 Colo. 552, 17 P.2d 308; Suburban Improvement Co. v. Scott Lumber Co., above.

[89]Postel v. Hagist, (1928) 251 Ill. App. 454; Moresi v. Burleigh, (1930) 170 La. 270; 127 So. 624.

[90]Bruce v. Mieir, (1932) 120 Cal. App. 287, 7 P.2d 1037.

[91]Madison Limestone Co. v. McDonald, (1956) 264 Ala. 295, 87 So. 2d 539; Russ v. Tuttle; (1910) 158 Cal. 226, 110 P.813; Price v. Town of Ruston, (1932) 19 La. App. 356, 139 So. 55; Kingston v. Anderson, (1940) 3 Wash 2d 21, 99 P.2d 630.

[92]Behrman v. Max, (1931) 102 Fla. 1094; 137 So. 120; Bayfield v. Defenbacker, (1932) 266 Ill. App. 385; First Nat'l Bank v. Corporation Securities Co., (1915) 128 Minn. 341, 150 N.W. 1084; Spitzli v. Guth, (1920) 112 N.Y. Misc. 630, 183 N.Y. Supp. 743.

[93]Baker v. Mulrooney, (1920) 265 Fed. 529; Copple v. Aigeltinger, (1914) 167 Cal. 706, 140 P. 1073; Prior v. Hilton & Dodge Lumber Co., (1913) 141 Ga. 117, 80 S.E. 559; Leadbetter v. Price; (1921) 103 Ore. 222, 202 P. 104; Baker v. Shaw, (1912) 68 Wash. 99, 122 P.611.

supported by a consideration is merely an offer that can be revoked by the optionor any time before it is accepted by the optionee.[94] A valid option, or an unrevoked offer, ripens into a contract for the sale of stock when the option is accepted according to the terms of the option or offer.[95]

Employee stock options. A corporation may grant its employees an option to purchase its stock at a bargain price. . . either by individual agreement[96] or under a general plan.[97] It's only an option. . . this means the employer does not become obligated to pay the purchase price until he elects to exercise the option. A valid option agreement or option plan must conform to the general legal principles governing option contracts.[98] The option grant also is subject to the general rules governing the conduct of corporate affairs.[99] Unless a statute or the corporate charter provides otherwise, the option agreement or option plan should protect any preëmptive rights of existing shareholders.[100]

Services as consideration for employee stock options. The usual purpose of an option agreement or option plan is to obtain the services of an individual or group for the corporation.[101] The tax benefit of certain stock options stimulated adoption of employee stock option plans.[102] Those benefits are now more limited . . . for example, restricted stock options, one of the types of tax-favored options, qualify only if they were granted before 1964 (with minor exceptions.)[103]

As in the issue of stock,[104] services can be adequate consideration for

---

[94]Thomas v. Birch, (1918) 178 Cal. 483, 173 P. 1102; Ankeney v. Brenton, (1931) 214 Iowa 357, 238 N.W. 71; Gillen v. Bayfield, (1931) 329 Mo. 681, 46 S.W. 2d 571; Brinley v. Nevins, (1914) 162 App. Div. 744, 147 N.Y. Supp. 985.

[95]Ankeney v. Brenton, (1931) 214 Iowa 357, 238 N.W. 71; Gillen v. Bayfield, (1931) 329 Mo. 681, 46 S.W. 2d 571; Moresi v. Burleight, (1930) 170 La. 270; 127 So. 624.

[96]Wyles v. Campbell, (1948) 77 F. Supp. 343; McQuillen v. National Cash Register Co., (1939) 27 F. Supp. 639; Sandler v. Schenley Industries, Inc., (1951) 32 Del. Ch. 46, 79 A. 2d 606; Milwaukee Sanitarium v. Swift. Under agreement saying (1) employee could exercise option in whole or part during its life and (2) it would expire within three months after death or termination of employment, holder can exercise option during three month period after termination; Army Corp. v. Nicholson (Fla., 1970) 249 So.2d 84.

[97]Clamitz v. Thatcher Mfg. Co., (1947) 158 F.2d 687; Kaufman v. Schoenberg, (1952) 33 Del. Ch. 211, 91 A.2d 786; Eliasberg v. Standard Oil Co., (1952) 23 N.J. Super. 431, 92 A.2d 862. See also Holthusen v. Edward G. Budd Mfg. Co., (1943) 52 F. Supp. 125, 53 F. Supp. 488, 2 opinions.

[98]Gottlieb v. Heyden Chemical Corp., (1951) 32 Del. Ch. 231, 83 A.2d 595.

[99]Steinberg v. Sharpe, (1950) 95 F. Supp. 32, aff'd without opinion, 190 F.2d 282; Wyles v. Campbell, (1948) 77 F. Supp. 343; Clamitz v. Thatcher Mfg. Co., see Note 97; Eliasberg v. Standard Oil Co., Abrams v. Allen, (1942) 36 N.Y.S.2d 174; aff'd without opinion, (1943) 266 App. Div. 835, 42 N.Y.S.2d 641. See also Greene v. Dietz, (1956) 143 F. Supp. 464.

[100]Gottlieb v. Heyden Chemical Corp., (1951) 32 Del. Ch. 231, 83 A.2d 595; Elward v. Peabody Coal Company, (1956) 9 Ill. App. 234, 132 N.E. 2d 549; Eliasberg v. Standard Oil Co., supra (Note 97); Milwaukee Sanitarium v. Swift, see Note 96.

[101]Spirt v. Bechtel, (1956) 232 F2.d 241; Clamitz v. Thatcher Mfg. Co., (1947) 158 F.2d 687; Kerbs v. California Eastern Airways, Inc. (1952) 33 Del. Ch. 82, 90 A.2d 652.

[102]Frankel v. Donovan, (1956) (Del. Ch.) 120 A.2d 311; Kaufman v. Schoenberg, (1952) 33 Del. Ch. 211, 91 A.2d 786; Eliasberg v. Standard Oil Co., (1952) 23 N.J. Super. 431, 92 A.2d 862.

[103]Internal Revenue Code, Sections 421-425. See Prentice-Hall, *Federal Taxes.*

[104]See pg. 526-527.

the grant of a stock option. A promise to assume an executive position,[105] continuation of employment after a proposed resignation,[106] and continuation of employment with disposal of outside interests,[107] have been held to be good consideration. In general, the corporation must be assured that the services will continue for a period of time, usually a year or more.[108] The value of the services must bear a reasonable relation to the value of the option at the time it is granted.[109] Usually the judgment of the board of directors, exercised in good faith, as to the value of the services or benefits received by the corporation for stock options is conclusive.[110]

Shareholder approval of employee option plans. Statutory provisions in some states regulate the adoption of employee stock option plans and approval by shareholders. Option plans have been attacked by dissenting shareholders as wasteful, fraudulent, and violative of preëmptive rights.[111]

It is advisable to submit employee stock option plans for approval by the shareholders even where not required by law.[112] This precaution is more important when directors receive the benefits of the plan, as directors, or as officers of the corporation.[113] If the shareholders have approved the plan, a dissenting stockholder must establish that the directors did not act in good faith. Without shareholder approval, the directors have a stronger burden of proving good faith.[114] A majority of shareholders cannot validate a stock option grant to employees that is without consideration.[115] The

---

[105]McQuillen v. National Cash Register Co., (1939) 27 F. Supp. 639.

[106]Wyles v. Campbell, (1948) 77 F. Supp. 343.

[107]Sandler v. Schenley Industries, Inc., (1951) 32 Del. Ch. 46, 79 A.2d 606.

[108]Holthusen v. Edward G. Budd Mfg. Co., (1943) 52 F. Supp. 125, 53 F. Supp. 488, 2 opinions. Kerbs v. California Eastern Airways, Inc., see Note 101; Eliasberg v. Standard Oil Co., (1952) 23 N.J. Super 431, 92 A.2d 862. But see Clamitz v. Thatcher Mfg. Co., see Note 99. Where options could be exercised at once, plans were held invalid in Frankel v. Donovan, (1956) Del. Ch. 120 A.2d 311; Kerbs v. California Eastern Airways, Inc., (1952) 33 Del. Ch. 82, 90 A.2d 652; Rosenthal v. Burry Biscuit Corporation, (1948) 30 Del. Ch. 299, 60 A.2d 106.

[109]Clamitz v. Thatcher Mfg. Co., (1947) 158 F. 2d 687; Frankel v. Donovan, (1956) Del. Ch. 120 A. 2d 311; Kerbs v. California Eastern Airways, Inc., (1952) 33 Del. Ch. 82, 90 A. 2d 652; Abrams v. Allen, (1942) 36 N.Y.S. 2d 174, aff'd without opinion, (1943) 266 App. Div. 835 42 N.Y.S. 2d 641.

[110]Some states expressly so provide by statute. See also Clamitz v. Thatcher Mfg. Co., see Note 97; Frankel v. Donovan, see Note 102; Kerbs v. California Eastern Airways, Inc., (1952) 33 Del. Ch. 82, 90 A.2d 652. See also "Employee Stock Option Plans — the Clydesdale Rule," 52 COLUM. L. REV. 1003.

[111]See Note, "Legality of Stock Option Grants to Officers," 49 COLUM. L. REV. 232. See also Krantman v. Liberty Loan Corp., (1957) 246 F.2d 581.

[112]Spirt v. Bechtel, (1956) F. 2d 241.

[113]Kaufman v. Schoenberg, (1952) 33 Del. Ch. 211, 91A.2d 786. See also 52 COLUM L. REV. 1003.

[114]Gottlieb v. Heyden Chemical Corp., (1951) 32 Del. Ch. 231, 83 A.2d 595, rev'd on other grounds, 33 Del. Ch. 82, 90 A.2d 660. Eliasberg v. Standard Oil Co., (1952) 23 N.J. Super. 431, 92 A.2d 862.

[115]Frankel v. Donovan, (1956) Del. Ch. 120 A.2d 311.

shareholders cannot validate an illegal option grant.[116] and some cases hold that, even under a judicially approved plan, individual option grants may be declared invalid.[117]

Stock option agreements among stockholders. Ordinarily a stockholder has the right to dispose of his shares as he sees fit. He may give an option for the purchase of his stock just as he may give an option for the purchase of any other property. There is no reason, therefore, why stockholders may not mutually contract with each other that, whenever any of them wishes to sell stock, the other stockholders or the corporation may have the exclusive right or option to purchase it during a limited time after notice of the wish to sell. Such an agreement is binding and enforceable.[118]

---

[116]Elward v. Peabody Coal Company, (1956) 9 Ill. App. 234, 132 N.E. 2d 549.

[117]Eliasberg v. Standard Oil Co., see Note 114. See also Kingston v. Home Life Ins. Co., (1917) 11 Del.Ch. 258, 101 A. 898, aff'd, 11 Del. Ch. 428, 104 A. 25. See also the discussion of employee benefit plans at page 352 in Chapter 11.

[118]Weissman v. Lincoln Corp., (1954) (Fla.) 76 So. 2d 478; Doss v. Yingling, (1930) 95 Ind. App. 494, 172 N.E. 801; Weiland v. Hogan, (1913) 177 Mich. 626, 143 N.W. 599; Model Clothing House v. Dickinson, (1920) 146 Minn. 367, 178 N.W. 957; Krieger v. Mazlish, (1955) 145 N.Y.S. 2d 815; Moses v. Soule, (1909) 63 N.Y. Misc. 203, 118 N.Y. Supp. 410, aff'd without opinion, 136 App. Div. 904, 120 N.Y. Supp. 1136; Nicholson v. Franklin Brewing Co., (1910) 82 Ohio 94, 91 N.E. 991; Coleman v. Kettering, (1956) (Tex. Civ. App.) 289 S.W. 2d 953. But see also pp. 616-620, infra. See Hardin v. Rosenthal, (1957) (Ga.) 98 S.E.2d 901 for an agreement held unenforceable as too indefinite as to price and payment terms.

Chapter 18

RESOLUTIONS RELATING TO RIGHTS TO SUBSCRIBE TO STOCK, STOCK PURCHASE WARRANTS, AND OPTIONS TO PURCHASE STOCK

Contents—Chapter 18

Options to Purchase Stock

STOCK SUBSCRIPTIONS

RESOLUTION OF DIRECTORS AUTHORIZING OFFER OF RIGHTS TO SUBSCRIBE FOR STOCK, SUBJECT TO EFFECTIVENESS OF REGISTRATION STATEMENT

RESOLVED, That, subject to the taking effect on or before ...., 19.., of the Registration Statement, No. ....., of .... Company, as amended on ...., 19.., and as it may be further amended, which Registration Statement was filed on ...., 19.., with the Securities and Exchange Commission under the Securities Act of 1933, as amended,

First. That the holders of record of the capital stock of .... Company as of the close of business ...., 19.., be offered the right to subscribe for one additional share of capital stock without par value for each four shares of such capital stock without par value held of record as of the close of business on ...., 19.., such subscriptions to be on the following terms and subject to the following conditions:

a. Written subscriptions for the shares to which stockholders are entitled to subscribe must be filed with the .... Trust Company, Subscription Agent, on or before ..... P.M., ..., 19.., and be accompanied by payment therefor at the rate of ..... ($....) Dollars per share for each share subscribed.

b. No subscription for fractional shares will be received.

Second. That the forms of transferable subscription warrants for capital stock and transferable fractional subscription warrants for capital stock, presented to this meeting and ordered filed with the records of the Company, are hereby approved and that such warrants be issued to each stockholder of .... Company of record as of the close of business ...., 19.., evidencing the right of subscription of such stockholder, on the terms and conditions authorized.

Third. That all of said shares of stock to which holders of subscription warrants are entitled to subscribe, which are not subscribed and paid for in accordance with the provisions thereof and the foregoing provisions of these resolutions, may be offered for subscription by the directors of .... Company to such persons and at such times and at such prices, not less than ..... ($.....) Dollars per share, as said directors may determine.

Fourth. That the issue of the shares of stock of .... Company subscribed upon said rights, or otherwise subscribed in accordance with the foregoing provisions of these resolutions, is hereby authorized, and upon the payment for the same, the President or a Vice President, and the Secretary or Assistant Secretary or the Treasurer or the Assistant Treasurer of ....

Company are hereby authorized to execute and deliver, or cause the delivery of, stock certificates therefor, to the persons entitled to receive the same.

RESOLUTION OF DIRECTORS AUTHORIZING ISSUANCE OF STOCK AFTER INCREASE, OFFER TO STOCKHOLDERS OF RIGHTS TO SUBSCRIBE SUBJECT TO EFFECTIVENESS OF REGISTRATION STATEMENT, APPOINTMENT OF SUBSCRIPTION AGENT, AND DELIVERY OF PROSPECTUS

[Issuance of stock after increase]

RESOLVED, That upon the filing in the office of the Secretary of State, of the State of ...., of the Certificate of increase of the number of shares, without par value, pursuant to Section ..... of the Corporation Law, authorized by the stockholders of this Company on ...., 19.., this Company issue a maximum of ..... (.....) shares of common stock, without par value, and

[Offer of rights to subscribe after effectiveness of registration statement]

RESOLVED FURTHER, That on or after the effective date of the Registration Statement of this Company, this Company offer to holders of record of common stock, without par value, at the close of business on ...., 19.., the right to subscribe, until ..... P.M. (Eastern Standard Time) on ...., 19.., to common stock, without par vlue, in the ratio of one (1) share for each four (4) shares held of record at the close of business on ...., 19.., at the price of ..... ($.....) Dollars per share, payable in New York funds to the order of .... Trust Company of ...., as Agent of the Company, at its main office, ... *(Street)*, ... *(City)*, ... *(State)*, or at its London office, ... *(Street)*, London, England, and

[Mailing of rights; fractional shares]

RESOLVED FURTHER, That transferable rights evidencing such subscription rights and to be surrendered to the said Agent upon the exercise thereof, be mailed on or about ...., 19.., to the holders of common stock of record as of that date; that rights in respect of fractional shares be issued entitling the holder upon surrender thereof, and of other fractional rights together aggregating one or more full shares, to subscribe to the number of full shares which such fractional share rights shall together aggregate, no subscriptions to be made for fractional shares, and

[Approval of form of rights]

RESOLVED FURTHER, That the form of rights and rights in respect of fractional shares submitted to this meeting are hereby approved, subject to such changes as may be advised by counsel, or as may be requested by the .... Trust Company of ...., as Transfer Agent, or the New York Stock Exchange, and

[Date to determine rights]

RESOLVED FURTHER, That in lieu of closing the transfer books of the Company, ..., 19.., is hereby designated as a record date for the determination of the common stockholders entitled to the right to subscribe to the aforesaid additional shares of common stock, without par value, within the time and upon the basis and terms in these resolutions set forth, and

[Letter and prospectus to be sent to stockholders]

RESOLVED FURTHER, That upon the effective date of the Registration Statement filed with the Securities and Exchange Commission, or as soon thereafter as practicable, a letter substantially in form presented to this meeting, together with a Prospectus substantially in form presented to this meeting, be sent to all holders of common stock and to all holders of preferred stock with warrants for the purchase of common stock attached, of record as of the close of business on date upon which the said Registration Statement becomes effective; and that said notices and Prospectus be continued to be sent to each holder of common stock or preferred stock with warrants for the purchase of common stock attached, who shall become such until the close of business ...., 19.., and

[Listing of additional stock on Exchange]

RESOLVED FURTHER, That an application be made to the New York Stock Exchange for the listing of the aforesaid ..... (.....) shares of additional common stock, without par value, and the aforesaid subscription rights of this Company, and that ...., ..., ..., and ...., or any one of them, hereby are designated to appear before the said Committee on Stock List of said New York Stock Exchange with authority to make such changes in said application or any agreements relative thereto as may be necessary to conform with requirements for listing, and

[Appointment of subscription agent]

RESOLVED FURTHER, That .... Trust Company of .... is hereby designated the Agent of this Company (1) for the purpose of issuing and mailing as soon as practicable after ...., 19.., but not later than ...., 19.., to the holders of common stock of record at the close of business on that date, the subscription rights referred to in the foregoing resolutions, together with a notice and Letter of Transmittal substantially in the form presented to this meeting, (2) for the purpose of splitting, grouping, and transferring subscription rights and rights in respect of fractional shares (including the splitting of full share subscription rights into fractional shares subscription rights) after the original issuance thereof and until the right of the said holders of common stock to subscribe has expired, and (3) for the purpose of the acceptance of the aforesaid subscription rights for exercise of the subscription privilege, and to accept payment for the shares of common stock to be issued upon the exercise of such rights and as such Agent, in behalf of this Company, to requisition the Transfer Department of .... Trust Company of .... for the required common stock in such names and denominations as may be necessary; to deliver such certificates for shares of common stock called for by the rights so exercised and upon receipt of such payment, to deposit the funds so received to the credit of said Company in its banking account with said .... Trust Company of ...., and to notify the Treasurer of this Company accordingly, and

[Issuance and delivery of stock certificates by transfer agent]

RESOLVED FURTHER, That upon the exercise of said subscription rights for common stock, ... Trust Company of ...., as Transfer Agent of this Company, shall issue, upon requisition of the Subscription Agent, and cause to be registered, and shall deliver certificates for common stock to such Agent in respect of the rights so exercised, and

[Delivery of prospectus with stock certificate to other than registered holders of rights]

RESOLVED FURTHER, That .... Trust Company of ...., as Subscription Agent of this Company, shall deliver a copy of the Prospectus with certificates for common stock when said certificates are issued to someone other than the registered holders of the subscription rights surrendered, and

[Subscription agent to act on advice of officers and counsel]

RESOLVED FURTHER, That .... Trust Company of ...., in carrying out its duties as such Subscription Agent in accordance with these resolutions, is hereby authorized and directed to act upon the instructions of the President or Vice President, or the Secretary or Treasurer of this Company, and to rely upon the advice of counsel for this Company, and

[Countersignature of certificates by Transfer Agent]

RESOLVED FURTHER, That .... Trust Company of ...., as Transfer Agent, is hereby authorized to record, countersign, and deliver to .... Trust Company, as Registrar, for countersignature as an original issue, in accordance with the resolutions of its appointment as Transfer Agent of the common stock of this Company, certificates for ..... (.....) shares of common stock, without par value, in addition to the number of shares specified in resolutions heretofore adopted appointing said .... Trust Company of .... as Transfer Agent, provided, however, that at the present time said Transfer Agent shall record, countersign, and deliver to said .... Trust Company, as Registrar, for countersignature as an original issue not in excess of ..... (.....) shares, the balance of said shares, to wit, ... (.....), to be issued upon further instructions of proper officers of this Company pursuant to resolutions duly adopted by the Board of Directors of this Company, and

[Countersignature by Transfer Agent of shares not purchased pursuant to subscription rights]

RESOLVED FURTHER, That .... Trust Company of ...., as Transfer Agent, is hereby authorized to record, countersign, and deliver to .... Trust Company, as Registrar, for countersignature as an original issue, certificates for such shares of the shares of common stock offered for subscription (the number of which will depend upon the number of holders of common stock at the close of business on ...., 19.., and which in no event will exceed ..... (.....) shares) as shall not be purchased pursuant to the exercise of the subscription privilege, hereinbefore referred to, in such names and for such number of shares as the President or Vice President of this Company may in writing direct, duly attested by the Secretary or Assistant Secretary, under the seal of this Company.

RESOLUTION OF DIRECTORS AUTHORIZING OFFER TO STOCK-HOLDERS OF ADDITIONAL COMMON STOCK AT FIXED PRICE

RESOLVED, First: That the ..... (.....) shares of common stock without par value of this Company, heretofore authorized, be offered to stockholders of record at the close of business on ...., 19.., for subscription pro rata according to their respective stockholdings on or before ...., 19.., at the price of ..... ($.....) Dollars a share, payable in cash or in New York funds at the time of subscription, or at the option of the subscriber, ... (.....%) per cent thereof at the time of subscription, and the remaining ..... (.....%) per cent on or before ...., 19..

Second: That the Board of Directors is hereby authorized and directed to cause proper transfers and subscription warrants to be prepared in accordance with this resolution and sent by mail as soon as practicable after ...., 19.., to stockholders of record at the close of business on that date.

Third: That the Board of Directors is hereby authorized to cause scrip certificates to be issued for fractional shares of new stock, containing provisions for exchange of such scrip certificates for certificates for full shares, and such other terms and conditions as to voting powers and dividend rates as the Board may deem advisable.

Fourth: That the Board of Directors is hereby authorized to cause to be done all such acts, and to adopt all such rules and regulations, as may seem necessary or proper for the issuance of the common stock without par value in substantially the manner above provided, and for the prompt retirement of such scrip certificates as may be issued.

RESOLUTION OF DIRECTORS OFFERING TO SELL ALL REMAINING UNISSUED STOCK TO STOCKHOLDERS

RESOLVED, That all the unissued authorized capital stock of this Corporation, consisting of ..... (.....) shares of common stock having a par value of ..... ($.....) Dollars each, be offered to the stockholders of record at the close of business on ...., 19.., for subscription pro rata according to their respective stockholdings on the date aforementioned, at par, payable in cash at the time of subscription, this offer to remain open until and including the .. day of ...., 19..; and that the President is hereby authorized to sell at par, any of the said stock remaining unsold after ...., 19...

RESOLUTION APPOINTING SUBSCRIPTION AGENT TO RECEIVE WARRANTS EVIDENCING RIGHTS TO SUBSCRIBE FOR STOCK

RESOLVED, That the .... Trust Company is hereby appointed Subscription Agent: (1) to receive Subscription Warrants evidencing the right to subscribe for one or more shares of the capital stock of this Company, in the form presented to and approved at this meeting, when accompanied by the subscription price of ..... ($.....) Dollars per share up to ..... P.M., E.S.T., on ...., 19.., on the offering of ..... (.....) shares of capital stock without par value of this Company, to be made in accordance with the resolutions of this Board as adopted on ...., 19..; (2) upon receipt of subscriptions in proper form, to requisition, when and as necessary, from the .... Trust Company, as Transfer Agent for said capital stock, the shares of capital stock to be delivered under the terms of said Warrants; (3) upon receipt of certificates for said shares of capital stock, to make delivery to or upon the order of the respective subscriber; (4) to surrender said Subscription Warrants to this Company for cancellation, and to remit to this Company the subscription price so received, and

RESOLVED FURTHER, That the .... Trust Company, as Transfer Agent, is hereby authorized and directed to countersign, issue, and record said shares of capital stock upon requisitions therefor, as hereinbefore provided, and

RESOLVED FURTHER, That ...., a Vice-President, is hereby authorized, in behalf of the Company, to furnish the .... Trust Company with such instructions and directions as may be necessary to carry out the purposes and intent of these resolutions.

RESOLUTIONS AUTHORIZING EXECUTION OF UNDERWRITING AGREEMENT FOR STOCK NOT PURCHASED BY HOLDER OF WARRANTS FOR RIGHTS TO SUBSCRIBE

RESOLVED, That ...., President of .... Company, is hereby authorized and directed, in behalf of .... Company, to execute the underwriting agreement in the form presented to this meeting and ordered filed with the records of the Company, addressed to .... & Co. and The .... Company, under the terms of which .... & Co., The .... Company, ..., Inc., ... & Co., and .... and Company, agree to purchase, upon the terms and conditions therein stated, the shares of capital stock of .... Company not purchased by the holders of subscription warrants evidencing the right to subscribe for such capital stock issued to the stockholders of .... Company, as authorized at this meeting.

RESOLUTION OF STOCKHOLDERS WAIVING THEIR PREËMPTIVE RIGHT TO SUBSCRIBE TO INCREASED STOCK AND AUTHORIZING SALE TO PRESIDENT

WHEREAS, the capital stock of this corporation was increased from ..... (.....) shares of common stock without par value to ..... (.....) shares of common stock without par value by authority of the stockholders given at a special meeting held on ...., 19.., and none of said ..... (.....) new shares of common stock without par value has been issued, and

WHEREAS, ..., President of this corporation, has submitted an offer to this corporation to purchase all of said ..... (.....) shares of unissued common stock for the price of ..... ($.....) Dollars per share, payable in cash, be it

RESOLVED, That the stockholders of this corporation do hereby waive their preëmptive right to subscribe in proportion to their respective holdings of the capital stock of this corporation to the ..... (.....) shares of unissued common stock without par value made available by the increase in the capital stock duly authorized at a special meeting of the stockholders held on ...., 19.., and they do hereby authorize the Board of Directors to accept the offer of .... and to issue to said .... (.....) shares of common stock without par value, and the certificate or certificates evidencing the same, upon full payment therefor.

RESOLUTION OF DIRECTORS OFFERING OPTION TO SUBSCRIBERS TO PAY IN INSTALLMENTS

Resolved, That subscribers electing so to do may pay for such stock in ten (10) monthly installments, at the rate of ..... ($.....) Dollars per share per month, with the exception of the tenth payment, which shall be at the rate of ..... ($.....) Dollars per share plus accrued dividends. The initial monthly installment should accompany the subscription application, and is payable on or before ...., 19... The remaining monthly installments will be payable on ...., 19.., and on the first day of each month thereafter. If subscribers paying in installments pay on the day fixed, they will be entitled to interest at the rate of five (5%) per cent per annum on the first nine (9) installments, to be credited at the time of paying the final installment. Certificates for such stock will be issued when the same is fully paid.

STOCK PURCHASE WARRANTS

RESOLUTION OF DIRECTORS AUTHORIZING CREATION OF STOCK PURCHASE WARRANTS AND RESERVING STOCK FOR ISSUANCE UPON EXERCISE OF WARRANTS

Resolved, That this Company create an issue of Common Stock Purchase Warrants, covering the right to purchase shares of Common Stock of this Company, all as set forth in the form of Common Stock Purchase Warrant hereafter adopted by this Board of Directors at this meeting, and

Resolved Further, That there is hereby authorized the issue of such Common Stock Purchase Warrants in temporary form covering the right to purchase ..... (.....) shares of Common Stock of this Company; that the President, or a Vice-president, is hereby authorized to sign, in behalf of this Company temporary warrants issuable on the transfer thereof or in exchange or substitution therefor; and that the proper officers are hereby authorized to cause to be delivered with and attached to the temporary certificates for ..... (.....) shares of $..... Cumulative Dividend Preferred Stock (heretofore authorized at this meeting to be issued and delivered) temporary Common Stock Purchase Warrants covering the right to purchase an equivalent number of shares of Common Stock of this Company, and thereafter, upon the transfer, exchange, or substitution of temporary certificates for any of said shares of Preferred Stock, to cause to be delivered therewith and attached thereto temporary Common Stock Purchase Warrants for an equivalent number of shares of Common Stock, and

RESOLVED FURTHER, That of the authorized but unissued shares of Common Stock of this Company, are hereby reserved for sale to holders of said Common Stock Purchase Warrants, or their assigns, ... (.....) shares thereof, which shall be used only for issuance upon exercise of the said warrants.

RESOLUTION OF DIRECTORS DETERMINING RIGHTS OF HOLDERS AND TERMS AND CONDITIONS OF STOCK PURCHASE WARRANTS

WHEREAS, this Company has agreed, in connection with the issuance and sale to .... and Company, of ..... (.....) 7% Cumulative Preferred Shares, to deliver to said .... and Company, Common Share Purchase Warrants, granting rights to purchase ..... (.....) Common shares without par value of this Company, and

WHEREAS, the form of the said warrants should be determined, and the rights of the holders thereof, and the terms and conditions of the said Common Share Purchase Warrants should be fixed, be it

RESOLVED, That Common Share Purchase Warrants conferring rights to purchase ..... (.....) Common shares without par value of this Company be issued and delivered in connection with the sale to .... and Company of ..... (.....) 7% Cumulative Preferred Shares, and that the terms, limitations, and conditions under which said warrants shall be issued, and the rights of the bearers thereof, and the form thereof, shall be as follows:

(Insert terms and form of the stock purchase warrants.)

and,

RESOLVED FURTHER, That the warrants conferring rights to purchase one hundred (100) shares shall be numbered W1 to W ....., and that the warrants conferring rights to purchase less than one hundred (100) shares shall be numbered WO1 to WO ....., and

RESOLVED FURTHER, That the price for which the ..... (.....) Common shares without par value of this Company shall be sold upon the exercise of the warrants heretofore authorized shall be as follows:

(Insert the prices.)

and,

RESOLVED FURTHER, That this Company sell or cause to be sold to the Bearers of said warrants, upon the exercise thereof, Common shares without par value of this Company for such price, and in accordance with the provisions of the warrants and the terms, limitations, and conditions thereof.

RESOLUTION OF DIRECTORS AUTHORIZING EXECUTION OF AGREEMENT APPOINTING WARRANT AGENT

RESOLVED, That this Corporation enter into an agreement with the President and directors of the .... Company, a copy of which agreement has been exhibited to this meeting, whereby this Corporation does hereby appoint said President and directors of the .... Company, Warrant Agent for Common Share Purchase Warrants conferring rights to purchase ..... (.....) Common shares without par value of this Corporation; and that the President and Secretary of this Corporation are hereby authorized to execute said agreement with said Warrant Agent in behalf of this Corporation, in the form as presented to said meeting, or with such modifications thereof as may be accepted by the President and Secretary, and to affix the seal of the Corporation thereto; and authority is hereby given to said President and Secretary to modify said agreement in such manner and in such particulars as to them may seem necessary or advisable, and

RESOLVED FURTHER, That all of said warrants shall be subject to said agreement, and that the rights of the bearers thereof shall be as expressed in said warrants and said agreement.

RESOLUTION OF DIRECTORS RESERVING COMMON SHARES TO SATISFY RIGHTS OF HOLDER OF STOCK PURCHASE WARRANTS

WHEREAS, the Company has heretofore authorized the issuance, in connection with the sale of ..... (.....) 7% Cumulative Preferred Shares, of Common Share Purchase Warrants conferring rights to purchase ..... (.....) Common shares without par value of this Company, and

WHEREAS, this Company, in said warrants and the agreement concerning the same, covenanted and agreed to reserve and set aside ..... (.....) Common shares without par value of this Company, for the purpose of satisfying the rights of the warrant bearers, be it

RESOLVED, That ..... (.....) Common shares without par value of the Company are hereby appropriated, reserved, and irrevocably set aside until ...., 19.., for the purpose of satisfying the rights of the bearers of said warrants by the sale to them of said Common shares in accordance with the terms and provisions therof; and that as and when said warrant rights are exercised by the bearers thereof, and the price for said Common shares paid, as provided in said warrants, the Company shall issue, out of said ..... (.....) Common shares, certificates for Common shares in satisfaction of said warrants.

RESOLUTION OF DIRECTORS AUTHORIZING ISSUANCE OF STOCK UPON EXERCISE OF STOCK PURCHASE WARRANTS, AND FIXING CONSIDERATION FOR SHARES TO BE ISSUED

WHEREAS, ... (.....) shares of common stock are authorized by the amended Certificate of Incorporation of this Company.

WHEREAS, ... (.....) shares of common stock have heretofore been authorized to be issued,

WHEREAS, ... (.....) shares of common stock have heretofore been reserved for sale to holders of Common Stock Purchase Warrants, be it

RESOLVED, That there is hereby authorized the issue of ..... (.....) shares of common stock, and

RESOLVED FURTHER, That said ..... (.....) shares of common stock be issued at any time or from time to time on or after ...., 19.., to or on the order of the persons purchasing the same as ..... ($.....) Dollars per share under the purchase privilege contained in the Common Stock Purchase Warrants of this Company now outstanding upon receipt of full payment of such purchase price.

RESOLUTION OF DIRECTORS AUTHORIZING EXTENSION OF TIME TO EXERCISE STOCK WARRANTS AND REDUCTION OF SUBSCRIPTION PRICE

RESOLVED, by the Board of Directors of the .... Corporation, a corporation of the State of ...., that the life of Stock Purchase Warrants outstanding under the Trust Agreement entered into between this Corporation and the .... Trust Company, as Trustee, dated ...., 19.., is hereby extended from ...., 19.., to ...., 19.., inclusive, and that during such extended life, the price of $42.50 to be paid for each share of Class A Common Stock purchasable with such warrants is hereby reduced to $30 per share, and

RESOLVED FURTHER, That the said Trust Agreement is hereby amended by changing to "........... .., 19..," the date therein of "........... .., 19.," which limits the life of the Stock Purchase Warrants provided therein, and further by changing to "$30" the amount therein of "$42.50," which limits the price to be paid for each share of Class A Common Stock purchasable in connection with said warrants, and

RESOLVED FURTHER, That upon the exercise at any time by any holder of any such warrant of any right hereby created, such holder thereby waives any right, conferred in Section ..... of the said Trust Agreement, or in any other section thereof, to any adjustment in price to be paid for any stock purchasable in connection with any such warrant, and

RESOLVED FURTHER, That except as hereinbefore provided, the said Trust Agreement shall remain unchanged and in full force and effect, and

RESOLVED FURTHER, That the proper officers of this Corporation are hereby authorized and instructed to do in the name of this Corporation all acts and things necessary to carry this resolution into effect.

OPTION TO PURCHASE STOCK

RESOLUTION OF DIRECTORS GIVING AN OPTION TO PURCHASE STOCK OF CORPORATION

WHEREAS, by appropriate action, the Capital Stock of this Corporation is being increased from ..... ($.....) Dollars to ..... ($.....) Dollars, to consist of ..... ($.....) Dollars Common Capital Stock (being the present authorized Capital Stock; viz., ... ($.....) Dollars and ..... ($.....) Dollars of the new stock) and ..... ($.....) Dollars ..... (.....%) per cent Cumulative Preferred Stock (being the balance of the new stock), and

WHEREAS, all the stockholders of this Corporation have duly waived in writing their rights to subscribe to any part of said ..... ($.....) Dollars of stock not yet issued, and

WHEREAS, "A" has asked this Board of Directors to grant him an option to purchase all of the said unissued stock for cash, at par, to continue for a period of ..... (.....) years from this date, and

WHEREAS, in the opinion of this Board, it is for the best interests of this Corporation to grant him such option, be it

RESOLVED, That, in consideration of the payment of ..... ($.....) Dollars on account of such option (receipt of which is hereby acknowledged by this Corporation), an option is hereby given, for a period of ..... (.....) years from the date hereof, to "A," his heirs, and assigns, to purchase for cash, at par, the entire amount of ..... ($.....) Dollars of the unissued stock of this Corporation, or any part thereof, with the understanding that such payment of ..... ($.....) Dollars, already made by him, shall be applied upon the purchase price of any stock purchased by him, his heirs, or assigns, under the terms of this option.

EXTRACT FROM MINUTES OF DIRECTORS' MEETING, APPROVING OPTION BY CORPORATION TO EMPLOYEE TO PURCHASE STOCK

The Secretary then submitted and read an option agreement with "X," giving "X" the right and option to purchase five thousand (5,000) shares of the common stock of this Corporation at ..... ($.....) Dollars per share at any time on or before ...., 19...

After consideration and upon motion duly made, seconded, and unanimously carried, it was

RESOLVED, That the option agreement with "X," submitted to this meeting, is hereby authorized and approved, and

RESOLVED FURTHER, That the Vice President and Secretary of this Corporation are hereby authorized and directed to execute the option agreement with "X" in substantially the form submitted to this meeting, and

RESOLVED FURTHER, That a copy of the said option agreement be inserted in the minute book following the minutes of this meeting.

RESOLUTION OF DIRECTORS AUTHORIZING EXERCISE, IN PART, OF OPTION TO PURCHASE STOCK

WHEREAS, a certain option agreement was executed under date of ...., 19.., by and among "A," "X" Corporation, and "B," Trustee, by which said "A" granted to "X" Corporation an option to purchase all or any part of fifty thousand (50,000) shares of the common stock of "Y" Corporation pursuant to the terms and conditions therein in said agreement set forth, and

WHEREAS, in the opinion of this Board it is desirable that "X" Corporation exercise at this time a part of said option and acquire a part of said common stock of "Y" Corporation, be it

RESOLVED, That "X" Corporation exercise at this time its option with respect to fifteen thousand (15,000) shares of said "Y" Corporation common stock, in accordance with the terms of the aforesaid option, reserving to itself the right from time to time to exercise said option as to the remainder of said fifty thousand (50,000) shares as provided in the aforesaid agreement, and

RESOLVED FURTHER, That a certified copy of these resolutions be transmitted to "A" and to "B," Trustee, and

RESOLVED FURTHER, That said "B," Trustee, is hereby authorized, upon transfer and delivery to "X" Corporation of fifteen thousand (15,000) shares of the common stock of "Y" Corporation, to transfer and deliver to said "A" nine thousand (9,000) shares of the common stock of "X" Corporation as payment in full therefor, and

RESOLVED FURTHER, That the executive officers of the Corporation, or any of them, are hereby authorized to do all such acts as may be necessary or appropriate to carry into effect these resolutions.

RESOLUTION OF DIRECTORS AUTHORIZING EXTENSION OF TIME FOR EXERCISE OF OPTION TO PURCHASE STOCK

WHEREAS, this Corporation entered into an agreement dated ...., 19.., with .... of the City of ...., State of ...., under the terms of which this Corporation granted to .... an option to purchase ..... (.....) shares of the preferred stock of this Corporation on or before ...., 19.., at a price of ..... ($.....) Dollars per share, and

WHEREAS, ... has notified this Corporation by letter dated ...., 19.., that he will be unable to exercise the said option within the time specified in the said option agreement, and

WHEREAS, ... has requested that the time within which he may exercise the option aforesaid be extended to ...., 19.., and has indicated his willingness to pay, immediately upon the granting of said extension, an additional sum of ..... ($.....) Dollars as consideration for the granting of said extension, and

WHEREAS, the Board of Directors of this Corporation deems it advisable to grant the said request for an extension of time to exercise the option aforesaid for the consideration offered, be it

RESOLVED, That the time within which .... may exercise the option to purchase ..... (.....) shares of preferred stock of this Corporation at a price of ..... ($.....) Dollars per share, granted to him under the agreement between this Corporation and the said .... dated ...., 19.., is hereby extended to and including ...., 19.., provided that .... shall pay to this Corporation on or before ...., 19.., an additional sum of ..... ($.....) Dollars as consideration for the extension of time herein provided, and

RESOLVED FURTHER, That the proper officers of this Corporation are hereby directed to do all things and to execute all instruments necessary and proper to carry out the foregoing resolution.

RESOLUTION OF BOARD OF DIRECTORS RECOMMENDING TO STOCKHOLDERS INCREASE IN OPTIONS UNDER RESTRICTED OPTION PLAN

RESOLVED, That in order to continue this corporation in a position to attract and retain strong management through the granting of options to present and prospective officers and employees to purchase common stock of the corporation by the award of Restricted Stock Options as defined in Sec. 421, 1954 Internal Revenue Code, this Board of Directors does hereby recommend to the stockholders of the corporation that they authorize and approve an extension of the Employees' Stock Option Plan approved by the stockholders at the annual meeting on ...., 19.., by increasing the total number of options which may be granted under the plan from ..... shares to ..... shares, the remaining provisions of the Plan to remain substantially in the form originally approved, and

RESOLVED FURTHER, That this recommendation be submitted to the stockholders at the annual meeting on ...., 19..

Chapter 19

CALLS FOR PAYMENT OF STOCK AND ASSESSMENTS

Contents—Chapter 19

Meaning of a "call." Strictly speaking, a "call" is a demand upon a shareholder for the balance of the purchase price of his shares, or some part of such balance.[1] The term "call" has, however, been applied to the resolution calling for payment, to the notice or demand for payment, and sometimes to the time when payment is due. The words "call" and "assessment" are frequently used interchangeably, for "assessment" also means that a fixed payment is required of the shareholder. "Call," however, is generally understood to apply to unpaid subscriptions, while "assessment" is used to designate demands for additional contributions on stock that is already fully paid.[2]

Generally, the completion of a valid transfer of stock imposes upon the transferee the existing liabilities of his transferor to the corporation, to the other stockholders and to third parties, including creditors.[3]

In most states it is the law, either common or statutory, that the transferee is liable for all calls made after the transfer, but not for those made before the transfer.[4] The liability is governed by the law of the state of corporate organization and not by the law of the state of the transferee's residence.[5] This liability, at common law is based on novation, that is, upon a substitution of the transferee in the place of the transferor as the debtor of the corporation for the balance unpaid on the stock.[6]

The date of call, not the date when it becomes payable, fixes the liability as between the transferor and transferee.[7] To escape liability for calls by a transfer of his shares, a stockholder must act in good faith.[8]

Necessity for calls for payment of stock. The time when stock must be paid for is generally determined by the provisions of the contract between the corporation and the purchaser of the stock.[9] Usually the

---

[1]Campbell v. American Alkali Co., (1903) 125 F. 207; Wall v. Basin Mining Co., (1909) 16 Idaho 313, 101 P. 733; Germania Iron Mining Co. v. King, (1896) 94 Wis. 439, 69 N.W. 181.

[2]Seyberth v. American Commander Mining & Milling Co., (1926) 42 Idaho 254, 245 P. 932.

[3]Gaffney & People's Trust Co., (N.Y. App. Div., 1920) 182 N.Y.S. 451, aff'd., (Ct. of App., 1921) 231 N.Y. 577, 132 N.E. 895; Geary St. P.L.O.R. Co. v. Bradbury Estate Co., (1918) 179 Cal. 46, 175 p. 457; Wichita Union Terminal Ry. Co. v. Kansas City, M. & O. R. Co., (1917) 100 Kan. 83, 163 P. 1067.

[4]Webster v. Upton, (1876) 91 U.S. 65, 23 L. Ed. 384; Sigma Iron Co. v. Brown, (1902) 171 N.Y. 488, 64 N.E. 194.

[5]Black v. Zacharie, (1845) 3 How. (U.S.) 483, 11 L. Ed. 690; Priest V. Glenn, (CA-8, 1892) 51 F. 400; McConey V. Benton Oil & Gas Co., (1906) 97 Minn. 190, 106 N.W. 900.

[6]Campbell v. American Alkali Co., (CA-3, 1903) 125 F. 207.

[7]Ibid.

[8]Rochester & K.F. Land Co. v. Raymond, (1809) 158 N.Y. 576, 53 N.E. 507.

[9]Hawkins v. Donnerberg (1901) 40 Ore. 97, 66 P. 691; Wood v. Universal Adding Machine Co., (1911) 166 Ill. App. 346; New Jersey Midland R. Co. v. Stuart, (1872) 35 N.J.L. 322. The contract may also govern who has to pay for the stock subscription. For example, it has been held that a surviving spouse has to pay the unpaid portion of a stock subscription, when the contract called for the stock to be issued in the name of husband and wife as tenants by the entirety; it didn't matter that the survivor didn't expressly agree to pay [Gum & St. Joseph Foods, Inc. (Mo. Ct. of App., 1973) No. 25—995, 5-7-73].

subscription contract, or contract of purchase, fixes the time of payment or indicates that payment shall be made in such installments as shall from time to time be called by the directors. Generally, in the absence of any indication in the agreement as to when payments are due, it is understood that they are due on call.[10] It has been held that if the agreement is silent as to the time of payment the subscription is due and payable at once.[11] However, the statutory provisions governing calls may be deemed part of the contract to be complied with before the corporation can sue for the unpaid amount.[12] A subscriber may agree to pay his subscription at certain times and in certain amounts, subject to statute or charter limitations.[13]

A call for payment must be made before the corporation can bring an action against the subscriber for the amount due.[14] A subscriber may waive the call and pay for his stock in full or in part at any time.[15] Some cases, however, hold that the subscriber may pay in full for his stock before payment is due only if the corporation accepts payment.[16] If the subscription contract requires specific payments the subscriber must pay the installments as they fall due; it is not necessary for the corporation to call for payment.[17] When the subscriber repudiates the subscription no call is necessary to charge him with liability.[18]

Who has authority to make calls. A call must be made by proper authority in compliance with any express provisions contained in the statute, charter, by-laws, or subscription contract.[19] The statute, charter, and by-laws usually confer the power of making calls for unpaid subscriptions upon the board of directors. Sometimes, the power is given to the stockholders. But in the absence of a provision conferring the power on others, the board of directors must make the calls for payment.[20] Calls made without proper authority, therefore invalid, may become valid if

---

[10]San Bernadino County Sav. Bank v. Denman, (1921) 186 Cal. 710, 200 P. 606.

[11]Harris v. Gateway Land Co., (1900) 100 Ala. 652, 29 So. 611.

[12]Vegetable Oil Corp. v. Twohy, (1927) 86 Cal. App. 409, 260 P. 813.

[13]Wark Co. v. Beach Hotel Corp., (1931) 113 Conn. 119, 154 A. 252.

[14]Glenn v. Marbury, (1892) 145 U.S. 499, 12 S. Ct. 914; Coast Amusements v. Stineman, (1931) 115 Cal. App. 746, 2 P.2d 447; Handley Inv. Co. v. Trenholme, (1916) 91 Wash. 146, 157 P. 472.

[15]Marsh v. Burroughs, (1871) 1 Woods (U.S.) 463; Wark Co. v. Beach Hotel Corp., (1931) 113 Conn. 119, 154 A. 252.

[16]San Bernadino County Savings Bank v. Denman, (1921) 186 Cal. 710, 200 P. 606; Welch v. Sargent, (1899) 127 Cal. 72, 59 P. 319; Wark Co. v. Beach Hotel Corp., (1931) 113 Conn. 119, 154 A. 252.

[17]Myrtle Point Mill & Lumber Co. v. Clarke, (1922) 102 Ore. 533, 203 P. 588; Commonwealth Bonding & Cas. Ins. Co. v. Hill,(1916) (Tex. Civ. App.) 184 S.W. 247; Columbus Institute v. Conohan, (1916) 164 Wis. 219, 159 N.W. 720.

[18]Shiffer v. Akenbrook, (1921) 75 Ind. App. 149, 130 N.E. 241. See, however, Cramer v. Burnham, (1928) 107 Conn. 216, 140 A. 477; Rockford Metal Specialty Co. v. Webster, (1926) 234 Ill. App. 260.

[19]Grafton v. Masteller, (1956) 232 F.2d 773; Wood v. Universal Adding Mach. Co., (1911) 166 Ill. App. 346.

[20]See Budd v. Multnomah St. Ry., (1887) 15 Ore. 413, 15 P. 659.

ratified by the corporate authority empowered to make calls. Calls may be made by others succeeding to the powers of a board of directors, such as a receiver for the benefit of creditors.[21]

Calls by directors. Where the directors have authority to make calls, a call must be made by a properly constituted board of directors at a regular meeting or at a special meeting regularly called.[22] If all the directors are personally present and participate in making the call, notice of the meeting is not required.[23] Whoever has authority to make calls has the right to determine whether a call is advisable; the action of directors who have authority to make a call cannot be questioned by the stockholders, if the call has been made in good faith.[24] The directors, of course, have no power to make calls at times and for purposes in violation of the agreement entered into with subscribers.[25]

If all the capital stock must be subscribed for before calls for unpaid subscriptions are made, the directors cannot make a valid call for payment until that condition has been met, or the subscriber has waived the condition, or is estopped from insisting that it be fulfilled.[26]

Amount of call. The body which has authority to make calls can determine the amount for which the call shall be made, subject to the limitations as set forth in the general laws, the charter, the by-laws, or the contract between the corporation and the shareholder. The call must be uniform and in ratable amounts, and any call that requires some shareholders to pay a higher rate than others is unjust and void.[27] However, the corporation has the right to call against the stock of certain stockholders for such an amount of their subscriptions as will produce enough to make their payments equal to the payments already made by other stockholders; no inequality results from such action.[28]

Resolution authorizing call for payment. The resolution authorizing a call for payment of stock should be carefully framed, for it lays the

---

[21]In re Phoenix Hardware Co., (1918) 249 F. 410; Carpenter v. Griffith Mortgage Corp., (1934) 20 Del. Ch. 132, 172 A. 447. State ex rel. Havner v. Associated Packing Co., (1929) 210 Iowa 754, 227 N.W. 627. In the Carpenter case the court denied a request for a general call to equalize the losses among the shareholders.

[22]Cheney v. Canfield, (1910) 158 Cal. 342, 111 P. 92.

[23]Minneapolis Times Co. v. Nimocks, (1893) 53 Minn. 381, 55 N.W. 546.

[24]Nashua Sav. Bank v. Anglo-American Land, Mortgage & Agency Co., (1903) 189 U.S. 221, 23 S.Ct. 517; Visolia & C.R.R. Co. v. Hyde (1895) 110 Cal. 32, 43 P. 10; Wark Co. v. Beach Hotel Corp., (1931) 113 Conn. 119, 154 A. 252: Budd v. Multnomah St. Ry. Co., (1887) 15 Or. 413, 15 P. 659.

[25]Grafton v. Masteller, (1956) 232 F.2d 773. See also Farmers' Lumber Co. v. Luikart, (1927) 36 Wyo. 413, 256 P.84.

[26]Haxtable v. Shumate, (1922) 79 Ind. App. 293, 134 N E. 896.

[27]Geary St., P. & O. R.R. v. Rolph, (1922) 189 Cal. 59, 207 P. 539; Great Western Tel. Co. v. Burnham, (1891) 79 Wis. 47, 47 N.W. 373. See also Germania Iron Mining Co. v. King, (1896) 94 Wis. 439, 69 N.W. 181.

[28]Imperial Land & Stock Co. v. Oster, (1917) 34 Cal. App. 776, 168 P. 1159.

foundation for recovery of payment if the stockholder does not respond to the call. The following information should be included in the resolution:

1. The stockholders to whom the call applies.[29]
2. The amount or percentage of the subscription required to be paid.
3. The time when payment is due.
4. The person to whom payment should be made.
5. The place at which payment is to be made.
6. Directions that notice of the call be given by the proper officer of the corporation.

From a legal standpoint, all of this information may not be necessary.[30] All that is required is that there shall be some act or resolution that evidences or shows a clear official intent to render due and payable a part or all of the unpaid subscription,[31] and that the terms of the call shall be definite.[32] The call need not show for what purpose it is being made,[33] unless that information is specifically required by statute, charter, by-laws, or agreement. The call may be valid, even though the resolution does not name the place at which or the person to whom payment is to be made, if the notice of the call gives this information.[34] A call that did not name the time, place, or person to whom payment was to be made was held to be a valid call, payable on demand, to the treasurer, at the corporation's place of business.[35]

While the courts have at times overlooked irregularities and informalities in resolutions, notices and the making of calls where there has been substantial compliance with the statutory, charter, by-law, or subscription contract requirements and the call has been otherwise adequate,[36] all the requirements of, and formalities incident to, the making of calls should be strictly followed, unless a strict compliance with these requirements and formalities has been waived by the subscriber either expressly, or impliedly by his conduct.[37]

For effect of transfer of stock upon liability for calls and assessments, see page 588 in Chapter 21.

Notice of the call. In some states, notice of the call must be given to subscribers; in others, notice does not seem to be necessary before the corporation can sue for payment.[38] A statute requiring demand for payment

---

[29]The corporation can look only to the list of stockholders on its books to determine who is liable to call. Prudential Petroleum Co. v. Peck, (1933) 132 Cal. App. 4, 22 P.2d 559. See also United States v. Cole, (1950) 90 F. Supp. 147.

[30]San Bernadino County Sav. Bank v. Denman, (1921) 186 Cal. 710, 200 P. 606.

[31]Budd v. Multnomah St. Ry., (1887) 15 Ore. 413, 15 P. 659.

[32]North Milwaukee Town Site Co. No. 2 v. Bishop, (1899) 103 Wis. 492, 79 N.W. 785.

[33]Budd v. Multnomah St. Ry., (1887) 15 Ore. 413, 15 P. 659.

[34]American Pastoral Co. v. Gurney, (1894) 61 F. 41.

[35]Western Improvement Co. v. Des Moines Nat'l Bank, (1897) 103 Iowa 455, 72 N.W. 657.

[36]Macon & A.R. Co. v. Vason, (1876) 57 Ga. 314.

[37]Graebner v. Post, (1903) 119 Wis. 392, 96 N.W. 783.

[38]See Germania Iron Mining Co. v. King, (1896) 94 Wis. 439, 69 N.W. 181.

does not apply to subscriptions contained in the statement of incorporation, unless the subscriptions were payable in installments.[39] When notice is required, any provisions governing the procedure must be followed. If a notice is statutorily required to be as provided in by-laws, a notice pursuant to a resolution is invalid even though no by-law exists.[40] Since some states still have no law on the point it would be well in those states to require or waive notice in the subscription agreement, by-law, or charter. Even if there is a statute, a detailed contractual provision may avoid future misunderstanding on such matters as, for example, frequency and amount of payments.

The notice of the call need not necessarily follow any particular form, unless a special form is required by statute, charter, by-laws, or contract. It should, however, contain all the information required by the statute, charter, by-laws, or agreements, and should also indicate to the recipient that a call has been made and that payment is required. A good plan to follow is to have the notice contain the same information that appears in the resolution authorizing the call. Reasonable notice is sufficient if no prescribed period is fixed by statute, charter, by-law, or contract.[41]

Remedies of corporation on failure to respond to call for payment. The statutes in most states contain some provision indicating the remedies available to the corporation upon failure of a subscriber to respond to a call for payment of his stock. Either under these statutes, or, in their absence, at common law, the corporation generally has some or all of the following remedies:

1. The corporation may bring an action at law against the delinquent subscriber to recover the amount of the unpaid call.
2. The corporation may sell at public auction such part of the shares as will pay the call due, plus expenses.
3. The corporation may sell the shares, apply the proceeds to the payment of the installment called for, plus expenses, and refund the excess to the original owner.
4. If the proceeds of a sale are insufficient to pay the installment due, plus expenses, the corporation may sue the delinquent stockholder for the remainder.
5. The corporation may declare the stock and all previous payments made thereon to be forfeited to the corporation.
6. The corporation may be given the right to purchase the shares through its secretary, its president, or any director, for the amount of the call, plus costs, if such amount cannot be obtained by a sale.

---

[39]Peoria Inv. Corp. v. Hoagland, (1939) 300 Ill. App. 54, 20 N.E. 2d 627, distinguishing Rockford Metal Specialty Co. v. Webster, (1924) 234 Ill. App. 260.
[40]See Note 32.
[41]Fairchild County Turnpike Co. v. Thorp, (1839) 13 Conn. 173.

In some states, the statutes permit the corporation to determine by its by-laws the manner of selling shares or forfeiting them for failure to pay calls. Remedies for nonpayment of calls may also be included in the corporate charter[42] or in the subscription contract.

The statutes generally require that notice be given to the subscribers of the proposed sale or forfeiture of their shares.

Right of corporation to sue for payment of call. A corporation generally has the privilege to sue for the amount called, even though the statute or the charter may give the corporation a special remedy, such as the right to sell or to forfeit the shares.[43] Such a statutory provision is additional and does not deprive the corporation of its common law right to sue to recover unpaid subscriptions.[44] After resorting to the remedy of forfeiture, however, the corporation cannot sue at law,[45] unless the right to do so is given by the statute.[46]

Forfeiture of shares for nonpayment. The right to forfeit or to sell shares for nonpayment is not an inherent power of the corporation; it must have the power delegated to it by statute or by its charter.[47] Without such delegation of power, a majority of the stockholders cannot pass a by-law permitting the corporation to forfeit shares.[48] Stockholders who have not assented to such a by-law will not be bound by it.[49] A subscriber, however, may make a contract providing that default in any payment shall forfeit previous payments, unless there is a statute, a charter, or a by-law provision prohibiting such a contract.[50] If the corporation is expressly empowered to adopt such a by-law, no question concerning its validity can arise so long as the by-law provision is general in its application and affects all delinquent stockholders alike.[51] Also, it would seem that a by-law with forfeiture provisions could be adopted by unanimous vote of the shareholders if not expressly prohibited by statute or charter.[52]

Forfeitures are not favored by the law, and the provisions of the

---

[42]Bessette v. St. Albans Co-operative Creamery, (1935) 107 Vt. 103, 176 A. 307.

[43]Nashua Sav. Bank v. Anglo-American Land, Mortgage & Agency Co., (1903) 189 U.S. 221, 23 S.Ct. 517; Imperial Land & Stock Co. v. Oster, (1917) 34 Cal. App. 776, 168 P. 1159.

[44]Campbell v. American Alkali Co., (Ca-3, 1903) 125 F. 207; State v. Associated Packing Co., (Iowa S.Ct. 1929) 227 N.W. 627; Mills v. Stewart, (1869) 41 N.Y. 384; Ohio Valley Industrial Corp. v. H.L. Seabright Co., (1931) 111 W. Va, 55, 160 S.E. 300.

[45]Buffalo & N.Y. City R.R. v. Dudley, (1856) 14 N.Y. 336.

[46]Mandel v. Swan Land & Cattle Co., (1895) 154 Ill. 177, 40 N.E. 462. See also Donman v. Country Club Realty Co., (1920) 143 Ark. 502, 220 S.W. 824.

[47]Denman v. Country Club Realty Co.,(1920) 143 Ark. 502, 220 S.W. 824.

[48]See Monroe Dairy Ass'n v. Webb, (1899) 40 App. Div. 49, 57 N.Y. Supp. 572. Cf. Hill v.Partridge Cooperative Equity Exchange, (1950) 168 Kan. 506; 214 P. 2d 316.

[49]In re Election of Directors of Long Island Ry., (1837) 19 Wend. (N.Y.) 37.

[50]Buffalo & N.Y. City R.R. v. Dudley, (1856) 14 N.Y. 336.

[51]Budd v. Multnomah St. Ry. C., (1887) 15 Ore. 415, 15 P. 659.

[52]Ibid.

statute, charter, by-laws, or contract governing forfeitures are strictly construed.[53] Those seeking to enforce a forfeiture must strictly observe all requirements that are necessary to enable them to exercise this strong power.[54]

If there are no provisions as to the details to be followed in enforcing a forfeiture of stock, the only requirement is that the method adopted be reasonable and just.[55] The statutes generally indicate the notice that must be given to delinquent subscribers before the corporation can forfeit the shares or apply the remedies permitted by statute. The statutory provision as to notice must be followed with strictness.[56] An irregularity or invalidity may be waived by the stockholder and the corporation to validate a forfeiture.[57]

Any action concerning the forfeiture of stock should be taken by a properly constituted board of directors, at a meeting called as required by statute, charter, or by-laws. The record of the meeting, as well as the notice of forfeiture to be sent to subscribers, should be checked against the requirements of the statute, charter and by-laws to see that the procedure prescribed has been correctly followed.[58]

Of course, if a stockholder is sued by the corporation on his stock subscription contract, he may use the ordinary defenses to a contract suit.[59] Following are some available defenses: fraud;[60] false representations that stock is non-assessable (which will also entitle the subscriber to rescind the contract);[61] agreement to repurchase;[62] failure to make call and give notice as required by corporate resolution.[63]

Following are not good defenses: lack of formal corporate resolution;[64] non-delivery of stock certificate;[65] corporation's failure to

---

[52]Ibid.

[53]Matter of N.Y. & Westchester Town Site Co., (1911) 145 App. Div. 623, 130 N.Y. Supp. 414.

[54]American Well & Prospecting co. v. Blakemore, (1920) 184 Cal. 343, 193 P. 779; Jent v. Friggeri, (1935) 141 Kan. 144, 40 P.2d 343; Jensen v. Northwestern Underwriters Ass'n, (1916) 35 N.D. 223, 159 N.W. 611.

[55]Crissey v. Cook, (1903) 67 Kan. 20, 72 P. 541.

[56]Nashua Sav. Bank v. Anglo-American Land Mortg & Agency Co. (1903) 189 U.S. 221, 23 S.Ct. 517; San Bernadino County Sav. Bank v. Denman, (1921) 186 Cal. 710, 200 p. 606; American Well & Prospecting Co. v. Blakemore, (1920) 184 Cal. 343, 193 p. 779.

[57]American Well & Prospecting Co. v. Blakemore, (1920) 184 Cal. 343, 193 p. 779; Crissey v. Cook, (1903) 67 Kan. 20, 72 p. 541.

[58]It is not essential that the resolution notes that the stock of a particular subscriber is being forfeited, if proper notice is given to the subscriber [Crissey v. Cook, (1903) 67 Kan. 20, 72 p. 541].

[59]Lex v. Selway Steel Corporation, (1925) 203 Ia. 792, 206, N.W. 586.

[60]Columbia-Knickerbocker Trust Co. v. Abbot, (Ca-3, 1918) 247 F. 833, cert. denied, 248 U.S. 558, 39 S.Ct. 6.

[61]Merchants' Realty & Investment Co. v. Kelso, (1920) 46 Cal. App. 218, 189 P 116.

[62]Tidewater So. Ky Co. v. Harney, (1917) 32 Cal. App. 253, 162 p. 664.

[63]In re Dickinson's Estate, (1916) 199 Ill App. 640, aff'd., Wicks Stone Co. v. Dickinson, 276 Ill. 590, 115 N.E. 176.

[64]Hanger v. Intern'l Trading Co., (1919) 184 Ky. 794, 214, S.W. 438.

[65]In re Hannewig, (Ca-3, 1925) 10 F. 2d 941; Axton v. Coca-Cola Co., S.Ct. Kan., 1929) 282 p. 579. However, a corporation must deliver its stock certificate to the one the articles name as a 50 percent stockholder upon payment of the purchase price, when the corporation has not strictly followed the statute on sale of unpaid stock [Scobee v. Continental Hotel Corp, (La. App. 1970) 242 So. 2d 610].

carry out the purposes for which the corporation was organized;[66] stock subscription contract sued on was made before the corporation came into existence;[67] corporate charter was obtained before the minimum capital stock was subscribed or paid for;[68] capital stock of corporation was increased subsequent to the organization of the corporation and the making of the subscription contract sued on.[69]

After forfeiture or sale of shares, the delinquent stockholder is divested of title to the stock. His liability for further payments to the corporation ceases and he is also relieved from liability to creditors for the amount unpaid, even though the debt was contracted with the creditor before the forfeiture.[70] If the stockholder has been discharged intentionally in order to defraud creditors, the forfeiture is of no effect and the stockholder is not relieved from liability.[71]

Meaning of assessments. As indicated on page 556, the words "call" and "assessment" are frequently used interchangeably. Strictly speaking, however, the word "assessment" means a demand upon stockholders for payment above the par value or contract price in the case of no par value shares.

Power to make assessments on fully paid stock. A corporation, in the sale and issuance of its stock, assumes a contractual relation with the shareholder.[72] One of the carefully guarded rights of the stockholder under the contract is that no demand for payment shall be made by the corporation above the par value or price contracted to be paid for the shares of stock.[73] In some states, the statutes specifically provide that stock for which the agreed consideration has been paid shall be nonassessable. In others, the assessment is indirectly prohibited, that is, the corporation is given the power to make assessments upon stock, not exceeding in the whole the balance remaining unpaid under the contract of subscription.[74]

Stockholders who have paid in full for their shares may not be called upon to pay an additional assessment (1) unless the statute or articles of

---

[66]Kennebec Housing Co. v. Barton, (1923) 173 Me. 293, 122 A. 852; Posey v. Citizens' State Bank, (1923) 93 Okla. 266, 220 P. 628; Badger Dairy Co. v. Hansen, (1926) 189 Wis. 547, 208 N.W. 477.

[67]Seacoast Packing Co. v. Long, (1921) 116 S.C. 406, 108, S.E. 159.

[68]Chappell v. Lowe, (1916) 145 Ga. 717, 89 S.E. 777; Drake Hotel Co. v. Crane, (1922) 210 Mo. App. 452, 240 S.W. 859; Jeffrey v. Selwyn, (1917) 220 N.Y. 77, 115 N.E. 275.

[69]Plankers' Warehouse Co. v. Sentelle, (1923) 148 Tenn. 353, 255, S.W. 589.

[70]Mills v. Stewart, (1862) 62 Barb. (N.Y.) 444, aff'd in 41 N.Y. 384; American Well & Prospecting Co. v. Blakemore, (1920) 184 Cal. 343, 193 P. 779.

[71]Ibid.

[72]Peters v. United States Mortgage Co., (1921) 13 Del. Ch. 11, 114 A. 598.

[73]Hill v. Partridge Cooperative Equity Exchange, (1950) 168 Kan. 506, 214 P. 2d 316.

[74]See Moore v. Los Lugos Gold Mines, (1933) 172 Wash. 570, 21 P.2d 253, for a constitutional prohibition of assessment.

incorporation[75] authorize an assessment upon fully paid stock,[76] or (2) unless an express and valid agreement for the assessment is made with the stockholder.[77] In some states a corporation may amend its charter to provide for the power of assessment.[78] In other states this privilege is not granted.[79]

Assessments under statutory or charter provisions. The statutes that permit assessment of fully paid stock vary in the several states. Assessments made under these statutes must conform to the requirement of the law,[80] for the courts strictly construe the provisions of the statute. Thus, the assessment must be made for the purpose described in the statute.[81] If the assessment is for a proper purpose, the directors' motive in levying it is immaterial.[82] If the statute fixes the maximum that may be called for, the assessment should be within the limit prescribed.[83]

The assessment, in order to be valid, must be authorized by those given the power by the statute or the certificate of incorporation to levy assessments and must be made in the manner prescribed. An improperly levied assessment may be declared void by the court.[84]

The directors are generally authorized to make assessments.[85] If the directors are empowered to levy an assessment, they must do so at a legal meeting, properly called.[86] As in the case of calls for unpaid subscriptions, an assessment on fully paid stock must be uniform; an assessment upon certain shareholders and not upon others is invalid.[87]

---

[75]Simons v. Groesbeck, (1934) 268 Mich, 495, 256 N.W. 496; Melville v. Rhodes, (1925) 136 Wash. 220, 239 P. 560; Good v. Starker, (1932) 207 Wis. 567, 242 N.W. 204.

[76]Schueth v. Farmers' Union Milling & Grain Co., (1927) 116 Neb. 14, 215 N.W. 458; Forsyth v. Selma Mines Co., (1921) 58 Utah 142, 197 P. 586; Huxtable v. Berg, (1917) 98 Wash. 616, 168 P. 187.

[77]Milton v. Bergstrom, (1916) 71 Fla. 197, 70 So. 1008; Big Creek Ditch Co. v. Hulick, (1929) 130 Ore 408, 280 P. 492; Child v. Idaho Hewer Mines, (1930) 155 Wash. 280, 284 P. 80. For a review of cases, see 39 YALE L.J. 580.

[78]Wilson v. Cherokee Drift Mining Co., (1939) 14 Cal. 56, 92 P.2d 802.

[79]Harris v. Northern Blue Grass Land Co., (1911) 185 F. 192; State ex rel. Brooks v. Overland Beverage Co.,(1949) 69 Idaho 126, 203 P.2d 1009; Hill v. Partridge Cooperative Equity Exchange, (1950) 168 Kan. 506, 214 P.2d 316.

[80]Schroeter v. Bartlett Syndicate Bldg. Corp., (1936) 8 Cal. 12, 63 P.2d 824; Rancho La Sierra v. Bixby, (1936) 12 Cal. App. 342, 55 P.2d 527.

[81]Koshaba v. Koshaba, (1942) 56 Cal. App. 2d 302, 132 P.2d 854; Kehlor v. Chesley Finance Corp., (1932) 123 Cal. App. 4, 10 P.2d 801.

[82]Clark v. Oceano Beach Resort Co., (1930) 106 Cal. App. 574, 289 P. 946.

[83]Sanderson v. Salmon River Canal Co., (1927) 45 Idaho 244, 263 P. 32.

[84]Koshaba v. Koshaba, (1942) 56 Cal. App. 342, 55 P.2d 527.

[85]See La Plante v. Hopper, (1932) 127 Cal. App. 146, 15 P.2d 525.

[86]Boswell v. Mount Jupiter Mut. Water Co., (1950) 97 Cal. App. 2d 437, 217 P.2d 980. See also Farbstein v. Pacific Oil Tool Co., (1932) 127 Cal. App. 157, 15 P.2d 766, for a valid assessment by de facto directors.

[87]Seyberth v. American Commander Mining & Milling Co., (1926) 42 Idaho 254, 245 P. 932; Omaha Law Library Ass'n v. Connell, (1898) 55 Neb. 396, 75 N.W. 837.

Assessments pursuant to agreements with stockholders. Even in the absence of a statutory or charter provision authorizing assessments upon fully paid stock, the stockholders may agree to pay an assessment on fully paid stock for the benefit of the corporation. If the voluntary assessment is supported by a valid consideration, the corporation can enforce the agreement of the assenting stockholders.[88] When stockholders voluntarily pay an assessment, although the stock is fully paid and nonassessable, they cannot later recover payment from the corporation or its officers.[89]

The consent of a stockholder may be given indirectly. If the shareholder purchases stock with knowledge of a by-law authorizing assessment, or if he participates in the enactment of the by-law, or pays an assessment under the by-law, he will be deemed to have agreed to its provisions.[90] If the stockholder received his stock before the passage of the by-law fixing the assessment, it cannot be said that he consented to the assessment if he did not concur in the passage of the by-law.[91]

Formalities in the levy of an assessment. The directors or stockholders, whichever body is authorized to levy the assessment, should do so by resolution properly proposed, seconded, and voted upon. A complete record should be kept of the action taken. If the certificate of incorporation authorizes the levy of an assessment only upon the vote of a certain percentage of the stockholders, the record should show that the required number of stockholders voted in favor of the assessment. An assessment has been held unenforceable because a full and proper record of the transaction was not made.[92] Oral evidence to supplement the record was not allowed. Notice of the assessment should be given to stockholders in strict conformity with the requirements of the statute or the charter.[93] In some states, publication of notice is required in addition to service upon the individual stockholders. In others, power to assess must be stated on the face of the stock certificate.

Enforcement of assessments on fully paid stock. The principles concerning the enforcement of assessments on fully paid stock are similar to those applying to enforcement of calls on unpaid subscriptions.[94] Stockholders become liable for the payment of valid assessments and the corpo-

---

[88]Good v. Derr, (1931) 46 F. 2d 411; Milton v. Bergstrom, (1916) 71 Fla. 197, 70 So. 1008.

[89]Speckert v. Bunker Hill Arizona Mining Co., (1940) 6 Wash. 2d 39, 106 P.2d 602.

[90]Jonas v. Frost, (1919) 32 Idaho 214, 179 P. 949; Big Creek Ditch Co. v. Hulick, (1929) 130 Ore. 408, 280 P. 492; Gowans v. Rockport Irrigation Co., (1930) 77 Utah 198, 293 P. 4.

[91]Sullivan County Club v. Butler, (1899) 26 N.Y. Misc. 306, 56 N.Y. Supp. 1.

[92]Corcoran v. Sonora Mining & Milling Co., (1902) 8 Idaho 651, 71 P. 127.

[93]Brown v. St. Paul Consolidated Oil Co.,(1929) 101 Cal. App. 263, 281 P. 646; Stivers v. Sidney Mining Co., (1949) 69 Idaho 403, 208 P.2d 795.

[94]See page 560.

ration may bring an action against them to enforce the liability. The corporation has no right to forfeit or to sell the shares of stockholders who have failed to pay a valid assessment, unless the statute or charter expressly so provides.[95] Where forfeiture and sales are permitted by statute or by charter, the provisions as to notice of the forfeiture or sale and the requirements as to the manner of conducting the sale must be pursued in exact conformance to the law.[96]

Power of corporation to assess stock marked "nonassessable." Many corporations issue stock that bears upon its face the words "full-paid and nonassessable." Such a provision becomes a part of the contract between the corporation and the stockholder, and, as between these two parties, the agreement may be relied upon and enforced.[97] But where the necessity arises to collect the assets of the corporation for the purpose of discharging its liabilities, the stockholders are obliged to pay whatever remains unpaid on their stock, despite the fact that the stock is marked "nonassessable."[98]

In some states the statute gives the corporation the power to levy an assessment against capital stock fully paid up, for the purpose of paying expenses, conducting the business, or paying debts. The fact that the certificates bear upon their face the words "full-paid and nonassessable" may render the shares represented by the certificates nonassessable even under such a statute.[99] An agreement between the stockholder and the corporation that the stock shall be nonassessable may be evidenced by the certificate of incorporation describing the stock to be issued, or by a provision in the by-laws, in the certificates of stock, in the subscription contract, or in the contract of sale. However, where a statute prohibits a distinction or preference between shares, unless such preference or distinction is stated in the articles of incorporation, a contract between a corporation and one of its stockholders that the shares held by such stockholder shall be nonassessable is void if the same freedom from liability to assessment is not accorded to all the stockholders.[100]

---

[95]Williams v. Lowe, (1876) 4 Neb. 382.
[96]Clark v. Oceano Beach Resort Co., (1930) 106 Cal. App. 574, 289 P. 946; Newhall v. Hunsaker, (1918) 38 Cal. App. 399, 176 P. 380; See also Castello v. Central Eureka Mining Co., (1948) 85 Cal. App. 2d 772, 193 P.2d 968.
[97]A.C. Frost & Co. v. Coeur D'Alene Mines Corp., (1939) 60 Idaho 491, 92 P. 2d 1057; Whicher v. Delaware Mines Corp., (1932) 52 Idaho 304, 15 P.2d 610.
[98]Norton v. Lamb, (1936) 144 Kan. 665, 62 P.2d 1311; Strong v. Frerichs, (1938) (Mo. App.) 116 S.W. 2d 533.
[99]Whicher v. Delaware Mines Corp., (1932) 52 Idaho 304, 15 P.2d 610.
[100]Martin v. Palmer Union Oil Co., (1920) 184 Cal. 386, 193 P. 950.

Chapter 20

FORMS RELATING TO CALLS FOR PAYMENT OF STOCK AND ASSESSMENTS

Contents—Chapter 20

Forms Relating to Assessments

FORMS RELATING TO CALLS FOR PAYMENT

RESOLUTION OF DIRECTORS FIXING TIME OF PAYMENT OF SUBSCRIPTIONS ALREADY OBTAINED

WHEREAS, various subscriptions to the common stock of this corporation do not fix the time for payment thereof but provide that payments shall be made thereon at such time or times and in such manner as called for by the Board of Directors, be it

RESOLVED, That all subscriptions to the common stock of this corporation, heretofore obtained, for which the time for payment has not been fixed, shall be payable in money in the following installments and at the following times—to wit:

..... (.....%) per cent, or ..... ($.....) Dollars per share on ....
.., 19..

..... (.....%) per cent, or ..... ($.....) Dollars per share on ....
.., 19.., and

RESOLVED FURTHER, That the Secretary is hereby directed to send notice of this resolution to each subscriber whose subscription does not indicate the time of payment.

RESOLUTION OF DIRECTORS FIXING TERMS OF PAYMENT OF SUBSCRIPTIONS TO BE OBTAINED IN THE FUTURE

RESOLVED, That all future subscriptions to the authorized capital stock of this corporation at present unissued shall be payable in money as follows: twenty (20%) per cent at the time of signing the subscription, twenty (20%) per cent in one month, twenty (20%) per cent in two months, twenty (20%) per cent in three months, and twenty (20%) per cent in four months from the date of the subscription.

RESOLUTION OF DIRECTORS CALLING FOR FULL PAYMENT OF STOCK SUBSCRIBED BY INCORPORATORS

RESOLVED, That an assessment of one hundred (100%) per cent be levied upon the shares of stock subscribed by the incorporators, and unpaid, as evidenced by the certificate of incorporation.

RESOLUTION OF DIRECTORS AUTHORIZING CALL FOR ENTIRE AMOUNT REMAINING UNPAID ON SUBSCRIPTIONS

RESOLVED, That a call be made upon all unpaid subscriptions to the stock of this company for the entire amount remaining unpaid thereon, and that the same is

hereby ordered to be paid to the Treasurer of the company, on or before ....,
19.., at the .... *City*), office of the company.

RESOLVED FURTHER, That the Secretary is hereby directed to mail a written
notice at least ..... days before the time for such payment to each stockholder
subject to this call.

RESOLUTION OF STOCKHOLDERS AUTHORIZING CALL FOR ENTIRE AMOUNT OF UNPAID SUBSCRIPTIONS, IN ANTICIPATION OF JUDGMENT RENDERED AGAINST CORPORATION

WHEREAS, a judgment for ..... ($.....) Dollars was obtained by the
.... Company against this Corporation in the .... Court on
...., 19.., and

WHEREAS, an appeal from said judgment has been taken by this Corporation to
the .... Court, and

WHEREAS, the outcome of said appeal is uncertain, and it is possible that the
judgment rendered against this Corporation may be affirmed, and the Corporation
may be required to pay an amount aggregating between ..... ($.....) Dollars and
..... ($.....) Dollars, and

WHEREAS, to avoid additional expense it is deemed best to be prepared to meet
such contingency, be it

RESOLVED, That a call be levied upon all unpaid subscriptions to the stock of
this Corporation for the entire amount remaining unpaid thereon, and that the same
is hereby ordered to be paid into the Corporation's treasury on or before ....
.., 19.., and

RESOLVED FURTHER, That the Secretary of this Corporation is hereby authorized
and directed forthwith to notify every subscriber to the stock of this Corporation,
whose stock has not been fully paid for, of the aforesaid call, by sending notice
thereof to such subscribers personally or by registered mail.

RESOLUTION OF DIRECTORS MAKING CALL FOR PAYMENT OF SUBSCRIPTIONS IN QUARTERLY INSTALLMENTS

RESOLVED, That, for the purpose of providing funds for the building of
additional plants, and for working capital, a call of ..... ($.....) Dollars upon each
share of the preferred stock of the company, not credited as fully paid, is hereby
made, said call to be payable at the office of the company in four installments as
follows: First installment, ... ($.....) Dollars per share, payable on ....,
19..; second installment, ... ($.....) Dollars per share, payable on ....,
19..; third installment, ... ($.....) Dollars per share, payable on ...., 19..;
and fourth installment, ... ($.....) Dollars per share, payable on ...., 19..,
and

RESOLVED FURTHER, That the Secretary is hereby directed to give notice of this call immediately to the registered holders of the preferred stock subject to the call.

RESOLUTION OF DIRECTORS PRELIMINARY TO FORFEITURE OF SHARES FOR FAILURE TO PAY CALL

RESOLVED, That the Secretary is hereby directed to send a notice to Mr. ...., in accordance with *(insert statutory, charter, or by-law requirement, designating the statute or article number of the certificate or by-laws)* requiring him to pay the call due on his shares with interest, and stating that, unless such call and interest are paid on or before ...., 19.., his shares will be forfeited without further notice.

RESOLUTION OF DIRECTORS CALLING FOR UNPAID SUBSCRIPTION AND AUTHORIZING FORFEITURE OF PREVIOUS PAYMENTS UPON FAILURE TO MEET THE CALL

WHEREAS, ... of the City of ...., State of ...., did subscribe for ..... (.....) shares, of the par value of ..... ($.....) Dollars each, of the capital stock of .... Company, the amount of his subscription being ..... ($.....) Dollars, and

WHEREAS, the said .... has heretofore paid on account of his said subscription the sum of ..... ($.....) Dollars, but declines and neglects to pay the balance thereof—to wit: the sum of ..... ($.....) Dollars although the same is past due and payable, be it

RESOLVED, That .... is hereby required to pay said unpaid balance on his subscription on or before ...., 19.., and that in the event that he shall decline or neglect to pay said balance on or before said date, said ..... (.....) shares of stock, subscribed for by him, and his payment of ..... ($.....) Dollars thereon, be forfeited to the use of the .... Company; and that a notice in writing be served upon him by depositing the same in the post office in the City of ...., State of ...., properly directed to him at .... *(Street)*, ... *(City)*, ... *(State)*, stating that he is required to make payment of said balance on or before ...., 19.., at the office of the .... Company, ... *(Street)*, in the city of ...., State of ...., and that if he fails to make the same, ... (.....) shares of stock and the said payment of ..... ($.....) Dollars thereon will be forfeited for the use of the .... Company.

RESOLUTION OF DIRECTORS AUTHORIZING FORFEITURE FOR NONPAYMENT OF CALLS, PUBLIC SALE OF SHARES FORFEITED, AND COLLECTION OF DEFICIENCY

WHEREAS, sundry persons in whose names the stock of this corporation stands are delinquent in the payment of calls ordered thereon, and

WHEREAS, at the meeting of stockholders held on ...., 19.., the following resolution was adopted, viz.:

RESOLVED, That the directors are hereby requested to take prompt and efficient measures for the collection of unpaid calls upon the capital stock of this corporation, and, so far as they think expedient, to sell all such shares as are not paid on or before ...., 19..,

BE IT, RESOLVED, That all stock on which calls shall remain unpaid on ...., 19.., shall be forfeited to the use of this corporation, and

RESOLVED FURTHER, That the Treasurer is hereby directed to issue a circular to be mailed to each delinquent stockholder, giving immediate notice of the above vote, and that all stock forfeited to the corporation by virtue of the foregoing resolution be brought to a public sale under the direction of the Treasurer, and sold at such times and places as he shall think expedient, and the Treasurer is hereby directed to enforce the collection of any deficiency that may remain unpaid on assessments after such sale by a suit at law.

RESOLVED FURTHER, That the minimum price of the stock be fixed at ..... ($.....) Dollars per share and that, if no offer is made at that price or more, the stock shall be bought in for the corporation.

RESOLUTION OF DIRECTORS AUTHORIZING SALE AT AUCTION OF SHARES FORFEITED FOR FAILURE TO PAY CALL AND PUBLICATION OF NOTICE OF SALE

WHEREAS, the persons named in the following list, holding the number of shares set against their names respectively, have neglected or refused to pay the calls due thereon, and

WHEREAS, proper notice was given on ...., 19.., to each stockholder named in the following list requiring him to pay the call due on his shares and stating that, unless such call were paid on or before ...., 19.., his shares would be forfeited, be it

RESOLVED, That the Treasurer is hereby authorized and directed to sell all such shares at auction, to the highest bidder, at the office of ...., in the City of ...., on ...., 19.., at ..... o'clock, .. P.M., for the nonpayment of the call due thereon, and

RESOLVED FURTHER, That the Treasurer is hereby directed to publish notice of the time and place of such sale and of the sum due on each delinquent stockholder's shares, for three weeks successively, once in each week before the sale, in the *(name of newspaper)*, and to mail a copy of such notice ot each delinquent stockholder at his last-known post-office address, at least ..... (.....) days before such sale.

(Insert the list of delinquent stockholders and number of shares held by each.)

RESOLUTION OF DIRECTORS AUTHORIZING PRESIDENT TO SETTLE UNPAID SUBSCRIPTION WITH SUBSCRIBER

WHEREAS, on ...., 19.., ... subscribed to ..... (.....) shares of common stock of this corporation and agreed to pay therefor ..... ($.....) Dollars upon the following terms: ..... ($.....) Dollars on ...., 19.., and ..... ($.....) Dollars on ...., 19.., and

WHEREAS, ..., on ...., 19.., made a payment of ..... ($.....) Dollars in accordance with the subscription agreement, and defaulted in the payment due on ...., 19.., and

WHEREAS, it is the opinion of this Board of Directors that .... is financially unable to make the payment of ..... ($.....) Dollars, and it would be to the disadvantage of this corporation to forfeit the stock of said .... because of his close relationship with certain valuable customers of this corporation, be it

RESOLVED, That the President is hereby authorized to negotiate with .... for settlement of the claim of this corporation for the unpaid balance of ..... ($.....) Dollars due on the subscription of said ...., upon the best possible terms, and to accept any sum offered by him, provided it be not less than ..... ($.....) Dollars, in full payment of his subscription to the aforesaid shares.

RESOLUTION OF DIRECTORS AUTHORIZING APPLICATION OF DEBT OF CORPORATION TO UNPAID SUBSCRIPTION OF CREDITOR

WHEREAS, this Company is indebted to the .... Company in the sum of ..... ($.....) Dollars for money expended, material furnished, and labor performed in the construction and operation of this Company's line of railroad, as shown by an itemized statement of account rendered on ...., 19.., by the .... Company to this Company and now on file with the Secretary of this Company, and

WHEREAS, the said .... Company is a subscriber to ..... (.....) shares of the common stock of this Company which stand on the books of this Company in hte name of ...., trustee, and

WHEREAS, the books of this Company and the Treasurer's account show that only ..... ($.....) Dollars in cash have been paid to the Treasurer of this Company upon said stock subscription, and that there is owing upon said subscription ..... ($.....) Dollars, and

WHEREAS, the .... Company has consented to permit the sum of ..... ($.....) Dollars of their claim to be applied in payment of the balance due on said stock so that said stock shall stand in the name of the owner fully paid and nonassessable, be it

RESOLVED, That ..... ($.....) Dollars of the amount owed by this Company to the .... Company be applied to the payment of the balance due upon the ..... (.....) shares of common stock subscribed for by the .... Company, and the stock is hereby declared to be fully paid and nonassessable, and this Company hereby acknowledges having received full value for the full amount of the par value of said stock.

WAIVER BY STOCKHOLDERS OF NOTICE OF CALLS

We, the undersigned, being all the subscribers to the Capital Stock with which this Corporation begins business, do hereby waive ..... days' notice of the time and place of the payment of our subscription to such stock, and we do also waive all the requirements of the laws of the State of .... as to notice of call and payment, and we agree to pay any part or all of the same to the Treasurer of the Corporation on demand, and at such time and in such amounts as the Corporation, by its Board of Directors, may direct.

Dated ...., 19..

....
....
....

NOTICE OF CALL

...., 19..

To ....

You are hereby notified that a call of ..... ($.....) Dollars per share on all the shares of the Common Stock of the .... Corporation, payable on ...., 19.., was made by a resolution of the Board of Directors of the said Corporation, duly passed on ...., 19...

The amount due upon your subscription dated ...., 19.., is ..... ($.....) Dollars, which you will please pay to the Company's Treasurer, at No. ...., City of ...., State of ...., on or before ...., 19...

When sending your check please forward this notice together with the form of receipt attached hereto.

By order of the Board of Directors.

....
Secretary

RECEIPT FOR PAYMENT OF CALL
of $..... per Share of
Common Stock due
...., 19...
.... CORPORATION

RECEIVED, from ...., the sum of ..... ($.....) Dollars, being the amount due on ..... (.....) shares of common stock in the above Corporation.

....
Treasurer

NOTICE TO SHAREHOLDERS OF POSTPONEMENT OF DUE DATE OF INSTALLMENTS ON SUBSCRIPTIONS

.... COMPANY
.... STREET
.... CITY, ... STATE
...., 19...

To Our Shareholders:

On account of the extraordinary financial condition existing at the present time, and for the convenience of prospective subscribers to the stock of .... Company, the Board of Directors, at a meeting held today, decided to defer the date when payment of the second, third, and fourth installments will become due, to ...., ..., and ...., respectively.

The first payment, however, will be payable on ...., in accordance with the original announcement.

Very truly yours,

....
President

NOTICE OF SALE OR FORFEITURE OF STOCK UPON FAILURE TO PAY INSTALLMENTS AS PROVIDED IN SUBSCRIPTION CONTRACT

To ....
....
(Address)

You are hereby notified that you have been in default for more than ..... (.....) days in the payment of the installment of ..... ($.....) Dollars, due under contract of ...., 19.., in which you subscribed to ..... (.....) shares of the capital stock of the .... Corporation.

Pursuant to the provisions of the law of the State of ...., a public sale of the said ..... (.....) shares of stock will be held on ...., 19.., at ....A.M., at the principal office of the said Corporation at .... *(Street)*, ... *(City)*, ... *(State)*. Said shares will be sold to the highest bidder for cash, but no bids will be accepted for an amount less than the balance due on said shares under the terms of the said subscription contract, plus the costs and expenses of sale. If insufficient or no bid is made, your entire interest in the said shares, including amounts paid on account thereof, will be forfeited to the said Corporation as liquidated damages.

...., 19..

.... Corporation

By ....

Secretary

NOTICE OF FORFEITURE OF PAYMENTS MADE UPON STOCK SUBSCRIPTION FOR NONPAYMENT OF CALL (WHERE SALE IS NOT REQUIRED)

...., 19...

To ....

....
(Address)

You are hereby notified that the Board of Directors of the ....
Corporation, at a meeting held on ...., 19.., duly passed a resolution forfeiting your rights to the subscription for ..... (.....) shares of the common stock of this Corporation, and, under the terms of such subscription, all payments heretofore made, because of your failure to pay the call of ..... ($.....) Dollars per share due thereon on ...., 19...

....
Secretary

NOTICE OF FORFEITURE OF STOCK FOR NONPAYMENT OF CALL

...., 19...

To ....

....
(Address)

You are hereby notified that the Board of Directors of the ....
Corporation, at a meeting held on ...., 19.., duly passed a resolution forfeiting the ..... (.....) shares of common stock having a par value of ..... ($.....) Dollars each, represented by Certificate No. ....., of which you are the record owner, because of your failure to pay the call of ..... ($.....) Dollars per share due thereon on ...., 19...

By order of the Board of Directors, said ..... (.....) shares of common stock will be sold at public auction to the highest bidder at the office of the Corporation, ... *(Street)*, City of ...., State of ...., or as many shares as will pay ..... ($.....) Dollars, which is the aggregate amount due on said shares, and also the costs of advertising and expenses of sale.

....
Secretary

PUBLIC NOTICE OF SALE OF STOCK FOR NONPAYMENT OF CALL

Public notice is hereby given that ..... (.....) shares of the capital stock of .... Corporation will be sold at public auction by the Directors of said Corporation at the office of said Corporation, ... *(Street)*, City of ...., State of ...., on ...., 19.., at ..... A.M.

Said sale will be made pursuant to the statutes of the State of ....., and the By-laws of said Corporation, in such case made and provided, because of the nonpayment by ...., subscriber for said stock, of a call for the payment of an installment on the same for ..... (.....) days after said installment was due and payable, due notice thereof having been given.

.... Corporation

By ....

Secretary

Dated at ...., ..., 19...

FORMS RELATING TO ASSESSMENTS

RESOLUTION OF DIRECTORS AUTHORIZING ASSESSMENT UPON FULLY PAID STOCK, UNDER STATUTE

WHEREAS, this corporation has become indebted to various persons, firms, and corporation, to the amount of approximately ..... ($.....) Dollars, as shown by the balance sheet of the corporation on ...., 19.., and

WHEREAS, current assets, as shown by the balance sheet on the date mentioned, are insufficient to meet the outstanding indebtedness of the corporation, and an increase in operating revenues sufficient to provide funds for paying said debts out of current earnings is not expected during the next six months, and

WHEREAS, this corporation has the power, under the laws of the State of ...., to levy and collect an assessment upon the fully paid capital stock for the purpose of paying debts, if more than one-fourth of the capital stock of this corporation has been subscribed, aand

WHEREAS, all of the authorized capital stock of this corporation is issued and outstanding and has been fully paid, be it

RESOLVED, That for the purpose of paying said indebtedness, an assessment of ..... ($.....) Dollars per share upon all of the fully paid capital stock of this corporation, issued and outstanding, is hereby levied, and that said assessment shall be payable to ...., Treasurer of this corporation, at the office of the corporation, ... *(Street)*, City of ...., State of ...., on or before ...., 19.., and

RESOLVED FURTHER, That if said assessment remains unpaid upon any stock on ...., 19.., such stock shall be declared delinquent and shall be advertised for sale at public auction, and, unless payment is made before ...., 19.., shall be sold on ...., 19.., at ..... A.M., to pay said delinquent assessment, together with the costs of advertising and expenses of sale, and

RESOLVED FURTHER, That the Secretary is hereby authorized and directed to give notice of this assessment, as well as notice of delinquency and notice of the sale of delinquent stock, as required by the provisions of the statutes of the State of ......

RESOLUTION OF STOCKHOLDERS LEVYING ASSESSMENT ON FULLY PAID SHARES TO COVER DEFICIENCY

RESOLVED, That, in order to pay the existing deficiency caused by the insufficiency of receipts to meet disbursements on account of the property and business of the .... Corporation, an assessment of ..... ($.....) Dollars is hereby levied upon each of the shares of the stock of the Corporation, making the total sum of ..... ($.....) Dollars, said assessment to be payable to the Treasurer within ..... (.....) days after notice thereof to each stockholder, with the results in case of nonpayment specified in Article ..... of the By-laws of the Corporation.

RESOLUTION OF DIRECTORS AUTHORIZING POSTPONEMENT OF SALE OF STOCK UPON WHICH ASSESSMENT IS UNPAID

WHEREAS, an assessment of ..... ($.....) Dollars per share upon the fully paid capital stock, issued and outstanding, of this Corporation was levied by resolution of the Board of Directors, passed at a meeting held on ...., 19.., and

WHEREAS, notice of said assessment was mailed to each stockholder, addressed to his last-known place of residence, and was published in the *(insert name and place of publication)* as required by law, and

WHEREAS, certain stockholders are still delinquent in the payment of the assessment, and

WHEREAS, ..., 19.., was fixed by the Board of Directors as the date for the sale of all stock delinquent in the payment of said assessment, and

WHEREAS, it is the desire of this Board of Directors to postpone the date of the sale of said delinquent stock in order to extend the time for payment on delinquent stock, be it

RESOLVED, That the date of the sale of stock upon which assessments are unpaid be, and the same hereby is, postponed from ...., 19.., to ...., 19.., at ..... P.M., and

RESOLVED FURTHER, That the Secretary is hereby authorized and directed to prepare and publish notice of the postponement of the sale of delinquent stock, as required by the provisions of the statutes of the State of ....

RESOLUTION OF DIRECTORS WAIVING STATUTORY PROCEEDINGS FOR COLLECTION OF DELINQUENT ASSESSMENTS, AND ELECTING TO PROCEED BY ACTION

WHEREAS, an assessment of ..... ($.....) Dollars per share upon the fully paid capital stock, issued and outstanding, of this Corporation was levied by resolution of the Board of Directors, passed at a meeting held on ...., 19.., and

WHEREAS, the following stockholders have defaulted in the payment of said assessment, and the stock held by them became delinquent on ...., 19.., in the amounts set opposite their respective names:

Name	Amount
....	....
....	....
....	....
....	....

and

WHEREAS, under the laws of the State of ...., this Corporation has the power at any time prior to the date set for the sale of delinquent stock to waive further proceedings under *(insert the section of the statute providing for sale of delinquent stock)* for the collection of delinquent assessments and may elect to proceed by action to recover the amount of the assessment, and the cost and expenses already incurred, be it

RESOLVED, That this Board of Directors hereby elects to waive further proceedings under the section of the statute aforementioned, for the collection of delinquent assessments, and does hereby elect to proceed to recover by action the amount of all such delinquent assessments, and the costs and expenses already incurred, and

RESOLVED FURTHER, That the President is hereby directed to take all steps necessary to enforce such delinquent assessments by action.

RESOLUTION OF DIRECTORS REDUCING ASSESSMENT ON FULLY PAID SHARES

RESOLVED, That this Board hereby waives the collection of one half of the assessment of ..... (.....%) per cent upon the capital stock of the Corporation, duly levied on ...., 19.., and hereby reduces the amount of said assessment to ..... (.....%) per cent of said capital stock—to wit: ..... ($.....) Dollars per share, and the Treasurer, the Secretary, and the President are hereby authorized and directed to collect and receipt for said ..... ($.....) Dollars per share of assessment in full satisfaction thereof.

NOTICE OF LEVY OF ASSESSMENT UPON FULLY PAID STOCK AND SALE UPON FAILURE TO PAY

.... CORPORATION
.... STREET
.... CITY, ... STATE

...., 19...

NOTICE is hereby given that, at a meeting of the board of directors held on ...., 19.., an assessment of ..... ($.....) Dollars per share was levied upon the shares of the corporation, payable to ...., at .... *(Street)*, ... *(City)*, ... *(State)*. Any shares upon which this assessment remains unpaid on ...., 19.., will be delinquent, and unless payment is made in the meantime, the shares, or so many of said shares as may be necessary, will be sold at .... *(Street)*, ... *(City)*, ... *(State)*, on ...., 19.., at ..... A.M., to pay the delinquent assessment, together with the costs of advertising and expenses of sale.

....
Secretary
....
(Address)

NOTICE OF SALE OF STOCK FOR NONPAYMENT OF ASSESSMENT

.... CORPORATION
.... STREET
.... CITY, ... STATE

...., 19...

There is delinquent upon the following-described stock, on account of the assessment levied on ...., 19.. (and assessments levied previous thereto, if any), the several amounts set opposite the names of the respective shareholders of the .... Corporation, as follows:

Name	Number of Certificate	Number of Shares	Amount
....	....	....	....
....	....	....	....
....	....	....	....
....	....	....	....
....	....		

And, in accordance with law and an order of the Board of Directors, made on
...., 19.., so many shares of each parcel of such stock as may be necessary
will be sold at .... *(Street)*, ... *(City)*, ... *(State)*, on ....
.., 19..; at ..... A.M., to pay delinquent assessments thereon, together with costs
of advertising and expenses of the sale.

....
Secretary

NOTICE OF POSTPONEMENT OF SALE OF STOCK FOR NONPAYMENT OF ASSESSMENTS

.... CORPORATION
.... STREET
.... CITY, ... STATE

...., 19...

By order of the Board of Directors, the date of the sale of stock for delinquent
assessment has been postponed from ...., 19.., to ...., 19.., ...
P.M.

....
Secretary

AFFIDAVIT OF SECRETARY UPON SALE OF STOCK FOR FAILURE TO PAY ASSESSMENT

State of ....
County of ....⎰ ss.:

..............., being duly sworn, deposes and says that he is the Secretary of
.... Corporation, a corporation organized and existing under the laws of
the State of ...., and having its principal office at .... *(Street)*,
.... *(City)*, ... *(State)*.

That, on ...., 19.., a notice of sale of delinquent stock, a copy of
which is annexed hereto and made a part of this affidavit, was duly served upon the
stockholders hereinbelow named, by mailing to each of them at his last-known
post-office address, a true copy thereof, and that, as appears from the affidavit of
..............., annexed hereto, said notice was duly published as required by law.

That, pursuant to said notice of sale, and at the time and place designated
therein, your deponent caused to be sold through ...., a licensed auction-
eer, the following shares of stock of said Corporation, represented by the certificates hereinafter set forth:

Certificate No.	No. of Shares	Standing in the Name of
....	....	....
....	....	....
....	....	

Chapter 21

TRANSFER OF STOCK

Contents—Chapter 21

Right of stockholder to transfer his stock. A stockholder has the right to transfer his shares of stock without interference by the corporation.[1] This right is based upon the inherent power of a person to dispose of his property.[2] It is a continuing right, existing from the time the subscription to the stock is made until the corporation is dissolved. A stockholder can sell his stock to another stockholder or to a stranger; he does not need to know the character or responsibility of the buyer.[3] In general this is also true even if the stockholder is a majority holder. As far as selling that stock is concerned, majority holders, whether one or a group, have no fiduciary relation to other stockholders, merely by virtue of ownership of stock.[4] Nevertheless, the right to alienate a majority of stock is subject to some restriction. For example, in selling his stock a majority stockholder cannot legally dominate, interfere with, or mislead other stockholders.[5] Nor can majority stockholders legally sell their holdings to persons who intend to loot the treasury or mismanage the corporation to its injury.[6] If the majority holders actually control and manage the corporation they cannot use their power to damage the corporation or injure minority interests.[7]

A stockholder who is a director has the same right as other stockholders to transfer his stock, provided, of course, that the transfer is not fraudulent or in breach of any trust. The fiduciary responsibility of directors to all of the stockholders will prevent their selling a controlling interest in the corporation, to the injury of the corporation, either knowingly or with negligent failure to investigate as to the possibility of such injury.[8]

Here are some examples of majority stockholder's fiduciary duty:
A bank that was majority stockholder of a corporation was liable for

---

[1]Farmers' Loan & Trust Co. v. Chicago, P. & S. R. R.R., (1896) 163 U.S. 31, 16 S. Ct. 917; Bd. of Comm'rs v. Reynolds, (1873) 44 Ind. 509. See also Sterling Midland Co. v. Chicago-Williamsville C. Co., (1929) 336 Ill. 586, 168 N.E. 655; Trisconi v. Winship, (1891) 43 La. Ann. 45, 9 So. 29.

[2]Howe v. Roberts, (1923) 209 Ala. 80, 95 So. 344; Hague v. DeLong, (1937) 282 Mich. 330, 276 N.W. 467; Gerdes v. Reynolds, (1941) 28 N.Y.S.2d 622.

[3]Curtis v. Beckett, (1943) 114 Ind. App. 221, 50 N.E.2d 920; Levy v. American Beverage Corp., (1942) 265 App. Div. 208, 38 N.Y.S. 2d 517; Gerdes v. Reynolds, see Note 2.

[4]Levy v. American Beverage Corp., see Note 3; Gerdes v. Reynolds, see Note 2; Stickells, "Stockholders' Duty in Sale of Stock," 31 B.U.L. Rev. 191.

[5]Roby v. Dunnett, (1937) 88 F.2d 68, cert. denied, 301 U.S. 706; 13 FLETCHER, CORPORATIONS §5805.

[6]Gerdes v. Reynolds, see Note 2; Insuranshares Corp. v. Northern Fiscal Corp.; (1940) 35 F. Supp. 22, noted in 25 MINN. L. REV. 525.

[7]Lebold v. Inland Steel Co., (1941) 125 F.2d 369, cert. denied, 316 U.S. 675, 62 S. Ct. 1045; Kavanaugh v. Kavanaugh Knitting Co., (1919) 226 N.Y. 185, 123 N.E. 148; Levy v. American Beverage Corp., (1942) 265 App. Div. 208, 38 N.Y.S. 2d 517.

[8]Perlman v. Feldman, (1955) 219 F.2d 173 (Ind. law); Soderstrom v. Kungsholm Baking Co., (1951) 189 F.2d 1008; Benson v. Braun, (1956) N.Y.S.2d 622. See also Southern Pacific Co.v. Bogert, (1919) 250 U.S. 483; 39 S. Ct. 533. Contra: Insurance Agency Co. v. Blossom; (1921) (Mo. App.) 231 S.W. 636 (harm to corporation no barrier to transfer of majority interest made in good faith).

breach of duty to minority stockholders when it secretly sold its stock to a purchaser who wasted the corporate assets. The bank could have reasonably anticipated the purchaser's acts and so it breached the duty of care it owed to the corporation and to the minority.[9]

The president and chairman of the board of directors who owned 74 percent of a corporation's shares jointly with his wife, breached his fiduciary duty to the corporation and its shareholders when he planned to financially destroy the corporation by lending it money from a joint account he had with his wife and then demanding immediate payment, since his motive was to deprive his wife of the use of such account and remove her from directorship. This was not done to promote the interest of the corporation and the shareholders.[10]

A corporation that was a majority stockholder could not use attorney-client privilege as a defense to a motion to compel production of documents in a securities law action by minority stockholders on the ground that documents resulted from studies made by its counsel; the majority stockholders owed a fiduciary duty to minority and privilege could not be used to block the required disclosure.[11]

Utilization of corporate profits to cover costs of unreasonable salary and living expenses of majority stockholder was breach of the fiduciary obligation owed by such shareholder to the corporation. The burden of proving unreasonableness lies with the minority stockholder.[12]

On the other hand, here are some examples contra:

A majority stockholder-director was not liable to a corporation's minority stockholders for breach of fiduciary duty when he sold his stock to a buyer who then looted the corporation, since at the time of sale no facts existed that would have put a prudent man on notice that the buyer's intentions were anything but honorable. Even the seller's continued position as director and his continued financial stake in the corporation did not charge him with knowledge of what the buyer was doing.[13]

A majority shareholder who was paid a premium for his stock because of the control that went with it had no duty to the corporation or minority shareholders to account for such additional profit.[14]

A parent corporation as majority stockholder did not breach its fiduciary duty to a subsidiary's minority stockholders, even though tax

---

[9]De Bann v. First Western Bank & Trust Co., (Calif. Ct. of App., 1975) Civ. No. 43994, 3-31-75.

[10]Thrasher v. Thrasher, (Calif. Ct. of App., 1972) 27 C.A. 2d 23.

[11]Valente v. Pepsico, Inc. (D.C.,D. Del., 1975) Civ. Action 4537, 8-25-75.

[12]Cole Real Estate Corp. v. Peoples Bank and Trust Co., (Ind. Ct. of App., 1974) 310 N.E.2d 275.

[13]Harman v. Willbern, (CA-10 [Kan.], 1975) 520 F.2d 1333.

[14]Thompson v. Hambrick, (Tex. Ct. of Civ. App., 1974) 508 S.W.2d 949.

election made in distributing gains after liquidating the subsidiary postponed the capital gains tax on the parent's gains while allotting a pro-rated share of the tax to minority stockholders. This is so, since tax liability remained the same and the parent should not be compelled to overlook income tax advantages.[15]

When the price paid to the controlling stockholder does not reflect any premium for the delivery of the board of directors, the buyer of such stock cannot void the purchase by claiming it included delivery of the board.[16]

Where the question of harm to the corporation is not present, the tests applied are those of good faith and reasonable care. If both are met, the holders of a majority of the stock are under no more restraint as to its transfer than holders of minority interests.[17]

Stockholders can transfer their stock when the corporation is in the hands of a receiver or in the process of liquidation.[18] The transfer carries with it any right that might accrue to the original owner.[19] Although shares cannot be transferred after dissolution, the stockholder may assign his right to share in the assets of the corporation, subject to any claims the corporation may have against the transferor.[20]

The situation referred to above in which the fiduciary duty of controlling stockholders comes into important play is when the controlling stockholders agree to deliver the board of directors to the buyers. There is no all-encompassing rule to delineate when this can be done.

In one case, the seller agreed to sell his 28 percent block of stock at a premium. But the buyer wanted control of the corporation, and said he would not take the stock unless the seller delivered the resignations of a majority of the board and caused the nominees of the buyer to be elected in their place. For an unrelated reason, the seller refused to go through with the sale. When the buyer sued for breach of contract, the trial court gave summary judgment to the seller on the ground, among others, that the agreement to deliver the board was illegal. The United States Court of Appeals, however, reversed the decision and sent the case back to the trial court to decide several issues, including the agreement to transfer control.

---

[15]Grace v. Grace National Bank of New York, (CA-2, 1972) 465 F. 2d 1068.

[16]Goode v. Powers, (Ariz. S. Ct., 1965) 397 P.2d 56.

[17]Nelson v. Northland Life Ins. Co., (1936) 197 Minn. 151, 266 N.W. 857; Smith v. Gray, (1926) 50 Nev. 56, 250 P. 369; Levy v. American Beverage Corp., (1943) 114 Ind. App. 221, 50 N.E. 2d 290; Adams v. Mid-West Chevrolet Corp., (1947) 198 Okla. 461, 179 P. 2d 147; Tryon v. Smith, (1951) 191 Ore. 172, 229 P.2d 251. For an excellent discussion of this entire problem, see Jennings, "Trading in Corporate Control," 41 CALIF L. REV. 1. See also 40 CORNELL L.Q. 786; 68 HARV. L. REV 1274; 54 MICH. L. REV. 399; 40 Va. L. REV. 195.

[18]Holingsworth v. Multa Trina Ditch Co., (1931) 51 F.2d 649; People v. California Safe Deposit & Trust Co., (1912) 18 Cal. App. 732, 124 P. 558; Curtis v. Beckett, see Note 3. .

[19]Ibid.

[20]James v. Woodruff, (1844) 10 Paige (N.Y. 541), aff'd, 2 Denio (N.Y.) 574.

It said that the *sale* of a corporate office is illegal, but the *transfer* of a corporate office, or even control of a corporation is not always illegal. If, for example, the *majority* stock is sold, there is nothing wrong in arranging for the resignation of the majority directors and filling the vacancies with the buyer's nominees. This, said the court, is simply a convenient way of accomplishing a foregone result. The trouble comes when, as here, less than a majority of the stock is sold. On this point, the three judges went separate ways.[21]

Minority stockholders have been able to bar majority stockholders of a corporation with shares listed on the New York Stock Exchange from issuing a new class of non-voting common stock. This is so, even though state law permitted the new class of stock, when its issuance would have resulted in the corporation's losing its listing, and the only purpose of the new class of stock was to keep the majority in control.[22]

Although the right to dispose of property is recognized by the courts, reasonable restrictions on that right have been upheld where the restrictions were imposed (1) by the certificate of incorporation, the by-laws, the contract of subscription, or any other contract between the corporation and the stockholder or among the stockholders themselves; (2) directly by statute; or (3) by the corporation under power given to it by statute.

Transfer of subscriptions to stock. A subscriber who has become a stockholder by the corporation's acceptance of his subscription has the right to transfer his subscription even before any payment has been made on the contract, whether or not a certificate has been issued to him, unless the statute, the charter, or the agreement between the subscriber and the corporation provides to the contrary.[23] In order to make the assignment effective, it must be accepted by the corporation and recorded upon its books. Until such acceptance and recording, the original subscriber continues liable for all calls made for the unpaid subscription.[24]

Usually, if the transfer is made by an original subscriber who is an incorporator and signer of the articles of incorporation, immediately after the corporation has received its charter, the acceptance by the corporation of the transferee as a subscriber in place of the original subscriber is voted toward the close of the meeting of the incorporators and is recorded in the minutes of the meeting. The acceptance may take place at any directors'

---

[21]Essex Universal Corp. v. Yates, (CA-2, 1962) 305 F.2d 572.

[22]United Funds, Inc. v. Carter Products, Inc., (Md. Circuit Ct., 1963) No. A-42888, Balto. Daily Rec., 9-23-63, p. 2.

[23]Roosevelt v. Hamblin, (1908) 199 Mass. 127, 85 N.E. 98.

[24]Butts v. King, (1924) 101 Conn. 291, 125 A. 654. See also Webster v. Upton, (1875) 91 U.S. 384; Campbell v. American Alkali Co., (1903) 125 F. 207; Geary St., P. & O. R.R. v. Bradbury Estate Co., (1918) 179 Cal. 46, 175 P. 457; Sigua Iron Co. v. Brown, (1902) 171 N.Y. 488, 64 N.E. 194.

meeting. It is not essential, however, that the acceptance of a transferee in place of the original subscriber be made by formal action of the corporation expressed in voting or otherwise. It may be implied from the acts and course of conduct of the corporation, and the continuing recognition of the substitution of the transferee in place of the original subscriber.[25]

Right of stockholder to transfer shares before payment. Even stockholders who have not paid in full for their stock have a right to sell and transfer their shares. The one restriction on such a sale is that a shareholder in an insolvent corporation, with actual or implied knowledge of such insolvency, cannot sell his shares to an insolvent or irresponsible person in order to escape liability on the stock.[26] Title to the stock passes to the transferee at once and is not affected by the subsequent action of the corporation in recognizing or refusing to recognize his title.[27]

Effect of transfer of stock upon liability for calls and assessments. A person who makes an absolute transfer of his stock in good faith is relieved of further liability for calls upon an unpaid subscription, provided the transfer is duly recorded on the books of the corporation.[28] In most states it is held, either under common or statutory law, that the transferee of the stock is liable for all calls made after the transfer, but not for those made prior thereto.[29] The law of the state in which the corporation is organized governs, and not the law of the state in which the transferee resides.[30] Under common law, the liability of the transferee is based on ''novation,'' that is, on a substitution of the transferee for the transferor as the debtor of the corporation for the balance unpaid on the stock.[31] The date of the call, not the date when it becomes payable, determines liability as between the transferor and transferee.[32]

A stockholder must act in good faith in order to be relieved of liability for calls by a transfer of his shares of stock.[33] If the transfer is made for the sole purpose of avoiding liability, the transferor remains liable; such a transfer is fraudulent and void.[34] The transferor also remains liable unless

---

[25]Butts v. King, see Note 24.

[26]Banta v. Hubbell, (1912) 167 Mo. App. 38, 150 S.W. 1089; FLETCHER. CORPORATIONS §6103, §6371.

[27]Manchester St. Ry. v. Williams, (1902) 71 N.H. 312, 52 A. 461; 14 C.J. §921.

[28]Webster v. Upton, (1875) 91 U.S. 384; Shaw v. Green, (1937) 128 Tex. 596, 99 S.W.2d 889.

[29]Geary St., P. & O. R.R. v. Bradbury Estate Co., see Note 24; Sigua Iron Co. v. Brown (1902) 171 N.Y. 488, 64 N.E. 194.

[30]Black v. Zachary, (1845) 44 U.S. 527; Priest v. Glenn, (1892) 51 F. 400; McConey v. Belton Oil & Gas Co., (1906) 97 Minn. 190, 106 N.W. 900.

[31]Campbell v. American Alkali Co., (1903) 125 F. 207; West Nashville Planning-Mill Co. v. Nashville Sav. Bank, (1888) 86 Tenn. 252, 6 S.W. 340.

[32]Campbell v. American Alkali Co., (1903) 125 F. 207.

[33]Rochester & K.F. Land Co. v. Raymond, (1899) 158 N.Y. 576, 53 N.E. 507.

[34]Bowden v. Johnson, (1882) 107 U.S. 521; National Bank v. Case, (1878) 99 U.S. 628.

the transferee accepts the transfer.[35] It has been held that the transferor remains liable after transfer to a minor.[36] A transferee has the right to assume that stock issued as fully paid is as represented, and is not subject to call, unless he has knowledge that the stock is watered.[37]

If paid-up stock is assessable,[38] the transferee is liable for assessments on the stock made after its transfer.[39] Generally, however, the statutes provide that a transferee is not liable for an assessment unless the power of assessment is stated on the face of the stock certificate.[40] If the transferee fails to have the stock transferred on the corporate record, he is liable to the transferor for any assessments the latter is compelled to pay after transfer.[41] A pledgee who has the stock transferred on the books to his name is liable.[42] A transfer of shares may be made even if there are unpaid assessments against the stock.[43]

In many states there are statutes giving the corporation remedies for the enforcement of unpaid subscriptions upon the failure of the subscribers to pay in response to a call for payment. Either under these statutes, or, in their absence, at common law, the corporation generally has some or all of the following remedies:

1. Bring an action at law for the amount of the unpaid call;
2. Sell at public auction such part of the shares as will pay the call due plus expenses;
3. Sell the shares in satisfaction of the amount of the call and expenses and refund any excess to the subscriber;
4. After sale, as in 2 or 3, sue the subscriber for any deficiency existing;
5. Forfeit to the company the shares and all previous payments made thereon; and
6. Purchase the shares itself through its secretary, president, or a director if the amount of the call and expenses cannot be obtained by sale as in remedy 2 or 3.

In some states the corporation may, by by-law provision, determine the manner of selling or forfeiting shares for non-payment of calls. Remedies for non-payment of calls may also be provided by the corporate charter or by the subscription contract.

---

[35]Russell v. Easterbrook, (1898) 71 Conn. 50, 40 A. 905.

[36]Hood v. North C. Bank & Trust Co., (1936) 209 N.C. 367, 184 S.E. 51.

[37]See page 463 in Chapter 15.

[38]See page 563 in Chapter 19.

[39]Porter v. Gibson, (1945) 25 Cal.2d 506, 154 P.2d 703; Libby v. Tobey, (1890) 82 Me. 397, 19 A. 904.

[40]Wilson v. Cherokee Drift Mining Co., (1939) 14 Cal.2d 56, 92 P.2d 802.

[41]Gaffney v. People's Trust Co., (1920) 191 App. Div. 697, 182 N.Y. Supp. 451, aff'd, memo dec., (1921) 231 N.Y. 577, 132 N.E. 895; Bell v. O'Connor's Executors, No. 2, (1940) 40 D. & C. (Pa.) 353.

[42]Greutzmacher v. Quevli, (1929) 208 Iowa 537, 226 N.W. 5.

[43]Craig v. Hesperia Land & Water Co., (1896) 113 Cal. 7, 45 P.10.

Statutory, charter, or contract remedies are generally held to be in addition to, and do not abrogate appropriate common law remedies.[44]

Example: A corporation has the right to sue for the amount of the call although by statute, charter, or contract, it may also have the right to sell or forfeit the shares.[45]

Unless the right to do so is given by statute,[46] the corporation cannot sue at law for the amount of the call after it has availed itself of the remedy of forfeiture.[47]

A corporation must deliver stock certificates to a person designated in articles of incorporation as a 50 percent stockholder upon payment of the purchase price, when the corporation had not used statutory means to dispose of unpaid stock.[48]

Contractual restrictions on transfer of stock. Provisions in the charter or by-laws of the corporation, or in the stock certificates themselves, restricting the transfer of stock are enforceable as contracts between the corporation and the stockholder.[49] The right of a stockholder to alienate his property is, however, a matter of public policy, and a stockholder is not free to contract away his privilege to any extent that he chooses. The restrictions agreed upon by the stockholder must be reasonable in order to be binding, and they are strictly construed.[50]

For example, transfer restrictions imposed by corporate articles on class A stock and requiring withdrawing stockholders to just offer stock to members of class, created first option rights and were not prohibited by law as resulting in a buy-sell agreement between more than 20 members of class, since provision in articles did not amount to agreement among members of class. Nor was incorporation of New York Stock Exchange rules on transferability of shares unreasonable, when the corporation was

---

[44]Campbell v. American Alkali Co., (CA-3, 1903) 125 F.207; State v. Associated Packing Co., (Iowa S. Ct., 1929) 227 N.W. 627; Mills v. Stewart, (1869) 41 N.Y. 384; Ohio Valley Industrial Corp. v. H.L. Seabright Co., (1931) 111 W. Va. 55, 160 S.E. 300.

[45]Nashua Sav. Bank v. Anglo-American Land, Mortg. & Agency Co., (1903) 189 U.S. 221, 23 S. Ct. 517; Imperial Land Stock Co. v. Oster, (1917) 34 Cal. App. 776, 168 P. 1159.

[46]Mandel v. Swan Land & Cattle Co., (1895) 154 Ill. 177, 40 N.E. 462.

[47]Buffalo & N.Y. City R.R. Co. v. Dudley, (1856) 14 N.Y. 336.

[48]Scobes v. Continental Hotel Corp., (La. Ct. of App., 1970) 242 So.2d 610.

[49]Vanucci v. Pedrini, (1932) 217 Cal. 138, 17 P.2d 706; Lawson v. Household Finance Corp., (1929) 17 Del. Ch. 1, 147 A. 312; New England Trust Co v. Spaulding, (1941) 310 Mass. 424, 38 N.E.2d 672; Penthouse Properties, Inc. v. 1158 Fifth Ave., (1939) 256 App. Div. 685, 11 N.Y.S.2d 416.

[50]In re Trilling and Montague, (1956) 140 F. Supp. 260; McDonald v. Farley & Loetscher Mfg. Co., (1939) 226 Iowa 53, 283 N.W. 261; Guaranty Laundry Co. v. Pulliam, (1947) 198 Okla. 667, 181 P.2d 1007; Citizens State Bank v. O'Leary, (1942) 140 Tex. 305, 167 S.W.2d 719; Pelton v. Nevada Oil Co., (1948) (Tex. Civ. App.) 209 S.W.2d 645; 23 Minn. L. Rev. 834.

a member of that exchange.[51] Absolute restrictions upon the sale of or transfer of stock, as distinguished from reasonable conditions precedent to transfer, will not be enforced.[52]

A distinction is sometimes drawn between restrictions imposed by charter and restrictions imposed upon an unwilling minority of stockholders through the by-laws. A provision that no stock shall be sold or transferred to a competitor was declared invalid as a provision in the by-laws, although the court held that such a by-law might have been valid if expressly authorized by the charter.[53] A provision in the certificate of incorporation that prohibited transfer of shares without just offering them to the corporation was valid; however, it was intended for the benefit of the corporation. So it cannot be enforced by a single stockholder acting in his individual capacity, but these restrictions were waived by resolution of the directors and the transfer was valid.[54] Where, however, the by-law restriction has been adopted by the unanimous vote of stockholders, a reasonable restriction is usually upheld, particularly where the question arises among the original stockholders.[55] Even if a restriction is void when considered strictly as a by-law, it may be enforced as an agreement entered into between the interested parties.[56]

Restriction requiring stockholders to give corporation option to purchase. A common contractual restriction on the transfer of stock is one requiring a stockholder to give to the corporation or to the other stockholders a first option to purchase his stock if the stockholder desires to sell it. That kind of provision is not an invalid restraint upon the alienation of corporate stock;[57] nor is it invalid as against public policy.[58] If for some reason the stock is issued in the name of a person other than the true owner,

[51]Ling and Co., Inc. v. Trinity Savings and Loan Ass'n., (Tex. S. Ct., 1972) 482 S.W.2d 841, reversing (Tex. Ct. of Civ. App., 1971) 470 S.W.2d 441.

[52]In re Laun, (1911) 146 Wis. 252, 131 N.W. 366.

[53]Kretzer v. Cole Bros. Lightning Rod Co., (1916) 193 Mo. App. 99, 181 S.W. 1066.

[54]First National Bank of Boston v. Sullivan (Mass. Ct. of App., 1974) 314 N.E. 2d 149.

[55]Krauss v. Kuechler, (1938) 300 Mass. 346, 15 N.E.2d 207; Weiland v. Hogan, (1913) 177 Mich. 626, 143 N.W. 599; In re Laun, (1911) 146 Wis. 252, 131 N.W. 366.

[56]Palmer v. Chamberlin, (1951) 191 F. 2d 532; Krauss v. Kuechler, see Note 55; Weiland v. Hogan, see Note 55.

[57]Warner & Swasey Co. v. Rusterholz, (1941) 41 F. Supp. 498; Lawson v. Household Finance Corp., (1929) 17 Del. Ch. 1, 147 A. 312; McDonald v. Farley & Loetscher Mfg. Co., (1939) 226 Iowa 53, 283 N.W. 261. Albert E. Touchet, Inc., v. Touchet, (1928) 264 Mass. 499, 163 N.E. 184; Model Clothing House v. Dickinson, (1920) 146 Minn. 367, 178 N.W. 957; Peets v. Manhasset Civil Engineers, (1946) 68 N.Y.S.2d 338; Wright v. Iredell Tel. Co., (1921) 182 N.C. 308, 108 S.E. 744; First Nat'l Bank v. Shanks, (1947) (Ohio Com. Pls. 73 N.E.2d 93.

[58]In re Trilling and Montague, (1956) 140 F. Supp. 260; Kromer v. Koepge, (1952) 118 F. Supp. 571, aff'd, (1953) 210 F.2d 655; State v. Sho-Me Power Co-operative (1947) 356 Mo. 832, 204 S.W. 2d 276; Allen v. Allen v. Biltmore Tissue Corp., (1957) 2 N.Y.2d 534, 141 N.E.2d 812; Wright v. Iredell Tel. Co., (1921) 182 N.C. 308, 108 S.E. 744.

owner.[59] Nor does it prevent a stockholder from selling his stock to another stockholder in the same corporation,[60] or disposing of it by will.[61]

The courts differ as to the validity of a by-law providing that stockholders must offer their stock to the corporation and other stockholders before selling it to outsiders, where the statute and the charter make no provision for the passage of such a by-law. Some courts have held a by-law passed for this purpose to be invalid, while others have held it to be valid.[62] The by-laws themselves have been interpreted in various ways in their application to stock transfer restrictions. Thus, a corporation whose by-laws restricted sale of its stock by giving its own stockholders the first option to buy could not prevent a stockholder's transfer of stock to his daughter as part of a divorce settlement. Such transfer was a gift, not sale, and did not violate the by-law.[63]

Further, the president of a close family corporation could not prevent transfer of stock to a present stockholder on the ground that such transfer violated a by-law restriction that the corporation had first option to the stock, when he did not show that transferee had knowledge of such restriction.[64] A close corporation's by-laws saying that shareholders can only transfer their shares to blood descendants, does not keep stock in the family, when a stockholder in a testamentary disposition makes no mention of shares. They are part of his residuary estate and go to the trustee for charitable purposes along with the rest of his property.[65] Also, a stock transfer from one stockholder-director of a close corporation to another is valid when, as by-laws required, the stock was first offered to the corporation and to other stockholder-directors at an informal meeting of all stockholder-directors. Allegations that by-laws did not allow transfer of the stock to just one stockholder-director fails when such a restriction was not specifically stated in the by-laws.[66]

In many cases, the courts have not considered whether the by-law is technically valid, but have decided the question on the ground that the terms of the by-law, printed on the face of the certificate, became a contract

---

[59]State ex rel. Cabral v. Strudwick Funeral Home, (La App. 1941) 4 So. 2d 760.

[60]Talbott v. Nibert, (1949) 167 Kan. 138, 206 P.2d 131.

[61]Stern v. Stern, (1945) 146 F.2d 870. Although by-law is valid, it will be strictly construed and held applicable only to voluntary sale. Hence legatee can force transfer on books. Taylor's Administrator v. Taylor, (Ky. 1957) 301 S.W.2d 579.

[62]*Invalid:* Brinkerhoff-Farris Trust & Sav. Co. v. Home Lumber Co., (1893) 118 Mo. 447, 24 S.W. 129; First Nat'l Bank v. Shanks, (1947) (Ohio Com. Pls.) 73 N.E. 2d 293.

Valid: Sterling Loan & Inv. Co. v. Litel, (1924) 75 Colo. 34, 223 P. 753; Evans v. Dennis, (1948) 203 Ga. 232, 46 S.E.2d 122; Nicholson v. Franklin Brewing Co., (1910) 82 Ohio St. 94, 91 N.E. 991.

[63]McLeod v. Sandy Island Corp., (S.C.S. Ct., 1975) 216 S.E.2d 746.

[64]Norman v. Jerick Corporation, (Ore. S. Ct., 1972) 501 P.2d 305.

[65]In re Estate of Martin, (Ariz. Ct. of App., 1971) 490 P.2d 14.

[66]Remillong v. Schneider, (N.D. S. Ct., 1971) 185 N.W. 2nd 493.

between the corporation and the subscriber for its stock.[67] An amendment of the by-laws to make all subsequent transfers subject to the restriction has no force unless printed on the face of the certificate.[68] The provisions of a consent decree supersede by-law restrictions on the transfer of stock.[69]

A sale or transfer of stock made in violation of a valid provision giving the corporation a prior option to purchase is void.[70] Directors may waive a provision of the by-laws requiring that stock be offered to the corporation before sale,[71] and a majority stockholder may vote his stock to prevent the corporation from making a purchase of stock under such a by-law provision.[72] When the by-law requirement is not observed over a period of years, a transfer without complying with it may be valid on the ground that the requirement is waived.[73] But some courts hold that a by-law restriction may not be repealed without the consent of the minority.[74]

Contractual restrictions held to be valid. The following contractual restrictions have been declared valid:

A by-law provision that all shares of stock are freely assignable, but that no owner shall sell to one who is not a stockholder without first offering the stock for sale to other stockholders.[75]

A by-law provision requiring stockholders to offer their stock first to the corporation at a price set by appraisers.[76]

A provision in the stock certificate, or the charter, that shares will not be transferred until all debts to the corporation from the record holder are paid.[77]

A contract between stockholders whereby they take out life insurance payable to a trust fund, so that if one dies, the stock shall be turned over to the surviving stockholders, or to the corporation, and paid for out of the insurance.[78]

[67]New England Trust Co. v. Abbott, (1894) 162 Mass. 148, 38 N.E. 432; Hassel v. Pohle, (1925) 214 App. Div. 654, 212 N.Y. Supp. 561; First Nat'l Bank v. Shanks, (1947) (Ohio Com. Pls.) 73 N.E. 2d 293.

[68]Peets v. Manhasset Civil Engineers, (1946) 68 N.Y.S. 2d 338.

[69]Weber v. Lane, (1946) 315 Mich. 678, 24 N.W.2d 418.

[70]Hassel v. Pohle, (1925) 214 App. Div. 654, 212 N.Y. Supp. 561.

[71]Blabon v. Hay, (1929) 269 Mass. 401, 169 N.E. 268.

[72]Kentucky Package Store v. Checani, (1954) 331 Mass. 125, 117 N.E.2d 139.

[73]Pomeroy v. Westaway, (1947) N.Y. Misc. 307, 70 N.Y.S.2d 449; Elliott v. Lindquist, (1947) 356 Pa. 385, 52 A.2d 180.

[74]Bechtold v. Coleman Realty Co., (1951) 367 Pa. 208, 79 A.2d 661.

[75]Deardon v. Deardon, (1948) 360 Pa. 225, 61 A.2d 348; In re Garvin's Estate, (1939) 335 Pa. 542, 6 A2d 796; Rychwalski v. Milwaukee Candy Co., (1931) 205 Wis. 193, 236 N.W. 131. See also Lewis v. H.P. Hood & Sons, Inc., (1954) 331 Mass. 670, 121 N.E.2d 850.

[76]Shumaker v. Utex Exploration Co., (1957) 157 F. Supp. 58, holding such a by-law provision is not invalid as an illegal agreement to arbitrate future disputes.

[77]Elson v. Schmidt, (1941) 140 Neb. 646, 1 N.W.2d 314.

[78]Bohnsack v. Detroit Trust Co., (1940) 292 Mich. 167, 290 N.W. 367; Welchman v. Koschwitz, (1952) 21 N.J. Super. 304, 91 A.2d 169; Greater N.Y. Carpet House, Inc. v. Herschmann, (1940) 258 App. Div. 649, 17 N.Y.S.2d 483.

A corporation that entered into an agreement with stockholders to remove restrictions on their shares and to include such unrestricted shares in a public offering had to issue to them new certificates without the restrictive legend and pay damages, plus accrued interest, occasioned by breach of agreement to include their shares in the public offering.[79]

A deceased stockholder's executrix could not have a corporation's repurchase option nullified on the ground it was an adhesion contract imposed on the deceased stockholder by the corporation's allegedly superior bargaining position. The option was proper since it protected the corporation against outside control.[80]

A corporation could repurchase stock from a former employee who was discharged after nineteen months of employment, when they agreed that the corporation would sell him stock at a nominal price, but that it could repurchase the stock at the same price if he failed to continue working for three years.[81]

Contractual restrictions held invalid. The following contractual restrictions have been declared invalid:

A by-law giving directors the right to refuse a transfer by one stockholder to another.[82]

A by-law giving directors power to refuse a transfer because they object to the transferee, or for any other reason.[83]

A provision in the certificate that stock may be transferred only to some person approved by the directors.[84]

A by-law prohibiting the transfer of certificates of stock except to the corporation.[85]

An agreement that no stockholder could buy or sell any share of stock in the corporation without the written consent of all the stockholders unless the sale was made between the stockholders themselves.[86]

A by-law declaring invalid a sale of stock to a competitor.[87]

A by-law authorizing directors and officers to refuse a transfer if they believed the transfer was sought in furtherance of a fraudulent scheme.[88]

A prohibition against an intra-family transfer of stock without permission of each shareholder was unduly restrictive and unreasonable. The test

[79]Bjork v. April Industries, Inc., (Utah S. Ct., 1977) No. 14620; 1-24-77.

[80]Yeng Sue Chow v. Levi Strauss & Co., (Ct. of App., 1975) 122 Cal. Rep. 816.

[81]Waldorf v. K.M.S. Industries, Inc., (Mich. Ct. of App., 1970) 181 N.W. 2d 85.

[82]Morris v. Hussong Dyeing Mach. Co., (1913) 81 N.J. Eq. 256, 86 A. 1026.

[83]Petre v. Bruce, (1928) 157 Tenn. 131, 7 S.W.2d 43.

[84]Douglas v. Aurora Daily News Co., (1911) 160 Ill. App. 506.

[85]Steele v. Farmers' and Mechants' Mut. Tel. Ass'n. (1915) 95 Kan. 580, 148 P. 661; Herring v. Ruskin Co-operative Ass'n, (1899) (Tenn. Ch. App.) 52 S.W. 327.

[86]People ex rel. Malcolm v. Lake Sand Corp., (1929) 251 Ill. App. 499.

[87]Kretzer v. Cole Bros. Lightning Rod Co., (1916) 193 Mo. App. 99, 181 S.W. 1066.

[88]Pelton v. Nevada Oil Co., (1948) (Tex. Civ. App.) 209 S.W. 645.

of reasonableness is whether restraint is so necessary to the enterprise as to justify the overriding general policy against restraints on alienation.[89]

An agreement requiring an employee, upon his discharge for cause, to offer his shares back to the company at the price he paid for them, violated a statute, since it unreasonably restrained the transfer of shares and permitted the company to repurchase at an unfair price.[90]

A repurchase agreement clause that stated "The Company, its officers, and/or subsidiaries agree to purchase from the purchaser . . ." was unclear as to whether corporate officers could be held personally liable when the corporation failed to buy back. A full-scale trial would have to determine the intent of parties in making the contract.[91]

Important considerations in drafting agreement. The above outlined cases indicate the guidelines that should be followed in drafting a buy-and-sell agreement. The following are the more important questions that must be answered:

(1) Shall the remaining stockholders or the corporation buy the stock?
(2) How shall the agreement be funded?
(3) If the agreement is funded by life insurance, who shall own the policies, pay the premiums and be the beneficiaries?
(4) Should the agreement be administered by a trustee?
(5) How should the stock be valued for the purposes of the agreement?

Pitfalls to watch. There are some pitfalls that can be avoided if you follow these suggestions when entering into a buy-and-sell agreement:

(1) Make sure the agreement has a clause binding the stockholder's executor or other legal representative; otherwise, the provisions against transferring the stock may not bind them when the stockholder dies.[92]
(2) Whenever possible, make the restrictions against transfer of the stock part of the articles and by-laws; that way, future stockholders and their successors will also be bound even though they are not parties to the agreement.[93]
(3) Make the corporation a party to the agreement; if you don't, a stockholder may later claim there was no consideration for the buy option to the corporation.[94]
(4) When you make provision for a retiring stockholder to offer his shares to the remaining ones in proportion to their respective holdings, include a clause that if any of the remaining stockholders don't elect to buy their

---

[89]Fayard v. Fayard (Miss. S. Ct., 1974) 293 So.2d 421.

[90]Systematics, Inc. v. Mitchell, (Ark. S. Ct., 1973) 253 Ark. Rep. 848.

[91]Hokama v. Relinc Corporation, (Hawaii S. Ct., 1977) 559 P.2d 279.

[92]Kolmer-Marcus, Inc. v Winer, (1970) 26 N.Y.2d 795, 309 N.Y.S. 2d 220; Vogel v. Melish, (1964) 196 N.E.2d 402.

[93]Tu-Vu-Drive-In Corp. v. Ashkins, (1964) 38 Cal. Rptr. 348; Peets v. Manhasset, (1946) 68 N.Y.S. 2d 335.

[94]Black & White Cabs of St. Louis, Inc. v. Smith, (1963) 370 S.W.2d 669.

shares, any of the other stockholders may do so. Failure to do so imposes a risk of the sale of such shares to outsiders.[95]

Necessity for stating restriction on certificate of stock. Under the Uniform Stock Transfer Act,[96] no restriction upon the transfer of stock was recognized unless the restriction was stated on the certificate of stock.[97]

A resolution passed by the board of directors placing restrictions on transfers, which were not printed on the certificates, would not be enforced.[98] A resolution or by-law of this type would not, by itself, justify the corporation in refusing to transfer on its books stock purchased in violation of the resolution or by-law, whether or not the restriction was reasonable,[99] and even though the transferee had notice of it.[100]

Effect of contractual restrictions on transferees. Valid restrictions on the transfer of stock are binding not only as between the corporation and the original stockholders, but also as against transferees with notice.[101] The restrictions are also binding on pledgees who accept stock as security with knowledge of the restrictions.[102] A provision in the stock certificate that shares will not be transferred until all debts due to the corporation from the record holder have been paid was held to be binding not only on the record holder, but also on his assignee.[103] A consent decree that restricts the transfer of stock is binding on the owner's assignee; the assignee is not entitled to a new certificate that does not include the condition imposed by the consent decree.[104]

---

[95]Helmly v. Schultz, (1963) 131 S.E. 2d 924.

[96]The Uniform Commerical Code, rather than the Stock Transfer Act, is now in effect in all states except Louisiana. However, it has not changed the former requirements of the Uniform Stock Transfer Act that restrictions be stated on stock certificates.

[97]Weissman v. Lincoln Corp., (1954) (Fla.) 76 So.2d 478; Weber v. Lane, (1946) 315 Mich. 678, 24 N.W. 2d 418; Costello v. Farrell, (1951) 234 Minn. 453, 48 N.W.2d 557. In Doss v. Yingling, (1930) 95 Ind. App. 494, 172 N.E. 801, a restriction was held binding on the president of the corporation, although it was not printed on a certificate he received after adoption of the Uniform Stock Transfer Act. And note that while the Uniform Stock Transfer Act was intended to make restrictions ineffective as to persons without notice, failure to note the restriction is no bar to enforcement against persons with actual notice. Erwin v. West End Development Co. (CA-10, 1973) 481 F. 2d 34.

[98]See also Larson v. Superior Auto Parts, Inc., (1956) 270 Wis. 613, 72 N.W.2d 316.

[99]Age Publishing Co. v. Becker, (1943) 110 Colo. 319, 134 P.2d 205.

[100]Sorrick v. Consolidated Tel. Co., (1954) 340 Mich. 463, 65 N.W. 2d 713.

[101]Warner & Swasey Co. v. Rusterholz, (1941) 41 F. Supp. 498; Citizens State Bank v. O'Leary, (1942) 140 Tex. 305, 167 S.W. 2d 719. See also Musler v. Homestead Bldg. & Loan Ass'n, (1934) (Mo. App.) 66 S.W. 2d 152. A reasonable restraint on alientation, inserted in the by-laws, is also valid against an undisclosed principal for whom the stock was purchased by an agent. Barrett v. King, (1902) 181 Mass. 476, 63 N.E. 934.

[102]Estate Funds, Inc. v. Burton-Fifth Ave. Corp., (1952) 111 N.Y.S.2d 596; First Nat'l Bank v. Shanks, (1947) (Ohio Com. Pls.) 73 N.E. 2d 293. See also Musler v. Homestead Bldg. & Loan Ass'n, see Note 101.

[103]Jennings v. Bank of California, (1889) 79 Cal. 323, 21 P. 852.

[104]Kund v. Fort Bedford Inn Co., (1942) 46 D. & C. (Pa.) 394.

An agreement between the original stockholders, restricting the sale of stock to them, is not binding on the corporation when the certificate of incorporation, the by-laws, and the certificates of stock are all silent as to the restriction. Under such circumstances, a transferee of treasury shares is not bound by the restriction, even if he knew about the agreement.[105]

Lien of corporation on shares of stock. A corporation has no lien on its shares of stock merely because the stockholder is indebted to the corporation, in the absence of statutory, charter, or by-law provision creating this lien.[106] In some states a by-law attempting to create a lien in favor of the corporation is invalid, unless the statutes or articles of incorporation give express authority to adopt such a by-law.[107] Stock may, however, be impressed with a lien in favor of the corporation by statute or contract, for debts owing to it.[108] Under the Uniform Stock Transfer Act, there was no lien in favor of the corporation unless the right of the corporation to a lien was noted on the stock certificate.

If the owner of the stock transfers it to a bona fide holder who has no notice of the lien of the corporation, the corporation cannot refuse to transfer the stock to the name of the transferee.[109] The courts are not in agreement as to what constitutes notice to the transferee. It has been held that the purchaser of shares is chargeable with notice of liens created under the statute or charter, but not with those arising under the by-laws of the corporation or under the custom of dealing between the corporation and its stockholders.[110] Notice of a lien imposed by a by-law must appear on the face of the certificate.[111] A notation on the face of the stock certificate of the existence of a lien has been held sufficient notice to a purchaser to put him on inquiry.[112]

When stock is sold or pledged, but the transferee does not have the transfer recorded on the corporation's records before the indebtedness of the record holder to the corporation accrues, the corporation's lien is valid.

---

[105]Peets v. Manhasset Civil Engineers, (1946) 68 N.Y.S. 2d 338.

[106]Central Sav. Bank v. Smith, (1908) 43 Colo. 90, 95 P. 307; Damron v. Denny, (1919) 149 Ga. 280, 99 S.E. 851; Iowa-Missouri Grain Co. v. Powers, (1923) (Iowa) 191 N.W. 363; Gemmell v. Davis, (1892) 75 Md. 546, 23 A. 1032; Boyd v. Redd, (1897) 120 N.C. 335, 27 S.E. 35.

[107]McKinney v. Mechanics' Trust and Sav. Bank, (1927) 222 Ky. 264, 300 S.W. 631.

[108]Bank of Searcy v. Mechants' Grocer Co. (1916) 123 Ark. 403, 185 S.W. 806; Sproul v. Standard Plate Glass Co., (1902) 201 Pa. 103, 50 A. 1003; First State Bank v. First Nat'l Bank, (1912) (Tex. Civ. App.) 145 S.W. 691; United Cigarette Mach. Co. v. Brown, (1916) 119 Va. 813, 89 S.E. 850.

[109]See Kress v. Tooker-Jordan Corp., (1930) 103 Cal. App. 275, 284 P. 685.

A provision on the stock certificate's face that the stock is transferable only on the company's books in accord with the by-laws is not sufficient notice to a transferee of the existence of a lien imposed by the by-laws. Chandler v. Blanke Tea & Coffee Co., (1914) 183 Mo. App. 91, 165 S.W. 819.

[110]Bankers' Trust Co. v. McCloy, (1913) 109 Ark. 160, 159 S.W. 205.

[111]Bank of Culloden v. Bank of Forsyth, (1904) 120 Ga. 575, 48 S.E. 226.

[112]Ibid.

It is superior to the rights of the purchaser or pledgee.[113]

Restrictions on rights of indebted stockholder to transfer his shares. Even if a lien is created in favor of the corporation, the stockholder has a right to assign his shares subject to the lien.[114] Limitations on the right of an indebted stockholder to transfer his stock have been upheld as contractual restrictions, where such restriction was provided in the charter[115] or by-laws of the corporation.[116] The statutes in some states also specifically provide such restriction. A bona fide purchaser of the stock, without notice of the restriction, has been held not to be bound by it.[117] Regardless of the restriction, the transfer of stock may be made to the executor or representative of a deceased stockholder.[118] However, the corporation can refuse to consent to a transfer by the representative while the stockholder's indebtedness remains unpaid.[119]

Statutory restrictions on transfers. Limitations upon the power of a stockholder to transfer his stock may be imposed by statute. The statutes may also authorize the corporation to place restrictions upon the power to transfer. The power to restrict the right of alienation, however, must be given to the corporation in express terms,[120] and such restrictions will be strictly construed.

Persons who become stockholders before passage of a statute restricting the transfer of stock are not bound by the restriction, for the power to transfer is an existing right that cannot be subsequently impaired.[121]

Method of transferring stock. Any means by which one person is divested of ownership of stock and another person acquires such ownership is a transfer of the stock.[122] In the absence of a provision in the statute or charter to the contrary, such a change of ownership may be brought about in any of the various ways of transferring personal property.[123]

The Uniform Stock Transfer Act,[124] was formerly the basic statute covering the transfer of stock certificates in the states in which it is in effect,

---

[113]Benson Lumber Co. v. Thornton, (1932) 185 Minn. 230, 240 N.W. 651.

[114]Milner v. Brewer-Monaghan Mercantile Co., (1916) (Tex. Civ. App.) 188 S.W. 49.

[115]Gibbs v. Long Island Bank, (1894) 83 Hun (N.Y. 92), 31 N.Y. Supp. 406.

[116]Costello v. Portsmouth Brewing Co., (1898) 69 N.H. 405, 43 A. 640.

[117]Brinkerhoff-Farris Trust & Sav. Co. v. Home Lumber Co., (1893) 118 Mo. 447, 24 S.S.W. 129.

[118]London, Paris & American Bank v. Aronstein, (1902) 117 F. 601.

[119]In re Starbuck's Executrix, (1929) 251 N.Y. 439, 167 N.E. 580.

[120]Howe v. Roberts, (1923) 209 Ala. 80, 95 So. 344. Manufacturers Trust Co. v. Bank of Yorktown, (1935) 156 N.Y. Misc. 793, 282 N.Y. Supp. 507.

[121]In re W.W. Mills Co., (1908) 162 F. 42, 54.

[122]Wallach v. Stein, (1927) 103 N.J.L. 470, 136 A. 209.

[123]Cliffs Corp. v. United States, (1939) 103 F.2d 77; Crocker v. Crocker, (1927) 84 Cal. App. 114, 257 P. 611; Young v. New Pedrara Onyx Co., (1920) 48 Cal. App. 1, 192 P. 55.

[124]As noted above the Uniform Commercial Code is now in effect in all states except Louisiana.

though now it is largely superseded by the Uniform Commercial Code (see below). That act provides:

> "Title to a certificate and to the shares represented thereby can be transferred only, "(a) By delivery of the certificate indorsed either in blank or to a specified person by the person appearing by the certificate to be the owner of the shares represented thereby; or
>
> "(b) By delivery of the certificate and a separate document containing a written assignment of the certificate or a power of attorney to sell, assign or transfer the same or the shares represented thereby, signed by the person appearing by the certificate to be the owner of the shares represented thereby. Such assignment or power of attorney may be either in blank or to a specified person.
>
> "The provisions of this section shall be applicable although the charter or articles of incorporation or code of regulations or by-laws of the corporation issuing the certificate and the certificate itself provide that the shares represented thereby shall be transferable only on the books of the corporation or shall be registered by a registrar or transferred by a transfer agent."

After execution and delivery of the instruments, they are presented to the corporation with a request to transfer, the old certificate is surrendered and cancelled, a new certificate is issued to the transferee, and the stock is registered in his name.

Mere physical delivery of the custody of the certificates, without a written assignment or power of transfer, does not constitute a valid transfer of the stock.[125] On the other hand, in the case of stock not subject to the Uniform Stock Transfer Act, physical delivery of the certificate is not necessary to transfer title to the shares.[126] Transfer on the books of the corporation, at the request of the record owner, takes from him all right, title, and interest in the stock thus transferred, and places it beyond his control. The corporation can no longer recognize his control of the stock.[127]

The transfer of stock is now mainly governed by the provisions of the Uniform Commercial Code.[128] That article amounts to a negotiable instruments law dealing with securities. It includes bearer bonds, registered bonds and stock certificates.[129]

Necessity for recording transfer of stock. Transfer on the books of a

---

[125]Zoller v. State Bd. of Tax Appeals, (1940) 124 N.J. L. 376, 11 A.2d 833.

[126]Simonton v. Dwyer, (1941) 167 Ore. 50, 115 P.2d 316; Copeland v. Craig, (1940) 193 S.C. 484, 8 S.E.2d 858. See also Helvering v. Kaufman, (1943) 136 F.2d 356; In re Penfield Distilling Co., (1942) 131 F.2d 694; Robbins v. Pacific Eastern Corp., (1937) 8 Cal. 2d 241, 65 P.2d 42. Under the U.C.C., there is a duty to deliver, (see §8-314).

[127]Copeland v. Craig, see Note 126.

[128]Article 8, "Investing Securities."

[129]U.C.C. Section 8-101, official comment.

corporation is the most efficient and effective manner of transfer and is the final step in the process of changing title to the stock from one person to another.[130] Under the Uniform Stock Transfer Act a transfer on the corporate books is not a prerequisite to the transfer of stock.[131] Even when the statute, charter, or by-laws specifically provide that stock shall be transferable only on the corporate books, registration is not necessary to the validity of the transfer between the parties.[132] (See page 629.)

In many states, however, the statutes specifically authorize corporations to make regulations concerning the transfer of stock. The by-laws of most corporations contain a provision requiring recording of transfers on the books of the corporation. These requirements for recording transfers are intended for the benefit and protection of the corporation,[133] so that it may know whom to recognize as a stockholder[134] in the payment of dividends,[135] holding of corporate meetings,[136] granting of voting rights,[137] and other matters relating to the internal affairs of the corporation.[138]

Although compliance with requirements of statute, charter, or by-law is necessary to make a transfer valid as against the corporation, a transfer may be valid as between the parties without such compliance.[139]

Effect as to corporation of failure to record transfer of stock. A transfer of stock is ineffective as against the corporation until actually made on the corporation's transfer books;[140] an unregistered transferee is not entitled to the rights and privileges of a stockholder in his relations with the

---

[130]Copeland v. Craig, see Note 126.

[131]Upson v. Otis, (1946) 155 F.2d 606; Snyder Motor Co. v. Universal Credit Co., (1947) (Tex. Civ. App.) 199 S.W.2d 792. However, the U.C.C. does impose on the issuer an obligation to transfer when certain requirements are not met (see Section 8-401).

[132]Rule v. Commissioner, (1942) 127 F.2d 979; Townsend v. Tatnall Bank, (1948) 76 Ga. App. 500, 46 S.E.2d 607. See also Drug v. Hunt, (1933) 35 Del. 339, 168 A.87; Patterson v. Fitzgerald McElroy Co., (1927) 247 Ill. App. 81; Dennistoun v. Davis, (1930) 179 Minn. 373, 229 N.W. 353; Green v. McKee, (1949) 361 Pa. 95, 63 A.2d 3.

[133]Bank of Commerce v. Bank of Newport, (1894) 63 F. 898; In re Giant Portland Cement Co., (1941) 26 Del. Ch. 32, 21 A.2d 697; York's Ancillary Adm'r v. Bromley, (1941) 286 Ky. 533, 151 S.W.2d 28; Mortgage Land Inv. Co. v. McMains, (1927) 172 Minn. 110, 215 N.W. 192; Chemical Nat'l Bank v. Colwell, (1892) 132 N.Y. 250, 30 N.E. 644; J.G. Wilson Corp. v. Cahill, (1929) 152 Va. 108, 146 S.E. 274; Lipscomb's Adm'r v. Condon, (1904) 56 W. Va. 416, 49 S.E. 392.

[134]In re Northeastern Water Co., (1944) 28 Del. Ch. 139, 38 A.2d 918; In re Giant Portland Cement Co., see Note 133; Application of Friedman, (1945) 184 N.Y. Misc. 639; 54 N.Y.S. 2d 45. See also Whitfield v. Nonpareil Consol. Copper Co., (1912) 67 Wash. 286, 123 P. 1078.

[135]Townsend v. Tatnall Bank, (1948) 76 Ga. App. 500, 46 S.E. 2d 607; Hale v. West Porto Rico Sugar Co., (1922) 200 App. Div. 577, 193 N.Y. Supp. 555. But see Lindner v. Utah Southern Oil Co., (1955) 3 Utah 2d 302, 283 P.2d 605.

[136]Hale v. West Porto Rico Sugar Co., see Note 135.

[137]See Morrill v. Little Falls Mfg. Co., (1893) 53 Minn. 371, 55 N.W. 547.

[138]In re Canal Constr. Co., (1936) 21 Del. Ch. 155, 182 A. 545.

[139]J.G. Wilson Corp. v. Cahill, (1929) 152 Va. 108, 146 S.E. 274; 12 FLETCHER CORPORATIONS, §5488; 53 MICH. L. REV. 620.

[140]Salt Dome Oil Corp. v. Schneck, (1945) 28 Del. Ch. 433, 41 A.2d 583; York's Ancillary

corporation.[141] Thus, payment on final distribution of assets to the shareholder of record, although not the actual stockholder, has been upheld.[142] The corporation may, however, waive the benefit of the requirement and consider someone other than the recorded holder as the owner of the stock.[143] If an irregular transfer is accepted and acquiesced in by the corporation, the corporation is bound by it.[144] Failure of a transferee to register his stock does not bar his claim to it as against an irregular transfer,[145] nor does it prevent him from maintaining a stockholder's suit against the management for waste of corporate property.[146]

If the corporation refuses without justification to make a transfer on its books, it is deemed to have waived the requirement, and it must recognize the person entitled to the transfer as the owner of the stock.[147] At the time of refusal to transfer stock on its books, the corporation must give its reasons for refusal, and any reasons not so given are waived.[148]

Effect between transferor and transferee of failure to record transfer of stock. As between a transferor and a transferee of shares of stock, the transfer is valid and effective without recording, even if recording is required.[149] An assignment duly executed on the back of a stock certificate, followed by delivery to the assignee, transfers the stock be-

---

Adm'r v. Bromley; (1941) 286 Ky. 533, 151 S.W. 2d 28; Double O Mining Co. v. Simrak, (1942) 61 Nev. 431, 132 P.2d 605.

Even if a transfer is recorded on the books, it may be shown that true ownership remains in the transferor. Swan v. Swan's Ex'r, (1923) 136 Va. 496, 117 S.E. 858. See also Allen v. Hill, (1860) 16 Cal. 113, in which it was held that a surviving partner could vote stock owned by the partnership even if the deceased partner appeared on the books as the record holder.

[141]Salt Dome Oil Corp. v. Schneck, see Note 140.

[142]Campbell v. Perth Amboy Mut. Loan, Homestead and Bldg. Ass,n, (1909) 76 N.J. Eq. 347, 74 A. 144.

[143]Johnson v. Moore, (1926) 31 Ariz. 137, 250 P. 995; Mortgage Land Inv. Co. v. McMains, (1927) 172 Minn. 110, 215 N.W. 192. Chemical Nat'l Bank v. Colwell, (1892) 132 N.Y. 250, 30 N.E. 644. American Nat'l Bank v. Oriental Mills, (1891) 17 R.I. 551, 23 A. 795; Stewart v. Walla Walla Printing & Publishing Co., (1889) 1 Wash. 521, 20 P. 605.

[144]Johnson v. Moore, see Note 143; Bassin v. Enock-Pearl Co., (1947) 140 N.J. Eq. 428, 54 A.2d 824; Stewart v. Walla Walla Printing & Publishing Co., see Note 143.

[145]Laden v. Baader, (1943) 134 N.J. Eq. 24, 34 A.2d 82.

[146]Rosenthal v. Burry Biscuit Co., (1948) 30 Del. Ch. 299, 60 A.2d 106.

[147]Bates v. United Shoe Mach. Co., (1914) 216 F. 140. See also Logan v. Crissinger, (1923) 290 F. 415.

[148]Hulse v. Consolidated Quicksilver Mining Corp., (1944) 65 Idaho 768, 154 P.2d 149.

[149]United States v. Rosebush, (1942) 45 F. Supp. 664; In re Giant Portland cement Co., (1941) 26 Del. Ch. 32, 21 A. 2d 697; In re Canal Constr. Co., (1936) 21 Del. Ch. 155, 182 A. 545; Bates v. Peru Sav. Bank, (1934) 218 Iowa 1320, 256 N.W. 286; Dennistoun v. Davis, (1930) 179 Minn. 373, 229 N.W. 353; State v. Druggists' Addressing Co., (1938) (Mo. App.) 113 S.W. 2d 1061; Double O Mining Co. v. Simrak, (1942) 61 Nev. 431, 132 P. 2d 605; Jones v. Waldroup, (1940) 217 N.C. 178, 7 S.E.2d 366; A. M. Law & Co. v. Cleveland, (1934) 172 S.C. 200, 173 S.E. 638.See also Bankers' Mortgage Co. v. Sohland (1927) 33 Del. 331, 138 A. 361; Hogg v. Eckhardt, (1931) 343 Ill. 246, 175 N.E. 382; Nicollet Nat'l. Bank v. City Bank, (1887) 38 Minn. 85, 35 N.W. 577.

tween the parties, even though stock is not transferred on the books of the corporation.[150] The fact that the assignor continues to receive dividends from the stock does not affect the validity of the transfer.[151] The corporation, however, is not compelled to recognize the possessor of the certificate as the legal owner, if the circumstances indicate that he may not be.[152]

An unrecorded transfer is valid against persons standing in the place of the transferor, such as administrators.[153] It may also be valid between a pledgor and a pledgee,[154] or between a donor and a donee.[155]

Stock transfer books. The work involved in transferring stock and in keeping stock transfer books may be performed (1) by an officer of the corporation, generally the secretary or treasurer; (2) by a separate department of the corporation under the supervision of one of its officers, usually the secretary or treasurer; or (3) by an independent transfer agent appointed by the corporation. The method pursued depends upon the size of the corporation, the extent to which its shares are distributed, and the facilities of the corporation to handle the transfer work. In any case, the transfers are generally recorded in a transfer record and in a stock ledger. The transfer record lists the various shares transferred from day to day from one person to another. The stock ledger contains the running account of each individual stockholder.

A corporation need not keep a special stock ledger and transfer record unless the statute or its charter requires them. In the absence of such requirement, transfers may be recorded in any book or record. An account in the stock ledger has been held sufficient.[156] Entries inserted on a subscription list,[157] and a notation made in the stock certificate book,[158] have been held to constitute sufficient compliance with a statute requiring the corporation to keep a record of transfers. In some states, the statute indicates what items must be entered in the stock records. Compliance with these statutory requirements is essential.

If, as is often the case, the statute requires that stock books or records shall be kept at an office within the state,[159] the statute must be followed. A

---

[150]Chatz v. Midco Oil Co., (1946) 152 F.2d 153; Dunn v. Wilson & Co., (1943) 51 F. Supp. 655; York's Ancillary Adm'r v. Bromley, (1941) 286 Ky. 533, 151 S.W. 2d 28.

[151]York's Ancillary Adm'r v. Bromley, see Note 150.

[152]Kund v. Fort Bedford Inn Co., (1942) 46 D. & C. (Pa.) 394.

[153]Shires v. Allen, (1910) 47 Colo. 440, 107 P. 1072.

[154]Bank of Steamboat Springs v. Routt County Bank, (1927) 80 Colo. 385, 252 P. 355; Townsend v. Tatnall Bank, (1948) 76 Ga. App. 500, 46 S.E. 2d 607.

[155]Dulin v. Commissioner, (1934) 70 F.2d 828.

[156]Cecil Nat'l Bank v. Watsontown Bank, (1882) 105 U.S. 1039.

[157]Stewart v. Walla Walla Printing & Publishing Co., (1889) 1 Wash. 521, 20 P. 605.

[158]Bank of Commerce v. Bank of Newport, (1894) 63 F. 898.

[159]See, for example, Florida, G.C.L. §608.39; Michigan, G.C.L. §450.36; New Jersey, G.C.L. §14:5—1; New York S.C.L. §10. These statutes will be found in Prentice-Hall *Corporation*.

penalty is generally imposed upon the corporation and its officers for noncompliance.

Liability of corporation for unauthorized transfers of stock. A corporation must exercise ordinary care and reasonable diligence to prevent its stockholders from being injured by unauthorized transfers of stock.[160] It is liable for negligence in making transfers,[161] and hence may refuse to make a transfer if it acts in good faith and has reasonable grounds for refusing to do so.[162]

As a general rule, a corporation is liable to the true owner for an unauthorized transfer of stock on its books. It is similarly liable to a transferee for refusal to record a legitimate transfer. As mentioned above, the Uniform Commercial Code specifically imposes that liability in Section 8-401. This section reads as follows:

DUTY OF ISSUER TO REGISTER TRANSFER

(1) Where a security in registered form is presented to the issuer with a request to register transfer, the issuer is under a duty to register the transfer as requested if

(a) the security is indorsed by the appropriate person or persons (Section 8-308); and

(b) reasonable assurance is given that those indorsements are genuine and effective (Section 8-402); and

(c) the issuer has no duty to inquire into adverse claims or has discharged any such duty (Section 8-403); and

(d) any applicable law relating to the collection of taxes has been complied with; and

(e) the transfer is in fact rightful or is to a bona fide purchaser.

(2) Where an issuer is under a duty to register a transfer of a security the issuer is also liable to the person presenting it for registration or his principal for loss resulting from any unreasonable delay in registration or from failure or refusal to register the transfer.*

---

[160]Geyser-Marion Gold Mining Co. v. Stark, (1901) 106 F. 558. See also Seymour v. National Biscuit Co., (1939) 107 F.2d 58, cert. denied, 309 U.S. 665, 60 S. Ct. 590; Clark & Wilson Lumber Co. v. McAllister, (1939) 101 F.2d 709; Kentucky Util. Co. v. Skaggs, (1943) 293 Ky. 622, 169 S.W.2d 808.

[161]Schneider v. American Tel. & Tel. Co., (1939) 169 N.Y. Misc. 939, 9 N.Y.S.2d 564.

[162]Winans v. Alpha Beta Food Markets, Inc., (1936) 11 Cal. App. 653, 54 P.2d 48; Soltz v. Exhibitors' Serv. Co., (1939) 334 Pa. 211, 5 A.2d 899; Mundt v. Commerical Nat'l Bank, (1919) 35 Utah 90, 99 P. 454. See also Western Union Tel. Co. v. Davenport, (1878) 97 U.S. 369, in which the court said that, if the officers "upon presentation of a certificate for transfer ... are at all doubtful of the identity of the party offering it with its owner, or if not satisfied of the genuineness of a power of attorney produced, they can require the identity of the party in the one case, and the genuineness of the

The officers charged with the responsibility of deciding whether or not the transfer should be made are not expected to decide legal technicalities.[163] Ordinarily, the corporation cannot decide the legality of the transfer, and base a refusal to record the transfer on that decision.[164] But a corporation is justified in refusing to transfer stock when there is a dispute as to the ownership,[165] or when a garnishment proceeding involving the stock is pending,[166] or when there is doubt as to the transferor's mental capacity.[167]

Before recording a transfer, the corporation should make sure that the signature on the assignment and the power of attorney are genuine, and that the person executing them had authority to do so.[168] The corporation is liable for conversion if it transfers stock upon the demand of an agent who, within the corporation's knowledge, has no authority to make such a demand.[169] Where the circumstances surrounding a transfer of stock are such as to put the corporation on inquiry, the corporation is deemed to have notice of all that an inquiry would reveal.[170]

A corporation cannot refuse to transfer and register a shareholder's newly acquired stock merely because a third party asserts a claim adverse to the shareholder's ownership.[171] Also, a corporation is liable to holders of stock warrants that required notice of dissolution, and so the corporation's failure to give such notice entitles holders to the amount they would have received upon distribution had they exercised their warrants.[172] A buyer of stock cannot compel an employee of the issuing corporation to issue stock certificates under a sales agreement that provided delivery of individual stock certificates would be made either (1) two weeks after a public stock

document in the other, to be satisfactorily established before allowing the transfer to be made, In either case they must act upon their own responsibllity ... Neither the absence of blame on the part of the officers of the company in allowing an unauthorized transfer of stock, nor the good faith of the purchaser of stolen property, will avail as an answer to the demand of the true owner.'' See further 12 FLETCHER. CORPORATION. §5549; Christy and McLean, ''The Transfer of Stock,'' (rev. ed., 1940); 38 MICH. L. REV. 726; 65 YALE L.J. 807.

[163]United North & South Development Co. v. Rayner, (1942) 124 F.2d 512.

[164]Commonwealth v. Camp, (1917) 258 Pa. 548, 102 A. 205.

[165]United North & South Development Co. v. Rayner; see Note 163; Baxter v. Boston-Pacific Oil Co., (1927) 81 Cal. App. 187, 253 P. 185; Leff v. N. Kaufman's, Inc., (1941) 342 Pa. 342, 20 A.2d 786.

[166]United North & South Development Co. v. Rayner, (1942) 124 F. 2d 512.

[167]Kentucky Util. Co. v. Skaggs, (1943) 293 Ky. 622, 169 S.W. 2d 808.

[168]Aronson v. Bank of Ameria Nat'l Trust and Sav. Ass'n, (1937) 9 Cal. 2d 640, 72 P.2d 548; Baker v. Atlantic Coast Line R.R., (1917) 173 N.C. 365, 92 S.E. 170.

[169]Aronson v. Bank of America Nat't Trust and Sav. Ass'n, (1941) 42 Cal. App.2d 710, 109 P.2d 1001.

[170]Baker v. Atlantic Coast Line R.R., see Note 168. See also West v. American Tel. & Tel. Co., (1939) 108 F.2d 347, rev'd on other grounds, (1940) 311 U.S. 223, 61 S. Ct. 179. But see Hiller v. American Tel. & Tel. Co., (1949) 324 Mass. 24, 84 N.E.2d 548.

[171]Jacobson v. The Fine Ivy Corp., (N.Y.S. Ct., 1973) N.Y.L. J., 2-8-73, p.16.

[172]Tisch Family Foundation, Inc. v. Texas National Petroleum Co., (D.C.D. Del., 1971) 326 F. Supp. 1128. On issue of damages for interest, see 336 F. Supp. 44.

offering or (2) after permission from the corporation's directors, since neither of these conditions occurred prior to the corporation's dissolution.[173]

Further, title to the shares did not pass to the attorney who was also the nephew of a decedent stockholder who had endorsed a share certificate in blank and given it to him, since evidence showed she had already over-compensated him for his services and her conduct showed she had not abandoned title to the shares.[174] Also a stock transfer agent was entitled to refuse to register the transfer of stock certificates, when it was shown that the purchaser knew that the certificates had been canceled before he accepted their delivery, that it was not a rightful transfer and that he was not a bona fide purchaser for value.[175] In another case, it was held that ownership of stock did not pass to a pledgee to whom it was transferred, when transfer was made to increase the value of the pledge by having dividends accrue to the pledgee.[176]

A sole stockholder of a holding company that owned stock of a second corporation did not make an effective assignment of corporation stock to his daughter, when he did not actually deliver the certificates and the holding company continued to vote the stock, collect dividends and treated the stock as its own.[177] Finally, approval by a state's corporation commissioner may be necessary to validate a transfer of stock. Thus, it has been held that a stock transfer is void when it accompanies payment of a broker's commissions, not approved by the state's commissioner of corporations.[178]

Transfer by life tenant; by trustee or executor. A corporation must frequently decide whether or not a requested transfer of stock is authorized when stock is willed to a life tenant and remaindermen. The stock should be registered on the corporation's books as "life tenant under will." Does the corporation have the right to transfer that stock upon demand from the life tenant? In deciding this question, the laws of the state of the testator and the laws of the corporation's domicile must be considered. However, the life tenant is not the owner of the shares and, therefore could not pass title under the Uniform Stock Transfer Act.[179] When a corporation has notice that a person is not entitled to a certificate indicating unlimited ownership, but only life tenancy, it is liable to the remaindermen if it transfers the stock

---

[173]Molinaro v. Frezza, (N.Y. App. Div., 1975; 49 A.D.2d 148.

[174]Feldheim v. Plaguemine Oil and Development Company (La. Ct. of App., 1972) 263 So.2d 382, affirmed (La. S. Ct., 1973) 282 So. 2d 469.

[175]Folsom v. Security National Bank, (Colo. Ct. of App., 1973) 507 P.2d 1114.

[176]Steiner v. Zammit, (La. Ct. of App., 1973) 279 So.2d 728.

[177]Hoffman v. Wanson Concrete Co., (Wis. S. Ct., 1973) No. 298, 5-14-73.

[178]Southern California First National Bank v. Quincy Cass Associates, (Calif. S. Ct., 1970) 91 Cal. Rptr. 605, 478 P.2d 37.

[179]Seymour v. National Biscuit Co., (1939) 107 F. 2d 58.

upon demand from the life tenant.[180] It has been held that when a corporation, knowing that the transferor had only a life interest, nevertheless issued new certificates, and delivered them absolutely to the transferee, it was liable in an action for conversion, because it breached its duty to the remaindermen.[181] Even those statutes that make the corporation liable for transfer by a fiduciary only under certain conditions do not authorize transfer of the whole title to the stock upon demand of one who has only a life interest in it.[182]

Ordinarily when a trustee is described as such on the face of a stock certificate, the corporation permits transfer of the stock at its own peril.[183] It is liable for a transfer on its books that deprives a trust of the stock. For example, the corporation knew that a trust provided that stock should be used for certain benevolent causes of a church. The church sold the stock and used the proceeds for a new church building. The corporation transferred the stock; it was, therefore, liable to the trustees of the benevolent causes.[184]

A corporation is not liable for transfer of stock by an executor in breach of fiduciary duty unless it had knowledge of the breach, or the transfer in bad faith.[185] The corporation is not bound to make inquiry, nor is the executor bound to give requested information. However, if the executor undertakes to supply requested information, he must state the facts fully and fairly. Otherwise, the corporation is justified in refusing to make the transfer.[186]

Appointment of transfer agent and registrar. Many large corporations with widely distributed stock follow the practice of employing transfer agents or registrars to assist them in the issuance and transfer of stock. The board of directors adopts a resolution of appointment, specifying the powers and duties of the transfer agent or registrar, and the class and number of shares for which the agency is created. Some trust companies that act as transfer agent and registrar issue a pamphlet indicating their documentary requirements and other regulations governing their relations with the corporation. The agency may be terminated at the will of the

---

[180]West v. American Tel. & Tel. Co., (1939) 108 F. 2d 347.

[181]Seymour v. National Biscuit Co., see Note 179. See 38 MICH. L. REV. 726. But see Middendorf v. Kansas Power & Light Co., (1949) 166 Kan. 610, 203 P.2d 156, holding corporation will not be charged with knowledge of a will and executor's authority, and can permit a transfer by an executor-life tenant, where the proposed transfer is apparently in the ordinary course of business for the purpose of paying debts or legacies.

[182]Seymour v. National Biscuit Co., (1939) 107 F. 2d 58.

[183]First Nat'l Bank v. Pittsburgh, F.W. & C. Ry., (1939) 31 F. Supp. 381. See also Klein v. Inman, (1944) 298 Ky. 122, 182 S.W.2d 34; "Liability of a Corporation for Registering Unauthorized Transfer of Shares in Name of a Fiduciary," 86 U. PA. L. REV. 653.

[184]King v. Richardson, (1943) 136 F.2d 849.

[185]Harris v. General Motors Corp., (1942) 263 App. Div. 261, 32 N.Y.S.2d 556.

[186]Ibid.

corporation or of the transfer agent or registrar. Usually, upon removal of the transfer agent by the corporation, the board of directors adopts a resolution terminating the agency, and designating an officer of the corporation to whom the transfer books and records are to be delivered.

Duties of registrar and transfer agent. The duty of the registrar is to see that the corporation does not issue its stock beyond the amount authorized. The registrar keeps a record of each share of stock issued and of each share of stock cancelled. It is not concerned with any of the details of transfer of stock. The transfer agent, on the other hand, not only attends to the actual transfer of the stock on the records of the corporation, and to the issuance of new certificates of stock, but it may also take care of stock subscriptions, preparation of stockholders' lists, payment of dividends, conversion or redemption of securities, and even mailing of notices to stockholders.

Liability of transfer agent and registrar. The transfer agent is the agent of the corporation employing it.[187] It owes no affirmative duty to the stockholders whose certificates of stock it issues and transfers, and incurs no personal liability in favor of such stockholders.[188] Thus it has been held that there is no direct liability of a transfer agent to the stockholder for wrongful nonfeasance in delaying or refusing to transfer stock.[189] The agent is answerable to the corporation for nonfeasance. The corporation is liable to the transferee. But the agent is not individually liable to the transferee.[190] The transfer agent is responsible to the corporation primarily for the following: (1) wrongful refusals to transfer stock;[191] (2) wrongful transfers of stock; and (3) failure to perform its duties as agent.[192] The statutes in some states impose a liability upon the transfer agent for failure to pay taxes due on transfers, or for allowing transfers to be made before required tax waivers have been obtained.

The registrar is liable both to the corporation and to an injured stockholder if it allows an overissue of stock. This liability is based on the principle that an officer or agent who issues unauthorized stock is liable to bona fide purchasers.

Issuance of new certificates of stock to transferees. Transferees of stock are entitled to new certificates upon surrender to the corporation of

---

[187]Nicholson v. Morgan, (1922) 119 N.Y. Misc. 309, 196 N.Y. Supp. 147.

[188]Palmer v. O'Bannon Corp., (1925) 253 Mass. 8, 149 N.E. 112.

[189]Mears v. Crocker First Nat'l Bank, (1950) 97 Cal. App.2d 482, 218 P.2d 91. See Christy and McClean, "The Transfer of Stock," 2d ed., §268, §281.

[190]Fowler v. National City Bank, (1934) 49 Ga. App. 435, 176 S.E. 113.

[191]Age Publishing Co. v. Becker, (1943) 110 Colo. 319, 134 P. 2d 205; Young v. Cockman, (1943) 182 Md. 246, 34 A.2d 428. See also Dewey, "The Transfer Agent's Dilemma: Conflicting Claims to Shares of Stock," 52 HARV. L. REV. 553; Van Antwerp, "Liability of Transfer Agents for Wrongful Refusal to Transfer Shares," 50 MICH. L. REV. 155.

[192]Nicholson v. Morgan, (1922) 119 N.Y. Misc. 309, 196 N.Y. Supp. 147.

the old certificate.[193] A corporation, for its own protection, should refuse to issue a new certficate without the surrender of the old.[194] It cannot be compelled to issue a new one until the old one is surrendered to it, except where the original certificate is lost or destroyed.[195] A certificate of stock properly issued by a corporation having power to issue stock certificates is a declaration by the corporation to all who may innocently purchase the certificate that the person to whom it is issued is the owner of the number of shares of stock specified in the instrument.[196] The corporation must make sure that the person to whom it issues the certificate is the true owner.[197] A bona fide holder of the certificate, that is, one who has acquired the certificate in good faith, for value, properly indorsed, has a claim to recognition as a stockholder.[198] Obviously, if the corporation issues a new certificate of stock without demanding the surrender of the old one, it incurs the risk of having to recognize bona fide purchasers of both certificates as stockholders. Cancellation of an old certificate on the corporation books when issuing the new certificate, without demanding the surrender of the old certificate, will not protect the corporation from liability to a bona fide holder of the old certificate.[199] The position to be taken by the corporation in case surrender cannot be made because the certificate is lost is disscussed on page 610 et seq.

It is not essential to the validity of a pledge that a new certificate be issued to the pledgee. However, the pledgee is entitled to a certificate and may demand it.[200] The corporation may require the pledgee to give satisfactory proof of his authority to demand the transfer and to receive the new certificate.[201] Reference to the pledge agreement should be made in the certificate. For example, the certificate should be issued to "John Smith, pledgee under agreement with Paul Jones, dated ......"

---

[193]O'Neil v. Wolcott Mining Co., (1909) 174 F. 527; Handy v. Miner, (1926) 258 Mass. 53, 154 N.E. 557. See also Morris v. Hussong Dyeing Mach. Co., (1913) 81 N.J. Eq. 256, 86A. 1026.

[194]Holly Sugar Corp. v. Wilson, (1938) 101 Colo. 511, 75 P.2d 149; Suskin v. Hodges, (1939) 216 N.C. 333, 4 S.E.2d 891.

[195]Knight v. Shutz, (1943) 141 Ohio St. 267, 47 N.E.2d 886. See, however, Danbom v. Danbom, (1937) 132 Neb. 858, 273 N.W. 502, in which it was held that a court could require a corporation to issue a new certificate to a purchaser at a sheriff's sale, without surrender of the outstanding certificate. Case is discussed in 86 U. PA. L. REV. 101.

[196]Manhattan Beach Co. v. Harned, (1886) 27 F. 484.

[197]Greasy Brush Coal Co. v. Hays, (1942) 292 Ky. 517, 166 S.W.2d 983.

[198]Rand v. Hercules Powder Co., (1927) 129 N.Y. Misc. 891, 223 N.Y. Supp. 383. Stock may be transferred to an officer or director of a corporation in the same manner as to any individual, provided that the transaction is not fraudulent or in breach of any trust. Du Pont v. Du Pont, (1919) 256 F. 129.

[199]Nowy Swiat Publishing Co. v. Misiewicz, (1927) 246 N.Y. 58, 158 N.E. 19.

[200]Hurley v. Pusey & Jones Co., (1921) 274 F. 487; Lawrence v. I. N. Parlier Estate Co., (1940) 15 Cal. 2d 220, 100 P.2d 765. For the right of a pledgee to have a new certificate issued in his name, see Foto v. Bussell, (1919) 45 Cal. App. 281, 187 P. 432, and Bankers' Trust Co. v. Rood, (1930) 211 Iowa 289, 233 N.W. 794.

[201]Palmer v. O'Bannon Corp., (1925) 253 Mass. 8, 149 N.E. 112.

Remedies of stockholder for failure of corporation to issue stock certificate. Upon refusal of the corporation to issue a certificate of stock when it is under obligation to do so, the person entitled to the stock certificate may pursue one of the following remedies against the corporation:

1. Compel the corporation to issue the stock certificate by a bill in equity.[202]

2. Compel the issuance of the stock certificate by mandamus proceedings.[203]

3. Consider the refusal as a conversion of the stock, and recover the market value of the stock at the time of the conversion.[204]

4. Treat the refusal as a breach of contract, and sue for damages.[205] However, a stockholder who disputes the price he is to be paid by the corporation for stock he sells in accordance with his stock transfer agreement, cannot demand access to the corporation's books and supporting documents, when the agreement fixed the purchase price as the proportionate value of assets as carried on the books, and attested to by the accountants' report. Another bookkeeping method might have produced a higher price, but the method used was agreed to by all the stockholders, and an audit would serve no purpose. Also, a corporation cannot subtract negative net earnings from base price per share to compute the price it must pay for stock under a restrictive stock agreement that employed the price formula of base price plus amount, if any, of accumulated net earnings per share.[206]

5. Consider the contract rescinded, and recover the money paid on the subscription.[207]

---

[202]First Nat'l Bank v. Pittsburgh, F. W. & C. Ry., (1939) 31 F. Supp. 381; Young v. Cockman, (1943) 182 Md. 246, 34A. 2d 428; H. M. Rowe Co. v. Rowe, (1928) 154 Md. 599, 141 A. 334; Virginia Pub. Serv. Co. v. Steindler, (1936) 166 Va. 686, 187 S.E. 353. This remedy is allowed only where the value of the stock cannot be readily ascertained with reasonable certainty, and where the recovery of damages would not give adequate relief. Falk v. Dirigold Corp., (1928) 174 Minn. 219, 219 N.W. 82.

[203]The decisions as to whether or not mandamus is a proper proceeding to compel a transfer are conflicting. Some authorities have held that mandamus will not lie. Spangerburg v. Western Heavy Hardware and Iron Co., (1913) 166 Cal. 284, 135 P. 1127; State ex rel. Cooke v. New York-Mexican Oil Co., (1923) 32 Del. 244, 122 A. 55; People ex rel. Rottenberg v. Utah Gold and Copper Mines Co., (1909) 135 App. Div. 418, 119 N.Y. Supp. 852. Others say that mandamus is an available remedy. In re Ballou, (1914) 215 F. 810; Hanna v. Chester Times, (1933) 310 Pa. 583, 166 A. 243. The general rule seems to be that mandamus will not lie when there is an adequate remedy at law (in damages), or in equity (by specific performance).

[204]Tobias v. Wolverine Mining Co., (1932) 52 Idaho 576, 17 P.2d 338; Young v. Cockman, see Note 191; Prudential Petroleum Corp. v. Rauscher, Pierce & Co., (1955) (Tex. Civ. App.) 281 S.W.2d 457; Beaumont Hotel Co. v. Caswell, (1929) (Tex. Civ. App.) 14 S.W.2d 292. See also Seymour v. National Biscuit Co., (1939) 107 F. 2d 58; cert. denied, U.S. 665, 60 S. Ct. 590.

[205]In re Ballou, (1914) 215 F. 810; De Lamar v. Fidelity Loan & Inv. Co., (1924) 158 Ga. 361, 123 S.E. 116.

[206]Baron v. Royal Paper Corp., (N.Y. App. Div., 1971) 36 A.D.2d 112.

[207]Texla Oil Co. v. Calhoun, (1927) 36 Ga. App. 536, S.E. 84; Beaumont Hotel Co. v. Caswell, see Note 204.

The court will not direct the issuance of stock if the certificates already outstanding represent the total amount that the corporation is authorized to issue.[208] The stockholder, in such cases, is relegated to his remedy of money damages.[209] In any case, before a stockholder may maintain any action for refusal to issue a certificate, he must make a demand for it.[210]

A stockholder may also have a right of action against a corporation for damages sustained because of delay in issuing a certificate,[211] but the officers of the corporation are not personally liable.[212]

Rules for transfer of stock. Corporations that handle their own transfers of securities, as well as transfer agents and registrars, often issue printed rules outlining their requirements for transfer of stock, as well as a set of rules to guide themselves in effecting the transfers. These rules generally outline: (1) the documents required for transfer of stock by individuals, corporations, fiduciaries, pledgees, bankrupts, and the like; (2) the manner in which the assignment of stock must be executed; and (3) the method of registration and issuance of new certificates of stock.

Actual delivery of the stock certificate may also be an important factor. Thus, for example, a purchaser was not held liable on promissory notes he gave in exchange for stock, when the corporate books merely contained unsigned stock certificates made out to the purchaser and no actual delivery was made, since without delivery there was no consideration for said notes. The purchaser's subsequent election as secretary-treasurer of the corporation, giving him the power to sign, did not fulfill the requirement that the seller complete the transfer.[213]

Lost, destroyed, or stolen certificates of stock. Since a stockholder is entitled to a duplicate certificate to replace one that has been lost, stolen or destroyed, most corporations make provision in their by-laws for replacing such certificates. The corporation will require evidence of the loss, usually in the form of an affidavit.

Where statutes regulate the issuance of duplicate certificates, they

---

[208]Selwyn-Brown v. Superno Co., (1918) App. Div. 420, 168 N.Y. Supp. 18. See, however, McWilliams v. Geddes & Moss Undertaking Co., 1936) (La. App.) 169 So. 894, in which it was held that a corporation could cancel the shares of stock wrongfully issued.

[209]Dupoyster v. First Nat'l Bank, (1906) 29 Ky. L. Rep. 1153, 96 S.W. 830.

[210]Swobe v. Brictson Mfg. Co., (1922) 279 F. 560; Teeple v. Hawkeye Gold Dredging Co., (1908) 137 Iowa 206, 114 N.W. 906.

[211]Rock v. Gustaveson Oil Co., (1922) 59 Utah 451, 204 P. 96. The measure of damages for delay is the difference between the selling price at the time delivery was due and the selling price on the market when delivery was actually made.

[212]Radio Electronic Television Corp. v. Bartniew Distributing Corp., (1940) 32 F. Supp. 431; Hulse v. Consolidated Quicksilver Mining Corp., (1944) 65 Idaho 768, 154 P. 2d 149.

[213]Wolf v. Sachse, (Wisc. S. Ct., 1977) 248 N.W. 2d 407.

usually permit the corporation to require a bond to indemnify the corporation against any future claim if the old certificate should show up. The amount of the bond may be left to the discretion of the board, or a maximum or minimum may be set. In addition to supplying an affidavit and bond, the stockholder or the corporation itself may be required to advertise the loss.

If the statute permits, the board may be given complete discretion in regard to the issuance of a new certificate. To the clause regulating the issuance of duplicate certificates may be added a provision for the replacement of mutilated or partly-destroyed certificates. No affidavit or bond is necessary in this case since the old certificate can be surrendered. Additional provisions may deal with the keeping of records on the issuance of new certificates and with marking the certificate "duplicate."

Resolutions providing for issuance of new certificates. A resolution is usually required to authorize the issuance of a duplicate certificate. The resolution may be in pursuance of the appropriate by-law or, in the absence of a by-law provision, it must conform to statutory requirements. A blanket resolution is often used in the absence of a by-law.

When a stockholder has supplied the affidavit and bond required by the by-laws, the directors may adopt a resolution authorizing the transfer agent and registrar to issue a new certificate. If the directors are convinced that the old certificate has been destroyed—as in a fire—so that there is no danger of its reappearance, they may approve the issuance of a new certificate without requiring a bond. But in such a situation, the corporation's transfer agent and registrar may require a resolution of indemnity. Further, the corporation may also ask the stockholder to agree to indemnify the corporation.

Provisions of the Uniform Commercial Code. Every state except Louisiana has adopted the Uniform Commercial Code. The provision of the Code that applies to lost, destroyed and stolen securities is Section 8-405. It reads as follows:

> (1) Where a security has been lost, apparently destroyed or wrongfully taken and the owner fails to notify the issuer of that fact within a reasonable time after he has notice of it and the issuer registers a transfer of the security before receiving such a notification, the owner is precluded from asserting against the issuer any claim for registering the transfer or any claim to a new security under this section.

> (2) Where the owner of a security claims that the security has been lost, destroyed or wrongfully taken, the issuer must issue a new security in place of the original security if the owner

(a) so requests before the issuer has notice that the security has been acquired by a bona fide purchaser; and

(b) files with the issuer a sufficient indemnity bond; and

(c) satisfies any other reasonable requirements imposed by the issuer.

(3) If, after the issue of the new security, a bona fide purchaser of the original security presents it for registration of transfer, the issuer must register the transfer unless registration would result in overissue, in which event the issuer's liability is governed by Section 8-104. In addition to any rights on the indemnity bond, the issuer may recover the new security from the person to whom it was issued or any person taking under him except a bona fide purchaser.

Note: "Overissue" here means the issue of securities in excess of those the issuer has the corporate power to issue (Sec. 8-104). Under that section, if registration would result in an overissue, the purchaser may recover from the corporation the price he or the last purchaser for value paid for the security, with interest.

Usual requirements for issuance of duplicate certificates. Following are the usual requirements for the issuance of duplicate certificates:

1. An order from the stockholder, directing the corporation to stop any transfer of the lost certificate.
2. An affidavit of the stockholder, setting forth the material facts surrounding the loss of the certificate.[214]
3. An indemnity bond by the stockholder, approved by the board of directors of the corporation, to protect the corporation against loss which may result from issuance of the duplicate certificate. The bond is often set at double the amount of the market value of the stock for which the new certificate is being issued. Many corporations cover these transactions by a blanket bond.
4. Usually the lapse of a specified period of time before issuance of the new certificate, to see if the old one will not turn up.

Rights of holders of lost certificates of stock. The rights of a bona fide holder of the old certificate of stock which allegedly has been lost,

---

[214]See Trust Co. v. Finsterwald, (1939) 188 Ga. 794, 4 S.E.2d 808, in which it was held that under the statute is was not necessary to state the "mode of loss."

destroyed, or stolen are not affected by the issuance of the new certificate. The corporation must recognize him as a stockholder, as well as the bona fide holder of the new certificate.[215] To protect the corporation against any loss which it may later sustain if the old stock certificate should reappear, the court directing issuance of a new stock certificate will require the person requesting replacement to furnish a bond to indemnify the corporation.[216] The court may order issuance of a new certificate without requiring a bond if the facts show that no danger of reappearance of the old certificate exists.[217] A corporation that issues a new stock certificate without court order will require an indemnity bond as a condition of issuance.

Replacement of lost certificates by transfer agent. Corporations that have a transfer agent and a registrar handling the issuance and transfer of shares sometimes authorize the transfer agent to replace lost certificates upon obtaining a satisfactory surety bond to such an amount as is provided by the by-laws. The board of directors is thus relieved of the necessity of handling each case of a lost certificate of stock. The authority may be given to the transfer agent by means of a separate resolution passed by the directors, or this duty of the transfer agent may be included in the general resolution covering the appointment. The registrar, whose duty it is to see that there is no overissue of stock and who is required to countersign every certificate issued, may wish to be protected against any loss, damage, or liability that may arise from complying with the request of the corporation or its transfer agent to register and countersign certificates of stock issued in place of those that have been lost or destroyed. In such a case, the directors will authorize by resolution the execution of an agreement between the corporation and the registrar to indemnify the latter against such loss.

---

[215]People's Bank v. Lamar County Bank, (1915) 107 Miss. 852, 67 So. 961.

[216]Davis v. Lime Cola Bottling Works, (1922) 18 Ala. App. 562, 93 So. 328; Will's Adm'r v. George Wiedemann Brewing Co., (1916) 171 Ky. 681, 188 S.W. 788; State ex rel. McCay v. New Orleans Cotton Exchange, (1905) 114 La. 324, 38 So. 204.

[217]Ibid.